"Natoma"

To The National Federation of Musical Clubs with all good wishes from Victor Herbert April 1917

VICTOR HERBERT

An eminent musicologist, Edward N. Waters is Assistant Chief of the Music Division at the Library of Congress. He was educated at the Eastman School of Music at the University of Rochester, where he received both the bachelor's and master's degrees. For many years Mr. Waters has been active in professional library and musical circles, as president of the Musical Library Association, Chairman of the Council of National Library Associations, and secretary of the American Musicological Society. He is also widely known as the author of numerous articles and book reviews.

THE MACMILLAN COMPANY
NEW YORK • CHICAGO
DALLAS • ATLANTA • SAN FRANCISCO
LONDON • MANILA

THE MACMILLAN COMPANY
OF CANADA, LIMITED
TORONTO

VICTOR HERBERT

A Life in Music

BY

EDWARD N. WATERS

1955

THE MACMILLAN COMPANY · NEW YORK

To
MY WIFE
who deserves a better book
than this one is

Foreword

AFTER years of inexhaustible and painstaking research, Mr. Waters has given us the most complete, factual, and honest history of Father's work that one could compile. He has brought out facets of Father's life which will come as a surprise to many, and he has interspersed his facts with interesting anecdotes which give glimpses of Father's human side as well.

Mr. Waters states his facts as he has found them, and has drawn his conclusions fairly and candidly. I do not agree with his evaluations in every instance, nor do I think every reader will, for that which is *best* in music, as in all forms of art, depends so much upon personal tastes and even on the circumstances under which one first hears or sees the piece in question. But none of us will quarrel seriously with Mr. Waters on this point; on the contrary, we owe him a debt of gratitude for reminding us of some of Father's great melodies which have, for the moment, escaped our memory.

It is not, I believe, as an exceptional cellist, nor as a fine conductor, nor for his work in the interests of fellow composers that Father will be remembered, but rather as a composer who had the unfailing capacity to touch the hearts of people with his fascinating music. He has left an eternal heritage in his music. Thomas Moore, in 1830, wrote in the autograph book belonging to my great-grandfather, Samuel Lover, a verse which I like to recall when I think of Father:

> The Dead are like the stars by day,
>   Withdrawn from mortal eye,
>   But not extinct, they hold their way
>   In glory through the sky.

New York, 1954   ELLA HERBERT BARTLETT

Preface

Victor Herbert—a name to conjure with! And a name to evoke memories, smiles, and musical contentment. Victor Herbert—whose name for a quarter-century and more was synonymous with Broadway and the best it had to offer in the way of musical theater. There was a man, indeed, one who composed a path into the heart of America which no one else can tread, which no one else has paralleled. But that path and the beloved figure it bore have become obscured by the passing years and the accretion of legends, by the exaggeration of faulty memory and the overindulgence of affectionate regard. They are obscured, too, by the simple fact that they are not known, never have been known, in all their brilliant entirety.

Victor Herbert not known? The creator of *Naughty Marietta*, of *Babes in Toyland*, a stranger? The conductor whose orchestra brought joy to millions, an unfamiliar person? Yet truly he is, for few indeed are the people today who see beneath or behind the glamour the Broadway stage cast over him. Few there are who know the Herbert of early years, the sterling young musician who brought new values to this country, the musical missionary who (like Theodore Thomas before him) took great art to colleges and towns and villages. Few there are today who appreciate the depth of Herbert's honor and his self-initiated struggle to defend it against commercial enslavement. How many Americans are there who know him as the champion of all composers, as the one individual above all others who bettered the lot of his *confrères* at a time when friends were scarce and sympathy silent?

And this is not all. Herbert has been forgotten as a composer of so-called serious music (to which his contributions were valuable), as a cello virtuoso (one of the greatest in the world), as a chamber music artist (bringing New York rare opportunities of listening), as a symphonic conductor (the peer of any man of the time). He was even more than this astonishing array indicates.

Herbert has become the "unknown" musician by the surpassing excellence of his operetta scores. His music lives on though most of the shows have died. In his music for the theater there was an immediacy and a permanency which America grasped at once, and which it now treasures as its own. And like his theater music his personality had an immediacy and a permanency which discouraged investigation and documentation. How could friends—they were legion—write about this warm, hearty, vital man whose talents were prodigious, and whose capacity for friendship was unlimited? They knew him, that was enough. What would tempt a historian to peer behind the scenes of a career which, thanks to publicity and public opinion, was seemingly concentrated in one endeavor? Circumstances and accidental development have conspired to shroud Herbert, if not from public view, at least from public understanding; and the loss has been ours.

He was a fabulous man. Only around the fabulous do myth and legend grow; and Herbert is now surrounded by both. Many apocryphal tales have grown up about him, for he was the kind of person who inspired them. Some of them were complimentary, others less so, but unquestionably they all were the result of personal affection and admiration. Musically he was incredibly gifted and versatile; socially he was gregarious and warmhearted; professionally he was tirelessly indefatigable; mentally he was sharp, witty, and possessed of shrewd intelligence; emotionally he was passionate and fiery, a true child of the romanticism on which he was reared. Lavish in giving of himself and his worldly goods in the service of art and to others less fortunate, he is one of America's greatest sons. Endowed with a grace of spirit and an integrity of soul rarely found together, he should be honored for his total achievement as man, artist, and creator.

The ensuing pages purport to tell the story of Victor Herbert, but I venture not to claim it is the whole story. His life was too rich to seize complete in a first attempt, too prodigal to capture all its beneficences and influences. It is time, however, to tell it as fully and plainly as possible; and, if there be any virtue at all in the tale, I expect many readers to say with me—there was a man!

Acknowledgments

IT GIVES me profound pleasure to thank the many individuals and institutions that proffered assistance and encouragement as this book laboriously took shape. Perhaps no author has ever been more dependent on the kindness and knowledge and resources of others. I like to believe it was the thought of Victor Herbert that motivated them primarily, although their innate generosity was, I know, exercised spontaneously. A number of those who aided me also enriched the holdings of the Library of Congress by presenting materials to the national Victor Herbert collection. I am happy to have been the mediator in such transactions.

My first expression of gratitude goes enthusiastically to my wife, who suffered and fretted, coaxed and wheedled until the job was done. She showed extraordinary industry in typing lists, copying data, and criticizing chapters. She was an indispensable co-worker; without her the book could not have been done.

Equally indispensable, though geographically separated from me, were Mrs. Ella Herbert Bartlett, the composer's daughter, and her husband, Robert Stevens Bartlett. The citations for each chapter eloquently attest the information and documents they supplied, but these offer only a meager reflection of their actual aid. They shared, to be sure, my great desire for an adequate and accurate account of Victor Herbert's achievements, and we truly worked together toward this end. I owe them an inextinguishable debt in which affection and gratitude are intermingled.

Special materials of great importance and invaluable assistance were supplied by the following: Mrs. John E. Beck, niece-in-law of Joseph D. Redding; Edwin Franko Goldman; Raymond Hubbell, last surviving founder of ASCAP; Wilmer M. Jacoby; Mrs. Gustav Klemm;

Fred L. Landau, long Victor Herbert's concertmaster; the Library of Congress and its staff (particularly Frank C. Campbell, William Crouch, Henry Dubester, Frank X. Dwyer, Werner B. Ellinger, Richard S. Hill, William Lichtenwanger, Richard MacCarteney and Harold Spivacke); the Museum of the City of New York (and May Davenport Seymour, curator of its theater collection); the New York Public Library and its staff (particularly Mrs. Elizabeth P. Barrett, George Freedley, John Tasker Howard, Philip L. Miller, Paul Myers, and Carleton Sprague Smith); the Carnegie Library of Pittsburgh (and Irene Millen, its music librarian); J. Cecil Prouty, last manager of the Victor Herbert Orchestra; RCA Victor (and Harold Desfor, director of its press division); G. Schirmer, Inc. (particularly Gustave Schirmer and Nathan Broder); Natalie Schmidt, who last saw Victor Herbert alive; Mrs. Frederik Stahlberg and her son, Herbert Stahlberg; Samuel W. Tannenbaum. I am profoundly grateful to each one.

I am no less indebted to these persons and institutions for furnishing invaluable information of a personal-historical-bibliographical nature: Sargent Aborn and Louis Aborn, of the Tams-Witmark Music Library; the Aeolian-American Corporation; the late Paul Althouse; the American Academy of Arts and Letters (Miss Felicia Geffen); the American Society of Composers, Authors and Publishers (especially Daniel I. McNamara and Richard Frohlich); the Art Society of Pittsburgh (especially Dr. Thomas A. Arbuthnot); the late Harold Bauer; Robert Russell Bennett; Arthur Bergh; Irving Berlin; the Bohemians (Clyde Burrows); Felix Borowski; the Boston Public Library (especially Richard G. Appel); the Boston Symphony Orchestra (especially John N. Burk and Leonard Burkat); Horace Britt; Gene Buck; Joseph Buffington, Jr.; Edward Childs Carpenter; the late John Alden Carpenter; Julian Caster; Gilbert Chase; the Chicago Public Library (Herbert H. Hewitt); the Cincinnati Symphony Orchestra (Martha M. Smith); Eric T. Clarke; the Columbia University Library (Mrs. Catharine K. Miller); the late Walter Damrosch; the Thomas Alva Edison Foundation (Norman R. Speiden); Leo Edwards; Philip Egner; Oscar Faber; Carl Fischer, Inc. (especially Gustave Reese); Major Ignatius Fischl; Miss Jessica Fredericks; Vinton Freedley; the Friars Club; Mary Garden; the late Archer Gibson; John Golden; Richard Franko Goldman; Scott Goldthwaite; Percy Grainger; Father Ralph Handron; R. J. Hayes; Sidney B. Hill; Frank Hornig; Philip James; Edward Johnson; S. Jay Kaufman; A. Hyatt King; Otto Kinkeldey; Victor Kolar; Fritz Kreisler; the Lambs (especially Emil Friedlander, the late Bert Lytell, and John F. Hamilton); Jerome Landfield; the Law Library, Appellate Division, Rochester, N.Y. (Fred E. Rosbrook); John W. Leahy; Ferdinand Lowack; John McClosky; the Manhattan

School of Music (Mrs. Janet D. Schenck); *Musical America;* the *Musical Courier* (Russell M. Kerr); New York Court of Appeals, Albany; the New York Philharmonic-Symphony Society (especially Arthur Judson); Mrs. John DeWitt Peltz; the Philadelphia Free Library (especially Arthur Cohn and Bernice B. Larrabee); Oscar Radin; the late Fritzi Scheff; Karl Schmid; George G. Schneider; Jean Schwartz; Schwartz and Frohlich, attorneys-at-law; Dr. Nathan Settel; Mr. and Mrs. Robert B. Smith; the Society of the Friendly Sons of St. Patrick in the City of New York (Richard C. Murphy); Otto F. Stahl; the Stamford, Conn. (Ferguson) Public Library (Mary Louise Alexander); Mack Stark; Dorothy Stone; the late Herbert Stothart; Broughton Tall; Deems Taylor; May Valentine; Walter Vincent; the late Ernest Wagner.

There were others who were equally helpful. If my memory and records are so faulty that their names are not preserved in these pages, I trust they will forgive me and be assured of my deepest appreciation.

I am also happy to thank a number of publishers, who generously permitted me to quote extended extracts from their publications. I offer my gratitude to: Charles T. Branford Co.; E. P. Dutton & Co., Inc.; Henry Holt & Co., Inc.; *The New Yorker* (and Robert A. Simon); W. W. Norton & Co., Inc.; Rinehart & Co., Inc.; G. Schirmer, Inc.; Charles Scribner's Sons; Simon and Schuster, Inc.; *Theatre Arts* magazine.

I also thank The Macmillan Company for patience and understanding, forbearance and lack of despair.

The persons, firms and institutions lending a helping hand are responsible for any merits this book may have. Its faults and errors are my own. Let us hope that, whichever predominate, the spirit of Victor Herbert will loom ever larger as America realizes more fully his contribution to our culture.

EDWARD N. WATERS

December 1, 1954

Contents

VICTOR HERBERT

Prologue

MORE than three-quarters of a century ago a great man was memorialized in Dublin. Lined in a margin of black, a tablet of white Parian marble was placed in the aisle near the north transept of St. Patrick's Cathedral. Encircled by a laurel in stone, elaborately and finely carved, the newly laid plaque informed the visitor or worshiper:

> In Memory of Samuel Lover, Poet, Painter, Novelist, and Composer, who, in the exercise of a genius as distinguished in its versatility as in its power, by his pen and pencil illustrated so happily the characteristics of the Peasantry of his country that his name will ever be honourably identified with Ireland. He died July 6, 1868, aged 72; in firm faith that, having been comforted by the rod and staff of his Heavenly Father, in approaching the dark valley of the Shadow of Death, he would be, through the tender mercies of his Saviour, gathered among the flock of the Good Shepherd.

Thus was a modest testimonial offered to the grandfather of Victor Herbert, who like his grandsire will always be honorably identified with Ireland, though America will always claim him as her own.

The two men had much in common—place of birth, pride of country, sharp intelligence, love of fellows, rare abilities, and amazing versatility. Both fought injustice, won early triumphs, became expatriates, and acclimated themselves to new surroundings. They had imagination and wit, of a kind to change garrulity to eloquence, and their innate gentleness attracted friends whose affection was lasting and immeasurable. They were unassuming men, happy and ambitious in their work, ready to acknowledge the merits of others. And they were proud, sure of the value of their own creations and quick to take offense at unfair charges or allegations. Finally, they were Irish and sociable, fond of

1

congenial company, partakers of life's amenities, dispensers of many pleasures. In these many ways their characters were parallel.

Ireland never produced more loyal sons than Samuel Lover and Victor Herbert. Though the older transferred his career to England, and the younger (willing to anathematize Great Britain) to America, they sang Hibernia's praises as long as they drew breath. Living in foreign lands, with new loyalties firmly established, they nevertheless inspired millions to love Ireland who otherwise might have given it no thought. Lover and his daughter Fanny nurtured Herbert in Irish romance and legend, and the boy flourished and grew strong on Erin's stories and tales and songs. He resented the persecutions of his country, hated its conquerors, gloried in its art and culture. He idolized his grandfather, and never ceased boasting of his racial origins. Could Lover have witnessed the boy's subsequent career, he too would have boasted of Irish genius, happy in its manifestation in his own close descendant. It is not possible for a stone to be prophetic; if it were, Herbert's name would likewise have appeared in St. Patrick's Cathedral.

Born on February 24, 1797, Herbert's grandfather grew up in a Dublin which was culturally at low ebb. It was inevitable that a man of his pronounced talents—in literature, music, painting and poetry —should seek a wider environment and a larger audience than the Irish capital afforded. In the middle of the 1830's therefore, Lover settled in London with his wife (Lucy Berrel) and his daughters, Meta and Fanny—the latter destined to be Victor Herbert's mother.

While Lover lived in England he was doubly bereaved, losing his wife after twenty years of happy marriage and his older daughter after a childhood and youth of brilliant promise. But Fanny remained, and she pleased her father by marrying happily and well. He felt her future was amply provided for. After marrying again (Mary Wandby) he settled down in his declining years to a life of contentment which was enhanced by pleasure in his grandson and by an official distinction from Queen Victoria.

Lover's last real home in England was in the small town of Sevenoaks, some twenty miles southeast of London in Kent. He lived in a lovely cottage called "The Vine," and it was here that little Victor listened as his grandfather ruminated on the glories and stories of their native land. Reasons of health forced Lover to seek other habitations, and he ended his days at St. Helier on the Island of Jersey. His strongest wish was unfulfilled—to visit his daughter and grandson in Germany; but his memory was alive forever in the heart of the young boy.

1

The Boy and the Youth

FEBRUARY 1, 1859, was the day on which Victor Herbert was born in the city of Dublin. All his life long he was proud of his birth-place; but his love for the Irish capital sprang from idealized imaginings far more than from personal acquaintance. He left the city in early childhood and had only the most tenuous connections with it thereafter. Dublin never knew what it lost, and still does not realize what a loyal and talented son it can lay sentimental claim to.

It was fortunate that the boy grew up elsewhere, for Dublin would have been a dispiriting place in which to develop. It had little to offer to a budding musical genius who was plagued with ambition, energy, and high spirits. At the time of Herbert's birth Dublin was no mean city, for it contained about a quarter of a million souls; but its size was decreas-ing, and so was its influence. It had a few beautiful streets and some admirable suburbs, and numerous trades and professions supplied the livelihood of thousands. There were several musical societies, "but very little music of a superior character is afforded to the citizens at large."[1] The merest handful of Irish peers, out of nearly two hundred, were satisfied to reside in the incongruous town which lacked beauty, modernity, and sanitation.

Like all communities, large or small, Dublin had its higher society: a professional group of doctors, lawyers, and judges. It can be assumed that Herbert's father came from this background, but practically nothing is known about him. The composer, boasting continually of his grand-father, declared repeatedly that his father was a Dublin barrister; he seems to have known nothing more about Edward Herbert except that he died when he himself was an infant of perhaps two or three years. The place of death is unknown, although Paris has been sug-gested. If Fanny ever told her son anything more, he never disclosed it

3

to his children or to his closest friends. It is possible, too, that Edward Herbert's death was in tragic circumstances. She loved him dearly and passionately, and Victor was conspicuously her favorite, because he was Edward Herbert's boy, even though she had a second son by a second husband. Fanny Lover Herbert Schmid allowed her German family no doubt about Victor's place in her heart.[2]

Fanny Lover married in Dublin, probably in 1850; in 1851 she was established at Holywell in Wales, where her father visited her as he recovered from the shock of Meta's death. When she returned to Dublin is unknown; but Victor was born there and lived there for several years. A pleasant legend from the early Dublin days is that an old gypsy fortune teller was accustomed to begging and receiving alms from Edward Herbert or his servants. Calling shortly after the boy's birth, she predicted he would become the greatest composer of his country—a prophecy that enthusiasts can interpret in favor of either Ireland or America. Years elapsed, however, before there was an indication he would be a musician.

With a two- or three-year-old boy on her hands Fanny Herbert faced real and pressing problems. She was in her early thirties, attractive, independent, and resourceful. She was proud of her Irish heritage, and she nurtured Victor on Irish songs and tales. Some Irish tunes he absorbed as soon as he could talk—perhaps before, because speech developed in him slowly; and when he was little more than two he knew Irish melodies by the score. Moreover, he could repeat them accurately in time and pitch.[3] Mother and son went to the grandfather's home in Sevenoaks, where the boy heard much more music between 1862 and 1865, and, in fact, received that inspiration which later decided his future career. It was a fine place for the boy, an environment which could fire his mind in many ways and awaken his susceptibilities to art and music. His grandfather's salon was wholly congenial, and so was the "old man" himself, who had had his own hard lot of struggle and loss—and gain.

Victor may have visited his grandfather in Sevenoaks more than once. In after years he spoke of going there as a boy after a trip to the Continent; but his longest and most eventful stay was surely the result of his father's untimely death. He was impressionable and sensitive at the age of three or four, and he readily absorbed the kindly companionship that Lover offered him. Often, after he had become a famous composer, he recalled the pleasures experienced in "The Vine." He had been a quiet boy, given over to daydreaming and reflection, and enjoyed the serene pleasures of Victorian adults. A favorite pastime was to watch his grandfather paint and draw. He would stand motionless for hours, fascinated by the artist's skilled strokes and steady hand.[4]

More fascinating still was music, music filling the house all day long. Lover's home drew a constant stream of distinguished writers, artists, and musicians; and among the music-makers, singers and pianists and violinists were active both afternoon and night. Responding to Lover's friendliness they sang and played to their (and his) hearts' content. One musician who came often made an indelible impression on young Victor: Alfredo Carlo Piatti (1822–1901), perhaps the greatest cellist of his generation, caught the boy's fancy and unconsciously dictated his future. Many years later, Herbert remembered him vividly at the height of his own fame: "The music . . . filled my soul with deep peaceful satisfaction. There was, I recall, a cellist, a well-known artist still unforgotten, named Piatti. Ah, his music was the supreme thing for me! Nobody in all the universe seemed quite as wonderful as he; nothing quite so glorious as his cello. I don't suppose I said much about it at the time. But the longing to play a cello was lodged then and there in my soul. It took root and awaited its time."[5]

Herbert estimated he had been seven years old at the time; but his memory may have played him false, for when he was seven he and his mother were established in Germany, where she was married to a German physician and Victor was entering a period of development considerably rougher than the idyllic period at Sevenoaks.

It has been said that Victor was "sent" to Germany for reasons of economy, that family reverses made English schooling too expensive, and that existence sought beyond the Rhine was cheaper. This can only be partly true. The death of Edward Herbert left Fanny in a difficult position, with a sturdy boy to care for, and with her father in rapid decline. Fortunately for herself and Victor, she fell in love again, with a Dr. Wilhelm Schmid whom she met in London,[6] and whom she married after a brief acquaintance. By spring of 1866 they were settled in Stuttgart, where Lover wanted so much to visit her; and here she bore her second son, Willy, who eventually rose to fame in the German theater under the name of Faber (the Latin equivalent of Schmid).

Wilhelm Schmid was descended from the nobility; but one of his ancestors, falling into difficulties, had renounced his heritage, with the result that Wilhelm lived as an ordinary subject of the King of Württemberg. In marrying Fanny he had failed to observe one of his civic duties—to obtain permission of his sovereign. Here perhaps Fanny's influence is to be detected. She proudly identified herself as a free daughter of Ireland and gloried in the independence that went with that fact. She hated constraint and convention, in traveling, in converse, in social observance. She was also a firm antimilitarist, and by stubbornly maintaining that Willy was the offspring of a free Irish-woman she saved him from wasting his time in military service.

When her German husband toyed with the idea of reclaiming his position among the nobility, she refused to let him carry it through. He could do nothing which would bring him closer to the army and army life.[7] He remained home, practiced his profession, and benignly watched over the two boys, who grew up to be the best of friends.

The equipment Fanny took to the Continent caused surprise and sometimes consternation (she would have loved twentieth century America's streamlined plumbing and ultramodern conveniences). It included two portable bathtubs, packed up and tied as trunks; and when she asked for soap and hot water she created a downright sensation. Victor remembered the amazement that followed her strange requests—hygiene through cleanliness being a concept not yet held by the multitude.[8]

Life in Stuttgart was normal, happy and healthy. German traditions were as rich and plentiful as Irish ones, and the special seasons of the year had their individual atmosphere and flavor. The boy never forgot the Stuttgart Christmas, the bells that pealed from the *Stiftskirche,* or the solemn chorales blown by the horn players who were perched tower-high.[8] Here he drank in the Teutonic legends, thrilled to the deeds of knights in armor, wandered through the woods of a romantic countryside. As he grew older and larger he became much more active and vigorous, combining with the dreaminess of the Sevenoaks days a delight in the rough-and-tumble ways of carefree boyhood.[9]

Education made its demands, and Victor was subjected to the usual training available to sons of professional parents. After learning the fundamentals he entered the local *Gymnasium,* where he struggled with Greek and Latin and looked forward to a career as a physician.[10] Luckily this failed to materialize: unexpected family reverses put medical study beyond reach.[11] Music was the natural and immediate alternative: a peculiar field, perhaps, for "making money," but the one in which Victor had decided gifts. It was a happy choice which apparently brought needed results within a reasonable time. They were glad of it afterward, he said, later, "for, very shortly, the lawyer of the estate ran away or something with the money, and we were up against it."[12]

Before adopting the cello as his instrument, Victor learned to play piano, flute, and piccolo. The last two enabled him to win a place in a newly formed school orchestra, though his mother, even this early, was urging him to take up the cello (she, too, remembered the tones from the bow of Piatti). An embarrassing mishap finally led him to abandon the winds. The young orchestra had scheduled a program including the gay overture to Donizetti's *La Fille du Régiment.* At the end of the slow introduction, in preparation for the main part of the overture the piccolo had to blow nine tones absolutely alone, a steady alternation of high C and the F below it. They must be crystal-clear, perfectly steady and even. For a measure and a half the audience would hear nothing else. When Victor, playing piccolo, came to the nine tones, which could make or break the whole performance of the overture, he fluffed them wretchedly! Nervousness, dizziness, stagefright—call it what you will—he botched the job and gave up the piccolo forthwith. He had another reason, quite as amusing as the first, which may awaken sympathy in the minds of flute-piccolo players everywhere. In after years he asserted, with characteristic gusto, that this was the compelling reason for his dropping the tiny instrument: "What really annoyed me was the smell of the oil, re-quired to clean and polish the ebony woodwork. You had to be always cleaning and polishing. It was an untidy business. I made up my mind to chuck it."[13]

In deciding to embrace music as a profession Victor met with no objections from the family. To be sure, some friends attempted to dissuade him, and his mother was a little hesitant in giving approval; but it was not difficult to win her over, when he turned to the cello. A short period of preliminary concentration enabled him to demon-strate the heights he might reach, and his first teachers realized he was ready for a master. He found one in Bernhard Cossmann, who re-sided and taught in Baden-Baden from 1870 to 1878. Victor left the *Gymnasium* at the age of fifteen, and it is presumed that he studied with Cossmann for the two years following, from 1874 to 1876.

Bernhard Cossmann (1822–1910) was one of the great cellists of the century. Mendelssohn secured his services for the famous Gewandhaus concerts in Leipzig, and Liszt appointed him first cellist of the orchestra at the Weimar court. A thorough musician of fine taste, he was a brilliant soloist and an excellent chamber artist. He had, moreover, a pedagogical instinct that could awaken the individuality of every student in his charge. His students profited musically, technically, artistically, and morally. They learned the cello repertoire and the literature of chamber music—and they obtained a foundation which could not be shaken or impaired.

Victor worked diligently with Cossmann, acquiring the elements of artistry and virtuosity with which he astonished America a few years later. He also absorbed all the musical impressions that fell his way. He would hear every artist who came to play or rest, and he retained vivid memories of what each one had to offer. It is curious that his strongest recollections from these years were of two pianists, for he was not overly fond of the piano and never learned to write well for it. The two were Hans von Bülow and Anton Rubinstein.[14]

At the conclusion of two years with Cossmann young Herbert began the arduous business of earning a living. He played in many cities during the next four years, becoming acquainted with the rest of Germany, with France, Italy, Switzerland, and Austria, and adding to his English and German fluency in French and Italian which he retained for the rest of his life. He played with orchestras and appeared as soloist, and he probably had more fun in this brief period than in all the years that lay ahead. It was a time of high experience and novel adventure, and he relished every incident.

Sometimes an adventure would turn into misadventure. In later years Herbert liked to refer to one that placed him in a most incongruous situation. He was in a traveling orchestra that became stranded at Bern, without work and completely without resources. Herbert lost everything he owned except the full-dress suit he was wearing and his cello. He managed to reach Montreux on Lake Geneva, where, conspicuous by day in evening dress, he aroused the wonder of the people as he wandered through the streets. A generous local musician relieved his plight, taking the young cellist to his own apartment, feeding him, and providing him with a new outfit and enough money to get back to Germany. Years later this event had a sequel. The musician of Montreux wanted to come to the United States, and Herbert was greatly pleased to help by finding him employment in an orchestra in Chicago.[15]

It is certain that Herbert made preparations for extensive travel at the age of nineteen. In the spring of 1878 he armed himself with an official document which he countersigned with his own little known full name and began making his way in earnest. The imposing paper was a British passport addressed to the German sovereign, reading as follows: "We, George Glynn Petre, Esquire, Her Britannic Majesty's Chargè [sic] d'Affaires to His Majesty the King of Württemberg Request and require in the Name of Her Majesty, all those whom it may concern to allow Victor August Herbert, a British Subject, residing in Germany—to pass freely without let or hindrance and to afford him every assistance and protection of which he may stand in need. Given at Stuttgart this 10th day of May 1878 . . ."[16] Home ties were not broken, but the young man was definitely on his own. Three years passed before Stuttgart again counted him among its residents.

Two of the years can be accounted for; one cannot. Presumably 1879 (perhaps the season 1879–1880) found Herbert a member of the fabulous establishment maintained by the still more remarkable Baron Paul von Derwies. This Russian baron supported his own orchestra and his own opera company, and he engaged only the best musicians to furnish him the best music. One of his orchestra players who became something of a celebrity in America was Charles Martin Loeffler, and it is not unlikely that he and Herbert were members of the Baron's musical retinue at the same time. Neither spoke of this in after years, however, and it is possible they were not friendly with each other. Their temperaments were so vastly different that the absence of friendship offers no surprise. Furthermore, the possibility remains that Herbert was with the Baron before Loeffler arrived.

Thanks to Loeffler and his reminiscing to Carl Engel, we have a glimpse of the Baron's extraordinary existence:

Upon Massart's recommendation as a gifted violinist [Loeffler] was engaged in the private orchestra of Baron Paul von Derwies, a Russian nobleman of fabulous wealth. The Baron, outside of his Russian estates, maintained two establishments; he spent the summers at his castle, Château Trevano, near the lake of Lugano, and the winters in his sumptuous villa "Valrose" at Nice. The Baron's orchestra numbered about seventy picked men. The conductor was Karl Müller-Berghaus, once the first violin in the famous quartet of the Müller brothers, second generation. Loeffler's deskmate—and in many passes of violinistic drill his model—was the concertmaster, César Thomson. But the latter remained only one year, while Loeffler stayed two years, until the death of Baron Derwies, at the age of seventy, broke up the orchestra.

The musicians rehearsed daily. At Lugano, concerts took place on Tuesday afternoons and Friday evenings. If no guests were present, the Baron would be the only audience—but a highly critical one. He would sit in a silk wrap, his hands folded over the gold top of his cane, and occasionally speed along a movement with a *"Sans reprise, s'il vous plaît,"* or bring the program to an end with a courteous *"Merci, messieurs."* The old gentleman was a good pianist. His playing of Mendelssohn and Weber, with the accompaniment of his orchestra, was flawless. One of his sons played the 'cello, another the violin. Young Loeffler often assisted in the performance of chamber music by the members of this musical household. Repeatedly he appeared as soloist with the orchestra. He was entrusted with Müller-Berghaus' difficult violin concerto. The repertory of the orchestra comprised —besides the classics—Berlioz, Saint-Saëns and Delibes, early Tschaikowsky, the overtures to "Rienzi" and "Lohengrin," Liszt, Dvořák (whose three Slavic Rhapsodies, Op. 45, composed in 1878, were dedicated to Baron von Derwies), and other "moderns" of the epoch.

Orchestral concerts were only a part of the Baron's musical hobbies. He had a mixed choir, consisting of about 48 singers, under the leadership of Karl Bendl. Like the leader, the singers were all Bohemians—Russians were unprocurable—but the Bohemians sang the Russian liturgical chants in Derwies' private chapels at Lugano and at Nice. They also formed the chorus on the operatic nights which were a regular feature of the Baron's entertainments at Nice. These operas were staged without regard to cost. It was nothing to spend fifty thousand francs for bells needed in Glinka's "La Vie pour le Czar." The solo singers were the best that money could obtain. The change of this princely court from winter to summer quarters, and back, required three special trains: the first for the family, the guests and the children's tutors; the second for the servants and the horses; the third conveyed the choir and the orchestra. Truly a genial picture of enlightened Plutocracy—but then, our democratic age has "progressed" to community music and the radio.[17]

In concluding his account of the Baron, Engel raised an observing, if cynical, eyebrow at our "beneficent" radio and community music. When Herbert talked of the Baron, he was equally impressed, equally observing, and equally cynical. He said, with more justification than Engel: "That is the way those Russian millionaires do things. And our Fifth Avenue hostesses expect the whole country to gape if they engage Caruso and two horn players for a single night."[18]

Herbert found service of the nobility interesting, but thought the life too soft. He moved on, to Vienna, and played a year in the orchestra of Eduard Strauss (successor of brother Johann as the Waltz King), who gave him the knack of conducting Viennese waltzes with grace and authority—an acquirement of no little importance. The sojourn in Vienna probably occurred in 1880 (possibly, again, the season of 1880–1881) and was his last semipermanent stay before he retraced his steps to Stuttgart.

Herbert had a stronger reason for leaving the Baron—he wanted more opportunity to play as soloist. If he found few chances in a privately supported orchestra, he would join a group which had a public, and which toured cities of varying sizes. He was not disappointed, for Eduard Strauss gave him frequent solo appearances which brought the desired experience. Strauss's orchestra was a large one. Though specially famous for its dance music and lighter classics, it also featured soloists in standard concertos and introduced them in towns accustomed to the best. When Strauss brought his soloists to Leipzig, for instance, they had to stand comparison with performances at the venerated Gewandhaus.

Two critics in Leipzig listened to Herbert's interpretation of a concerto by Goltermann and were eminently satisfied with his performance. He was a "magnificent master" of the piece, one who knew how to treat the cantilena expressively and to execute the passage work correctly and with bravura. The orchestra, indeed, could not be praised enough, for it had soloists who could "completely satisfy the most pampered audience of the Gewandhaus concerts." As an unknown, Herbert caused great surprise by the sweetness of his tone, his ingratiating playing of a melody, and the brilliant finish with which he tossed off the thirds and sixths in the last movement. One of the critics noted his youth, said that he aroused the highest hopes, and wrote one bit of advice: "Since he is still very young . . . he should direct his attention, in the more rapid passages, to a quieter manner of bowing."[19] His career as virtuoso was auspiciously begun.

The season with Strauss ended, Herbert toured through Germany and Switzerland and came back to Stuttgart as soloist at a Lieder-kranz concert. He was warmly received, and had the offer of a position in the Court orchestra. It was a favorable moment to stay, and he accepted. He had gained a world of experience already; as soloist he had had his "baptism of fire"; he wanted to study composition, and his mother was there to keep house for him. So he settled in Stuttgart for the next five years.

2

Stuttgart to America

STUTTGART was a beautiful city of varied attractions, cultural and physical. Neither large nor cosmopolitan, it had advantages that many a greater town could envy. As capital of the small kingdom of Württemberg it enjoyed a political prestige that stimulated nonpolitical events—concerts, opera, theater, and so on. The ubiquitous Baedeker claimed for it the most beautiful situation of all German capitals and came close to rhapsodizing over the wooded slopes and vine-clad hills surrounding it. The region was scenic, the climate healthy.[1]

In this busy and charming little metropolis of nearly 120,000 souls[2] Herbert settled down as a court musician. He lived with his mother, their address being Tübingerstrasse 17, 2. The city directory gave his profession as "Hofmusikus" and gave Fanny Schmid simply as "Doktors Frau."[3]

What kind of town was Stuttgart for a musician—or a music student? A "Stuttgart Letter" in the New York *Musical Courier*, February 1, 1888, from its Paris correspondent, H. Woellhaf, who was touring the neighboring country to gather data for potential students, characterizes the town largely as Herbert knew it.

First of all, Woellhaf declared, a music student in Stuttgart could be assured of a sound and many-sided education; more than that, the town had advantages over nearly every other European music center. Living was cheap, comfort was attainable; the surroundings were quiet and congenial, and distances to lessons, concerts, and the opera were short. A student with good preparation, a reasonable amount of cash, good digestion, and, of course, musical talent could obtain a first-rate musical schooling in Stuttgart.

It was best to be independent and live alone. Specially desirable was a new and handsome quarter of the city where housewives favored a stu-

12

dent clientele and, through the columns of the local paper, it was easy to find a large single room or a small apartment which was airy and well lighted and very likely commanding a fine view over the encircling vine-clad hills. A student might well find himself the landlady's only lodger and, as her protégé, receive all sorts of comfort-making services for two or three marks a month. A student living on one of the desirable, secluded streets could walk to the other end of the town in twenty minutes; fifteen minutes would take him to the Conservatory, ten to the business center on the Königsstrasse, and eight to the theater.

The town was not inferior musically. The music heard was excellent and was plentiful, but there was no surfeit of it as in Berlin. This, Woellhaf thought, was an important consideration. The orchestra was superb, and gave a fine series of subscription concerts. The Verein für klassische Kirchen-Musik provided oratorios and the Kammer-Musik Soiréen brought forth the best in chamber music. Stuttgart prided itself also on its opera, which occupied the stage of the leading theater three to four times a week. The presentations maintained a uniformly high standard. Many European cities supported more pretentious establishments, but few mounted productions that were artistically or musically superior. Stuttgart was too small to venture into the "star" system or to vie with Paris or Vienna in huge glittering ballets. Yet it had a well drilled ballet corps of about twenty, a fully reliable chorus of about forty, and an expert régisseur. The soloists, if not world-famous, were more than adequate. With such facilities, directed by the admirable musician Karl Doppler (1825–1900), the Stuttgart opera boasted a large repertoire and supplied invaluable experience to both performers and students. Moreover, the auditorium of the theater was celebrated for its excellent acoustics, a fortunate circumstance, again, for both student and performer.

The Stuttgart Conservatory drew students from near and far. Under the patronage of the King it enjoyed an enviable reputation for its faculty and its instruction. Here students could take courses designed to be difficult, in composition, the usual theoretical and historical subjects, and the string and keyboard instruments. There were also opportunities for ensemble playing and chorus singing, and one who was mechanically inclined could learn the principles of organ manufacture. There seems to have been only one deficiency—the orchestral wind instruments were not taught (though they were supposed to be); as a result it was impossible to form a students' orchestra. The court orchestra had masters of all the orchestral instruments, and so this neglect was peculiar, to say the least. One explanation may be that persons desiring to study flute or clarinet or trombone went to larger cities, where immediate employment would be easier to obtain. The musical personnel of Stuttgart was relatively stable, so that the turn-over of musicians was fairly slow.

Woellhaf was obviously dissatisfied with one other thing: singing. On Stuttgart's vocal instruction he refused to comment, contenting himself with the biting observation that Americans rarely came to Germany to study voice.

Herbert entered a favorable musical atmosphere when he joined the cello section of the Court Orchestra of Stuttgart. Although he was never the principal cellist, as has often been alleged, he was prom-inent from the start, receiving opportunities and recognition as a soloist which would only be granted to a musician of outstanding ability. He was not yet twenty-three years old and was a rank newcomer in a band of experienced players; only remarkable talent could win such recogni-tion during his first season.

Herbert was as eager to learn as he was to play. He not only strove for mastery of his own instrument, but also sought to penetrate the secrets and intricacies of theory, harmony, composition. Many a fine executant has been handicapped by lack of theoretical knowledge, and Herbert was determined to leave the group of musically illiterate musicians. He had much to learn, as he himself confessed later, having devoted the years preceding almost entirely to performance on his instrument. Determination to become a composer followed close upon the decision to study; it was strengthened by the encouragement of his teacher.

A full-fledged instrumentalist, the young man approached the Conservatory as a student. Here he had the good fortune to fall into the hands of Max Seifriz (or Seifritz, 1827–1885), who knew what he needed and perceived his latent possibilities. Seifriz, a composer of stature, a conductor, and a violinist, had come to Stuttgart in 1869 and had been appointed Königlicher Hofmusikdirektor in 1870. He was a friend of Liszt and Wagner and thus in the forefront of modern romanticism; and he exercised a great influence over students, who considered him to be a progressive force in musical art.

Herbert was always happy to acknowledge his debt to Seifriz, whose influence carried beyond the classroom into the orchestra pit. On two occasions in particular he related benefits received, confirming the fact that his theoretical studies had been retarded prior to his joining the Stuttgart orchestra:

I cannot be too grateful to Herr Seifritz for coaxing by encouragement and kindly criticism the best that was in me musically. While I was only a 'cello player in the royal orchestra at Stuttgart and not far advanced in harmony studies, he suggested that I try my hand at composing. Timidly I made an attempt, whose result was meagre enough, but sitting down to the piano he explained why my little composition sounded so wretchedly. On second trial I fared better, and one day, under this system of corrective criticism, I appeared at an orchestra concert to perform a 'cello concerto of my own composing. I had learned to distinguish well sounding from poorly sounding harmony, and by degrees was developing a sound musical judgment.

Then again I cultivated early the art of scoring for the orchestra, and during the intervals that my 'cello was silent in the orchestra I listened acutely for the effect of the various instrumental combinations. When results were unsatisfactory I learned at once the reason. In this way I developed my instinct for orchestral coloring, and gained practical knowledge of the possibilities of the various instruments.[4]

The composer admitted that he became a student upon beginning his orchestral duties, that is, in 1881. He remained with Seifriz for several years, very likely to the older man's death. Interesting is his account of listening for the effects of instrumental combinations, which must have been with the deepest concentration, to judge by the results of later years. Herbert was to be a master of the art of orchestration, which he evidently learned without formal instruction.

On another occasion Herbert said:

My teacher gave me a few simple melodies, with the request that I harmonize them, and this before I had gone very far in my theoretical studies. First I wrote them for a male quartet, then for mixed voices, next for strings and finally for a cello solo with string accompaniment. Of course, my first work was crude. On paper the harmony seemed all right, but in playing it the sound was awful. And why? Well, my instructor pointed out why. The parts were too far apart, the progressions were wrong, the skips were large or the parts crossed. The evils were pointed out, and corrected, and so before I had even partly mastered harmony or counterpoint I could treat a theme quite satisfactorily. Next I was allowed to invent my own melodies, and early exercise the power of fantasy.[5]

He trod a familiar path that was onerous enough, no doubt. But it had to be: there is no short cut to creative mastery.

The Stuttgart orchestra gave ten subscription concerts per season. Herbert's first big chance as soloist came at his second concert, unexpectedly, on October 25, 1881. This was both an advantage and a disadvantage, for it meant that he had to play without the usual preparation. The announced soloist was a pianist, Martha Remmert, who intended to play Liszt's *Fantasy on Ruins of Athens* and his fourteenth *Hungarian Rhapsody*; but illness prevented her from appearing. Two members of the orchestra were chosen to fill in: a flutist by the name of Koch, and Herbert. Herbert played the A minor Concerto by Goltermann, then a part of the standard cello repertoire. Two printed criticisms of his performance are almost diametrically opposed to each other, one finding considerable fault with his playing, the second being wholly laudatory. The adverse critic stated that the technic was not adequate for certain difficult passages which consequently sounded unclear and indistinct. He admitted, however, that the player's tone in the singing melodies was beautiful and sympathetic.[6] The admiring critic reported that the "appearance of the newly engaged cellist, Herbert, afforded real joy," that he exhibited an "excellent technic and fine firm tone," and that he reaped abundant applause.[7]

If Herbert's playing lacked something on this important occasion, it seems reasonable to set it down to the emergency nature of his appearance. Furthermore, the second critic may have been quite correct— probably was, in fact—for Herbert continued to appear as soloist throughout his stay in Stuttgart. This would hardly have been so had he played badly in his début.

A few months later Herbert played in a concert of religious music which occasioned considerable acrimonious dispute. He probably had no part in the strife itself, nor any interest in the "principles" from which it rose; but he was a member of the concert party which was driven from pillar to post in the name of religious propriety.

The question was whether art should conform to denominational fitness. When opportunity arose to continue structural work on the great cathedral in Cologne, the ultramontane Catholics had raised a hue and cry because a Protestant architect was placed in charge. Now a smaller storm blew through Stuttgart, with its orthodox Protestants adopting a similarly narrow view. The Neuer Singverein, directed by a Professor Krüger, wanted to give a concert for the benefit of the building fund of the Friedenskirche, a Protestant church. They planned to give it in the Leonhardskirche, another Protestant church, which had granted the necessary permission. Then the directorate of the latter received the program and objected to two pieces because they were based on Catholic texts. One, incredible though it be, was the famous Bach-Gounod *Ave Maria*; the other was a *Salve Regina* by Ludwig Stark, a founder of the local Conservatory, celebrated as composer and editor. So the good fathers of the Leonhardskirche withdrew permission for the concert even though the receipts would go to a Protestant church in need of aid. The vexed Professor Krüger then turned to the Stiftskirche, where he received the same decision; but finally a compromise allowed the concert to proceed. The concession? The Bach-Gounod song was dropped, and the Stark opus retained. After all, Stark lived and worked in the city; he had influence, and the public must have the "enjoyment of the beautiful atmospheric piece." The program as a whole was a peculiar mixture of instrumental and vocal music, choral and solo. Herbert himself played only an Adagio by Golter-mann and the cello part in Schubert's *Des Tages Weihe*, Op. 146. All the performers acquitted themselves well except one male singer "whom we do not name since he is a dilettante." The little episode was a tempest in a teapot, but it was quickly reported beyond the confines of Stuttgart for the amusement and "edification" of all Germany.[8]

In the summer of 1882 Herbert had one of the greatest experiences of his life. He treasured its memory as long as he lived and recounted the event with passionate enthusiasm. Musicians of a later day can only envy him for what he heard and saw.

An elaborate music festival was held in Zürich the second week of July. Franz Liszt was in attendance and received all the honor due to unsurpassed genius. An extraordinary announcement[9] proclaimed that the "Tonkünstler-Versammlung des Allgemeinen Deutschen Musik-Verein in Zürich" would take place July 8 to 12, and outlined the activities of the five days. The festival director was Fritz Hegar, of Zürich, who had drawn up an enticing schedule of events. Perhaps the biggest single attraction was the performance, on July 9, of Liszt's oratorio, *Die Legende von der heiligen Elisabeth;* but the first chamber music session on July 11 was of more interest to Americans, because Edward MacDowell was invited to play a piano suite of his own composition. MacDowell's appearance, bearing out what Herbert was to write many years later, resulted from Liszt's direct intervention, for the young American had played for the master only a short while before. An augmented orchestra was needed for the festival, and thirty selected members of the Königliche Hofkapelle in Stuttgart as well as a few from the grand ducal orchestra in Karlsruhe were invited to participate. Herbert was among those favored.

The precious memory preserved by Herbert centered on the festival's last day. The morning session, beginning at eleven o'clock, did not end until two, and the musicians and audience were distressed because rain interfered with a prompt luncheon. Some of them, moreover, had to be present, at half past three, at an important *Kaffeegesellschaft* arranged in Liszt's honor by the Bodmer-Trümpler family. It was held on the family estate, "Seeburg," outside Zürich, a location made more inconvenient by the steady shower. One of the invited guests, Herbert was blissfully unconscious, after the party was over, of any difficulties in reaching it; for, though the gathering was social, though Liszt was swamped by idolaters, there was music, too, with the seventy-year-old master playing as if in the first flush of youth.

Marie Breidenstein, a well known contralto and a favorite of Liszt's, sang his *Die Loreley* with the composer at the piano—she, by the way, had acquired some fame for her interpretation of the part of Sophie in *Die Legende von der heiligen Elisabeth,* and in 1880 Liszt had dedicated a short work to her.[10] Then a Herr Dingeldey declaimed Liszt's peculiar and extravagant recitation, *Lenore,* again with the composer at the piano. After this Liszt and Saint-Saëns together played Liszt's four-hand arrangement of his own *Mephisto Waltz* (the second) with electrifying effect. There was more music yet to come, notably Saint-Saëns playing with the violinist, Ysaÿe,[11] but those who followed Liszt must have seemed definitely anticlimactic.

Herbert never forgot this meeting with Liszt or the tremendous effect of the playing with Saint-Saëns. He described it rapturously as he paid a heart-felt tribute to the great composer:

You should have heard that playing. We were afraid every moment the piano would go to smash under Liszt's gigantic hands that came down like very sledge hammers. He played primo and St. Saens secundo, and though St. Saens had the more powerful end of the piano Liszt soon overpowered his bass notes completely.

The occasion was the "Allgemeines Deutsches Musikfest." Liszt was the star guest, a large number of his compositions were played, and the great pianist was fairly worshipped by all present. I was playing cello in the Royal Orchestra of Stuttgart, which had been engaged upon recommendation of Brahms, and never will I forget the impression Liszt made upon my youthful mind.

I see his kindly, beaming face yet, his long white locks, as sitting in a box listening to the orchestra and choruses, he would fall into a short doze, then suddenly wake up again.

Liszt was a grand old man, the idol of all who knew him, generous to the extent of prodigality, and a musician in every fibre of his body. Few people wholly realize how much musical art owes to him, not only for his own direct work, but for that done indirectly in championing worthy composers, notably the great Wagner.[12]

The Zürich music-making gave Herbert also his first opportunity for hearing Ysaÿe, and another novel impression he never forgot. "At Zurich on this occasion I . . . for the first time saw a telephone. Indeed, I will always remember how we marveled at this telephone, and every few minutes set the bell ringing just for the pleasure of hearing the voice at the other end."[12]

Before the trip to Zürich, and regularly afterward, Herbert made frequent appearances as a chamber music artist, playing at concerts sponsored by both the Liederkranz and the Tonkünstlerverein. He appeared successfully in duos, trios, quartets and quintets, sometimes performing works which are still landmarks in the classical repertoire, at other times works of contemporaneous composers which have not survived. This was the mark of progressive musicianship to which he addressed himself zestfully.

Two years after his début as solo cellist Herbert had the rare opportunity of appearing as composer-soloist in a work of large dimensions and major importance. The occasion was the second regular concert of the subscription series (October 23, 1883), and the work was the Suite for cello and orchestra, Op. 3. The piece was splendidly played and received, the composer scoring a double triumph in his dual rôle. One movement struck the public's fancy so forcibly that it had to be repeated.[13]

More than cursory attention must be paid to this suite, Herbert's first known attempt to write in one of the larger forms. Although numbered 3 it is his earliest known work, the preceding works being completely unaccounted for. With it he accomplished at least three things: he proved himself, at the age of twenty-four, a finished composer of skill and substance; he justified Max Seifriz's confidence in his creative ability; he discharged a sentimental indebtedness to his former cello teacher by dedicating the work to the good Professor Cossmann.

The Suite is in five movements: Allegro moderato, Scherzo, Andante, Serenade (Andantino grazioso), Tarantelle. Each movement is rich in melody, sharply rhythmic, finely orchestrated. Each has a distinctive character, maintained from beginning to end. The music is romantic—Herbert never learned or wished to write any other kind— but cleanly so, with none of the contemporary exaggeration of pathos or *Schwärmerei* which was so typical. By exact definition the work is not a suite; that is, it is not a succession of dance movements (except possibly the last). Neither is it in a symphonic form, and the title chosen is as good as any other. The five pieces are concise, well shaped, and most expressive. The Serenade had to be repeated at the first performance, and it has gone on delighting millions ever since. Its easy, mellifluous flow proved to be so popular that its detachment from the whole was foreordained, giving it a separate life (and its composer a separate fame) which may or may not have been advantageous. The "Herbert Serenade," in no way related to his opera, *The Serenade*, is deservedly known the world over; but this excessive popularity has exacted a toll—forgetfulness of the suite whence it came. Other movements are just as good, probably better, than the Serenade, but they have receded in favor of the eloquent trifle. The Scherzo, for instance, is exceedingly effective, with a delicate vigor enhanced by the lightest orchestration. The woodwinds especially are used with great deftness.

The brilliant Tarantelle provides a tumultous finale that is both breath-taking and tuneful.

The solo cello part in this suite gives a fine measure of Herbert's ability as a virtuoso. It exploits the instrument to the utmost and makes exacting demands on the player. For an effective performance a master cellist is needed; and, from the success Herbert had with it, this is what he was. Singing tones in the instrument's most effective range, flashing scales, double stops, octaves—he utilized them all, with idiomatic ease.

The following year, at Christmas time, Herbert was again soloist with the orchestra. He selected a cello concerto by the recently deceased Raff and "once more showed himself to be an outstanding artist on his instrument."[14] A year later, however, a much more important occasion brought the young soloist before the subscription audience: the fourth concert of the season (December 8), at which he introduced his first cello concerto, in D major (unfortunately, still unpublished).

The event, of course, stirred up special interest. Herbert was now well known to the concert public, and it looked forward to his offerings. A local critic wrote, "From the talented young musician we have already received many pearls of his exquisite art," and he went on with enthusiasm: "we are happy to assert that the work performed yesterday can be counted among the best compositions in violoncello literature." He was impressed with the clarity of its structure and with the easy, graceful flow of its melody—qualities which reminded him of the virtues of French music. "Herr Herbert played his Concerto himself and gave us repeated opportunity to admire his large, full, and noble tone and his brilliant technic."[15]

Finished possibly in 1884, more likely in 1885, the first cello concerto was scored for a larger orchestra than the suite and labeled Opus 8. It was also a much more ambitious work, its three movements being broadly conceived as the composer manipulated his materials to fill out an expansive frame. The movements are entitled Allegro con spirito, Andante—Scherzo (Vivace), Allegro fantastico. Special interest attaches to the second, an unusual instance of combining a usual slow movement with a usual scherzo. After the animated middle portion is over, there is a brief return to the slow beginning, the result being a reminder of the slow movement in Tchaikovsky's first Concerto for piano.

As a whole this cello concerto is a laudable achievement. The themes of the first movement are attractive and well developed. Occasionally an episode seems to be a bit protracted; but a variety of orchestral color prevents tediousness, and several climaxes afford ample dynamic contrast. The piece is well integrated. The slow movement is a romantically conceived poem of convincing sentiment, and its scherzo interlude has verve and charm that are quite individual. The third movement is a brilliant, energetic finale which, to be wholly effective, should be tossed off with éclat and abandon. Throughout, the piece has some very fine touches of the woodwinds, and the solo part itself demands all that the cello can give. Like the earlier suite, it requires an unqualified virtuoso for a satisfying performance.

While living with his mother, Herbert received plenty of encouragement from her toward further composition. Occasionally she would submit to him a poem she considered apt for musical treatment. An interesting example is preserved among the Herbert papers in the Library of Congress: a small two-leaf manuscript in his mother's hand bearing two stanzas in German with her own English translation. The author was Carl Weitbrecht (1847–1904), writer and literary historian and an eminent teacher in Stuttgart. On the first page Herbert's mother wrote, "A song for my Vic to compose if he likes." The stanzas run:

Erinnerung

Was am Tage längst vergessen
Kehrt im Traum mir oft zurück,
Altes Leid! vergang'nes Glück!
Was nur je das Herz besessen.

Und erwachend halb mit Bangen
Tröst' ich mich: "Das liegt nun weit!"
Und doch nach der alten Zeit,
Fasst mich heimlich ein Verlangen.

The skillful translation is unusually attractive:

Remembrance

What by day was long forgotten
Comes in dreams to me again.
All that once my heart so treasured,
Ancient rapture! ancient pain!

Then I wake, my heart appeasing
With the thought: "All this is o'er!"
Yet a secret yearning thrills me
For the joys and griefs of yore.

The little manuscript is undated, but it testifies to Fanny Schmid's desire to stimulate her son. (In this particular case he deferred composition apparently for some time, the result being a really charming song that was published in 1915.)

Chamber music playing continued to occupy much of Herbert's time, and over the years in Stuttgart he played many works in many combinations. On one occasion, it is interesting to note, he played a Brahms sonata with Percy Goetschius at the piano.[16] Or he would appear in trios[17] (Mozart, B flat, Schubert, B flat), Beethoven sonatas, quintets, and other works.

Herbert played in string quartets also, but one fact calls for special notice: whenever he played in a string quintet (calling for two cellos), he played the second cello part—evidence that another cellist had priority or seniority over him. This "rival," who may have been the best of friends, was Julius Cabisius (1841–1898). Cabisius, an excellent cellist at the height of his career, had been in Stuttgart since 1877.[18] As an instrumentalist in Stuttgart the younger man had little chance of early promotion. It seems more than probable, therefore, that Cabisius' presence contributed to Herbert's early departure. But first Herbert tried to extend his activities beyond the scope of the usual orchestral and chamber music circles.

He joined the faculty of a new music school which was founded in Stuttgart in the fall of 1885. The Neue Stuttgarter Musikschule announced its opening for October 15, and it solicited the patronage of "Künstler und Dilettanten." Its directors were two pianists, Alwens and Morstatt, and its subjects of study were: piano, singing, violin, violoncello, composition and theory, score reading, choral music, aesthetics, and music history. The prospectus was free and would be sent post-paid. The violin and cello teachers, respectively Künzel and Herbert, apparently did not have to relinquish their posts in the Royal Court Orchestra—they were the only professors listed in the advertisement whose names were preceded by the proud title "Hofmusiker." Herbert held this position through the 1885–1886 season and was announced as a faculty member for the summer semester beginning April 12;[19] but his placid existence in Stuttgart was nearly over, and under the influence of another he would set out to conquer new worlds.

In the summer of 1885 the Royal Opera of Stuttgart found it necessary to freshen its roster. Seeking out young and promising talent, the management early announced that the following season would see "two distinguished youthful powers" on its stage.[20] One was Herr Luria, a bass-baritone from Vienna who had made a good impression in Der fliegende Holländer and L'Africaine. The other was Therese Förster, a dramatic soprano who had recently had great success at the Dresden opera as Aida and had aroused particular enthusiasm with her interpretation of the dusky heroine. Of the two, only the young lady is of interest here.

Therese Förster was born in Vienna in 1861. She showed out-standing musical talent as a child, and her clear girlish voice excited general admiration. She was committed to the studies that are the lot of all beginners. With these behind her she entered the class of the famous artist Marie Luise Meyer-Dustmann, under whose tutelage she rehearsed most of the rôles the great teacher had essayed on the stage of the Vienna opera; and for success so shortly after her student period she owed much to excellent instruction. Besides winning warm approval in Dresden and in Stuttgart, she made guest appearances in Frankfort, Mannheim, and other noted German cities where her impressive voice, dramatic ability, and physical beauty were fully appreciated.

When she came to Stuttgart, Victor Herbert fell immediately des-perately, hopelessly in love with her. Perhaps it was an ideal case of love at first sight, but the young composer-cellist had to be more than usually resourceful in making a contact with the young soprano which would close the gap between orchestra pit and stage. How did he go about it? Very simply—at first with a short formal note of September 1, 1885, beginning,

"Sehr verehrtes Fräulein":

I have learned through Herr Luria that you need an accompanist to rehearse your parts, and I venture to inform you it would afford me very special pleasure if you would accept my services for this purpose. In the pleasant hope of receiving an affirmative answer as soon as possible I remain

> With greatest esteem
> Respectfully
> Your
> VICTOR HERBERT
> *Kgl. Hofmusiker*
> Archivstr. 15, II[21]

The answer was prompt enough but, alas, in the negative: Fräulein Förster already had arranged for an accompanist. On September 7 Herbert wrote to her again, not withdrawing his suggestion, but pro-posing an enlargement to it. Quoting Akiba ben Joseph, the ancient Jewish philosopher, to the effect that there is nothing new under the sun, the young man said that surely, at some time or other, a singer must have had two rehearsal assistants—need had made him inventive, and, like a drowning man, he clutched at a straw. Then he begged for permission to call on her, for he could plead much better in person; in this pleasant hope ("it is unfortunately my last") he would remain her respectfully and wholly devoted Victor Herbert.[21]

In a short time Therese's reserve was gone, and so, apparently, was the first accompanist. The few remaining letters between Victor and his idol indicate a fond intimacy in which mutual affection and music were the staples of their daily life. He was miserable away from her, and a twenty-four-hour separation was a torture. He also had the temerity to watch over her career, to listen for constant improvement, to select songs suited to her voice and temperament. On one occasion he wrote that she had sung beautifully the night before, that the most dangerous places had been smoothly done, especially the phrase

For the first time, he told her, it was perfect, and she had every right to be satisfied with herself—as he observed she was. On the following day he was going to select some *Lieder* by Schubert and Schumann for her, and they would run them through in the evening.

When Therese left Stuttgart to make a guest appearance elsewhere, as in Mannheim, the young man ardently followed her every move. Naturally he delighted in her success; but beyond that he observed her fellow artists in an operatic cast, knowing who could help her and who could not. On one occasion he wrote: "I am very happy that your partner in the Dutchman [i.e., *Der fliegende Holländer*] is the baritone Knapp. He is a very good artist who will be able to improve your own performance."[21]

Again, when Therese was out of town, her lover would go to one of the city's leading restaurants and write her the news of the day. "I have just come from the Opera and am sitting in Hiller's . . . The singer Schaumann was simply terrible. Not a clear tone the whole evening, always ¼ to ½ a tone too low . . ."[21]

On another occasion he tried to concentrate on music, was diverted at once to love, and then, foolishly happy, recollected that his thoughts had strayed. This, too, was written in Hiller's: "And now to business! You sang very beautifully yesterday, never before so straight into my heart. I was so happy in thinking the while 'she who is singing is your kind and loving Therese.' Then my heart leaped madly, and if ever in my life I realized how much I loved you . . . it was yesterday. Oh dear! that wasn't business, after all."[21] It was much more essential than business, and the two of them knew it.

The year passed rapidly. Both the artists were busy, both constantly improving, and both presumably looking for greater opportunities. Herbert felt that Therese was not sufficiently appreciated in the Stuttgart Opera, and he was not hesitant in saying so. When an inferior singer like Schaumann gave general disappointment, vexing the management as well as the public, Herbert wrote: "I am not sorry for the Stuttgarters, for they deserve nothing better, and certainly not you."[21] Youthful ambition was straining at the leash—an invariable phenomenon when talent and energy combine forces.

The leash snapped in the summer of 1886. The Metropolitan Opera Company of New York had finished its first season of opera in German. It needed worthy recruits and fresh blood for the coming season. Three men—Edmond C. Stanton, Walter Damrosch, Frank Damrosch—were charged to scour Europe for the proper material. After visiting Munich and the Starnberger See, Frank Damrosch found himself in Stuttgart whither he had gone to investigate a tenor. This tenor failed to impress, but the young New Yorker encountered Fräulein Förster whom he considered a genuine discovery. When he visited her in her hotel, he enjoyed another new acquaintance, the singer's fiancé, Victor Herbert. Damrosch was looking for singers and wanted Therese. The betrothed pair wanted joint employment in America so they might marry. The youthful impressario, only twenty-seven himself, was soon convinced that he wanted both of them for the New York house and engaged the two forthwith: Therese to sing, Victor to play in the orchestra.[22]

So Therese Förster and Victor Herbert were married in Vienna on August 14, 1886,[23] and came to America in the autumn. New friends, new customs, new triumphs awaited them, as well as experiences which were truly bewildering in their kaleidoscopic variety.

3

Artist par Excellence

JUST a fortnight before leaving Europe, Herbert went to Vienna for a day or so. Therese stayed home in Stuttgart, doubtless preparing feverishly for the adventure in America, and so her husband paid the respects to her family and friends. Her sister, Elise, was immediately pressed into service as a shopping expert, for the young musician was determined to take his bride a lovely gift. With Elise he visited several modistes; but his critical, prejudiced eye found nothing suitable, and he was glad enough to leave the choice to the agreeable sister. He wrote to Therese on September 29 that he would inform her on the following day of the time of his return; now he had many things to attend to and could write no more.[1]

Then came two weeks of preparation for the voyage—which was far from pleasant. The good ship *Saale* left Bremen on the 13th, touched at Southampton on the 14th and Cherbourg on the 15th, then headed for the open sea and an extraordinary siege of foul weather which sapped the strength of the thousand-odd passengers sailing into New York on Sunday October 24.[2]

The *Saale* carried several personages to the Metropolitan Opera. Easily the most prominent were the conductor Anton Seidl and his wife, the singer Auguste Seidl-Kraus. Others were Silvia Franconi, Wilhelmina Mayer, and Rudolph von Milde.[3] When an enterprising reporter from the New York *Herald* called on Herr Seidl Monday morning some of the singers were already there paying respects to the maestro; but the chief topic of conversation was still the storm at sea. The artists had not yet recovered from exhaustion and alarm.

Then the reporter went to the Belvedere House at Fourth Avenue and Eighteenth Street to seek out Therese Herbert-Förster. Her husband, as an obscure member of the orchestra, had none of the glamour

26

attached to a newly engaged prima donna; but the scribe was completely smitten by Therese and her charms. He found her a striking beauty, German in type but delicate in feature, with luminous blue eyes and a crown of thick blond hair. She had a fine, commanding presence which could lend considerable *vraisemblance* to the rôle of the Queen of Sheba, who was supposed to be both compelling and seductive. Frau Krämer-Wiedl, her predecessor in the part, had left much to be desired. The newcomer told the reporter that the management had selected this rôle for her, though she had never done it before, and that she personally wished her début might have been as Aida. The admiring interviewer shuddered at the disfigurement that would be required to transform the Austrian beauty into the dusky African heroine; and he spiced his story with this observation.

Therese—youthful, confident, radiant—was joining the still infant Metropolitan Opera. The season 1886–1887 was only its fourth; yet some of the most illustrious names in operatic history were already on its roster, including Max Alvary, Albert Niemann, Lilli Lehmann, and Marianne Brandt. The company was German, and all operas were sung in German. Its repertoire was limited; but it was the American center of opera activity and was a busy, thriving organization that challenged the leading establishments of Europe. The New York *Tribune* of March 7, 1886, had summarized the energetic season of 1885–1886 in a manner which today seems fresh and novel, giving a picture more detailed, and consequently more penetrating, than can be found in the 1950's.

In the regular series of presentations only nine operas had been given; but they totaled fifty-two performances. Goldmark's *Die Königin von Saba* was by far the most popular, being staged no fewer than fifteen times; Wagner's *Die Meistersinger von Nürnberg* and *Rienzi* came next with eight and seven performances respectively. The least popular was *Carmen,* which audiences looked at only twice. No Verdi opera—in fact, no Italian opera at all—was performed, although *Aida* was prepared and "ready to go."

Of course the *Tribune* mentioned the great hopes and expectations held for the following season, which were to be realized for the most part—fourteen operas achieving a total of sixty-one performances. The program was better balanced, too, for the opera staged most frequently, *Tristan und Isolde,* was on the boards only eight times.[4]

The two conductors who functioned in both these seasons as well as later were Anton Seidl and Walter Damrosch. Seidl (1850–1898), senior by some years, was a genius in opera and symphony alike. He had studied at the Conservatory in Leipzig, won the favor of Hans Richter, served as secretary and assistant to Wagner himself. He idolized the master of Bayreuth and spread the Wagnerian gospel as ardently as humanly possible. He was handsome and hearty, with a personality that attracted multitudes of admirers. He offered the rare instance of a conductor both loved and respected by his men.

Seidl and Herbert quickly became the closest of friends. They had much in common—musical enthusiasms, warm natures, liking for social intercourse, and wives who were professional singers. Moreover, the helpfulness shown by the older man cemented the firmer the union between them. His early death, at the age of forty-seven, was a tragedy of national dimensions, for his art and his name had kindled the imagination of millions. On this sad occasion the greatest musicians of the day poured out glowing tributes; but none of them excelled Herbert's in eloquence, sincerity, or understanding, which took as its point of departure Seidl's characteristics as leader of German opera in New York City:

When I first came to the United States, in 1886, I had known Anton Seidl only by his great reputation as a Wagner disciple, then so widespread in Europe. He was at that time in the second year of his work at the Metropolitan Opera House. The musicians comprising his orchestra had readily come to appreciate his profound knowledge of Bayreuth tradition, alike of the stage and the orchestra. They had found in Seidl a man thoroughly imbued with Wagner's ideas, both in the general conception and in the smallest detail of each opera. He fairly bristled with animated energy, and was ever alert to right the minutest of errors. His thorough knowledge of this work, which with him was a life passion, enabled Seidl to make incredible progress with both players and singers in the preparation of his superb productions. The great presentation of *Tristan and Isolde* at the Metropolitan Opera House in the year mentioned was accomplished with but five rehearsals with the orchestra, including the one set apart for correction of the orchestral parts.

But our conductor never took to himself any credit for such remarkable achievements. Always anxious to ascribe honor where honor was due, he attributed this, the greatest success of the season, to perfection of discipline in the orchestra, the ready perception of its members and their fine routine in orchestral work. To his soloists he was ever anxious to accord a full measure of praise. In 1886, for instance, the principals included Lehmann, Auguste Kraus, Marianne Brandt, Niemann, Robinson, Anton Schott, Alvary and Herbert-Foerster, whose artistic contributions to these great operatic performances were graciously recognized by the conductor, his characteristic modesty invariably placing them and the orchestra before himself.

The musicians frequently saw that the music affected Seidl most profoundly. He was a man of deep emotion. Certain passages in *Siegfried* and the wonderful closing scene of *Tristan* always made him cry like a child, so that by the time the curtain had dropped he would be in a state of emotional collapse.

Seidl was universally admired and loved by the members of his orchestra. He never showed the faintest trace of false pride. His players were his companions, his helpers; he was simply one of them. It was through this strong bond of fraternity that he came to acquire a powerful personal influence over the instrumentalists which was entirely distinct from the musical magnetism exerted in rehearsals and public performances. This all-powerful, impelling yet unfathomable power of control imperiously commanded his followers in the orchestra by first awaking their entire interest and then spurring them on to efforts that they could make under the bâton of no other master. The graceful, incisive, clean-cut movements of his stick were intelligible at all times. And, for his part, Seidl always relied implicitly upon the quick perception of his musicians, never wasting time in unnecessary explanations of what was to be brought out in this bar, or avoided in that. We always knew by a glance from his eye just what was expected of us.

Mr. Seidl was a man little given to words. As it was once so aptly remarked of von Moltke's position in the realm of scientific warfare, so it may be said of Anton Seidl as a musician and conductor, that he was "der grosse Schweiger" (the great silent). Yet he never failed to say the right thing in the right place, and many anecdotes are related of his quick wit and dry humor. When he talked it was because he had something to say; and as many of his friends can attest, he was exceptionally apt in his remarks.

Some years since, after a performance of his orchestra at Brighton Beach, a few of us sat down towards midnight for a lunch with Mr. Seidl in his favorite café. There were present in the little party several musicians, and among the enthusiastic amateurs of music a prominent New York manufacturer, who was an ardent admirer of Italian opera. For twoscore years or more had this gentleman faithfully attended all of the Italian opera presentations in New York; he had fraternized with all the famous artists who sallied forth from their Milan stronghold to make conquests of New World audiences. As one would naturally expect, during the course of the evening he turned the drift of conversation upon the subject of his favorite hobby. Niemann was present, and, if I mistake not, there may have been another singer or two in the little gathering. All save Seidl had something to say about the decadence of the ultramontane school of opera. Finally, when the subject seemed to have been exhausted, the conductor made a few remarks.

He was known to be very fair in his judgment of men and their works. He admired all that was good in Italian operatic music, but was ready to condemn what was rubbish. Many of the singers from sunny Italy he regarded as great; Campanini's glorious voice and superb vocal art were his especial admiration. But his profound regard for the eternal fitness of things appeared to instigate this brief succinct expression of his views on the topic under discussion.

"In the property room of the Metropolitan Opera House, gentlemen, there is a helmet." He paused for a moment, reflectively puffed at his cigar, and then resumed: "It may be tarnished now, but a year or two ago it was brightly burnished. If you were to hunt it up you would find that this specimen is much like other helmets save for the 'Schwannritter' emblem which it bears. It was made for *Lohengrin*, and my dear friend Campanini wore it in a truly magnificent performance of the rôle. Yet if you were to find that helmet to-day you would discover that in addition to the prescribed dimensions and insignia of this piece of knightly headgear Mr. Campanini had put on a blue plume, probably three feet in length. That, my dear gentlemen, is Italian opera."

Seidl's death was the pathetic termination of a career which had just fairly realized its highest ambitions. He had just come into the acquisition of all that he hoped for. Strong influence had secured for Seidl a substantially permanent orchestra. This was a well-deserved recognition of his merits and talents. He had the Philharmonic Society, and the Metropolitan Opera House German productions. He had the promise of regular work at Bayreuth festivals; and a permanent engagement at Covent Garden, in London. And in the midst of all this, the ripe harvest of a busy life, Seidl was stricken down.[5]

With Seidl on the podium the Metropolitan opened its 1886–1887 season on November 8 with Carl Goldmark's *Die Königin von Saba*, a spectacular opera combining musical lushness with the splendor of oriental settings, and an excellent piece with which to start the year. It was familiar—there had been fifteen presentations the year before —it was modern, it was decidedly effective. The pageantry of the stage gave added inducement for pageantry in the audience as society flocked to the great . house on Thirty-ninth Street. One reporter, excitedly surveying the female auditors, was convinced that the Queen of Sheba had lived too soon, that the gowns and jewels and flowers he beheld were beyond the dreams of the eastern ruler. The auditorium provided a fitting background for what he saw. The great expanse of white and gold was bathed in soft illumination, and the color and design of the vari-tinted robes added a radiancy which "paralyzed the senses and reduced reason."[6] Outside the house, as the crowd gathered, the effect was similar though probably less breathtaking. Flashing electric lights threw into relief the jam of traffic and press of throng. It seemed, indeed, "as if every stable in the city, private and public, had turned out its full line of equipages" to bring the faithful back to their accustomed haunt.[7]

On the stage a gala performance was effectively produced. Careful rehearsing of singers and orchestra and the studied plotting of the *mise en scène* assured the achievement of a memorable presentation. No more impressive opera performance, reported the New York *Times* the next day, had ever been seen in the New World. Into this maelstrom of glory and glamour Therese Herbert-Förster injected herself most auspiciously, not at all intimidated by the responsibility of a new rôle. Reviews of her appearance were laudatory to such a degree that newspaper readers had the right to conclude that another vocal immortal was demanding recognition.

Metropolitan music critics in the 1880's, though well known and with partisan followings, wrote without benefit of by-lines—a custom which endured for many years. Presumably the regular critics reported personally on their various assignments; but if they ever sent an assistant or substitute to cover a performance the reader was none the wiser. It is hazardous, therefore, to attribute particular reviews to certain individuals, even though the temptation to do so occurs often enough. It is known that 1886 found H. T. Finck with the *Evening Post*, H. E. Krehbiel with the *Tribune*, W. J. Henderson with the *Times*, J. T. Jackson with the *World*, and Albert Steinberg with the *Herald*;[8] whether they wrote all the music reviews their papers published is another matter. In any case they were practically unanimous in praising Therese's Metropolitan début.

The *Times* was a bit reserved, but positive. It said that she was received with favor, and that her mezzo-soprano voice had strength and resonance. It commented on her physical attractiveness and archly admitted that only now was it possible to understand how the Queen of Sheba (Therese's rôle) had captured the love of Solomon's courtier, Assad. The *Tribune* reviewer—was it Krehbiel?—cast reserve to the winds and forthrightly described Therese as "a newcomer and a most welcome addition to the Metropolitan Company. She was the *Queen*, and the first pleasure that she caused was due to the fact that her features saved the spectators the unpleasant necessity which they have been under heretofore, of accepting the beauty of the Arabian charmer who plays such sad havoc with Assad's mind, on the *lucus a non lucendo* principle. Frau Herbert-Förster is handsome; more than that, she is really a fine dramatic singer, one who will make her compatriots look sharply to their laurels. And she is an actress of decided gifts. Mr. Stanton and the public are to be congratulated on her acquisition."

The *Musical Courier* had a reviewer in the house who reported similarly on November 10. The judgment of this journal a decade later must be open to question; but on Therese's début it had no reservations. She was "a perfect revelation," a Queen "both handsome and stately" whose acting was dignified and impressive. Best of all was the encomium on her voice: "a rich, dramatic soprano, of fine quality and sympathetic, pure timbre, and her enunciation, as well as her phrasing, is of that finished and artistic kind which denotes the true and cultivated musician."

So the youthful Therese brilliantly passed the test of an opening night in a new rôle—in a work which the cognoscenti practically knew by heart. Four days later she had a more difficult task when she sang the part of Aida.

Verdi's classic opera had been rehearsed and prepared in the preceding season, but had not reached production. The November 12 presentation, in which Therese appeared, was the Metropolitan's first of one of the greatest of all operas. This, too, is an exotic piece, the African settings and Egyptian ceremony easily rivaling the court of Israel and Solomon's glory. The stage designers capitalized on their opportunity. Their *Queen of Sheba* had been reported as the most splendid spectacle ever seen in the New World; only half a week later the entirely new *Aida* was rapturously referred to as the most elaborate and superb *mise en scène* ever looked upon in New York City.[9] As a matter of fact, great expectations had been raised by rumors and unverified reports, and the audience swept into the hall in joyful anticipation. They were not disappointed. The astonished *Tribune* critic—again, perhaps, Krehbiel—admitted he had not been ready for the "extraordinary sumptuousness" the stage revealed. The images seen that night, he said, stood first in picturesqueness and scenic grandeur among the operas the city had been privileged to hear. It would be rash to attempt a description of the stage and the costumes, but surely "the glory of Goldmark's Solomon pales before the magnificence of Verdi's Pharaoh." Seeming to foresee the products of Hollywood around 1950, he added: "And the brilliancy of the spectacle extenuates, if it does not justify the departures from strict archeological accuracy." Though tremendously impressed with the stage pageantry, he did not neglect the music, which he found finely interpreted throughout. Seidl could conduct Italian opera, as well as Wagner, appreciatively, and Therese "intensified the good impression made on the opening night."

Other critics, hearing Therese for the second time, were just as cordial, although with an occasional remonstrance. The most enthusiastic review appeared in the *World,* which said: "The second appearance of Mme. Herbert-Forster [sic] confirms the very favorable impression she created on Monday night as the Queen of Sheba. The music of 'Aïda' is well suited to her voice and she sang with fervor and true dramatic feeling. Her singing of the great aria and prayer at the end of the first act won her enthusiastic applause and three recalls. In conjunction with Fräulein Brandt (Amneris), she also received a similar compliment after the great duel [!duet] in the second act. Indeed Mme. Herbert-Forster has already secured a firm place in the hearts of Metropolitan audiences."

The enthusiasm of the reporter from the *Sun* was modified by two reservations: he thought that Therese's acting needed more experience; and he found that her voice lost its color in delivering tones of lower range. However, far from altering his opinion of her vocal abilities, she "confirmed the good impression she had made on the occasion of her début. She is already a singer of excellent accomplishments, and in a few years, when she has matured, in an histrionic sense, she ought to take a front rank among prime donne. For her voice, colorless as it is in its lower register, is one of uncommon strength, endurance and brilliancy. Frau Foerster sings with feeling and occasionally with passion, and she seemed besides to have had admirable vocal training, as was seen in her skillful use of mezzo and sotto voce effects. Her success with the audience was complete."

The reviewer for the *Times* expressed an opinion so different that he might have been listening to another singer. Yet he was not unfriendly, simply persuaded to point out Therese's failure to meet his own conception of the rôle and to suggest where she would probably give more pleasure as her career continued. "Frau Herbert-Förster, who portrayed Aïda, shared with Fräulein Brandt, at those stages of the action in which the two women are beheld together, the honors of the night. It cannot be conceded that Frau Herbert-Förster was an ideal Aïda; in her two solos, in which as much *mezza voce* as *piena voce* singing is called for, there was no medium between a bad pianissimo and a vigorous forte, and throughout the opera the nicer shades of expression were habitually missed from the lady's delineation. Frau Herbert-Förster, however, revealed the possession of a voice of considerable strength and vibrancy, and showed that in a more dramatic rôle, demanding less lyric and histrionic finesse, she might easily rouse her hearers to enthusiasm."

Singing the first Aida in Metropolitan Opera history, albeit in German, was a great honor that Therese carried well; but she did not rest on this alone. Three more important rôles fell to her that season, and in each of them she won praise. Some critics confessed irritation with her performances, objecting chiefly to her failure to develop more rapidly in acting ability. Others continued to find satisfaction in her appearances, and said so. When she sang Elsa in *Lohengrin* on December 15, the *Times* critic remarked that "she supplied an intelligent delineation of Wagner's heroine, and sang with considerable power." He was even more pleased when, substituting for Lilli Lehmann, she impersonated Irene in Wagner's *Rienzi* on February 12, 1887: ". . . yesterday's representation showed no falling off from its forerunners. Frau Herbert-Foerster's fresh and vibrant voice coming forth with abundant effect in the finale of the second act, and the songstress meeting the requirements of the score quite acceptably at the remaining stages of the action." The man from the *Herald*, ever a connoisseur of pulchritude, proclaimed that Therese was an admirable Irene who sang beautifully and looked very handsome. And when she sang Elizabeth in *Tannhäuser* on February 21 the *World* was moved to comment that she "was warmly applauded for her singing of the song in the beginning of the second act, 'Dich Theuer [sic] Halle.' She was in fine voice, and was heard to great advantage in the rôle of the lovely Thuringian princess."

During that season at the Metropolitan Therese made twelve appearances in five operas: Sheba and Aida, four times each; Elsa, twice; and Irene and Elizabeth, once. The *Musical Courier* of February 23 carried her portrait on its cover and supplied a commentary which seems wholly veracious. Of the Viennese belle it said: "Her charming appearance and artistic temperament bear witness to the truth of the reputation the ladies of the old Kaiserstadt have for beauty and vivacity. . . . Her style is queenly, her singing shows fine culture and her general appearance is prepossessing in the extreme."

Then something happened, or began to happen, which led to Therese's almost immediate retirement from the Metropolitan Opera company and, within a few years, her retirement from professional singing. Scarcely the slightest hint of the cause can be found. Her youth, her personality, her beauty, her voice had been lavishly praised by astute critics. There was every reason to expect a notable career in which the artist would gain steadily in maturity and finesse. As the public became familiar with her powers, it also recognized her limitations (all singers have them); but her first year's engagement had justified, it would seem, indefinite retention. Yet that season was practically her only one at the Metropolitan: she was on the roster for 1887–1888 but made only one appearance—on February 14, when she again sang Elsa in *Lohengrin*. Then she was through, though she sang successfully elsewhere for several years. Her early departure remains unexplained.

Meanwhile Victor Herbert was obscurely buried in the orchestra pit. His introduction to America had been very different. Fortunately placed in the Metropolitan orchestra, he was still only one of a multitude of orchestra players and faced an uncertain future of anonymity and modest income. Players at the German opera, earning from $40 to $50 a week, were better situated than their colleagues in theaters or other ensembles who averaged from $25 to $30; but at best the work was seasonal, and social amenities were a drain upon the pocketbook.[10] As a class they were looked at askance, and probably with great envy; they were considered as spendthrifts, known to be careless in business, reputed to be generous drinkers, and accepted as the warmest of friends.

Café life was popular in New York, in a way which has long since disappeared, and musicians flocked to colorful restaurants where food was choice and beer plentiful. It was particularly true of the German colony in which the Herberts established themselves immediately. It must be remembered, however, that the cafés and restaurants were not drinking places as such; they were meeting places for natural and necessary intercourse, the equivalent of clubs, the center of professional coteries and artistic confraternity. They exerted an irresistible attraction upon Herbert and his wife, especially in their younger days, and offered unequaled opportunities for meeting the musical élite of the city. James Gibbons Huneker's autobiography, *Steeplejack,* affords wonderful glimpses of these animated cafés, wherein he began his life-long friendship with the Herberts. He himself had come to New York to live early in 1886, so that his career there was really coëval with the Irish composer's.

Huneker, that unique connoisseur of both music and musicians, that startlingly original critic of music-drama-art-literature, loved his cafés and the gifted persons he found in them. One of his favorite haunts was Lienau's, on Fourteenth Street east of Fourth Avenue. Facing famous Steinway Hall, it was restaurant, bar, and aesthetic salon all in one. A room in the rear sheltered a piano where, to regale their friends, artists of the caliber of Joseffy, Friedheim, and Rosenthal would play to perfection. It was here that Huneker found the Herberts as well as William Steinway, Anton Seidl and wife, Wilhelmj, Scharwenka, Theodore Thomas, and others—an assemblage he referred to as "the very cream of the musical aristocracy."[11] Other eating places of equal appeal were Lüchow's, only a few doors removed from Lienau, Billy Moulds' café (celebrated for bean soup, free lunch, and no tips), and Werle's, another artistic center of wide renown. Living near Werle's, Huneker finally found himself in a house at Seventeenth Street and Irving Place "where at any time before midnight the sound of pianos, violins, violoncellos, even the elegiac flute might be heard, and usually played by skilled professionals. . . . Across the street was . . . the pretty Washington Irving house, and at another corner lived Victor Herbert. From the vine-covered entrance of Werle's I often heard string music made by Victor Herbert, Max Bendix, . . . and others."[12]

Free (of dues) they might be, but these cafés presented their own problems of acceptance. Huneker knew what he was talking about when he wrote: "In New York, as in Paris, the café is the poor man's club. It is also a rendezvous for newspaper men, musicians, artists, Bohemians generally. It is the best stamping-ground for men of talent. Ideas circulate. Brain tilts with brain. Eccentricity must show cause or be jostled."[13] Herbert was neither roistering nor loafing during the hours spent in the stimulating cafés. To be sure they were enjoyable; but they were also soul-stirring, pricking the imagination to heated activity, enlivening the artistic temper, forming rich friendships based on musical and intellectual sympathies.

Huneker took special note when Herbert appeared among the cellists of the opera orchestra, but knew him for a few months at least only as the husband of that "handsome Viennese woman, who sang with a sumptuous voice."[14] He had to make his own way, independent of his wife's charms and talents. One of the first things both husband and wife did upon arriving in this country was to acquire professional cards denoting their respective occupations. Herbert's card, pointing at once toward a separate career, announced that he was the solo cellist from "the Royal Orchestra of his Majesty the King of Würtemberg" and that he was ready to give instruction on his own instrument as well as in vocal music and harmony.

In a surprisingly short time Herbert was brought before the public as composer and performer; and in both capacities he made an impressive début. On Saturday January 8, 1887, Walter Damrosch conducted the third concert of the Symphony Society in the Metropolitan Opera House. The usual public rehearsal had occurred the day before. Two soloists were featured: Herbert, playing the Andante, Serenade, and Tarantelle from his Suite, Op. 3; and the excellent pianist Adele Aus der Ohe, playing Chopin's Concerto in E minor.

Critical response to Herbert's appearance was all that could be desired. The sober *Tribune,* obviously accepting him as a typical German artist, said that he proved himself "a good, solid musical violoncellist, one who produces a fine volume of tone and plays without the extravagant sentimentality which so many of his colleagues affect." It lavished no great praise on the Suite, but neither did it disparage it, resting content with the phrase that it exposed "a refined fancy."[15]

More enthusiastic, yet not extravagant, was the report of the *Herald's* critic, who was captivated by Herbert's music and playing. The three movements of the Suite, he thought, showed considerable invention and were "distinguished" by "good writing." Observing that Herbert had made an impression such as few cellists had made before him, he explained why this was so: "His style is infinitely more easy and graceful than that of most 'cello players, just as his tone is more liquid, more melodious and of a more noble quality, simply because he never forces the tonal capacity of his instrument beyond its natural limits."[16]

A few days after his fine début with the Symphony Society Herbert found himself in a situation quite common in the musical life of sixty-odd years ago; in fact it has not disappeared today. Budding aspirants for solo honors—boys and girls, vocalists and instrumentalists—would prepare a recital program, hire a hall, and engage a mature artist to share the program. On January 11, 1887, Augusta M. Fischer, youthful pianist from Brooklyn, appeared in Steinway Hall, and with her was Victor Herbert. The latter played beautifully, "with admirable technic and a breadth and sweetness of tone that are seldom found combined in one and the same artist." Among his offerings were two pieces of his own, a quiet *Berceuse* and an effective *Polonaise*. Augusta did not fare so well, one reviewer suggesting that if Anton Rubinstein merited a mark of 95 for playing, the girl might receive between 52 and 53![17]

Herbert had promptly become active and successful his first winter in New York. His wife had completed a satisfactory season at the Metropolitan. In the summer of 1887 they returned to Europe for a visit and some music making, but the extent of their activities is a closed book. The only thing certain is that Therese sang at the Vienna opera,[18] and that they were ready to sail back to America, from Bremen, in the middle of August.[19] They sent word ahead that both were "prepared to accept engagements here."

Again in New York, Herbert immediately displayed his characteristic energy and briefly engaged in an activity which carried promise of things to come. He formed an orchestra for entertainment purposes only and appeared with it in different places. The New York public first heard this sizable ensemble in Koster and Bial's famous concert hall on Twenty-third Street, an institution quite superior in the variety of offered pleasures. It was built on German models, featuring generous musical programs and a refreshment service second to none. Opening in the spring of 1879, it had met with success at once and drawn such a clientele that expanded quarters were quickly needed. Musical artists and entertainers of top rank were engaged. If the music was not profound, it was brilliantly and unforgettably done, by artists like Wilhelmj and Remenyi. The hall became celebrated in two continents and was one of the important shrines for the city's visitors.[20]

After "the wholly respectable attraction of Victor Herbert and his orchestra of forty"[21] won applause at Koster and Bial's September 12 to 17, they traveled to Boston and gave a highly successful concert of light character at Music Hall. The popular prices of ten, twenty, thirty cents resulted in a large audience that gave approval to a Sunday evening program of extraordinary variety. The manager of the Music Hall, Austin by name, advertised the occasion as the "first appearance in this city of the latest New York success, Mr. Victor [photograph] Herbert, the eminent European Conductor and Cello Soloist to His Majesty the King of Wurtemberg, and his MAJESTIC ORCHESTRE INTER-

NATIONALE" composed of forty solo instrumentalists. They were to play "the most popular repertoire ever presented at any Sunday evening concert in this city," and the program confirms the superlative statement. Herbert appeared as both conductor and soloist, a practice he was to maintain until he became the leader of a genuine symphony orchestra a decade later.[22]

This first excursion into musical entertainment was short-lived. Perhaps the recruitment and maintenance of an orchestra proved too troublesome; possibly the number of engagements was too small. In any case the *Musical Courier* soon announced that Herbert had abandoned his concerts at Koster and Bial's and was seeking engagements elsewhere. He was also ready to accept a few cello pupils, and anyone interested could reach him through the magazine. In the same issue Herbert inserted a professional notice: "Mr. VICTOR HERBERT, Violoncello Virtuoso, will accept engagements for Concerts and Solo work; also a limited number of Pupils . . ." Evidently he was not prepared to concentrate on the cello to the exclusion of most other activity.[23]

Meanwhile Therese Herbert found her way to a new and quite possibly a more congenial stage for 1887–1888. She sang opera at the Thalia Theatre, which was completely German. Drama, comedy, and opera all were given here, and the achievements were notable. The season just opening, the last under the management of Gustav Amberg, was particularly brilliant. The New York stage annalist, Odell, ventures to say that the season was "generally conceded to be the most brilliant sequence of stars and plays ever given here in German, or, perhaps, in any other language."[24]

The opera season opened on October 17 and extended through December. The audience was German, persons too poor to pay the Metropolitan prices but probably far more discriminating than the society folk uptown. The first production of the year was Verdi's *Der Troubadour*, in which Therese sang the part of Leonora opposite Heinrich Bötel doing Manrico. Bötel was the featured star of the season. He had been brought to New York from the Stadttheater in Hamburg and contributed much to the Thalia's happy flourish.

Therese and Bötel made a fortunate stage couple, appearing together often and arousing the spectators to real enthusiasm. On December 8 they both sang in Meyerbeer's *Die Hugenotten*, as Valentin and Raoul respectively, and received tumults of applause, even bravos. This pair was simply splendid, reported the *Herald*; and, as for Therese, "she sang superbly as Valentin. Her fine presence, her impassioned delivery and intelligent acting were well worthy of the recognition they received from the large audience."

This was the season in which Herbert made another début in New York—as a chamber music player. He joined three other young men to form the New York String Quartet. All were excellent musicians, and saw an opportunity to provide something lacking in the city's musical life. The others were Sam Franko, originator and first violin of the group, Henry Boewig, second violin, and Ludwig Schenck, viola. Franko, of an astonishingly musical family which has served America well for three generations, was an adventurous spirit. He had served six whole weeks in the Boston Symphony Orchestra when Gericke was its conductor, only to drop out when the rehearsals became unbearably dull. He admitted that Gericke gave performances which were finely nuanced and full of subtleties; but they were dispirited and lifeless and conducive to boredom. He found his opinion corroborated by Herbert who loved to refer to the Boston band as the "Viennese Ladies' Orchestra."[25]

In chamber music the very essence of music seems to be brought out in highest relief. Perfection is never achieved, and practice is always insufficient; new ideals must be formulated, of musical values, of cooperation, of blending musical personalities. Probably the most satisfying of all forms of music-making, it is also the most thankless. Individual interpretation and virtuosity must be cast aside; so, too, must thoughts of wild applause and lucrative returns. With respect to the last consideration Franko, testifying to the generosity of the house of Steinway, confessed that his quartet gave all its concerts in Steinway Hall and had to pay not a cent of rent—furthermore, he even persuaded the firm to furnish the programs.[26]

It is not strange, therefore, that New York seldom heard first-class chamber music concerts, and that such as it did were practically never limited to string quartets. The fare would have been entirely too strict, too ponderous, for even the elite public to take. Almost always variety was supplied by assisting artists, or members of the ensemble offered solos. When the New York String Quartet gave its first concert of the 1887–1888 season on December 8 in Steinway Hall, two assisting artists shared the program: Max Vogrich, pianist, who played Schumann's F sharp minor Sonata, and Charles Kaiser, who sang several songs by Grieg. The string players offered Grieg's String Quartet in G minor and, Vogrich taking the place of a violinist, Rubinstein's Piano Quartet, Op. 66.

The reviews were critical, appreciative, and judicious. The *Sun* asserted that for musicians no treat was rarer than a good concert of chamber music, that the men played well together, that the "cultivated listeners" derived "no little gratification." The Romanza in the Grieg Quartet was singled out as specially satisfying, but lacking in precision in the striking of chords. The *Tribune* seemed to echo this sentiment, attributing some of its dissatisfaction to "the leader's want of incisiveness and breadth." Nevertheless the group had high capabilities, and the program was well selected, "dignified in every part." The *Times* very definitely found the concert a success, and the *Herald* and the *Musical Courier* were particularly pleased with Herbert's rendition of the solo passages allotted to the cello.

Two more concerts were given by the New York String Quartet that season—both affording real musical satisfaction. Among the major works performed were: Haydn's String Quartet, Op. 64, No. 5; Mendelssohn's String Quintet, Op. 87 (with Nahan Franko); Schumann's String Quartet, Op. 41, No. 1; Goldmark's Suite for cello and piano, Op. 11 (played by Herbert and that fabulous pianist, Rafael Joseffy); and Rubinstein's Sonata for cello and piano, Op. 18 (played by Herbert and Conrad Ansorge).[27]

Herbert, of course, had no idea of curtailing his solo activities; and he had an exceptional opportunity for these late in 1887. On Saturday afternoon December 10, he played his own violoncello Concerto at one of Theodore Thomas's matinées for young people. Thomas, so important in the development of musical America, was leading two series of concerts with his own orchestra: a regular symphonic series, and the matinées for the younger generation, which were considered by some to be superior to the symphonic series in freshness, novelty, and general attractiveness; and Herbert's appearance was a fortunate event. As usual his playing was more than satisfactory, although the *Tribune* critic thought he had been heard earlier to better advantage. More interesting was the critical reaction to the Concerto, which New York had not heard before. Even the *Tribune* admitted that it deserved praise: "It is neither meretricious nor commonplace in thought and workmanship." The equally authoritative *Times* was pleased to say that, "though far from being profound, [it] contains many good ideas and some delightful instrumental effects. The final movement is humoresque in spirit and moves with briskness. Mr. Herbert plays well, and his interpretation . . . was decidedly commendable."

The day was not yet over for Herbert: that night at the regular concert of the New York Philharmonic Society, which was also conducted by Theodore Thomas, he was called on to play the Concerto again! When the scheduled soloist, Emil Fischer of the Metropolitan Opera, was suddenly indisposed and unable to appear, Thomas summoned the artist he had accompanied a few hours earlier. This alone tells how well Herbert had played at the young people's concert; but it remained for the *World* to print the best eulogy of the day. The reporter was full of enthusiasm as he referred to the "admirably written and very interesting concerto" which the composer played "with so much beauty of tone and such skilful and brilliant execution as to make his efforts not only entirely worthy of the high standard of performance of the Philharmonic, but so as to hold the audience bound in closest attention during his long solo."

Because Herbert's appearance was in the nature of an emergency, his name did not appear on the program. Nevertheless, a New York musician had had a piece performed, and the *Musical Courier* was prompted to observe: "Thus the hitherto unheard of thing came to pass that the work of a local composer invaded the sacred precincts of the Philharmonic Society. May the success which attended this chance invasion encourage the board of directors to repeat the experiment."[28]

Exactly how much and how often Herbert played with the Philharmonic at the time remains unknown. The Society then was a cooperative organization. It had started in this fashion in 1842 and did not change until its sixty-first year. The orchestra members paid their respective shares of concert expenses; they made good any losses, and divided any profits.[29] It was an honor and a distinction to belong to the Philharmonic Society, achieved by election. Herbert was a nonmember when he made his début as a Philharmonic soloist. Office records show that he played with the orchestra for eleven consecutive seasons, 1887–1888 through 1897–1898. He was proposed on November 27, 1889, as an "actual member to play violoncello," and presumably was accepted into the Society shortly thereafter.[30] However, and perhaps erroneously, Krehbiel's history of the Society does not list Herbert's name earlier than 1892 among the performing members.[31] Whenever he achieved membership, Herbert's 1887 appearance initiated a long and fruitful association which lasted far beyond the eleven seasons mentioned.

The year 1888 continued to favor Herbert as both composer and performer. New York became better acquainted with his fine capabilities, and neighboring communities were pleased to hear him for the first time. Before the year was out he was far richer in experience, more familiar with American geography and much closer to the American people.

It could easily become monotonous to relate all the commendations Herbert received from his various solo appearances; but another concerto performance demands attention by virtue of one newspaper's method of criticizing it. The second week of February brought Theodore Thomas and his orchestra into Steinway Hall for one of their numerous concerts, and Herbert was engaged to play Rubinstein's second cello Concerto, Op. 96. The public rehearsal, which most of the newspapers reviewed, occurred on the afternoon of the 9th. On the evening of the 8th the Boston Symphony Orchestra had appeared in New York and had also featured a cello concerto, Robert Schumann's, played by its own first cellist, Fritz Giese. The New York *Times* thought it unfortunate that Thomas should advance a cello soloist on the very next night; the inevitable comparison could only be invidious (for someone). Luckily it turned out well for Herbert:

> The [Rubinstein] concerto as a whole is not a very serious work, but it is sufficiently interesting to be offered as a means for displaying a 'cellist's ability. The suspicion seems reasonable that Mr. Thomas exhibited his solo 'cellist yesterday to invite comparison with Fritz Giese of the Boston Orchestra, who appeared the night before. Such experiments are not always attended with happy results. However, if Mr. Thomas wants comparison he shall not be disappointed. Mr. Victor Herbert, yesterday's soloist, acquitted himself much better than the player of the previous evening. The Rubinstein concerto bristles with rapid passages in high positions, and is prolific in harmonics. Mr. Herbert surmounted the obstacles with a fine command of technique and, moreover, played with a good tone and no little expression.

The genial reporter, who willingly fell into the Thomas trap, ended by saying that Herbert was, and deserved to be, warmly applauded.

The *Tribune* agreed completely with its rival on the quality of Herbert's accomplishment, but had a higher regard for Rubinstein's work. It was, said the paper, "a beautiful one, appealing almost equally to a severe and an easy taste, utilizing to the full the few good qualities that the violoncello has as a solo instrument, and affording ample opportunity for display."

Only a month later, on March 16 and 17, Herbert played still another concerto (by Raff, Op. 193) in Brooklyn, again under the baton of Thomas. Truly the Thomas-Herbert team was giving New York and vicinity unusual opportunities to learn the modern cello repertoire. As usual the performance brought the artist a triumph and plentiful applause.[32]

With approach of summer, Herbert found a new means of employing his time and talents. He went to Brighton Beach to play in Anton Seidl's season of summer concerts, the announcement of which in the spring had created quite a sensation. As the opening date neared, Saturday June 30, the public was informed that Seidl would have a picked orchestra of eighty men, would give two concerts daily for ten weeks, would present music of the masters from Bach to Strauss, and would have Victor Herbert as assistant conductor.[33] Music lovers welcomed the news and hoped the season would be a stunning success. Others looked upon it as frankly experimental. There was a new hall at Brighton Beach, but classical music at the seashore was not calculated to draw crowds. The betting fraternity seized an opportunity, and wagers flourished that fewer than 5,000 persons would hear Seidl throughout his ten-week stay. Not far away was Manhattan Beach, which offered Gilmore's Band and tasty chowder, both of proven popularity, and their followers believed that Wagnerian music was weak in comparison.[34]

It was quickly demonstrated that the Seidl experiment would be completely successful, and those who gambled to the contrary were sore chagrined. And it may be presumed, and hoped, that Gilmore and chowder lost none of their devotees. Seidl arranged programs which were appealing in variety and excellence—overtures, symphonic poems, a goodly number of symphonies, novelties, American works—with occasional outstanding soloists among whom was Therese Herbert-Förster. More than 50,000 people came to the concerts, and New York's music colony made Brighton Beach its summer headquarters. An observer from the *Musical Courier* remarked that scores of familiar faces were always in evidence, notables like Joseffy, Burmeister, Krehbiel, Sternberg or Henderson.[35]

The closing concert called forth a frenzied ovation from the audience, which was loath to release either Seidl or his men. Not a little of the tribute was for Herbert, who had conducted a number of the lighter compositions throughout the series. The applause had an ardor and a spontaneity too frequently lacking in the response to present-day performance. "Women vied with men in their applause, using umbrella handles and waving handkerchiefs vigorously. A more enthusiastic and delighted audience never left a concert hall."[36] Pelted by rain, the train left the island with a cheerful load of passengers returning to the city; their clothes were dampened, but their spirits sparkled.

Plans were immediately laid for another season the following summer. The public was assured that the Brooklyn and Brighton Beach Rail Road would provide every facility for the comfort of transient guests, and unaccompanied ladies would have the protection of a special car. The hotel at Brighton Beach would also have improved accommodations, notably the addition of a reading room where patrons could while away the time between concerts or take refuge from inclement weather. The music pavilion, too, would be rearranged: reserved seats would be installed, and obnoxious smokers would have to sit in a designated section. Too many ladies had suffered annoyance from this vice and had been forced to take undesirable seats to escape the weedy fumes. Nothing, in short, would be left undone, for the Seidl concerts had most certainly "raised the tone" of the resort by augmenting the attractions for persons of "refinement and culture."

This much is sure: Seidl strengthened his hold on the masses; Herbert was initiated as a symphonic conductor; a new public was exposed to the influence of good music, be it light or heavy. This much may be surmised: The experience and observations of the summer probably gave Herbert his first realization of popular music-making. Here he may have first sensed the values pertaining to music for mixed (i.e., informed and uninformed) audiences and have apprehended the social benefits related thereto. The people clamored for more and more, and he may well have divined the opportunity for popular conducting. This was, after all, long prior to the unsatisfactory Victrola and the tyrannical radio.

Once the summer orchestra season was over, Herbert's restless energy sought a new outlet. He knew how to relax, but he could never be idle. His new activity provided him with novel experience, amusement, and the chance to bring music to audiences different from any yet encountered. In the 1880's the concert party was an important feature of musical life. Musicians of divers talents would band together, tour the inland cities and towns, and present programs of astonishing variety. The groups sometimes included artists of exceptional ability who presented solo and concerted numbers of distinctive quality; other concert parties left much to be desired in performance and selection. Herbert joined one concert party, in fact was more or less in charge of it, and toured a wide area in the Middle West.

The company was organized by the famous American soprano Emma Juch, and Herbert was its music director. It was one of the best such companies ever formed. Some of its members were first-class, while the others were more than amateurs or novices. Juch and Herbert were outstanding, and fully matching them was Adele Aus der Ohe, the pianist, who had studied several years with Liszt. Additional members were Rosa Linde, contralto, W. J. Lavin, tenor, and Clemente Bologna, bass. The company presented a wide variety of vocal and instrumental music, especially when visiting a town large enough to contribute its own orchestra. Even without this, orchestra music was somehow rendered, for the main offering was an operatic scene with the singers donning the proper costumes. As music director Herbert had plural responsibilities—conducting, coaching, playing cello solos, and supplying piano accompaniments for Juch's vocal selections.

The variegated musical family opened its western tour in Milwaukee in the beginning of October, 1888, and played up and down the region for a solid month—Duluth, Dubuque, Des Moines, Kansas City, Cincinnati, Atchison, St. Joseph—spreading a delight and pleasure which more formal organizations seldom give. Emma Juch's name had great drawing power. Though only twenty-five, she had been an opera prima donna for seven years, and the Metropolitan had vainly tried to secure her services.[37] Her voice was remarkably lovely and of pure quality, enhanced by an enunciation that was a joy to hear. She had, too, a fondness for the road and the unfrequented towns along its edge, greatly favoring the audiences there over the audiences in established opera centers.[38]

The company aroused great enthusiasm wherever it appeared. The singers presented concert songs and opera arias; Aus der Ohe played pieces by Chopin, Mendelssohn, Schumann, and Liszt; Herbert used movements from concertos and attractive single pieces (he had another accompanist) and sometimes played cello obbligatos to Juch's selections; the entire group closed an evening with a costumed opera scene or act, most often the second act of Gounod's *Faust*. The provincial critics were sometimes amusingly lavish with praise, at other times disconcertingly honest. The three artists who never failed to please were Juch, Aus der Ohe, and Herbert, and the second and third made a Cincinnati critic especially happy. He preferred the pianist in a Liszt Rhapsody rather than in Schumann's *Carnaval,* which he found uninteresting. Herbert, he wrote, furnished excellent accompaniments for the vocalists and, in playing a cello fantasy by Servais, proved himself "the most brilliant cellist in this country." The critic was probably right, just as he was in congratulating Miss Juch on obtaining such an accomplished musician as her music director; but, with the exception of Emma herself, "the vocalists of the company do not deserve special mention."[39] The most perceptive or, shall we say, sensitive critic seems to have been the one in St. Joseph, Missouri, who perpetrated an understatement of classic hue. After listening to the second act of *Faust* he reported that it "was well sung, although 'Faust' in the piano accompaniment is somewhat weak."[39]

During the fall and winter of 1888–1889 Therese Herbert continued to make concert appearances in New York and Brooklyn, generally in mixed programs presenting a variety of artists. After the jaunt to the Middle West her husband was sometimes heard with her—for instance, on November 11, when they both delighted audiences in Brooklyn's Amphion Academy at a sacred concert by the Zöllner Männerchor.[40] She appeared again in Brooklyn with Rafael Joseffy on December 19; but perhaps her most satisfying appearance of the season was on November 20, when she was one of the soloists at the Metropolitan Opera House in a benefit orchestra concert conducted by Seidl to raise funds for the Aguilar Free Library.[41]

The Aguilar Free Library existed from 1886 to 1903, when it was consolidated with the New York Public Library. Its main objective was to provide, without cost, high types of literature to the underprivileged Jewish population. Sponsoring the plan were the Young Men's Hebrew Association and the Hebrew Free School Association, each of which presented a book collection to the several circulating branches.[42] The reading habits of clients were carefully watched, and a secretary expressed pleasure which every librarian can understand: "The tables accompanying this report will illustrate the gratifying statement that the *character* of the reading is constantly changing for the better, and that the demand for books other than *fiction* is increasing. While good fiction is wholesome, the library proposes to further a taste for instructive reading, and it is pleasing to record a growing taste for historic and scientific works among our readers."[43] The musicians who aided the library in expanding its nonfiction holdings must have been happy with the results of the concert. A clear profit of more than $2,000 was realized, and the performing artists were roundly applauded.

On December 1, 1888, Herbert enjoyed another personal triumph which was twofold. Anton Seidl conducted his second orchestra concert of the season, in Steinway Hall, and he brought to audition two important novelties: Vincent d'Indy's symphony trilogy, *Wallenstein*, and Herbert's Serenade for String Orchestra, Op. 12. It is unfortunate that neither piece is heard today. Critics handled D'Indy's work roughly, finding in it all the alleged unpleasantness of contemporary art. The Herbert score, however, stimulated a quite different reaction and apparently saved the concert from being a dismal failure. This was owing not alone to the fact that the composer, who conducted his own première, bore no resemblance to his French colleague. His score was a good one and merited the approval it received.

Herbert's string Serenade is a series of five short pieces which, by their nature and sequence, deserve the title of Suite more than did his Opus 3. The opening Aufzug (Procession) is a spirited march wherein delicacy prevails over Teutonic weight. The Polonaise shows the same lightness, as the characteristic rhythm supplies sparkle and verve. The Liebes-Scene (Love Scene) is a highly emotional fragment which, though lushly romantic, can be extremely effective. The Canzonetta approaches cuteness in its lighthearted manner, and the Finale, another brilliant tarantella, sweeps the hearer along to an exciting close. Krehbiel spoke of the work in this fashion: "Less interesting for its melodies (some of which have familiar faces) than for the manner in which they are handled, the serenade is nevertheless a composition which deserves to be played again. The vivid and varied dashes of color which Mr. Herbert threw into the score, notwithstanding that he had only five stringed instruments of the orchestra at his command. were most effective. One movement, the third, I should like to see taken out of the set by Mr. Herbert and rewritten for full band. It is denominated a 'Love Scene,' and in it Mr. Herbert develops an intensity of feeling which, though eloquently expressed by the voices of the quintet, deserves a larger and more telling apparatus."[44]

As the year drew to a close a new form of chamber ensemble caught

Herbert's attention. With Max Bendix, violinist, and Reinhold L. Herman, pianist, he organized a group that called itself the Metropolitan Trio Club and gave its first concert in New York, at the indispensable Steinway Hall, on December 13. The artists played two trios, by Raff and Godard respectively, while the ever present assistant (Emily Winant) sang French and German songs. The *Musical Courier* of December 19 praised the new and youthful ensemble and offered only one bit of censure that players of chamber music today will understand: Whenever Herbert and Bendix were heard, their playing was clear, precise, artistic; but in this new trio the pianist would have to sub·ordinate himself more, else the desired musical blend would hardly result.

The very next issue of the *Musical Courier* bestowed more praise on Herbert, a fact worth remembering in view of subsequent developments. Its cover bore an impressive portrait of the composer, and a carefully prepared statement briefly summarized his career and accomplishments. It concluded with a panegyric which nobody could deny: "His compositions . . . all show a refined taste, abundant melodic invention and great skill in the handling of the orchestra. As a violoncellist Mr. Herbert ranks with the foremost alive, his cantabile being superb and his technic most facile. He is the prince of good fellows, a most genial friend and companion, and is one of the most popular of our metropolitan musicians."[45]

Theodore Thomas, in New York and later in Chicago, had a happy penchant for introducing important new works to American audiences. On January 5, 1889, his listeners had their first experience with the great and formidable "Double Concerto," Op. 102, by Johannes Brahms, which the modern German master composed for violin, cello, and orchestra. Chickering Hall in New York was the scene of the American première, and the soloists on whom the responsibility was thrust were Max Bendix and Victor Herbert. With their conductor they shared the privilege of bringing to America one of the most difficult masterpieces of the century. Their task was not easy, either from an executive or from an aesthetic standpoint.

Even today Brahms's massive work lacks a popular following. Its austerity, its difficulties (musical as well as technical, with no concession to virtuosity), its brooding introspection offset, to a high degree, the very real beauty that informs its pages. In presenting it to New York—the world première on October 18, 1887, in Cologne was not long past—Thomas, Bendix, and Herbert surely had no hope of increasing their own popularity. The two soloists, aged twenty-two and twenty-nine, realized their assignment was out of the ordinary. To do justice to the music, a different kind of practice was necessary, a kind calling for personal discipline which, though brief, had to be rigorous. Consequently the high-spirited young men vowed that, while they were learning the ungrateful concerto, they would forgo shaving. With unkempt beards they would not be tempted to time-wasting parties and could master the music without interruption.[46] Master it they did, playing it from memory and earning the praise the critics were inclined to give.

The weather was particularly bad on the night of the concert. Another handicap was the fact that Seidl was simultaneously conducting a concert in Steinway Hall. Although the audience was far from capacity, it compensated by the warmth of its response. The reviews suggest that the soloists were better appreciated than the composition.

The *Musical Courier* of January 9 "sincerely congratulated" Bendix and Herbert "for the exquisite finish with which they played each one of the three movements, for their wonderful ensemble, their beauty of tone and absolute beauty of intonation, the almost marvelous technic with which they performed the 'vivace non troppo,' to say nothing of the difficult feat of memorizing and playing faultlessly from memory a work of such complexity and of such large dimensions. That the audience was not quite capable of appreciating their efforts must not discourage these two artists, for it was not their fault, but the audience's, for whom a Brahms composition of so much intricacy is not the most catchy thing imaginable."

The *Times* felt that the first and third movements had "an abundance of energy and some good thematic material. The treatment, however, is involved, and far from easy to follow. The solo parts bristle with formidable difficulties, particularly the 'cello part, and they result in small effect. The andante, however, is one of Brahms' happy inspirations and is a really lovely movement. Masterly use is made in it of the singing qualities of the violin and 'cello, and the orchestral background is such as might have been expected of the composer. Indeed the orchestra is treated with much freedom throughout the composition and is not relegated to the position of a mere accompaniment. Messrs. Bendix and Herbert performed their somewhat thankless task in a careful and generally effective style, for which they were warmly applauded."

The most perceptive notice of the music, with full appreciation of the soloists' contribution, was supplied by Krehbiel, who was pleased that Thomas had programmed the concerto: "The Concerto is no more remarkable and unique because of the vehicle chosen for it than it is as a piece of music. . . . In Europe, Joachim, the violinist, and Hausmann, the 'cellist, have practically monopolized it, and they are not likely to have many rivals in its performance. It is highly intellectual music, and sincere and full enjoyment of it is reserved for highly cultured publics. Yet intellectuality is not its only characteristic. The second movement is an exquisitely beautiful and noble instrumental lyric, and there are passages in the first and last movements that awaken the keenest sensations of delight. Both solo parts bristle with technical difficulties, which were conquered in so masterly a manner by Mr. Bendix and Mr. Herbert that their skill held the attention whenever it threatened to desert the music."[47]

Another interesting activity at this time was Herbert's participation in the work of the New York Composers' Club, which had just completed one year of existence. In spite of its name it was not primarily a society of composers: its members were musicians and music lovers banded together to study the art of the masters. It had begun as a group of seven who met in private homes to indulge in music for purely personal satisfaction. By the beginning of 1889 the set limit of fifty members had been reached, and some two hundred more were clamoring to enter. The initiation fee was two dollars and dues were a dollar a month. Only artist members were allowed to perform at meetings, which were generally devoted to the music of a single composer. Schubert and Beethoven, for example, had already been "studied"; Brahms was to be investigated in February, and Schumann was the center of attention on January 8. The audience, which was assembled by invitation, now numbered several hundred.[48]

The Schumann *Abend* took place with great success in the Crescent Hall, recently opened by the piano firm, Hardman, Peck & Co. Herbert played in two chamber compositions, the String Quartet in A minor and the beautiful Piano Quintet in E flat major. The pianist in the latter work, a local artist named Lucie E. Mawson, won the esteem of her colleagues. The other artists in the string quartet were Sam Franko, Charles S. Schmidt, and Nahan Franko. With Herbert they rendered a performance that was highly acclaimed and satisfactory.[49]

To record all Herbert's performances and the approval they elicited would be downright superfluous. Enough testimony has been evoked to justify calling him the best cellist in America and one of the best in the world. His enthusiastic sorties into chamber music stamped him as an artist more interested in musical values than in personal glamour. He continued his appearances with the Metropolitan Trio Club; and his departure from the city to travel westward and finally to Chicago with Theodore Thomas prompted the *Musical Courier* on February 20, 1889, to expressions of great regret. Thomas continued to present him as soloist, and always with the happiest results. Herbert distinguished himself on January 17 in the cello obbligato of Volkmann's D minor Serenade, and again, in Brooklyn, on February 15 and 16, in a concerto by Reinecke.[50] Hastily reassembled, the Emma Juch concert company gave a concert at Vassar College on February 5. Herbert officiated as before and impressed the girls as a highly "romantic figure."[51] His innate charm, handsome features (beardless again), and excellent playing made him irresistible to his feminine audience.

Another important engagement this season for Herbert and his wife was a huge musical festival at Pittsburgh, on May 21–24. It was under the general direction of Anton Seidl, who gathered around him the usual group of distinguished artists. Lilli Lehmann and Emma Juch were on hand, and so was Giuseppe Campanari. Herbert and his friends Adele Aus der Ohe and Max Bendix were soloists. The program announced an orchestra of one hundred men, and a chorus of five hundred.

The occasion for the festival was the inauguration of the new Exposition Building, of which the city was inordinately proud. Elaborate preparations were made, and carpenters, electricians, decorators, and workmen were busy up to the hour of opening. An enthusiastic local reporter described the edifice as a beautiful palace of song. He watched the boxes receiving their final touches and rhapsodized over their trimmings of satin and velvet. Two thousand lights were to blaze in glory, and magnificence and elegance impressed all beholders.[52] James G. Huneker (who had just begun his unique "Raconteur" column in the *Musical Courier*) experienced a different reaction: "I noticed the interior decorations of the festival building were so discordant as to actually put some of the instruments out of tune. Greens on light yellow, bright scarlet on delicate pink, and this, combined with the steam whistles on the river, made up a curious—but not an harmonious—ensemble."[53]

The festival was a great success, even Huneker admitted; but whether it was musically significant is open to question. The only event that he singled out for comment was Herbert's solo, which won an ovation. Notwithstanding the success, however, certain conditions caused discomfort, musical and physical, and these in turn prove that perfection was lacking. The hall was very large, with a seating capacity of more than 4,700 persons; only about 3,500 attended on opening night,[54] and this must have had a dampening effect upon the performers. The size and peculiar shape of the arena were such, indeed, that the unabashed Huneker commented twice, the first time lapsing into baseball jargon: ". . . but the exposition building was so large and so crooked that sweet Emma Juch said she had to use in singing some of Buck Ewing's ball curves to get her voice around the corners. Oh!" And again: "One French horn player in the orchestra was so impressed by the size of the building that he blew with such might and main as to blow his horn out straight."[55] It was also cold in the hall, sufficient proof that gaudy decoration was deemed more essential than the audience's well-being.

Finally, there were musical hazards, in the river-boat whistles. A classic incident (or accident) happened on opening night, in the course of the Bach-Abert Prelude, Choral and Fugue. As the brass choir was intoning the Choral a steamboat sent out a whistle exactly in tune with an instrument. It blended so well that, when the orchestra stopped, the audience thought the music was still continuing. So wrote our reporter, who naïvely added that Seidl, the conductor, seemed annoyed.[56] Huneker again gave a more flavorsome account of the weird occurrence; he was quite conscious of the dangers wafted up from water level. "One paper printed the following: 'Manager Locke also requests that rivermen will refrain from blowing steamboat whistles for the balance of the week. The noise impairs the harmony of the music.' Impaired harmony is good. But the evening the Abert-Bache prelude, choral and fugue were performed, one big whistle chimed in with the orchestra in perfect accord, a genuine drone bass or river pedal point *à la* 'Rheingold,' and the audience were delighted until Seidl rapped and the orchestra stopped playing, so as to give the whistle a chance."[57]

After a well deserved rest Herbert turned to a new activity, as associate conductor of the Worcester Music Festival of 1889. The Worcester festivals, with a record of rich accomplishment, were the outgrowth of conventions inspired by Lowell Mason two generations earlier. The pioneer educator set the pattern of the conventions in Boston in 1836 and 1840, when, after giving instruction in singing and note-reading, he organized a formal concert; then all would join in singing the music which had just been studied. Such conventions were very popular. Worcester's first was in 1858. The activity was vigorously promoted, and the Worcester County Music Convention, in which twenty-five villages and towns participated, was formally established in 1863. Enthusiasm was high, and private subscriptions made it possible to purchase a fine organ and install it in the hall of the Mechanics Association. Two years later Carl Zerrahn began his long term as conductor and produced the first complete oratorio, with the new organ and an orchestra of six. In two more years the orchestra had grown to eighteen, and by 1871 the modern festival was ready to emerge.[58] By 1872 the annual festivals were under way, sponsored by the newly named Worcester County Musical Association.[59]

The festival of 1889, September 23–27, found the sixty-three-year-old Zerrahn in need of aid. He was no longer able to perform single-handed the exhausting duties of directorship, and an assistant was engaged. The qualifications were not light. The desired person had to be one who could take charge of most of the rehearsals, carry through the concerts if necessary and appear as a soloist in his own right. After long and careful deliberation the administration selected Herbert, who immediately showed that the choice was fortunate. His execution of his duties aroused hearty approval, and he willingly shared the burden of playing piano accompaniments for solo singers.

The instrumental soloists at the 1889 festival were M. Sautet, oboe, E. Heindel, flute, Frank Taft, organ, Adele Aus der Ohe, piano, Franz Kneisel, violin, and Herbert, who made his first appearance with a solo on Wednesday September 25, playing Servais's brilliant *Fantaisie carac-téristique*. On the following day he contributed a group of three short numbers of widely varying styles: a Sarabande by J. S. Bach, a *Mélodie* by Massenet, and the popular *At the Spring* by Davidoff.[60] It is pleasant to read of Herbert's general effect upon the festival, for even the pro-vincial critics were accustomed to elevated standards of musical achieve-ment:

Victor Herbert's 'cello playing was another delightful feature of the con-cert. Mr. Herbert's number was a "Fantaisie Caracteristic" of Servais, well adapted for winning the audience on a first appearance, and Mr. Herbert understood it.

He settled himself to his work with a confidence and air of satisfaction which indicated that he knew his own powers, and in the most graceful way, began his selection. Rapid fingering and careful bowing made sharp demands at times, which he met with an ease delightful to witness. The audience felt another flush of enthusiasm, and despite elaborate bows, continued to applaud until he hesitated, and then, Mr. Zerrahn adding his solicitation, he repeated the concluding part of the number he had played.

It is time something was said about Mr. Herbert's great success in the present Festival. He came here with both 'cello and baton and unquestion-ably his engagement was one of the best strokes that the management has made.

His work with the 'cello had already been noticed in detail. As associate-conductor he has been doing a great deal of work which has not been seen by the public.

In private rehearsal with the artists, and in other ways, he has been able to lift much of the burden off Mr. Zerrahn's shoulders.

Personally he is an ornament to the Association. Pleasant and obliging, he has succeeded in making friends with everybody, from the ladies in the chorus, most of whom are now worshipping at his shrine, to the artists and the orchestra.

People will differ on the question of his being a greater 'cellist than Giese, but certainly he is more of a man.[61]

It was also probably in the fall of 1889 that Herbert joined the faculty of that remarkable National Conservatory of Music of America which had been founded four years earlier by the equally remarkable Jean-nette Thurber. Mrs. Thurber (1851–1946), one of America's greatest music patrons, one of her great visionaries, one of her most imaginative cultural leaders, is all but forgotten today, lost in the obscurity of a once bold enterprise, an eventual failure, which brought Dvořák to this country and made America conscious of her musical racialism. Huneker, a teacher at the Conservatory and later Mrs. Thurber's secretary, asserted that she achieved more by her failures than others do by their successes! His secretarial assignment he described as "a daily visit at her residence, where I sat for an hour and admired her good looks. She was a picturesque woman, Gallic in her 'allures,' but more Spanish than French in features. She spoke French like a Parisian, and after thirty years I confess that her fine, dark eloquent eyes troubled my peace more than once. But I only took it out in staring."[62]

The National Conservatory actually flourished for years, boasted a truly brilliant faculty, offered comprehensive curricula, and proved itself a vital force in the country's musical development. To this day no institution of musical instruction in America can be said to have surpassed it in potentialities. Whether the musical youth of the land was ready for it, of course, is a different question.

Mrs. Thurber's prime and noble purpose was to establish a conservatory where talented and deserving students could obtain every type of musical training right through to the highest degree of professional expertness. At the very beginning, training in voice and opera monopolized attention; but the teaching staff was rapidly expanded to include every branch of musical practice or adjunct then conceivable, even fencing: "It is a pretty and striking sight to see M. Senac facing a dozen young ladies drawn up in a row, assuming various attitudes, and brandishing and thrusting their rapiers at the teacher's word of command."[63] Vocal work was always stressed, and solfeggio was prescribed, even for the instrumental students. Naturally piano students soon predominated, the leading teacher of the household instrument being Rafael Joseffy. Tuition was purely nominal, and gifted students paid none at all, provided that, "having completed their education, they shall aid others as they were themselves assisted, by a contribution to the general fund, for the first five years, of one quarter of the emoluments they receive over and above one thousand dollars a year."

In spite of her magnanimity, perhaps because of it, Mrs. Thurber was always faced with many problems. A pamphlet for the third (1887–1888) season of the Conservatory emphasized the need of a permanent endowment. Since the institution was patterned after the Paris Conservatoire, why should it not receive Government aid? Consequently the uninhibited founder sent a petition to Congress asking for an appropriation of $200,000 to "be used under the direction of the trustees . . . in extending [the school's] usefulness, and upon condition that each Senator and Member of the House of Representatives shall have the privilege of nominating one pupil, who, upon passing the requisite examination as to talent, shall be taught free of charge." This ingenious attempt failed to bring a flood of congressional appointments to the student body, or to convert the school into a musical West Point. However, Mrs. Thurber was only strengthened in her determination to nationalize her institution, and in 1891 she actually succeeded in obtaining from Congress a charter of incorporation which seemed to promise a glorious development in the future. It is a curious document, meriting contemplation and consideration today. All of one woman's hopes were bound up in it, and many felt that it was the greatest step forward in the annals of American music.

CHAP. 558.—An act to incorporate the National Conservatory of Music of America.

Be it enacted by the Senate and House of Representatives of the United States of America in Congress assembled, That Jeannette M. Thurber, William G. Choate, Chauncey M. Depew, Abram S. Hewitt, Frank R. Lawrence, of the State of New York; William Pinkney Whyte, Enoch Pratt, of Maryland; Fitzhugh Lee, William H. Payne, of Virginia; Olive Risley Seward, John Hay, S. P. Langley, Anthony Pollock, C. R. P. Rodgers, John M. Schofield, of the District of Columbia, and such others as may be associated with them, are hereby constituted a body politic and corporate by the name National Conservatory of Music of America, with perpetual succession, with power to sue and be sued, complain and defend in any court of law or equity, to make and use a common seal and alter the same at pleasure; to acquire, take by devise, bequest, or otherwise, hold, purchase, and convey such real and personal estate as shall be required for the purposes of its incorporation; to appoint such officers and agents as the business of the corporation shall require, and to make by-laws not inconsistent with any law of the United States for the admission and qualification of members, the management of its property, and the regulation of its affairs. Said corporation is hereby empowered to found, establish, and maintain a national conservatory of music within the District of Columbia for the education of citizens of the United States and such other persons as the trustees may deem proper in all the branches of music. The said corporation shall have the power to grant and confer diplomas and the degree of doctor of music or other honorary degrees.

SEC. 2. The power to alter, amend or repeal this act, is hereby reserved. Approved, March 3, 1891.[64]

Fifteen days after the enactment an editorial in the New York *Evening Post* reflected the anticipation of future effects:

On the same day that the International Copyright Bill was passed in the Senate, another bill of importance from an intellectual point of view was signed, incorporating the National Conservatory of Music . . . The last provision is of special importance as, to our knowledge, no American conservatory has hitherto had the power of legally conferring the degree of Doctor of Music; and the bill is also of interest as being perhaps the first instance of anything done by the National Legislature in behalf of music. That the National Conservatory will not abuse the privilege may be hoped from the high character of its instructors, which at present include such eminent names as Rafael Joseffy, Camilla Urso, Signor Sapio, Bruno Oscar Klein, Victor Herbert, Otto Oesterle, etc. Hereafter the National Conservatory in New York will be nominally only a branch of the central establishment at Washington, but in reality it will continue, for some time at least, to be of more importance than the Washington school.

The Washington school, alas, never materialized, and our Capital's most exciting musical adventure remained frozen in New York. Incorporation was one thing; the provision of physical resources, quite another. Supporters of the cause were hopeful when a bill was introduced into Congress in 1894 to provide a Washington site. Unfortunately it was, of necessity, referred to the Committee on the District of Columbia, which reported adversely,[65] dooming the glorious project.

From the very beginnings of the National Conservatory, Mrs. Thurber inspired her colleagues by her ideals and objectives. The faculty subscribed wholeheartedly to her strivings and voluntarily endeavored to further her efforts. An exchange of letters printed in the *Musical Courier* of January 8, 1890, illustrates this feeling and at the same time establishes Herbert's early connection with the distinguished institute.

New York, December 24, 1889

To Mrs. Jeannette M. Thurber, President of the
National Conservatory of Music of America:

Dear Madame—Appreciating the efforts you have made to advance the art of music in America, and knowing how hard and successfully you are laboring to establish a United States conservatory which shall be truly national in character, and which has for its object the advancement of art and not pecuniary profit, we, the undersigned professors of the National Conservatory of Music, desire to contribute our mite to its success, and to this end offer our services for a grand concert, the proceeds of which shall be devoted to the establishment of free scholarships. Hoping that you will approve and aid us by making the necessary arrangements, we remain, dear madame,

Very respectfully,

RAFAEL JOSEFFY   THEOPHILE MANOURY
LEOPOLD LICHTENBERG   ADELE MARGULIES
CHRISTIAN FRITSCH   JESSIE PINNEY
                    VICTOR HERBERT

The patroness, probably lobbying in the Capital, responded:

Washington, D.C., December 31, 1889

To Mr. Rafael Josefly and other Members of the Faculty
of the National Conservatory of Music:

I am deeply touched by your letter evincing so much sympathy and interest in the progress of the educational work in which we are all engaged. The success of any such work depends as much upon the interest and sympathy of the faculty as its friends. The trustees cordially accept your generous offer for a grand concert, the proceeds of which shall be devoted to the establishment of a free scholarship, as you suggest, and we will gladly cooperate with you to this end.

Faithfully yours,
JEANNETTE M. THURBER, President

Charles Inslee Pardee, dean and secretary of the Conservatory, sent these letters to the *Musical Courier* with a note to the editor announcing that the concert would take place in the Metropolitan Opera House on March 27, 1890. I have not discovered that this momentous concert was ever given, or why it may have failed to materialize. The offer of the artists to present it is evidence enough of the splendid spirit instilled by Mrs. Thurber in her promotion of musical education.

Herbert's association with the National Conservatory was happy and fruitful. It was tacit recognition as the country's leading cellist, and it gave him a new ensemble group for the performance of chamber music. Herbert with two prominent colleagues—Adele Margulies, pianist, and Leopold Lichtenberg, violinist—organized the National Conservatory Trio Club and appeared at the Berkeley Lyceum on January 16, 1890. As usual their program was incredibly varied, each artist playing solos and only one trio (Godard's second, in F major) being heard.[66]

The new trio ensemble only made Herbert busier than ever, and at the very time when his duties with the Thomas orchestra were increased. Now he began officiating as Thomas' assistant conductor. His first known appearance in this capacity was on January 2, 1890, at a gala concert opening the popular Lenox Lyceum.

It sometimes happened that Herbert had two engagements the same evening. This occurred on February 13 when he played in Brooklyn, then scurried back to Manhattan to play a solo at a concert by the Rubinstein Club in Chickering Hall. He almost failed to make it, for he rushed into the hall just in time to see the exodus of the disappointed audience; but he was ready to play, and Conductor Chapman called the crowd to their seats for the instrumental feature. It is not surprising to find Huneker writing that he played "in his usual musical fashion, but he looked very tired."[67]

With the advent of summer Herbert resumed his work with Anton Seidl at Brighton Beach and increased his popularity in New York. He was already, indeed, a marked man, to such an extent that the press commented on his shaving off his beautiful Irish mustache. The irrepressible Huneker again, as "Raconteur," sketched a likeness of the happy Irishman in a few telling phrases:

I came up from the island with the celebrated "Vic" Herbert, the Irish 'cellist, and Otto Oesterle . . . and had a quiet chat about music, the difference in readings of orchestral conductors and such.

Herbert, whose massive head is probably the largest of any musician in the country (*vide* his white hat, in size a perfect cerebral barn), can also lay claim to being one of the best looking of the guild.

His ruddy color, bright eyes and general facial make-up all proclaim him to be a son of the Green Sod—Erin. His grandfather wrote one of the most rollicking, jovial books ever penned—"Handy Andy"—and his talented grandson writes good music.

He has improved greatly in his conducting, and will be the assistant conductor at the [1890] Worcester Festival.[68]

The Worcester Festival took place on September 22–26, and Herbert functioned as in the year before. His main contribution as a composer, his string Serenade, Op. 12, was warmly praised; but in offering a group of cello solos he unfortunately included his own *Petite Valse*. It was never intended as a pretentious composition, yet the pundits of Worcester denounced it as trivial and far below the standard of festival selections. One critic went so far as to write that, "compared to his reception of the previous year, Victor Herbert was received as solo 'cellist with far less enthusiasm in the 1890 festival," and then asserted that Boston had several 'cellists who were better in every way.[69] Herbert may have erred in programming a piece of only slight importance, but he scarcely deserved the buffeting received.

It probably made little impression upon him. Back in New York he continued his indefatigable music making and scored another triumph in playing the Saint-Saëns concerto, winning praise for his fine technique, tone, intonation, and general musicianship. These were the characteristics "for which he is so favorably noted."[70]

The Worcester Festival, possibly America's best, was far from being unique. Many towns and cities sponsored festivals, some of them extremely ambitious, and audiences were attracted from a wide surrounding area. In the Springfield, Massachusetts, festival of May 6–8, 1891, the Boston Festival Orchestra participated, under Herbert's direction. This now-forgotten ensemble had been formed in 1889 by George W. Stuart, primarily to furnish accompaniments for festival-sponsoring choral societies. A festival might allow instrumental music to be heard, but choral music was its staple. In addition to such appearances the Boston Festival Orchestra, embracing many musicians from the Boston Symphony, gave concerts and presented soloists through the New England and Middle Atlantic States. In the words of a latter-day observer: "I don't imagine they introduced many purely orchestra novelties, but they probably had a good many first performances to their credit in various communities. They were the broadcasters of fifty years ago."[71] In 1891 Herbert led the orchestra on its second tour; on its first the conductor had been his old festival associate, Carl Zerrahn.

Under the general direction of that fine musician, George W. Chadwick, the Springfield festival combined a chorus of nearly two hundred voices with Herbert's orchestra. Herbert appeared twice as cello soloist, scoring a triumph each time. He first appeared playing a Goltermann concerto in the concert of May 7. This was allegedly covered by a reviewer for the Boston *Herald*; but his article aroused the ire of the correspondent of the *Musical Courier,* O. F. (probably the editor, Otto Floersheim), who wondered what on earth had happened to the writer from the Massachusetts capital when he failed to mention either Chadwick or Herbert and at the same time praised W. H. Rieger for singing *Celeste Aida* and H. W. Parker for conducting his own *The Kobolds.* After noting that Herbert had played finely, O. F. stated that Rieger had sung a substitute aria and Chadwick had conducted *The Kobolds* instead of Parker, who was unable to leave New York. Whereupon O. F. justly observed: "What can be said in defense of that writer for one of the biggest papers of the music-proud Hub? He must have been either drunk or he shone through absence, in either of which cases he had no right to telegraph to his paper."[72]

After the Springfield festival Herbert and the orchestra toured southwestward. The illustrious composer Peter Ilich Tchaikovsky joined them as guest conductor in Baltimore and Philadelphia on May 15 and 18. On his first and last visit to America the fabulous Russian was conducting only his own works, which were acclaimed and appreciated; but he was desperately unhappy and maintained the mood that characterizes the brooding Slav. His melancholy diary[73] reflects his depressed state of mind, and there is no evidence that even the ebullient Herbert enlivened his spirit.

What Tchaikovsky expected is not disclosed, but he was set back at his Baltimore hotel by "indifference and neglect, as usual." He felt extraordinarily "pitiable and unhappy," and was vastly irritated by a Negro waiter who had difficulty in understanding his breakfast order. He felt better when he met the pianist, Adele Aus der Ohe, who was to play his B flat minor concerto, and went with her to the hall for rehearsal. Here he drooped again; and he tells us why, revealing only a slight effort to appreciate the problems of Herbert's exhausting schedule:

Went . . . to the rehearsal in a carriage. The final glory took place on the stage of the Lyceum Theater. The orchestra turned out to be small (there were four first violins in all!!!) but not bad. There was not even a thought of the Third Suite. We decided to play in its stead the Serenade for Strings, which the musicians did not know at all, while Mr. Herbert (the conductor) did not even think of playing it through beforehand, as Reno had promised me. The Concerto with Aus der Ohe went well at once, but it was necessary to fuss considerably with the Serenade. The musicians were impatient, and the young concertmaster [Emil Mollenhauer] was not particularly courteous, for he displayed too vehemently that it was time to finish. True, this unfortunate touring orchestra is very tired from traveling about.

The first impression from this tirade, that Tchaikovsky had little respect for Herbert's handiwork, is unwarranted. He found the orchestra too small, yet it was not bad; he found it also worn out from the rigors of touring. Just how or when Herbert could have tried the Serenade, which the musicians had not expected to play, Tchaikovsky did not explain. It is conceded today that Tchaikovsky was not a competent conductor, and it may be surmised that Herbert's men were as annoyed by him as he was by them.

If the Russian maestro was gloomy over his first encounter with the orchestra, he was satisfied with the concert itself. Now, however, the audience displeased him:

After the rehearsal went home with Aus der Ohe again. We changed in a half hour and drove at once to the concert. As is customary at concerts during the day, I conducted in a frock coat. Everything went perfectly well, but I did not notice any unusual enthusiasm in the audience, at least, in comparison with New York.

In an evening concert by the orchestra that same day, Tchaikovsky had no part; there were other soloists, and Herbert played the cello. The critics were extravagant in their praise of the two programs given, according to the Baltimore *American* of May 16, by "one of the best organizations of musicians that has ever visited this city"; the *American* offered this peculiar description of the Russian composer:

[He] is also a czar among musicians and directors. His personal appearance alone shows him to be a great man. As he stands to direct, he looks as if the commander of all the armies in Russia had for the moment laid aside the sword of conflict and destruction and taken up the baton of harmony and peace. He has, indeed, a "front like Mars" and "an eye to threaten or command." In fact, he does more directing with his eye alone than other directors do with all the means at their command.

. . . it is hard for any one to be unmusical in his presence. His magnetic personality sways all who are about him. Yet he does nothing for effect. He directs, and all follow; he commands, and all instinctively obey; as though grateful in their serfdom, art governs him, and all whom he can govern. If he makes them slaves, they delight in his chains.

Herbert received his share of praise, but naturally the international celebrity attracted the greatest attention.

On May 16 Tchaikovsky went to Washington, where the orchestra had played on the 14th, and where he lost a front tooth. The resulting hiss in his speech caused him considerable embarrassment, but it did not prevent his attending a fancy dinner in his honor at the Metropolitan Club. Then on the 18th he hastened to Philadelphia for another appearance with Herbert and his men at the Academy of Music. Here the orchestra had only one concert, with solos by Adele Aus der Ohe, pianist, Rose Stewart, soprano, Myron W. Whitney, bass, Felix Winternitz, violinist, and Herbert himself, cellist. The long and heterogeneous program[74] follows:

Vorspiel to "Lohengrin"	Wagner
Aria: "I'm a Roamer"	Mendelssohn
Mr. Whitney	
Le Dernier Sommeil de la Vierge	Massenet
Intermezzo from "Naila"	Delibes
Mad Scene from "Lucia"	Donizetti
Miss Stewart	
Concerto in B flat minor	Tchaikovsky
Miss Aus der Ohe	
Composer conducting	

INTERMISSION

Fantaisie Characteristique for 'cello	Servais
Mr. Herbert	
Aria from "The Magic Flute"	Mozart
Mr. Whitney	
Fantasy on Airs from "Othello"	Ernst
Mr. Winternitz	
Songs with piano	
Thou Art So Like a Bird	Chadwick
A Bird in the Wood	Taubert
Miss Stewart	
Suite for String Orchestra*	Tchaikovsky
Composer conducting	
Overture to "Der Freischütz"	Weber

* Probably: Serenade for Strings.

Again Tchaikovsky was the center of attention, though the orchestra was lauded and the entire concert conspicuously successful. There was some comment on the small size of the audience lured to the hall by his only appearance in Philadelphia. From the account in the *Public Ledger* it would seem that the feud between the composer and the concertmaster had not ceased! In any case Tchaikovsky was

an energetic and authoritative conductor, and under his direction the men evidently felt the spirit of his music as they could not have felt it under another leader. The orchestra, organized on a basis of three double basses and six [sic] first violins, was notably well balanced and satisfactory in volume and quality of tone except in the Tschaikowsky suite [Serenade ?], where the principal and another of the first violins dropped out for some reason not readily apparent. With Miss Adele Aus der Ohe at the piano, almost uniformly at her best in her execution, the concerto had unsurpassable interpretation, with the composer to emphasize its character and bring out its inmost beauties. This was done with a brilliancy, boldness and delicacy that stirred the audience to genuine enthusiasm. Miss Aus der Ohe and Tschaikowsky were called before the house three times and almost overwhelmed with applause, and each deserved it all the more because each endeavored to put the other most prominently forward as the deserving recipient of the honors.

If the Russian master felt the orchestra was weary in Baltimore, he was probably aghast at learning it was to begin a three-day festival in Providence on May 19. This was organized by the Arion Club under the leadership of Jules Jordan. It had done much for the city in its eleven years' existence, and Mr. Jordan was entitled to his townsmen's gratitude. The only trouble was that he sometimes conducted pieces better left to others. A discriminating observer who described the results rather shrewdly was William A. Potter; he first pointed out the peculiarly warm relationship maintained by Herbert with his men:

In reviewing the whole festival it may be said to have afforded us the pleasure of hearing some excellent artists, chorus singing of a high order and a well chosen variety of the best music. The orchestra, while furnishing good accompaniments to the choral works, played very unevenly in the purely orchestral numbers. When Mr. Jordan conducted they seemed to be half asleep or not trying. As soon as Mr. Herbert assumed the baton they came to life again. Whether this was intended to accentuate their preferences in the matter of a conductor, or owing to some other unknown cause, the writer does not profess to know. The fact, however, was so noticeable that every musician with whom we talked commented on it.

Of course, Mr. Jordan does not assume to be a Nikisch or a Thomas, as he only sees an orchestra three or four times a year. But he probably studies his scores thoroughly, and with his successful record in the handling of large choral works ought to be able to get good work out of an orchestra. If he found that he could not do so, either from lack of experience or from want of con-

fidence on the part of the men, he had better have put the whole—instead
of a part—of the orchestral work upon Mr. Herbert, with whom the players
seemed thoroughly *en rapport*. In fact, the orchestra was advertised as being
his.[75]

During the summer Herbert's main activity again was with Seidl
at Brighton Beach. He played and conducted and enlivened the general
musical scene. The orchestra had its loyal following, and Seidl found
that good music was by no means despised in hot weather. The ten-
week season opened on June 27, and the programs promised so much
healthful musical fare that the *Musical Courier* urged music students
to come here for edification alone. Indeed, it declared, students could
hear as much good music in ten weeks of Seidl's orchestra as they
could in ten years on the European Continent.[76] This was an exaggeration; but a great quantity of music was available, and not a few
music-hungry persons took advantage of it.

This summer with Seidl did not preclude Herbert from keeping
other engagements. Early in July he was cellist in the sixteenth national
Sängerfest at Newark, New Jersey, of the northeastern singing societies,
with Frank Van der Stucken as the main conductor. It was a gala
event, for which more than five thousand German singers assembled.[77]
Herbert collaborated in a series of free concerts at Castle Garden in
New York, sponsored by the *Morning Journal* with Sam Franko as
organizer and director. At first only four concerts were planned; but
they proved to be so popular that sixteen were given, the average
attendance (chiefly laborers and clerks) amounting to 5,000. Other
artists collaborating with Franko in this praiseworthy enterprise were
the Scharwenka brothers, Franz Rummel, Arthur Friedheim, and
Leopold Godowsky. The first concert took place on September 2, and
Franko later declared that he had never seen a more enthusiastic or
reverent audience.[78]

Herbert's keenest anticipation during the summer of 1891 was unquestionably of the Worcester Festival (September 21–25), where he
would officiate as usual and, much more important, produce his
dramatic cantata, *The Captive*. He would also play, impeccably, the
Saint-Saëns concerto.

Undisturbed by the criticisms of the preceding year, he threw himself heart and soul into his work; but he could not make friends with
everyone. It is amazing, indeed, to what lengths a critic would go in
harshly judging an action which could only be called inevitable. In
the second festival concert Herbert was conducting the orchestra for
Mrs. S. C. Ford's singing of Mozart's *Bella mia fiamma*. Somewhere
in the audience a child began to cry, so forcefully that the critic

admitted it "sounded as if the oboe had broken loose and gone off on a spree with one of the clarinets." The singer tried to ignore it; but Herbert quite properly stopped the performance and waited until quiet was restored. Whereupon the splenetic critic observed: "Bad as the infant's yell was, Mr. Herbert seemed to make the matter worse. He is such a pleasant chap that it is unfortunate that it should be necessary to speak of the matter."[79] The critic at least made clear who had the more sensitive ears!

The first performance of *The Captive,* a large and important work for solo voices, chorus, and full orchestra, was on September 24. Based on a narrative poem by the contemporary German poet, Rudolf Baumbach, it was the most ambitious score Herbert had written; and it remains one of his strongest compositions. It is impressive, fluently contrived, and orchestrated with the skill and imagination ever at his command. The portions for chorus are considerably more effective than the passages for soprano and baritone solo, which, though highly acceptable, are not out of the ordinary. Because it was intended as a choral work and was composed especially for the occasion, Herbert undoubtedly concentrated on the choral sections. Musically there are many felicitous touches of melody, harmony, and atmosphere. It was not a forward-looking work in the sense of artistic innovation, yet it was romantically modern and expertly done. It would be well worth hearing today; but a choral society contemplating a revival would have to face difficulties, particularly the need of a first-class orchestra.

The text, not too happily rendered into English by E. Buck, tells of a knight captured by a band of warriors. As he is led away to execution he passes beneath the window of a noble lady who is moved to pity, compassion, and tears—also love. She is so highly placed that she can, and does, command his immediate release, making it clear that the knight is to marry her and belong to her forever. But the captive tells the lady that his heart is already promised to another, that even to save his life he will not break faith with his betrothed. There is no other means of rescue, and the knight continues on his way to death. For this simple incident Herbert developed an elaborate score which lasts nearly an hour in performance. The dramatic significance of the tale is slender, and the composer achieved quite a feat in maintaining the musical interest.

The best and briefest summary of the work was by "Raconteur" (Herbert's admirer, Huneker), who engaged in prophecy at the same time.

I wish to say right here . . . that Herbert has composed an extremely strong work, picturesque as to coloring and incident and extremely dramatic.

It is all so easy, so unforced, so free from the "agony" and "pumping up" processes of many modern composers, that it is a welcome and an agreeable task for me to predict for the young composer a brilliant future. With his graceful lyric gift, delicate harmonic sense and that beautiful style of orchestration almost Gallic in its touch, there is no reason why Victor Herbert shouldn't write a very successful opera. He has plenty of Celtic fancy, passion and humor in his mental make-up, and his orchestral sense is finely developed, having that feeling for the subtle correspondence and combination that are latent in the orchestral family. Therefore there is no reason in the world why he shouldn't do some big things, except the trouble of a good libretto, and that, let me sadly add, is a bar that genius itself halts before, or behind, and often goes off limpingly. Just think of Schubert's, of Beethoven's, of Weber's . . . and Schumann's librettists! What overflowing genius it took to surmount the cacophonic barriers of speech erected by these misguided individuals? A Lorenzo da Ponte is not born every day, and Mozart was a lucky fellow.

Rather than see Herbert's lovely music saddled with a poor book I will, being in a modest vein to-day, write a libretto for him myself, and my sympathies being at the present time realistic, and agreeing with Mr. Boston Howells that in contemporary life may be found lots of mud, mortar and building material for a young ambitious literary Buddensieck, I will construct my music drama of things now transpiring in this goodly city of cable construction.[80]

Huneker's vision of Herbert as a musical dramatist would soon materialize, albeit in the field of operetta. His comment on the weakness of the cantata "book" was true enough, and it may be wondered if the two debated the matter. As a matter of fact, he was pointing out the weakest aspect of the composer's whole career; for it must be acknowledged that Herbert was never a good judge of operatic librettos, light or serious. He was intensely loyal to his librettists, both light and serious, but the number of "books" he misjudged as to dramatic quality was appalling. His subsequent triumphs on the stage were generally in spite of plot and drama, and his failures were often because of them. Huneker's facetious proposal—perhaps serious at the time—to concoct a libretto for Herbert gives rise to speculative regret. Together they might have done a lustier, gustier, opera than any that was to fall from Herbert's pen.

On December 9, 1891, Herbert again performed in two places in the same evening. With Sam Franko, Emil Fischer, Mme. Fursch-Madi, and other artists he participated in a grand concert at the Madison Square Garden concert hall to aid immigrants from Russia. Then he had to rush to Hardman Hall for the first of a series of concerts by the Schmidt-Herbert String Quartet—an undertaking which vastly enriched New York's musical season. This new ensemble had organized but five weeks before; yet its playing was hailed with delight, and its future concerts were keenly anticipated. The artists in the group were Louis Schmidt, Jr., and Henry Schmidt, violins, Franz Kaltenborn, viola, and Herbert, cello. The program was: Schumann's Quartet in A minor, Op. 41, No. 1; two movements from Raff's *Die schöne Müllerin*, Op. 192 (*Declaration* and *The Mill*); Boccherini's Cello Sonata in A; Rubinstein's Quartet in F, Op. 17, No. 3.

The *Musical Courier* of December 16 said that the names of the artists alone guaranteed the excellence of the playing; but it remained for the *Times* to render praise that was downright lavish: The group excelled in every respect, playing with "a full and resonant tone, of vibrant quality, precision of attack, intelligent phrasing, a discreetly forceful vigor and delicacy of sentiment, and admirably graduated light and shade." It was a pleasure to welcome the group, which would henceforth be heard with more than common interest. The *Times* took note of Herbert's "inimitable and captivating style"; but the *Herald* was even more impressed, for it reported: "Mr. Herbert's exquisite playing of the Boccherini sonata was the feature of the evening. This excellent player, who stands at the head of our resident cellists, is not heard often enough this season."

Three more concerts were given by the group in January to March, 1892. The programs, which were on a consistently higher level than those offered by Franko, are reproduced here:[81]

January 8: Haydn, Quartet in D, Op. 20, No. 4; Bach, Chaconne (violin); Chopin, Prelude in B minor; B. Scholz, Minuet, from Quartet in G; Bazzini, Quartet in D minor, Op. 75.

February 11: Beethoven, Quartet in E flat, Op. 74; Herbert, Legende and Scherzo (cello); Tchaikovsky, Andante Cantabile, from Quartet, Op. 11; Grieg, Quartet in G minor, Op. 27.

March 16: Schubert, Quartet in A minor, Op. 29; Chopin, Nocturne, and Brahms—Joachim, Hungarian Dance (violin); Mozart, Andante, from Quartet in D; L. Schmidt, Jr., Scherzo Tarantelle; Beethoven, Quartet in F minor, Op. 95.

After the concert on January 8 it was the *Tribune's* turn to wax enthusiastic: The presence in New York of the Schmidt-Herbert String Quartet had materially strengthened the weakest aspect of the city's musical life; the artists revealed high aims and lofty standards, fine taste and unfailing intelligence; they knew how to imbue the Bazzini work with color and vitality, while Haydn received "a performance of beautiful fluency and refinement, one, in fact, that quite caught the simple and gracious spirit of the composition"; the entire concert was characterized by "much smoothness and a noteworthy unanimity of feeling."

On January 13 Herbert played two of his own shorter pieces and the cello part in a Trio by Titus d'Ernesti at one of the private concerts of the famous Manuscript Society (the evening also provided a special reception for Emma Eames); and on January 21 he appeared in Buffalo as soloist with the local orchestra. The upstate conductor was the well known John Lund, who as one of Herbert's dearest friends and closest colleagues was delighted with a characteristic act of the cellist. After playing his first solo, excerpts from his Suite, Op. 3, Herbert simply joined the other cellists in the orchestra and played along with them. He had already dazzled the audience with his playing, and this unpremeditated act of friendliness called forth a new demonstration. As one reporter put it: "Mr. Herbert made two thousand friends on the occasion of this visit, 'all unbeknownst to his self.'"[82]

Spring saw, or heard, the production of another piece of Herbert's which, to its own detriment, became too popular. This was the lively *Irish Rhapsody*, which was written for and first heard at the annual Feis Ceoil agus Seanachus of the Gaelic Society on April 20. Herbert directed the performance in the Lenox Lyceum. Again the tireless Huneker burst forth with loud praise—for Herbert, whom he called the "Irish Wagner," and for the piece, which he said would become a concert favorite.[83] This prediction was, if anything, too accurate, for the Rhapsody became so popular that it was played to death, and separated from the composer's serious music. It was so brilliant and facile, so associated with Irish festivities, and so adaptable to various ensembles that it killed itself as an independent concert number. This was unfortunate, for it was skillfully wrought and deserved the kind words that Huneker attached to it.

Late in June, Herbert appeared alone as cellist and with the Schmidt-Herbert Quartet in Syracuse at the meeting of the New York State Music Teachers' Association. He and his colleagues acted here as missionaries of music, and were readily admitted and appreciated as such. "The average country teacher does not get many opportunities during the year of hearing ensemble selections, hence it is most praiseworthy on the part of the program committee . . . to introduce more and more of just such music."[84]

Meanwhile Herbert composed several new pieces that appeared at this time. They were all smaller efforts and foreshadowed his later addiction to music in the lighter vein. He was already a consummate master of the style which was to make him America's best loved composer. Playing under Seidl on December 4 at the Lenox Lyceum,[85] he brought forth his romantic *Pensée amoureuse* for cello accompanied by string orchestra. It had charm and exquisite refinement, and the audience responded with warm approval. Then an entirely different audience welcomed two short pieces for cello and piano, *Tristesse* and *A la Mazurka,* which the composer played at a Schmidt-Herbert Quartet concert on December 20.[86] (Flanking them on the program were Schumann's Quartet in A major and Dvořák's Quartet in E flat major.) Presumably about this time, Herbert wrote *Badinage,* a carefree, spritely orchestral confection which has become a salon classic —at least, family records show that it was written prior to 1893. Curiously enough, no one today knows Herbert's original version, for it was never published and the autograph has long since disappeared. It was first printed in 1895 as a piano arrangement by Alexander Rihm; then in 1897 Otto Langey made an orchestral version (his band version came a year later) which was universally accepted, and which undoubtedly had Herbert's sanction. Presumably, too, therefore, the composer's original vanished at a very early date.[87]

Late in 1892 a rather unpleasant experience came to Herbert. It had its origin in an anonymous letter to the *Musical Courier.* Seeing a good story, the journal exploited it to the full and was responsible for the subsequent disclosures, after which it compelled the composer to be an arbiter in a curious case of musical plagiarism.

Orchestral transcriptions were as popular then as now, and Max Spicker, one of New York's most prominent musicians, offered his arrangement of Chopin's A flat Polonaise to Anton Seidl, who duly played it. The standard and older arrangement of the piece was by Müller-Berghaus. Suddenly this alarming letter appeared in the *Courier*:

Editors Musical Courier:

In your last number you jokingly allude to a "tampering with a score of Mueller-Berghaus." Now, why not state the facts, which are that Mr. Max Spicker deliberately copied the orchestration of a Chopin A flat polonaise by Mueller-Berghaus and palmed it off on Mr. Seidl as his own work. One of your staff was present when this musical swindle was discerned, but as Mr. Spicker belongs to the charmed circle it is kept quiet. Had some other unfortunate young composer shown but the slightest similarity in his ideas with someone else you would have cut him to pieces, but as this party belongs to the "gang" he necessarily must be shielded. Come now, practice what you preach and expose this musical kleptomaniac and charlatan.

VERITAS[88]

First of all the *Courier* deprecated resort to anonymity; then it expressed a desire to expose fraud of any kind. It stated that Spicker was reputed to be an excellent musician and his orchestral arrangements had found wide favor. Finally it admitted that a member of its editorial staff had compared the two versions of the Chopin transcription, in the presence of Victor Herbert, John Rietzel, and Henry Schmitt. Although the comparison had shown how damaging the charge was, it refused to make a judgment. Spicker should have his say and an opportunity to clear his name. The implication was that the three men named must make public their opinion.

Meanwhile a representative of the *Courier* interviewed the unhappy Spicker, who tried to toss the affair off, saying that he himself had disliked the Müller-Berghaus score and had tried to write a better one, that he had written every line of it, and that both Seidl and Van der Stucken knew it. If there was any resemblance between the two, it was purely accidental.[89] Then the *Courier* encouraged further comment by saying the matter was now too serious to drop, and urged the formulation of signed charges. Herbert and his friends interpreted this as a direct challenge, and they accepted it, protesting their innocence respecting the anonymous letter. Their statement, probably written by Herbert, left little room for doubt.

New York, November 18, 1892

Editors Musical Courier:

In your last issue you take exception at the receipt of an anonymous letter charging Mr. Max Spicker with boldly appropriating the Müller-Berghaus orchestral arrangement of Chopin's A flat polonaise, and after mentioning our names in connection with the charge against Mr. Spicker you ask us to prove our assertion, or rather, to formulate the charge.

We the undersigned accept this challenge and are prepared to prove absolutely that Mr. Max Spicker has with several very significant and irrelevant changes copied Müller-Berghaus' arrangement of the polonaise in question. But first we wish to heartily disclaim the authorship of the anonymous letter which we saw in the office of THE MUSICAL COURIER. It was not written by us nor do we know from whom it emanated, nor yet again do we approve of such a letter. We have absolutely no animus in the matter, but are assured that Mr. Spicker, in denying the impeachment in your last issue, is under a misapprehension. One of the members of your editorial staff, Mr. J. G. Huneker, was present when the two scores were compared and must verify the truth of this assertion.

We therefore ask any fair minded person to compare these two scores and to say if there is not a plagiarism pure and simple.

With a recapitulation of the statement that in this matter there is no personal feeling whatsoever, we hereby affix our names.

VICTOR HERBERT
JOHN C. RIETZEL
HENRY P. SCHMITT[90]

By naming Huneker, Herbert threw the responsibility directly back to the *Courier,* which in turn asserted it had discovered a song composed by W. Groeschel (1884), but subsequently appropriated by Spicker as his own. It tried to inject a bit of humor into the situation by reporting that Seidl, in programming the polonaise arrangement, had spent $30 for the copying of parts when he could have purchased the Müller-Berghaus parts for $2.70. It attempted to close the case by announcing that both Huneker and Seidl had inspected the score, which seemed so like the earlier transcription that "nothing short of the miraculous could explain away the similarities. It is a plagiarism pure and simple, as was the song, and the matter is now forever dismissed with the sorrowful thought that, for a musician of Mr. Spicker's supposed capacity, these plagiarisms are inexcusable." Spicker tried to defend himself, but the *Courier*, with a bluntness which always exceeded its taste, accused him of falsehood and said he should have let the scandal die out.[91]

Enjoying its best season, the Schmidt-Herbert String Quartet brought New York some undisputed masterpieces of chamber music. On January 13, 1893, it played Haydn's D major quartet, Op. 64, No. 5, and Beethoven's quartet in F major, Op. 59, No. 1.[92] On February 10 its main offerings were the C major quartet by Mozart and Schubert's quartet on *Death and the Maiden*.[93] And on March 24 it performed Schubert's *Quartettsatz* in C minor, Haydn's variations from the *Kaiserquartett* and Beethoven's quartet in A minor, Op. 132—probably the noblest program it ever played.[94] The artists continued to alternate in presenting solos between the more formidable chamber selections, for an enthusiastic audience for chamber music alone did not yet exist.

After the concert on March 24 Herbert was visited by a young man in his late teens who was to attain distinction in American letters— Percy MacKaye. He came to discuss a project of seemingly terrific importance[95] which, promising and impressive, was nevertheless doomed to failure.

On October 21, 1892, the President of the United States had proclaimed that a celebration of the four hundredth anniversary of Columbus' discovery of America would take place at the Chicago World's Fair. Planning was started at once, but the magnitude of preparations delayed the official opening until the following May. The most ambitious scheme was advanced by that stormy petrel and undisciplined genius of the American stage Steele MacKaye, father of Percy, whose grandiose visions were simply impossible to realize (or finance). Perhaps Percy did not exaggerate in describing his father as the only person who "dared to propose and demonstrate, for a great World Exposition, a commensurate dramatic art to interpret it."[96] For Chicago he dreamed his biggest dream; and collected a vast amount of money to finance it—but not enough. The dreamer's health was shattered by disappointment and frustration, and he died shortly afterward.

His vision embraced the construction of a huge auditorium called a "spectatorium" in which would be presented a breath-taking "spectatorio" entitled *The Great Discovery* or *The World Finder*. This was to portray, depict, and interpret the physical and spiritual adventures of Columbus as he daringly sailed westward to find the New World. It was to be scenic, dramatic, pantomimic, and it needed all the resources which musical and dramatic art could supply. Steele MacKaye's plans included the tossing billows of the sea, the conflict of saints and demons, the fear and awe of the impressionable sailors, and the steadfast faith of the worthy captain. Two composers were to furnish the music: Dvořák (recently come to this country to teach at Mrs. Thurber's National Conservatory) and Herbert. For the former, MacKaye had unbounded admiration. He placed the Czech composer and the Genoese explorer together as having surmounted the most discouraging obstacles to reach hard-won goals.

Dvořák's lively interest and promise of cooperation were obtained with the help of Mrs. Thurber. He was to compose a "majestic orchestral portion" of the "new dramatic art-form"[97] which Seidl would perform with a full symphony orchestra. The musical interpretation of a vast new world appealed strongly to the Bohemian master, and, although the project failed to materialize, it is not unlikely that the immortal *New World Symphony* had its inception here.

Herbert was to provide the pantomimic music for the "spectatorio," and he was busy writing it in the early spring of 1893. Young Percy MacKaye heard him play extended passages of it, and praised its picturesque qualities. He long remembered his conference with the "slim, black-haired" Irishman on March 24 and the zest with which Herbert illustrated what he was writing. Percy reported to his father (in Chicago) the fine impression Herbert's music made, and the elder MacKaye replied: "I am delighted to hear such good news of Victor Herbert's music. I am trying to arrange to have Seidl, Herbert, [Frederick] Archer and Percy here for a couple of weeks in the early part of April."[98]

But, alas, MacKaye's optimism was promptly quenched. His gigantic project was a financial fiasco, and the public never had a chance to judge its effectiveness. It is not known exactly how much music was written for it; but one orchestral movement by Herbert unquestionably resulted from the ill starred venture. Among his autographs in the Library of Congress is the orchestra score of *The "Vision" of Columbus*, dated at the end, "June '93." Years later Herbert found a use for it and, with a slightly different title, made it the finale of his *Columbus* suite. He also made choral settings of a couple of Percy's texts.

Herbert, like so many others, had a great affection for the unhappy Steele MacKaye, as the son makes clear in his biography. In 1916 Percy endeavored to memorialize his father, and he asked Herbert to be among the friends participating. Herbert answered: "Having known your dear father very well indeed, I consider it a great honour to have my name added to those on the committee." Others participating were Walter Damrosch, John Drew, Thomas A. Edison, Daniel Frohman, Childe Hassam, William Dean Howells, and Augustus Thomas. Eight years later the composer and Percy MacKaye lunched together at The Lambs, where Herbert said: "I am going to write you a tribute of my heart to your father's genius. I am rushed now, but I'll mail it to you within three weeks." Less than three weeks later he was dead, and the promise remained unfulfilled.

4

The Band and the Stage

In 1893 Herbert was thirty-four, respected, esteemed, and loved. But he was also restless and ill at ease, chafing under the monotony of orchestra playing and wanting more opportunity to assert his individuality. He was also plagued by melodies and shorter phrases which he knew should be turned to account. If augmented income and increased popularity resulted, so much the better.

Thus the thought of composing operettas occurred to him at a relatively early date. He was not reticent about it, for he confessed his desire to some orchestra colleagues. His early wish to approach the stage resulted in a piece which apparently was never produced—which, in fact, seems to be irretrievably lost and is completely unknown. Enough people mentioned it, however, including the composer himself, for its former existence to be unquestioningly accepted.

Under the title *La Vivandière*, two successive issues of the *Musical Courier* in the late summer of 1893 referred to it.[1] Allegedly finished, it was reported as having been read and accepted by Lillian Russell, then playing at New York's famed Casino. In 1894, when Herbert's first known operetta was produced, an unidentified critic wrote: "Nearly a year ago I inspected an operetta by Victor Herbert and Francis Neilson called 'La Vivandiere,' and it was easy to recognize merit of no ordinary kind in the work."[2] Herbert played great portions of it to his friend Huneker, who praised it warmly, finding the music light and dainty and the whole score filled with humor and enthusiasm.[3] And it may have been Huneker that lamented, six years later, that Herbert's best light opera would never be produced, suggesting that La Russell's failure to appear in it came from her fear of using a work by a man unknown to the operetta stage.[4] A Buffalo reporter, who told the composer of hearing that he had written two works for the stage,

72

quoted him as saying: "Why, it's all the same opera. The only one I have completed is 'La Vivandiere,' which has been accepted by Lillian Russell and probably will be put on when 'Princess Nicotine' in which she is now playing at the Casino is withdrawn. I can't say when that will be."[5] At the same time he admitted that a second operetta was under way, to a libretto also by Francis Neilson.

In view of Herbert's subsequent achievements the mystery of *La Vivandière* may be minor; but it is tantalizing. After all, one person called it his best, when such brilliant scores as *The Serenade* and *The Fortune Teller* had been taken to heart; and so the desire to estimate the loss is irresistible.

However, association with the stage had to wait while Herbert embarked upon an activity far different from any he had yet attempted. He became a bandmaster—a wise decision though the occupation was a novel one. It relieved him of the monotony of orchestra playing; it did not interfere with solo work or composing; it made him still more popular with more people; and it sharpened his appreciation of the value of music *qua* entertainment. Incidentally, his acceptance of the post saved a notable organization from collapse and, according to available reports, led to unprecedented standards of band performance.

If any reader feels that Herbert hereby took a retrogressive step, let him correct his thinking at once. Generally speaking, the great concert bands are no more; but with them have disappeared their audiences. These democratic ensembles of music brought their message to the common man. Indoors and out, winter and summer, a huge following responded wholeheartedly to the bewildering variety of their programs. Having their origin in military pomp, they supplied to listeners the thrill of patriotic joy, and they offset their novelty selections with pieces of deeply moving beauty.

America's premier bandmaster in the nineteenth century was Patrick Sarsfield Gilmore, who, born in Ireland in 1829, had come to America as a young man with an increasing reputation as a musician and organizer. Before, during, and after the Civil War his bands attracted wide attention. He was a good showman, and his men loved him for a rare personal integrity. His name was already a household word in 1872, when he moved from Boston to New York to form and direct (for twenty years) the band of the Twenty-second Regiment of the New York National Guard.

The Twenty-second Regiment came into being in the spring of 1861. With zeal and ardor it equipped a band of forty-four pieces and engaged F. B. Helmsmuller as its leader. The band was mustered into service with the regiment, and they went to war together in 1862. This, of course, proved to be a mistake, but experience is ever a dear teacher. The foreigners in the band—perhaps the Americans, too—had no liking for military strictness, and none of them was satisfied with the niggardly government pay. In order to keep the band, therefore, the officers of the regiment had to contribute money from their own pockets—a heavy drain from which they saw no relief. With respect to behavior, General Wingate tells the story:

> During their service [in the campaign] not a few breaches of discipline of a minor character were committed by the musicians, whose knowledge of military usages at the front was generally in the inverse proportion of their skill in music. They apparently never could understand why they should not be out of camp after tattoo, nor why, if they were, they should not return by the shortest line, instead of going round by the guard tent. Neither could they be made to understand the object of the countersign, or its use.
>
> Night after night the sentries would be heard calling "Halt! who goes there?" and the reply, "I ish de band."
>
> Finally, in July, 1862, the band was sent home, and the Twenty-second thereafter depended upon its drum corps for its military music during this campaign.[6]

But when the regiment itself came home, the band went to Philadelphia to meet it, blowing its loudest welcome in Helmsmuller's *Twenty-second Regiment March*. Infractions were forgiven, annoyances forgotten as officers and men vociferously cheered the wayward artists.

Dying in 1865, Helmsmuller was succeeded by Dodworth, then by Rehm; but the band failed to fulfill the wishes of the regiment. Deciding it must have only the best in the way of leadership, it called upon Gilmore in 1872 and prevailed upon him to head a revitalized Twenty-second Regiment Band. Agreement was reached on financial responsibility, and the new leader was encouraged to make it nationally prominent. In 1878 the band toured Europe with brilliant success and then delighted all America with its prowess. Two observations from John Philip Sousa attest the abilities of Gilmore's Band and the service it rendered to the American public:

> Gilmore organized a corps of musicians superior to any wind-band players of his day, many of them coming from the leading orchestras of the world and possessing a virtuoso's ability on their respective instruments. He engaged his musicians regardless of expense and paid them salaries commensurate with their talents.

The second was prompted by Gilmore's death:

> The passing of Patrick Sarsfield Gilmore in the autumn of the previous year . . . saddened the musical world. Mr. Gilmore had organized and

gathered together the very best wood-wind and brass players of both Europe and America. He had gone into the highways and byways of the land, playing Wagner and Liszt, and other great composers, in places where their music was absolutely unknown, and their names scarcely more than a twice-repeated sound.[7]

Gilmore died almost without warning on September 24, 1892, in St. Louis, where his band was playing an engagement of several weeks at the Exposition. His death was a blow to the country and the cause of profound grief among his men. It posed the problem of selecting a successor—quickly, for the future of the band was in jeopardy. Gilmore, ever concerned for the permanency of his band, had called his men together before the tour of the previous season and asked them to name their next leader: he knew that the success of a band unendowed and unsustained depended upon the director's skill and personality. But no action had been taken, and now the band members were in a quandary.[8]

Knowing some one had to be found promptly, they took hasty action, that they would regret before the season was over. They chose D. W. Reeves, director of Reeves' American Band (of Providence, Rhode Island) which was playing an engagement in Portland, Oregon:

St. Louis, October 12
Mr. D. W. Reeves:
    At a meeting of the band you were unanimously elected leader and conductor of Gilmore's Band. Knowing you to be the only man in America worthy of keeping the band up to its high standard, and following in the footsteps of our lamented Mr. Gilmore, we extend to you, sir, a hearty welcome and support, and beg you to name a day when you can meet the band.

> C. W. Freudenvoll
> E. A. Lefebre
> A. Bode
> Carl O. D. Chiara
> John Sheridan
> *Committee appointed by the Band.*[9]

Reeves, responding at once to the message, promised to join his new ensemble in St. Louis as soon as his Portland engagement terminated on October 23.

Unfortunately for the Gilmore Band, the prosperity did not continue. Some of its members left to join Sousa, who was in his first season as a conductor outside government service and was intent on forming a band of the best possible quality. His autobiography boasts that he secured the services of about nineteen of Gilmore's finest players immediately after Gilmore died. Among them was the cornetist, Herbert L. Clarke. The Gilmore group had the further misfortune of issuing a public statement which combined with an appeal for support a polite excusing of Sousa (but not of all his motives) and a severe condemnation of the men who had joined him. The *Musical Courier* of March 15, 1893, printed it in full:

GILMORE AND SOUSA

An Open Letter

To whom it may concern—Gilmore's Band speaks

Gilmore's Band, the band of the famous Twenty-Second Regiment N.G.S.N.Y., is none the less the greatest band in the world at the present time than it was under the guidance of its great organizer. It has been so conceded hundreds of times recently, and we feel that the sentiment of the hundreds of thousands of people who have been entertained and made happy under the spell of its matchless music is that the famous organization should be perpetuated. It is well known that Mr. Gilmore possessed the finest library of music extant, embracing thousands of the finest specially arranged pieces and played by only his band. Mr. Reeves' library also is celebrated as being extensive and containing many valuable MSS. pieces arranged by himself. The two great libraries are now combined, and Mr. Reeves has the exclusive use of the entire collection through the active and earnest cooperation of the family of the late Mr. Gilmore, and who heartily second the efforts of Mr. Reeves. A persistent effort is being made by interested and unscrupulous parties, who do not hesitate to resort to doubtful methods in order to silence this great name, to create the impression that Gilmore's Band is no more, and we warn all the friends of the late bandmaster and of his world famous band of the fact that they may take the reports for what they are worth. Gilmore's Band is here to stay and they will prove to all who attend their concerts the fact as asserted above.

In explanation of the above it is proper to state that a syndicate was formed, headed by a man whom Mr. Gilmore repudiated for reasons. A gentleman and a musician was induced to leave a prominent position under the Government, and a band selected haphazard from various parts of America was hastily formed, purporting to hail from Chicago, for the avowed purpose of running Mr. Gilmore from the field. The aforesaid musician was placed at the head of "this band from Chicago." This leader, being too much of a gentleman to enter into any doubtful operations, is acquitted of any intents except to make as good a band as possible. It was called the New Marine Band, trying plainly enough to steal the honors from the band made famous by Mr. ———, the leader aforesaid. Warnings from Washington caused the name to be changed to the World's Fair Band, in hopes of capturing the world's exposition business. Failing in that, a concert tour promising fifty weeks was "wound up in nine." Failing in that, this "syndicate" set to work to induce Gilmore's Band to join their party, that they might perhaps share in their great reputation. This was not so much of a failure, for some men who have played with Mr. Gilmore were induced to join this "band from Chicago." Probably 2,000 musicians first and last could claim "that honor" of having played with Gilmore "some time," and as the band numbered 100 when Mr. Gilmore died, and fifty of that number have been dropped, it would be easy enough to organize quite a large band composed of men who had played with Mr. Gilmore, and that quite recently. So from first to last this famous band has relied on some "other fellow's reputation." First, the Marine Band; next, world's fair, and now on a few fossiled and worn out members of Gilmore's Band, and strange to say that, armed with the last named evidences of their genius, they have actually convinced men of standing and judgment that even a few men that "fit with Gilmore" are better than their whole band "from Chicago." It now remains to be seen whether the reputation of an organization twenty years under the baton of the greatest leader of the century, followed by a leader of thirty years' experience, is to suffer "even to death" by the unscrupulous methods of speculators, whose only object in connecting themselves with a musical organization is to make money. Gilmore's Band is still marching along in the path laid out by its great founder, firm in their determination to perpetuate the name, and your attention is called to the results of the coming tour, surrounded as we are by a well-trained corps of vilifiers whose efforts seem directed more to Gilmore's Band than to their own.

Gilmore's Band

Some parts of this strange statement were true, such as the passages about the formation of a syndicate—Sousa himself bought a $1,000 share in it[10]—and the loss of several men to his newly formed band. Other parts were not true, especially the allegation that the men in question were "fossiled and worn out." The *Musical Courier* was right in saying that it exhibited bad taste and showed only resentment over loss of engagements to the rival organization. Never one to discourage a controversy, the journal gave the "fossiled" musicians an opportunity to reply, on the same page with the statement:

A CARD

The undersigned, late solo members of Gilmore's Band, but now members of Sousa's Band, have observed with amazement the circular issued to the public, signed "Gilmore's Band," attacking Sousa's organization in general and the undersigned in particular, and characterizing us as "fossiled and worn out members of Gilmore's Band." Perhaps no person on earth, were he living, would be more astounded and indignant than Mr. Gilmore himself to see such an attack made upon the men who occupied his first chairs when he died, and whom he took pleasure in advertising as his great favorite soloists. Mr. Reeves, the present leader of Gilmore's Band, who has written this circular and who claims to be Mr. Gilmore's friend, could hardly have inflicted a deadlier insult to his memory than to stigmatize him as having chosen and led, up to the time of his death, what Mr. Reeves characterizes as "fossiled and worn out men." This is sufficient to say of this part of Mr. Reeves' circular.

The undersigned left Gilmore's Band and took an engagement with Mr. Sousa because his band had been chosen to succeed Gilmore's Band for the long engagements of the St. Louis Exposition, the Manhattan Beach and the World's Fair, and in addition long tours of concerts, thus affording his musicians a continuous and extended engagement. It was also a great pleasure for us to enroll ourselves under the leadership of so thoroughly accomplished and exceptionally successful a leader as John Philip Sousa, whose brilliant band it is an honor to any musician to belong to.

It only remains to question the right of Mr. Reeves to sign the name of "Gilmore's Band" to any circular, or in any connection, considering the fact that the band is now not only destitute of its late brilliant and lamented leader, but most of its soloists who aided him in making it famous, and of the engagements which had been so long identified with his successful career. These soloists and these engagements being now in possession of Sousa's Band, and its management being the same as that which piloted Gilmore as successfully through the last five years of his great career, it would seem as if the question might be an open one whether Sousa's organization, if he wished it, could not lay greater title to being "Gilmore's Band" than the organization whose leader, by his wanton and gratuitous attack upon the favorite musicians of Gilmore, has so belied the latter's character as a competent judge of the qualifications of the musicians whom it was his pleasure to employ.

> M. RAFFAYOLO, euphonium soloist
> E. A. LEFEBRE, solo saxophone
> A. BODE, first cornet
> H. L. CLARKE, cornet soloist
> F. W. WADSWORTH, first flute
> A. P. STENGLER, first clarinet
> F. URBAIN, first clarinet
> J. LACALLE, first clarinet
> THOS. F. SHANNON, bass saxophone
> HERMANN CONRAD, tuba-helicon
> ERNST MUELLER, drum and timpani

This goaded the unhappy successor to Gilmore into another statement, confusing, defiant, and on the whole pointless, in the *Musical Courier* of March 22, 1893:

GILMORE AND SOUSA

Editors The Musical Courier:

Of the eleven signers of a card in last week's issue of THE MUSICAL COURIER four have not been members since my advent. Of the remaining seven four occupied "first chairs;" three were soloists. When the open letter was published some of these persistently declared that they were not going to leave Gilmore's Band, but I now believe that at that time they had contracts in their possession. These seven highly sensitive gentlemen, being a part of the famous 100 that selected me as their leader, swearing, figuratively, that the name of Gilmore was dear to them, that they would never desert me as his representative, by their own admissions in "the card" say they joined the other band because they got a better "job."

They assume much when they assert that they aided Mr. Gilmore in making his band famous. Mr. Gilmore made his own great reputation and what fame these men have is simply his reflected glory. Whatever these seven men may be called, I am willing to submit to the public their final judgment of men brought into prominence by association with Gilmore's Band (four at least of whom signed a contract to play with the band and immediately after signed another to play with Sousa's), who at the first opportunity deserted, so to speak, to the enemy. The absurdity of questioning my right to sign the name of Gilmore's Band is apparent, when I state that out of 100 men I have fifty. Mr. Sousa has seven, who have no more right to the name than deserters in the face of the enemy have for mercy.

D. W. REEVES,
Leader, Gilmore's 22nd Regiment Band

March 18, 1893

The publication of this exchange showed the extent of public interest in great bands of the period, and the unfortunate plight of the once noble Gilmore group. Reeves had failed, and he gave up without a struggle—though his contract was effective until January 1, 1894, he resigned in the early fall so that a new conductor could more easily be chosen.[11] The men settled upon Victor Herbert during the summer, confirmed his election in early autumn, and were ready to regain their former glory in the season just ahead. The closely observant *Musical Courier* expressed an opinion it is well to remember: "Mr. Herbert is in every way qualified for the position, and will doubtless infuse some of his vitality and musical enthusiasm into the performances of his organization. We congratulate both the band and Mr. Herbert."[12]

In taking over the band Herbert was confronted with more than musical problems. It had lost some of its best men, and there was prestige to be recovered. The remaining faithful were discontented and looked to the new leader's spirit to bolster lost morale. When the season opened, the band had only twenty-eight men who had played under Gilmore,[13] and there was some question as to whether it should go under his name. However, the players wanted the name preserved and insisted on its legitimacy, affirmed by the fact that Mrs. Gilmore still had a financial interest in it. The best omen for the future was Herbert's successful effort to reengage most of the outstanding artists who had left when Gilmore died.[14]

After intensive rehearsing Herbert made his début with the band Sunday evening November 26, 1893, at the Broadway Theatre in

New York before an enthusiastic audience. One box was occupied by three persons who, more than all others, longed for a brilliant success: Mrs. Herbert and Mr. and Mrs. Anton Seidl. They were not disappointed. The program:

Overture to Tannhäuser	Wagner
Träumerei	Schumann
Intermezzo from Naïla	Delibes
Grand aria from Mahomet II	Rossini
Chevalier Luigi Colonnese, baritone	
Badinage	Herbert
Nocturne in E flat	Chopin
Tarantella	Cossman
Victor Herbert, cello	
Aria, "Thou Brilliant Bird," from La Perle du Brésil	David
Charlotte Maconda, soprano	
Hungarian Rhapsody No. 2	Liszt
Twenty-second Regiment March (first time)	Herbert
Romanza from Maria Padilla	Donizetti
Chevalier Luigi Colonnese	
Pizzicato Polka	Strauss
Loin du Bal	Gillet
" 'Twas April"	Nevin
"Les Filles de Cadix"	Delibes
Charlotte Maconda	
Duo for cornet and trombone	
Herbert L. and Ernest H. Clarke	
American Fantasy	Herbert

The band was resplendent in new blue and red uniforms, and it was noticed that Herbert, so appareled, looked handsomer than ever. He was deluged with flowers as the crowd vented its approval, and Herr Seidl positively beamed upon his erstwhile protégé. The attendance was smaller than anticipated (both Sousa and Damrosch were conducting concerts that same night), which led the *Staats-Zeitung* to call it a "mehr ein leeres, als ein populäres Konzert," but the demonstration left nothing to be desired.

More important were the press criticisms, which were practically unanimous in praising the conductor and his results. Harking back to Gilmore, the *Recorder* exclaimed: "The King is dead; long live the King!" and then declared the band played with great élan and brilliancy. The *World* observed that the band was really Gilmore's in name only; in personnel and appearance it was so different that a new identity was gained. Herbert's leadership had already produced a marked precision, and his new march was a melodious and stirring piece. The staid *Tribune* was gratified with the effects obtained, and its ever-present admiration for Herbert was actually increased: It was obvious that he set his men a high standard of performance; and his striving for excellence made one forget the conventional prejudice against bands as a concert medium.

So was launched a notable band career which lasted through the spring of 1900, when Herbert (with less and less time for it) was succeeded by Paul Henneberg.[15]

The début was followed by numerous engagements and tours, and the conductor was sore beset at first to keep his various dates in an orderly way. Unusual demands were made upon him for benefit appearances in noble causes, with disconcerting frequency. On November 29 Herbert and his men played a benefit for the newly organized New York Letter Carriers' Band, which was in need of instruments. On January 3, 1894, a concert had to be given at a charity ball. And on February 4 he combined forces with Seidl in an extraordinary affair at Madison Square Garden for the benefit of the Free Clothing Fund being raised by the New York *Herald*.

In spite of Herbert's popularity and reputation for probity, the *Musical Courier* disseminated a sleazy rumor in the fall of 1893 which aroused his ire and called forth a sharp denial and statement of principle. The rumor was primarily directed against Reginald de Koven, but that did not soften the cellist's righteous anger. (Let it be said once for all that the continuous annoyances from the *Courier* seem to have emanated from its editor, Marc A. Blumenberg, who pathologically could not resist sowing seeds of altercation. Views, judgments and reports by his staff members remained free of bias and personal spleen.)

On page 17 of its November 1 issue the magazine displayed this astonishing passage:

Rumor this time attaches Victor Herbert's name with "The Algerian," the new operetta by Reginald De Koven and Glen MacDonough, which was produced last Thursday night at the Garden Theatre. Certainly the music is unlike much that we have had from Mr. De Koven, and the orchestration is evidently made by a practical musician. Possibly this is mere hearsay about Mr. Herbert. We do not believe that a composer of his ability would do such a thing. We know that he made the piano score for "The Knickerbockers," and if we mistake not also for "The Fencing Master." But a piano score and an orchestral score are two widely different things. Mr. De Koven, if he wrote the music of "The Algerian," must have done a lot of hard studying, for it is vastly superior to "The Knickerbockers," although not as tuneful as

"Robin Hood." . . . "The Algerian" is not destined for a long life. The most interesting thing about it is, after all, the question which it provokes, Did Mr. De Koven score the work? It is full of Delibes and other composers, but the musical pie is better baked than usual. Who did the baking?

De Koven's reaction to this nasty innuendo is not known; but it drew a tart reply from Herbert at once. This may have been all that the nefarious editor desired; he printed it in the next issue of his paper under the conspicuous heading, "VICTOR HERBERT'S DENIAL":

New York, November 3, 1893

Editors Musical Courier:

I was surprised to read in your issue of November 1 that rumor attaches my name with "The Algerian." I most emphatically state that I have never seen a note of "The Algerian." I have never even heard the work.

It must have been an enemy—unknown to me—that started such a report. My indignation is surely pardonable, for I deem the man who would do such work as base as the one who would accept.

For Messrs. Schirmer I arranged a selection and dances for orchestra and a fantasie for piano and violin from "The Knickerbockers," and that is all. I met Mr. De Koven once when filling an engagement as 'cello soloist at one of the sacred concerts of the Vaudeville Club.

I hope you will do me the justice of publishing this letter in your next issue.

Yours respectfully,

(Signed) VICTOR HERBERT

With great solemnity the pious editor of the *Musical Courier* deplored the taint of suspicion lodged against De Koven's piece and hoped the composer would do something to banish it. Then he declared that the Herbert rumor was doubtful from the first since it showed such an "artistic mésalliance." His parting observation did nothing to assuage the really injured man's feelings: "We wonder when Mr. De Koven will write an opera that the world will acclaim as Reginald De Koven's!"

Vexed by such unnecessary association with De Koven and largely occupied with his band, Herbert continued the rest of his musical activity in normal fashion. On December 7 he was again among his friends in Buffalo where, with the local symphony, he played the Goltermann A minor concerto. This trip was marked by an incident which was nearly tragic, for it well-nigh cost him his instrument, a modified Rogeri. Going to the morning rehearsal with the orchestra Herbert slipped and fell on his cello. When he arose and looked at it he found a crack on the left side extending from the bottom to the F hole, and both he and the conductor (Lund) were in despair.

Fortunately an expert craftsman in the orchestra was able to glue the break so that the fine mellow tone was not affected, and the concert proceeded as planned.

Back in New York, Herbert appeared as soloist under Frank Van der Stucken at an orchestral concert of the Arion Society on December 17; he played his Suite, Op. 3, in its entirety, giving New York its first opportunity to hear all five movements.

About this time, he achieved real distinction in the famous Aschenbrödel Verein on East Eighty-sixth Street. The center for German-American musicians in New York, with the greatest musical celebrities among its members, it owed its existence to semisocial, semiprofessional reasons. Here at their best were good nature, good fellowship, good food, and good drink, the last being memorable to Huneker because of the magnificent assortment of imported beers. Life offered no greater pleasure to Huneker than to haunt the Aschenbrödel Club and argue with musicians about the tempi of Beethoven symphonies, the daring orchestration of Richard Strauss, the Seidl interpretation of *Tristan und Isolde,* and the Irish quality of Victor Herbert's harmonizations. Those he encountered there, he apostrophized: "Ah, me! a merry crew and earnest worshippers of their art!"[16]

The club had everything for the physical and artistic comfort of its members. The Bierstube was in the basement. On the ground floor were the office, a billiard room, a card room, library, bar, and lounge. A parlor and retiring rooms were on the second floor, and still higher was an excellent concert hall where most unusual performances were heard. It was a place of bustling activity with an atmosphere never duplicated anywhere else.[17]

On December 26, 1893, an exclusive and small dinner party forgathered in the clubhouse to render homage to three celebrated opera conductors, Anton Seidl, Enrico Bevignani, and Luigi Mancinelli. The two Italians were enjoying their first season at the Metropolitan. The table, set for only fifteen, was gaily decorated with the colors of the United States, Germany, and Italy, and the food also represented the cuisines of those nations. Spicing the elaborate menu were the finest of wines—champagne and Chianti, Rhenish and Bordeaux. The guests of honor were placed at the head of the table, with Victor Herbert at one side, Nahan Franko at the other. It was a jolly assemblage, and the enjoyment was enhanced because there were no formal speeches, only the pleasantest of musical and personal recollections. Herbert and the three guests were heard to special advantage, but the rest of the company suffered little in comparison.[18]

The American Symphony Orchestra, organized by Sam Franko, was another valiant enterprise which Herbert helped to launch, at least to the extent of appearing in its first concert, in Chickering Hall on February 24, 1894. Franko's idea was a good one at that time. The New York musical scene was dominated by foreigners, and the opinion prevailed that a first-class orchestra could not be formed from native talent alone. A formal declaration was issued which defined the orchestra's aims and objectives, at the same time asking no favors because of its national limitations.[19]

A measure of Franko's success, perhaps unappreciated by him, can be noticed in his complaint that every year for five years he was compelled to assemble and train a practically new group. Invitations from other orchestras annually depleted his ranks.[20]

Herbert had neither the desire nor the eligibility to play in the American Symphony Orchestra, but he was glad to play with it. As soloist, at its first concert he gave the first performance of his *Légende* for cello accompanied by harp and strings, another work which is today unknown.

A fortnight later he produced a much more important work: his second Concerto for cello and orchestra, Op. 30. Naturally he was the soloist, on March 9 and 10, as Seidl conducted the première with the Philharmonic Orchestra. He had been working strenuously on the piece since the summer of 1893, devoting to it all the skill and crafts-manship at his command. The time and effort were well spent, for the resulting composition was an outstanding contribution to cello litera-ture, a creation of real merit which deserves more hearings than it gets today. It is quite different, both in style and in concept, from the Suite and the first Concerto, both of which were fine virtuoso pieces but lacked unity and cohesion.

When Herbert played the work (which he dedicated to the New York Philharmonic Society), an elaborate description was printed in the program annotations:

A glance at the score . . . reveals the fact that it is symphonic in character. The orchestra is not merely a meaningless adjunct to the solo instrument, with an occasional *tutti* as a source of relief, but the two supplement each other and are closely allied in publishing the composer's ideas. The thematic structure, too, is symphonic, for the component parts of the different themes are exhaustively made use of in the course of the work. The three move-ments are closely connected, growing as it were the one out of the other. The principal subject of the first and the third movements, a vigorous rhythmically emphatic theme, is given out by the orchestra without a prel-ude. It consists of two motives. The first of these is heard in the bass in-struments and is at once followed by the second in the woodwinds and strings accompanied by crescendo chords of the trumpets and trombones. The minor seventh is a distinguishing characteristic of the latter. After these motives have been repeated three times the 'cello takes up the first theme *Lento* in rhapsodical fashion. The opening *tutti* is repeated and then the 'cello announces the complete subject. This, as will be readily noted, is an enlargement of the motives heard in the introduction. It is not difficult to trace the component parts of this melody throughout the movement even in the rhythmically and harmonically disguised forms in which they appear. With admirable skill the composer has made them serve the purposes of the contrast and brilliant passages for the solo instrument. The transition to the second movement by means of the first motive, now given to the clarinet and oboe, is a lovely conceit. The principal subject of the *Andante* is a touching melody, the first two measures of which furnish material for effective dialogue between the 'cello and orchestra. The plaintive character of this theme is relieved by an episode of a more impassioned nature, the gist of which is a short frequently recurring motive. The first theme then returns accompanied by variations in the 'cello. It gradually dies out into a faint echo until the soft trembling harmonies lead into the Finale. The theme of the first movement which is also part of the last is heard *pianissimo* in the bassoons. Very gradually it gains strength. One instrument after the other joins in until a powerful *tutti* proclaims it in all its energy. This subject is now made to appear in an entirely new light. The virtuoso has an opportunity to display his digital skill in scintillating arabesques and double stops while the orchestra persistently adheres to the original motives. Then the composer pays a tribute to his knowledge of counterpoint by giving to the 'cello the melody of the *Andante* without checking the orchestra in the course. Soon the tables are turned. The orchestra takes up the subject of the *Andante* and the 'cello that of the *Allegro*. The latter again gains the ascendancy and finally brings the concerto to a brilliant close. These brief outlines can give but an inadequate idea of the skill with which from a limited number of motives the composer has constructed a work as harmonious as it is replete with effective contrasts.[21]

Failing to approach the musical essence of the work, this passage likewise failed to stress sufficiently the remarkable unity Herbert obtained by thematic derivation and manipulation. He was, moreover, highly successful in striving for what he wanted—a compact, closely knit score in which each part should be logically related to the others. To integrate it still more, he wrote the work without division into separate movements (though they exist and are perceptible), obviously influenced by Liszt and his piano concertos. The net result was that he produced a composition of real vigor and charm—melodious, dramatic, direct—with a minimum of basic material. This is a test for any musician, and the composer passed it triumphantly.

The reaction of the critics was mixed. None condemned the work or failed to discover virtues in it, but they disagreed as to what the good qualities actually were. The *Times* reporter seized the opportunity to protest against cello concertos in general, basing his argument on the instrument's comparative unwieldiness. Perhaps this thesis can be sustained, but its appearance was not appropriate to the occasion. Moreover, the writer had to conclude his peroration with a compliment tinged with regret: "All that need be said here is that if a man feels driven to the verge of composition, it is well that he understands the technics as well as Mr. Herbert. It is a pity that the gods did not bless him with a violin."

The *Tribune* was complimentary without meaning to be so, and expressed a doubt which arouses equal doubt today. Apparently the critic was thinking of concertos only in terms of virtuosity, not musical values; and his suggestion that Herbert failed in his intent can be roundly disputed:

The new composition was a concerto . . . by Herbert, who played the solo. It is an ambitious work, the creation of a musician rather than a mere virtuoso, but concerning its effectiveness . . . we are somewhat in doubt. It would seem as if, in his desire to keep away from the light-waisted style which is only too common among composers for the violoncello, Mr. Herbert has gone to the opposite extreme, and has composed an orchestral piece with obligato violoncello. Much of the music is dignified, and there is one touch, at least, of a dainty fancy, but, on the whole, we doubt that the concerto is what Mr. Herbert fondly intended it to be.

The *Herald* gave its usual rhapsodic praise to Herbert, but the *World* printed the most intelligent and just appreciation of the work. Special interest attaches to this review because it was written by Reginald de Koven:

It is, on the whole, an interesting and effective composition; effective for the orchestra, which is happily used as an important factor in the organic whole rather than as a mere accompaniment, and effective also for the solo instrument, although by emphasizing the importance of the orchestral side of the work the composer has run the risk several times of dwarfing the interest and importance of the solo part. The concerto is in the conventional three movements, which are closely connected, and grow the one out of the other into a very close organic unity. . . .

The principal subject, which is the same for the first and third movements, is vigorous, rhythmic and emphatic, and in it a characteristic and strongly marked interval of a minor seventh plays an important and effective part. The first movement, somewhat in the style of a free fantasia, strikes one as somewhat sought after, or, as the Germans say, "gesucht"; but the second movement is melodious, fluent and full of charm, while in the last movement several happy effects are made by contrasting the two themes of the first and second movements, which are taken up alternately in contrapuntal fashion by the solo instrument and the orchestra.

As a whole the composition is one which will undoubtedly grow with repeated hearings, and is certainly one which gives striking evidence of the composer's skill and musicianship.

Not only had Herbert produced a notable work; his concerto exerted an immediate influence upon Antonín Dvořák, director of the National Conservatory of Music, who was delighted with his friend's score. There is little reason to doubt that it was the stimulus for Dvořák's cello concerto, Op. 104, which was written during the fall and winter of 1894–1895. A Bohemian compatriot, the cellist Hans Wihan, was eager to have a concerto from Dvořák, but it might never have been written if Herbert had not done his first. It is known that Dvořák heard the première and expressed delighted admiration for Herbert's distinguished music.

Herbert had the greatest affection for Dvořák, at the same time realizing fully the genius of the Bohemian. In December of 1893 the New World Symphony was presented by the Philharmonic Society, and the musicians and composers of the country debated its importance and whether it would be the start of a national school of composition. Herbert was second to none in his enthusiasm for the work, and he made probably the wisest of all remarks about it. When asked if he thought it would be an influence on composition in America he simply laughed and said: "Yes, if the composers are Dr. Dvoraks."[22]

Herbert left one of the best and most intimate pictures of Dvořák, a pencil portrait which has never been previously published. In 1922 Hans Schnoor, a German critic in Dresden, wrote to Carl Engel, Chief of the Music Division in the Library of Congress, in search of materials for a Dvořák biography. Engel, knowing no one in a better position than Herbert to reminisce on the Czech master, conveyed the appeal to him.

The New York composer thereupon drafted in pencil a fine sketch which is of prime importance to all Dvořák students, and which is now in the Music Division of the Library of Congress:

Dear Dr.
  Mr. Carl Engel (Chief of the Music Division, Library of Congress, Washington, D.C.) has asked me to give you some details as to my recollections of my association with Dr. Antonin Dvořák.
  I was head of the Cello-Class of Mrs. Thurber's National Conservatory when this enthusiastic lady managed to persuade Dr. Dvořák to accept the directorship of this Conservatory. It was my pleasure to see the doctor practically every time I gave lessons at the Conservatory. He took great interest in my pupils as he was most anxious to have them join the orchestra class, which he directed, although it was, to my mind, the "enfant terrible" of the institution. With the exception of some excellent violin pupils of that master,

Leopold Lichtenberg, few of the players were advanced enough, to play in the orchestra—and what they "didn't do" to Mendelssohn's "Midsummer-night's Overture" (the Dr. might have chosen a simpler piece) is beyond description. However, Dr. Dvořák seemed to enjoy these orchestral orgies.

One of my pupils, a very charming girl and rather advanced player, acting as Solo-Celliste, often had fainting spells when the Dr. got very excited.

Dr. Dvořák, when he was not teaching Composition, was always busy composing and often I heard him playing, even singing, in the front room of the conservatory. I had the pleasure of playing the cello part of his beautiful Trio "Dumbka," which he had just completed, with him, Michael Banner taking the violin part. Dr. Dvořák was not a great pianist, but his playing was intensely musical, of course. We liked the composition immensely and I asked him what "Dumbka" meant in bohemian—He thought for a while—shook his head and said, to our surprise: *It means nothing*—What *does* it mean?

Dr. Dvořák was most kind and unaffected, took great interest in his pupils, one of which, the very talented Harry Burleigh, had the privilege of giving the Dr. some of the thematic material for his Symphony—"From the New World." I have seen this denied—but it is true. Naturally I knew a good deal about this Symphony—as I saw the Dr. two or three times a week—and knew he was at work on it.

The first orchestral rehearsal of it took place under the great Anton Seidl, then Conductor of the Philh. Society of N.Y. in the Chamber-music hall in Carnegie Hall—and I was Solo-Cellist.

A few years afterwards, after I had played my (2d) Cello-Concerto in one of the Philh. Concerts—Dr. Dvořák came back to the "Stimm-Zimmer" —threw his arms around me, saying before many members of the orchestra: famos! famos!—ganz famos!

We all loved him, for he was so kind and affable—his great big beautiful eyes radiated warmth—and of such childlike simplicity and naturalness—and when he left us, we lost not only a master-musician whose presence had had a marked influence on musical activities in N.Y. but a most admirable, lovable friend.

V. H.

P.S.

Dear Dr.

As Mr. Harry Burleigh (one of Dr. Dvořák's best pupils in composition) probably knows much about him, I have asked him to send you a "résumé" of his recollections.

Burleigh (a Negro) was thought much of by Dr. Dvořák and has written many beautiful songs, etc. etc.—showing the Dr.'s judgment was right.

Wishing you success

[scrawl]

V. H.

It was probably in the fall of 1893 that Herbert severed his connection with the National Conservatory of Music and abandoned his efforts to secure private cello students. His professional card seems to have appeared last in the *Musical Courier* for October 25; the following week it was replaced by a notice of the well known Fritz Giese. As early as September 13 the *Courier* had announced that Herbert would again teach at the National Conservatory, but on November 8 it informed its readers that Giese was joining the faculty. The activities with the band, the preparation of the second Concerto, and numerous cello engagements throughout the season no doubt convinced Herbert of the impracticality of maintaining a regular teaching schedule.

On April 5, 1894, he played at the Academy of Music in Brooklyn.[23] On April 8 he shared the honors in one of the Sunday afternoon chamber concerts of the Aschenbrödel Verein, playing in the D flat Trio by Rubin Goldmark and the Septet, Op. 74, by Hummel.[24] April 22 and 30 found him in the Carnegie Chamber Music Hall, and April 26 in Madison Square Garden.[25]

With the advent of summer—late spring, in fact—Herbert and his band had a seasonal concentration which was not of the happiest; yet it resulted in a not unimportant composition and so cannot be neglected. They were engaged to provide music at Eldorado, a popular amusement resort across the Hudson from New York and accessible by ferry from Fourteenth Street or Forty-second Street. It had attracted large crowds in 1892 and 1893, with Nahan Franko furnishing music, but the spectacles were so lavish, apparently, as to cause financial difficulties. In September, 1893, at any rate, the enterprise had gone into the hands of a receiver.[26] Evidently undaunted by any risk involved, Gilmore's Band—by now it was just as likely to be called Herbert's Twenty-second Regiment Band—began giving Sunday concerts there on May 12. After two weeks, on May 27, he played his new march, *Eldorado,* which proved extremely popular and had to be repeated several times.[27] But the real trouble lay ahead.

Each summer one specially striking spectacle was presented daily to the throng of entertainment seekers, and in 1894 it was *Benamela, or Summer Night's Dream,* a figment of the imagination of Vincenzo Romeo, with music by Carlo Brizzi. This was supposed to be given every night except Sunday, beginning June 9, and elaborate preparations were made for producing it in the park's amphitheater. Herbert, of course, was supposed to conduct the music.

It would be difficult today to conceive of anything more amateurish, more unintelligible, more absurd than this "spectacle." Some of the music and a typed libretto can be inspected in the Library of Congress. In this incredible creation an Egyptian Sultan is thwarted in trying to add to his harem of one hundred forty-four wives the daughter of his Vizier. The intervention of a good fairy sets everything right after unbelievable complications threaten disaster. What Herbert felt when he was confronted with this hodgepodge of bad music and bad drama can hardly be imagined; but he manfully helped whip it into shape for a first production on June 13, and composed a finale of which the Library of Congress has an autograph copy in piano-vocal form. That the finale is the best piece of music in the spectacle—so bad that one reporter, sympathetic to Herbert, suggested he "must have laughed in his military sleeve at all this musical drivel"[28]—is no particular compliment to Herbert; but it was a highly respectable march and chorus which he later used (with different words) in his operetta *The Idol's Eye.* Fortunately, however, it was not sufficient to save poor *Benamela,* discontinued after July 7.[29]

Herbert and the band continued to play at Eldorado until August 20, when they refused to proceed with the expected concert. The reason was simple: they had received no remuneration for the two previous weeks. The magazine making this announcement berated the Eldorado management severely for treating the band so shabbily, and insisted that the decision to stop playing should cast no discredit upon Herbert and his men.[30] Obviously the financial hazards of 1893 were still alive and finding new victims.

Irritated by the experience, Herbert refused to let it dampen his enthusiasm for the band. In the fall he was again giving weekly concerts in New York and introducing new works—his own and others'. One, apparently a commissioned piece, was the *New York Herald Waltz* by Johann Strauss, dedicated to James Gordon Bennett. When it was played for the first time, on October 14, the *Herald* made the most of it; but it was not one of the Waltz King's happiest inspirations. The newspaper announced that Herbert received the manuscript from Europe the night before the concert and had to arrange it for band at once. He also composed a special introduction for it.

Newspapers of the period used music to court public favor, and the *Sun* was responsible for Monroe H. Rosenfeld's *The Sun March and Two-Step,* dedicated to Charles A. Dana, which Herbert arranged and played on October 7; but its purpose and dedication failed to give it a long life.

Before the year was out Herbert acted with Hugh A. Clarke and Charles C. Converse to judge in a song contest sponsored by the *Dominant.* The winning songs were "Old Glory," by Homer N. Bartlett, and "Sons of America," by J. Remington Fairlamb. The sponsoring journal announced apologetically that it could not publish the names of the winners until its January issue; so many manuscripts had been received, and one of the judges had so many urgent private affairs! It is a foregone conclusion that this last phrase was a reference to Herbert, "the greatest musician among the bandmasters of the United States."[31]

The *Dominant* was not alone in being aware of Herbert's multiple activities; the public was also concerned about them. Late in 1894 the Wolfsohn Musical Bureau (managing Herbert's cello appearances) published an advertisement to allay one of the public's fears: "Victor Herbert has not abandoned his 'cello playing. Although his time is very much occupied in finishing several comic operas and attending to the rehearsals of the Gilmore Band, he has a large number of engagements during the next month. He is as popular as ever and it is hoped he will also be heard in this city some time during the season."[32]

It was time that something like this appeared, if only to show that Herbert was not too rapidly turning away from one occupation to another. A new one was looming large. His first known, or earliest preserved, operetta had its first performance at the Broadway Theatre, New York, on November 20, 1894. It was *Prince Ananias*.

With this "comic opera" (as the printed score calls it) Herbert invaded a field far more competitive, in a way, than it is today, when mechanization enables motion picture musicals and individually popular musical comedies of the stage (which may or may not leave New York) to overrun the country. In 1894 this was accomplished by touring companies able to endure hard schedules or by theaters specializing in musico-dramatic entertainment. New York avidly consumed light opera and, between 1882 and 1892, enjoyed thirty-five such works at the Casino alone. These included the masterpieces of Strauss and Offenbach as well as numerous fine works by Millöcker, Sullivan, and Lecocq.[33] Some fourteen comic opera companies were touring America during the 1894–1895 season, without counting companies that offered burlesque, variety, and musical comedy.[34]

Herbert's first dramatic creation was presented by the Bostonians, a touring company justly famous for its popularity, competency, and artistic excellence. The origin of the group was implicit in its name. In 1878, when *H.M.S. Pinafore* was becoming the rage, a Boston newspaper had suggested that an *ideal* cast be assembled from the city's talented church and amateur singers so that Sullivan's score could be ideally sung. The management of the Boston Theatre liked the suggestion and asked Miss Effie H. Ober, already operating a bureau for concert singers, if she would form the company. Thus was assembled the Boston Ideals, which gave a sensationally successful performance of *Pinafore* in the spring of 1879. Thus was launched, too, the best operetta company of its time, one which was to be a household word for a generation to come.

After several years of great success, a new policy was needed. The repertoire had to be refurbished; some singers had to be replaced; and a new impetus had to be discovered. So Tom Karl, William H. Mac-Donald, and Henry Clay Barnabee (a uniquely beloved comedian and the real leader of the company) effected a reorganization and changed the name to Bostonians in 1887.[35] The new name, not strikingly original, was proposed by a friend and admirer, the journalist Henry Watterson.[36] Thereafter they continued to delight the country for many years, striving to find American works of exceptional value, and taking the best of American musical entertainment from the eastern to the western seaboard.

How or when Herbert met the Bostonians is not known; but it may be assumed that his fortunes with them developed rapidly after he and W. H. MacDonald became friends in the spring of 1894.[37] The actor was much interested in the composer's work and induced him to let them produce *Prince Ananias*—of which a substantial portion may already have been written, for Herbert had told the Buffalo reporter in December that he had a second operetta under way. In any case, the Bostonians and the composer quickly reached an agreement, and "Raconteur" Huneker proudly announced on the 4th of July:

> The Bostonians signed a contract Tuesday of last week with Victor Herbert and Francis Neilson, binding themselves to produce the latter's comic opera, "Prince Ananias," next season. The composer is of course very well known. Mr. Neilson is a young man who has had considerable theatrical experience under the late Dion Boucicault, and has written several librettos. This one is particularly clever, and in conjunction with Herbert's music should be a great success.[38]

Huneker reported the facts accurately—maybe he had witnessed the signing of the contract on the preceding Tuesday. It is important enough to reproduce in its entirety because it shows Herbert's insistence on certain conditions and details the responsibilities of the contracting parties.[39]

> *AGREEMENT* made this twenty-sixth day of June in the year one thousand eight hundred and ninety-four between *Victor Herbert* and *Francis Neilson* of the City, County and State of New York, parties of the first part, and *Henry Clay Barnabee, Tom Karl* and *William H. MacDonald* representing an organization called "The Bostonians" parties of the second part.
> *WHEREAS* the said parties of the first part do hereby agree to write, to compose, and to deliver a new and original comic-opera (the scenario of which is entitled "Prince Ananias") on or before the first day of December

in the year one thousand eight hundred and ninety-four (December 1st, 1894) and

WHEREAS the said parties of the second part are desirous of producing the said opera in the United States of America and in the Dominion of Canada.

NOW THEREFORE the said parties of the first part and the said parties of the second part respectively agree as follows:—

1st. The said parties of the first part agree to sell, assign and transfer and hereby do sell, assign and transfer to the said parties of the second part the exclusive right to produce and to represent the said opera in the United States of America and in the Dominion of Canada for which sale, assignment and transfer the said parties of the second part agree to pay to the said parties of the first part or to their authorized agent as follows:—

The sum of five hundred dollars ($500.) on the signing and execution of this agreement which sum shall be in advance of royalties and to be deducted from first royalties.

2nd. Also on completion and delivery of score and book by the said parties of the first part, to the said parties of the second part the said parties of the second part shall pay to the said parties of the first part or to their authorized agent the further sum of five hundred dollars ($500.) which sum shall also be in advance of royalties and to be deducted from first royalties.

3rd. Also the further sum in royalties as follows; Five percent on the first eight thousand dollars ($8,000.) gross weekly receipts and six percent (6%) on all gross weekly receipts above for all performances of the said opera in the United States of America and in the Dominion of Canada.

4th. The said parties of the first part agree to rebate royalties to the amount of fifteen hundred dollars ($1,500.) as part payment of the cost of production; the said sum to be deducted from the first royalties.

5th. The said parties of the second part agree that the said opera shall be produced on or before the first day of June in the year one thousand eight hundred and ninety-five (June 1st, 1895).

6th. The said parties of the second part agree to announce the said parties of the first part as sole authors of the said opera on all programmes, posters and other advertising matter connected with the said opera.

7th. The said parties of the second part and the said parties of the first part agree that they shall mutually superintend the rehearsals of the said opera and that the production shall be given under their mutual direction, and that no changes shall be made in the libretto or music without the consent of the said parties of the first part.

8th. The said parties of the second part agree that the orchestra in New York will not consist of less than twenty-five pieces and the said parties of the second part also agree that *Mr. Herbert* will conduct said opera upon the first performance in New York and as often thereafter as mutually desired.

9th. The said parties of the second part agree that all rights of publication of libretto and musical score belong to the parties of the first part.

10th. The said parties of the second part agree to furnish weekly statements of the gross receipts of the said opera in the United States of America and the Dominion of Canada to the said parties of the first part or to their authorized agent and to make weekly payments or royalties according to the terms of this agreement to the said parties of the first part or to their authorized agent when such payments shall become due according to this agreement.

11th. The said parties of the first part agree to and with the said parties of the second part that they are the sole authors of the said opera and that they have not assigned and that they will not assign to other than the said parties of the second part their rights in the said opera in the United States of America and the Dominion of Canada, and that they will assist the said parties of the second part in the protection of their rights thereto, and will execute any and all pleadings and will give to any judicial magistrate or any other person appointed their testimony on every matter concerning the said opera and furnish any evidence that may be necessary to protect the rights of the said parties of the second part in the said opera.

12th. The said parties of the second part agree that the said opera will be adequately produced and all scenery, costumes, supernumeraries and effects will be of first class standard.

13th. The agreements hereto are binding upon the heirs, executors, administrators or representatives of the parties hereabove mentioned.

IN WITNESS WHEREOF the parties here below named have set their hands and seals the day and year first written above.

VICTOR HERBERT (s)

FRANCIS NEILSON (s)

BARNABEE KARL & MacDONALD by Kirke LaShelle (s)

A bit of caution may be detected on Herbert's part in the wording of the contract. He promised to deliver a score not later than December 1, 1894, and this work was to be produced not later than June 1, 1895. Yet, when the former date actually arrived, the opera had been running nearly two weeks; surely a phenomenal instance of being ahead of schedule. In spite of Herbert's capacity for rapid writing, it must be surmised that much of the score was done when he signed the contract, and that in this, his first operetta venture, he was intent on "playing it safe" by fixing a terminal date which could be approached in leisure and with peace of mind.

The two-act *Prince Ananias* tells a story of sixteenth century France. Its slight content includes an outlaw in love with a nobleman's daughter (Mirabel), an impecunious poet (Louis—Prince Ananias) loved by a leading lady, a village belle ready to flirt with anyone. Banded together in a company of players, they arrive at court and find they must bring laughter to the King or suffer dire consequences. Their presentation is a failure, but the poet unexpectedly dispels the King's melancholy, and everyone is forgiven and saved. The happily mated lovers share the joy of the vastly relieved actors and courtiers.

The printed program on opening night announced the following cast:

```
Boniface, King of Navarre............George B. Frothingham
Cerdic, Duke d'Angers...................William Castleman
Killjoy, Chamberlain to the King.................Peter Lang
Louis Biron, a vagabond poet and adventurer. .W. H. MacDonald
George Le Grabbe, an outlaw ................Eugene Cowles
La Fontaine, manager of a band of
      strolling players....................Henry Clay Barnabee
Eugene, his assistant ......................Joseph Sheehan
Jacques, an innkeeper......................James E. Miller
Ivon, a villager.................................Mr. Boyle
Felicie, Countess of Pyrennes, sister to Killjoy. .Josephine Bartlett
Mirabel, daughter to Killjoy....................Mena Cleary
Ninette, a village belle....................D. Eloise Morgan
Idalia, La Fontaine's leading lady..........Jessie Bartlett Davis
        Lords, Ladies, Heralds, Pages, Halberdiers, Players,
                  Villagers, Attendants, etc.
```

The musical director was S. L. Studley, but Herbert conducted the première with notable briskness and gusto.

The leading theatrical journals of the day were the *Dramatic Mirror* and the *Clipper,* and both gave fair reviews of the production on December 1. The former pointed out that for some years the Bostonians had been trying to find a successor to *Robin Hood,* De Koven's unique triumph which they had produced in 1890; that *Prince Ananias* fell short of this, but was a show with considerable merit. It sagely observed that the librettist had a fine theme to start with, then failed to develop it in a satisfactory manner. It offered as an example, which was all too true, the device of persuading the King to laugh not by having the stage comedians do something funny, which the audience could appreciate and share, but by a reminiscent song outside the experience of everyone concerned. The critic noted that the music was ambitious though uneven. The composer's gift for melody was obvious in the several marches and waltzes, just as his skill was apparent in the harmony and orchestration.

The *Clipper* also was pleased, similarly commenting on the librettist's lack of skill. The first act was far too long and the second was wanting in form and substance. The music, however, was delightful throughout, the score being notable for its dainty qualities and for special instrumental effects which emphasized the humorous situations. The show had shortcomings, but the music would live despite them. It was, on the whole, the best work acquired by the Bostonians in the past two years.

The daily press received the show warmly enough, though some of the reviewers may have read more into it than any of the producers intended. On the other hand, maybe not. Before the première the *Tribune* of November 18 discussed the plot and intimated that some of the evils of the stage were healthily satirized. Nothing like this appeared in the paper's review of the performance—which, though long, left the audience unwearied, because the music was good regardless of the quality of the lyrics. Herbert had "composed some ingenious dramatic music to give color and expression to characters and situations. There are moments when the music sounds labored, but they are all in the first act, which is expository." The second act had music welcome for its "idyllic prettiness, its warmth of sentiment and its farcical form."

Another reviewer[40] also dwelt on what might be extra-relevant factors. After damning the book as one of the worst in contemporary comic opera, he doubted that the public would be pleased with a text so full of references to professional stage work; they could only be appreciated by actors familiar with the problems of exits and make-up and life behind the scenes. One of his stringent criticisms was most curious. He wrote that the gowns worn by the admirable Jessie Bartlett Davis were exact copies of costumes worn by Lillian Russell in *La Cigale, Apollo,* and *The Grand Duchess.* Not only that; the Davis make-up imitated La Russell's so clearly that it might have been taken directly from a volume of Russell photographs freely distributed as a souvenir just a year before. Imitation, he felt, was not in this case the sincerest form of flattery; and he accused the Bostonians of bad taste in such a slap to the reigning queen of the American musical stage.

The judicious *Times,* after reporting the need for abridgment, remarked that the show had elements that could lead to either success or failure. The libretto had to be cut appreciably. If success ensued, it would be owing to the music, which was always interesting to a trained ear, with a scoring full of variety and refinement. By implication, however, the critic pointed out that the trained ear was not always to be found in an operetta audience, that when Herbert became more familiar with operetta requirements "he will make his melodic framework smaller, and will stick to the elementary song form, which is easily within the grasp of operetta audiences."

Both the *Sun* and the *Post* criticized the libretto adversely and the music favorably. They felt that Herbert's talents had produced a score on a somewhat higher level than the operetta public was accustomed to (which was undoubtedly so); but they also called attention to the fact that the music contained real operatic characterization which appropriately supported the leading rôles.

The elaborate choral finales with which Herbert often closed his acts have aroused frequent comment. The opening scene of a Herbert operetta can be just as varied and vigorous, however, and *Prince Ananias* begins with an animated picture of musical breadth, charm, and piquancy. There are irresistible melodic phrases, snatches of song which continue the dramatic action without interruption, dances of fetching grace, and nicely placed choral responses. The duo sung by Louis and Ninette ("It Needs No Poet") is a specially effective number, the fine phrases of which contrast oddly with the inane words. There is some excellent descriptive writing in the scene between Ninette and La Fontaine, and the girl has some coloratura roulades and scales that call for the highest skill. The sweetly sentimental "The Hamlet of Fancy," sung by Idalia, is the most pretentious solo in the opera, though it is not the best. The most impassioned is Idalia's and Louis' duo, "I Am No Queen," a love dialogue ending in a slow waltz of climactic force. The first act culminates in a complex finale of surprising skill and contrast. If one part can be singled out for comment, it is the waltz section, "Ah! He's a Prince," wherein Idalia thinks she cannot wed Louis because of his supposed royal lineage.

The gem of the opera, and one of the gems of all light opera, is "Amaryllis," at the beginning of Act II. The wistful melancholy of Idalia's song, the delicate accompaniment and the interpolation of a dainty minuet make this a truly extraordinary selection. Herbert never attempted anything quite like it afterward, and he may have felt it was too fragile a thing for the operetta stage. In the same act other noteworthy numbers are Eugene's solo, "Ah! Cupid, Meddlesome Boy!" the quintet, "Ah! List to Me," and Idalia's short solo, "Love Is Spring." Strangely enough, the "punch" song of the entire opera, the one which had to make King Boniface laugh, gives the impression of being neither good nor clever, and there must have been a modicum of pantomimic action in its rendition in order to make it the least bit plausible.

Were the Bostonians satisfied with their new vehicle? The answer seems to be Yes and no, according to their leader, Henry Clay Barnabee, who recalled that it had an unpromising title, some musical merit, and a "bushel or more of libretto chaff." But it was good enough for them to take it on the road as the companion to the still unparalleled *Robin Hood* and display it across the country as far as California.[41] Two years later they were still playing it, though with no perceptible degree of regularity.

The comparative success of *Prince Ananias,* however, quickly determined the composer to follow it with more operettas. It also influenced librettists to approach him with texts in the hope that he would select one of them for his next venture. One specific instance proves that Herbert was eager to examine anything that seemed to have a reasonable dramatic prospect. Late in 1894 he penned a short note:

> New-York City
> 1126 Park Ave.
> Dec. 16th
>
> Mr. G. A. Townsend
>   Dear Sir
>   I would like to see your libretto very much.
>   Will you send it on to the above address or are you coming to this city shortly? I have been out of town concertising and didn't get your letter in time.
>
> Sincerely yours
> Victor Herbert[42]

This brief exchange had no results; at least, George Alfred Townsend of Washington, D.C., fails to appear among the Herbert librettists.

5

The Theater's Beckoning Hand

THE fears that Herbert might abandon his cello playing because of other pressures soon vanished. As a solo artist, early in 1895, he was more distinguished than ever, and appeared in both usual and unusual places. On January 21 he played, perhaps for the first time, at one of the famous and élite Morning Musicales which A. M. Bagby sponsored at the Hotel Waldorf.[1] Engagements elsewhere followed fast, and occasionally a failure to appear caused more comment than Herbert's accustomed performances. When the Aschenbrödel Verein gave its third Sunday afternoon concert of the season (February 24) it was reported that other performers were heard because "the two leading men of the club, Victor Herbert and Sam Franko, were absent."[2]

So popular was Herbert as a cellist at this time that he was singled out for a rare distinction: Funk & Wagnalls used a portrait of him, with his instrument, to illustrate the definition of "violoncello" in *A Standard Dictionary of the English Language*. For more than half a dozen editions this reference work presented Herbert's likeness to seekers after knowledge; but the man who gazed so pleasantly from the page was never identified, living there in lexicographical anonymity. Thousands of the dictionary's users must have wondered who the handsome artist was as they compared the picture of the cello with its textual description. By 1913 the likeness had disappeared from the book.

Besides appearing regularly as cellist Herbert was also composing, or at least working on, another operetta. How definitely it had taken shape is unknown—it may not have progressed beyond sketches—but it was stolen from him and apparently never recovered. The sympathetic

99

Huneker published the loss in his "Raconteur" column[3] and mingled compliments with regrets in his animated style.

The most urgent call upon Herbert's attention came from the Twenty-second Regiment Band, which, under his leadership, had to regain the national prestige first won by Gilmore. This meant extensive tours and, whenever possible, long engagements at expositions. The people had not forgotten Gilmore's organization; but, unless the band went back to them, there was danger that they might.

Herbert took his band responsibilities with the utmost seriousness. To be sure, a band had to provide entertainment, often frivolous and sometimes empty; but it also had a chance to ennoble or edify its audience, and he took full advantage of every opportunity offered. He did this by writing as well as by conducting and traveling. When that rather fantastic two-volume *The Music of the Modern World* (published by D. Appleton & Co., 1895–1897) was in preparation Anton Seidl as editor-in-chief asked Herbert for a statement on "Artistic Bands." Here is the result:

ARTISTIC BANDS
By Victor Herbert

The important part that military bands have taken in the development of musical knowledge in America can not be overstated. In this land of the free a musician can seek engagements where he will, and is not compelled to accept enforced service. This freedom has drawn to our country the best musicians of the world, and has fostered native talent. In consequence of these conditions a band conductor has at his disposal artistic material, which has so stimulated public taste that to-day we have concert military bands bidding for the appreciation and support of music-lovers of every degree of culture. It would be interesting to analyse the popular preference for bands over orchestras, if space permitted, but the fact can be clearly demonstrated. There are to-day large and expensive concert bands which travel from State to State over the entire continent, while orchestras have to limit their *tournées.*

From the old bands which depended on the local brasses and drums, all forced to their utmost to make the most noise possible, to the bands of the present day which interpret the works of the greatest so as to satisfy even the most exacting musician, has been a hard but glorious struggle up the steeps of Parnassus, and to Patrick Sarsfield Gilmore belongs most of the glory. Mr. Gilmore knew men and music, and through his knowledge of both he held the masses and led them. In each programme there was something that made each auditor a better man musically, and prepared him for another step ahead. The compositions of Wagner lend themselves readily to the transition from orchestra to band, a quality due to the prominence given wood and brasses in all his works. A remarkable example of this may be noted in "Elizabeth's Prayer," where the wood-winds are used alone; and in many of the most beautiful passages in the "Nibelungen" the strings are not used at all. Wagner was the first composer to recognise the possibilities of these sections of the orchestra, and to him is due the credit of enlarging them. For this reason, since Gilmore's time, every band conductor makes a feature of his great overtures, and a year's programmes will show many concerts exclusively devoted to Wagner. As the repertories of bands have increased, the demand for new tone-colour effects has caused new instruments to be made, so that to-day the composer or adapter has a wide range of registrating. The use of compositions originally written for orchestras has caused a great increase in the wood-wind section of the bands—flutes, oboes, clarinets, and saxophones—of which every band should have a quartet— bassoons and contra-bassoons. These additions make the repertory of the band universal. The greater sustaining power of the wood-winds gives a beautiful richness of harmony, and relieves one from the torture of listening to the scratchiness of poorly played strings.

Taking his band so seriously, Herbert was doubtless happy in the early discovery that the spring, summer, and fall of 1895 were to be extremely active. The February 20 issue of the *Musical Courier* announced that Gilmore's Band had been engaged for several spring festivals as part of a long tour through the South and the Midwest as well as for longer expositions later in the year. The tour was typical of the burdens borne by such organizations. Contemplation of it awakens admiration for the musicians' fortitude and endurance.[4]

March 16, Sat.	Grand Opera House, Wilmington, Del. (mat.)
	Music Hall, Baltimore, Md. (eve.)
17, Sun.	Albaugh's, Washington, D.C.
18, Mon.	Opera House, Lynchburg, Va. (mat.)
	Academy of Music, Roanoke, Va. (eve.)
19, Tues.	Staub's Theatre, Knoxville, Tenn.
20, Wed.	Grand Opera House, Atlanta, Ga. (eve.)
21, Thurs.	Grand Opera House, Atlanta (mat. and eve.)
22, Fri.	Exposition Building, Augusta, Ga.
23, Sat.	Savannah Theatre, Savannah, Ga.
24, Sun.	Park Opera House, Jacksonville, Fla.
25, Mon.	Academy of Music, Macon, Ga.
26, Tues.	Opera House, Americus, Ga. (mat.)
	Springer Opera House, Columbus, Ga. (eve.)
27, Wed.	Montgomery Theatre, Montgomery, Ala.
28, Thurs.	O'Brien's Opera House, Birmingham, Ala.
29, Fri.	Academy of Music, Selma, Ala.
30, Sat.	Mobile Theatre, Mobile, Ala.
31, Sun.	Grand Opera House, New Orleans, La.
April 1, Mon.	Grand Opera House, New Orleans. (Also Tues., Wed.)
4, Thurs.	Temple Opera House, Natchez, Miss.
5, Fri.	Opera House, Vicksburg, Miss.

	6, Sat.	Hexter's Opera House, Greenville, Miss.
	7, Sun.	Grand Opera House, Helena, Ark.
	8, Mon.	New Lyceum Theatre, Memphis, Tenn. (Also Tues.)
	10, Wed.	Morton's Opera House, Paducah, Ky.
	11, Thurs.	Exposition Music Hall, St. Louis, Mo.
	12, Fri.	Opera House, Jefferson City, Mo. (mat.)
		Wood's Opera House, Sedalia, Mo. (eve.)
	13, Sat.	The Auditorium, Kansas City, Mo.
	14, Sun.	Atchison Theatre, Atchison, Kansas (mat.)
		Tittle's Theatre, St. Joseph, Mo. (eve.)
	15, Mon.	New Funk Opera House, Lincoln, Nebr.
	16, Tues.	Peavey Grand Opera House, Sioux City, Iowa.
	17, Wed.	Mankato Theatre, Mankato, Minn.
	18, Thurs.	Metropolitan Opera House, St. Paul, Minn.
	19, Fri.	The Lyceum, Minneapolis, Minn.
	20, Sat.	The Lyceum, Duluth, Minn.
	21, Sun.	Metropolitan Opera House, St. Paul.
	22, Mon.	Opera House, Oshkosh, Wis. (mat.)
		Crescent Opera House, Fond du Lac, Wis. (eve.)
	23, Tues.	Academy of Music, Milwaukee, Wis.
	24, Wed.	Central Music Hall, Chicago, Ill.
	25, Thurs.	Opera House, Niles, Mich. (mat.)
		Academy of Music, Kalamazoo, Mich. (eve.)
	26, Fri.	The Lyceum, Detroit, Mich.
	27, Sat.	Music Hall, Buffalo, N.Y. (Also Sun.)
	29, Mon.	Massey Music Hall, Toronto, Ont. (Also Tues.)
May	1, Wed.	Rochester, N.Y. (Also Thurs.)
	3, Fri.	Academy of Music, Northampton, Mass.
	4, Sat.	Worcester Theatre, Worcester, Mass.
	5, Sun.	Boston Theatre, Boston, Mass.
	6, Mon.	Odd Fellows Hall, Lynn, Mass.
	7, Tues.	Gloucester, Mass. (mat.)
		Salem, Mass. (eve.)

This was a grueling schedule to maintain—sixty-two concerts in fifty-three days, plus the problems posed by ceaseless travel, different and indifferent food, and public relations (including interviews, which Herbert neither could nor would avoid). The success of the tour depended so much upon the conductor's inspirational and musical qualifications. A brief glimpse of his zeal and unique temperament, which guided the tour through a series of continuous acclamations, was provided by one of the band members talking to a Florida reporter. "He is one of the finest men that I have ever met; such a jolly good fellow, you know, and he never thinks he is above any of the other members of the band. Why, do you know we do not feel as though we are working when we are playing? It becomes a positive pleasure under his leadership. He seems to go at it in such an enthusiastic way that the time passes rapidly, and we forget all about being tired until the performance is over. And he knows how to get all the music there is out of the players. If there is any music in a man, it has got to come out—he couldn't keep it back if he wanted to."[5]

This encomium was delivered in Jacksonville, where the concert crowd was small, probably because it was Sunday. Now, if ever, the men had a right to be disgruntled, for they had tried in vain to secure sleeping-car accommodations from Savannah. A few of the players finally obtained a single berth for Herbert, but when he learned that his band couldn't share such comfort he refused it and sat up with them in the day coach. Of such stuff are heroes and beloved persons made.

It is more than instructive to follow a tour of this kind with particular attention. The receptiveness of audiences, their degree of musical appreciation, their inclinations and prejudices (as reflected in provincial criticisms sometimes uncommonly acute)[6] form a vital picture of the America Herbert was trying to reach. They presented to him problems which he solved with enviable ease, and if some of the solutions were cheap music these were countered by fare as solid as the public could take.

There were the inevitable soloists, a motley group of varying abilities. Herbert had his cello and played regularly, always to everyone's amazed delight. Wind virtuosos in the band frequently demonstrated their agility and skill, especially the Clarkes, Herbert and Ernest. Mme. Louise Natali, an opera coloratura who had seen better days, could still give much pleasure. (Herbert's piano accompaniments aided her greatly.) Aldis J. Gery was a young man exhibiting a new instrument, the autoharp, which never became a standard product of the concert hall. And alternating with Mme. Natali was little Frieda Simonson, a piano prodigy who apparently deserved the fulsome praise lavished upon her.

Frieda, called a "little princess of the piano," was born in Germany in 1884.[7] She was compared favorably with the youthful Josef Hofmann and had enough juvenile charm to bewitch all hearers. Her selections on the tour with Herbert's band were musicianly, yet popular, and nowhere did she fail to reap extravagant applause. An extra-special feature was a duo which she played frequently with Herbert: Chopin's brilliant Introduction and Polonaise, Op. 3. It was a display piece for both performers, impressing the listeners; but even more attractive was the tremendous contrast of person—the large-framed thirty-six-year-old cellist and the demure eleven-year-old pianist. Greater opposites can hardly be imagined, and they swept the audiences off their feet by fine playing and enjoyment of it.

The tour began with great éclat. Many of the cities had welcomed the band when Gilmore was at its head, but had not heard it under the direction of Herbert. Consequently they awaited the musicians with expectancy and curiosity. The Baltimore *Herald* proclaimed that the city held Gilmore's name in greatest reverence, that his band was his monument; yet under Herbert—who was scholarly, practical, and experienced—it was more efficient than ever. The new leader, moreover, showed his higher aims promptly, for the program contained better selections than formerly.

In Knoxville a reporter was happy in listening to a band that could really play. When he heard the familiar *Tannhäuser* overture he joyfully wrote: "But it was not butchered this time." The music from Grieg's *Peer Gynt* which was "so odd and so difficult to execute . . . was better received than it usually is, possibly because it was rendered better." He was highly pleased with the band's *pianissimo* effects—a crucial test for any wind ensemble—and he marveled at two of the largest tubas he had ever seen. In a novelty composed especially for them "they went down, down, until it seemed as if a plank or two would have to be taken out of the floor to accommodate the last note."

A music festival, opened by the band on March 20, was responsible for its comparatively long stay in Atlanta. The Atlanta *Constitution* was simply amazed by its tone color and perfection: it sounded just as effective as Theodore Thomas' orchestra, and Victor Herbert was surely the most versatile musician in the United States.

Rushing on to Augusta, Herbert was overjoyed by a display of sheer friendliness: George A. Oates, a resident, approached him in the Arlington Hotel to present Samuel Lover's manuscript of "The Low-Back'd Car," explaining that many years before on a visit to Britain he had met the poet, who had given him this token. A representative of the Augusta *Evening Herald* witnessed the ceremony and rejoiced with Herbert, who "pressed the precious paper to his heart and happiness and joy lit up his every feature." (The manuscript has disappeared; if it comes to light again it may be in no stranger place than Augusta, Georgia).

Herbert may have been irritated at Augusta by naïve queries. To the question whether the band's music wouldn't be rather loud for the opera house, he replied: "No, indeed; we can play as softly as a string orchestra when the occasion demands, and then when we choose, we can make the rafters ring." He finally said: "Now, treat me right—and don't write a criticism of the music until you hear the band." Thus admonished, the critics listened, then rhapsodized over what they heard. One of them with a feverish imagination chronicled his reactions to the music in passages of deep purple: A local chorus joined the band

and rendered "a maelstrom of melody"; the program as a whole, wildly successful, provided a "banquet of harmony"; for the trained and discerning ear there was classical music, but also there were "choice morceaux . . . which appealed to the proletariat."

Such conditions and reactions were repeated in practically every town along the route, and even blasé New Orleans capitulated to Herbert and his men. Swinging northward, they "for the time being placed the Vicksburg concert stage upon an equality with that of the gayest and wealthiest capitals." But on Sunday April 7, they struck a snag in Helena, Arkansas, a community of some 5,000 souls dominated by rigid Protestant parsons.

The band had been advertised for a full two weeks. Excursion rates tempted the people of the country around to come by rail and river. A huge crowd was indicated. However, the concert was to be on Sunday; and on the preceding Thursday the Protestant pastors petitioned the City Council, "praying for such steps to be taken as would prevent the desecration of the Sabbath." The Council at once referred the matter to the law-enforcement officers. On Friday the Reverend Mr. Corrigan of the Methodist Church and the Reverend Mr. Opp of the Baptist persuasion called on the county's assistant prosecuting attorney, John T. Lowe, asking him to inform a magistrate that "the aggregation known as Gilmore's Band, Victor Herbert, conductor, was coming to the State for the purpose of violating a law of the State by accepting money . . . for a concert performance" on Sunday. That official promised to take action when the aggregation arrived and actually engaged in receiving money for opera-house seats. By Saturday the managers of the opera house began to worry. They wired to the approaching band in Vicksburg that trouble was brewing and asked for a release of contract. Ignorant of the Sunday law, John Mahnken as the band manager naturally refused; but the band would have been money ahead if he had given the release.

On Sunday, Helena was full. Hundreds of visitors came from all directions, hungry for music, eager to see the famous aggregation, and curious to see the officers prevent the concert. The band arrived by a special train in the afternoon and found five hundred persons at the station to give them welcome. Together they all trooped to the opera house, where Sheriff Burke appeared as soon as the box office was opened and served his writ. Consultation led to a decision to give a free concert at once. It was the regular program, and a huge crowd expressed its delight. Then it was announced that a collection would be taken; ushers passed hats, and the audience responded liberally. At night another free concert was played, and another offering collected. Herbert dropped a generous amount into the hat, and the members of the band did likewise. Both collections were then turned over to Chief of Police Clancy, to be used for Helena's poor and needy. Herbert, with his manager in close agreement, let it be known that he wished to take no Sunday money from the town against the wishes of its law-abiding citizens. The band departed sadder, wiser, and poorer—but, as usual, richer in friends.

In St. Louis, the city where Gilmore had died, the men in the band wanted to do something appropriate; and a ceremony was organized at which the former leader was eulogized, and the current leader praised. In addition, the men presented to Herbert a specially designed medal as a token of their affection and esteem. Frieda, the little princess of the piano, brought it in on a white cushion, and Louise Natali pinned it on Herbert's broad and already much decorated chest. The band played "He's a Jolly Good Fellow." The ladies of St. Louis also wanted to honor the popular conductor, but were too late. They caught up with him in Kansas City, where they forced him to accept a wondrous floral harp eight feet high. Three days afterward in Sioux City another floral piece, magnificently conceived with the letter B conspicuously displayed in white flowers, was bestowed upon Herbert. The Sioux City *Journal* explained: "The Beethoven Club, most of the ladies in full dress, occupied the front rows in the balcony."

So the tiring tour continued to its end, a success in every sense of the word. It established Herbert as the premier band leader of the country, and it reestablished Gilmore's Band in the hearts of the American people. It also heightened public anticipation of the band's appearance at large expositions, where band music was peculiarly suited to the temper and character of the festivities.

The late summer and early fall brought the band two important exposition engagements, the fulfillment of which shed new luster on Herbert and his men. Near the end of August it was reported that Herbert was rehearsing his group daily for the concentrated efforts ahead, and that exceptional programs would be given in the two cities where they would stay longest. These were Pittsburgh, September 4 to 14 (the Western Pennsylvania Exposition), and Atlanta, September 18 to October 20 (the Cotton States and International Exposition).[8] For the occasions Herbert composed, in accordance with custom, three bright and cheerful marches: Pittsburgh was honored by *The Belle of Pittsburgh*; Atlanta, by *Salute to Atlanta* and *The Gate City Guards*.

When the Pittsburgh engagement opened, twelve thousand people listened to what was temporarily called "Gilmore's Grand Exposition Band." The musicians were in fine fettle, having "warmed up" on August 31, September 1 and 2, at Philadelphia in Washington Park on the Delaware, where the three-day throng had been estimated as approaching two hundred thousand.[9] The band won its customary plaudits there and at Pittsburgh, and then played its way to Georgia, stopping over at Columbus, Ohio, on September 15, Louisville on the 16th, and Nashville on the 17th.

The five weeks in Atlanta won a continuous round of popular approval as the result of hard work and finished execution. A typical day for the band consisted of four one-hour concerts—two in the afternoon and two in the evening—leaving little time for leisure. The music of a complete day's program[10] was widely varied, with something to suit every taste:

Afternoon, 2:00–3:00

March from Prince Ananias	Herbert
Overture to Rienzi	Wagner
Come Back to Erin (piccolo solo)	Noritto
<div align="center">S. De Carlo</div>	
Lolita, Spanish Serenade	Langey
Artist's Life, Waltz	Strauss
Grand March from Le Prophète	Meyerbeer

Afternoon, 4:00–5:00

Overture to William Tell	Rossini
Spring Serenade	Lacombe
Peer Gynt (two movements)	Grieg
Souvenir d'Espagne (trombone solo)	Desormes
<div align="center">Ernest H. Clarke</div>	
The 22nd Regiment March	Gilmore

Evening, 7:30–8:30

Overture to Robespierre	Litolff
Badinage	Herbert
Duet for cornet and trombone	Campana
<div align="center">Herbert L. and Ernest H. Clarke</div>	
Airs de ballet from Faust	Gounod
Annie Laurie (solo for autoharp)	
<div align="center">Aldis J. Gery</div>	
The Belle of Pittsburgh March	Herbert

Evening, 9:30–10:30

Overture to Tannhäuser (requested)	Wagner
Fantaisie (cello solo)	Servais
<div align="center">Victor Herbert</div>	
Scènes napolitaines	Massenet
Inflammatus (cornet solo)	Rossini
<div align="center">Herbert L. Clarke</div>	
Hungarian Rhapsody No. 2 (requested)	Liszt
American Fantasy	Herbert

While the band was playing in Atlanta a rumor spread abroad which excited his men and intrigued the public. In the spring the composer had told a St. Paul reporter that he was writing an operetta called *The*

Wizard of the Nile. Now rumor had Herbert leaving the band to become director of the company producing his opera. Herbert made an emphatic denial: There was no truth to the rumor at all; he would stay with the band, which held his enthusiastic interest. He would, naturally enough, conduct the opera for the opening performance, then return to the band and the tour.[11] But the rumor showed how imminent was the production of his second stage work and how eager his admirers were to learn more about *The Wizard of the Nile.*

Harry B. Smith, the librettist of the new work, described its origins in his autobiography many years later[12] when his memory was faulty, so that much of the account is inaccurate. Nevertheless, the following may be assumed from it.

Smith, already the author of several librettos (including the popular *Robin Hood* with music by De Koven), had an oriental story which seemed to be suitable for an operetta; and he offered it to Kirke LaShelle, who was manager of the Bostonians when *Prince Ananias* was produced. LaShelle liked Smith's ideas. About to embark on independent managing with his friend Arthur F. Clark, he wanted Smith's book as a vehicle for the celebrated comedian, Frank Daniels; and he suggested Herbert be asked to compose the music. Smith demurred, feeling that *Prince Ananias* had been an extravagant failure, but yielded to LaShelle's persistence, never dreaming that he was entering an association which would flourish for many years. He wrote the first act of *The Wizard of the Nile* and gave it to Herbert for musical treatment. Within two weeks the music was ready, and the composer himself first played it to Smith, Daniels, LaShelle, and Clark. They were all delighted, Smith making the rather naïve assertion that Herbert showed an unusual facility for setting words to music.

When the preliminary negotiations took place is uncertain; but Herbert contracted[13] on January 16, 1895, to compose the music for a comic opera entitled *The Wizard of the Nile,* to be produced by LaShelle and Clark. The management promised to produce the work on or before January 1, 1896, and guaranteed to present it at least one hundred times during the 1895–1896 season. The composer agreed to attend rehearsals before production, as well as performances and rehearsals after production, if his presence was required. His financial return from the work was to be 2½ per cent of the first $8,000 of each week's gross receipts and 3 per cent of additional weekly gross; but the first two weeks were to be exempt from royalty payments.

Public announcements of the venture began to appear early in March, 1895. On March 2 the *Dramatic Mirror* stated that Frank Daniels would be seen in a new opera next season. The following week it declared that Daniels would be at the head of a company which had secured a new comic opera by Smith and Herbert; the subject was Egyptian, and it would be called either *The Wise Man of the Nile* or *The Kibosh*. On March 23 the title was announced as *The Wizard*, but from June 1 on it was always *The Wizard of the Nile*.

Considerable curiosity was evinced over Daniels' appearance in the production. A comedian with a host of admirers, he had not hitherto played in operetta or comic opera—whatever the difference may be— and the engagement was eagerly anticipated. Early in the summer the public was informed that his entire tour was booked for next season, and that he was beginning his operatic career under "most favorable auspices." It was predicted that he would quickly become a comic-opera favorite without going through the usual probation. At the same time it was stated that elaborate preparations were under way for spectacular scenic effects, costumes, and all manner of stage embellishments. Most of the cast and chorus had been engaged by the middle of June, and the arrangements had been made for the New York opening in the fall, in the Casino. The completed company numbered about 70, and its musical director was Frank Palma. Rehearsals were to start on August 19, also at the Casino.[14]

The arrangements worked out beautifully and according to schedule, but *The Wizard of the Nile*, unlike *Prince Ananias*, opened outside of New York. The first performance on any stage occurred at the Grand Opera House in Wilkes-Barre, Pennsylvania, on Thursday September 26, 1895. Before it reached New York it played in several Pennsylvania cities including Pittsburgh, then in Buffalo, Detroit, and Chicago (two weeks), everywhere creating a warm reaction. It opened in New York at the Casino on November 4, with Herbert waving the baton before a delighted throng. The New York program gave the following cast:

Kibosh, a Persian magician, making a professional tour
of Egypt.................................Frank Daniels
Abydos, his apprentice........................Louise Royce
Ptolemy, King of Egypt......................Walter Allen
Simoona, Ptolemy's second wife.................Mary Palmer
Cleopatra, a princess who knows naught of love..Dorothy Morton
Ptarmigan, Cleopatra's music teacher............Edwin Isham
Cheops, the royal weather bureau..............Louis Casavant
Obeliska, captain of the Amazons..............Helen Redmond
Netocris, lieutenant of the Amazons..........Claudia Carlstedt
Merza, first maid-of-honor to Cleopatra..........Grace Rutter
Royal Guards, Nobles, Citizens, Pages, Maids-of-Honor,
Dancing Girls, Galley Slaves, etc.

The stage manager was Napier Lothian, Jr.

Smith was wrong in calling *Prince Ananias* a failure, because it wasn't; but he was right in implying that *The Wizard of the Nile* was by far the greater success. It may, indeed, be considered as the work which won for Herbert national recognition as an important operetta composer and as a major figure in the American musical theater. The score was cleverly executed; its exotic background stimulated pseudo-oriental effects; and its songs and choruses were fluently contrived. Neither the best nor the worst of Herbert's music is found in its pages; but they do contain much that is characteristic and easily assimilable. The book is an implausible farce in which ancient times and modern customs mingle freely and the lyrics offer little in inspiration. They are simpler than the lyrics in *Prince Ananias,* but also more common.

The incredible story takes place in ancient Egypt, which is suffering from drought. Kibosh, an impudent and itinerant magician, happens by, and through sheer good luck seems to save the country by conjuring up a storm. It doesn't stop as soon as it should, however, and the poor fellow is sentenced to die. The King conducts Kibosh to a tomb where the victim is to be sealed in alive; but the fatal stone is put in place before the monarch can get out. He is rescued by some fortunately placed pages, and he is so happy that he issues pardons to all, including Kibosh. Rather unusual is the fact that the usual lovers (Ptarmigan and Cleopatra) are not united at the close. He can continue to give her music lessons, but she chooses to wait for Mark Antony and the place in history that is reserved for her.

The music was less ambitious than in *Prince Ananias,* but it was consciously Oriental in descriptive scenes and properly mellifluous and dramatic. The King's march was intentionally pompous, and Kibosh's boastful song about his powers was broadly effective. "Pure and White Is the Lotus," a lovely part-song with solo responses, describes Cleopatra's innocence. The refrain of the waltz-quintet, "Star Light, Star Bright," became the most popular number, the very short air having an attractive lilt and a delicious turn of phrase which completely caught the public fancy. The rescue of the apparently doomed men was heightened in effect by an excellent chorus, "To the Pyramid." Always conscious of unusual instrumental effects, Herbert wrote the accompaniment to the cheerful "Stonecutters' Song" for piano and xylophone, a glittering, chipping combination.

The plots of comic opera are, by their very nature, impossible and often anachronistic; but they can be fast-moving, witty, satirical, and brilliant, particularly with respect to the lyrics of the songs. *The Wizard of the Nile* has none of these characteristics; it is tedious, absurd, pedestrian. The success it enjoyed, which was considerable, was surely due to the charm of the music and the near-burlesque, slapstick comedy of the uninhibited Daniels. The critical reception in New York was widely varied, but the attractiveness of the music earned it firm approval. In 1895, however, the book was judged to be exceptionally good!

The astute reviewer for the *Dramatic Mirror* (November 16) had difficulty in classifying the show. The program referred to it as a comic opera, but he thought this was a misnomer; at best it was on the border line between comic opera and burlesque, because "no performance can be ranked as genuine comic opera when the librettist places its locale in ancient Egypt while the chief comedian indulges in sayings and doings of modern America." It was, in fact, only a slight framework for operatic drolleries, ballads, and concerted numbers. But the whole production had been treated artistically, especially from the musical point of view. As far as stage writing was concerned, Herbert had profited from his experience in the too musicianly *Prince Ananias*. Now his music, always melodious and skillfully wrought, was more consistently appropriate; it was frivolous or sentimental, as occasion demanded, but never badly fitted to the author's text.

On the morning after the New York première the conservative *Times* delightedly told of the huge crowd at the Casino witnessing a success like the best days of old. The new opera was exceptional: its book had life, originality, and humor, and in its singing and acting it was definitely superior to any similar entertainment of recent date. Whatever defects it had were far outbalanced by its merits. The costumes were tasteful, the Egyptian settings were handsome, and the girls had pretty faces and figures—"a fact which they revealed with charming frankness." Herbert's ability was long since recognized, and the music was the best part of the production. The ringing choruses were effective; some of the songs would be immediately popular; and parts of the music were complex enough to escape being catchy. Naturally Daniels was the most prominent of the cast. He was adroit and droll, with the ability to seize every opportunity and to earn all his applause. Dorothy Morton, however, made the greatest impression. She acted ably and sang extremely well. Even in operetta she portrayed Cleopatra as a living being, as an innocent young thing whose candor wholly disconcerted her various impassioned suitors.

The *World* gave the shrewdest estimate of the music, which was on a lower level than the strains of *Prince Ananias*, but intentionally and happily so. Herbert had struck a popular vein and had judged this libretto better than the earlier one. If the music had no great value, at least it had no dull moments; and it was leavened with local color, minor intervals and harmonies, muted horns and blasts of trumpets. It was noticeable how sparingly he used waltz rhythms in the score.

Martial airs predominated, perhaps under the influence of his new work as bandmaster.

The Wizard of the Nile remained at the Casino for thirteen weeks, and then on the road for an indefinite period. Before December was over there were rumors that the entire company might go to Europe in the summer;[15] but this dream failed of realization. In January there was a report that Herbert and Smith had sold the French rights to Pol Plançon, the famous French opera singer, who contemplated presenting it in Paris in July.[16] (No record of such a performance has come to light. There are no Gallic traits in the opera, and the Parisians would probably have been apathetic toward it.) It found its way to Europe, but under different auspices.

Before it left the Casino, a touching tribute to Herbert offered as much of a spectacle as the pageantry on the stage. On Thursday night January 30, 1896, more than five hundred members of the Twenty-second Regiment of the New York National Guard attended the theater to hear their bandmaster's latest work. He conducted the second act. At its close Captain W. B. Smith presented him with a silver and ebony baton, and waves of applause drowned out Herbert's words when he tried to acknowledge the gift. Following the performance there was a special banquet at the Hotel Metropole.[17]

The Wizard of the Nile pleased America for the next ten years, first through the company surrounding Daniels, then through other companies of equal caliber and competence. Less than a year after the New York opening the Daniels company displayed it in New York again. In the middle of November, 1896, at Philadelphia, they performed it for the three hundred and fiftieth time. The five hundredth presentation occurred early in the following May at New York.[18] In April and May, 1900, the show enjoyed six consecutive weeks in the famous Tivoli Theatre at San Francisco; and it continued to be a strong attraction in various cities down to 1905.[19] In view of better Herbert scores which had appeared meanwhile, it had an astonishing vitality; and it clung to the boards tenaciously.

During the first New York run it had been rumored that *The Wizard of the Nile* would go to Europe. This came true largely through the efforts of Alexander Neumann, who traveled on the Continent in the summer of 1896 in the interests of Herbert and Smith. Two letters from him, dated June 9 and 26 and written to the composer and the librettist jointly, are preserved in the Library of Congress. They disclose the zeal that was necessary to effect an European production.

Neumann tried Berlin first; but the sober North Germans had no sympathy for such "phantastische Geschichten." The initial inquiries in Vienna were no more encouraging, but finally the enthusiasm of Franz von Jauner, director of the Carl Theater, revived Neumann's spirits.

There was some haggling over financial details, and it was necessary to employ a theatrical agent who charged a 10 per cent commission. Neumann was equal to everything, however, and proudly told Herbert and Smith that the matter was practically settled. He begged them to rush over copies of the music, score and parts, photographs—anything which would facilitate immediate production of the oriental drama.

Although Herbert could not help being pleased, he accepted Neumann's results in a rather calm manner. In July he wrote to his friend and publisher, J. F. H. Meyer (head of E. Schuberth), the following, also in the Library of Congress, which reveals other traits besides an attention to business.

As to Neumann I suppose he had to make a contract with some representative and I also think that 10 percent is customary in Vienna and that other authors have to pay the same. I have no hard feelings against Neumann; I am glad to get a fine performance at one of the finest European comic opera houses and with all the chances for a big success we shall not be too small, where Neumann certainly feels proud of his having placed the Wizard. I don't want to be mean enough to buy Smith's rights as I will take special delight in seeing him make piles of European money in the future. Ten percent for our European representative is not so much, if you consider that Miss Harbury here takes and gets 8 percent for doing nothing.

You had better cable Neumann that the score was shipped a week ago and (if that is unnecessary) that the chorus parts must be copied from [the] piano score. It was and will be quite impossible to get the German translation into the score; it is too closely written; it isn't necessary either for the conductor.

I send today money order for $112\frac{50}{}$ as I am not sure about my bank acc. Don't take Englaender's works before the[y] are given and are successes. I only say that for your benefit. Come down next week sure.

Apparently arrangements for the Vienna *Wizard* were accomplished without difficulty. It was produced at the Carl Theater on September 26, 1896,[20] the first American comic opera to find its way to German-speaking lands,[21] and was a success, eliciting the praise of the director himself, although it probably failed to meet the composer's and author's hopes and expectations. On December 4, 1896, Jauner wrote to Herbert thanking him for a photograph of the Twenty-second Regiment Band and reporting that the Viennese had enthusiastically welcomed *Der Zauberer vom Nil*. Unfortunately conditions in the Vienna theaters just then were far from satisfactory, and receipts were on the meager side. Nevertheless he would present the work again during the Christmas holidays. The principals of the Austrian cast sent the composer their best greetings and photographs. At some future time Jauner hoped to present another of Herbert's operettas.[22]

In the next spring the Vienna company took the work to Prague; but a far more curious aftermath occurred in the United States. The German version was staged in New York on May 19, 1897, at the popular Terrace Garden, with Herbert again as conductor. The town's German population flocked to it and enjoyed it to the full. The greatest changes from the initial production of 1895 seem to have been in the style of presentation, the German conception being generally superior; the amusing features were made more prominent, and a good share of the buffoonery was eliminated; also, more respect was paid to the music. But even the dignified *Tribune* conceded that nothing in the new version compensated for the loss of Frank Daniels' rollicking fun. The production was another landmark in the history of Herbert and of operetta: according to the *Musical Courier* this was the first return home of an American work, as adapted for and produced in a foreign country, in the garb and language of that country.[23] The statement was only partly true, because the scenery and the costumes were borrowed from the Daniels entourage.

Still another foreign adventure awaited the opera—in London, where it was produced at the Shaftesbury Theatre on September 6, 1897. The music was well received, but the book was not, with the result that the anticipated run failed to develop. This intelligent criticism characterized the British reaction:

> *The Wizard of the Nile* starts with a droll idea and a fairly amusing first act. But the author's ingenuity carries him no great length, and the two succeeding acts fail to fulfill the promise contained in their predecessor. The dialogue which is not exactly a marvel of wit, teems with Americanisms appealing doubtless with greater force to playgoers beyond the Atlantic than to ourselves. Very slight, moreover, is the plot, but it possesses the advantage, rather unusual in comic opera libretti, of being tolerably coherent and intelligible. . . . Its best feature is unquestionably Mr. Herbert's music, which, if not strikingly original, is at any rate exceedingly tuneful, graceful, and occasionally worthy of a better use than that to which it is put.[24]

The *Musical Courier* of October 6 briefly reported the London production as a failure and placed the blame on the company. It indicated that the well known Adèle Ritchie (apparently the only American in the cast) was chiefly responsible.

6

The First Masterpiece

WHILE *The Wizard of the Nile* was enjoying its first New York run, the New York *Journal* induced Herbert to write *The American Girl* march, piano solo version, which it issued as a Sunday feature on January 5, 1896, in its series of popular musical compositions. Herbert's popularity as a creator of comic opera made him a natural choice to provide such a musical offering. Aside from its publicity value the piece was not important.

Incomparably more important in 1896 was Herbert's election to membership in The Lambs,[1] a confraternity of men of the theater that has vigorously affected the American stage and dramatic development. This famous club appealed strongly to him, and he gave it many hours of time, talent, and affectionate service.

Entertainment, recreation, and edification were provided by members to members, and Herbert spared himself not at all in contributing to the "gambols." His personal appearances were generally restricted to serious music-making, as cellist or conductor—sometimes as accompanist; but he composed many a sparkling skit or parody to top off a brilliant evening.

At the time of joining The Lambs, Herbert must have been engaged on a minor theatrical venture which remains to this day very much of a mystery. He provided the incidental music to *A Midnight Bell,* one of the light comedies of Charles H. Hoyt, but the extent of his labor is totally unknown. The earliest program known that mentions Herbert's music is for a performance at Togus, Maine, on April 9, 1896.[2]

Hoyt was an important figure in the development of American comedy. He created his situations from homely incidents in the lives of everyday people who may seem to be somewhat stilted now but had the virtue of individuality. His characters were drawn from every class and

115

profession, and they stimulated a satire which was comical, kindly, and widely applicable. His best known work was the farce *A Trip to Chinatown,* which set something of a record for consecutive performances.[3] Hoyt himself was no musician, and whenever his plays needed musical elaboration his friend Percy Gaunt supplied it.

A Midnight Bell had been first produced in San Francisco on April 4, 1888, and had come to the Bijou Theatre in New York[4] on March 5 of the following year, when the program noted that the overture and a song in the third act were composed by Gaunt.[5] It had been reasonably successful, the New Yorkers liking the rural New England characters and the combination of homespun comedy and village melodrama. When it reappeared in 1896 with "complete new music by Victor Herbert" the company was headed by two favorites of American comedy, Digby Bell and his wife, Laura Joyce Bell.

It is tantalizing to ponder on the nature of the music, to wonder how much was original and how much arranged. Some arrangements were unavoidable, for the school children sang "Jingle Bells" and the church choir intoned the hymn, "There's a Land That Is Fairer Than Day."[6] But there were other moments when music fitted into the background, and it would be interesting to know what Herbert supplied. It is quite possible that only arrangements were used. Bell and company toured with this production, and later programs (Washington, May 4, Brooklyn, November 23) emphasized "music arranged by Victor Herbert."[7] Probably nothing important has been lost.

Herbert of course still had his band; and by the middle of April he was drilling it daily. Ahead lay a strenuous summer and fall which demanded an extra large repertoire and executive perfection. He had planned to go abroad,[8] obviously wanting to follow more closely the fortunes of *The Wizard of the Nile,* but the popularity of the band forced him to give up the trip. The concerts began in May, and by the 30th he was embarked on a better than three-month engagement at Philadelphia's Washington Park.

Additional activities were largely operatic. Herbert had revised and rescored some of *The Wizard of the Nile* for the forthcoming presentation in Vienna. He had written more than half of a new opera, *The Serenade,* based on a book by Harry B. Smith. And he had completed the music of a musical comedy which New York was expecting in the early fall.

The musical comedy, ill-fated from the beginning and of bitterly short duration, was *The Gold Bug,* which opened in New York at the Casino on September 21, 1896, proved a failure before the week was out, and was withdrawn after the performance of September 26.[9]

No piano-vocal score of the work was published, and the only excerpts printed were two songs ("One for Another" and "The Owl and the Thrush") and *The Gold Bug* march. How these fitted into the drama, and what the rest of the music was like, must be conjectured. The march was spirited and full of verve, bright enough to enjoy great popularity whenever Herbert programmed it in one of his band concerts. "One for Another" was a rather ordinary waltz song, but "The Owl and the Thrush" was decidedly attractive. It was quaint and tricky, moralistic in tone, and ended in a mood of genuine charm. The early collapse of the show must be attributed chiefly to a flat story and inadequate preparation.

The spirit of the whole enterprise now seems to be somewhat foreign to Herbert's temperament, and it may be wondered how enthusiastic he was about it. The names of the characters provide a clue to the lightness of the work. The weak political, diplomatic, and naval satire had little influence upon the composer's best talent, which lay in the direction of romantic effusion.

The Gold Bug, according to the program "a new musical blend" in two acts, had a libretto by Glen MacDonough, derived from a story by G. A. Pierce. It was produced under the direction of Max Freeman, and the well known Gustave Kerker was in charge of the music. The first act unfolded in Washington, on the lawn of the residence of the Secretary of the Navy; the second took place on the deck of the cruiser *Gold Bug.* The cast was:

```
Lotta Bonds, the banker's daughter............Virginia Earle
Hon. Willet Float, a man with a past............Max Figman
Wawayanda, the girl he left behind him..........Molly Fuller
Penn Holder, the private secretary...........Frederick Hallen
Lady Patty Larceny, a celebrated case..........Marie Cahill
Doolittle Work, a social highwayman..........Henry Norman
Constant Steele, the politician................Robert Fisher
Lingard Long, one of the shadows of a great city..Charles Wayne
The Mysterious Stranger, a dark secret............Harry Kelly
Pauncefort, a limited male...................Matthew Ott
Lord Tudor Clare, a gilded fool.............Philip H. Ryley
The French Minister, a gay Parisian.............John Slavin
The Spanish Minister, the Squire of Dames........Daniel Baker
Bandmaster............................'..Arthur Etherington
Boatswain.............................Talmadge Baldwin
```

Essie ⎫
Bessie ⎪ daughters of Lingard Long......⎰
Jessie ⎬   ⎱
Tessie ⎭

Ada Dare
Babette Rodney
Rose Figman
Sallie Randall

Lobbyists, Athletic Girls, Office-Seekers,
Naval Reserves, Marines, etc.

Besides these discouraging personages the program carried further announcements or promises. It called the production "a harvest of autumn fun, as colorful as the gayest tints of fall-prank't wildwoods," then defined it as "a rattling blend of the supremely engaging qualities of comic opera, burlesque, comedy, extravaganza, farce, spectacle and ballet." Such fantastic entertainment could scarcely emerge from the pitiful story in which Willet Float, once an Indian agent and now the Secretary of the Navy, is more or less blackmailed by his deserted Indian daughter (of Vassar) into permitting a young couple to achieve their romance.

Weak as it was, the show suffered still more by two postponements of the première, a fact which led people to anticipate far more than what they finally received. A third postponement threatened on opening night because some necessary costumes failed to arrive on time, but eventually the curtain went up. When it fell at the end, many of the audience had departed, and the remaining faithful gave no sign of approbation.

One event was important, however, and had unforeseen results. The producers of the show were Thomas Canary and George W. Lederer. Once preparations were under way Canary went for a holiday to French Lick, where he was much impressed by a pair of Negro comics who were performing in the hotel. He sent them to New York the next day, instructing his partner to put them into *The Gold Bug* as a specialty. They could not save the show; but they embarked on a metropolitan career in Herbert's third stage work, which was fabulously successful. They were Bert Williams and George Walker.[10]

The Gold Bug was designed as one of a series of lighter entertainments then being presented at the Casino. Herbert was doubtless disappointed in its fate, but not unduly disturbed. His band work continued as usual, and so did the public adulation. The concerts at the St. Louis Exposition, September 9 to October 3, won an unprecedented ovation, and the band was unanimously chosen to play again the following season.

Herbert and his men returned to New York on November 8, happy and tired. They had been away since May 30, averaging two concerts a day in that long interval. Another tour began on November 12 and lasted until five days before Christmas. Herbert's activity with the band was characterized by the ceaseless industry which marked his every interest and undertaking. Occasionally an untoward incident would threaten him with idleness; but it was somehow circumvented so that the "show would go on."

An accident at Erie, Pennsylvania, on November 22 caused serious damage. As the baggage car was being sidetracked, a fast train from the West rammed it, and the band's instruments were caught in a jumble of trunks and luggage. Several were ruined, and at the concert that night five members of the band were unoccupied because they had nothing to play on.[11]

The year 1897 began well for Herbert. He was still the cellist, delighting an audience with the magic of his bow. Two weeks later, as bandmaster, he announced that his organization had won the privilege of supplying the music for the inauguration of President McKinley on March 4. But first another happy event occurred—the première of his operetta *The Serenade.*

This was, and is, a real masterpiece of light opera, first presented to a Cleveland audience on February 17, 1897, by the tried and true Bostonians. The undeserved neglect into which it has fallen should not blind companies of the present day to its musical and dramatic possibilities.

The Bostonians had long sought a successor or alternating companion piece to De Koven's phenomenally popular *Robin Hood.* They found it in *The Serenade* which, however, was far more than a parallel production. It was a sensationally fine operetta with music brilliantly suited to the action and the characters on the stage. The libretto by Harry B. Smith, notwithstanding some situations of confusion, was much better than his book for *The Wizard of the Nile.* The score was one of the best Herbert ever did, and he never surpassed some of its concerted and dramatic numbers.

Barnabee and his Bostonians were overjoyed. Years later the comedian told with relish what pleasure and profit accrued to his troupe from Herbert's music. They found *The Serenade* to be "a score of surpassing loveliness." Its merits brought to the Bostonians a renewal of prosperity which lasted for years as they spread it before the public from coast to coast and back again. Barnabee thought it "the best American contribution to genuine comic opera—as distinguished from musical comedy, which I consider 'Robin Hood' to be—up to now revealed."[12] The distinction he was trying to make is largely meaningless today, and may have been meaningless when he wrote it. It was certainly superfluous, for there is nothing in De Koven's work to match the skill, cleverness, and variety of Herbert's best pages.

In *The Serenade* Herbert was challenging the best of Sullivan, Strauss, Offenbach, and Suppé—unaided by a superior libretto. He would do this again in some of his subsequent operettas, and again he would be under the handicap of words which did not sparkle and situations which did not develop. Some of his most remarkable operetta music is wholly unknown today because it can be heard only in stage presentation—which is highly unlikely to happen in view of contemporary taste and practice.

But Smith exerted himself in *The Serenade,* and his efforts were sufficient to the day thereof. He planned his text carefully and tried to fit it to the Bostonians' recognized abilities. As the title implies, a prominent feature of his scheme was a recurring melody of importance to the plot, a device employed differently in Genée's *Nanon,* which was familiar to the New York public. Smith feared he might be unfairly charged with borrowing this idea, and so he informed the public (in the printed program) that his book was drawn from an Interlude by Carlo Goldoni, famed comic author of the eighteenth century. Though no such interlude is known to exist, the statement was perfectly plausible, and probably no one cared, but H. E. Krehbiel of the New York *Tribune* took it seriously, declaring in true pundit fashion that the author probably had gathered his material from a French version of Goldoni, because he did not think Smith could read Italian![13] Thus are hoaxes perpetrated and rash victims captured.

The contract settling the details of the opera was signed on June 16, 1896. Much of it was conventional enough, but a few clauses were decidedly unusual. They reveal an extraordinary amount of caution on the part of the Bostonians, who had been deluded too often in finding *Robin Hood*'s successor, and they posed a peculiar criterion whereby success should be determined.

The parties of the first part were Henry Clay Barnabee and William H. MacDonald of the Bostonians; of the second part, Harry B. Smith and Victor Herbert. Among other things the contract provided:

1. The parties of the second part hereby agree that they will fully complete an opera entitled "The Serenade" (which title is subject to change by mutual consent) and deliver the manuscript words and music to the parties of the first part on or before the first day of October 1896.

3. The parties of the first part agree to produce the said opera in a first class manner, with a cast including all members of the Bostonians, who may be provided with roles, on or before February first, 1897, and further agree to present the opera at least twenty-five times during the ninety days immediately following the first performance of said opera. Such twenty-five performances may be given with costumes selected from the repertoire stock of the Bostonians, provided such costumes are not in condition absolutely detrimental to the success of the opera. But it is understood and agreed that the opera shall not be performed in New York, Boston, Philadelphia or Chicago until new and appropriate costumes are provided, together with all the accessories which contribute to what is known as a first-class production. It is understood and agreed that the scenery shall be newly painted and constructed expressly for the opera and shall be ready for the first performance wherever given. It is further agreed that under no circumstances shall the

opera be performed in New York, Boston, Philadelphia or Chicago until at least fourteen out of the twenty-five trial performances shall have been given elsewhere.

4. Said parties of the first part agree that the said twenty-five performances shall be given, as above agreed, without regard to the success or failure of the opera. The success or failure of the opera shall be determined by ten performances which the parties of the first part agree shall be given within sixty days of the last of the twenty-five trial performances. If the gross receipts of such ten performances average eight hundred dollars or more then shall the opera be considered a success. If the gross receipts of such ten performances average less than eight hundred dollars, then shall said opera, at the option of said parties of the first part, be, in their opinion, a failure. If said opera is a success according to this text, said parties of the first part agree to present it at least three times a week during the remainder of the season of 1896–97, and further agree to perform said opera at least three times a week (on an average) during the season of 1897–98, according to the terms and conditions of this contract. If said opera is a failure according to the applied financial test, in that case parties of the first part may at option return all manuscripts to said parties of the second part, who in that case agree to relieve parties of the first part from all obligations in this contract; in which case all rights of parties of the first part shall cease; or said parties of the first part may at their option continue to present the said opera an average of at least one performance a week during the remainder of the season of 1896–97.[14]

Rumors and reports of the new opera circulated early; but only toward the end of the year did it begin to take shape as a production. Late in October the Bostonians met at the Murray Hill Theatre in New York for a first reading of the work; and a few weeks later their manager, Frank L. Perley, arranged with Walter Burridge, Ernest Albert, and Alfred Williams for scenery and mountings.[15] There was still some doubt about the title, *The Serenaders* being presumed to be the solution. Rehearsals started forthwith, but the Bostonians were a traveling company and had to adapt their time to the demands of the road. Early in January an announcement came from Washington that rehearsals were progressing satisfactorily and that Herbert and Smith had appeared on the scene to work out final details.[16] The first performance was scheduled for Buffalo on January 14; but such optimism could not be justified, and Rochester was suggested. This, too, fell through, with the result that final rehearsals took place in Montreal, followed by still more changes in Albany.[17]

The great event at last occurred in Cleveland where the Bostonians appeared February 15–17, playing *Robin Hood* the first two days.[18] *The Serenade* was launched on the 17th, and was immediately successful. Thoroughly tested in Chicago, it opened in New York at the Knickerbocker Theatre on March 16. According to the terms of the contract the Ohio première was somewhat tardy; but the company lost no time in bringing the opera to the center of theatrical activity. Herbert conducted the New York opening.

The audience in the Knickerbocker Theatre found this cast:

The Duke of Santa Cruz.............Henry Clay Barnabee
    A self-made nobleman, in love with
    Dolores, and pursuing the singer of
    the serenade.

Carlos Alvarado........................W. H. MacDonald
    Baritone of the Madrid Opera, who
    loves Dolores as he has quite rarely
    loved before; a fugitive from his credi-
    tors—also from Yvonne, whom he has
    jilted.

Romero....................................Eugene Cowles
    President of the Royal Madrid Brig-
    andage Association, Limited, the head
    of an influential syndicate of robbers.
    He commits crimes one day and re-
    pents them the next as a monk in a
    monastery.

Lopez, Secretary of the same corporation.......William E. Philp

Gomez.............................George Frothingham
    A tailor in love with Dolores, and try-
    ing to learn the serenade in order to
    win her affections.

Colombo....................................Harry Brown
    Formerly a grand opera tenor, now re-
    duced to playing the devil in panto-
    mime.

Yvonne....................................Alice Nielsen
    His daughter, a ballet dancer at the
    Madrid Opera, in love with Alvarado,
    for whom she is looking with a wealth
    of devotion—and a stiletto.

The Mother Superior of the Convent of
    St. Ursula...........................Josephine Bartlett

Juana   ⎫   ⎧ Marcia Van Dresser
Isabella ⎬ schoolgirls............⎨   Leonora Guito
Mercedes ⎭   ⎩   Louise Cleary

El Gato, a brigand......................Charles R. Hawley
The Abbot of the Monastery of St. Benedict.....James E. Miller
Fra Anselmo...............................Harry Dale
Fra Timoteo...............................A. Warmouth

Manuelo, the Duke's cook..................Bertha Lovejoy
Dolores, the Duke's ward, in love with
    Alvarado.........................Jessie Bartlett Davis

The stage direction was vested in W. H. Fitzgerald, and the musical direction in Samuel L. Studley. The stage manager was R. H. Burnside, later famous in New York. Act I revealed "the main office of the Royal Madrid Brigandage Association, near a haunted castle in the mountains"; and Act II, "the garden of the Monastery of St. Benedict, adjoining the Convent School of St. Ursula." Act III reverted to the opening scene.

The story[19] is of Alvarado's courtship of Dolores, who is jealously guarded by the Duke. The young couple have fallen in love at the opera when the handsome singer captured her heart with a wondrous serenade. Alvarado also is escaping from Yvonne, who feels she has been jilted. They run afoul of Romero, the brigand chief, who is bad one day and repentant in a monastery the next. Adjoining the cloistered retreat is a convent where the Duke establishes his ward; but love triumphs over all obstacles, and the lovers (Alvarado and Dolores, Lopez and Yvonne) are finally united. The real hero, however, is "The Serenade," which permeates the entire countryside, including the dwelling place of the contemplative monks.

It is all a farrago of nonsense; but for it Herbert supplied music brilliantly picturesque, clever, adroit, and extremely melodious. He made the scenes plausible, at times hilarious, and for special incidents he created an uncannily fitting atmosphere.

The opening chorus of brigands and Romero's "Song of the Carbine" are vigorous and direct. The quivering chorus of the Duke's attendants ("Peering Left, and Peering Right") scoots along to a shuddering climax, and Alvarado's swaggering, galloping postilion's song ("With Cracking of Whip and Rattle of Spur") soars bravely over the pounding of horses' hoofs. The Duke's first song ("The Funny Side of That") is sprightly and innocuous, quite in keeping with his character and mode of thought. The famous serenade appears initially as the second part of an elaborate duet between Alvarado and Dolores ("I Love Thee, I Adore Thee") where they sing of how they first met. The serenade itself is not presented as a solo; it is an impassioned love song recalled by Alvarado, and Dolores adds comments of agreement as she listens to it again. The remainder of the duo is an animated musical dialogue closing as the lovers sing the serenade in unison.

"The Singing Lesson," wherein Yvonne and Colombo try to teach poor Gomez how to sing the serenade, is a gem of comic musicality. Full of delicious phrases, rapid *parlando* interchange, and the grotesque buffoonery of the pupil, it is enhanced by special figures in the accompaniment and by frequent shifts of tempo. Of special difficulty is Gomez's task—singing deliberately off key while his instructors try to keep him on. The purely musical humor of the piece is a notable achievement in comic opera writing.

The opening of Act II is another triumph of operetta skill. The artfully simple strain of the pious monks ("In Our Quiet Cloister") and the convincing imitation of churchly-choral style are irresistible. They have their counterpart in the ecclesiastical phrases of the Convent novices. When the monks have a chance to change to gleeful rumination, the novices continue the solemn chant, but the position is soon reversed, the monks resuming religiosity while the girls spiritedly sing of youth and love. It is extraordinary how the composer combined and contrasted these two styles. Once in the Monastery, Yvonne and a monkish chorus indulge in a dancelike piece that is a riot of color and rhythm ("In Fair Andalusia"), and immediately afterward the repentant Romero sings feelingly of the pleasures of the flesh ("The Monk and the Maid"). Again the churchly idiom is brought in with telling effect. When the Duke brings his ward to the Convent, he sings about women as the source of all trouble ("Woman, Lovely Woman"), and when Dolores is left in her new surroundings she succumbs to spiritual awe and sings "The Angelus." Expanded by chorus, orchestra, and organ, this solo was immediately effective and extremely popular; but it did interfere with the action and was foreign to the spirit of the score. It is not the best piece in the opera, but audiences were thrilled by its placid serenity. Much more fitting and certainly more natural is Yvonne's leisurely waltz ("Cupid and I") with an ingenious syncopation in the second part, following which comes the absolutely unique and hilarious chant version of the serenade sung by the monks *a cappella*.

The last act opens with a fine unaccompanied chorus. Then Dolores and Alvarado sing the sparkling duo "Don José of Sevilla," which is just as gay as it is cynical. Lopez at last has a chance to sing a love song inspired by Yvonne, and he delivers an effective "romance" entitled "I Envy the Bird." Close to the end the Duke, Yvonne, and Gomez present a trio ("Dreaming, Dreaming") which, after a rather ordinary start, develops into one of Herbert's most characteristic waltzes, a piece in which an unpromising beginning is followed by a most sensuous, caressing air. It was one of the most popular numbers of the show, also practically the last, for the cast had only a brief closing chorus in which no new music was heard.

The music alone made *The Serenade* what it was; but the rendition of the music was a vital factor. It was difficult and made real demands upon the vocalists. The Bostonians were equal to it, of course, but it eventually cost them their two best singers and hastened their foreseeable disorganization.

Jumping into stardom with *The Serenade,* playing the part of Yvonne, was the best and most intelligent prima donna Herbert ever had—Alice Nielsen. She was only twenty, relatively inexperienced, and a new member of the troupe; but she had remarkable ability, a vital personality, and a mind. Her story of securing the rôle forms an important chapter in Herbert's career as well as her own. Born in Nashville, living in Kansas City and San Francisco, she quickly disclosed her extraordinary voice and talent. When the Bostonians visited the West Coast she was struck by their presentations and their voices; and she decided then and there to go with them. She practically forced herself upon H. C. Barnabee, persuaded him to grant an audition, and after days of waiting obtained an engagement to sing *ingénue* rôles and understudy the parts for lyric sopranos. With some complacency she indicated later that she was not so popular with other members of the company and incurred the special disfavor of the well established Jessie Bartlett Davis. Individually the Bostonians were large people, and some of the female contingent seemed to resent Alice Nielsen's youthful figure, small feet, praiseworthy ankles, and general daintiness. Yet their vocal ability? She wrote: "But sing? Mother of Heaven, how they could sing!" And again: "I doubt very much whether any opera company—grand or comic—has ever had more beautiful voices."[20] With the company, too, was Hilda Clark, a lyric soprano with a lovely voice, and soon Hilda and Alice were alternating in lyric rôles.

At this time the Bostonians realized their repertoire needed refurbishing, and they arranged with Herbert for *The Serenade.* Presumably the composer was wholly unaware of Alice Nielsen; but on one occasion Mrs. Herbert heard her and ("bless her gentle heart") rushed home to tell him that the ideal Yvonne had been found. Herbert himself then went to hear her, and found her in good voice and spirit.

When the score of the operetta was finished, the parts were assigned. Herbert stipulated at the outset that, regardless of other assignments, he alone would select the Yvonne. Both Hilda and Alice learned the music, and one afternoon both girls sang it to the composer. Alice confessed that on that particular day Hilda sang it better—her voice was excellent, she had poise, and she demonstrated Bostonian dignity. Following her, Alice added a bit of burlesque and clowning, injected a little fire into the characterization, and completely won the composer's heart. Herbert announced that Alice would sing the part. Insistence by the management that Hilda at least had a legal right to alternate in the rôle had no effect on him. In fact he threatened to take his score away from the Bostonians if the part were denied to Alice.

Apparently the alternating possibility could not be completely ignored, and Alice, finally accepted as the chief Yvonne, was asked which of three cities she preferred to open in: New York, Boston, or Chicago. She chose to open in all three, and did, creating a sensation in each. On certain occasions Hilda was heard as Yvonne; but her performances were not memorable.

Herbert's judgment, and his wife's, was more than vindicated. In the next two years Alice played the leading roles in two more stellar Herbert productions (*The Fortune Teller* and *The Singing Girl*), but apart from the Bostonians. She was at the head of the Alice Nielsen Comic Opera Company, which also had the Bostonians' famous bass, Eugene Cowles. It is reasonable to suppose that their defection did irreparable damage to the older group.

There is not much point in reviewing the reviews of the New York production of *The Serenade*. Almost without exception the critics lavished praise and eulogized its inspiration. Most of them, too, found the book and lyrics unusually good. Perhaps they were, compared with the ordinary run of comic opera fare; but one astringent scribe deprecated the show's tomfoolery and regretted seeing the Bostonians in "an almost altogether ridiculous piece." Even he, however, found the music fitting and attractive, and was astonished to discover Alice Nielsen's winning ways.[21] The *Tribune*, though fooled by Smith's misleading reference to Goldoni, reported handsomely on the whole production, saying the composer here had surpassed all his previous efforts. Another paper, unhesitatingly hailing Herbert as a "musical genius," described the music as having "virility, vivacity, versatility," then suggested that with a few more comic operas like *The Serenade* America would liquidate the debt to Offenbach, Lecocq, Planquette, Suppé, and Sullivan.[22]

One criticism which sparkled in its own right, seeming to catch the verve of the opera it reported, came from the pen of Huneker, who had once thought of collaborating with Herbert in a musical drama. It was a jocular masterpiece of praise and approval.[23]

Inevitably the question of European production arose, and in 1903 Herbert was practically certain that it would take place. In the summer it was reported that Otto Weil, of Witmark's Music Library, had completed arrangements for a brilliant presentation in Vienna.[24] At the same time Herbert wrote to the publisher of the music and made this protective declaration: "The opera will be performed without any interpolations. In case an extra number should be needed, I will write a new number and in that case it shall be incorporated in the German score."[25] Unfortunately the production failed to materialize, and the autobiography of the librettist suggests why, explaining that the second act was found objectionable on religious grounds. The contiguity of convent and monastery, the "propinquity of schoolgirls and monks," which the stage hilariously revealed, was frowned upon by the authorities, and the performance was forbidden. This decision seems astonishing, but it was not without logic. The carefree parody of monastic and cloistral life had barbs in it, although it was neither licentious nor suggestive. We can only be thankful that America's puritanism differed from the European Catholic brand.

Just as *The Serenade* was beginning its unique history the attention of the country was fixed upon the inauguration on March 4, 1897, of William McKinley and Garret Augustus Hobart as President and Vice President of the United States. The celebration in Washington was elaborate and featured the festal characteristics of the military band. The executive committee in charge of arrangements had to engage the finest band in America, and from nearly two hundred organizations it unanimously chose Herbert's.[26]

The inauguration band had no prosaic duties such as marching and parading. It was to give concerts in the most impressive of surroundings, to entertain (if not edify) throngs of visitors, tourists, and curious onlookers. In three days Herbert conducted six programs, as follows: Thursday evening March 4, Friday morning, afternoon, and evening, and Saturday afternoon and evening. All of them belonged to the general festivities, but the first was doubtless the most important; next in order was the one of Friday night, given in honor of the United States Congress.

The concert on March 4 preceded the inauguration ball. The scene was the incredibly decorative Pension Building, still standing, the like of which is to be found nowhere in the country. Impressive in its daily dress, it had been transformed for the climax of the day into a hall resembling a palace plucked from the Arabian Nights.[27] On the south side of the central court an orchestra stand—for dance music—not for the band—glistened in white with trimmings of yellow. The picture was completed by rich-hued flowers, greenery, and golden wreaths. Blazing on high was a national shield which surmounted a banner flaunting the names of McKinley and Hobart.

The arrangement of the bandstand, at the east end of the ballroom, furnished the most striking effects in the huge enclosure. Beneath a great golden gateway, it was supported on fluted columns, and rose in terraced layers so that Herbert and his white-coated men could be seen from afar. Soaring over them was a spacious arch in the center of which was a three-colored star; and this framework in turn provided space (also above the band) for a dozen or so ladies in elegant array.

The band began playing at nine o'clock on the evening of March 4, but it is doubtful if the music made much impression. The crowd was there for another purpose: to welcome the new President and to eat and dance. A prosperous crowd milled around the hall awaiting the arrival of the Chief Executive, but it was not especially exclusive. There were only three requirements for admission, and love of music was not one of them. It must have been a Republican reporter that defined the requirements as the possession of five dollars and a decent suit "together with an honest reputation."

The presidential party appeared shortly before ten o'clock. Then ensued the promenade across the dance floor to the west end of the building, where, in a special room, the President and his friends partook of supper. They approached and entered their private refectory as Herbert's band blew *Hail to the Chief*.

Music remained extraneous even after the President was at table. It was now time for the public to eat, in the several rooms so arranged, and they flocked to the food as in a panic. The dinner, at one dollar per person, attracted so many that it had to be served to the consumers as they stood; but the pressure of diners only led our reporter to discover another national virtue. "The good natured way in which the throng consented to feed itself was characteristically American, sometimes the scrabble growing so vigorous that there seemed danger of a general grab game with a survival of the fittest." No doubt many a decent suit was ruined that night—and many a fragile gown. The dance was still to come, scarcely beginning before midnight and gyrating to the strains of Professor Will Haley's orchestra.

The concerts on Friday and Saturday drew crowds which were more attentive to Herbert, but they, too, found music of secondary interest. They were celebrants at a change in government, not seekers after art's solace and comfort. True, Herbert and his men were soundly praised for the concert in honor of Congress; but the feature of this concert was the Republican Glee Club of Columbus, Ohio, whose singing "surpassed anything in the way of a male chorus Washington has ever heard."[28] The program also featured Herbert's new march, *McKinley Inauguration,* which he dedicated to the President; but it failed to win special acclaim.

After the inauguration Herbert pursued his band work without interruption, except by an unexpected trip to Buffalo where he was again soloist with the local Symphony on March 18.[29] Concerts continued in the New York area, ending at the Old Homestead Garden on July 30. Then the men took to the road, going directly to Nashville, Tennessee.[30] For almost two months they remained in two cities for prolonged stays. A later advertisement of the band[31] explained the tour: From August 2 to September 7 they played in Nashville for the Tennessee Centennial Exposition; from September 8 to October 23 they were at the St. Louis

Exposition; on October 24 they were heard in Louisville, and thereafter they worked their way eastward in daily stages.

Herbert returned to New York at a favorable moment, for his fifth operetta was at the height of its popularity. It had been produced, tested in the provinces, refined, and brought to the metropolis. Herbert was not present to conduct the New York première. The production was in familiar and competent hands, however, since it had been written for Frank Daniels and company, and Harry B. Smith had again supplied the libretto. In three acts, described as a comic opera, it had the title *The Idol's Eye.*

The theater-going public was made aware of the new opera by mid-summer at the latest. An early announcement was made that Smith and Herbert were creating a sequel to *The Wizard of the Nile.* The scene was oriental, and Kibosh, the luckless wizard, was the central figure.[32] Smith's published recollections fail to corroborate this. He states that Frank Daniels needed a new vehicle after playing *The Wizard* for two seasons, and that he and Herbert set about providing one; the plot was derived, at least in part, from an old Chinese law that had come to his attention—that anyone who saves the life of a would-be suicide assumes full responsibility for that person's actions.[33] In any case, a merry hodgepodge resulted, and Daniels was in possession of another popular farce.

The first performance on any stage occurred at Rand's Opera House in Troy, New York, on September 20, 1897, and the New York première was at the Broadway Theatre on October 25 under the direction of Julian Mitchell, one of the most distinguished directors of the time; the music was conducted by the company's regular leader, Frank Pallma. The cast at the New York opening was as follows:

Abel Conn, an aeronaut who seeks and finds adventure	Frank Daniels
Ned Winner, an American novelist in search of material and Maraquita............	Maurice Darcy
Jamie McSnuffy, the last of the McSnuffys of Castle McSnuffy, a kleptomaniac, drummed out of a Highland regiment....	Alf. C. Whelan
Don Pablo Tabasco, a Cuban planter, traveling in India in search of big game.......	Will Danforth
Corporal O'Flannagan, devoted to the Colonel	Sinclair Nash
Chief Priest of the Temple of the Ruby....	Newton Westbrook
First Brahmin ⎫ Emissaries from the Rajah ⎧	Arthur Carleton
Second Brahmin ⎬ of Japalpur in search of ⎨	Lee Latta
Third Brahmin ⎭ the stolen ruby........ ⎩	Wensley Thompson

Damayanti, favorite Nautch girl of the Rajah of Japalpur.......................		Norma Kopp
Maraquita, daughter of Don Pablo, in love with Ned.........................		Helen Redmond
Bidalia, oldest daughter of Corporal Wattles, nurse to her brothers and sisters; looking for the "right man" to release her from domestic bondage.....................		Belle Bucklin
Chief Priestess of the Temple of the Ruby..		Claudia Carlstedt
Second Princess [i.e., Priestess] of the Temple of the Ruby......................		Jane English
Lieut. Desmond.......................		Claudia Carlstedt

Viola		Jane English
Blanche	Officers' daughters..........	Mae Emmons
Berenice		Florence Ritchie
Mollie		Edith Joyce
Dollie		Nellie Hughes
Pollie	Housemaids in Officers'	Eva Palmer
Ollie	families	Dora Zephlin

Soldiers, Brahmins, Priests, Hindoo servants, Officers' wives and daughters, Nautch girls, Priestesses, etc.

The time was the present, the place was India, and there were two scenes: Acts I and III, officers' quarters of an English regiment; Act II, interior of the Temple of the Ruby.

The story[34] of this fantasy, which offered quite as much opportunity as *The Wizard of the Nile* for Daniels' burlesque, is weak and puerile. Yet it had its advocates, and the music had its admirers.

A sacred ruby has been stolen from an Indian idol. It is a gem of love, and whoever possesses it wins the love of everyone around him. The thief is a mean little Scotchman, McSnuffy, who has been saved from suicide by Conn, an adventuring balloonist. In India at the same time are Maraquita, a Cuban beauty, and Ned, her American suitor, who must find one hundred thousand pounds (the exact value of the stolen gem) to win her hand. Deep in the Indian jungle is a companion ruby—a stone of hate; and there is a concerted rush to secure this, too. The interchange of precious stones, the shift of personal attraction as the jewels go from one to another, and Ned's final gaining of Maraquita's hand are the elements of the nonsensical book.

The music of the opera is attractive, tuneful, effective, but not exceptional for Herbert. Compared with that of *The Serenade* it is pallid, lacking in characterization, refinement, and shapeliness. The score has some pleasant and interesting aspects, but not many; and they miss distinction.

Don Pablo's "Cuban Song" in Act I deserves attention, and so does the "Entrance of Brahmins"—the imposing chorus salvaged from the ill-fated *Benamela* of three years earlier. The obvious oriental atmosphere is heavily effective. Two numbers are extraordinary by reason of their very triteness: Bidalia's cockney lament, "Minding the Baby" (unimportant for the action of the drama), and Abel's foppish "I'm Captain Cholly Chumley of the Guards" are remarkable imitations of English music-hall songs with all their commonness and vapidity, excellent parodies of the empty British ditty that Herbert may have written with his tongue in his cheek. Damayanti's "The Lady and the Kick" is almost as good. An elaborate finale closes the act, and it is fairly dramatic. Its most effective feature is the sudden interpolation of an *a cappella* chorus. This supplies a sharp, and sweet, contrast which is all too soon forgotten when an ordinary galop rushes in the end.

The weightiest of the oriental strains open the second act, but they sound labored. The best, in fact the only, love song—the first part of which requires an extremely low contralto voice—follows next. This probably lost some of its deserved effect on the audience because the Chief Priestess ("Song of the Priestess") addresses it to the idol and the expected lovers' duets or solos are absent. The remainder of the score is adequate and calls for no special comment.

The reviewing corps reacted in amazingly diverse ways. Some critics liked the production tremendously; some tolerated it; and some condemned it roundly. One disappointed spectator stated flatly that the music was unworthy of Herbert, that most of it was exceedingly commonplace and lacking his well known "delicacy of treatment and musicianly skill."[35] A more neutral opinion conceded that the music was popular and tuneful, and emphasized the merits of a few individual numbers.[36] One usually conservative organ (the *Tribune*) was almost enthusiastic, finding that the music had excellent life and spirit; and it commended the audience for demanding a repetition of the gem of the show, the *a cappella* chorus near the close of the first act. But the person who most enjoyed himself was the (unfortunately, anonymous) critic of the *Evening Post*, who went into raptures over the music: It was "by far the best" work New York had seen in several years, and Herbert, now at the head of the American school, had a score which could be heard a half-dozen times with increasing delight. "Indeed, now that Suppé is dead, Sullivan written out, and Strauss practically quiescent, he has no superior in Europe."

The drolleries of Daniels and the support of his company gave unfailing satisfaction for seven weeks in New York,[37] and then on tour. Most important, perhaps, was the fact that Daniels now had a companion piece to *The Wizard of the Nile*. In the following season he was able to alternate them as he traveled all over the country; and his manager freely admitted that the Herbert comedies gave him the busiest season he had ever enjoyed.[38]

Approximately half a year elapsed between the opening of *The Serenade* and that of *The Idol's Eye*, during which Herbert contemplated another operetta which apparently was never written. In the United States Copyright Office at Washington is a small sheet of paper with typing that resembles a conventional title page, indicating that *Lafitte* is to be a comic opera in three acts, that Herbert is to be the composer, Louis DeLange the author. The registration by the two creators, presumably seeking protection before they started on the book and music, was on April 14, 1897.[39] Beyond these meager facts nothing is known of the operetta.

In spite of a growing attachment to the stage and multiple interests elsewhere, Herbert still found time for his beloved Aschenbrödel Verein. On Sunday afternoon January 30, 1898, he was in charge of a concert there[40] which attracted unusual attention, and about which all too little is known. The program was highly miscellaneous, including a performance of Beethoven's Kreutzer Sonata by Maud Powell and Xaver Scharwenka, and a Quintet which Bruno Oscar Klein had written for soprano, violin, cello, horn, and piano. A more interesting novelty, however, was heard in a pair of pieces by Herbert himself, who chose this strange combination of instruments: three flutes, two oboes, soprano and alto saxophones, four clarinets, two bassoons, bass clarinet, and contrabass clarinet. Not only was this grouping of timbres extraordinary, but the lowest-pitched instrument was unusual and excited much speculation. Herbert's two pieces, both short, remain a mystery—only their titles have been preserved, *Einsamkeit* and *Humoresque*—and so does his interest in the contrabass clarinet; but he used the new instrument so effectively that the *Humoresque* had to be played a second time.[41]

Not long after this strange musical incident Herbert was profoundly saddened by the sudden death, on March 28, of his friend Anton Seidl, the great conductor. In his passing Herbert lost one of his staunchest companions and supporters. Seidl had so entrenched himself in the hearts of the public that the funeral took on the appearance of a municipal event, final services being held in the Metropolitan Opera House on March 31. There was a private service first in the Seidl home on Sixty-second Street, then, shortly after noon, the cortège moved down to the home of opera. At Fortieth Street and Fifth Avenue it was met by one hundred members of the Musical Mutual Protective Union who volunteered their services as a tribute. Preceding the hearse to and from the Opera House, they played funeral music under the direction of Herbert (also a pallbearer) and Nahan Franko, and thrilled the multitude that lined the streets as they intoned the funeral march from Beethoven's piano sonata, Op. 26.[42]

On the 1st of May Herbert suffered a broken nose when he was thrown from his bicycle in crossing the cable-car tracks at Seventy-second Street and Columbus Avenue.[43] He recovered in time to take part, with his band, in the touring Lambs Gambol later in the month.

For neither the first nor the last time the club needed money. The amusement committee hit upon the novel device of organizing a touring party from the membership and offering their unique and stellar talents to the public of several receptive cities. The proceeds— $50,000 was the goal—were to be applied to liquidation of the club's irritating debt. Nine press agents, all willing Lambs, were sent out in advance, and a parade of the participants, headed by Herbert and the musicians of the Twenty-second Regiment, was promised to each city.[44] Augustus Thomas was director of the tour, which was laid out as follows: Monday May 23, evening, New York City (Metropolitan Opera House); Tuesday matinee, Springfield, and evening, Boston; Wednesday matinee, Brooklyn, and evening, Philadelphia; Thursday matinee, Baltimore, and evening, Washington; Friday evening, Pittsburgh; Saturday matinee and evening, Chicago; Monday May 30, evening, New York City (Wallack's Theatre).

The variety and entertainment values which the Lambs could command were incomparable. A minstrel show, songs and dances, comic skits, a serious monologue or scene—nothing was beyond them. And they boasted the country's greatest stars. On this tour they presented to the public DeWolf Hopper, Stuart Robson, Nat Goodwin, Jefferson De Angelis, H. C. Barnabee, Chauncey Olcott, Eugene Cowles, Digby Bell, Willie Collier, W. H. MacDonald, Vincent Serrano, and many more. They marched and sang under Herbert's direction, and they performed two pieces which he wrote for the occasion: "Mary's Lamb," a song followed by dances, and "Columbia," which the Lambs adopted as their anthem.

It may be assumed that this glamorous troupe enjoyed the experience as much as the auditors. The week was spent in comparative comfort, and sociability reigned supreme. One inquiring reporter ascertained that "the congregation of celebrities will travel in a special train, the beauties of which will run the full gamut of luxuries, from a clean towel to a mysterious section where glassware and varicolored liquids, for medicinal purposes, form the most pronounced fixtures."[45]

They all returned from the escapade safe and sound, and the Lambs found themselves richer by $38,000 (by no means disappointing, even if $12,000 short of the goal), which was used to reduce the mortgage on their building. They had grossed more than $61,000 from the eleven performances. When the last show was over, in New York, Herbert and his band proudly led the entire company up Broadway to the clubhouse, where they were welcomed and regaled by the members who had stayed behind.[46]

7

An Orchestra at Last

THE summer of 1898 was for Herbert a prelude to one of his most brilliant triumphs as well as to a remarkable change of occupation. The triumph was manifested in the production of another inspired operetta; the change of occupation, in his acceptance of a post as a full-fledged symphonic conductor. During the summer and early fall, however, he continued with his band to please the thousands that flocked to hear it. The main engagement was at metropolitan Manhattan Beach, from June 27 to September 11.[1] In October it played for several weeks at the Pittsburgh Exposition, closing the festival amid thunderous applause.[2]

September brought forth a work which at once captured the country's heart and favor, and proved to be more than a successor to *The Serenade*. Much of its music is still known and loved. It was *The Fortune Teller*, a gorgeously romantic spectacle of gypsy love, flashing uniforms, Magyar fire, and delectable tunes. It was thrilling and moving and exotic—and the star was the bewitching Alice Nielsen.

Alice had glorified herself and the composer with her memorable performance in *The Serenade*. Though young, she knew her own value; and she was partly responsible for the creation of Herbert's next masterpiece. After her success in *The Serenade* she left the Bostonians; and Frank L. Perley, who had been business manager of that group, formed around her the Alice Nielsen Opera Company. Intimations of the new venture were given in January of 1898 when it was announced that an as yet unnamed opera was being written for her.[3] In the course of a few weeks the public learned that Victor Herbert and Harry B. Smith were writing the new vehicle, and the title was soon disclosed as *The Fortune Teller*.[4]

Alice was canny as well as attractive. Her intention to star under

135

Perley was proclaimed in January, but her real break with the Bostonians waited until April 23. Many members of the troupe still regarded her as a newcomer, and they scarcely welcomed the announcement of her ambitious plans. She admitted she felt uncomfortable—no doubt happily so—and she resented instructions to avoid interviewers from the press. The 23rd of April brought the climax when Barnabee gave her, in her own words, "a very pointed and obvious affront on the stage, and I promptly and very emphatically resigned."[5]

Rehearsals for the new opera began in the first part of August.[6] In professional music circles advance knowledge of the music caused considerable excitement, which had important results for the composer. A number of publishers were trying to secure his new works, and the successful bidder was the young but energetic firm of M. Witmark & Sons.[7] The firm issued a bulletin called *The Witmark Monthly*, which made the important announcement in August, 1898. As soon as the contract was signed, Herbert and Isidore Witmark repaired to the Gilsey House to drink toasts to the occasion. The new relationship had actually been established by Herbert's friend Otto Weil, manager of the Witmark Music Library and a schoolmate in Vienna of Mrs. Herbert's. He was very close to the composer for a number of years.[8]

The Witmark-Herbert alliance gave rise to one comment of considerable importance, in the *Musical Courier*: "It is apparent that M. Witmark & Sons, in publishing the music of Victor Herbert's new comic opera, 'The Fortune Teller,' are certainly making strides to identify themselves with publications of a higher class of music than that they have achieved their fame with. They are certainly to be congratulated."[9] This notice can be evaluated only in the light of subsequent events.

The new operetta, meanwhile, went through its preparatory stages and was presented initially to an audience in the Grand Opera House of Toronto on Wednesday evening September 14. It was produced in New York on Monday evening September 26, at Wallack's Theatre. The program announced that Frank L. Perley was presenting the Alice Nielsen Opera Company in *The Fortune Teller*, produced under the stage direction of Julian Mitchell. The cast was as follows:

Musette, a gypsy fortune-teller Irma, a pupil in the ballet school of the opera at Buda-Pesth...................... }	Alice Nielsen
Fresco, ballet master and stage manager at the opera house.............................	Richard Golden
Count Berezowski, a Polish composer and pianist..	Joseph Herbert
Sandor, a gypsy musician..................	Eugene Cowles

Captain Ladislas, a Hungarian hussar......... Frank Rushworth
Boris, a gypsy, father of Musette............. Joseph Cawthorn
Mlle. Pompon, a prima donna.............. Marguerite Sylva
Vaninka............................... Marcia Van Dresser
Rafael................................... Jennie Hawley
General Korbay.......................... Paul Nicholson

Wanda			Fanny Briscoe
Etelka	} Pupils of the ballet school....... {	May Boley
Vera			Frances Sears

Matosin, a gardener......................... William Brown
Waldemar, prompter at the opera house........ E. Percy Parsons
Lieut. Almir............................... Jennie Hawley
Lieut. Timar............................... Annie Clay
Jan, a tailor's boy........................... Fanny Briscoe
Paul, a baker's boy.......................... Nelly Marsh
A violinist................................ P. J. Worthington
A pianist................................. John T. Gray
A trombone player....................... Wm. C. Deusing
First detective............................. J. B. Henrichs
Second detective........................... W. H. Grimke
A wounded hussar.......................... J. Smith

Chorus of ballet pupils, Hungarian hussars, drummers,
cadets, tradesmen, etc.

The musical direction was in the capable hands of Paul Steindorff.

When the curtain went up on the metropolitan première the audience was expectant, attentive, and soon enthusiastic. The music was masterly, and Alice Nielsen, in her first individual starring effort, did not disappoint. The supporting cast, some of whom fairly shared honors with the star, was excellent. The book alone caused confusion and discontent, but not enough to spoil the evening's pleasure. The severest criticism appeared in the *Tribune* whose caustic reporter said of the great applause that one-tenth was for the persons on the stage, and nine-tenths for the music.

The story[10] is fairly well known and calls for little comment. Irma and Musette bear an uncanny resemblance to each other. The former, a lost heiress, is loved by Ladislas; the latter, by Sandor. Irma must avoid an unhappy marriage with the Count, and Musette runs into all sorts of complications as she helps the other girl out of her difficulties. Both of the lovers are confused in the mixing of identities, but a Hungarian military victory helps straighten things out in the end.

Herbert wrote some of his finest and most fluent music for the inane plot. The opening scene is a delight to hear, and Irma's "Always Do As People Say You Should" is a happy expression of injured innocence. Quite opposite in vein is the stirring hussar chorus, as brave as the men who sing it. Sandor's "Ho! Ye Townsmen" paints an attractive picture of gypsy life, but the most famous gypsy music in American operetta literature is, of course, the remarkable quintet which includes "Romany Life" and "Czardas." The fire and ardor of imaginary Magyar existence make this piece unique. One of the best love songs in all operetta is here, too: Sandor's "Gypsy Love-Song," which has a stanza melody as haunting as its refrain. Less well known, but just as effective, is the duet "Only in the Play" (Pompon and Ladislas), which has a sparkling musical dialogue and a waltz refrain of genuine charm.

Throughout the score, moreover, the music fitted the dramatic action well, and there was scarcely a number that failed to propel the play along. The music was good enough, indeed, to make *The Fortune Teller* a household phrase all over America. What more could a composer desire?

Most of the critics agreed on the music and the inimitable Alice Nielsen. The *Times* praised her rather sedately:

And she does it without any startling display of histrionic ability, yet with genuinely fascinating manner and with some very pretty touches of stagecraft. She has the invaluable faculty of always looking pretty and always being refined, while she sings her music excellently with a small but pure and true voice."

The reviewer wrote further that Herbert

shared the honors of the evening with her. At the end of the second act he was called for with tremendous enthusiasm, and in response to shouted demands, took the baton from Paul Steindorff and conducted his own stirring march which brings the curtain down. Mr. Herbert fully deserved the warm applause which he received. He has written a score which is rich in all varieties of delightful operetta music. There are numbers grave and gay, light and serious, catchy in the most popular manner and musicianly in a thoroughly praiseworthy style.

Mr. Herbert's command of National coloring is shown in the fine Czardas air of the first act and in the serenade medley of the second. The hussar song and chorus and the brilliant march at the end of the second act show his skill in military music, while the finale of the first act is one of the most admirable pieces of writing ever heard in operetta.

With the music causing cheers it is astonishing how short a time *The Fortune Teller* stayed in New York—only five weeks.[11] The company was organized as a traveling unit, and binding commitments took it away. In quick succession it played in most of the large cities of the East, then toured inland as far as Chicago. Everywhere there were approval, applause, and acclaim.

Soon there were the inevitable rumors of a European production, the first hint suggesting that London's Shaftesbury Theatre would house it in the spring of 1899.[12] However, Herbert and the Nielsen Company had more to offer America before satisfying European curiosity, and two years passed ere they attacked London, with results that are still debatable. Because these were important in one of Herbert's later adventures, it is pardonable to jump ahead and examine the English undertaking, which also marked Alice's retirement from the operetta stage.

In London *The Fortune Teller* turned out to be neither a sensational success nor a dismal failure. It opened auspiciously, and the public liked it. The critics were divided, but none proved to be as enthusiastic as the New York reviewers. Some seemed to be purposely antagonistic, while others failed to appreciate the qualities which endeared Herbert to Americans.

On March 20, 1901, the Alice Nielsen Opera Company with Frank Perley at the head sailed for Europe.[13] It was already known that Alice would leave Perley's management at the end of the London season, but it was hoped this would be far distant.[14]

The London première occurred on April 9 at the Shaftesbury Theatre, and the public response was more than gratifying. Herbert was in Pittsburgh awaiting the news, and the first message was a wire from Alice saying the opera had won cheers and tremendous applause.[15] Other messages followed fast, giving the impression that a permanent triumph had evolved. Even the critic of the staid London *Times* conceded the enthusiasm of displayed approval; but he added that the demonstration spoke ill for English taste, which was being vitiated through American importations of operetta; and he reminded the public of the virtues of other comic opera composers—not forgetting Sullivan. He spoke well of Alice but felt her songs were not very good, either in words or in music. What little enthusiasm he could raise was for Eugene Cowles in Act III when he delivered "O Sing the Praise of the Sword," a vigorous song which Herbert produced in time for the London performance.

Another song new to this score was "Cupid and I," from *The Serenade*;[16] but it was interpolated without Herbert's knowledge or consent, and he probably would have forbidden it.[17]

By far the friendliest opinion appeared in the *Pall Mall Gazette*, expressing a real sympathy for the music and marred only by a slight touch of condescension.

The weeks rolled by, and *The Fortune Teller* was presented night after night for approximately three months. Then excessively hot weather set in, and *The Stage* announced on July 11 that Alice Nielsen was forced by doctor's orders to take a rest. The theater was to be closed for a short vacation, but Herbert's operetta would be there when it reopened. Also promised were new effects, fresh costumes, and pleasing novelties. Only a week later the same journal notified its readers that *The Fortune Teller* had closed "last Saturday," to be followed by a Japanese variety company.

The Fortune Teller did not reopen in London. Though the manager of the Shaftesbury seemed to be sincere in wanting to attempt a fall season, the members of the company were unwilling to remain; and further arrangements were pointless.[18] When Eugene Cowles returned to America he implied that the early demise of the show had resulted from inadequate publicity and advertising. There were also rumors that Alice had become autocratic and impossible, but the popular basso refused absolutely to discuss them.[19] The venture was over, the company broken up, and Alice's stage association with Herbert was finished.

Prior to the original production of *The Fortune Teller* Herbert had committed himself to a new career to which he hoped to devote his life. He became conductor of the Pittsburgh Symphony Orchestra, a new ensemble of which the citizens were inordinately proud, and in which the whole of the country was keenly interested.

In 1873 the Art Society of Pittsburgh had been founded, according to its charter,

for the purpose of cultivating and promoting music, painting, and other fine Arts, among its members and the public at large, by holding and supporting, with or without admission fees, public and private meetings, receptions and entertainments, with lectures, discussions, concerts, exhibitions and other exercises or features appropriate to the purpose aforesaid . . .

Eventually it sponsored the formation of a symphony orchestra to be governed by the Society's Orchestra Committee. The orchestra was organized in 1895 and gave its first concert in Carnegie Music Hall on February 27, 1896. The conductor, for three years, was Frederick Archer (1838–1901), an English organist and composer who was more popular than substantial. Herbert became conductor in the fourth season. His stay with the orchestra, far from being for life, lasted only six years, which brought him some of his greatest joys and some of his most vexing irritations. For a share of the latter he may have been partly responsible, because he was ill suited to understand the pettiness and meanness he finally encountered.

When it was necessary to find a new conductor the Orchestra Committee consisted of W. N. Frew, chairman, H. C. Frick, William McConway, Reuben Miller, and Jacob Slagle, who were among the town's leading citizens, prominent in social life and in business, and in the professions. They were proud of their orchestra and unstintingly gave their time to it. As chairman Frew was very active, so much so that he occasionally presumed to render artistic as well as administrative advice to the conductor. This was ominous for Herbert, yet Frew on the whole remained friendly to him. Herbert's real trouble began when Frew relinquished the chairmanship. If Frew's musical experience was more than a bit circumscribed, it was broader than his successor's.

Archer's best was not good enough, and the Orchestra Committee had to engage a new director. Rumors of difficulties were widespread, and there were numerous candidates. Beginning on January 10, 1898, Frew made approximately the same reply to each one, thanking him for his application and assuring him that his application would be fully considered in the event of a change of conductors. Among those interested were John Lund (Buffalo), Ross Jungnickel (Baltimore), Joseph Otten (St. Louis), William H. Reussenzehn (Cincinnati), Johannes Miersch (brother of Paul Miersch, Philadelphia), Bernhard Ulrich (Chicago), Adolph Rosenbecker (Chicago), Carl Retter (Pittsburgh), A. L. Rothmeyer (New York), and Gustav Hinrichs (Philadelphia).

The records available in the Carnegie Library of Pittsburgh (invaluable for documenting Herbert's Pittsburgh experiences) fail to show Victor Herbert among the aspirants for the position. He may have expressed an interest in it in the fall of 1897, or he may have been thrust upon the committee early in 1898.

Frew, obviously knowing that Archer would not be reengaged, thought that Emil Mollenhauer of Boston would be a suitable conductor, and he asked the famous critic Philip Hale to make inquiries: the matter was to be strictly confidential, the engagement was for one season, the salary would be $2,000. Hale put Mollenhauer and Frew in touch with each other—and then suddenly Herbert appeared in the picture as the likeliest and finally the successful candidate. There is strong evidence for believing that Herbert was Hale's preference. On October 10, 1898, when Herbert's first concert was but a few weeks off, Frew wrote to Hale: "I hope very sincerely you will strain a point or even two to come on and see or *hear* the outcome of your advice last winter."

Presumably Frew went to Boston late in January of 1898 and talked with Hale. On January 31 Herbert received a contract in duplicate, with instructions from Frew to sign both. If he was chosen as the conductor the Orchestra Committee would fill in the contract accordingly, and the decision might be expected within the week. On February 10 an official communication from the chairman to the guarantors of the orchestra explained the Committee's careful study of the problem, asserted that the future of music in Pittsburgh was at stake, revealed consultation with the country's leading conductors and music critics, and declared that many able and well known persons had been considered; after weighing the advice received and the qualifications of the leading applicant (musical and technical ability, local adaptability), the Orchestra Committee had elected Victor Herbert the conductor for the coming season. On the next day Frew sent Herbert a letter of notification:

February 11th, 1898

Mr. Victor Herbert,
    164 West 92nd Street
        New York
Dear Sir:—

It gives me great pleasure to notify you that, at a meeting of the Orchestra Committee, held yesterday afternoon, you were elected Conductor of the Pittsburgh Orchestra for the season 1898–9, being selected out of fourteen able conductors, who were under consideration, and all of whom had signified their willingness to accept the position if elected. The action of the Committee was formally endorsed by the guarantors of the Pittsburgh Orchestra, at a meeting held subsequent to that of the Committee. I enclose herewith duplicate copy of contract executed by myself as representing the Orchestra Committee.

I enclose also clippings from this morning's Pittsburgh papers. In one publication, as you will notice, $2,000 is mentioned as the amount of salary to be paid. This statement has not been authorized by the Committee. We have not made the salary public, and think it better that it should be kept between ourselves. It is not part of the public's business.

Allow me to assure you most heartily that every assistance possible will be rendered you by the Orchestra Committee to make the next season of the Orchestra a notable success in every way. Our interests are identical and we will see to it that nothing we can do for you is lacking to make your first season in Pittsburgh successful in every way. The plans for next winter's season should be mapped out well in advance and, before any players are engaged, we will of course have to pass upon the items of expense referred to in the contract and many other details should be discussed.

Hoping to hear from you soon, I remain

W. N. FREW
Chairman, Orchestra Committee

Months later, but before his first concert with the Pittsburgh Orchestra, Herbert reflected to an interviewer his pleasure in the appointment. In Europe, he said, state subsidies made it possible to "rehearse as frequently and as many times as seems desirable":

The only drawback to the highest art in our public performances is the need of more rehearsals. In that particular, America falls behind, because of the necessary relationship between the artistic end and the business end of musical enterprises.

Continuing, he remarked that his association with the great orchestra, which was "making an art center" of Pittsburgh, might well "become my life work":

I have not given up my house in New York yet, but I can see a future for myself in the new work which is likely to identify me with it permanently. . . . Think of an inland city—not even a capital—supporting an orchestra that can engage such soloists as Moriz Rosenthal, Giuseppe Campanari, H. Evan Williams, Luigi M. von Kunitz, Josephine Jacoby and Johanna Gadski![20]

In choosing Herbert the Orchestra Committee in Pittsburgh showed considerable courage. In spite of his experience under Seidl and Thomas and at the Worcester festivals, his conducting for several years had been limited to a band—even though the best in the country—with activities far different from those of a symphony orchestra, and a following likewise different. Moreover, the committee made its decision after the *Musical Courier* had launched a series of personal attacks on Herbert—who, for some years, became the victim of as venomous, vitriolic, and unjust an onslaught as may be found in the annals of professional music.

There is no proven origin for the magazine's hostility toward Herbert. It may be that he refused to advertise in its pages, or that it wanted to persecute a person of unparalleled popularity in order to quicken reader interest. For years the *Musical Courier* had lavished praise on Herbert. Its reportorial praise never stoppel, but its editorial utterances made an about-face, growing more and more vindictive and ridiculous. (The present-day *Musical Courier* is a different institution from the one that belabored Herbert, and should suffer no stigma for the misdeeds of its forerunner.)

An early onslaught,[21] months before Herbert was engaged for Pittsburgh, blasted him both as cellist and as conductor: the Twenty-second Regiment Band had given a concert in New York which the journal characterized as appealing only to the most ordinary taste; other bands then prominent in the country were, by strong implication, much finer, and the spiteful writer remarked: "Some of the interior towns may be satisfied with a performance such as Herbert and his band gave, but after hearing the Banda Rossa and Innes and the great Sousa, New York demands something of a different character." As usual, Herbert played cello solos in this concert. His playing was called "puerile": waving a baton had harmed his bowing arm, and the critic concluded that when the cello is "played with continual vibrato and affected sentimentality its effect is unhealthy."

Less than a week after Herbert's engagement in Pittsburgh was announced the thoughtful journal proclaimed:

. . . In the selection of Mr. Herbert to succeed Mr. Archer we cannot conscientiously congratulate the chairman of the Art Society, nor indeed Pittsburg.

Herbert is anything you like but a good conductor. He is not even a successful band conductor, as his recent tours have proved. And he has had absolutely no experience with symphony orchestra conducting; indeed with any orchestra. As a 'cellist he was proficient before he stopped practicing, and he is a highly successful composer of comic opera. Personally, we have not the slightest fault to find with this Irishman, but to put a raw man—in the sense of a conductor—at the head of a well equipped orchestra seems a pity. Certainly music will not be benefited in Pittsburg. When we speak of Mr. Herbert as not being an adept conductor we mean just what we say. As a leader of band music his beat is wild and amateurish, musical conception commonplace, and he lacks the greatest of all requisites of a conductor: He has no personal magnetism. As a musician we admire Mr. Herbert, as a 'cellist we applaud, for his tone is sympathetic and magnetic, yet, strangely enough, when he gets up before an orchestra with a stick in his hand all magnetism, all sympathy, all mastery vanishes. He is simply awkward. It is the same with Walter Damrosch, who, in addition to being a sound, practical musician, is a piano accompanist of the first rank and, as good accompanists are rare and mediocre conductors plentiful, we should like to keep Herbert at his 'cello, Damrosch at the piano.

However, Pittsburg will find out about Victor Herbert for itself.[22]

Just a week later with a deliberate disregard for logic, it blandly printed the following:

The versatility of Victor Herbert is admirable to behold. Last Saturday night he played among the 'cellists of the Philharmonic. This week he may stand in a bandmaster's uniform directing a military march played by a brass band. He may also be at work on a comic opera, and then be called to Pittsburg to conduct his Philharmonic concert. Any musician who can do all these things and do them all well would do one of them well enough not to be obliged to do any of the others.[23]

When the spring tour of The Lambs, including Pittsburgh, was announced the curious scribe of the *Musical Courier* was tempted once more:

The people of Pittsburg will get a first-class idea of how Band Leader Herbert will conduct Beethoven symphonies next season at their Philharmonic concerts, when he heads the parade of the Lamb's Club with the Twenty-second Regiment Band, N.G.N.Y., as the procession passes through Wood street, Fifth Avenue, Penn Avenue and other Pittsburg thoroughfares. He will open up the marching program with the now celebrated "All coons resemble," followed by the dirge in the "Idol's Eye," when the other fellow blackened it. After this he must give the Pittsburgers a touch of his 'cello by playing it seated on the bass drum as it is held by other Lambs. He will conduct with one hand, play the 'cello with the other, in the meantime constantly composing in his own mind. He can do these things. . . . At the end of the march the club will sing the "Lambs' Fry Anthem," one of Herbert's hottest compositions, and the procession will finally be dismissed with an imitation on four cornets and a trombone, accompanied by a flute, of Richard Wagner's "Ride of the Valkyries," arranged for the mounted officers of the Twenty-second Regiment N.G.N.Y., by Band Master Herbert.[24]

Three weeks earlier the *Courier* had reached what it considered to be a hilarious conclusion from a statement by Herbert to Pittsburgh newspapers that it was not the salary as conductor that attracted him to Pittsburgh: he was financially independent and only wished to make the orchestra the equal of any in the world.[25] Then in the middle of May the non-signing foe vented his spleen in this vein:

Bandmaster Herbert, like a good soldier, marched at the head of his Twenty-second Regiment Band as the regiment went to camp last week, but the band did not encamp. The musical people of Pittsburg have the great distinction of possessing a symphony conductor who can demonstrate his patriotism in more than idle talk; he can march to the ferryboat and see the boys off and then go home and study symphony scores for the next Pittsburg season.[26]

Such was the ceaseless stream of invective which the *Musical Courier* poured on Herbert's head. It was augmented by anonymous contributions from Pittsburgh, signed "X," "Honestas," and "Traumerie." Who these persons were, or who this person was, was a puzzle to the Pittsburgh Orchestra Committee. The first Pittsburgh friend to dare support Herbert in the *Courier's* pages was Arthur Wells, who entertained a reasonable apprehension of Herbert's conversion to a symphonic conductor. After Herbert's band performances at the Pittsburgh Exposition of 1898 Wells sent this understandable statement to the slandering journal:

Victor Herbert closes the Pittsburg Exposition for the season of 1898. He has with him his famous Twenty-second Regiment Band of New York, one of the finest and best trained bod[ies] of musicians now playing under the name of a band. His reading of classical music shows a true appreciation of the better ideals, while at the same time the dash and vigor of his performances of the "Stars and Stripes Forever" is enough to win the admiration of the most severe critic. His happy intermingling of popular and classical music has made him more appreciated than ever in Pittsburg . . .

The experiment of allowing a bandmaster to assume the leadership of a full-fledged symphony orchestra is to be tried in Pittsburg the coming winter. The orchestra has been improving steadily since its inception, and while it is to be hoped that not only will Mr. Herbert prove himself capable of leading it on to a still greater degree of perfection, but demonstrate as well his own fitness for the more exalted musical position, yet as a matter of principle we are opposed to a bandmaster being offered such a post, although in this instance it may be shown that Mr. Herbert has been merely undergoing a natural course of training, gradually working his way upward, until he now approaches his rightful position.

Mr. Herbert is really a higher type of musician than the average bandmaster, and it is possible that his keen appreciation of classical forms, his great personal magnetism, his wonderful control of musicians, and his own genius, will combine to make him a success in this new role. The venture has elements of success as well as failure. . . . Upon the success of this season's concerts may depend the future existence of the orchestra.[27]

Headed by Frew, the Orchestra Committee chose to ignore the stand taken by the *Musical Courier*. The chairman gave assurances that Herbert was solely responsible for the musical results, and he explained that the Art Society as such did not govern the Orchestra. The Orchestra Committee was the court of last appeal. He also begged Herbert to hasten the final arrangements for the season's opening. The conductor, who had his own countless affairs to manage, occasionally procrastinated in making decisions, a fact which worried the good chairman not a little.

At first Herbert's contact in Pittsburgh was only W. N. Frew; but soon he began to transact most of his business with the orchestra manager, George Henry Wilson. Wilson (1854–1908), a native of Massachusetts, had drifted into music by way of newspaper work where he had attracted some attention as a chronicler of musical events. He aspired to cultural and social prestige and kept himself in the good graces of the Orchestra Committee regardless of his personal relations with others. Pedantic, finicky, superficial, faithful to the committee as a dog to its master, he lacked the heartiness and sincerity essential to friendship. He discharged his duties punctiliously, had no imagination, and was small-spirited if not mean. His personality was as different from Herbert's as night from day, and a clash between the two was inevitable. Herbert made every effort to win Wilson's friendship but failed, and the clash eventually arrived. Unfortunately Herbert's want of tact widened the breach and hastened his departure from Pittsburgh.

On the last day of May, Wilson wrote to Herbert that he had just been elected manager of the Orchestra for another season and promised

to do his utmost to make the conductor's efforts a success. He also
sent information on players and their contracts. Herbert was encountering a little difficulty in settling such matters, and occasionally
his patience wore thin. An indication of the problems and salary
scale is preserved in his letter of August 17 to Wilson:

> I enclose new contract for Vater (tymp.) for $33.00. I hope this will be
> the last of this.
> Will you please send for Rothleder and ask him if he will accept engage-
> ment at 25$. I will place him on one of the first stands but can't promise
> him a certain place or second concertmaster chair as I am corresponding with
> a gentleman about that position. If he refuses 25.00, the sum Sauerwein,
> Kaltwasser, Stelzner receive, you could go as far as 27.00 but this is the limit.
> I hope he will accept at once.
> The list of members I will send you end of this week; also my curriculum
> vitae.

The orchestra at Herbert's disposal was not large. As the season
opened, it included: 1st violins, 10 (L. von Kunits, concertmaster);
2nd violins, 8 (E. N. Bilbie, principal); violas, 6 (J. B. de Backer,
principal); cellos, 4 (Louis Heine, principal); double basses, 4; flutes
and piccolo, 3; clarinets, 3; oboes and English horn, 2; bassoons, 3;
horns, 4; trumpets, 3; trombones, 3; tuba, 1; tympani, 1; drums, cymbals,
etc., 1; harp, organ, piano, 1 each. The tympanist served also as
librarian. Small as the orchestra was, with the obvious weakness in
the strings, it had five more members than in the year before and eight
more than in the initial season of 1895–1896. The total cost for the
coming season of twenty concerts (ten programs) was estimated at
something over $30,000—a substantial sum for an inland city in 1898.
Herbert conducted his first concert with the Pittsburgh Orchestra on
Thursday evening November 3, 1898. During the day Manager Wilson
sent him a note purporting to convey the final instructions from the
Orchestra Committee. The only encores to be allowed were of soloists
who might arouse the audience to extreme enthusiasm; orchestral
encores were out of the question. The players were to be on the stage
by 8:13, the conductor at 8:15; the ushers would then close the doors,
but the conductor must wait until the people in the aisles were seated.
The players were forbidden to go into the hall before the concert or
during the intermission. The concern of the manager for these points
of decorum must have amused Herbert, the veteran of many a concert
of equal or greater propriety.
The program was thoroughly representative, with Giuseppe
Campanari, one of the vocal idols of the day, as soloist:

Leonore Overture No. 3	Beethoven
Aria, "Non più andrai," from Le Nozze di Figaro	Mozart
Symphony No. 5, in E minor	Tchaikovsky
Symphonic poem, Le Rouet d'Omphale	Saint-Saëns
Aria, "Dio possente," from Faust	Gounod
Prelude to Die Meistersinger	Wagner

At the end of the concert the audience, including H. C. Frick, Charles M. Schwab, and Andrew Carnegie, was jubilant; and the newspapers the next morning vied with one another in praise and adulation. A few of the critics, as if fearing to declare that absolute perfection had been achieved, tried to point out minor flaws; but this only accentuated the encomiums bestowed upon the new conductor and the largely new orchestra: Pittsburgh had brought to light a new conducting genius, and the orchestras of New York, Boston, and Chicago had best look out or the inspired local organization would wrest their laurels away. No doubt the critics were prejudiced, no doubt they lacked the experience and competence of their confrères in New York; but their enthusiasm cannot be questioned, and their unanimity suggests that Herbert's début in Pittsburgh was a triumph well deserved and based on merit.

Perhaps the most perceptive criticism appeared in the Pittsburgh *Dispatch,* which praised the conductor, the soloist, the program, and the audience and then discussed the affair in more detail:

Herbert has grace as he wields the baton . . . [and] the power to bring from the instrumentalists all that is in them. The arrangement of the desks, while not radical, was unique in some ways, and the outcome showed that the judiciousness with which this had been done was an innovation in the line of genius. . . .

The woodwind and brass choirs of the orchestra are improved, most of the musicians in these divisions having been transferred from Mr. Herbert's band . . . For the strings as much can hardly be said. Mr. Luigi von Kunits, restored to his old position of concertmeister, displayed the efficiency of his fine musicianship in the uniform bowing of the violins, but in total strength the strings do not show up well in proportion to their increased numbers. The violas are better than before . . . but the cellos are generally overpowered. However, an improvement in the contrabasses tends to help them out.

The discipline of the players is perfect. Their work plainly evidences arduous training under an experienced master of the orchestra, whose slightest look or gesture evokes instant response. . . . From the most delicate breath-like pianissimo by steady crescendo, the tone volume grows into a well-rounded, evenly balanced fortissimo, and, on the contrary, as in the close of the first movement of the symphony, the tone is allowed to fade.

Mr. Herbert's directing is never dry. The Beethoven classic he reads with perfect understanding. The Saint-Saens tone poem he interprets with the daintiest finesse. The wonderful symphony . . . is worked out by the man with the baton after a compelling fashion. It may be that Victor Herbert's native Celtic fire, his German scholasticism and abundant artistic experience have taught him how to understand Tschaikowski. In the Wagner prelude Mr. Herbert's players delineated the medieval pomp and ceremony with which the score bristles.

The concert and its attendant success were repeated on Saturday afternoon November 5. Everybody was happy, Pittsburgh was congratulating itself, and Chairman Frew was overjoyed. On the following Monday he sent an enthusiastic note to Herbert which was decidedly complimentary and said that he would like to address the orchestra the next morning when it assembled for rehearsal.

Standing before the musicians Frew announced that his appearance was authorized by the Orchestra Committee, which wanted the men to know how deeply it appreciated the musical results of the first program. They were also to be complimented for their exemplary deportment, for tuning their instruments before entering the stage, for the undivided attention given to their conductor, and for the efforts of each to do his very best. He ended by bestowing special praise on Herbert, whom he compared favorably with Paur, Gericke, Thomas, and Richter. He stressed the praise by remarking it was not his alone—it was shared by the committee and by many others who were fortunate in hearing the opening concerts.[28] The future looked golden and the possibilities seemed limitless.

8

A Double Career

IN ONE quarter, the news of Herbert's successful début as an orchestra conductor was decidedly unwelcome—the office of the *Musical Courier*. Yet it made a pretense of fairness by printing a short letter of praise from Myron R. Stowell of Pittsburgh who, on November 5, asserted that the opening concert was marvelous, that there were no dissenting opinions, that the city was feverishly enthusiastic. He concluded: "We think Herbert is great, and so will you."[1]

Immediately after this hearty endorsement the same issue of the paper printed an excessively long diatribe from the Orchestra's unidentified foe, "Honestas." The intemperance and extravagance of the language were such that no reader could take it seriously, but it defined the stand of the *Musical Courier* and showed that peace was an unobtainable goal:

Happy Pittsburg! Unfortunate Boston, New York and Chicago, who have to be content with inferior men. Considerable curiosity was aroused by the preliminary flourish of trumpets, and an expectant audience was on hand . . . to witness the début as a serious symphonic conductor of "the brass band leader and comic opera king" (as he was named in advertisements), who had already won renown at the Exposition as the exponent of "Tossing the Pickaninny," "Champagne Galop" and other classical works whose high tone and educational value cannot be denied. The experiment was by no means a success.

The whole remarkable expression, so savage as to be ridiculous, was but the first of a series by "Honestas." They had no appreciable effect upon Herbert, the orchestra or the Orchestra Committee. The last named only issued a statement that the frantic attempts by the *Musical Courier* through a Pittsburgh correspondent to deride Herbert and

150

the orchestral organization had utterly failed. Asserting that the character of the journal was now meaningless, it admitted a certain humiliation that any resident of the city would stoop to such a low conspiracy.

Meanwhile the season continued according to plan, with concerts on Thursday afternoon and Friday evening, November 10 and 11. The soloist was Johanna Gadski, who was the second most expensive soloist of the year, receiving $500 for her engagement as compared with Campanari's $350. She sang arias from Weber's *Der Freischütz* and Wagner's *Tannhäuser*, and Herbert offered Schumann's *Manfred* overture, Beethoven's Fifth Symphony, and two Wagnerian excerpts. Again there was a brilliant triumph, press and public joining in praise of the new conductor. It was an especially proud night for Herbert because his mother, in America on her first and only visit, sat in a box with his wife.[2]

The more perceptive critics once more noticed the weakness of the strings, but Herbert was well aware of their insufficiency. Two conditions were necessary before the lack could be remedied: money and men. Chairman Frew found the former, and Herbert the latter, helped by the disbanding of the Seidl orchestra and the financial failure of Emil Paur's attempt to establish an orchestra in New York: string players, good ones, could be had in abundance. Frew wanted Herbert to have all the personnel he needed, and called a special meeting of the committee to authorize the necessary expenditure. Paul Henneberg, first flutist of the Pittsburgh Orchestra, went to New York and enthusiastically announced, on his return November 18, the acquisition of four first and four second violins, two violas, three cellos and two double basses.[3] Herbert was elated, and so were the local music lovers.

Two days after Christmas, Herbert conducted a special concert for the members of the Pittsburgh Art Society, which had just sponsored an award for "the best original work in overture form, by composers living in Pittsburgh and vicinity,"[4] the judges of the contest being Herbert, Walter Damrosch, and Arthur Foote.[5]

Two compositions were deemed worthy of recognition: a symphonic piece, *Faust*, by Adolph M. Foerster, and an overture, *Richard III*, by Fidelis Zitterbart. Both received prizes, and both were performed at the Society concert.

There must have been some consternation over the award to Foerster. Though Frew had placated him the preceding season, he was again clamoring for a performance. On the other hand he had begun to write letters against the Orchestra—sending them to the *Musical Courier*, of all places!—and the Orchestra Committee can be pardoned for not responding warmly to his request for a hearing. It might even be pardoned for trying to identify Foerster as the writer of the scurrilous anonymous attacks against Herbert; but it carefully refrained from such a suggestion.

Herbert's name appeared in the controversy on December 8, when Frew chid Foerster for suggesting the conductor ought not to resume his band career at the close of the orchestra season. He went so far as to say that Foerster found the matter a bigger bugbear than others did, and that Herbert would gladly surrender the band when all the people of Pittsburgh supported the Orchestra as they should. This was sound sense—and so was his message to Foerster on December 17, agreeing on the undesirability of a "praise racket" and denying knowledge of any arrangement to secure continuous praise for the Orchestra. The most he would concede was that severer criticism might be in order when the orchestra was more fully established.

Some suspicion of this discord must have reached the ears of others, and Foerster was the subject of some curiosity when the Art Society concert was presented. He and his work were well received by the audience, and he "said privately that he was very well satisfied with the care that the orchestra had given his production."[6]

The last pair of concerts occurred on January 20 and 21, 1899—a splendid program. The major symphonic work was Beethoven's seventh, and Moriz Rosenthal as solo pianist played Chopin's first Concerto. He was the most sensational star of the season and the most expensive, receiving a fee of $1,000. Orchestra, conductor, and soloist outdid themselves, and the audience trooped from the hall lamenting that the end of the season had come. Happily they could look forward to next year. Herbert's reengagement had already been announced, with the promise of nearly twice as many concerts.

On January 21, as soon as the season was over, twenty-five members of the orchestra furnished the music of a farewell concert for Herbert in the Hotel Schenley. Conducted by Paul Henneberg, they played nothing but Herbert's compositions. The creator beamed, and finally rose to lead a special selection. This caused Herbert's local enemies (or enemy) to burst into print again with two vicious onslaughts in the January 25 *Musical Courier.*

Then, curiously enough, the *Musical Courier* of February 15 printed a letter from a Pittsburgh citizen who came to Herbert's support. It was from Arthur Wells, once apprehensive about the conductor's success and now convinced of his sterling qualities, and quoted opinions from the season's soloists to buttress his own views:

. . . But "Honestas," "Traumerie" and others of like perverted vision to the contrary notwithstanding, the writer is pleased to consider that the season just ended has demonstrated the justness of the Pittsburg Orchestra's claim to recognition as one of the orchestras of this country. . . . The unstinted praise which has been bestowed upon the Pittsburg Orchestra by visiting artists of international fame . . . proves beyond controversy the absolute truth . . . that the orchestra has improved steadily since the opening of the present season, and that it has developed, under the leadership of Victor Herbert, a capacity for intelligent rendering of classic music . . .

Evan Williams, Mrs. Josephine Jacoby, Willy Burmester, Miss Aus der Ohe, Campanari and Moriz Rosenthal have each in turn expressed to the writer personally their high opinion of both Victor Herbert and the body of musicians of which he is now in control . . . and they failed not to praise Mr. Herbert for his successful handling of a practically new organization. . . . These statements were not made on account of any warm personal regard for Mr. Herbert, nor were they spoken out of courtesy to the local management—but they were given as true and unbiased expressions of candid, personal opinion, and made from an entirely unprejudiced standpoint.

It was the writer's good fortune to meet Mr. Rosenthal and Mr. Burmester in Chicago last week . . . Once again they both praised Mr. Herbert and his men very highly, Rosenthal stating that he considered Herbert a "musician of a high order," and they both agreed that the accompaniments given them in Pittsburg by Mr. Herbert were as good as any they have had in this country. Burmester was surprised when told that Herbert had formerly been a brass band master. He replied, "He doesn't belong in that class, and should never have been there."

There was the rub, the supposedly weak chain in Herbert's armor which his jealous and vindictive foes could not forgive. He had led a brass band; he had been on a lower rung of the musico-social scale; he had come from beyond the pale of polite society. But honest folk knew better, and so did Herbert, who looked forward to constant improvement of the orchestra he deeply loved.

The orchestra season was over, but its business continued. Early in April, Chairman Frew expressed alarm on reading that Herbert, back in New York, was in serious difficulties with the Musical Mutual Protective Union. Herbert's light treatment of the matter failed to reassure him; and he wrote on June 5 that it was quite possible that Herbert might be prevented from conducting next season, and then it would be senseless to engage the Orchestra's players. Next, he voiced a sentiment which is heard perennially—the Union was unfair, but its strength could not be ignored.

For a while the problem was bothersome. The Union suspended Herbert on charges by several of his band players that he owed them salaries for a tour some years back. Herbert countered with the explanation that he himself was on a fixed salary and had no responsibility for the remuneration of his men. He, too, had had difficulties with his management and had broken connections with it, whereupon he assumed personal responsibility for the organization.[7] A bitter dispute arose in the union, and feeling was high for about two months, the opposition being headed by members who were not musicians. Eventually Herbert won, after resorting to counsel and threatening to form a band wholly his own. The Union then decided he had been suspended illegally, without sufficient notice, and with no chance to prepare an adequate defense. The consensus was that Herbert had won a major victory.[8]

Nevertheless, the experience was annoying, for it interfered with Herbert's resumption of activity in New York. At the annual review of the Twenty-second Regiment (April 3) he was permitted to lead the band at drill and maneuvers; but another person took the baton for the concert which came after.[9] And when the Lambs presented their famous annual gambol in the Fifth Avenue Theatre on the afternoon of May 19, Herbert was forbidden to direct the music he had composed—*Hula-Lula*, "a territorial operetta"—for the occasion,[10] although the program bore his name. DeWolf Hopper explained the situation to the audience as Jesse Williams took Herbert's place.

The disturbing quarrel with the union came at a most inconvenient time. In the spring, summer, and early fall of 1899 Herbert was at his busiest, with no fewer than four operettas flowing simultaneously, or in extra-quick succession, from his pen: *Cyrano de Bergerac; The Singing Girl; The Ameer;* and *The Viceroy.*[11] *The Ameer* was of indifferent quality and added nothing at all to Herbert's reputation; but the others, although varying in degree of success, contained excellent music.

The music of Herbert's *Cyrano de Bergerac* has suffered the undeserved fate of complete oblivion; yet some of its pieces are extraordinary, and the score was soundly praised. He was probably ill advised to set Rostand's great play to music, for the result failed to supply either comic or romantic entertainment. Moreover, the quality of the original play, and the impact it had on the public, foredoomed to failure conventional operatic treatment. The drama still resists the addition of music, in spite of scenes which are usually enhanced by it.

Rostand's play, sensationally triumphant from the time of its first production in Paris on December 28, 1897, was already well known to American theatergoers. Through some error or oversight he had failed to claim a United States copyright, and it was fair prey for anyone wishing to capitalize on its qualities. The American stage idol Richard Mansfield presented an authorized version to New Yorkers on October 3, 1898—and on the same date Augustin Daly's company, headed by Ada Rehan, produced an unauthorized version in Phila-delphia.[12]

Exactly one month later Weber and Fields' Music Hall in New York presented an unsuccessful burlesque of the play with music by John Stromberg and text by Harry B. Smith and Edgar Smith, entitled *Cyranose de Bric-a-Brac* and unwittily described as "a prominent feature, amputated from the French, and disfigured without per-mission."[13]

By 1899, therefore, the American theater public was thoroughly acquainted with Rostand's masterpiece. When it was announced in mid-July that Herbert had finished the score for a musical version, curiosity was rampant, increased by the accompanying statement that Francis Wilson, a really great comedian, would produce it.[14]

This comic opera in three acts with book by Stuart Reed and lyrics by Harry B. Smith had its world première in Montreal at the Academy of Music[15] on September 11, 1899, and opened on September 18 at the Knickerbocker Theatre in New York with the following cast:

Cyrano de Bergerac, a soldier of fortune..	Francis Wilson
Christian de Neuvillette, of the Cadets of Gascony	Charles H. Bowers
Ragueneau, pastrycook, devoted to the muses	Peter Lang
Captain Castel-Jaloux, Commander, Cadets of Gascony......................	John E. Brand
Count de Guiche, Christian's rival.......	Robert Broderick
Montfleury, an actor of the company of the Hôtel de Bourgogne A Friar	A. M. Holbrook
A Captain of the Musketeers............	Joseph M. Ratliff
Roxane, Cyrano's cousin................	Lulu Glaser
Lise, wife of Ragueneau................	Josephine Knapp
Duenna	Josephine Intropidi
An Actress, of the company of the Hôtel de Bourgogne....................	Bessie Howard
An Actor, of the same company.........	F. S. Heck
A Young Lord.....................	William Laverty
A Doorkeeper.......................	Charles F. Dodge
A Pickpocket.......................	Fred Scott
First Cadet.....................	Bessie Howard
Second Cadet.....................	Stella Koetter
Third Cadet.....................	Martha Stein
First Poet........................	Karl Stall
Second Poet.......................	Thomas de Vassey
Third Poet........................	H. L. Owen
Page	Clara Hollywood

First Cook's Boy	Lotta Watson
Second Cook's Boy	Laura Wise
Third Cook's Boy	Edith Scott
Musketeers	F. S. Heck Carl King H. L. Owen Karl Stall

The production was staged under the direction of A. M. Holbrook; the director of the music was John McGhie.

At the end of opening night, the audience was in a state of wonderment. And they never made up their minds as to whether they had seen a great play travestied or a mediocre burlesque almost ennobled. Familiar with Rostand's story about the long-nosed warrior who sacrificed his happiness for love, they had come unprepared for the strange mixture of serious romance and rough comedy beyond the footlights. Some of the scenes seemed to have been taken directly from the French drama; others were hopelessly bizarre and resisted all efforts to make them plausible.

While mutilating Rostand's carefully designed poem, the operetta seemed to have possibilities for serious treatment. Unfortunately Wilson tried to be both a slapstick comedian and a romantic lover, and he failed between the two extremes. A victim of Rostand's magic, he was unwise enough to believe he could unite buffoon and gallant in the same character. The press praised his aspiration to act on a higher level than low comedy, and even admitted that his delivery of serious, romantic lines was surprisingly good; but, the more he satisfied his penchant for refinement, the more ludicrous was the contrast with rough buffoonery.

The reception of the music was vastly different. It was felt that the opera's success depended on Herbert's contribution, which was "of an exquisite beauty" and affirmed that he was in the forefront of American operetta composers.[16] Another perceptive critic labeled the music delightful and added: "There is much of the daintiest and most picturesque instrumentation that has been heard in operetta since the palmy days of Sir Arthur Sullivan."[17]

In only one respect—but so important—was the musical part of the show deficient. Most of the critics noted in no uncertain terms that the singers were not equal to Herbert's demands. Wilson and Lulu Glaser could not cope with the songs. The reviewer for the *Times* wrote, "So far as the solo numbers went, one had to guess what most of them would sound like if they were well sung"; but he heartily commended the work of the orchestra and chorus.

H. E. Krehbiel denounced the operetta as a miserable failure,[18] but long afterward the review of *The Singing Girl* in the *Tribune* by that formidable arbiter of musical taste (it was surely his) implied extraordinary praise of *Cyrano.* He still recalled too easily the vocal effects, and how they had spoiled Herbert's efforts and intentions:

> How necessary the co-operation of the singers is to the composer who cherishes such an ideal [i.e., operetta worthy of those who appreciate good music] was demonstrated in the first of Mr. Herbert's new operettas brought forward this season. Mr. Wilson's wish to have his "Cyrano de Bergerac" treated with dignity, or at least as a "respectable perversion" of the original subject, as Mr. Gilbert defined his "Princess Ida," was heartily seconded by Mr. Herbert, much of whose music might be conveyed as it stands into a genuine opera comique based on M. Rostand's play; but it will never make that impression upon the public until it is given to good voices, or good voices are given to it.[19]

The music of the operetta was not misjudged. It was vital and animated, vigorous and dramatically fitting. It was, within legitimate operetta style, entirely on the level Wilson was trying to reach, and it suggests the belief that it was Herbert's chief effort to date. The lively opening scene, the rapid recitative, the touch of a French minuet afforded an auspicious beginning. Roxane's "I Am a Court Coquette" and Cyrano's rustic "I Come from Gascony" are excellent, but they do need singers! The languorous trio, "Since I Am Not for Thee" (Roxane, Cyrano, Christian), was most effective, and the first finale was extended, complicated, and thrilling.

The second act opened with an ingenious chorus ("In Ragueneau's Café") followed by the "Chorus of Poets" with a hilarious burlesque ending. The stirring chorus, "Cadets of Gascony," came next, whereupon Roxane sang her waltz, "I Wonder," one of the best and least appreciated that Herbert ever wrote.

The first vocal number in the last act was for male chorus, unaccompanied ("In Bivouac Reposing"), a real gem of sentimental tenderness. Still more attractive, though entirely different, was the second trio for Cyrano, Christian, and Roxane, "Let the Sun of My Eyes," which was also exceptionally clever, for it illustrated the balcony scene where Cyrano utters the first phrases of love and Christian imitates him with the same words and same tones. A delightfully syncopated middle section brings the three principals together in a lilting refrain of utter charm.

Throughout the opera the music was of the best; but it was unhappily associated with a questionable stage conception, and it suffered the same fate—quick extinction. After only twenty-eight performances in New York[20] the production took to the road, where audiences derived much the same impression. Wilson tried to save it by abandoning his ambition toward legitimacy for a consistent burlesque interpretation; but success never came.[21] Herbert was the victim of a dramatic misapprehension.

If hopes were high for the musical *Cyrano de Bergerac* they were even higher for Herbert's second offering to Alice Nielsen and her company. Nearly a year in advance a simple announcement was made that Alice would appear next season in a new Herbert opera.[22] With the advent of summer more news was available. The book was the product of Stanislaus Stange, the lyrics were furnished by the inevitable Harry B. Smith. Rehearsals were to begin in August. The only uncertainty was the title, there being three possibilities: The Singing Girl; The Street Singer; and The Little Minstrel. Manager Perley disliked the word "Girl," thinking it smacked of musical comedy and burlesque, whereas the new work was nothing less than "a high-class comic opera."[23] He found no substitute for it, however, and Herbert's admirers cared little for titles as they flocked to hear *The Singing Girl.*

The first performance on any stage took place in Montreal on October 2, 1899, at Her Majesty's Theatre. After moving to Toronto and Buffalo, where it was warmly received, the opera opened in New York on October 23 at the Casino, inaugurating the light opera season on the stage "so long recognized as the centre of comic opera productions."[24] The producer was the eminent Julian Mitchell, and the director of the music was the competent Paul Steindorff. The program gave the following cast and incidental information:

Duke Rodolph, Governor of Linz............Eugene Cowles
Count Otto, looking for his "well-beloved".......Richie Ling
Prince Pumpernickel, one whom age cannot wither,
    nor custom stale....................Joseph W. Herbert
Aufpassen, Minister of Police..............Joseph Cawthorn
Stephan, brother of the Singing Girl..........John C. Slavin

Frederick			Edward F. Metcalfe
Francis			Louis Kelso
Felix	Officers of the Austrian army		Albert McGuckin
Karl			George Tennery
Ludwig			H. W. Humphreys
Ferdinand			Frank Edwards
Oelrich			William Bechtel
Herman	Peasants..................		R. Wallace
Fritz			Albert Busby*
Hans			M. H. Lorenz

Marie, sister of Duke Rodolph..............Lucille Saunders

* J. A. Wallerstedt.

Elsa ....Jennie Hawley
Mina.................................Ursula Garrett*

Alma		Cara Isham
Elizabeth		Eunice Drake
Margaret		Louise Hilliard
Katrina		Lillian Samuels
Lena		Nellie Marsh
Freda	Girls of Linz............	May Boley
Netta		Winifred Williams
Tolfta		Louise Lawton
Xesia		Nellie Devere
Vida		May Devere
Paula		Ruby Capen

and

Greta, The Singing Girl.....................Alice Nielsen
Villagers, peasants, etc. 16 girls, 9 boys

Synopsis of Scenery

Act. I: Noonday in Linz, Austria, July 1st, 1820. The Haupt
Platz, or Public Square, rising from the river Danube.

Act. II: Evening of the same day. Bridal apartments in the
palace of Duke Rodolph at Linz.

Act. III: Daybreak on the following morning. Schloss and convent overlooking Linz.

The plot hinges on a law recently promulgated by the Duke of
Linz, who has been jilted by his betrothed: all lovers must have a
license before they can court and woo, and if a boy and girl are
caught kissing each other they must marry at once or be imprisoned
for life. Greta and Otto circumvent the strictures and restore romance
to the people of the village.

The most impressive number was the dramatic "The Song of the
Danube," in which Greta portrayed the great river in calm and in
storm. She also sang "Love Is Tyrant," an exquisite waltz song that
is one of Herbert's gems. In the last act a charming septet, "Lovely
Nature, Fare Thee Well," was notable for its grace and texture, and
the finales showed how the composer could speed the action along
by sheer musical power and skill.

It was Herbert's music, again, that brought success and merited
popularity. His score, of exceptional charm and skill, dramatically
effective, romantically lush (possibly too much so) and vocally demanding, remains a superior work. The only reservation arises from
comparison with *The Serenade* and *The Fortune Teller,* two works
without precedent in the field of American operetta. *The Singing Girl*

* Gurnett?

did not surpass them, nor did it equal them in certain points of musical originality or brightness. Krehbiel even thought the music, *qua* music, lagged behind the score of *Cyrano de Bergerac,* and he may have been right; but *The Singing Girl* needed no apologists.

For the most part the press reviews varied from warm commendation to raving enthusiasm. The single sour-minded critic, in the *Sun,* disposed of the music as being "unrecognizably commonplace"—the "least melodious and the most mechanical" Herbert had yet written. This was obviously not so. A critic at the other extreme found that the music sparkled in variety and originality and smacked substantially and praiseworthily of grand opera; he was thoroughly entranced by the effects in the Danube song, and proclaimed the waltz song "a veritable feast for the genuine music lover." Other numbers were but little inferior, and it was certainly the music which carried off the honors of the work. La Nielsen, to be sure, was her graceful charming self, but even she had been "studiously and ambitiously" supplied with songs fitting her voice and personality.[25]

Again the conservative papers rendered the best balanced opinions, reflections which were penetrating enough to please Herbert profoundly. The reviewer for the *Times* asserted: "The greatest merit of the operetta is to be found in the score of Mr. Herbert. This gentleman possesses an apparently inexhaustible fund of pretty melody, and his thorough musicianship, combined with rare taste and fruitful fancy, enables him to dress it in the most attractive orchestral and vocal garb. There are a dozen numbers in 'The Singing Girl' which would make the reputation of a new-comer in this field of composition, but which are accepted as matters of course from the facile pen of Mr. Herbert."

The essay in the *Tribune,* typically Krehbiel in phrase and viewpoint, was more analytical. The writer was thoroughly entertained at the show in spite of the book's "paucity of incident," for Nielsen was charming, the comedians mirth-provoking, the stage pictures brilliant, and the music captivating.

The Singing Girl continued at the Casino for eleven weeks (eighty performances), then had to leave at the height of its popularity.[26] It toured widely and gave infinite pleasure, and with it the Nielsen Company occasionally alternated *The Fortune Teller,* which the public refused to forget or ignore. The little prima donna was blessed with two of the best scores of the modern stage, and her adoring public knew it.

The 1899–1900 season was Herbert's most prolific as a composer of comic opera, but it was not his most successful. Two productions followed fast upon *The Singing Girl,* neither of which brought him much credit. Ironically enough, the first was enormously popular for a while with lovers of burlesque and slapstick, and contained the less important music. The second enjoyed but scant popularity, and had some really beautiful music. The texts of both were nonsensical, utterly incapable of saving Herbert's pages.

The genial comedian Frank Daniels had been fortunate with *The Wizard of the Nile* and *The Idol's Eye*. He began negotiating for another work from Herbert early in 1899.[27] Herbert signed the contract on the 4th of April and agreed to have the orchestra score completed by the first of June, for production not later than January 1, 1900.[28]

The public first heard of the opera as *The Ameer of Afghanistan*. The last two words of the title were soon dropped, and *The Ameer* was first staged at the Lyceum Theatre in Scranton, Pennsylvania, on October 9, 1899, to the complete joy of the audience. Herbert was present and responded to the cheers, and Daniels felt secure in a new spectacle of oriental fantasy, comedy, and incredibility. The text was the work of Frederick Ranken and Kirk LaShelle, neither of them even the equal of Harry B. Smith.

After the successful opening a tour took the play to Canada and as far west as St. Louis before New York received it on December 4 at Wallack's Theatre. The *dramatis personae* in the program too clearly reveal the character of the action:

Iffe Khan, Ameer of Afghanistan..............Frank Daniels
Heezaburd, Lord Chamberlain..............W. F. Rochester
Crackasmile, the Court Jester...............William Corliss
Blakjak, Chief of Brigands for Cut and Slash....Will Danforth
Ralph Winston, Captain of the British Guards....George Devoll
Knifem, a bad brigand.......................J. J. Martin
Slicem, another...........................Frank Ranger
Lieutenant of the British Guards..............Sadie Emmons
Benjaboo, a peasant.......................Harry L. Arthur
A Weaver................................Robert Delius
A Dyer................................Howard Lawrence
Constance, an American girl................Helen Redmond
Fanny, her friend..........................Norma Kopp
Mirzah, an Oriental slave.......................Kate Uart
Sereza ⎫
Nana ⎬ Peasant girls.................. ⎰ Mae Emmons
Ayall ⎭ ⎱ Jane Mandeville
                                     ⎱ Virginia Karroll
A Dressmaker.............................Tunnie* Leslie
        Peasants, Nobles, Brigands, Soldiers, Palace Guards,
                    Pages, Nautch Girls, etc.

* Tennie.

The scenic synopsis: Act I: Morning, Public Square, Cabool, Afghanistan; Act II: Afternoon, woods adjoining business house of Cut and Slash; Act III: Evening, Throne Room, Ameer's Palace.

The stage director was John Stapleton, the music director, L. F. Gottschalk.

The extravaganza[29] tells of the dilemma of the Ameer, who must marry a wealthy maiden in order to pay the annual tribute to the British. His selection is an American girl, who is in love with the English commanding officer. The western couple outwit the Orientals, and the Ameer finds a native girl with all the money he needs. A subplot almost costs the Ameer his throne, but the treachery is exposed in time to preserve order.

After watching the strange drama one critic understated the fact when he declared that it was novel in conception, lacking in continuity, weak in development, and remote from probability; whatever jokes or humor it had would seem "lame in a kindergarten series," and only the music gave "refreshing relief from the tedium of the book."[30] Such opinions, of course, did not affect the popularity of Frank Daniels, who had just the vehicle he wanted for his cavorting personality. He gave fifty-one performances in New York, then took the opera to the road for the rest of the season and all the next.

Friends of Daniels may have been happy, but Herbert's admirers were not. The musical pieces he furnished to *The Ameer* were below his standard. The melodies lacked his customary grace; the choruses were wanting in his customary richness; and one commonplace waltz dominated the score. Even the finales and the opening scenes were oversimplified, perhaps because the company was not qualified to have better. It is impossible to define Herbert's frame of mind as he wrote this music. One charitable observer suggested that he recognized the book as plain burlesque and gave it the music it deserved, thus lending a degree of respectability to the commonplace measures;[31] and little more can be advanced today.

The Ameer was not Herbert's happiest product. Neither was his next light opera, *The Viceroy*; but it contained some excellent numbers, in spite of its rapid failure. It was first produced by the Bostonians in San Francisco, February 12, 1900, at the Columbia Theatre; and they introduced it to New York at the Knickerbocker Theatre on April 9.[32] For better or worse—it was worse—the librettist was Harry B. Smith. His story was just as fantastic as that of *The Ameer*. Smith's autobiography cheerfully admits it was a failure; but he seems to be reluctant to assume any responsibility for the failure, and he has nothing to say about the opera's musical virtues.[33] In this respect he is inferior in generosity to Bostonian Barnabee who admits: "And then we were caught with two more operatic 'dead ones,' 'The Smugglers' and 'The Vice-Roy.' The latter justified the first syllable of its name, so far as the attributes of its leading character went. The music, by Victor Herbert, was worthy of its name."[34]

When the work was presented to New York, Herbert himself conducted the orchestra. The production was lavish, with costumes superb and scenic effects magnificent. The cast was as follows:

The Viceroy of Sicily	Henry Clay Barnabee
Corleone, Captain of Militia	William H. MacDonald
Bastroco, Sergeant of Militia	George B. Frothingham
Barabino, Minister of Police	William H. Fitzgerald
Luigi, a fisherman	Frank Rushworth
Ruffino, a jailor	John Dunsmure
Tivolini, a pirate chieftain	Helen Bertram
Fioretta, the Viceroy's daughter	Marcia Van Dresser
Beatrice, for whose hand the Viceroy and Tivolini are rivals	Grace Cameron
Ortensia, wife of Bastroco	Josephine Bartlett
Stiletto ⎱	Harry Dale
Vermicelli ⎰ Tivolini's men	Adam Warmouth
Spaghetti	David J. White
Macaroni	James E. Miller
Waitress	Edith Hendee
First citizen	Arthur T. Earnest
Second citizen	Henry Miller

The scenes were: Act I, the Lido, the public promenade on the sea wall, Palermo; Act II, a public square in Palermo; Act III, the pirates' cave. William H. Fitzgerald was stage director, and Samuel L. Studley had charge of the music.

In the sixteenth century, a false Viceroy fears the loss of his throne; the pirate chief Tivolini, who is his cousin, is the rightful claimant. Tivolini regains his ruling power and the girl of his heart (Beatrice), and magnanimously permits his unethical relative to share the government.

Such a plot would have handicapped any composer, but Herbert supplied a score "so melodious and delightful that it almost robs the melancholy book of its terrors."[35] There is some exaggeration in this, but not much. While the composition as a whole was inferior to *The Serenade* and *The Fortune Teller*, it included a number of pieces of real individuality and musical excellence. Because of their gloomy auspices they have failed to enjoy the independent existence they thoroughly deserved.

One of these gems is Tivolini's Serenade ("Hear Me"), with a languorous stanza and a lilting refrain. Another is Luigi's passionate song to Fioretta, "Just for Today." Still another is Beatrice's surprisingly serious "The Robin and the Rose" which was quite out of operetta style. Probably the most captivating piece is Tivolini's " 'Neath the Blue Neapolitan Skies," one of the type which Herbert did so often and so well: the stanza (changing in words, but not music) is really the refrain, and the refrain is different each time, in national flavor, dance style, or what not. And this was one of the best.

A few choral numbers also were out of the ordinary; but, in spite of what he poured into the score, Herbert failed to make the operetta a success. The book was bad, and the music was uneven. The Bostonians presented the work twenty-eight times in New York[36] and realized they could do nothing with it—even though it was worthy of the composer's name.

9

A Symphonic Future

READY to begin his second season as head of the Pittsburgh Symphony, Herbert was more celebrated than ever. His feat of writing four operettas within a year had won national attention, but he claimed no special credit: "No, I found no difficulty in writing four operas in less than a year. I compose rapidly, almost without effort, as soon as the atmosphere of the work takes possession of me. It is the scoring and the orchestration that keeps me plodding week after week and month after month at my desk." A query about his unique accomplishment brought the genial reply: "I have done my best, but who has not aspirations? What do I hope for the future? I like the old toast, 'May the greatest of my desires be the least of what I may obtain.' "[1]

Ardent ambition now dominated the composer. Once the four operas were out of the way, he took a long rest from the musical stage, to concentrate on the orchestra and return to the more solemn forms of artistic creation. With Manager Wilson he had to work out innumerable details regarding players, programs, dates, and so on; and a special objective raised a challenging head. Arrangements were completed in the summer for the Pittsburgh Orchestra to make its début in New York, at Carnegie Hall on January 23 and February 27, 1900.[2] The anonymous Maecenas promoting this venture was none other than Andrew Carnegie, who had completely fallen under Herbert's spell during the latter's first year in Pennsylvania.

Herbert's second season opened far more auspiciously than the first. The orchestra was larger and was thoroughly acquainted with his manner. The first year's success provided a measure for achievement. New York beckoned attractively, and impressed the Pittsburgh public.

Yet a few annoyances cropped up which were probably not unexpected. Some players wanted an increase in salary and were not unwilling to take advantage of the leader's good nature. They soon discovered that Herbert could be as firm as he was affable, and that he accepted no insolence from petitioning musicians.

Another irritation came from the previous year's troublemaker, Adolph Foerster, who, although probably innocent of wrongdoing, inadvertently aroused Herbert's wrath. Moreover, Manager Wilson was unclever enough to worsen the situation.

Four years earlier, Foerster had written a *Dedication March* for the opening of Pittsburgh's Carnegie Music Hall. It had been played by the New York Symphony Orchestra under Walter Damrosch on November 7, 1895, in the midst of a week of festival significance. In 1899 Foerster thought that it was time to hear the march again, and that the opening concert (which celebrated Founder's Day) was the most appropriate occasion. On July 26 he wrote to Wilson asking that it be performed.

Wilson, without consulting the conductor, unfortunately encouraged Foerster to think his request would be granted—a careless act for which Herbert reproached him in a letter from New York: The letter, dated August 5, touches also on other matters of interest:

Dear Mr. Wilson:—

Yours of Aug 3rd received. I will be in New-York and you can meet me any time you come by advising me one day in advance. I have decided to keep the dates for the [New York] concerts, only be careful not to accept anything for those two weeks. Wcek commencing Jan 22nd and Feb 26th because I think we can book another concert here and one in Brooklyn, you might work Phila. Speaking of Philadelphia reminds me that you ought to put in a bid for Willow Grove Park next summer. I hope you will make a great display in Pittsburg and all towns where we are to play this winter of the fact that we will play NEW-YORK, this ought to be one of your strong points in advertising. I am sorry you wrote Mr. Foerster that you hoped I would play his (Rotten) march at the opening concert, hope you did not mean it. Luckily most of the programmes have been made and are too good to be spoiled. Don't forget to notify me when you are to arrive in NEW-YORK that I can arrange to give you my attention, I am a very busy man and cannot afford to be disappointed thereby losing time.

With kind regards,

Very truly yours,
VICTOR HERBERT

Seeming to regret his intemperate adjective, Herbert wrote to Wilson on August 21:

The opening number on the first programme ("Overture Sakuntala") I might change and substitute Foerster's march. I have written Foerster to send me the score of his march, will write you my decision after I have looked it over. If after you have waited until the last minute before sending the programmes to the printer you fail to receive my decision Sakuntala will be the opening number.

It is significant that Goldmark's *Sakuntala* overture launched the season on the 2nd of November.

A message from Herbert on September 28 is of importance because it reveals his musical standards and a flair for shrewdness. A soloist had to be secured for the second New York concert (Marie Brema was already engaged for the first), and Herbert offered suggestions. He wrote to Wilson:

I am in favor of Madame Gadski as soloist at the second New-York concert providing she does not sing all over New-York before then. If you can secure her be sure to have this in the contract. As for Sherwood I am opposed to having him at all not if he offers to play for nothing.

As events turned out, neither of the artists appeared at the concert in question.

Herbert opened his second season as symphony conductor with concerts on the evening of Thursday, November 2 and the afternoon of Saturday the 4th.

Then a quick and arduous tour took the orchestra to Ann Arbor, Michigan, November 6; Oberlin, Ohio, November 7; Elyria, November 8, and Cleveland, November 9. An unquestioned success musically, the tour produced rumors which reflected on the manager's skill and diplomacy. Some of the players were dissatisfied with food and accommodations; others asserted that Wilson had handed each one the munificent sum of twenty-five cents for his evening dinner. The Pittsburgh *Leader* of December 3 had a prominent story on the affair in which the manager laid the blame on chronic kickers. When asked specifically about the quarter dinners he huffily said the matter was no concern of the public's and refused to speak further.

The third pair of concerts occurred November 17 and 18, the soloist being the English contralto Clara Butt. Herbert's offerings were Berlioz's *Carnaval romain* overture, Tchaikovsky's Sixth Symphony, Wagner's "Good Friday Spell" from *Parsifal,* and Massenet's ballet music from *Le Cid.* After the concert of the 17th there was a party in the Hotel Schenley, to which the critic of the *Post* accompanied Andrew Carnegie, eliciting this statement from the steel king:

I am greatly pleased with the excellent work done by our orchestra to-night. Their performance shows most marked progress, and is of the highest standard. We need not be ashamed to take this orchestra to New

York. In fact we can look forward to such an event with pride. I think it is the best orchestra, with the exception of possibly the Boston Symphony, in the United States. There is nothing like it in the country. New York has no permanent orchestra. Now, isn't it strange a great city like that wouldn't have a permanent orchestra? But it is true. Yes, I know that the Damrosch Orchestra comes from New York, but it is not permanent. I don't know what date has been fixed for its visit to the metropolis, but I hope it will be soon, as it would be one of the proud moments of my life to hear our glorious Pittsburg organization play before a New York audience. Now, while on the subject of New York audiences, I have to say that the assembly present to-night was as fine in every way as the performance of the musicians. I would just like to see that audience go to New York with the orchestra. It would certainly create a most favorable impression. Our best, most refined and most highly cultured people were in the music hall to-night. That is certainly most gratifying. All showed their appreciation by their genuine outbursts of applause. Now, don't ask any foolish question about whether or not I was well pleased. I could not be otherwise. I am delighted. I would like to go to my room and think it all over, but I promised my friend, John Bindley, to drop in on this banquet for five minutes or longer and I will keep my word.

About this time Herbert began expressing his musical thoughts to Pittsburgh, chiefly in interviews by Gustave Schlotterbeck of the *Post*.

In spite of his adoration of Wagner and Tchaikovsky, Herbert revealed a catholic taste and a wide range of knowledge in preparing his regular symphonic programs. As the season wore on he performed the following major works: Haydn, Symphony in D major, No. 2; Saint-Saëns, *Phaëton*; Schumann, Symphony No. 3; Mozart, Symphony in C major ("Jupiter"); Dvořák, Symphony in E minor ("New World"); Liszt, *Les Préludes*; Mendelssohn, Symphony in A minor ("Scotch"); Haydn, Symphony in E major; Saint-Saëns, *Danse Macabre*; Beethoven, Symphony No. 6; Liszt, *Mephisto Valse*; Schubert, Symphony in B minor ("Unfinished"); Hadley, Symphony No. 1; Beethoven, Symphony No. 8; Dvořák, Symphony No. 4; Beethoven, Symphony No. 9 (without choral finale); Liszt, *Mazeppa*. Such works, in addition to excellent shorter selections (overtures, excerpts from opera and ballet, suites, etc.), gave the Pittsburgh Orchestra a repertoire of breadth and variety.

The soloists engaged conformed to an exceptionally high standard, and so did their presentations. Besides those already mentioned, the following appeared: Alexandre Petschnikoff, Tchaikovsky's Violin Concerto; Pol Plançon, aria from Verdi's *Don Carlo*, and selections by Gounod and Schumann; Mary E. Hallock, Saint-Saëns's Piano Concerto No. 2; Marguerite Hall, Berlioz's *La Captive*; Clarence Eddy,

Bossi's Organ Concerto, Op. 100; Mark Hambourg, Rubinstein's Piano Concerto No. 4; Frances Saville, arias by Rossini and Gounod; Luigi von Kunits, Vieuxtemps's Violin Concerto in D minor; Leonora Jackson, Bruch's Violin Concerto in G minor; Antoinette Szumowska, Schumann's Piano Concerto; Fanny Bloomfield Zeisler, Grieg's Piano Concerto; Marie Brema, Wagner's *Götterdämmerung* (finale). One of them, the pianist Mark Hambourg, appeared with the orchestra January 5 and 6, 1900, on his first American tour; but he reached Pittsburgh before Christmas, and his early arrival allowed him to enjoy Herbert's famous hospitality. Many years later his memoirs referred to this event with grace and gratitude.

Even before the first concert the acknowledged highlight of the season was the orchestra's début in New York City. Then as now the metropolis was the country's musical center. New York performances set the standard, and critical acclaim from New York was most valued. Every conductor wants to take his orchestra to New York when it has reached a certain stage of proficiency; every city likes to have its orchestra go to New York when it has become a factor in local cultural growth.

It cannot be said that Herbert was ill advised in taking the Pittsburgh Orchestra there on January 23; but it was probably not advisable to play a second concert there a month later. The first was listened to with care and concern: men and leader were subjected to honest criticism; shortcomings and faults were pointed out; virtues, discovered; and achievement, praised. There could be little change within a month, however, and the second concert received scant attention.

The orchestra office had many details to arrange for the first New York concert. Manager Wilson thought it should be a week later, and wrote on November 27 to Chairman Frew a fairly direct complaint against Herbert for not changing from January 23 to 30, which, he stated, was better for business reasons; but he did not explain them, and he seemed to forget that the earlier date had been announced in August.

On January 3 Wilson wrote to Andrew Carnegie in New York that first-tier boxes 33 and 35 would be placed at his disposal with the compliments of the Orchestra Committee—a rather superfluous observation when the concert was possible only through Carnegie's sponsorship, which he was careful to acknowledge. Evidently the sponsor wished to see some results from his anonymous philanthropy, for Wilson promised he would do everything possible to secure financial returns.

On January 4 Wilson wrote to H. E. Krehbiel that the New York concerts were being promoted in the most dignified way, and that his help would be appreciated.

The great day came at last—Tuesday January 23—and Herbert presented to New York the following excellent program:

Overture, Carnaval Romain	Berlioz
Air de Télaire, and Menuet Chanté, from Castor et Pollux	Rameau
Marie Brema	
Symphony No. 5, in E minor	Tchaikovsky
Mephisto Valse (after Lenau)	Liszt
Six Chansons à Danser (1st time in New York)	Bruneau
Marie Brema	
Prelude to Die Meistersinger	Wagner

The newspapers reveal to what extent satisfaction was rendered. Some raved, some had reservations—all seemed to be pleased. The *Tribune*'s review (surely by Krehbiel) was one of the briefest, and one of the best:

The visit of the Pittsburg Orchestra might have been a surprise had we not known how zealously the city at the confluence of the rivers which make the Ohio has been striving to encourage art in all its forms for several years —to put it plainly, since Mr. Carnegie has undertaken to help along culture in the city in which he won his capacity to figure as a Mæcenas, to which no poet could do justice had he the zeal of a hundred Horaces. As it is it must be said that the Pittsburg Orchestra distinguished itself particularly by the readings which it gave its numbers under Mr. Herbert. We knew most of its musicians, but we did not know what they could do under the conditions in which Pittsburg's public spirit has placed them. We must admire the spirit which they exemplified in their performance, for it was in every respect most admirable, and it may not be out of place to say that last night's concert demonstrated that Pittsburg is entitled to rank with the foremost cities of the country—Boston, New-York, Chicago and Cincinnati—in respect of orchestral music.

This was reassuring, but strangely nonspecific. The *Times* remedied the vagueness by printing a review of contrasting, but not conflicting, opinions:

It was to be expected that sooner or later the Pittsburg Orchestra would come to this city for dress parade and review. The visit was welcome, and the orchestra will return home with a creditable record. The performance was not one to call forth expressions of ecstasy, and it is wholly improbable that its projectors expected it to do so. But it was one to call for the conveyance of felicitations to the flourishing and enterprising city at the junction of the Allegheny and Monongahela Rivers. It is a happy thing for that city to possess so good an assembly of musicians, evidently inspired with ambition and seriousness of purpose and conducted with enthusiasm by so capable a musician as Mr. Herbert. With such an agency to labor for it the cause of good music has made progress in Pittsburg, and will make more.

It may be ungracious to comment on the present shortcomings of the orchestra and it certainly is ungrateful; yet such comment may be accepted merely as a suggestion as to ends yet to be reached. While the orchestra has made a considerable advance in the direction of a good ensemble, there is yet wanting a solid, rich homogeneity of tone, without which its utterance can never attain the highest nobility of instrumental speech. The strings can be improved in smoothness and sonority as well as in quality—in the latter particular especially in the 'cellos—and the brass will admit of much polish. The oboes, clarinets and flutes are fairly good, and the bassoons have a poor tone. The attack of the whole orchestra yet lacks muscularity, and there are evidences of timidity in the treatment by the conductor of rests.

But when all is said and done, it is a more than ordinarily good orchestra, and has in it the promise of better things to come. Mr. Herbert has plainly worked hard with his men, and there could be no question that last night's programme had been carefully rehearsed.

The *Evening Post* summarized things very sensibly:

It would be easy to pick out a weak spot here and there, to note an occasional roughness and want of balance . . . among the instrumental groups; but it is more important to note that Mr. Herbert has a good orchestra of seventy men—and the usual woman harpist—which has obviously been subjected to a thorough drilling. . . . Mr. Herbert shows in his conducting the same excellent qualities that made him America's leading violoncellist—thorough knowledge, sympathy, confidence, and above all enthusiasm. He is the embodiment of buoyancy itself, and as all his players are young like himself, they "just make things hum," to use a popular expression. Sometimes there is, indeed, too much storm and stress, as in the "Meistersinger" overture, which was somewhat too strenuous. . . . Apart from this there is little but praise for the conductor whose conception of Tchaikovsky's inspired symphony was particularly interesting. Pittsburgh had better look out or New York will be trying to win back Victor Herbert. We need such a man badly.

The reviews quoted are representative of the general reaction. There was a wide latitude of critical judgment, but everyone seemed to be genuinely pleased to hear the new orchestra invading from the West. One more review calls for attention. A host of onlookers and listeners must have been waiting for the opinion of the *Musical Courier,* and it satisfied their impatience on January 31. In view of the paper's past hostility to Herbert the review is astonishingly favorable—to such a degree, in fact, that it can scarcely have come from the same pen as the earlier scurrilous attacks. Conceding that the Pittsburgh Orchestra had weaknesses, that all its choirs could be better, that the tone was brilliant but brittle, that it was lacking in sonority, and that the strings were less opulent than those of the Boston Symphony, the writer noticed individual shortcomings and really had a good word only for the first-horn player.

All this was credible enough, but the critic added phrases which were significant and were opposed to the *Courier*'s Pittsburgh policy: "Yet the orchestra plays with fire and freedom, if not finish; amazing withal, when one considers the short time Mr. Herbert had directed it. . . . his unlimited capacity for hard work—here is an object lesson for lazy home organizations—has produced undeniable good. . . . What he wanted he did not always get, though his force responded to the best of its ability." The conclusion is positive: "The début of the new orchestra may be pronounced a satisfactory one."

Special dispatches were wired to Pittsburgh after the concert, for the home town was waiting for reports of triumph. One observer saw Krehbiel, Carnegie, and President Hyde of the New York Philharmonic Society in earnest discussion during the intermission. It was imperative to have a statement from the steel king, and Carnegie was quoted to this effect: "Unanimous verdict! This is Pittsburgh's night. She stands now with Boston and Chicago in her orchestra, and with New York's Philharmonic—one of the great quartet. The Tribune tomorrow will prove this, I am sure, for Mr. Krehbiel pronounced the orchestra immense. Mr. Hyde said he had been behind the scenes to congratulate Herbert who he said was one of the few great conductors."[3]

Also after the concert there was a banquet for the orchestra and a few friends—and the host was Victor Herbert. It was held in Lüchow's famous restaurant in Fourteenth Street, and joy was unconfined, speeches, toasts, and genial fellowship continuing into the small hours of the morning. The entertainment of his men was characteristic. Full credit for the concert's success, he said, must go to "the boys"; they had acquitted themselves out of personal pride, and every man had offered the best that was in him.[4]

When Herbert returned to Pittsburgh he found himself more than ever an object of adulation. The papers recounted the New York triumph, and friends overwhelmed him with felicitations. One party staged for him stirs even today the envy of the socially inclined.

Among the hearty group of men who called themselves the Caribou Hunters was Emil Winter (1857–1941), who eventually became one of the city's legendary steel millionaires and was already well on his way to a reputation for extravagance and eccentricity. On Saturday evening January 27 he gave a dinner to his fellow Caribou Hunters —all, men of prominence—at which Herbert was a specially privileged guest. There was an invisible orchestra which immediately caught the musician's ear. The first selection was played in tolerable fashion; in the next, glaring faults caused him to bite his lip. Then came a selection from *The Serenade*, and every guest hoped there would be no mishap. But suddenly "there was a hesitation, a trembling, a pause, a fresh start, a wavering wild and frantic screech, then silence."[5] They had actually broken down! No one dared look at Herbert, whose face reflected surprise, pain, vexation, wonder. He jumped up from the table and swept back the portieres that concealed the players—disclosing fifteen of the best players of his own orchestra, as skilful in their simulated bad playing as in their good. Once the secret was out, the music was resumed on a professional level of highest competence, and joyfulness was restored.

Another sumptuous dinner on the following Thursday, at home, celebrated Herbert's forty-first birthday. This was given by his wife, known far and wide as a past mistress of culinary art. It was an eventful day, the constant stream of visitors including a delegation from the orchestra to present a silver loving cup in expression of their affection and esteem.[6]

The next day (February 2) was even more important, for at the evening concert Herbert conducted the first performance of his new orchestral suite. *Episodes Amoureuses*, Op. 31, was the title printed in the program; but it was published the next year under the title *Suite Romantique*, the four separate movements being labeled, Visions, Aubade, Triomphe d'Amour, and Fête Nuptiale. Scored expertly for large orchestra, it was Herbert's most ambitious work to date in the field of "serious" music. The local critics hailed it with delight, and some said it was his best musical achievement. The artificial barriers of the time—they are still obstacles today—forbade their accepting or considering *The Serenade* and *The Fortune Teller* as his best. This is not to belittle the suite, which is a charming and sumptuous work, but to point to the critics' failure to define Herbert's uniqueness. There may be a doubt, indeed, as to whether Herbert himself realized it.

The suite is colorful, passionate, rich, exotic. The four movements are moods as well as episodes, and Herbert painted each one with a characteristic freedom from restraint. It is not as closely knit as the second cello concerto; but, as a suite, it was not supposed to be.

One criticism of the suite clamors for reproduction. It was written by Huneker, still the delightful "Raconteur," who traveled to Pittsburgh to hear it and who stamped every sentence he wrote with his individual, extravagant style. As a matter of fact, he used his trip to the smoky city as an excuse for a miniature essay that is a classic example of his wit and charm.[7]

Herbert performed his new suite when he took the Orchestra to New York for its second concert—on February 26 instead of the 27th, in order to avoid a conflict with the Metropolitan Opera Company. The main orchestra work in the program was Mozart's "Jupiter" Symphony, and this performance seemed to lack the finesse and grace so essential to that composer's art; but there was nothing discouraging in the reviews. They merely reiterated the faults already perceived, and rightly prescribed years of practice and refinement. Krehbiel was the severest critic and the fairest: "They are an exceedingly commendable company," he wrote in the *Tribune,* "and they have twice displayed a spirit that must make for the good of musical culture in the community in which they are active. The discipline of the band is excellent, and Mr. Herbert's zeal is as warm as his knowledge is broad and well based."

After the return to Pittsburgh the orchestra quickly finished its season. The last pair of concerts were played on March 9 and 10, with Marie Brema singing the closing scene from *Götterdämmerung.* Herbert offered Liszt's symphonic poem *Mazeppa* and, very curiously, Beethoven's ninth symphony without the choral finale. The program made a tremendous impression, and conductor and soloist shared honors at the end. Herbert, in fact, received a laurel wreath from the musicians in his charge.

Simultaneously the Pittsburgh papers of March 9 seized the opportunity to announce Herbert's engagement for a third season, drawing their news from an official communication by Chairman Frew: the Orchestra Committee had voted unanimously to retain the conductor and expressed deep gratification over his acceptance of another term.

A copy of the contract for the 1900–1901 season which was tendered to Herbert still exists. It carefully specifies the extent of Herbert's responsibilities and probably differs little from the agreements of the first two seasons, which have not come to light. One advance, however, is certain—Herbert was now to receive $3,000 a year (five payments of $600 each) for the thirty-six regular concerts. For each additional concert and attendant rehearsals he was to have $100 more; and this fee was increased by traveling and hotel expenses when the concert was out of town.[8] Thirty-three such concerts took place under the contract, and so it is easy to compute Herbert's conducting income for the season at $6,300.

The contract obligated Herbert to conduct eighteen evening and eighteen afternoon concerts (with all preliminary rehearsals) in the regular season. He had to certify the accuracy of the weekly pay roll.

He had to "organize, conduct and assume entire charge of the musical department of said Orchestra"; to "select, engage and discharge, subject to the approval of the Orchestra Committee, all orchestral musicians and . . . soloists required . . . under the auspices of the Art Society"; to "select and order all orchestral music and scores required, the total cost not to exceed the amounts estimated" by the conductor and approved by the committee; to "advise and consult with the press agent or manager as to newspaper paragraphs and analytical matter to be inserted in the programme books." During his engagement Herbert was required to obtain the express permission of the Orchestra Committee before connecting his name with any similar organization in Pittsburgh or with any music school or conservatory in the city. The contract ran from October 15, 1900—or as much earlier as might be necessary to assemble the orchestra and begin preparations—to March 15, 1901.

Financial estimates of the coming season are also preserved. Under prevailing conditions the committee expected the total cost to be $64,689. Players' salaries would amount to $45,880, and soloists' fees to $6,475; conductor's and manager's salaries were $3,000 and $1,500 respectively. This left approximately $8,000 for office and miscellaneous expenses. The committee estimated the season receipts at $46,100 and looked to the guarantors to make up the inevitable deficit. The cost of the orchestra had more than doubled over a five-year period, but the guarantors made no complaint: it was a period of healthy expansion, and civic pride fully endorsed an increasing budget.

Herbert's third season with the Pittsburgh Orchestra was probably his happiest and most productive; but it was impossible for him to realize it at the time. He worked with terrific energy to improve the orchestra; he brought forth his most important orchestral composition; and at the end of the season it looked as if he had achieved permanent association with Pittsburgh.

Throughout the summer of 1900 Herbert was in close touch with Wilson and Frew, forming plans for programs in the near and not so near future. In June, from Lake Placid, he wrote to the manager a letter full of high spirits and enthusiasm, and expressing the friendliest feeling:

Dear Mr. Wilson   June 9th 1900

Yours of June 7th at hand. As to the Buffalo Expo. 4 or 5 weeks would be very acceptable. It would be best to get September and October time, in one way, on the other hand if the Expo. is not a great financial success it is much better to get time in the early part of the affair; you're sure of your money then.

I have had experiences of this kind. You will always have to figure in R. R. exp. *both ways,* no matter what part of the engagement you take.

If you charge them $3000. a week on a minimum 4 weeks engagement, as you suggest, it's about right. That's the sum we received in St. Louis the first year we played there. As to St. Louis I personally hope we will not get it, it's *so* hot there, but for the Best of the Band, allright, here goes.

I think you are quite right in what you say about Gabrilowitsch and the Everett piano. I guess we'll pass him untouched. I enclose letter from [Arthur] Whiting. I think it would be nice to have an American Composer and Soloist for a change. I saw his Fantasy: a very good work. As to his 2d Part numbers *all Brahms—no.* If Mr. Frew is in favor of having him, (Whiting) will you please communicate with Whiting, telling him that I turned the thing over to you now, and that we *must* have selections of a popular or *brilliant* character in the 2d Part of our program. Tell him that we don't believe in forcing the *Brahms-pills* down our audience's throat as long as we can give them pleasant and more exhilarating doses of morphiness. (read more-Finesse!) ha! ha! To be serious, Whiting is certainly one of the best American composers and a fine pianist.

Will we get Sternberg for nothing? He wants to play Liszt E flat. This meets *with my approval.* I am having a great time here. Come up soon; it is simply divine!

With best regards to everybody

Yours

VICTOR HERBERT

In September, Herbert was asked to conduct a concert on October 29 for the benefit of the Pittsburgh Police Pension Fund. Noting that this was just three days before the official opening of the season, Herbert wired to Wilson on September 14 that he would gladly appear if a date could be selected after the first regular concert. Chairman Frew evidently intervened, convincing Herbert that nothing should interfere with the plans of the guardians of the peace. On September 20 the conductor wired to him: "All right if you and Orchestra Committee consider it good policy to give concert in question. As far as I am personally concerned the police are always welcome to any protection they need."

The police benefit concert took place in Duquesne Garden as planned, with astonishing success; but Herbert's orchestra had already played a series of popular concerts the week of October 15 in Boston, where they earned the gratitude of the New England Conservatory of Music by playing gratis at the school for the students on Saturday morning October 20. The Boston *Herald* of that date stated that the concert resulted from the close friendship between Herbert and George W. Chadwick, director of the Conservatory. On November 1 Chadwick wrote the official note of thanks:

My dear Mr. Herbert:

This is to convey to you officially, as well as personally, our thanks for the delightful concert you so kindly gave our pupils at this institution. I hope that you will also express to the members of your admirable Orchestra our sense of obligation to them.

Wishing you and them the greatest possible success,

Very truly yours,

G. W. Chadwick

For the Management

The engagement of the full Pittsburgh Orchestra in Boston was, to say the least, unusual. The real reason for its appearance, in the Mechanics' Building, was the Merchants' and Manufacturers' Twentieth Century Exposition; but rumors promptly emanated that Boston music lovers were tired of the classical fare presented by the local orchestra and the Pittsburgh group had been invited to play a week of ragtime. Home again in Pittsburgh Herbert was visibly annoyed when a reporter asked him about it. He answered:

The whole story was the invention of a single enterprising reporter on a Boston paper, who was overzealous and knew nothing whatever about music. The orchestra played the entire week before a critical, highly-cultured audience, and it seemed to me the more classical and difficult the selections played, the more popular they were with the audience. I know not of a single request made to me asking for ragtime selections. The Pittsburg orchestra does not play such light, frivolous stuff, and the people that listened to the orchestra in Boston did not desire such music. Only one night did we play any light music. That was one evening set apart as "Harvard night," and then the selections chosen were of the lighter order, although ragtime was not indulged in. We have no time for such nonsense.[9]

Nor was any nonsense in evidence as Herbert conducted the first regular concert of the season on November 1. The orchestra had been enlarged again (1 second violin, 2 violas, 1 clarinet—total strength now, 78), and it had had a short period of intensive playing. The socially distinguished audience was out in force, rapturously applauding everything that Herbert did. He interpreted Beethoven's overture to *Fidelio,* Tchaikovsky's fourth symphony, Wagner's prelude to *Lohengrin* and Siegfried's Rhine Journey from *Götterdämmerung,* and Liszt's sixth Hungarian Rhapsody. The soloist was an excellent baritone named Scotti, from the Metropolitan Opera Company.

After the first two pairs of concerts the orchestra embarked on a highly successful tour—to Ann Arbor, Detroit, Oberlin, and Akron. The Oberlin concert was on the afternoon of November 14, the program being overly long in view of the Akron concert to follow in the evening. Arthur S. Kimball, who reviewed the concert for the Oberlin *News*, was well enough pleased except toward the end, which he ironically described as follows: "It is to be regretted that the most evident thing about the last few numbers of the program seemed to be the fact that Mr. Herbert was trying to make the five o'clock train. He was undoubtedly successful."

The next year Oberlin again wanted the Pittsburgh Orchestra; but this time Herbert had something to say to his manager about arranging the details. Oberlin was to have the afternoon concert; Cleveland, the evening affair. Smarting under the happenings of the last two years, Herbert vented his feelings to Wilson on October 6, 1901:

I must in this connection call attention to the fact, that we never have been able to get away from Oberlin in time to reach the town for the evening concert in good time for supper and the proper other arrangements. It looks right on the *time table*, I know, but last year and the year before the Oberlin concert had to be given in a disgraceful hurry. Dinner at the Hotel there was terrible also. I think you might ask them to give us a *simple* but *substantial* meal (if we *have to dine* there). Say Roast Beef, baked Ham, Potatoes and vegetables and a cup of coffee, *but enough of it!* That wouldn't take too long and would satisfy the boys better. It is very hard to work with an empty stomach. Will you kindly bear this in mind when you make arrangements in that *terrible little place?*

Thus Herbert in his early forties was already the paternal protector of his "boys"—and thus, too, he was more disturbed over the haste of the concert than the unhappy Mr. Kimball.

The orchestra returned from the first tour of the season in time to give a surprise to Andrew Carnegie. A hotel banquet was arranged for the doughty little Scot on November 15, he being in town to explain future plans for his Institute. While the diners were finishing their repast, the musicians assembled in the ground-floor lobby, encircled by the regular guests aquiver with excitement. Herbert slipped out of the banquet hall unnoticed, dashed down to his men, jumped up on an improvised podium and led some spirited dance music by Massenet. Astonished, Carnegie walked to the stairs to view the sight, leaving the dining room just as the orchestra swung into Herbert's specially arranged version—he had done it since six o'clock—of *The Blue Bells of Scotland*. Then came *The Star-Spangled Banner* and a short new piece by Herbert, *Punchinello*. Carnegie sang the national anthem lustily and beamed as he listened to the music. When it was over he begged for more. Herbert refused; he knew it was a tribute only, and should not be made into an importunate concert. Learning the music was over, Carnegie beckoned Herbert to him and said: "Mr. Herbert,

I wish to thank you for this music. It was a complete surprise, and a sweeter compliment could not be conceived."[10]

As the season progressed Herbert brought new and old music to the city. The new encountered the same raised eyebrows, the same opposition that it meets with today; but one letter to a newspaper reveals a difference which may or may not have been typical of its time. This doubter of contemporary music at least attributed to it virtues which listeners in the 1950's fail to find in the works of their contemporaries. Herbert in giving the first Pittsburgh performance of Strauss's *Tod und Verklärung* had created a sensation, strange as it may seem now. How well it was apprehended is anyone's guess; but it prompted a letter to the *Post* of November 25 expressing the peculiar sentiment that the modern work was on a cultural level that towered far above the classics!

On November 30 and December 1 the listeners had a feast. Herbert conducted Beethoven's *Eroica* symphony, and young Fritz Kreisler played the Bruch G minor violin concerto. The youthful violinist—he was only twenty-five and commanded a fee of $350—stirred up a furore, but it may be wondered how many of his hearers recognized him as one of the most important musicians of the new century. Herbert did, and a peculiarly warm friendship sprang up between them which changing circumstances never altered. In the second half of the program Kreisler dazzled the audience with his Fantasy on Paganini's *Non più mesta* and then astonished Herbert by playing, as an encore, and on the piano, his delightful Serenade from the Suite, Op. 3.

The very next week Herbert's chosen American composer and pianist, Arthur Whiting, appeared; but neither his music nor his execution impressed the local critics. One wonders whether the Pittsburgh reviewers were really perspicacious or whether they, too, were enslaved by foreign names. American composers have pretty much come into their own today, even though they still doubt it; but in 1900 the native creators of serious music were in a less favored position. They were also fewer, and their proponents were scanty. Herbert was anxious to play any American works that he found worthy of attention. He had presented a major score by Henry Hadley the season before, and had scheduled it just in time to help Chairman Frew answer a complaint from J. Robert Wright at the absence of American music from the programs. Frew wrote on February 10, 1900, that Herbert was seeking the best music obtainable, foreign or American, and was less opposed to American music than Wright seemed to think.

An examination of Herbert's six seasons in Pittsburgh amply confirms Frew's assertion. In that period Herbert presented twelve American works, exclusive of his own—not a great number, but a very respectable one. It was a formative period for American orchestra music, and a leader like Koussevitzky was still a generation away. And so, to a large extent, was American music! Herbert's record of American performances in Pittsburgh follows:

1. Henry Hadley, Symphony No. 1 ("Youth and Life"), February 16–17, 1900. First time in Pittsburgh.
2. Arthur Whiting, Fantasy for Piano and Orchestra, December 7–8, 1900. First time in Pittsburgh; composer at the piano.
3. Arthur Foote, Serenade for String Orchestra, Op. 25, January 4–5, 1901. First time in Pittsburgh.
4. Henry Hadley, Concert Overture "In Bohemia," February 15–16, 1901. First time in Pittsburgh.
5. George W. Chadwick, Symphony No. 2, in B flat, November 29–30, 1901.
6. Henry Holden Huss, Concerto for Piano and Orchestra, January 10–11, 1902. First time in Pittsburgh; composer at the piano.
7. Henry Hadley, Suite Orientale, Op. 32, March 14–15, 1902. First performance.
8. Edward A. MacDowell, Indian Suite, Op. 48, November 14–15, 1902. First time in Pittsburgh.
9. Arthur F. Nevin, Suite "Love Dreams," December 12–13, 1902. First time in Pittsburgh.
10. Horatio W. Parker, Concerto for Organ and Orchestra, Op. 55, February 27–28, 1903.
11. Frank Van der Stucken, Festival March, Op. 12, November 13–14, 1903. First time in Pittsburgh.
12. Henry Hadley, Symphony No. 2 ("The Four Seasons"), Op. 30, November 27–28, 1903. First time in Pittsburgh.

The disappointment occasioned by Whiting, a sterling musician, must have been shared by Herbert; but it pointed up the problem of the American composer when it was really acute. It is difficult to see how Herbert could have done more to solve it. At least, he was aware of it when, for many conductors, it just did not exist.

Another quick tour was tossed off before Christmas, and then two more remarkable soloists came to Pittsburgh in quick succession: Pol Plançon ($1,000 fee) on December 21 and 22, Teresa Carreño ($400 fee) on January 4 and 5, 1901. A most important concert on January 18 and 19 was practically a dress rehearsal for a tour which would take the orchestra back to New York for the revised judgment of metropolitan critics. The program included Beethoven's fourth piano concerto, played by that phenomenal musician, Ernst von Dohnanyi ($375 fee); but he of course did not play in New York. The rehearsal aspect centered in the two major orchestral numbers, Dvořák's New World Symphony and

Herbert's new symphonic poem, *Hero and Leander*, Op. 33. Herbert had learned the former from Dvořák himself; the latter was but recently completed and was having its first performance.

Let it be stated emphatically that *Hero and Leander* is Herbert's most important instrumental composition. In writing his most serious and unrelieved score he was pursuing an ideal; and he spared no effort. No one knows the work today—the more's the pity, for it is skillfully wrought, of burning sincerity, artful description, and tonal beauty. It is scored for a large orchestra, and the performance lasts a good thirty minutes; but it has moments of grandeur and surges of romantic imagination. A revival of it, either complete or with judicious cuts, would be a service to American music. Unfortunately it has never been published, and the only known copy (the autograph has disappeared) is in the Victor Herbert collection of the Library of Congress.

Herbert was asked to recount his experience in writing the poem. His statement reflects his hopes and aspirations for the work:

This is not the kind of thing that one can sit down and write by contract. I do not expect that "Hero and Leander" will at all gain popularity. But it is the gratification of an ambition to do something that will live in musical literature—an ambition that every sincerely musical person has. If there is any reason for writing it, that ambition is the reason. It will have no commercial value, I know, for the sales will never realize the amount that it costs to produce such a work. But if I have written something that will find commendation with critical and serious-minded musical people it is a source of far greater satisfaction to me than any light popular suite or any comic opera can ever be. There is really no reason for writing "Hero and Leander." It is something that one feels within one and it comes forth without the bidding. I couldn't write this just when I wanted to. I had to wait until I felt the spirit upon me.

As to why I chose the theme, I suppose that is a natural result of a classical education. My Irish birth did not prevent me from receiving an education in Germany, and in the universities of Germany the students live more in the Rome and Athens of ancient times than anywhere else. The musical resources of the story of "Hero and Leander" had often impressed me, and it is a topic that has not been worn out. I believe there are one or two works upon the subject, but they have never gained a wide musical fame and are not well known. I do not believe it has ever been treated in this style as a symphonic poem.

The fact that no comic opera has engaged my attention this year, and that when I went away for my summer vacation I gave up all work at composition, gave me time for meditation upon this work. While I was at Lake Placid, in the Adirondacks, my thought upon the work bore fruit, and the time came when I went to work upon it. That was in July. The themes were, of course, natural promptings, and were evolved in the early days of my work. Through the summer there were various times when I was attracted to the manuscript, and when I came home I had gone a good way upon the composition. I continued my work at home, and about five weeks ago I finished, consuming in all about six months upon the symphonic poem.[11]

The Pittsburgh program carried the usual analytical notes by Manager Wilson; but they were prolix and complicated. A more compact interpretation with mythological background, written by H. E. Krehbiel and printed in the program book of the New York Philharmonic Society, January 29, 1904, is more appropriate here:

Hero was a priestess of Aphrodite, who lived at Sestor, on the Thracian coast; Leander, a youth, whose home was at Abydos, on the Asiatic shore, beyond the Hellespont. The pair met and loved, and Leander was wont to swim across the strait every night, while Hero held a torch at her tower window to direct the bold swimmer to her side. One night there arose a tempest and Leander was drowned, and his body was cast up by the waves at the foot of the tower. Then Hero threw herself upon the jagged rocks beside him, and the lovers were united in death.

That tale is old, but love anew
May nerve young hearts to prove as true

sang Byron, after he had put discrediting doubts to shame by swimming the Hellespont himself, and catching an ague for his pains. A simple tale, but with what a lovely fervor have the poets sung it over and over again! Byron could smile at his own quixotic feat in the lines which he wrote six days after its accomplishment, but in "The Bride of Abydos" he did not attempt to conceal the affection which he felt for the tale, or his pride in the thought that Helle's buoyant waves had borne up his limbs as well as Leander's: and who can call up, without emotion, Keats' picture of

Young Leander toiling to his death,

pursing his weary lips for Hero's cheek, and smiling against her smiles until he sinks and

Up bubbles all his amorous breath.

Right nobly, too, did Schiller hymn the lovers, and two centuries of opera composers—Italian, German, French, English and Polish—have sought to weave their pitiful story into a lyric drama. . . .

Mr. Herbert's symphonic poem is a frank piece of programme music which aims to give musical delineation to the scenes and incidents of the pathetic story, as well as the emotions of the actors and the agencies which bring about the catastrophe. It begins (*Molto tranquillo*) with what is designed to be at once a depiction of externals and a delineation of moods. The Hellespont smiles in the moonlight with a "smile innumerous," and we may imagine Hero gazing expectantly across its shimmering surface. The device of organ point is employed, and three solo violins interweave their voices over the divided body of strings. An oboe sings (*Semplice*) of the wrapt gaze of Hero, and a clarinet breathes out her love. Meanwhile there are ominous mutterings of a melodic symbol of Fate, and there enters the melody of

Leander, filled with eagerness by its propulsive triplets, having its full proclamation by violins, violoncellos and wood-winds choir (*Allegro con fuoco*). There is a suggestion of the flux and reflux of the water in the accompaniment as the themes associated with Hero are reiterated, and a love scene which follows the meeting is presaged. A *fermata* precedes the moment of union. The Love Melody is sung, first by the oboe and English horn and repeated more and more passionately as the sweet pair exchange their protestations (violas and violoncellos on the one hand, violins on the other). Into the climax of the ecstatic utterances the Fate theme hurls its threatening voice, foretelling the woeful end of the lovers' happiness, which is not delineated, however, until the next section—a storm scene—is reached. In this (*Allegro moderato*) the themes of Fate . . . [are first] sent hurtling through the realistic din, which dies away toward the close, and permits the exhausted swimmer audibly to exhale his last sigh in a reminiscence of the Love Melody— Leander dying as Tristan dies, in Wagner's love tragedy, with the name of his mistress on his lips—"Up bubbles all his amorous breath." The orchestra sings its mournful threnody (*Andante espressivo*), and at the last comes the apotheosis (*Un poco animato*), the celebration of the sweet passion of the lovers, the bliss of their union, superimposed on the sinister comment of the symbol of Fate.[12]

The Pittsburgh critics hailed *Hero and Leander* as a masterpiece, and it was undisputedly a notable achievement. It was nobler and far more serious than the *Suite Romantique,* in every way a larger conception and a more sustained effort. Herbert was thoroughly justified in presenting it at the New York concert on January 22, 1901; but it was a lengthy work, and he should have been less generous with the rest of his program. The concert was overlong, and his listeners were already handicapped when his music was played. Any reader will agree with this when viewing the entire program:

Leonore Overture No. 3	Beethoven
"Dove Sono" from Le Nozze di Figaro	Mozart
Dorothy Harvey, soprano	
Symphony No. 5, "From the New World"	Dvořák
Hero and Leander	Herbert
Mignon	Liszt
Serenade	R. Strauss
Dorothy Harvey, with piano accompaniment	
Caprice Espagnol	Rimsky-Korsakoff

The metropolitan critics were practically unanimous in noting the improvement within twelve months. Indeed, one even suggested that this was probably the reason for the extended program. There were still faults to be found, but the observed progress of a year and the confidence in Herbert's leadership led to a prediction of ample achievement. The orchestra was now compared more directly with the Boston Symphony, naturally to the advantage of the New England band; and only special weaknesses were singled out for comment. Special areas for betterment were also singled out, but there was no question about the favorable impression created. Two of the severest criticisms appeared in the *Tribune* (Krehbiel?) and the *Sun* (Huneker?), and they were in close agreement. The former remarked:

The band has made admirable progress since its first visit. Plainly Mr. Herbert is a painstaking drill master, and knows how to fire his men with zeal and ambition. A perfect orchestra it is not, but a most commendable one. Its tone in general is somewhat acrid and garish, and there is little homogeneity between the different choirs. But the men have attained a high degree of precision, and it is a delight to note how earnestly all the men strive to do their best.

The *Sun* commented:

It may be said without fear of contradiction that the playing showed a year of severe drilling. The overture was well done and so was the symphony —though there were slips in wood and brass. The strings are more homogeneous in quality, more solid in attack; but the wood-wind choir leaves much to be desired, as excellent individually as are some of its members. For its massed attacks the orchestra deserves particular praise.

More important to Herbert, as creative artist, was the reaction to the new symphonic poem. Here opinion was divided; most reporters thought it too long, but it attracted keen attention and was most carefully described. The two soberest judgments appeared in the *Tribune* and *Times,* as might be expected. They may not have made the composer too happy, but they were eminently fair and unbiased. Of *Hero and Leander,* Krehbiel wrote:

The music exemplified some of the best traits of Mr. Herbert's character as a creative musician. It was better than his romantic suite in that it never became trivial in theme, but it was overburdened with passages which made for color effect and nothing else. It is less a pity that the work is overlong than that so much of it is remplissage which might easily be eliminated. A device, neither strikingly beautiful nor effective, but which captivated the composer's fancy, is so exasperatingly exploited in the introduction that interest is dulled before the real subject matter of the composition is reached. There is also a deal of panoramic, or scenic, music in the beginning and at the end, which might be spared to the benefit of the genuinely emotional music which comes between, music built out of themes at once expressive and plastic and proclaimed with real eloquence and power. Mr. Herbert had a sympathetic audience, and his work was joyfully acclaimed.

It was probably W. J. Henderson who, after lauding Herbert's interpretation of the Dvořák symphony, wrote in the *Times*:

> Mr. Herbert's own symphonic poem . . . is thoroughly modern and well sustained in style. The opening passage, ingeniously scored, is intended to establish a picture, the moonlit, lovely sea, and the solitary figure of the expectant Hero. This passage might well be shortened; the flute figure becomes monotonous. Following a part devoted to a musical presentiment of Hero's emotions come the arrival of Leander and a love scene, which, momentarily interrupted by a warring of fate, is developed with all the resources of the orchestra to a forcible tutti, designed to embody the throbbing passion of the lovers. Later come a storm and the drowning of Leander, after which the coda sets forth a sort of idealization of the love of the unhappy pair. While it cannot be said that the work gets at one's heart, for the thematic material is too fragmentary, it nevertheless establishes the proper moods and is very gorgeous in its instrumental color scheme. It was well played.

In 1901 Huneker was critic for the *Sun,* and it will surprise no one that this paper's description and estimate of *Hero and Leander* were the most enthusiastic of all. In his eyes the Irish composer was a giant, and he never swerved in either friendly or musical allegiance. He could take Herbert to task when necessary, directly or by implication, but he loved the genial artist and could rarely do other than praise him. His panegyric on the symphonic poem makes one long to hear the work today, though it, too, mildly warned against its length:

> The chief impression gleaned . . . is that the composer has left far astern all of his previous efforts. His suite played here last season seems noisy, even tawdry, in comparison to this well-knit, if lengthy work. The style from the first F major bar to the last is of one pattern; there are no discordant departures from the mood key, nothing to disturb the weaving of the tale. . . .
>
> Mr. Herbert has clung to the barest outline of the story—the woman, her love, her lover, the perilous passage across the stormy waters, the death. The psychology is not complicated, the expression of passion and pain evoked by poet's vision, ample but intense. That is thematic simplicity, for the whole formidable apparatus of the modern orchestra and modern orchestration, even unto the very hell gates of Richard Strauss, are made captive.
>
> It would be folly to deny Mr. Herbert's musical forbears. He stems from Liszt, Wagner, Tschaikowsky and Richard Strauss, and add to this an orchestral coloring that has all the languorous and fainting richness of the Orient—Goldmark, for an example. He has an individual style of his own; a past master of scoring, his manner often blinds one to his matter; and there is at least one theme in the poem that may be fairly called commonplace. This same accusation has been brought against Strauss. The Irish composer

employs but four motives—for his *Hero* theme is really bifurcated—and with these he paints and relates, chiefly the latter. Hitherto his devotion to the purely external side of his art caused his admirers to wonder if he would ever explore other regions besides the prettily romantic or the picturesquely sensual.

The question was satisfactorily answered last night. "Hero and Leander" has a strong passionate climax, an almost brutal climax, dramatic withal, and its tunes are good, virile and full of sentiment. But what is more desirable, the composer has contrived atmosphere, poetic atmosphere, and, despite fairly well-founded critical objections as to the length, the prelude creates definite images. Its trailing flute passages, always beginning on an anticipation with a shuddering nebulous background, put one in the key of the legend. What follows is full of promise.

The interweaving of the themes, the constant play of ingenuity to avoid conventional assonances, harmonic commonplaces, trite rhythms, coupled with boldness of tinting, all these reveal the breadth and depth of the composer's studies during the past year. Even the storm episode is not banal because of its suppression of old-fashioned screaming chromatics and other banalities. And it does not last long. At the close the tragedy was adumbrated with polyphonic mastery and the ear saturated with tone is not left in suspense. The ending is inevitable.

But "Hero and Leander" must not be heard on a two and a half hour programme of music.

Such was New York's second reaction to Herbert as composer-conductor. It was amplified on Sunday January 27, when F. N. R. Martinez recapitulated the event in his musical column in the *World*. He wrote nothing that had not been expressed previously, but his brief remarks called forth an interesting rejoinder from Chairman Frew. Martinez spoke warmly of *Hero and Leander*, which in spots he found more illustrative than expressive: "But when the note of passion is sounded, when Hero's emotions at fever heat surge with excitement, when the storm's fury breaks and the tragedy supervenes, . . . [the] music throbs with passion and its dramatic intensity is overwhelming." Again he compared the Pittsburgh Orchestra with the Boston, and said that time alone could make the former equal to the latter. He hoped that Pittsburgh would not resent praise which was thus only relative; Rome was not built in a day, and an orchestra was not perfected in a season or two. Herbert had drilled his men "carefully, assiduously and intelligently," and he kept them stimulated by his buoyancy and optimism. He was an admirable man for his post, intensely earnest, a thorough musician, an indefatigable worker, and an amiable, magnetic personality.

In Pittsburgh, Frew read this criticism and liked it; and on the 1st of February he wrote his appreciation to Martinez, telling him that the Pittsburgh Orchestra was not sent out in a boastful spirit, that it should benefit from playing to different audiences and in different atmospheres, that it would surely benefit from "candid expert criticism" which was not always obtainable at home. In fact, he admitted that some of the Pittsburgh criticism was "amateurish and even absurd." He freely admitted also that the Pittsburgh Orchestra was by no means equal to the Boston Symphony, the pride of musical America, and he referred to Herbert as a leader of very great promise who would continue to develop as he "separates himself farther from the lighter forms of music."

For a while it looked as if Frew's hopes and objectives would be gained, and never more so than on February 12 when the orchestra played again in New York. Fannie Bloomfield Zeisler performed Grieg's piano concerto, and Herbert conducted Goetz's F major symphony (a fashionable work of the period), Strauss's *Don Juan,* and excerpts from Wagner's *Die Meistersinger*. This time the critics largely ignored the orchestra's weaknesses and dwelt on the audible virtues.

More momentous on February 12 than the concert was a luncheon at the Manhattan Hotel. It was a luncheon such as musicians would never forget—and musicians partook of it. The printed menu announced that it was given to Victor Herbert and the Pittsburgh Orchestra; and it may well be wondered how the men recovered to give the concert in the evening. The prodigal supply of food and beverage (a luncheon, remember) would equal a banquet today:

Blue Point oysters; Hochepot à l'Eude, celery, olives; mignon of beef béarnaise, stuffed artichokes, new peas, potatoes fondant; Imperial salad; omelette soufflée, petits fours; Gruyère and Roquefort cheese, toasted crackers; coffee; Piesporter, Chablis, Pilsner, cigars, cigarettes, Cognac, liqueur.

The host was William S. Hawk, one of the hotel's proprietors and vice president of the Carnegie Music Hall Company. He declared two reasons for offering the luncheon: the pleasure afforded him by the Pittsburgh Orchestra at its earlier appearance; and a constant interest in Herbert's career as cellist and conductor—he lamented that Pittsburgh's gain was New York's loss.

Herbert responded graciously, explaining that he and the orchestra owed their achievements to the man who had given Pittsburgh the fabulous Carnegie Institute. William N. Frew was present, and he echoed Herbert's praise of the best citizen Pittsburgh ever had. It was not strange that Andrew Carnegie too was a guest; before the festivities were over, the host introduced him as "the star-spangled Scotsman," whose hobby was "mind upbuilding and soul uplifting."

Carnegie arose and confessed his one worry was not what to say, but what to leave unsaid. He told of his dreams and air castles, and how surprisingly they had been realized: all his flights of fancy and imagination paled before the reality of the Institute in Pittsburgh. Then he warmed to his task:

I did not know what I was building. I built gropingly, little dreaming how it would develop in my life time and surprise my dreams.

In Victor Herbert Pittsburg is doubly fortunate. He appeals to the soul in you who are the members of the orchestra and you express the soul in music. I used to dream that I would one day be as mad as the mad King of Bavaria and have an orchestra. The Pittsburg orchestra has exceeded my dreams.

You speak of Pittsburg's materialism and the part that I have had in its business development, but I regard these as only the foundations upon which the structure has to be built, with towers reaching to the skies. Unless we build things spiritual we build in vain. The Pittsburg orchestra is one of the city's chief assets because it is working in that higher, far higher domain of spiritual uplifting.

You who are members of the orchestra have the right conductor. How far you go depends upon yourselves. I have just been speculating about my castle in Scotland, and I have thought that some day we would just take ship and go over to London, Paris, Vienna and Berlin, and when you have played there you would come back by way of Scotland and stop at my castle.[13]

Carnegie's enthusiasm was intense, and it seemed lasting. He wrote a letter two days later to the Pittsburgh *Post,* which published it in facsimile, affirming his faith in the orchestra and joyfully looking toward the future:

Feby 14th
Not what I say of our Orchestra, but what the highest musical critics say, is what counts.

When Mr. Finck of [the] Evening Post declares that it plays Dvorak's New World Symphony fifty percent better than the justly celebrated Boston Orchestra & more than one good judge elsewhere speaks in similar strain no word of mine is needed—

The Pittsburgh Orchestra has already become one, & not the least, of the three musical organizations which distinguish this continent—and, as I dream, is an orchestra destined some day to make every Pittsburgher proud & happy travel through the world where he may.

Mr. Herbert and his associates have only begun.

Truly yours
ANDREW CARNEGIE

Nor can there be any question about Carnegie's fervent admiration for Herbert. His support of the Orchestra and his remarks about Herbert prove this. The most extravagant fancy of this nature he ever uttered may date from the 1901 New York concerts. He was leaving the hall and appeared to be moodily preoccupied. Pressed for a reason, he explained: "I'm thinking of heaven, and my idea of heaven is to be able to sit and listen to all the music of Victor Herbert I want to."[14]

Carnegie's dream of a European tour for the orchestra did not materialize, and eventually he lost some of his ardor. In course of time, too, Frew's hopes were dimmed, and Herbert's ambitions thwarted. The full explanation for these shifting phenomena is lacking. I like to think that Herbert was too independent to become enslaved by money power. One point is certain: the troubles just ahead could only handicap his career in Pittsburgh, and it is reasonable to suppose that Carnegie was not pleased.

After the New York adventure, little remains to be told of the season. Evidently celebrating Herbert's *Hero and Leander* and his birthday at the same time, the members of the orchestra gave him a handsome bust of Beethoven and begged him to write his first symphony. He promised to do his best. Then on February 17 Ethelbert Nevin died. Practically a native of Pittsburgh, he was mourned by the whole city, and Herbert hastened to orchestrate his famous *Narcissus,* playing it as a memorial at the concert of February 22. Finally, the penultimate concert of the season was a request program, and the town's music lovers voted overwhelmingly to hear *Hero and Leander* again. Herbert was a very happy man.

Simultaneously, the Pittsburgh papers of March 1 announced, with appropriate headlines and hearty rejoicings, that Herbert had signed a new contract—for three years, not just one, so that it was reasonable to look upon him as a permanent feature of the city's cultural life. The terms were fundamentally the same as those which had bound him for his third season; no financial increase was involved. Chairman Frew, in giving out this news, expounded his satisfaction convincingly.

At the same time George H. Wilson had been reelected orchestra manager because of his "enthusiastic and faithful work . . . in a trying and laborious position," and William B. Clayton again had been chosen assistant manager. The latter, of course, had been brought to Pittsburgh by Herbert whom he served as close personal friend, general assistant, and amanuensis.

Then, or shortly thereafter, a tragic happening occurred which left the entire future in doubt and threatened the fate of Herbert, Wilson and even the Orchestra. Wilson and Herbert quarreled. The reasons remain clouded and obscure, though the irony of the situation lay in the precipitation of the quarrel so soon after Herbert had signed his first three-year contract.

The disagreement must have been a bitter one, for Herbert was goaded into urging the Orchestra Committee to rid itself of Wilson at once. Some reflection would have told him this was impossible, but since he failed to reflect (at least sufficiently) Frew had the unpleasant task of flatly refusing his request. Herbert had asked for a special meeting of the committee to consider the matter, and on the 1st of July Frew wrote that the committee was scattered and the meeting could not be held. Furthermore, Frew reminded him that Wilson had again been elected the Orchestra's manager and had signed a year's contract. The committee could not abrogate that contract without paying a full year's salary ($1,500) which it obviously did not intend to do. He ended his note by expressing sorrow over the violent difference of opinion between the two men and fear that it would lead to unpleasantness for all.

Only two days later Frew was impelled to write Herbert again. The press, eagerly seizing rumor and scenting conflict, announced that Fred Ranken (Herbert's friend and joint author of *The Ameer*) was to be manager next season. Obviously, wrote Frew, this was a serious mistake. Wilson alone was the manager of the Pittsburgh Orchestra. Moreover, if Herbert wished to free himself from the Pittsburgh management for a tour the following spring—and this points to some, at least, of the disagreement—he should do nothing to hurt the orchestra's touring business during the regular season. The closing portion of the letter disclosed another impulse which Herbert was about to yield to. He intended to use the orchestra as constituted and solicit engagements for it on new stationery which would disclaim any connection with the sponsoring Art Society. This plan really alarmed Frew, and he informed Herbert frankly that the new stationery would be very distasteful to the Orchestra Committee. The Orchestra belonged to the Art Society; if Herbert started out for himself next spring the word "Pittsburgh" must be dropped from his letterheads, advertisements, and prospectuses. He ended his message by begging Herbert to exercise caution and by saying that his advice was offered in a friendly spirit. It undoubtedly was.

There were probably a number of contributory reasons for the rupture between conductor and manager. Fundamentally two men of vastly different temperament had come to a parting of the ways. Herbert had tried to be friendly with Wilson, had repeatedly urged him to visit the summer retreat at Lake Placid. There is no evidence that Wilson ever reciprocated this cordiality, or wanted to. Wilson was not the mechanically perfect manager (he could forget to have a piano ready at a concert); he was not adroit in correspondence; he was not skillful in caring for the men (the Oberlin arrangements, for example, and the probability of twenty-five-cent dinners). The two men had nothing in common, and the break could have resulted from countless annoyances and infinite exasperation. The three years they had worked together in apparent harmony were, perhaps, cause for astonishment; more aston-ishing is the fact that they worked together three years more before they finally separated. At the end of that time Wilson proved to be the vin-dictive one, and Herbert the forgetter.

Herbert was, in the vernacular, mad through and through. During the summer of 1901 he was not immune to temptation and occasionally upbraided Wilson for interfering with personal matters. Herbert's mes-sages of this nature have not come to light, but one of them piqued Wilson sharply. He was trying to make an engagement for the orchestra in Chicago, and he wrote on September 11: "I earnestly hope that after reading my letter of September 6th . . . you will understand for once and for all that I am not assuming anything regarding your personal affairs." By itself the sentence is not wholly illuminating; but it indicates that the altercation arose from something deeper than spring tours. For that matter, so does Herbert's original protest to W. N. Frew.

Business continued as before, although Herbert's letters to Wilson developed a colder tone and there were no more invitations to Lake Placid. He rose above the situation; but Wilson did not, and there is some reason for believing that the manager began subtly to undermine Herbert's position with the Orchestra Committee. Long after Herbert had left Pittsburgh, however, with Wilson solidly entrenched there, the manager found he had made a mistake. The disruption of the or-chestra finally came, caused by the very man Wilson advocated as Her-bert's successor. There was a poetic justice in the dénouement, but the entire city of Pittsburgh was the victim.

10

The Courtroom

ANOTHER blow fell at the same time.

For a long while the editor of the *Musical Courier* had left Herbert in peace. Each passing year found the conductor more solidly entrenched in Pittsburgh, and his achievements were readily acknowledged in New York. He seemed inclined, moreover, to abandon the field of operetta and determined to deploy his talent in the composing of serious music. The *Musical Courier* was at a loss in contriving to heckle him further. But its nefarious motives were freshened when rumors reached New York about the quarrel between Herbert and Wilson, and the editor took full advantage of the opportunity offered.

The issue of July 17, 1901, contained a speculative account of the break (already referred to). Some of the implications were uncomplimentary, but on the whole the article was not reprehensible. The editor of the *Musical Courier*, Marc A. Blumenberg, in the same issue supplied all the personal animus which the more conventional article lacked. He wrote, in fact, one of the most vitriolic, prejudiced, and untrue attacks ever directed against a prominent musician. Feeling secure in his rôle of critic, he wielded a pen which dripped venom as it spewed forth the following:

A cablegram from London states that Victor Herbert's "The Fortune Teller" made a most lamentable failure at the Shaftesbury Theatre and that it is doubtful whether American plays would hereafter be given that theatre. Our standards of taste are based upon European decisions and we are compelled to bow meekly to this conclusion regarding this comic opera; but it is necessary to say that this paper—THE MUSICAL COURIER as it is known—long since declared not only that the "Fortune Teller" had no merit whatever, but that all of Victor Herbert's "written to order" comic operas were pure and simple plagiarisms. There is not one single aria, waltz move-

192

ment, polka, gallop or march in those operas that has touched the public ear, and the street pianos and organs have ignored them—the best evidence that the people do not find them palatable. The whole Sousa repertory is alive and pulsating; the whole Herbert repertory is stone dead, and London merely acted on rhythmic impulse when it rejected this agglomeration of puerile piracies and refused to countenance them.

But what has all this to do with Pittsburg? We refer our readers to an article on another page giving some curious conditions revolving about the orchestra and Victor Herbert.

From the very outset it could not be understood by equipoised minds how a writer of comic operas (and American comic operas at that), and a conductor of brass bands accustomed to parade at the head of militia and processions, could possibly be the director of a symphony orchestra. The greatest of the composers of classic comic operas—Offenbach, Lecocq and Von Suppe —could not have been suggested by the wildest fancy as directors of symphony concerts for the simple reason that the genre is not only distinct but separate, and that the artistic impulse that drives a man to write "La Grande Duchesse" or "La Fille de Mme. Angot" drives him out of the atmosphere of classical music.

Everything written by Herbert is copied; there is not one original strain in anything he has done, and all his copies are from sources that are comic or serio-comic. He became popular suddenly by attaining command of a brass band and joining a rollicking club of actors and Bohemians known as the Lambs, who, removed entirely from any musical comprehension, accepted the good natured band leader as their musical dictator, and American fashion immediately paralleled him with serious minded composers. It was never a serious matter in itself.

How Pittsburg intelligence could ever select this clever bandmaster as its symphony director passes comprehension, unless indeed the people there never really appreciated the true significance of the artistic movement a permanent symphony orchestra represents. Geo. H. Wilson could never have had any real sympathy for the Herbert craze, for he is too deeply versed in the theory of the symphony and its application as a means of public culture to have sincerely adhered to the claim that Herbert could possibly be a permanent success as such a director. Possibly Mr. Wilson's candor finally crupted, and as a result the change is announced to which the article we reprint elsewhere refers.

Custom is the forerunner of law, and in the particular field of symphony custom has placed at its interpretative head such musicians only as are clearly identified with the pursuit of classical music. The Leipsic Gewandhaus had Reinecke recently, who was succeeded by Nikisch; the successor to the Berlin Philharmonic to Bülow was Nikisch. Seidl succeeded Thomas here, and Paur, of the Boston Symphony, succeeded Seidl. The great symphony conductors are not drafted from the ranks of the composers of the shoddy American farce operas, alias leg shows, nor are they taken from the leaders of the parading military bands who are specialists, and who develop in that direction solely. If Mr. Herbert were a symphony conductor he *could not* write the music for these American farce operas. It would be impossible; his mind would rebel, and his musical constitution would protest, but as he is not per se a symphony conductor, he amiably drops into the condition best fitted for his mind and his aesthetics, and hence he writes "Fortune Tellers," "Wizards of the Nile," "The Idol's Eyes," &c., and this is the reason why he and Geo. H. Wilson could not very well remain permanently adjusted. The dislocation was bound to come.

This was too much for the long-suffering Herbert, who for three years had been the target of Blumenberg's virulence. He sued the *Musical Courier* for libel, and the trial constituted one of the most remarkable cases in musical jurisprudence. Herbert won a complete victory, which was celebrated by honest musicians everywhere, and Blumenberg was ridiculed and humiliated, but not put out of business. While it lasted— late in October of the following year—it was front-page news which rocked the country with laughter as readers watched the weak defense of the hapless slanderer. Quite unintentionally Blumenberg turned the trial into a circus as he and his witnesses were routed by Herbert's counsel and rebuked by Herbert's stanch musical (and friendly) experts. Blumenberg's colleagues were a thoroughly discredited lot by the time the trial was over.

The full import of the trial can only be realized from some knowledge of Blumenberg himself. His career was colorful, and he was incredibly audacious. He could write, he could bluff, he could terrorize. He was a hypocrite who rendered lip service to great music and gouged money from its practitioners. By virtue of his journal he exerted a power completely out of proportion to his ability, and he intimidated untold musicians into parting with their hard-won earnings.

Blumenberg was born in Baltimore on May 21, 1851, and died in Paris on March 27, 1913. He had risen to be editor-in-chief of his paper and president of the Musical Courier Company. His father a merchant, the boy was reared in a musical atmosphere, but (said his paper on April 2, 1913) "early acquired sound commercial intelligence." He took music lessons, played organ in church, taught piano; eventually he turned to journalism "in which he was to distinguish himself so signally." Apparently he became a man of universal knowledge because after much reading and study he developed into "one of the best known and most competent dilletant [*sic*] judges of painting, sculpture and architecture to be found here or abroad." In the 1880's he went to New York and bought an interest in a then small paper called *The Musical Courier and Dramatic Weekly*. He dropped the dramatic department and injected the remainder with "a new initiative force" and "a potent personality" which impressed the profession. His "musical perspective and ideals were of the highest"; he championed Wagner and then Strauss; he based his musical credo on Bach, Beethoven, and Brahms.

The second of the three B's was his god, and his eyes could fill with tears when he talked of Beethoven's music. He was well posted on philosophy, literature (especially Goethe, Shakespeare, and the ancient authors of Greece and Rome), even Egyptology. His memory was so retentive that he dictated articles "without any reliance whatsoever on reference books for a date or a name; he despised reference books and bantered those who used them because of their lack of memory." As a writer he "was master of a peculiarly cosmic style and large authoritativeness. His praise was as decisive as his censure. He had the ability to marshal his facts into imposing masses and drive them home like literary battering rams. Whatever the Blumenberg pen handled was sure to be thoroughly viewed from every possible angle and always the subject ended in an instructive deduction or an exposition of principle."

He was, continued this obituary, forceful and aggressive and militant. He had no superior as a financial authority or as an expert in business and banking in the world of music. He labored for the cause of American music and musicians, but "popular" American music was repugnant to him. The *Courier* admitted he was a great soul destined to make a few important enemies. He was soft-spoken and witty, a brilliant conversationalist when stimulated; indeed, "the Blumenberg naturel [*sic*], when not roused to combat, was gentle, winning, even irresistible."

This fantastic obituary reads as if Blumenberg had prepared it himself, and perchance he did; stranger things came from his fevered imagination. Naturally it forgot or overlooked certain things, among them the Herbert suit of 1901 and 1902, an editorial by John C. Freund in *Musical America*, October 29, 1898, and another editorial by Freund in *The Music Trades*, April 10, 1909. They tell a different story and reveal a different man. Even when allowances are made for Freund's utterances in journals competing with Blumenberg's they are sufficiently damning to exclude the latter from the circles of respectable professionalism—but they did not, for righteousness is soon forgotten in the marts of business.

Freund's earlier editorial dwelt on "Organized Blackmail" as practiced by a "certain notorious musical paper." There was no doubt about its identity. Freund wrote that unhappy conditions had prevailed for some years. How? Very simple to describe. The unnamed journal would send a representative to an artist newly arrived in New York. The artist would be asked for a sum of money: if paid, favorable criticisms would result; if unpaid, the artist could expect the opposite. Occasionally something would cause the annoyance of the less than honorable critic. Freund told of one instance where a critic roundly abused a singer who refused to pay the assessment—but the critic had "reviewed" a concert which did not take place!

Freund described another method. The unnamed journal would induce a professional artist to insert an advertising card in its columns for three months. The cost would be $100 or $200, but the promised benefits seldom appeared. At the end of another term another bill would be sent, although no order had been given to continue the card. This would go on until the poor victim was billed for several hundred dollars. When he refused to pay, the journal would threaten the prevention of engagements, and bad reviews or no reviews at all. Its agent—generally a woman—would persuade the victim of the stupidity of fighting the organization, then would offer to settle for $200 in cash and a note for the balance. The artist, frequently with a family to provide for, usually capitulated.

Freund was quite willing—nay, eager—to have *Musical America* known as the trade journal with ethical standards, and in the issue of November 5, 1898, a symbolic cartoon appeared. His paper was represented as a female draped in an American flag carrying the staff of "Honest Journalism" in an attack upon "Blackmail Castle."

His editorial of 1909 was entitled "Journalism vs. Commercialism." Here he referred to Blumenberg by name, and in scathing terms, as he explained how aroused public opinion forced the nation officially to repudiate the *Musical Courier*'s editor. As Freund put it, the practically unanimous verdict "rendered against him must for all time to come determine his status both as a citizen and as an editor."

Freund explained the facts in the following manner. The Government of Austria-Hungary decided to celebrate the centenary of Joseph Haydn's death in May of 1909 and invited various countries to send official representatives. Blumenberg learned of this and offered his services (paying his own expenses) to the poverty-stricken State Department. No other candidates volunteered, the matter was not deemed overly important, and Blumenberg's credentials were made out. (This may have been America's first opportunity to participate in international musicology.) But when Blumenberg's appointment was announced the State Department and members of Congress were deluged with letters and telegrams denouncing it as totally improper. The New York *Tribune* termed the appointment indecent and demanded a worthy replacement. Secretary of State Root had accepted Blumenberg's offer; Secretary of State Knox felt the reaction, ordered an investigation, and rejected Blumenberg. Oscar G. T. Sonneck, Chief of the Music Division in the Library of Congress, was chosen in his place.

This was the peculiar person—the *Musical Courier*'s great soul—whom Herbert battled in court. It is no wonder that, seven years before Freund's bitter denunciation, the conductor's victory delighted thousands who despised Blumenberg and his paper.

The battle lines of litigation were quickly drawn, but the trial (held in New York) did not take place until October, 1902.[1] Herbert's first lawyer was Julius Lehman, who died before the trial began and was replaced by Nathan Burkan, Herbert's close friend and attorney for the rest of his life. The examining lawyer for the plaintiff, however, was Arthur C. Palmer. Attorneys for the *Musical Courier* were the notorious firm of Howe and Hummel, with Gilbert Ray Hawes doing most of the examining.

The Supreme Court Justice who heard the trial (by jury) was Charles H. Truax.

Full of wrath, Herbert drew up his bill of complaints in October of 1901. He stated first that the defendant was a corporation publishing a periodical in the City of New York called the *Musical Courier*. He stated secondly that the plaintiff had composed the music of *The Fortune Teller, The Wizard of the Nile, The Singing Girl, The Viceroy, The Ameer, The Idol's Eye, The Serenade,* and numerous other works, and was the conductor of the Pittsburgh Orchestra. He stated thirdly that the journal in question had published on July 17 wrongful, wicked, and malicious matter concerning the plaintiff (and he reproduced the entire insulting editorial). He stated fourthly that the matter so published was false and defamatory, that the thousands of copies circulated throughout the world worked to the plaintiff's great injury and damage. He stated fifthly that he was harmed in his profession and community to the extent of $50,000—wherefore he sought damages of this amount from the defendant as well as costs and disbursements of the action.

The defendant's answer began naïvely. It admitted Herbert's first allegation; but of his second it blithely denied "any knowledge or information sufficient to form a belief, as to the allegations contained" therein. It denied the publication of any wrongful, wicked, or malicious matter or any false or defamatory statements pertaining to Herbert. It denied every other allegation by Herbert, claimed to be a weekly journal devoted "to music and the musical trade" and to inform the public of newsworthy events. It declared one of its duties to be the criticizing of composers' music and operas; hence, "in its duty which it owed to the public, the defendant in a fair and proper manner, and without any malice towards the said plaintiff, criticised and discussed the composition of the said plaintiff . . . and that among other things, according to the opinion and judgment of the writer . . . Victor Herbert's 'Fortune Teller' had no merit whatever and that many of the comic operas which the said plaintiff wrote and presented for public criticism, were plagiarisms . . . that the airs of some of the said comic operas, instead of being invented by the said Victor Herbert, were taken from the works of other persons." Finally the defendant claimed that its statement of July 17 was published in good faith as proper criticism "solely for the purposes of discussing with the public the said compositions of the said plaintiff and the comparison with the work of other authors."

The trial began on October 22, 1902, and before many minutes it was apparent that every conceivable kind of question would be asked. Contracts, aesthetics, personal beliefs, superstitions, foibles, and comical ignorance bubbled forth in a constant stream. Primarily the plaintiff's witnesses testified that Herbert could and did write original music; the defendant's witnesses, that he did not. From the final results it is difficult to see how the latter group remained members of a professional musical community.

Herbert's Mr. Palmer called Otto Weil as the first witness. He was manager of the firm, M. Witmark and Sons, had known Herbert for sixteen years and had watched him write some of *The Fortune Teller,* also some of *The Wizard of the Nile.* Cross-examined by Abe Hummel, Weil denied having any money interest in Herbert's operettas, but admitted that his firm had. He was asked why he had been with Herbert when the operas were being written, and he explained that he called on him frequently as a personal friend.

Blumenberg's first appearance on the stand was very brief. He identified himself and his paper, and insisted he was ignorant in matters pertaining to business and circulation. He listened as Palmer read several excerpts from the *Musical Courier* highly complimentary to Herbert. Pressed by Palmer, he admitted that, prior to the suit, he had received a letter asking for a retraction of the July 17 editorial but had published none.

When Herbert was called, he furnished the usual identification and then spoke of his compositions. He denied that *The Fortune Teller* had failed in London; quite the contrary, it was a great success. He refuted the editorial vigorously. "I have written in all lines of so-called classical writing—that is, numerous works for orchestra, songs, part songs, concertos . . . I was in the serious field only until the year 1894. This article is wrong in saying, 'There is not one single aria, waltz movement, polka, gallop or march in those operas that has touched the public ear, and the street organs have ignored them, the best evidence that the people do not find them palatable' as these operas were all great successes. There are some running now. . . . The operas that I have mentioned were not copied by me. The statement in the article 'There is not one original strain in anything he has done,' is very false. And the statement that 'All his copies are from sources that are comic or serio-comic' is false. My comic operas were no pure and simple plagiarisms nor any part of them."

Replying to Hummel, Herbert reiterated: "I have not carried the airs and the melody from any other composer into those pieces of music. No, nor the themes." He described many of his activities in America, even to his playing several summers in John Lund's orchestra at Saratoga's famed Grand Union Hotel (beginning in 1892 or 1893). Hummel's further questioning indicated an ignoble train of thought. (The following and ensuing testimony is from the trial record.)

Q. After that you were the leader of the brass band of the 22nd Regiment, were you not?
A. A brass band is not a regimental band.
Q. Is the music of that regimental band brass and drum?
A. It consists of wood and brass.
Q. And you marched through the streets?
A. Yes, sir.
Q. Is there any difference between what is known as a string band and a brass band?
A. Oh, yes, we call a string band an orchestra.
Q. And what would you call a band attached to a regiment marching through the streets?
A. A military band.
Q. And you led that?
A. I did.
Q. Marching through the streets?
                    (Objection; sustained)
Q. Did you lead the band of the 22nd Regiment through the public streets of the City of New York?
                    (Objection; sustained)

Here Palmer explained to the Court that Herbert did not consider this a libelous act.

Hummel next questioned Herbert about some of his operas and how they were faring, trying to trip the composer up on the subject of inspiration, a word which was given a very broad interpretation. It came out that several of the operas had been performed at the Tivoli Theatre in San Francisco, the majority since the printing of the Blumenberg editorial.

Q. With success?
A. I hope so.
Q. Well, you know from the standpoint of your communications regarding your property?
A. I get a certain lump sum from those operas.
Q. And you have gotten that lump sum from those operas as they have been performed?
A. Yes.
Q. Speaking of those operas, let me begin with the first, "The Wizard of

the Nile"; did you not write that opera under an arrangement or a contract with Mr. LaShelle?

A. LaShelle, yes.

Q. And that music that you wrote then was as you claim, inspired?

A. Yes.

Q. By understanding or agreement with Mr. LaShelle?

A. No.

[Q.] You said the music was inspired by an agreement with Mr. LaShelle?

[A.] Oh, no.

Q. You composed the music by reason of the fact that you had agreed with Mr. LaShelle to write the music for the opera for him?

A. Yes, by reason—

Q. Then it was inspired?

A. It was inspired by Mr. Harry B. Smith's libretto.

Q. Nothing else inspired it—you agree that the best music is written by inspiration?

A. Yes.

Q. Our greatest composers who have written our greatest music have written their music by inspiration?

(Objection; sustained)

. . . . .

Q. For whom did you arrange to write the opera "The Serenade"?

A. Mr. Frank Perley.

Q. Under contract?

A. Yes.

Q. Receiving from Mr. Perley a sum of money therefor?

A. No.

Q. Well, do you mean that you wrote that opera under contract with Mr. Perley for no money?

A. No money down.

Q. I did not ask you money down; that was not my question.

A. I am ready to answer anything if you put the question properly.

Hummel extracted from Herbert the titles of his next few operas, including one called *Peg Woffington* which was never issued and has disappeared (it just preceded *The Fortune Teller*); and the composer consistently claimed they were "inspired" by the librettos, not by the contracts. He also freely admitted that his operetta music was not classical, that there was no symphonic music in comic opera. He testified as to his present occupation, said he lived in Pittsburgh and had signed his three-year conducting contract before the editorial appeared. Whereupon Hummel asked, "No attempt has been made by your employers to vitiate the contract?" The question drew a vigorous objection which was sustained.

Herbert's testimony established what was probably his first year (1902) as a conductor in the famous Saratoga resort. Just before this engagement he had led his orchestra three weeks at Willow Grove Park in Philadelphia (his first engagement there also). "We are laying off now," he explained to Hummel, "and commence in two weeks again at Pittsburgh. I played in some other places on my own personal risk. When I go on a tour and play an engagement of two weeks, that is my own personal risk. In the spring two weeks in Buffalo—I made a spring tour, two weeks in Baltimore and two weeks in Buffalo. In other words, I have been actively engaged, spring and summer, since the publication of this article."

It was time for Hummel to try another approach. He turned his attention briefly to Sousa.

Q. Do you know Sousa's music?
A. Some of it.
Q. Have you heard some of it?
A. Oh, yes.
Q. You have played some of it?
A. One march, "Stars and Stripes." . . .
Q. Do you not know Sousa's repertory is lively and pulsating?
(Objection; sustained)
Q. Describe the character of Sousa's music.
(Objection; sustained)
Q. Do you consider that Offenbach, Lecocq and Von Suppe are great composers?
(Objection; sustained)

Herbert was finally allowed to leave the stand. One of his witnesses, Frederick M. Ranken, was called. Examined by Palmer, Ranken admitted he was the librettist of *The Ameer*. The defense objected when Palmer asked the witness if he had written the entire libretto, and Palmer explained that he would show how the librettist changed his script from time to time, the composer thus being forced to change the music accordingly.

Herbert's next witness was the thirty-year-old Henry Hadley (destined to be one of America's leading musicians), who testified that Herbert could write music without assistance. He had seen him do it! Said Hadley: "Mr. Herbert was actually engaged in writing music while I was in the room. I was present at least two hours when he was doing it. . . . I would speak to him occasionally when he would turn to me and make some comments about his music or score."

At last Blumenberg reached the stand. On direct examination by Hawes he began with pomp and righteousness:

A. . . . I wrote the editorial which has been complained of, every line of it. I studied piano and organ, musical theory, harmony, counterpoint, but for the last 25 years I have been engaged in musical criticism. . . . I have what might be called a universal acquaintance with the whole classical musical field. I have studied music abroad from a literary and critical point of view. I have seen and heard original compositions by the great classical authors, that is one of my pursuits and that is my specialty. . . . I have known Victor Herbert since he was in this country. I have never had any ill feeling against him, none whatever. No grievances against him on the part of myself or The Musical Courier so far as I know.

Hawes then gently led him to the expression of his beliefs and superstitions, using the damning editorial as a springboard.

Q. Mr. Blumenberg, as a musical expert, let me ask you whether in your opinion it is true that "The Fortune Teller" has no merit whatever, and that all of Victor Herbert's "written to order" comic operas are pure and simple plagiarisms?

A. Yes.

Q. Now, give us the grounds of that opinion.

A. From the standard of criticism of The Musical Courier, the compositions of that nature do not enter into the field of a serious classical criticism—these compositions, especially of that kind which are written to order, where a libretto is furnished for the purpose of getting a musical entertainment, because it is not music in the sense of educational music. It is music in the sense of public entertainment—it is not anything in connection with classical music, and nothing with music as an art. It is only in reference to public entertainment in conjunction with singers and dancers. These are the ordinary, common American operas—but they are not exactly operas, they are operettes, something of that kind—and the music of that kind written to order, it is not considered as eligible as music under the regime of classic interpretation. It may be written correctly, but it is not original; it has no creative character; it is common-place in order to reach the taste of the public, because the public is not educated in classical music. And one of the reasons why it is not, is because this music which is written to order, most of it, is put before the people. One of the greatest effects of the Courier is to educate people in classical music, and to discourage this kind of music that Mr. Herbert has written. It was only after he got into business of writing music to order that he fell from that high stand, and for that reason the paper protested that a person who lives in that atmosphere of comic opera music cannot legitimately aspire to do that which men do who devote themselves to the study of classical music.

This rather confused utterance seemed to provoke the Court to a special line of thought. Blumenberg was asked if a good composition

was any different because it had been specifically ordered, and he replied it could only be great "when it is inspired by the aesthetic senses."
When reminded that some of the world's greatest operas resulted from
orders, he tried to divert the implication by saying they were written
for certain occasions.

Q. Well, that was to order, was it not?
A. For honor—for the honor of it—a great musician receives a great commission to write for a great occasion—for the consecration of an opera
   house or a temple of music, or for a great national event. Richard
   Wagner wrote for the Centennial Exhibition in 1876, a march called
   "The Centennial March." It was written to order for money and it
   decreased his reputation at that time in the estimation of musicians, in
   the first place because he wrote it for money to order, and because it is
   ordinary business.* But men like Meyerbeer and Verdi, when they received a commission it was for a national event for the consecration of
   an opera house or temple of music, which were connected with the art
   life of the people. There are many operas and other works written to
   order, but they have no standing whatever. They do not stand in the
   classical field as worth anything. They do not figure on the programs of
   symphony concerts, and are not placed in the great opera houses of the
   world. I do not call them opera houses in Elmira and Wilmington, etc.
   —we make a distinction between opera houses and opera houses.

. . . . .

Q. And were any of these great works of classical authors written to order?
A. No, sir. There may have been some overtures for dedication—I believe
   Beethoven wrote an overture for the dedication of a house, but it was
   not for money.
Q. What has become of that?
A. It is occasionally played. It is a study and an orchestral director takes
   it out of his library sometimes.
Q. With those few exceptions, how were these great works produced?
A. 99 out of 100 were direct inspiration.
Q. Were they inspired by any contract?
A. No contract with Bach or Beethoven.
Q. The inspiration of a libretto?
A. It was the genius of music.

It was time for the trial to touch upon the most important point:
whether Herbert's music was original or plagiarized. Blumenberg chose
a peculiar way to sustain his charge of the latter (he was still in the
merciful hands of Hawes):

* Blumenberg failed to add that Wagner was an ignoble creature who had sent
a bad march to the Exhibition authorities.

Q. You say further, "Everything written by Herbert is copied"?
A. Yes, sir.
Q. That is true, is it?
A. Yes, sir.
Q. "There is not one original strain in anything he has done, and all his copies are from sources that are comic or serio-comic," is that true?
A. Yes, sir.
Q. State the ground for your belief in that respect.
A. Copied music is music taken from preceding sources. It is not necessarily copied—not necessarily copied mechanically—a musician carries any quantity of airs in his mind—a musician carries from 500 to 5,000 themes and airs in his mind and he recalls at once a phrase or musical theme. It is not necessary for him to look at the composition. He knows it. If a piano were here, a musical expert could tell at once the source of any air. There is no original air in the Herbert compositions. Much of the music Mr. Herbert has written is good music, legitimate music. Honest music but not original. It is copied music.
Q. Can you illustrate that from Mr. Herbert's music in court?
A. I have here some of his music which I can show is direct copies.

Blumenberg now offered his illustrations. He alleged that the trio of Herbert's *President's March* was copied from the trio of a *Clio March* by one J. Guernsey issued in 1891. Not only were the melodies similar, they were in the same key; but he hastened to add: "It is not necessary in copying to keep the same key. A man may unconsciously copy by an entirely different key. There are twelve major keys and twelve minor keys, and he has a chance in each, but it happens to be in the same key. That may have been unconscious. I have no doubt it was."

Then he charged that a waltz theme from *The Serenade* was taken from a waltz song, *Grace O'Moore*, by Max S. Witt (1895), "one of these disreputable songs we have here in America by the million that help ruin public taste." Another of Herbert's copies was supposed to be a harmonic progression in *The Singing Girl* which had its prototype in Faure's famous song, *The Palms*. Still another was a theme in *The Wizard of the Nile,* allegedly copied from William J. Scanlan's *Molly O* —and the most surprising was an atmospheric passage in *The Wizard of the Nile* which Blumenberg attempted to identify with the opening of Beethoven's Ninth Symphony. Finally he declared that the Serenade movement in Herbert's Cello Suite—at least, its introduction and theme—derived directly from Moszkowski's popular Serenata.

Satisfied with these musical illustrations, Hawes led Blumenberg to expand on other statements in the editorial. The journalist explained that a symphony conductor should not march through the streets at the head of a band, that he should never separate himself from classical music—examples of propriety were Reinecke, Nikisch, Seidl, Thomas, Paur—that the character of comic opera had changed since the days of Mozart's *Don Juan*. Operas like that were now performed as serious music; they had helped to develop the orchestra field. They were far removed from the "rag time tunes and coon songs and comic operas" of the present. Indeed, Mr. Herbert simply couldn't write such music if he were a real symphonic conductor.

Palmer, the plaintiff's attorney, now cross-examined the complacent Blumenberg and quickly had the editor in floundering confusion. The Court and jury promptly learned what kind of spirit directed the country's leading musical paper. After opening formalities Palmer warmed to his task:

Q. Now, this Musical Courier, then, is a paper engaged in trying to educate the people of this country to enable them to understand the higher classical music?
A. That is one of its functions.
Q. That is the principal one?
A. Yes. . . . My purpose is to turn the public to the classical field as against the comic opera, not radically—gradually. That is the principal purpose of this paper. . . .

Suddenly Palmer veered off in a different direction, changing the subject to advertising which the *Musical Courier* carried. Blumenberg thought that Herbert had advertised at one time, but he was not sure; he knew nothing about the nature of this advertising. Under pressure he admitted knowing that Herbert's advertisements had ceased prior to July 17, 1901. This led to an interesting exchange.

Q. And did you say to Mr. Weil that, if he [Herbert] did not continue to advertise, you would pound him, because it was business?
(Objection; overruled)
A. Never in my life—I never made a remark of that kind.
Q. You were trying to get Victor Herbert to advertise again?
A. Never.
Q. Never to anybody?
A. Never.
Q. Not to any one acting on his behalf as manager or otherwise?
A. No one.
Q. And you never said to Mr. Weil in substance that it was business and you were going to pound Herbert?
A. Never in my life; I never could use such a remark as that.
Q. Why do you say you could not do it?
A. Because I never do and never did.

Having drawn the jury's attention to an important possible motive for the editorial, Palmer wanted to explore further the question of musical inspiration. In a short while Blumenberg found himself in very hot water.

Q. Do you remember Aida?

A. Yes, very well.

Q. At whose order was that written?

A. That was written for the dedication of an opera house at Cairo.

Q. Was it written at the command of the Shah of Persia?

A. No, it was written for the opening of an opera house for the Khedive of Cairo.

Q. Do you mean that if a man is inspired to as great a degree as any person you have ever known is told by a person who wants him to write an opera, and that he can take any time to write his music, and the price is fixed, that he cannot be inspired after making that contract?

A. He could be inspired.

Q. Then where does your "written to order" proposition come in?

A. I mean a musician that gets a theme at night and gets out of bed and writes it down—I mean by that that a musician gets an inspiration suddenly at any moment and retains it and uses it for the basis of his work, whether a song or a sonata, whatever it may be, just as a poet gets one. It is a question of aesthetics.

Q. Do you think if a man that that kind of contract I mentioned that was inspired, that simply the making of that contract would kill all his inspiration?

A. Very apt to.

Q. And you speak understandably on the subject?

A. I hope so.

Q. In other words, you feel that your inspiration and artistic ability is such that you understand the different minds of the different artists in the world?

A. Not at all.

Q. Then what are you speaking from?

A. I am speaking of general knowledge of musical composition and musical art. Before I started in my criticism I used the expression in my testimony that Herbert had written some good, legitimate, honest music; I meant that; I could not say how much.

This statement gave Palmer a beautiful opportunity to confound Blumenberg further, and he made the most of it. The editor was ill prepared, even musically, to parry the thrusts which came his way.

Q. Had you not even taken pains to find out before you wrote this article in which you say he never wrote an original line—taken pains to find out how much, good honest music Herbert had written?

A. Yes.

Q. Tell the jury how much.

A. He wrote that suite for the cello; that is good music; it is not original, but it is good music.

Q. Whom did he steal that from?
A. I did not say he stole anything.
Q. Whom did he plagiarize when he wrote it, what you have just mentioned?
A. The suite?
Q. Yes; whom did he plagiarize?
A. From hundreds of sources.
Q. Tell the jury some.
A. From the German composers.
Q. Well, which ones?
A. I can't specify now.
Q. What compositions?
A. I can't specify now—I only know it is not original music.
Q. Do you want [it] to be understood that you are a sufficient expert in music, based upon the experience you have had, so that the moment you hear what is claimed to be original you can tell whether it is copied from anything in the world?
A. Yes.
Q. You cover the whole field?
A. Yes.
Q. You testified that upon the hearing of the rendition of a theme claiming to be original, you can tell instantly whether any portion is copied or not?
A. I can tell whether it is original.
Q. Copied?
A. Copied from hearing and experience.
Q. Do you mean from common sense you can tell it?
A. From common sense.

. . . . .

Q. If you heard any piece played you could tell instantly whether it was copied or not?
A. Yes, sir.
Q. You can?
A. Yes, sir.
Q. Do you know whether anybody else can?
A. Ten thousand musicians in this country can do it; Mr. Herbert can do it in a moment.

Palmer was making progress and was ready to concentrate on more specific problems. Blumenberg was no better off than before.

Q. Now, you say as to Herbert's first composition [the march] that the key was the same?
A. Yes, sir.
Q. What do you mean by that?
A. The same key.
Q. What do you mean musically?
A. There are twelve major and twelve minor keys—the keys are the same.

Q. Don't you know the key is the same in thousands of original productions?

A. The key is the same in thousands, yes, sir.

Q. Do you mean to state as a musical man that because it was in the same key it was plagiarized or copied?

A. I never said it; I said it happened that the two compositions are in the same key.

Q. Was there anything significant in that?

A. Being in the same key it looks like a copy.

Q. Don't you think that original productions are frequently in the same key?

A. Of course, each production has its own key.

Q. Do you mean to say that two original productions, they cannot both be in the same key?

A. Certainly.

Q. Then being in the same key it was not significant?

A. It was significant, as the theme was the same.

Q. I ask you whether you don't know that original productions concededly so, are frequently in the same key—original compositions are in the same key?

A. There must be, because there are only twelve major and twelve minor keys.

Q. There is nothing significant about that?

A. Not if the theme is not the same; it is only when the theme goes with it.

Q. What is the theme?

A. It is usually the opening phrases. It depends upon what the composition is.

Q. Give the different instances in which the different compositions will give you the different themes—give us one illustration. You say the theme differs according to the composition?

A. I mean if you have got a waltz you begin with a certain theme, and with a concerto it is different.

Q. So that you would write one theme for one composition and another for another?

A. Yes.

Q. You have stated that it started off with one theme and changes?

A. The theme develops.

Q. You say his theme developed different from the other?

A. Yes.

Q. Was it not original?

A. The development was original.

Q. That is the actual music after its development from the theme was original?

A. I mean the development from that theme was different from the other one, and was not copied from it.

Q. What you mean to say is that Herbert began at the same point, but diverted from it?

A. Yes.

Q. When he got away from it was it not original?

A. No, it was commonplace or ordinary music.

Q. When he diverted from the theme did not it become original with Herbert?
A. It did not become original music.
Q. Did it not become original with him so far as you know?
A. It became an original development of his, but not original music.
Q. Take the instances in which you have shown, as you claim, that Herbert copied and your general statement that you know, from your skill and ability, that everything he has produced is copied, is there anything else that justifies that statement?
A. The general consensus.
Q. Is this article where you made the attack, what you wrote, is that what you call a general consensus?
A. Yes, sir, those things go to a general consensus—the position of an artist is fixed by general consensus.
Q. The opening phrase is the same, is that what you mean?
A. The opening of the theme.
Q. When he opened did he get away soon—when he opened with the phrase the same?
A. I don't know how soon he got away.
Q. You have made no comparisons?
A. Yes.
Q. When he got away was it original?
A. Original in getting away, but not original music . . .

Poor Blumenberg was not yet through. Under persistent questioning he assumed that 300,000 persons a week read his magazine, to which there was nothing comparable anywhere in the world. He could not remember clearly whether he had written previous articles (praise-worthy or blameworthy) about Herbert. And he confessed that the bulk of reports printed in his paper never passed before his eyes. He tried weakly to uphold Herbert as a good musician, asserted he was out of place as a symphony conductor—but certainly did not want him dis-lodged—and endeavored to distinguish a pirate from one who commits piracy.

The dialogue grew funnier as it went along. Blumenberg's next aston-ishing disclosures were that Herbert's music could not come up to the editor's standards because the composer was still living, and that Herbert, after all, was a good composer! Conceding that Herbert had written serious classical or romantic music, Blumenberg was confronted by new problems.

Q. Well . . . would you class it as objectionable?
A. It is not objectionable.
Q. It had not got up to your standard?
A. It could not be, because he is living. It takes longer than his life to fix itself.

Q. The artistic man cannot be imbued with the musical inspiration while he is alive?

A. Yes.

Justice Truax was sufficiently interested in this topic to ask about Wagner, Verdi, and Mozart. Blumenberg admitted the first two were exceptions to the rule ("Verdi became very old and outlived it"), and Mozart gained only slight recognition in Austria. Palmer returned to the problem at hand.

Q. Now, in this romantic field of Herbert as you were in touch with the musical world, how had he gotten on in that middle field?

A. He stood very still.

Q. That was a little bit above the comic opera even?

A. Yes.

Q. Then Herbert had, as you knew, on the 17th of July, 1901, some artistic ability, hadn't he?

A. He was a good musician.

Q. But in this romantic field . . . he had some ability as a composer?

A. He had the ability of a good musician as a composer, but not the ability of a composer of quality.

Q. He had the ability of what?

A. As a composer as a good musician.

Q. But the reverse of that was not true—he was not a good composer as a musician?

A. He was not a good composer as a composer, but he was a good musician as a composer.

Q. You mean that, do you?

A. Absolutely, that is right.

Q. And you understand exactly what your answer has expressed?

A. I really hope I do.

It was time for other witnesses to be summoned. The first to be called for the defendant was one Platon Brounoff (1863–1924), a Russian composer-conductor-teacher, who boasted of his study with Rubinstein and Rimsky-Korsakoff. He also boasted of a broad knowledge of musical literature: "I am quite familiar with the classical composers, both ancient and modern, Bach, Beethoven, Wagner, Richard Strauss, Tschaikowski, Gounod, Verdi and also American authors. I am familiar with the music composed by Mr. Victor Herbert . . . In my opinion the music of Mr. Victor Herbert is not original and not classical." Asked to be more specific Brounoff avowed that Herbert's Serenade theme (Cello Suite) was taken from Moszkowski's Serenata. He modestly explained that "it is possible for an expert musician like myself to tell at once, either by looking at the music or reading it or hearing it, whether or not it is an original composition."

The next witness for the defense was an Italian opera conductor, Augusto (or Auguste) Vianesi (1837–1908), who was far from unsuccessful in his profession. He had been on the staff of the Metropolitan Opera Company for the seasons 1883–1884 and 1891–1892, and had directed musical drama in every country under the sun. He was more boastful, also more naïve, than his Russian colleague. "No conductor in the world can name the theatre where I have not been conductor— all over England, all over France, all over Germany and Russia and in the United States in all the principal theatres." In 1902 he was living in New York as vocal teacher and operatic coach. He was a voluble talker and an unconscious comedian.

Hawes examined him first. He had looked over *The Fortune Teller,* *The Wizard of the Nile,* and *The Idol's Eye* as well as other pieces by Herbert. He was asked to express his opinion of them in his own language. "If I am to express my personal appreciation, I would say I don't like any of them."

When asked if he knew Herbert's Suite for Cello and Orchestra, Vianesi spouted forth: "I saw open a piece of music and at the first bar I said, 'Oh, who is this composer?' They said to me, 'Victor Herbert.' No. The second bar there is a little change, two notes changed, but the first bar, the key, everything; the time, tune, everything the same as the Serenade of Moszkowski, which was played when I was five years old." It was not necessary to point out that Vianesi was five years old in 1842, and Moszkowski was not born for another twelve years!

Poor Mr. Vianesi was made for cross-examination, and Palmer had a field day with him. He seemed at least to be without guile, which is more than can be said for the bluffing Blumenberg. Palmer and Vianesi launched into their exchange:

Q. Who asked you to examine the three operas of Herbert?
A. I had them at the office of Mr. Blumenberg and I saw these three operas and he said, "Do you know them?" "No." "Will you look?" I said "Yes." I took the operas at the time, and as I can read music as you read the paper, immediately, in the opening I had a poor opinion.
Q. We are not discussing the question whether you thought they were poor. The question is whether you were able to say after you examined these three operas as to whether they were copied from some other music.
A. Little bits everywhere.
Q. How long have you known the gentleman, Mr. Blumenberg?
A. Oh, 15 years—more than that.
Q. Do you know him pretty well?
A. Good friend, nothing else.
Q. . . . How long a time did you spend in examining them?
A. After dinner—afternoon.

Q. How many hours did you spend in going over the three operas?
A. Two hours.
Q. Going over the three?
A. And playing them.
Q. I open at page 76 and 77 of the "Wizard of the Nile." Tell me what that is copied from, the music that you find on those two pages?
A. I can't say.
Q. Well, now, I open at pages 102 and 103 at random, in "The Fortune Teller." Tell me what that is copied from?
A. Why do you choose—
Q. Open anywhere in that book. Open anywhere and tell me where you can put your finger upon anything.
A. Give me "The Idol's Eye."
Q. Will you open anywhere in "The Wizard of the Nile" and tell me any part that was copied and what it was copied from?
A. I can tell you all that I heard before, but where it is copied from I cannot.

. . . . .

Q. Give me the name of a composer where you have found in that book any theme or any music that was his work, give me the name of a single composer in all this field that you know.
A. Offenbach, Lecocq.
Q. Tell me where there is anything in that from Offenbach?
A. The same thing over.
Q. Point it out.
(Witness produces and points at a page)
Q. Do you mean page 120 or 121?
A. It is a page—have not a piano here.
Q. Which do you mean, page 120 or 121 copied from Offenbach?
A. 120.
Q. What are Offenbach's works it is copied from?
A. "The Brigands"—the same thing—am I permitted to sing?
[At which point the Court came out with an emphatic "No!"]

. . . . .

Q. Is that copied in body from Offenbach?
A. In body, no.
Q. How much of it is from the "Brigands" of Offenbach?
A. The form.
Q. When you speak of the form to what special thing do you refer?
A. I can't make out what you mean.
Q. When you say "form" what special thing do you mean?
A. Do you know what means phrasing?
Q. Yes. The notes are not the same, are they?
A. No.
Q. Is the air the same?
A. Nearly.

Q. Is it the same?
A. Nearly.
Q. Is it dissimilar in any respects?
A. It is a little dissimilar.

The defendant's next witness was another Italian, Arturo Buzzi-Peccia, who composed and taught voice in New York. He was not very helpful to Blumenberg's cause, for he failed to name a composer from whom Herbert had pirated themes. On the other hand he confessed to having no liking for Herbert's music. When Hawes asked him if he knew Herbert, he replied, "I have not the pleasure"; and when Palmer asked him if he had no sympathy for comic opera, he blithely answered: "I like it very much. I enjoy it—why not?"

Buzzi-Peccia had familiarized himself with *The Singing Girl* and *The Fortune Teller*. He did not think their music was very original, and it did not appeal to him; but when Palmer asked if he could say it was copied from any other composer, he replied, "Oh, no; I don't take that trouble . . ."

Blumenberg surely pinned high hopes on his next witness, Alfred John Goodrich, teacher at the Guilmant Organ School. Goodrich (1847–1920) was a well known American theorist and musical author. In describing his qualifications he said he had written *Analytical Harmony, Theory of Interpretation, Complete Musical Analysis, Synthetic Counterpoint,* and *Guide to Practical Musicianship.* (In 1904 he would bring out a *Guide to Memorizing Music.*) Under Hawes's gentle questioning he testified he had very recently examined some of Herbert's music and found it to be not original.

Palmer, however, was not so lenient, and he hammered the poor witness without respite. It was fortunate that he did, for he thus caught Goodrich in the most egregious musical error of the trial. Goodrich maintained that a page in *The Wizard of the Nile* was taken literally from the opening of Beethoven's Ninth Symphony, and he maintained it steadfastly, much to his discomfiture later. It was an opportunity which Palmer did not neglect. Goodrich was shown a copy of the Herbert opera and remarked:

A. . . . I know the score of Beethoven. (Looks at *Wizard*) That is the passage I observed, that is note for note from Beethoven. Every musician knows that. The motif is the one thing.
Q. Do you refer to the entire music upon the entire page?
A. No, it only means the text.
Q. That is the motif of this music and the motif of the music you have mentioned, is where you claim the similarity to exist?
A. As far as I looked—beyond that I did not look.

Q. That is as far as you are able to go?
A. That is as far as I did go.
Q. What do you understand motif is?
A. It is the text; it is the germ of the music.
Q. Are the notes the same?
A. Yes.
Q. The notes are exactly the same?
A. Note for note the same; even the key, the form of the rhythm.

. . . . .

Q. You haven't got it [Beethoven's Ninth Symphony] here?
A. I haven't got it here.
Q. Will you return after recess and have it here?
A. Very well.

Recess was not yet at hand, and the questioning continued for some time. Goodrich was willing to cite any number of pages by Herbert which he thought were taken from another's music, but when pressed for the source he could never recall it. Palmer asked him if he had ever heard of Ebenezer Prout, the English theorist and pedagogue who had made a comparison of Mozart's *Requiem* and Händel's *Joseph*. Goodrich was familiar with Prout, but not with his comparative study. Of Prout, Palmer asked: "He is a well known authority, is he not?" Goodrich replied, "I would not call him an authority," which prompted the lawyer to inquire tartly, "His books do not compare favorably with yours?"

Hawes took over again and treated Goodrich with more respect. The witness followed the general line of his predecessors regarding Moszkowski and Offenbach, then unburdened himself of a rather remarkable sentiment: "One who has acted as a critic for music goes to a concert and hears a piece of music. He isn't any critic unless he knows whether he has heard it before. He does not say that is from so-and-so, but he says it is original or not original when he hears a piece of music, he sees it himself, it is original or it is not. If it is not original of course he does not care for it. Those are mostly impressions, but the impressions of a good critic are of course infallible."

Before leaving the witness stand Goodrich found a Waldteufel waltz to be one of Herbert's melodies, and he defined Dvořák as an unoriginal composer because he was one of those "who develop other people's ideas."

The next witness for the defendant was William C. Carl (1865–1936), organist and church musician, and director of the Guilmant Organ School. Perhaps he was to lend an air of sobriety to the defendant's team. However, he was not a good witness. He substantiated what his colleagues had said, but he did it in a rather half-hearted man-

ner, and Palmer tied him in knots in forcing him to explain how the
twelve chromatic tones could be changed around without altering the
character of the music. He admitted he had been advertising in the
Musical Courier for nine years.

Palmer had not forgotten the advertising angle, and he summoned
Blumenberg back to the stand. Though the editor denied everything,
the dialogue was significant:

Q. Do you remember being asked on the redirect examination, as to what
length of time ensued between the time Herbert stopped advertising in
the *Musical Courier* and the time when adverse criticisms commenced
being put in the paper, and your putting it at five or six years?
A. Yes, sir.
Q. I hand you a copy of the Musical Courier, and ask you whether in
August, 1896, page 20, of the paper of that date Victor Herbert was
not advertising on that date?
(Objection; overruled)
A. I see an advertisement here of Gilmore's famous band with Victor Herbert's picture.
Q. I hand you a copy of the Musical Courier of December 10th, 1898, and
ask you whether that was a copy of the paper circulated by the de-
fendant in this case?

Hawes objected to this evidence, but the Court allowed it because
it showed animus on the part of the defendant.

A. Yes, sir.
Q. Now, isn't it a fact, Mr. Blumenberg, that Mr. Victor Herbert did not
take charge of the orchestra in Pittsburgh until that very month preceding, November, 1898?
A. I don't know anything about that.

* * * * *

Q. Did you at one time have a lawyer by the name of Lellman?
(Objection; overruled)
A. Yes.
Q. He was your lawyer during the years 1898 and 1899?
(Objection; overruled)
A. Mr. Lellman had charge of some legal business of the paper.
Q. Did you ever authorize Lellman to say to Mr. Weil if Herbert would
pay $2,000 you would stop pounding him?
(Objection; overruled)
A. I never used any such language in my life to anybody.

The trial up to now had featured the side of the defendant, who was
faring badly. The defense had been a consistent attack upon Herbert
by denying either quality or originality in his operatic music. Now it

was Herbert's turn, and Palmer called the plaintiff's chief musical witness. It was Walter Damrosch—and Herbert needed no one else. Damrosch was handsome and accomplished, a national idol, a thorough musician whose word carried authority and prestige, and a man of broad general culture. He liked Herbert, musically and personally, and he had himself suffered from Blumenberg's spiteful gibes. His testimony was exemplary, for it was based on keen intelligence which appreciated Herbert and Blumenberg according to the merits of each.

In his preliminary remarks Damrosch implied how extensive Herbert's conducting experience was. "I have known Victor Herbert . . . ever since he came to America. I don't know the exact date he entered the orchestra as first cellist of the opera. Every musician in my orchestra has played under him. I know solo players outside of my orchestra who have played in his orchestra in Pittsburgh. I have heard him conduct . . . the symphony orchestra; four or five times; even oftener."

In a lengthy examination of Damrosch, Palmer quickly obtained from the conductor a clarification of the mysterious terminology Blumenberg's henchmen had used:

Q. Tell me what the difference is, Mr. Damrosch, if there is any, between motif, as applied to music, and motive, as applied in the ordinary accepted sense.

A. The one is a foreign word and the other English. Motif was brought into prominence more especially through the Wagner operas and the word used to designate the theme—musical theme—which Wagner used throughout his operas to designate a certain grammatic [dramatic?] idea. The English word motive very well translates itself, as if a preacher would select a text, "God is great," and another should take the same text and preach a different sermon on it. The musician can confuse the layman's mind by using such terms, but actually, after all, the intention and purposes, the meaning of the two, is the same.

Q. Now, I hand you the vocal score of "The Serenade," . . . I hand you also a piece of music, "Grace O'Moore," and I ask you what, if any, similarity there is from a musical standpoint between those two pieces?

A. They are both waltzes.

Q. Is there any similarity?

A. None that I can discover that is prominent enough to be worthy of mention. The fact is that all comic operas—

Here the defense attorney interposed an objection. The Court overruled it and directed Damrosch to proceed with his exposition.

A. —the fact of it is that comic operas are of necessity, and because of the nature of the subject on which they are written, generally written in certain well recognized dance rhythms, such as waltzes, polkas, jigs, or any of the national or well known dances. They are not intended for the serious edification of the highly educated musical people, but for the entertainment of people who want to go and hear music too, but music which may not occupy their mind to a great extent. And in this way it can happen that not one, but a dozen similarities to others may occur. They have to use polkas and to use the well recognized dance themes, and in so far they are similar.

Q. Is that the only way?

A. All my musical knowledge can perceive.

Q. If the music which is produced upon page 8 of "The Serenade" it is charged was copied or that a part of the music was taken from "Grace O'Moore," and that is the only criticism made of it except that some experts say that they have in their mind some recollection that somewhere they heard something very like the whole opera, "The Serenade," would you say that that was original work of Herbert's or not?

A. I should say that was original.

Q. Is there anything peculiar about Victor Herbert and is characteristic of him?

A. Yes.

Q. What is it?

A. It is hard to define it.

Q. As you know him, through his comic operas?

A. I should say Mr. Herbert's music had a distinctly original coloring to it. He has written thousands of pages, and you can't say that all of them have the same amount of originality, but that there is a great deal in the compositions of his I have heard. I am glad to testify to it, although we are rival conductors.

Q. Take page 43 of "The Singing Girl," and take the little slip of music that is there and tell me what similarity you find between those two— take Defendant's Exhibit J [*The Palms*].

A. There is a decided resemblance in the bar which is quoted as being the one taken from the other, but it is absolutely of no consequence whatever, because the one bar they have taken is the second of two introductory bars to the theme proper which follows it. It is as if you would begin a story and say "It was November, 1862."

Here Damrosch's remarks were not too clear. If he was referring to the excerpt from *The Palms* he located them erroneously; but his principle was basically sound. It is astonishing that none of the defendant's experts were expert enough to detect his slip!

Q. Or "Once upon a time?" (This by the Court)

A. Yes, and then begins the story. These are introductory and become of no importance.

. . . . .

Q. Compare page 43 of "The Singing Girl" with this piece marked Defendant's Exhibit J. Would you say that the music of "The Singing Girl" found upon that page is original or otherwise?

A. Do you mean the part that is not in discussion.

Q. No, I mean the part that is in discussion.

The Court was much interested in the new development and interposed: "Take the whole of it and say if it is original. The whole of that page." Damrosch willingly resumed.

A. Well, I can see no resemblance to any composition I know.

. . . . .

Q. Take page 147, Act III, introduction in Defendant's Exhibit B, "The Wizard of the Nile," Mr. Goodrich has said that that and the theme which follows on shows that it was taken from the piece which he has designated "The Waldteufel Waltz;" are you familiar with it?

A. I am.

Q. Is it copied from it?

A. I don't think it is copied. I think it is similar . . .

Q. Take "The President's March" . . . is there any other similarity that you find between the march of Herbert and the march with which they compare it, "The Clio March?"

A. I can perceive a similarity between the first two bars which consist of exactly three notes of which the first two are identical—something not even worth mentioning.

Q. Of what importance is that from a musical standpoint in determining whether the composition is original or not?

A. Absolutely none.

The most important part of Damrosch's testimony was now to come. In the midst of it he delivered a couple of little lectures on musical similarities, denied that *Grace O'Moore* had influenced Herbert, and exposed the unreliability of Alfred Goodrich's memory. Herbert could not have had a better ally.

Q. Mr. Damrosch, "The Wizard of the Nile," on page 10, Act I, has been characterized by the experts on the other side as being a copy or imitation of the Ninth Symphony of Beethoven; I hand you the Ninth Symphony and ask you to make a comparison of those two and tell me in what particulars, if any, there is any resemblance between the two compositions?

A. No possible comparison could, or should, be made between the two. Both are in the same key.

Q. In music has that any signification at all?

A. As much as the location of a story in New York or Paris.

Q. Has it no more significance than that?

A. None at all.

Q. Now, proceed and tell me in what particulars they are similar, if at all.

A. They are not similar in any particulars. It is incorrect that the similarity which experts on the other side of this case say they found in the works of Herbert never occurred among the great masters. There are hundreds of resemblances. Gounod wrote an oratorio called "The Redemption," the principal theme of which is symbolic of the Saviour, and this theme is virtually identical with that of Mendelssohn's Italian Symphony, which is virtually identical with The Heroic Symphony. There is a hunting chorus in Weber's Freischutz, which is virtually identical with a theme from Schumann's "Gipsy Life." There is a sonata by Clementi, written before Mozart's Flute, which is absolutely identical. . . . I have heard a great deal of Mr. Blumenberg's testimony. I heard Vianesi testify. As an expert, I think it is impossible for an expert carrying in his mind a recollection which would enable him to testify as Vianesi did, that he had in his mind enough, without being able to recall the composer or when it was composed or where he had heard it or by whom, but that by what he carried in his mind he could say that all of Herbert's operas here in dispute in the comic opera field were copied or were airs that had been suggested by something some one else had done.

. . . . .

Q. Now, state the fact as to the comparison . . . ?

A. Beethoven's Ninth Symphony is written in two-quarter time and the first sixteen bars . . . do not contain the theme at all. There are a few technical terms absolutely necessary in this case. There is a tremolo in the violins and violoncellos on the empty fifth—a confused murmur—to create the feeling of mystery and indecision, and in this little accompaniment there are little notes which follow each other at certain intervals for sixteen bars, and it is only after the sixteen bars that the real theme of the Ninth Symphony comes in. In Mr. Herbert's introduction the action is supposed to take place on the banks of the Nile, and before the curtain rises we are supposed to be taken into the eastern atmosphere, which is characterized by this empty fifth by a great many composers who have adopted it from Oriental music, as any one who has heard the music can testify. Those that in the Ninth Symphony occur on the interval of the fifth in Mr. Herbert's introduction occur on the fourth and represent the cries of the Egyptian boatmen, heard as the curtain goes up. In other words, the introduction is carefully written to carry us into the eastern atmosphere of the story.

Q. Is there any such similarity . . . with reference to the two notes?

A. Absolutely none.

. . . . .

Q. Is the statement . . . concerning the similarity an actual fact from comparison?

A. It is the very reverse.

A slight diversion in the questioning elicited from Damrosch his opinion on the two Serenades (from Herbert's Cello Suite and by

Moszkowski): "They are both of them written on similar harmonies in the accompaniment, each of them developing an independent and original melody on this accompaniment, but the harmonies, which are simple, resemble each other and are often used in simple song form." Abe Hummel wanted the last statement struck out, but Justice Truax refused his request. When Palmer asked if the acknowledged harmonic similarity had any significance in view of possible plagiarism, Damrosch replied: "It is of no significance, because harmonies are common property and have been used by a great many composers of conceded merit." But they were not through with Beethoven.

Q. I now hand you Defendant's Exhibit L, Mr. Goodrich, their expert having testified that what appears there is a copy of the Symphony which you hold in your hand; I ask you whether it is a copy?
A. It is not.

During the recess aforementioned Goodrich had evidently made his own copy from memory. After Damrosch's emphatic answer Hummel protested, saying: "I object to the question. He did not so testify; he testified from memory to the Symphony, as the record shows." But the lawyer received no comfort from the Court, who seemed to be closely attentive as he replied: "The effect of his testimony was that it was a copy. He said that he testified from memory, and we want to see how good his memory is." Whereupon Damrosch promptly chimed in: "His memory is sadly at fault, your Honor."

Damrosch's good opinion of Herbert never changed. In a private statement in 1939, repeated to me in 1947, he proved his unswerving admiration for the composer—and he also shed a sidelight on the trial of 1902: "I cannot claim to have been Victor Herbert's closest friend, although I had the highest regard for him as a musician, and liked him very much as a man. . . . I did help him as a friend and so-called expert witness to win a libel suit which he brought against a musical journal of that period which at that time was in 'unclean hands.' "[2]

The trial had to go on, and Herbert was brought back to answer musical questions posed by Palmer. Hummel objected to this, but the Court overruled, saying that Herbert was now testifying as a musical expert. It takes little effort to imagine the composer's denial of all the charges of plagiarism and copying. Occasionally a flash of wit would issue from his remarks. Palmer's inquiry about *The President's March* brought out one example.

Q. When you wrote the President's March did you know the music of the Clio March?
A. Never heard of it in my life.

Q. Did you see any part of it until you came into this trial?
A. No, sir, never, and I don't suppose anybody else had.

Parenthetically it may be remarked that the *Clio March* is a rather mysterious entity today. No copy has been found in the Library of Congress, and the title seems to be absent from the records of the Copyright Office. Even the spelling of the composer's name takes on different forms in the trial record: Gernet, Gurnet, Guernsey, etc. It was probably by John Gernert who died in Pittsburgh on February 25, 1938.[3]

As the trial neared its end, Palmer flaunted a neat dramatic effect. He summoned Otto Weil back to the stand and had him recall a meeting with Blumenberg in May of 1898:

Q. Did Mr. Blumenberg say to you—
                    (Objection; overruled)
Q. Did Mr. Blumenberg, upon that occasion that you mention, say to you
    that he knew that Victor Herbert was a good musician?
A. An excellent musician, were his words.
Q. Did Mr. Blumenberg, on that occasion, say to you that personally he
    admired Mr. Herbert?
A. He did.

The trial was over, but there was more excitement, or at least amusement, to come. The case was closed about noon on Monday October 27, and the two lawyers delivered their addresses to the jury. Hawes, for the defendant, spoke first. He chose a peculiar approach, one scarcely foreseen in the light of Blumenberg's own assertions. He said:

There is one point where we can agree with our learned adversary, and that is that this case is a very serious one. The complainant in this action asks you to take $50,000 out of the treasury of the Musical Courier Company and . . . that would be a very serious thing indeed. Now, gentlemen, Mr. Herbert is not on trial in this action. His musical compositions are not on trial. It is not incumbent with us to show that Mr. Herbert is not an original composer.

Just what was incumbent with him, Hawes had difficulty in explaining. He tried to show that Blumenberg's editorial had no intention of accusing Herbert of theft—it was only a matter of reminiscences. Then he recited selections from Shakespeare, Keats, Byron, and Longfellow to illustrate how individual styles could immediately be perceived. He tried to do the same in music and hummed a strain from the *Blue Danube Waltz*, but this "served to amuse more than to elucidate." The following astonishing remark, with a strange mixture of sentiments, was about the best he could offer, and it was not good enough:

We have the kindest and best feelings toward Mr. Herbert personally. We would like him as a friend. But we detest his music and say it is rot. And we earnestly say that the Pittsburgh Art Society disgraced itself when it took him as its musical director.[4]

Not so with Herbert's Palmer, who held his audience spellbound as he blistered Blumenberg with scorn, irony, satire, and ridicule. He spoke to Herbert's twelve peers with intense earnestness; his peroration was masterly.

Your Honor and Gentlemen of the Jury:—

If the editor of the *Musical Courier* sitting there should accuse me in his next issue of plagiarism because in beginning my address to you I employed a phrase that has often been used before by other lawyers under similar circumstances, his charge would not be more absurd than the accusation of plagiarism that he made against Victor Herbert.

We will let Shakespeare sleep in his silent grave with the recommendation given him by Mr. Hawes who recites well. What has it all to do with the attempt of that man there [pointing to Blumenberg] to blast the character and destroy the life work of the plaintiff in this action?

There have lived in times past masters of music, men of inspiration, who have preferred to live and die in humble surroundings in order to enrich the field of Art. . . . You have learned also of men who are marching in the footsteps of those old masters. Do you believe that this man, Blumenberg, is one of that sort? Did you believe him when he sat in the witness chair and told you that the chief mission of the *Musical Courier* is to uplift the people into the atmosphere of high art? Did you believe him when he said that he didn't know the circulation of his own paper? Did you believe him when he swore that he had nothing to do with the advertising department of his paper? Did you observe how when he started to read an article, which he first said he wrote and then, when he found something that would be damaging to his case, how he suddenly decided that he did not write it and that he knew nothing about it? Do you believe that he is the great philanthropist that he pictures himself to be, laboring to elevate the Art of music, or do you believe he has a shrewd, misdirected mind that plans to turn to commercial account everything that he does?

Look at him! Does he look like an inspired man? If I ever saw the embodiment of the commercial spirit I see it in him! There is only one question regarding the field of music that interests him, and that is: "How much is there in it for me? How much can I get for advertising?" [Roar of applause from spectators; judge warns room will be cleared if repeated.] He has told us of his beautiful inspirations. Let us suppose that a musician came to him with an advertising contract for his paper and the money to pay for it and that he should find Blumenberg visited with an inspiration; do you suppose that he would forget to take the money? Did he strike you as that sort of a man when he was on the stand?

The idea of the opposing counsel coming here to apologize when their client, in a single hour, did more to blast the reputation and good name of Victor Herbert than he could undo if he occupied himself in the effort until the day of death! They suggest that Blumenberg may have made a mistake when he wrote this alleged criticism, which is the worst example of vicious, gibbering English that I ever expect to see in a journal of standing. Don't be deceived, gentlemen; he made no mistake. He wrote in that article exactly what he intended to write. He wrote it with the thought that he would have Victor Herbert deposed from the directorship of the Pittsburgh Orchestra unless he came back into the fold of his advertisers. What he was after was a divvy!

This man, Blumenberg, knows that musical men are keenly sensitive by nature; he deliberately formulated plans to turn this knowledge of their susceptibilities to commercial account. That was his impulse when he sat down in his office and wrote this article. But he found a musician for once with the courage to say to him: "I am going to make you answer for the lies you have printed about me." Then he commenced to scurry about to find experts who could sustain him in his position, based solely upon falsehood. Blumenberg said on the stand that there are 10,000 musicians in America who can tell at first hearing that Mr. Herbert's music is not original. Where are they? Where are the 10,000? I find upon counting that they produced five. And you recall the kind they were! All that God has ever endowed upon the brain of man was wrapped up in their anatomies!

This point gave Palmer an opportunity to ridicule the defendant's witnesses, to expose their empty pretensions and their egotism. By contrast he praised Damrosch's rational and clear testimony and the general deportment of Herbert's allies. Then he was off on poor Blumenberg once more:

And then Blumenberg, who could not tell upon the stand when an inspiration was coming on, claims that in the midst of one, he sat down and wrote this scurrilous article, and now joins hands with his counsel and tries to apologize. Blumenberg on the stand under oath told you that Victor Herbert composed good, honest, original music. When he wrote his villainous attack he said that every line of music he ever wrote was copied. Was not that a false statement, pure and simple? He knew it was a lie when he wrote it. He sat in his office, like a snake in the grass with its hollow tooth filled with poison ready to spring upon the unsuspecting passer-by, and wrote a scurrilous, villainous article calculated to destroy the reputation of this man who had worked a life-time to win a place of recognition for himself. And this Blumenberg claims inspiration! The only inspiration he will ever feel is derived when he receives cash.[4]

Justice Truax made his charge to the jury after Palmer's explosive description of Blumenberg. His words were especially important because they actually took away the editor's last hope. Blumenberg still wanted to escape unscathed on the ground that his article was "privileged," was a form of public criticism wherein adverse opinions could be freely vented. The judge told the jury that the article was distinctly libelous, but at the same time he pointed out what they should consider as they deliberated for a verdict.

Lawyer Hawes asked the Court to emend his charge in several respects, pleading that the judge should charge "that the words, published as they were in a musical paper as part of a musical criticism, were privileged." Hawes also told the Court that Herbert had proved no loss of money resulting from the article. The judge merely replied that this was unnecessary. Again Hawes pleaded that the article was written in good faith as a piece of musical criticism; consequently it was privileged, and "the verdict must be for the defendant." To this the Court made strong answer: "I decline so to charge. I know of no law that gives the publisher of a paper a right to say an untruthful thing about a private individual or a public individual."

One of the jurors asked if the plaintiff had to prove damages. Justice Truax instructed him carefully and not without some grim humor: "As I told you, the question of damages is for the jury. You are to say as sensible men, if the plaintiff has been libeled, what sum will compensate him for the injury that he has sustained. A man gets his leg cut off; you can't value a leg by so much a pound and give a big man more damages because his big leg has been cut off than you can a little man because his little leg has been cut off. It is a question for you to take hold of and consider as reasonable men. Has the defendant maliciously injured the plaintiff? If he has, give the plaintiff compensation; if you think it is malicious, do more."

The jury retired and was out about two hours. It returned with a verdict in favor of Herbert and awarded him damages of $15,000. (To this was added $158.40 costs.) The defendant immediately moved for a new trial, which was denied. Of course he appealed; but on July 7, 1903, the Appellate Division of the Supreme Court upheld the original decision, although Blumenberg obtained some financial satisfaction. The judgment against him was reduced to $5,158.40. Carried still further, to the Court of Appeals, the case was argued on December 30, 1904, but the defendant (the appellant) lost again. He immediately asked for a reargument, which, on January 24, 1905, was not granted.[5] The case was closed.

Herbert's great triumph, of course, was on October 28, 1902, when the favorable verdict was returned. He had completely discredited his opponent, and the amount of damages was liberal—for that matter, so was the reduced amount, because no attempt to prove financial injury was ventured. His friends and reputable musicians everywhere rejoiced, hailing the outcome as a glorious victory of right over wrong, and the musical press had a topic that was good for at least a week. H. E. Krehbiel's feature article in the *Tribune* for November 2, *"Thematic Coincidences,"* took as its starting point Goodrich's testimony on Beethoven's Ninth Symphony. "It was a silly device," wrote the critic, "and so bunglingly done that it was easy for Mr. Walter Damrosch to testify that the alleged quotation from Beethoven was not within a mile of the Ninth Symphony." He also remarked: "The contention of 'The Musical Courier's' professor has served its purpose in amusing musicians and helping Mr. Herbert to win his case."

Herbert was lionized, in fact. Everyone was happy because he had won, and everyone admired his courage in bringing suit. The ill repute of the *Musical Courier* was extraordinary, but no one had dared to attack it or correct it: "Herbert is the only one who has taken this sort of thing into a court house and the effect of the verdict must be considerable upon musical journalism and upon the people who patronize it."[6] A journal in the Middle West commented that the *Musical Courier* had exceeded its "usual reserve" and would have to pay money for its recklessness. The editor slyly added: "The unfortunate circumstance is that it costs it so seldom."[7]

The big celebration took place on Monday night November 10, when a festive banquet was tendered to Herbert in Berger's restaurant. It was, in every way, a remarkable tribute. The committee on arrangements was distinguished, the guest list was notable, the speeches were incisive and memorable. The committee was comprised of Damrosch, Palmer, Weil, Krehbiel, Alexander Lambert, and August Spanuth. Among the guests—musicians, patrons, music merchants, and instrument manufacturers—were E. Francis Hyde, Augustus Thomas, Frank Damrosch, Henry Hadley, Max Bendix, Sam Franko, the Witmark brothers, Richard Burmeister, Arthur Whiting, George Maxwell, Andreas Dippel, Nathan Burkan, Dr. Emanuel Baruch, Elkan Naumburg, Richard Aldrich, W. J. Henderson, Edward Ziegler, Raoul Martinez, Arthur Mees, Julian Edwards, Gustave Kerker, and Harry Rowe Shelley.

Walter Damrosch officiated as toastmaster. He declared that the composer's action against the paper had "done more to break the miserable power of the *Musical Courier* than anything that has ever happened," and that "this gathering shows that the better element of the musical profession is determined to suffer no longer from the attacks of this disreputable sheet." Calling Herbert "the courageous man who with one blow defeated this dragon, this hydra," he proposed as a toast "Hoch soll er leben!"[8] The banqueters sang it to make the rafters ring.

In response Herbert made no great speech. His remarks were modest, subdued, and good-natured. He was happy for the chance to punish the foe of all musicians; he gave full credit to Palmer and his witnesses —Damrosch chief among the latter; he was sorry for Blumenberg, because "I pity a man who sits in a courtroom with a guilty conscience, for I felt badly enough at times with a clear conscience." Damrosch's testimony had been so clear and effective in proving the falsity of the charges, he said, that he had detected tears in a policeman's eyes—"and an Irish policeman at that!"

William J. Henderson gave several accounts of the *Musical Courier's* infamy, and William Dalliba Dutton (president of the National Piano Manufacturers' Association) described how the paper unethically gouged money from the group he represented. Frank Damrosch, who had brought Mr. and Mrs. Herbert to America, was most denunciatory of all as he castigated Blumenberg and all he represented.

The speech by Krehbiel shared the sentiments of others present; but he had prepared a little surprise. He referred to Blumenberg's contention that Herbert's music was not popular enough to find its way to hand organs. This was the signal for a real hand organ, concealed behind a screen, to blare forth with some of Herbert's best known tunes —and pandemonium broke loose! It was also disclosed that so much Herbert music had found its way to the inside of such boxes that the composer was considering a suit against the Hand-Organ Syndicate of New York City for nonpayment of royalties.[9]

And what of the *Musical Courier* all this time? It was frantic. The issue of November 5 was filled with editorials pleading for freedom of criticism. It predicted a dark future for musical journalism if courts would not allow the feelings of composers to be hurt. It condemned the act of permitting a jury of the musically ignorant to decide, in dollars and cents, how much a musician had been injured. It implied that it could not change its attitude toward unoriginality, for "What will become of New York and the United States, musically speaking, if THE MUSICAL COURIER should throw itself into the arms of the enemy?"

This rhetorical question was too much for another musical magazine then flourishing. It could not answer categorically, but it suggested a probability: "Well, we can't say what would become of New York and the United States under those circumstances, but the 'enemy' would probably pass along its armful of refuse to the garbage plant and have itself disinfected."[10] The last word was marvelously misprinted; it appeared as "pisinfected"! Clearly it was a typographical error, but one wonders (from the meaning of the sentence) if the editor mischievously passed over its correction.

11

Pittsburgh's Loss

WAGNER and Beethoven "are beyond all doubt the greatest composers of all time."[1] With this firm avowal of musical faith Herbert plunged into his fourth year as head of the Pittsburgh Orchestra. It was to follow the pattern of previous seasons, but it opened the second half of his symphonic career and proceeded under a tension which increased to the end. Nevertheless his programs remained excellent, and the quality of the orchestra did not suffer. There was a rumor that he would soon be composing a new light opera for the Bostonians, based on the legend of Alfred the Great, but it was not borne out.[2]

The new tension resulted from the quarrel with Wilson, and Herbert's notes to him now often had a tone of impatience and acerbity. This was especially true in the summer of 1901. Herbert spent practically all of this period at Lake Placid and had to counsel Wilson in many things, some of which the manager should have understood better.

Wilson tried to do as much as he could independently, and occasionally exposed a woeful lack of diplomacy. Desiring to perform more works by contemporary Americans, Herbert thought that Henry Holden Huss should be soloist in his own piano concerto and instructed Wilson to negotiate. On the 6th of August the manager wrote to Huss inquiring his fee and was tactless enough to say: "You will recognize of course that your drawing power before this public is not very great." Huss was supposed to agree with this and fix his price accordingly—which he probably did, for he appeared in Pittsburgh on January 10 and 11, 1902, and received only $150.

Two out-of-town engagements caused considerable trouble. The first was for a series of concerts at the Pan-American Exposition in Buffalo, which had been under consideration for a year. Well in advance of the October engagement, Herbert wrote for it his popular and clever *Pan-*

227

americana, calling it a "morceau caractéristique." He wrote to Wilson: "The piece is of the more popular order and will make a hit. The first part is 'supposed' to be 'Indian' the second part 'ragtime' (modern America) and the trio 'Cuban' or Spanish character."

The great tragedy of the Exposition was the assassination of President McKinley who was shot on September 6. Herbert wrote to Wilson on September 14: "The deplorable death of the president will certainly settle that one extra week in Buffalo. Under the circumstances we can't expect to get it. They are certainly getting it 'in the neck.'"

Eleven days later Herbert included in another letter to Wilson a few phrases which were really admonitions:

As to the Buffalo engagement I want to say this: Lund with his orchestra played from 2–4 and 8–10. I hope this will be our time too. Since we can't play in the open air, I don't see how or why they could shift us around much. I will send you the program tomorrow. I've had a terrible cold and was unable to do anything but cough and sneeze. I hope you will see that we get all the advertising we ought to have there *before we* arrive and *when we get there.* I know that the Buffalo Expo. people are *very hard up,* and that several of the organizations had the devil's own time to collect the money due them. They are perfectly honest all right enough, but they *don't seem to have it!* I hope however they will do some business from now on and that we will *have no trouble of that kind.*

Wilson evidently replied that the Buffalo engagement could still be broken; but Herbert would have none of this. On October 1 he expressed to his manager his conception of the problem and settled the matter:

What I said about Buffalo was that I *knew* they had had hard times paying their attractions, but that they *did* finally. I don't see how we could ask them now "if the money was all right" at this time. All we can do now is to hope for a better attendance at the fair, and to insist upon prompt payment . . . when the time comes.

The other specially troublesome engagement was for a pair of concerts in Chicago on the 9th and 10th of December. This city was the stronghold of Theodore Thomas, and a spirit of competition whetted the desire to play there. The Chicago management made two requests: (1) a new popular piece by Herbert; (2) two soloists at each concert. Herbert was not too happy about the first, but agreed, declaring emphatically that it would not be a two-step; he disliked the idea of including it in the first concert. He finally instructed Wilson to inform the Chicago people "that I have written a 'Grand Festival March' (or some other title of the kind) in honor of the 12th anniversary of the

[Chicago] Auditorium. Please make them understand that it is *not a two-step,* but an elaborate Grand March. I have introduced in the piece 'Auld Lang Syne.'" When it was performed on December 9, at the first concert, it was programmed as *Auditorium Festival March,* Op. 35.

Herbert was furious over the plan to have two soloists at each of the Chicago concerts. He wrote to Wilson on October 1:

> Just rec. your last letter. For heaven's sake don't let us have more than *one* soloist at our Chicago concerts. I never heard of having *two soloists* in a concert of that character in my life. Where does the Orchestra and I come in? Must we have somebody to draw (!) again? *Bispham I refuse to have* anyway. *He is rotten!* You know he sings *flat* all the time!

Herbert's annoyance seems to have been perfectly justified, but Wilson completed the arrangements and allowed the four soloists. His excuse was that there was no other way of getting into Chicago, the goal of two years' striving. Herbert's sole consolation was that Bispham did not sing.

In spite of difficulties the season opened on November 7 and 9, 1901, with the usual brilliance. Society turned out on Thursday evening, and Andrew Carnegie arrived for Saturday afternoon. The main work was Beethoven's Fourth Symphony. The orchestra was better equipped than ever before; it had just acquired a double bassoon, paid for by Herbert out of his own pocket.[3] And it still had the full enthusiastic support of Carnegie, who said on November 8:

> I was glad to hear the Boston Symphony Orchestra last night. It is one of the great musical organizations of the world. The instrumentation and ensemble work were magnificent, and the orchestra sent forth a flood of music as if it were one mighty machine and not 60 or more performers.
>
> But I am frank to tell you that I prefer to hear the Pittsburg Orchestra play. They may not be so perfect in instrumentation, nor so smooth in execution, but they play with more enthusiasm and enter more fully into the true interpretation.
>
> Victor Herbert is one of the great, if not the greatest, orchestra leaders in this country. He shows fine taste in his interpretations and much spirit and life in his playing. There is lots of color in his conception [and] he is a master musician. I think he is superior to the Boston leader; at least, I enjoy his selections much better. The Muses seem to be present when he plays in order to inspire him.[3]

Off to its usual good start the orchestra embarked on a short trip after its second pair of concerts.

Accustomed as Herbert was to tours, he had some apprehension over this one; and it turned out to be well founded. He had prepared his programs a month and a half in advance and sent them to Wilson.

Nordica was to be the soloist in Cleveland, but he worried not about her. He wrote on October 6: "If we receive the music for Mad. Nordica's aria *in time to rehearse it here,* we will certainly *not need* a rehearsal with her in Cleveland. Mad. Nordica knows me and will without doubt *not insist* upon a rehearsal."

He did worry, however, about Akron and Oberlin. "So far all our concerts in Oberlin were a perfect disgrace!" he wrote to Wilson on October 7. "We had to get through an enormous program in about 1 hour." Arrangements must be better this time. They also had to be better in Akron; but here the problem was different—that of sharing the program with a local choral group. He continued quite logically:

As to *Akron* I don't see how I can make a program without knowing *what numbers* that Singing Society is going to sing! Anyway who conducts those two numbers? Is it that same woman of two years ago? If so, remember that *Mr. Frew* said (at the time) she should never have had the chance to conduct our Orchestra.—Am I to share the honors on that occasion with that lady? Would you think of offering Mr. Theod. Thomas or Mr. Gericke such a partnership? Is *anybody* good enough to stand up before an orchestra like the Pittsb. Orch? I sincerely hope there is no foundation for my fears, and will be pleased to hear from you on this subject.

These fears proved to be groundless. Charles E. Clemens was now in charge of the Akron "Singing Society"—the mixed chorus of the Tuesday Musical Club—and he was acknowledged to be better than the unfortunate lady. The real and totally unexpected trouble arose in Cleveland, where Nordica contradicted Herbert's prediction about rehearsal.

The impresario of the Cleveland concert was Adella Prentiss (Mrs. Hughes), who for many years was a creative force in the city's musical affairs. She, too, expected Nordica to forgo a rehearsal with orchestra; but the great soprano was adamant when she arrived in Cleveland: she absolutely insisted on trying her aria with the orchestra. To find the time was difficult for the Orchestra; though it passed through Cleveland on the way to Oberlin, its equipment had to be transported, set up, and taken down in the most disconcerting manner. Miss Prentiss was resourceful. She met the train carrying the musicians, she had transfer wagons ready to do the hauling, she steeled herself to meet a disgruntled conductor. Hoping to minimize the annoyance, she forced him to drink a champagne cocktail before nine o'clock in the morning and drove him to the rehearsal. All went well, and the Orchestra reached Oberlin in time for its concert.[4]

The Pittsburgh concerts of December 6 and 7 were specially important because they featured the first performance of another new work by Herbert: *Woodland Fancies,* Op. 34. It was a suite, programmatic in the sense of being pictorial and symbolic of natural phenomena, and dedicated significantly to Andrew Carnegie.

The "nature aspect" of the piece came from no passing fancy. The composer was entranced by Lake Placid and the Adirondacks, and the time he spent there refreshed and invigorated him. The suite was the direct result of his affection for the region which he loved to wander through and labor in. His fondness of exercise, indeed, was well known and called for occasional comment.[5]

The program book for the concert carried a lengthy description which was specially prepared by G. Schlotterbeck. The four movements of the suite were titled respectively Morning in the Mountains, Forest Nymphs, Twilight, and Autumn Frolics, and the whole was characterized by the phrase "mountain life and its moods."

The music was charged with color and life; but it was less ambitious than *Hero and Leander,* and less concentrated and sustained. It was really an elaboration of Herbert's best popular vein, and the audience responded warmly.

Herbert took the new suite to the Middle West, but, alas, his two concerts in Chicago met with a generally cool reception. The local critics were by no means so fair and objective as the New York reporters, and it seemed to offend them that their local pride—Theodore Thomas —was not officiating at the Auditorium's twelfth birthday celebration. The first concert occurred on December 9, and the *Daily Inter Ocean* of the 10th remarked rather grudgingly, it would seem, that "Mr. Thomas himself was not discoverable at the concert, but several of his admirers were, and even they grew careless at times and applauded." The second concert was scarcely better received.

Herbert must have been disappointed with the effect his men reportedly made. Moreover, he had to share each program with *two* soloists—an arrangement which he properly resented. Pittsburgh observed the state of affairs calmly and judged it for what it was worth. Schlotterbeck, the leading local critic, noted that the Chicago reviews "were so colored with partisanship as absolutely to defeat themselves and make the critics ludicrous. A criticism passed by one competent, and bearing the stamp of fairness and honesty is acceptable at all times, even though it hurt a little. But fairness is one thing, and viciousness quite another."[6]

He scarcely exaggerated, and New York proved it when the Pittsburgh Orchestra played there on January 21, 1902—Wilson having failed to secure a fall engagement. The criticism was judicious, appreciative, and intelligent.

The program contained only three works: Tchaikovsky's First Symphony, Rubinstein's D minor piano concerto, and the conductor's *Wood-*

land Fancies. Most of the critics condemned the opening number, but Krehbiel (who again in the *Tribune* expressed his admiration) wrote of the suite: "Here there were many pretty touches of color and exquisite nuance. It is in part a poetical work; in part an example of ingenious and experienced construction. There is dainty beauty in the second movement, and eloquent expression of mood in the third; but the first is labored and the last elaborately developed dance music. It was played con amore, and the audience found much delight in it."

Josef Slivinski was to have played the concerto; but at the last moment he quarreled with the manufacturer of his piano and refused to appear, reporting himself indisposed. A replacement was found quickly—Julie Rivé-King, who attacked the work in its place on the program. She showed plenty of pluck, the critics acknowledged; but they could not admire her execution. One charitable reporter explained that, since she "undertook at the last moment to replace another pianist, comparisons would be not only odious but also ungallant."[7] At the same time Slivinski was subjected to some censure, for he came to the concert, sat in a conspicuous box, and chatted contentedly throughout the music he was supposed to play!

Between this New York concert and the next (on March 4), Herbert's birthday again was the occasion for festivities in which all the orchestra shared. Last year the men had given their leader a bust of Beethoven; this year they gave one of Wagner. Luigi von Kunits made a handsome presentation speech, and the conductor almost wept as he expressed his pent-up feelings.[8]

The rest of the season passed with increasing satisfaction to Pittsburgh. It was hailed as the most active season the orchestra had yet enjoyed, eighty-one concerts being played as contrasted with sixty-nine the year before.[9] Then a long spring and summer tour lasted until September. In the quarrel with Wilson, Herbert must have gained some points, because he took the "Pittsburgh Orchestra" on the road at his own financial risk. Neither Wilson nor the Orchestra Committee was connected with the venture; but the governing board watched it with intense interest[10] and found no cause for alarm.

It was a most important departure, for it brought Herbert to two places with which his name would henceforth be indelibly associated: Willow Grove Park in Philadelphia (until the end of his life), and the Grand Union Hotel in Saratoga (for a number of years). His association with the first could almost be called the opening of an era; with the second, the beginning of an end.

The first Victor Herbert orchestra concert at Willow Grove Park occurred on June 16, 1902, when the public was informed he would be there for three weeks.[11] The park was actually a few miles north of Philadelphia. Here was developed America's greatest outdoor music center in the first quarter of the twentieth century. The musical fare was light and wholesome—as it should be in the summer; but the attractions were excellent and their presentations distinguished. Built up and managed as a recreational and amusement resort by the Philadelphia Traction Company, which also provided transportation to it, it was one of the country's show places. The first concerts were given in 1896;[12] Sousa (also a perennial favorite) came in 1901; and Herbert, the following summer.

The park was beautifully laid out, with lakes, promenades, and flower beds. One could dance or stroll or row, be thrilled with scenic devices or left breathless from mechanical contraptions, attend a theater, and eat the fanciest or the plainest food. The most celebrated enticement was the music at the Pavilion, seating 3,500 persons with space around its periphery for 10,000 more to listen with full enjoyment.[13]

On the Fourth of July, 1902, Herbert and the Pittsburgh Orchestra began the first of a series of annual engagements in Saratoga, at the fabulous Grand Union Hotel. He had played and conducted there before, but this was evidently his first appearance at the head of such a large ensemble.

An old friend, John Lund, who conducted an orchestra of some twenty-five men in the Grand Union, had introduced Herbert to this hostelry ten years earlier. Lund used to say that he shared his own salary with Herbert, and recounted other experiences which hardly square with the known facts of the early nineties.[14] But it probably is true that the attractions of Saratoga too often persuaded Lund to neglect his obligations, and that Herbert assumed charge of the music in his stead. The change was made at the instigation of the hotel management, Messrs. Gerrans and Woolley.*[15]

In Saratoga, Herbert was part of a picture that has now vanished from the American scene. Willow Grove was more important; but the New York spa was infinitely more glamorous, and the Grand Union Hotel was a miracle of spacious luxury.[16]

Even by present-day standards the building was huge and incredible; and it exuded atmosphere. A casual passer-by seeing it for the first time would stare at it in astonishment and dream of that gilded age when some Americans felt they deserved a throne room simply because they had untold wealth. It was overpowering in its ornamentation and size. The Broadway front was eight hundred feet long, and it was graced by an iron piazza three stories high. The main dining hall, sixty by two

---

* Woolley was the uncle of the actor Monty (Edgar Montillion) Woolley, who as "Little Edgar" would once a year solemnly conduct Herbert's orchestra on the hotel piazza.

hundred and seventy-five feet, was covered with exotic frescoes and glittering mirrors. The central rotunda, eighty feet in diameter, was overlooked by five spacious balconies—one on each of the five floors—from which guests commanded a majestic view of the entrance, the offices, and the grand saloon (lobby). In 1900 it was announced: "Three elevators are now in operation, and guests are conveyed to and from the five floors with the utmost ease and dispatch."[17]

In this fairyland of the *haut monde* Herbert became something of an institution; but he dispensed pleasure only. There was nothing on which to exercise an influence. Morning and evening concerts regaled the pleasure seekers, and the night affairs were brilliant beyond belief. The morning concerts were given on the piazza; but "no American resort ever has had anything which would quite compare to his evening concerts. The stand was under the huge elms in the garden of the Grand Union. Bejeweled ladies and white-tied men crowded the piazza and the cottages to listen. Farther away, where the shadows reached, would be even greater numbers of those who had neither jewels nor white ties."[18]

During the season Saratoga was flooded also by sportsmen, gamblers, and celebrities of the stage. The country's premier race track was here, and so was Canfield's famous casino. Herbert was no gambler, and his relationship with Canfield was, if anything, one of rivalry. His concerts drew as many people after the races as the gaming house. Occasionally he would place a bet at the races; but he was a poor judge of horses and almost invariably lost. His irritation was extreme and understandable. One of his great pleasures at Saratoga was to forgather with other men of note in the Grand Union café after his evening concert over a stein of Pilsner.[19] The talk would be lively, the company spirited—and Herbert's friends liked his personality as much as his music.

As Herbert prepared for his fifth season in Pittsburgh he received his final papers of American citizenship. He had so identified himself with the life of the country, had so frequently referred to himself as an American, that most persons thought he had long since achieved this status. However, it was on October 14, 1902, that he became a citizen of the United States—before Judge Joseph Buffington of the United States District Court, Western District of Pennsylvania.[20] Buffington, one of America's most eminent jurists, was deeply attached to Herbert and, when the composer finally decided to leave Pittsburgh, wrote him one of the rarest expressions of affection ever penned.

Long before the season opened, in September indeed, the conductor knew that conditions were changing in Pittsburgh, and not for the better. W. N. Frew, his critical but stanch supporter, was no longer chairman of the Orchestra Committee—in fact, he had ceased to be a member. H. C. Frick also had dropped off. The new chairman, on the committee for the first time, was J. B. Shea, and he began his tour of duty with a distinct hostility toward Herbert. He was a dollars-and-cents man, apparently convinced that expenditures in Pittsburgh alone were justifiable. It is doubtful if he knew the meaning of artistic endeavor.

The first display of animus was shown in considering the possibility of more concerts in New York. Herbert naturally wanted to play there again. He had presented to the metropolitan critics a highly commendable, if not perfect, orchestra, and every concert there was a broadening experience for himself and his men. Frew knew this and was in hearty sympathy with the idea. New York concerts were costly, however, and Andrew Carnegie had evidently not volunteered assistance. Was he waiting to be asked? In any case $6,000 was needed in addition to the desire for the concert.

Shea was not in favor of going to New York, and on September 19 he wrote Wilson his views. Not only did he use terms strongly antipathetic to Herbert, but he took measures to prevent any possibility of Herbert finding support from other committee members:

I have yours of the 16th. I am now, as I have been since I understood the matter, opposed to any New York concert this year. What Mr. Herbert says cuts no ice. The point is that we are not justified in spending $6,000.00 of the Guarantors money on any such outside affair. If Mr. Carnegie chooses to put up the six thousand I will be glad to authorize the trip, but *I* shall not ask Mr. Carnegie to do so. Furthermore *I* would consider it a lowering of self-respect of our Guarantors to ask Mr. Carnegie to give such sum to so many well off men. I wish you would see some others of the Committee— say Mr. Smith & Mr. McConway—& so forestall any effort Mr. Herbert might make to convince them of the correctness of his views. You can show this letter.

This letter was harsh, particularly in its resentment of the players' receiving any additional fees, but it accomplished its purpose. It was not publicized—and George Wilson was not inclined to side with Herbert. The remainder of Herbert's stay in Pittsburgh was not going to be pleasant.

In spite of inevitable misgivings Herbert opened his season on November 6, and the concerts proceeded with the usual success. After a month a new annoyance arose. The manager revealed that he was under instructions to effect new economies; he was also trying to pay all bills more promptly than a year ago. He so informed the conductor and added that the committee wanted to keep the expenses as low as possible.

He assured Herbert that his planning was not to be circumscribed, but he should think carefully before running the music bill too high.

A bright event occurred at the fourth pair of concerts (December 5, 6); but its real culmination was in the future, unsuspected by both conductor and audience. The soloist was a twenty-three-year-old Viennese soprano, uniquely vivacious and charming and beautiful, named Fritzi Scheff; she had been on the roster of the Metropolitan Opera Company since 1900, for which she sang leading rôles in such operas as *Fidelio, La Bohème, Don Giovanni, Le Nozze di Figaro, Die Zauberflöte, Carmen,* and *Faust,* even the shorter, lighter parts in Wagner's *Ring,* with conspicuous success. Unknowingly (?) she was waiting for the opportunity which would make her the toast of a continent and the queen of America's musical stage—of course in Victor Herbert's operettas. But in 1902 all this lay ahead, and with the Pittsburgh Orchestra she sang "Non so più cosa son" and "Voi, che sapete" (both from Mozart's *Le Nozze di Figaro*), a Cradle Song by Ries and a Serenade by Brahms.

Her vocal art, her dramatic ability, her archness and twinkling personality were not lost on the Pittsburgh critics. They succumbed completely. After the evening concert the *Dispatch* printed: "Miss Scheff in opera was one of the most fascinating soprani Mr. Grau ever brought here. On the concert stage she is not less brilliant and more attractive. In addition to the sweet purity of a soprano voice, rare in range and flexibility, she is a consummate actress." The writer for the *Times* recalled that she was "wildly encored," and that she was "in bright red with a feather boa that she used to advantage during her appearance on the stage." Even the serious Schlotterbeck of the *Post* could not resist her: "Little Fritzi Scheff, the ideal of simple, charming grace, yet almost ready, top-like, to spin, or, quicksilver-like, to elude the touch, is in many ways a wonder." And he was struck with her entrance, appearance, and demeanor.

As the season waxed and waned Herbert began to think once more in terms of operetta; but his thoughts at this time had no room for Fritzi Scheff. They were induced by the firm of Hamlin & Mitchell which agreed to produce a new work in Chicago during the summer of 1903. On Sunday March 1 he was visited by two men intimately connected with the enterprise, Julian Mitchell and Glen MacDonough, who was destined to be the librettist. Some years had passed since Herbert's last operatic venture, and if he returned to this field he wanted to do something ambitious and unprecedented. When asked to expound the matter he was still somewhat vague, but his response showed how seriously he viewed it.[21]

Thus was *Babes in Toyland* beginning to take shape and make more likely Herbert's departure from western Pennsylvania. On the other hand, it is doubtful that he had any premonition of how wholeheart-edly he would return to the theater. In addition to leading the sym-phony he was still composing "serious" music, and the first pair of concerts of 1903, on January 2 and 3, brought to first hearing another new suite: *Columbus*, Op. 35. (The opus number was the same as that attached to the *Auditorium Festival March*: probably he had decided that the smaller, earlier piece did not deserve such designation.)

Part of *Columbus* had been written ten years and more ago. The rest was newly composed in order to make a four-movement work of dignity and weight. The titles of the separate sections were Sunrise on Granada, At La Rabida (At the Convent), Murmurs of the Sea, Tri-umph. Once again the program book carried a special description written by Schlotterbeck:

The "Columbus" music performed to-day for the first time in its present form, recalls the World's Fair of 1893 at Chicago and the great Spectatorium planned by Steele Mackaye, for the presentation on unheard of scale of grandeur of the spectacle "Columbus, the World-Finder." Dr. Antonin Dvorak, in first instance, had been commissioned to write appropriate music, but a multiplicity of other duties preventing, Victor Herbert was entrusted with the important task, Anton Seidl commending him as the one composer equal to the occasion. Many months were devoted to the work of composi-tion, but the Mackaye enterprise proved too gigantic of realization and the music was never given hearing, at least not in its entirety. Two of the numbers so impressed Mr. Seidl that he programmed them repeatedly at the New York concerts of his famous orchestra, scoring flattering approval at each rendition. These two selections Mr. Herbert has taken for the first and last movements respectively of the "Columbus" suite, performed at to-day's concert, while for the second and third movements he has composed music entirely new.

. . . Purely descriptive and impressionistic are the first and third, while in the second and fourth the elements of determination and despair, so prominent in Columbus' struggles for recognition at the court of Spain, alternate and contend with the soothing voice of Hope as suggested by the stately choral of the church organ.

This was the last work of symphonic character Herbert was ever to write; like his similar productions, it is regrettably unknown today. It was an important score, for itself, for its subject matter, and for its origin with MacKaye and the World's Fair.

It was unfortunate that the season practically closed on a note of dissension. Herbert's friends and followers would be undisturbed by it, but a new and less than friendly Orchestra Committee was displeased. It was unhappy over rumors of dissatisfaction with the general character of programs the season had brought. This feeling was hardly justified by the compositions played. Ten of the standard symphonies were rendered, plenty of standard suites and overtures and symphonic poems, and a fine array of concertos and arias. Among the soloists were such established luminaries as Mme. Schumann-Heink, Lillian Blauvelt, Campanari, Witherspoon, Gabrilowitsch, Hambourg, Hugo Heermann, and E. H. Lemare.[22]

Manager Wilson also declared publicly that it was the best financial season the orchestra had enjoyed, that the patronage of out-of-town concerts was steadily increasing.[23] One significant fact emerges, however —the out-of-town concerts had alarmingly decreased to 29 from 45 the preceding year. It may well be that Herbert's independently sponsored spring tours were usurping some of the towns on the Orchestra Committee's schedule. This question was subsequently raised, though indirectly, and it was then too late to solve the problem in an amicable way.

Herbert's last season with the orchestra—his last full year as a full-fledged symphonic conductor, but far from his last appearance as such—was turbulent, gratifying, amusing, and annoying. He received great honors and great affection, was the victim of chicanery and double dealing, and witnessed operations which were stupid and deplorable. The comedy of human errors was seldom so fully exposed, even to the American visit of Richard Strauss whose advent completely disrupted the placid state of West Virginia.

One more glimpse of Herbert's unique temperament and personality as a conductor is afforded by the pianist Harold Bauer. This great artist, who died in 1951, gave me a remarkable statement on one of his solo appearances with Herbert in Pittsburgh. Penned on October 11, 1947, it reveals all Herbert's traits as a conductor, as a man, as a hater of fraud. Bauer's little sketch, indeed, is a masterpiece of characterization. The performance of the Tchaikovsky Concerto it refers to occurred in Pittsburgh on November 27 and 28, 1903:

My acquaintance with Victor Herbert was not intimate, but it was very cordial. I am sure I must have played with him at least half a dozen times, in Pittsburgh and in other cities when he was on tour with the orchestra. I dined at his house several times and I remember being impressed by the lavishness of his hospitality and the enormous quantities of food and drink that were served. It reminded me of a prosperous German household, the more particularly, perhaps, for the reason that he seemed to enjoy speaking German more than English, although on the other hand, nothing could be more natural than his occasional lapses into Irish, sometimes with lots of "brogue."

As a conductor, I should say that nobody ever gave me the impression of *understanding* the orchestra and the technique of each instrument more perfectly than did Victor Herbert. I don't remember that his interpretations ever seemed in the least subtle or refined, or even original. I think that on the rare occasions when he played music that was not sympathetic to him, he took very little trouble, and the result was dull. He liked music that was hearty and straightforward like himself, and he became terrifically excited with dramatic works. On one occasion (I believe in Pittsburgh) I was rehearsing the Tschaikowsky Concerto with him and he worked himself up to an almost uncontrollable frenzy of musical ardor with the result, since the piece was spinning along fluently, that the orchestra and the soloist became equally excited. Finally the pace and the fortissimo was too much for me. I felt that I was being completely submerged, and I roared for mercy. He did not hear me for some seconds, but at last my shouts of "Stop for God's sake," reached him. He was quite breathless when he asked me, almost indignantly, what was the matter. "Your tempo and your dynamics," I retorted. "I can't possibly cope with them." Herbert wiped his streaming face and said rather disappointedly: "Is that all? All right." Then, raising both his hands high in the air, he yelled at the orchestra: "Let her go, me bhoys!" and we were off again, just as before. The performance that evening was a huge success and my fingers were paralyzed and bleeding. This, of course, was over 30 years ago, and since then the Tschaikowsky concerto has been played faster and louder by many pianists. But up to that time I feel pretty sure that nobody had delivered it with the frantic excitement of Victor Herbert.

His Irish humor was very comical sometimes. I happened to be in Detroit when he came to lunch at Ossip Gabrilowitsch's home. Herbert entertained us all with his adventures on the orchestral tour he was then making, and spoke of the conductor of a local orchestra in one of the large cities he had passed through. He had attended one of the rehearsals. "The man certainly had an illegant baton," he said reflectively, "and it was a fair treat to watch his hands. Give it to me, gintlemen, he seemed to be saying all the time. Give it to me for the love of Christ. I don't know what I want, but do, do, do please give it to me!"

This anecdote makes one regret that Herbert never tried his hand at musical criticism. He would have punctured many an inflated ego.

A minor musical adventure happened to Herbert late in October of 1903. N. C. Goodwin revived in New York Shakespeare's *A Midsummer Night's Dream,* and he engaged Herbert to adapt Mendelssohn's incidental music for the production. It opened on October 26—inaugurating and dedicating the New Amsterdam Theatre—and was an immediate failure. The effects of stage and color were admittedly beautiful, but dances and songs and spectacular features had been inserted to such an extent that the production was condemned as a "circusing of Shakespeare."[24] The music, drawn chiefly from Mendelssohn's instrumental music as well as from his incidental pieces for the drama, found favor at once; but more than music is needed to keep Shakespeare alive. Herbert's efforts were gratefully noted, and they called forth the observation that they were worthy of a better cause.

The greatest honor which Herbert ever received as a symphonic conductor was unquestionably centered in the invitations he received to direct the New York Philharmonic Society. His début as leader of the celebrated orchestra occurred on January 29 and 30, 1904, at a time when it was having difficulty securing a permanent conductor. It was decided to have no one person conduct during the 1903–1904 season, but to have several world-famous leaders exhibit their prowess. (This method, as a matter of fact, prevailed for three seasons. Herbert was so successful on his first appearance that he was recalled for two pairs of concerts during 1905–1906: December 1 and 2 and March 2 and 3. The conductorship was finally awarded to Vassily Safonoff.) No outright competition for the post was announced, but it is rather obvious that such was the idea. The other conductors during 1903–1904 were Edouard Colonne, Gustav F. Kogel, Henry J. Wood, Felix Weingartner, Vassily Safonoff, and Richard Strauss.[25] A report was circulated to the effect that Herbert was a stopgap for Felix Mottl whose change of plans prevented his accepting an invitation. This was not true. Mottl was unable to accept, but the Philharmonic management wanted an American and Herbert was its choice. He was a selection who caused no regret.

Curiously enough, Manager Wilson seems to have initiated the trend toward Herbert. He was undoubtedly thinking of the prestige that would accrue to the Pittsburgh Orchestra, not acting from friendship for its conductor; in fact he was so eager to be rid of Herbert that he probably hoped the Philharmonic would take him permanently. In the early summer of 1903 Wilson was in Paris, where he talked with the influential New York impresario, Wolfsohn. The latter took action immediately, and Wilson informed his own committee. The committee, in a rather roundabout way, informed Herbert on July 3, 1903, that he might accept the invitation if extended, but warned him that he must not put the Pittsburgh Orchestra under any financial obligation. This meant that Herbert would have to pay for his own substitute at any Pittsburgh concerts missed.

The formal invitation was issued on August 19, 1903, by one of the Directors of the Philharmonic Society.

Dear Mr. Wilson:—

Referring to our previous correspondence and to your interview with Mr. E. Francis Hyde in Paris, I would say that it affords me great pleasure to extend to the Conductor of the Pittsburgh Orchestra, Mr. Victor Herbert, the Philharmonic Society's invitation to conduct the Society's Public Rehearsal and Concert on January 29 & 30, 1904. The acceptance of the invitation would involve Mr. Herbert's obligation to conduct three private rehearsals on the mornings of Jan. 26, 27 & 28. I should be extremely obliged to you, to let me know at your earliest convenience if Mr. Herbert is still free to accept on the above dates. In that case I shall, in compliance with your previous suggestion, apply directly to Mr. Herbert, formally offering the invitation and inquiring for his terms. With many thanks for your kind offices and the courtesy of the Orchestra Committee of the Pittsburgh Orchestra I am

Yours very sincerely

AUG. ROEBBELEN

Herbert was only too happy to accept, and the details were quickly worked out. A few bits culled from the New York *Sun* afford interesting reflections. On December 30 this notice appeared: "One of the oldest members of the Philharmonic retired because Victor Herbert and not he was invited to conduct the concert . . . There is so much feeling of this kind in the orchestra against Victor Herbert that he probably could not be called to the conductorship." Thus was it ever! Many a victim, too successful, has fallen prey to the jealousy of former colleagues. The same notice had an additional compensating feature—it revealed that Herbert was contributing his entire honorarium to the Philharmonic's pension fund.

The *Sun* also reminded its readers on January 24 that "It was only on the urgent request of the Executive Committee that he included one of his own compositions in the program." The audiences which heard Herbert, therefore, listened to the following works: Schubert, Symphony in B minor (the "Unfinished"); Liszt, Piano Concerto No. 2, in A major; Herbert, *Hero and Leander*, Op. 33; Dvořák, *Carnaval* Overture, Op. 92. The soloist was the brilliant pianist, Alfred Reisenauer, who was making his American début on this occasion.

There is no need to dwell on Herbert's performance. The reviews were eminently favorable, and his symphonic poem was more warmly appreciated than when the Pittsburgh Orchestra had played it.

The Pittsburgh press and public hailed the event as a new triumph for their fellow citizen. While Herbert was away from home he missed one pair of concerts and the soloist whom, above all others, he should have accompanied, the cellist Pablo Casals. Manager Wilson had encountered some difficulty in finding a substitute for Herbert. He tried to get Franz Kneisel and failed. He tried to get the Englishman Frederic Cowen, and failed. Finally he had to appeal for suggestions to Herbert, who wrote on September 28, 1903:

I note carefully what you say regarding the available conductors to substitute for me January 29–30. In this connection I should advise for consideration of the Orchestra Committee to invite Mr. Walter Damrosch.

I am sure Mr. Damrosch would conduct for me if he is not otherwise engaged, and in this country.

Damrosch did conduct for Herbert, with great success, and thereby made himself the leading candidate to follow Herbert at the head of the Pittsburgh Orchestra. But the Pittsburghers grossly mishandled the situation and lost the opportunity of engaging him.

The musical climax of the Pittsburgh season arrived on March 11 and 12 when Mr. and Mrs. Richard Strauss appeared with the orchestra —the former as composer and guest conductor, the latter as soloist in her husband's songs. (Just before the Pittsburgh concerts, the Strausses and the Orchestra were in Cleveland together.) A year earlier Herbert and Wilson had decided to bring the Strausses to Pittsburgh if possible. The three-month tour from February to April, 1904, was the great composer's first visit to America, and his fame as a radical innovator made him a much sought attraction. He was not to be had cheap, and the Orchestra Committee had to pay a fee of $1,500 for Richard and Pauline de Ahna Strauss together. The success in Pittsburgh was doubtless worth it, for the two audiences were delighted with the artists, and Strauss said the right thing to the right reporter: "The one mistake of this, my first American tour, is that I did not engage the unapproachable Pittsburg orchestra for every one of the concerts I was engaged to conduct, including those in Philadelphia, New York and Boston."[26]

The program of the Strauss-Herbert concert in Pittsburgh was:

Symphony No. 7	Beethoven
Songs with orchestra:	Strauss
Das Rosenband	
Morgen	
Cäcile	
Till Eulenspiegels lustige Streiche	Strauss
Songs with piano:	Strauss
Ein Obdach	
Traum durch die Dämmerung	
Heimliche Aufforderung	
Tod und Verklärung	Strauss

Herbert conducted the symphony to everyone's satisfaction and then retired from the program. Strauss conducted the rest of the evening and played the piano accompaniments for the second group of songs. On Saturday night March 12 the Strausses were dinner guests of the Herberts, and the two artists fortified themselves for the strenuous experience awaiting them in Morgantown, West Virginia, on March 14.

The West Virginia episode is hilarious because of the zealous, never-say-die spirit of an appealing "madman," dean of the school of music at West Virginia University, 1902–1904. He was Sydney Lloyd Wrightson, who was born in England in 1869 and died in Washington in 1922. In the nation's capital he founded, and for a decade was president of, the Washington College of Music.[27] He was a Richard Strauss idolater and managed to appear three times with the composer in 1904. He declaimed the text of *Enoch Arden* while Strauss played the keyboard accompaniment.

Wrightson wanted to bring Strauss to West Virginia—and he did, with a roar and a tumult heard far beyond the confines of the little college town. He engaged the Strausses early, in the summer of 1903, and then learned they were to be in Pittsburgh on March 11 and 12 of 1904. Why not have Herbert and the Pittsburgh Orchestra, too, and have a concentrated one-day festival? His letters to Wilson (preserved in the Pittsburgh Carnegie Library) are extraordinary effusions of zest, ambition, frustration, and rancor.

At first he had secured the Strausses for March 10, and on August 18, 1903, he wrote to Wilson of his intentions:

. . . I am going to make it the biggest musical event in West Virginia. Business men and banks will close at noon that day & I shall run special trains from Fairmount (South) and Uniontown (North).

What can I get the orchestra for, for the same evening? I'll arrange about Strauss conducting his own compositions, & I'd want a mixed program with Victor Herbert for the balance. I can sleep all your men in single beds . . . On Oct. 4th, 1902, you made me a proposition of $275 a night with Herbert, & I to pay expenses. Is this the best you can? Make me a proposition *for this night, you paying R.R. transportation* and I providing all the rest, meals, accommodations, advertising, etc. . . .

Send me the *best* you can do & if it's anywhere reasonable I'll sign the contract & cordially invite you to come down & see what we can do in half a day here.

P.S. My contract with Strauss is for the evening, but I can arrange it for the afternoon & have a double header.

Wrightson was quickly informed that March 10 was out of the question; nothing daunted he wrote again, on the 20th of August:

I am dead set on my Strauss plan & can bring it about, orchestra and all. I know the pulse of the musical people of this State better than anyone & want your first appearance here to be a "cracker jack." Can you give me the orchestra *March 14?* I am determined to make a big day & I want your immediate answer.

The weeks went by, and the orchestra date was made. On September 28 Wrightson informed Wilson he was coming to Pittsburgh with a very important Colonel Frazer. Wrightson, Frazer, Wilson, and Herbert simply had to dine together—there were so many things to discuss. As for the concert, "The Governor has consented to be present & I am stirring up a regular hornets nest in the State. This dinner means a *good deal* to me, but by no means misunderstand me, it is at *my* expense."

More weeks passed and Wrightson heard nothing from Pittsburgh. He complained he was being forgotten. Then on December 5 he sent a "bombshell" to the Orchestra office:

. . . Of course Mr. Herbert's resignation [just announced] will in no way interfere with his appearance here.

I have engaged Wm. Sherwood March 14th also. Strauss, Madame Strauss, Sherwood, Herbert & Pittsburg orchestra. What do you think of that? I want Sherwood to play a concerto with the orchestra in the evening. When can he practice with them for this? He has to play here in the afternoon.

Wilson obviously explained to the blundering Wrightson that Herbert detested Sherwood and would not countenance his playing with the Orchestra. The college dean testily replied on December 11:

I am sorry if I have made a mistake about Mr. Sherwood, but I am surely entitled to choose my own artists for a concert, & as Sherwood is a man of national reputation & has played several times with your orchestra I cannot see the objection to his doing so now. He recently gave a concert for me & made such a hit that one of my prominent & rich men instructed me to re-engage him, & he'd foot the bill. It's to my advantage to make Mch 14th as attractive as possible & I want to get in *all* I can.

The Pittsburgh office tried to be tactful as it remained firm on Sherwood, reasonably pointing out that no rehearsal time was available. But a minor matter of this sort would not trouble Mr. Wrightson. He wrote again on January 6, saying he would not start the concert until 8:45; the orchestra and Sherwood could rehearse in the hall from 7:30 to 8:15! But Sherwood was going to play, said Wrightson:

. . . Although I have no desire to be arbitrary I must request that my wishes regarding this matter shall be granted, as under any circumstances, whether Mr. Herbert wishes and desires it or not, Mr. Sherwood will appear sometime during the evening even if I have to prepare a special program during the intermission.

Sherwood did not play with the orchestra—but Wrightson's troubles were only beginning. His letter of February 22 disclosed a new dilemma, something rarely thought of in the propagation of music on the road:

The following is the position I am in. After working & *pleading* for accommodations at my two best hotels, lo & behold last week the grand jury *closed* up one for illegally selling liquor, as this is a prohibition town. In this hotel I had 28 beds engaged, in another 20 & in another 10. Can you imagine my feelings? I am doing all I am for the town, & no one but one or two appreciate it.

My violin teacher informs me that when travelling with the Boston Symphony Orchestra for over a year, often the men doubled up, & surely your men have been enough to-gether to know each other well enough to pair off at a pinch. It seems ridiculous to me, but after past experiences with you I feel how fruitless it is to appeal for any assistance. I shall meet the difficulty *somehow*. . . . *Never* will your orchestra play before a prouder, more unique, or appreciative audience. By the way, what is the *minimum* size of *stage necessary* to seat your seventy men?

Somehow difficulties were overcome as the concert day drew near. On March 4 Wrightson announced that the great Colonel Frazer himself would entertain Herbert. The orchestra men could change into their evening clothes in the college gymnasium and, if they wished, they could take a swim in the tank. Three days later the dean had taken in $1,796.50 in advance ticket sale, but not $25 had come from out of town. A platform was ready to seat ninety men.

The great day came and went, and two concerts took place—a song recital by Pauline Strauss in the afternoon, the orchestra concert at night. Schools, banks, and business closed, and the Governor kept his promise to attend. The State Cadets donned full uniform and acted as escort and guard of honor. Strauss received a key to the city and all the honors imagination could devise. A long account of the incredible affair appeared in the *Musical Courier* of March 23 (mentioning the Pittsburgh Orchestra, but not Victor Herbert). Strauss compared Morgantown with Bayreuth—to the detriment of the latter!—and praised the zeal of the festival's organizer, telling the townsfolk:

But Bayreuth has not as much material as Morgantown from which to construct a Mecca. Morgantown has immense enthusiasm, a sincere desire toward music, and an intelligent comprehension as to the relation of music to life. It has, too, infinitely more money than the German town, a beautiful location, and a world of country about from which to draw sympathy and audiences. But all this might be without the rara avis, the "leading spirit," suited by various qualities of head and heart and personality, to promote unusual endeavor. Such a person is Sydney Lloyd Wrightson, who has practically raised the plane of music in this section of country a decade in a couple of years. I do not speak of this affair, of course, as an ultimatum in progress, flattering as it is to myself, but of the extraordinary power of musical flame and intelligence and energy which have made such an affair possible under the circumstances.

So Wrightson had his moment of reflected glory as he promoted the art of the great German composer in America's hinterland.

The story of Herbert's departure from Pittsburgh and the sequence of events leading up to it bring out several important things: Wilson's divided sentiments, the Orchestra Committee's stubbornness, Herbert's willingness to compromise, and the unique affection which Herbert could inspire.

In the spring of 1903 the committee asked Herbert if he wished to continue as conductor after the following season. Still having one year under his contract, Herbert replied that he could not answer the question until fall. If he should stay, he said, he would want a salary of $10,000 a year; but he was not yet ready to have his name considered. In the fall of the same year he remained outwardly undecided;[28] but there is little doubt that his mind was made up. Then on November 26 he penned the following statement, with a covering note, to the new chairman of the Orchestra Committee, James I. Buchanan:

Dear Sir:—

In a conversation at Saratoga last August, with the manager of the Pittsburg Orchestra, I said that I could not afford to continue my connection with the Pittsburg Orchestra, with justice to myself and fair consideration of other demands upon my time unless the committee could see its way clear to pay me a straight salary of $10,000.

Since that time the demands of my profession have been so many and varied that I do not feel that I can afford to sacrifice them. I am therefore reluctantly compelled to ask the committee not to consider me as a possible conductor of the orchestra after the expiration of my present contract.

While taking this step I wish to assure the committee that it is based upon the broadest view I can take of my professional future, and not upon any small or local considerations. The difficulties I have met have been the ones usually inseparable from the task of establishing a new orchestra in a new place, and it has been a labor of great interest and pleasure to me to overcome those difficulties.

The pleasure of this labor has been due partly to the fine orchestra I have been able to organize and to conduct here, and partly to the loyal support of the music loving public of Pittsburg. In severing the relation which has existed for six years between myself and the Pittsburg Orchestra, I wish to express my hearty appreciation of everything that has been done by the committee, the public and the newspapers to make my stay here pleasant to myself, and, I sincerely hope helpful to the best interests of the orchestra, for the future success of which I most sincerely hope.

Very truly yours,
VICTOR HERBERT

Buchanan sent an immediate response which carried some faint glimmer of a possible settling of difficulties:

November 27th, 1903

Victor Herbert, Esq.,
No. 519 Aiken Avenue,
East End.

My dear Mr. Herbert:

I have your esteemed letter of the 26th inst. and regret to say that I have been confined to my house for a week past with a very severe cold and I have been unable to attend to business matters for some time. I will promptly refer your letters to the committee and I know that they will cause them a great deal of regret. I have made one or two ineffectual attempts to see you personally this season and will try again as soon as I am out, when we can talk the matter over to our mutual satisfaction.

Yours very truly
J. I. BUCHANAN

If the two men met and discussed the matter, they agreed only to part. On December 3 the following message was sent to the conductor:

My dear Sir:—

The Orchestra Committee of the Art Society beg to acknowledge your letter of November 26th, 1903, wherein you ask them not to consider you a possible Conductor of the Orchestra after the expiration of your present contract which terminates March 19th, 1904.

The Committee received this letter with regret and surprise as they were without intimation of your intentions in this respect. But your reasons for removing to New York at the end of the present Orchestra season in Pittsburgh are expressed in so sincere a manner that the Committee feel that your attitude is positively determined.

In reluctantly accepting the situation the Committee unanimously tender you their gratitude for the splendid work you have accomplished with the Pittsburgh Orchestra as a medium. You will always be remembered in Pittsburgh as the principal factor in a campaign for music education covering a pivotal six years.

During this time the appreciation by the community of music as an art form has largely increased and the musical standard has been greatly advanced. This is largely because of the wisdom shown in the selection of your programs, the zeal and enthusiasm of your interpretations of both classic and modern masters, and the unprecedented loyalty of the players to you as their Conductor, which is but a reflection of your own earnestness and devotion to the art you serve.

In leaving Pittsburgh you will create a void difficult to fill,—a task towards the accomplishment of which the Committee have of course taken no steps. Wherever your future may lead you will take with you the goodwill of ourselves and that also of the entire cultivated public of this community, and all the success you are sure to achieve in the future will be shared by us and them.

We are, dear Mr. Herbert, for the Orchestra Committee of the Art Society

EDWIN Z. SMITH, President, The Art Society.

JAMES I. BUCHANAN, Chairman, Orchestra Committee of the Art Society.

Faced with the realization of losing Herbert, the signers were no doubt largely sincere in voicing their feelings; yet their message contained some inaccuracies. The reference to the wisdom of the programs ignored the fact that the guarantors were grumbling. One of these wrote to a colleague that he had not enjoyed the concerts either this season or last: the music Herbert was "dishing up to us" was not acceptable; it might be high class, but it was never pleasing.[29] (Evidently Herbert's programs were still too rigorous for the cultured steel barons!) And Buchanan himself had been willing to look for Herbert's successor as early as last summer, when he heard that the conductor might not remain a seventh year.[30] The committee was scarcely "without intimation" of Herbert's decision.

In one respect, however, the writers of the letter understated the case: the loyalty of Herbert's men. The players were thunderstruck by their leader's action, and they pleaded with him to change his mind. After weeks of consideration they sent a formal-personal statement while they were on tour which speaks for itself:

Hamilton, Ont.   Feb. 15th. 1904

To Victor Herbert, Esq.

  Conductor of the Pittsburg Orchestra

Sir:—

Since the announcement was made by you that you would at the close of the season resign your position as Conductor of The Pittsburg Orchestra, you must have heard on every side expressions of the great regret which that resignation caused. No matter how great or sincere those regrets might be on the part of the guarantors or the Management or the great public of Pittsburg, they would be small in comparison with the regrets of the individual members of the Orchestra.

During the years of our connection in which you have raised the organization to the position it now holds in the musical world, the members have come more and more to reverence and admire you as a large hearted whole souled man. To us one and all it would be a deep personal loss to have no more your guiding and directing genius and grateful personality. Further than this when we think of the wonderful artistic successes which you have enabled us to achieve, we feel as artists, that it would be nothing short of a calamity if by your withdrawal the efficiency of our organization, gained at so hard labor should be impaired.

Would it not be possible for you to reconsider your decision? If you would only do so it would be a cause for heartfelt gratitude to every one of us. We would rejoice to look forward to years of work with you, under the happy relations that have always existed between us, and with the high ideals in view which you have always impressed upon us.

Will you not take into your thought this earnest and united appeal from us, and if possible withdraw your so much regretted resignation?

Signed on behalf of the members of the
Pittsburg Orchestra.

The musicians were not satisfied with this. On the same day they sent the following:

To The Music Committee
  of The Pittsburg Art Society.
Gentlemen:—

Ever since the announcement of Mr. Victor Herbert's resignation was made, there has been a steadily growing feeling of regret among the members of the Orchestra, and increasing desire that if possible he should be induced to remain in Pittsburg as Conductor of the Orchestra. Especially has this been borne in upon us during our present tour by reason of the magnificent artistic successes which the Orchestra has been achieving under his direction. Your Committee know well the personal affection and esteem felt by the individual members of the Orchestra for our Conductor and even on this ground alone we would desire to have him stay with us,—but we feel that it is on the artistic side of the matter that there would be cause for even greater regret. By his genius and industry Mr. Herbert has raised the Orchestra to a state of efficiency which is everywhere openly spoken of as the very highest. His withdrawal from Pittsburg might involve some changes, possibly more than a few, in the personnel of the Orchestra, and a consequent impairment of its efficiency. It seems to us a pity that if possible this shall be allowed to happen. So strongly do we feel that we have ventured to address to Mr. Herbert a letter expressing the unanimous desire of the Orchestra that he reconsider his decision and a copy of our letter is enclosed herewith.

We would with all respect ask your Committee to aid us in our appeal to Mr. Herbert, and to join with us in requesting him to reconsider the matter of his resignation.

In the hope that you may approve of the course which we have taken and may give us all the assistance which you can,

We are,
Yours respectfully,
Signed in behalf of the members of The Pittsburg Orchestra,
PAUL HENNEBERG   HENRI MERCK
HENRY BURCK

It is impossible to exaggerate the importance of these two letters as testimonials to Herbert's influence, personality, and leadership. That they failed to achieve their purpose is beside the point. They may be without precedent in the history of orchestra conducting. How many conductors of today, or yesterday, can claim over their men the hold which Herbert exerted over his?

In this connection there is an unauthenticated anecdote, probably apocryphal, which Herbert admirers would like to believe in principle if not in detail. After a strenuous rehearsal Herbert and some of his players strolled across the street to the Schenley Hotel for a glass of beer. A socialite backer of the Orchestra chanced to pass, witnessed the conviviality and reproached the conductor. He told Herbert that fraternizing with his players was beneath the social position the conductor should maintain. Herbert was instantly furious and exclaimed: "I'd rather be seen with them than with you!" Then he resigned forthwith.[31]

Quite different, but equally warm and deep, was a tribute dated December 4, just as Herbert heard from the Orchestra Committee. It came spontaneously from Judge Buffington, who had welcomed the conductor to American citizenship. The discerning jurist, who died in 1947 at the age of ninety-two—after forty-six distinguished years on the Federal bench—was a profound admirer of Herbert as man and artist, and a special eloquence winged his words:

My dear friend:
I cannot get down to work this morning until I have unburdened myself. We are to lose you. My head says you are right but my heart wants something else. As I have grown to know you better and better and realized what you were I have been drawn to you, my dear Herbert, in a way that men are not often drawn in mature life. My little "drop ins" for your companionship in walks was showing me how much I found in you that I wanted. Last night when I came past your place at twelve o'clock and saw your light I could not resist the inclination to give a boyish "too whoot" hoping it might draw you to the window and I might have some excuse for dropping in at that unseasonable hour and spending some time with you. I only speak of these little things as straws to show how much I found that was congenial and companionable in your good self. Now that you are going away I feel that I have let slip what to me was really the foundation for a really deep seated friendship—I only write this to say how sorry and really pained I am you are going.
Our thoughts and interest will go with you. You have done a great work here. How much your heart was in it and how deep a work you were doing was I think not appreciated. But are you alone in that? All really deep natures are in a measure alone in aspiration, hope and work. I am sorry to see you go in that I feel I will be out of touch with you. I have felt you were broadening and deepening in a way you did not yourself suspect.

Successful as your work has been I cannot but feel you have a reverence and aspirations within you that you do not realize and that as these features find vent you will reach heights of development you do not suspect. Art is the attainment of reality and therefore of truth: truth is truth because it is of God and I can conceive of no great artist who is not in time and accord with the great master and creator of harmony, the eternal, invisible, unheard harmonies to which some day our ears will be opened when we shall see Him and know Him as HE is. If this note conveys to you the feeling and assurance that while I feel you ought to go, my heart is really pained you should, it will have served its mission.

Your friend
Jos. Buffington

To Victor Herbert
Personal[32]

Herbert's withdrawal of his candidacy was reported in the Pittsburgh papers of December 4. There was immediately vast consternation, but the full realization of loss was not yet apparent. The *Dispatch* sought Herbert out and persuaded him to make a statement:

I have been desirous of retiring from the orchestra for some time past and have only remained as long as I have as a matter of sentiment, and to the detriment of my business interests. It is a pretty hard matter to conduct an orchestra like the one we have here in Pittsburg, keep the men in hand, write operas and look after the production of them. In fact, my duties have been so arduous that I found that I would soon be a physical wreck if I did not relinquish some of them, and I decided to leave the orchestra, as the work of writing and producing plays is more congenial to me.

At the present time I am engaged on three new operas . . . Two of my operas are running on Broadway, "Babette," with Fritzi Scheff as the star, and "Babes in Toyland." I am encouraged by the fact that they are two of the great successes of the season in New York. I think that it would be unfair to myself to remain in Pittsburg longer than the present season, as I believe that the field of my labor lies in the metropolis.

I have received the very best of treatment at the hands of Pittsburgers. It is with the deepest regret that I leave here, but I feel that I cannot further sacrifice my own interests. But I shall never forget Pittsburgh for the kind treatment I have received.

The Pittsburgh *Times* of that date, in announcing Herbert's resignation, bluntly referred to his disagreements with the manager, G. H. Wilson; it explained that Herbert's salary was $3,000 a year, that fees for out-of-town concerts raised this to between $6,000 and $7,500, that the conductor and Wilson were less than friendly to each other. It suggested that the manager neglected opportunities for more out-of-town concerts, with a consequent financial loss to the conductor. With respect to Wilson it remarked: "For weeks the manager . . . who knew as early as last August that Herbert intended to resign, has been saying that the orchestra was in a dilemma and that this was the critical season."

The implication was obvious, so obvious that Wilson was aggrieved and unwisely wrote to the editor:

Again, in my opinion, have the columns of The Times been used to hurt me personally. The article in your paper of December 4 regarding Mr. Herbert's removal to New York contained such references to the manager of the orchestra as would indicate a personal motive. The attack on me I do not care about only as any self-respecting person deplores the fact that he has an enemy; I do regret exceedingly the injury to the orchestra cause that must result.

The misstatements, therefore, that are possible at present in The Times because of the privileges of at least one individual in its columns, make me decide not to send your paper any information regarding myself or my plans that under natural circumstances I would send to all the newspapers.

You would do the same yourself if you were hit a blow from behind, your opponent being invisible.[33]

The editor replied at once, and easily, to Wilson's foolish outburst. He declared simply that the article referred to "was an accurate recital of facts which persons clearly familiar with the affairs of the orchestra have pronounced a fair and impartial statement." He said further that only Wilson had tried to inject a personal element into the situation, and he surprisingly disclosed that Wilson had "made a vain effort to have a reporter for The Times suppress one of the most important parts of Victor Herbert's letter to the orchestra committee." He closed with the assurance that "The Times will continue to publish the ungarbled news, which might not be the case if the information came from G. H. Wilson."

The manager, it must be admitted, had developed a real disdain for Herbert; but he tried to keep it concealed. Occasionally, however, he yielded to impulse, as when he wrote to Carlo Fischer of Cincinnati, on December 14: "Herbert has withdrawn his name as a candidate for the Conductorship of the Orchestra after this season as he wants to be a Bohemian only. The Rialto and the Lambs Club will now cover him up." This was not meant to be flattering.

Wilson's note gave no indication of Herbert's successor, but speculation was rife as to who it might be. The name of Walter Damrosch was bandied about, and reporters in New York approached him only to learn that he had heard nothing from the Pittsburgh committee. An article in the Pittsburgh *Dispatch* advanced the names of Damrosch and Emil Paur as possibilities, calling attention to the very reasonable salary figure Herbert had mentioned: Theodore Thomas in Chicago was receiving $15,000 a year; in Boston, Gericke's salary was $18,000; Nikisch had turned down the New York Philharmonic post because he demanded a salary of $25,000 plus a bonus of $100,000.[34] The inference was clear.

Because of Herbert's renewed interest in the theater, rumors circulated to the effect that he was totally giving up conducting. He quickly stopped such reports by declaring his intention to maintain an orchestra in New York which should be second to none, and to continue his spring and summer engagements as usual. His orchestra would have a New York office (William B. Clayton in charge) beginning March 20, 1904.[35]

And what of the Pittsburgh Orchestra? Financially the 1903–1904 season was not good; but this condition was nation-wide. The committee had two problems to solve concurrently: securing guarantees for the future, and selecting a new conductor. No money meant no orchestra; but no conductor was apt to mean no money. Names considered were Henry J. Wood, Alfred Hertz, Emil Paur, and—Walter Damrosch. Damrosch seemed the most promising, and he was conducting in Pittsburgh while Herbert led the Philharmonic in New York. Perhaps something could be worked out with him. On January 15 Manager Wilson wrote to Damrosch explaining that Pittsburgh was recovering from a business paralysis, and money was hard to obtain; but the committee was trying to secure $35,000 for a one-year guarantee. Would Damrosch be willing to come for one year with the understanding that he would be wanted for two more if the financing was successful? He wrote again the next day in the same vein, reporting a conversation with four committee members. It was not an offer, but the next thing to it.

On January 15 also Wilson wrote a most peculiar letter to W. N. Frew which belittled Damrosch and practically slandered Herbert. He began by saying that nothing could be done until after Damrosch's appearance on January 29 and 30. Damrosch was known to be available, and the public reaction to him should be closely watched. Finding Herbert's successor was no easy task. A foreigner would be difficult: his traditions would be different and so would his programs. Herbert's programs, "which I have come to think are so admirably fitted for the purpose," left little to be desired. The manager wanted a better conductor than Damrosch, but none was available. Evidently Damrosch was superior to Herbert in one respect only: his personal qualities "would make him welcome in the best houses in Pittsburgh (which is not the case with the present Conductor), and this you will admit would mean much to the Orchestra." This sentiment contrasts strangely with Judge Buffington's fond farewell.

Damrosch conducted as planned, and the public gave him a cordial reception. On January 30 the Orchestra Committee tendered him a banquet at the Union Club at which details and possibilities were discussed at length. The affair was reported in the next day's papers, but Chairman Buchanan stated that no definite offer had been made—it could not be until the guarantee fund was assured.[36]

Negotiations with Damrosch fell through, and the handsome German never went to Pittsburgh. The Pittsburgh public thereupon seized a chance to agitate for the retention of Herbert. The attempt began about the middle of February, and in a short time practically all the Pittsburgh papers were demanding that ways should be found to keep Herbert from leaving. It was a valiant effort, which might have been successful; but the Orchestra Committee was divided, and G. H. Wilson, obviously in a position to influence opinion, was opposed.

Herbert's friend Schlotterbeck, of the *Post,* took the initiative in a long article published on February 14. Franker than he had been in past writings he admitted that Herbert was not perfect and had a violent temper; still, the conductor was a man who "LOVES HIS WORK," a real distinction among artists, and his achievements with the orchestra had been astonishing. The writer also pointed out a great weakness in the local situation. "And the orchestra committee might do worse than arrange a conference with Victor Herbert for friendly consultation on ways and means toward arousing a more widespread interest in orchestra music in this city. If there has been one drawback to success more serious than another it is the utter absence of these heart to heart talks with the conductor." If this was true (there is no reason to doubt it), it is amazing. That the conductor should be excluded from discussions pertaining to the orchestra's very existence is an incredible situation. The other papers followed Schlotterbeck's lead, and for several weeks the call to draft Herbert was loud and insistent. Herbert all the while maintained a dignified silence.

The clamor had some effect, however, and on March 16 the Orchestra Committee drew up a set of conditions to which Herbert should accede if he were to remain in Pittsburgh:

1. Standard of programs at out-of-town concerts to be as high as those of Pittsburgh. Very few encores at out-of-town concerts.

2. No use of Pittsburgh Orchestra name on so-called "Spring Tours," or anywhere outside the control of the Committee.

3. No competition for business between the "Spring Tour" management and the management of the Regular Season: the Regular Season management to say what field or cities it will not visit in a given season. Conductor to exercise control of all encores of singers.

4. While the Committee welcome occasionally compositions by its Conductor it does not approve of the general use of his compositions, in either the home programs or those abroad.

5. The Committee require fewer if any encores by the Orchestra.

6. The Committee to exercise supervision over all musical matters whenever in their opinion it becomes necessary.

Point No. 6 was totally unacceptable to any conscientious musician. Point No. 4 was insulting and unnecessary. Herbert was remarkably chary in the use of his own music on regular symphonic programs, both in and out of Pittsburgh; only his more popular programs were studded with his own selections. The people loved them—and still do. The other points were reasonable.

On March 25 Herbert countered with a list of conditions to be fulfilled if he stayed in Pittsburgh:

1. Mr. Herbert would require the present manager to be superseded by another satisfactory to both the Committee and himself.

2. Salary to be fixed as $10,000 for the season to consist of twenty weeks and prorata for extra of four or five weeks.

3. The right to engage players for twenty-five weeks instead of twenty weeks.

4. The use of the name "Pittsburgh Orchestra" to be entirely under the control of the Committee.

5. Standard of out-of-town concerts must be left to the judgment of the Conductor.

6. Will agree that there shall be no competition for business between the "Spring Tour" management and the management of the regular season. The lowest price for the orchestra to be fixed by the Committee. The regular management to say what fields or cities it will not visit in a given season. The conductor will exercise control of all encores of soloists when made part of contracts with soloists.

7. The Conductor will welcome frequent meetings with the Committee to discuss plans to enlarge the money making scope of the orchestra and other features, but reserves the right to settle all artistic questions.

Sensible as this presentation was, the Orchestra Committee rejected it; and on March 26 Herbert was informed accordingly. The final word from the committee assured the conductor that his great service to the city was deeply appreciated; they also regretted that "circumstances have necessitated the severance of your relation to the Orchestra."

All this time the orchestra management was trying to find a permanent conductor. Communication was established with Emil Paur in Vienna, who was widely known in America from his service at the head of the Boston Symphony, 1893–1898. As early as March 10 Wilson wrote to Paur one of his malicious denunciations of Herbert, explaining that no offer could yet be made because the guarantee fund was not yet secure, but that Paur was the most likely candidate. He also said that the friends of Herbert were trying to hold on to the genial Irishman, who was not man enough to step aside. Herbert had no chance at all, thought Wilson, for the committee did not want him. And then: "If he is reelected I leave Pittsburgh as he is too low a man in character for me to continue even an official connection with." Paur was soon chosen as conductor and received a three-year contract with an annual salary of $10,000. The announcement was made late in March.[37]

Wilson anticipated a happy future; but his pleasure was short-lived, and vanished in a sudden flowering of poetic justice. It is true that Paur, more than any one individual, ruined the Pittsburgh Orchestra which staggered through the 1909–1910 season and then collapsed. Wilson died on March 18, 1908—but he knew the end of the orchestra was coming. He had resigned as manager on December 24, 1906, taking this step in order to keep his self-respect. Why? The new conductor was responsible. Wilson's letter to Chairman Buchanan asserted that the twelve best years of his life had been devoted to the orchestra, his pride and pleasure in it

have all constrained me during the past two years to bear with the personal idiosyncrasies, the superficiality of his musical faith, the narrowness of his musical horizon, the indifference to the success of the out-of-town concerts, the hazard (to Orchestra business) of an uncontrolled temper, the frequent distrust of my motives, and the peculiar and ever-shifting focus of the stupidity, of the present conductor . . . these things are characteristic of the man, not passing symptoms.

Can there be any doubt that Wilson often longed for the past when the orchestra had been directed by the "low" Herbert?

12

Toyland and Vicinity

THERE was no uncertainty or indecision about Herbert's return to the stage. He threw himself into the venture with wholehearted zeal, determined to outdo all his previous efforts. He announced his intentions to the Pittsburgh press in the spring of 1903, and the eventual results proved the lack of any exaggeration. With *Babes in Toyland* he scored one of his greatest triumphs—and America gained one of her happiest products.

In January of 1903 Fred R. Hamlin and Julian Mitchell produced in New York a musical play entitled *The Wizard of Oz* (music by Paul Tietjens and A. Baldwin Sloane). It was derived from the immortal book by L. Frank Baum; and in this respect it had an advantage over any of Herbert's shows. It was tremendously successful, and the producers were at once eager to try their luck with something similar. The music of *The Wizard of Oz* was not outstanding, but the book and the spectacle were. If the right composer could be found, the next achievement might be incalculable. The producers approached Herbert and won his collaboration; Glen MacDonough wrote the libretto, which was largely meaningless; and Julian Mitchell personally supervised the staging. The latter, who developed a marvelous skill in scenic effects and imaginative action, was a wizard of stagecraft;[1] and in *Babes in Toyland* he was in his element.

Arrangements for the work were quickly completed, and the public knew, early in the spring, its title and general character. It was to be a spectacular extravaganza[2]—which could only mean that fancy, *bizarrerie, grotesquerie,* unimpeded by plot or logic, would be the dominant elements. Max Hirschfeld, a reliable conductor, was appointed musical director at Herbert's request,[3] and Chicago was to be privileged with the first performance on any stage. *The Wizard of Oz* was prospering in New York, and *Babes in Toyland* was to be ready as its successor.

Rehearsals began in New York in May, although some of the music was not yet finished: the date June 9, 1903, appears in the composer's hand at the end of a most important instrumental section in the autograph score.[4] At the end of the month Julian Mitchell took the entire company of one hundred and twenty-three to Chicago,[5] where intensive work led to the première in the Grand Opera House on June 17.

The critics in Chicago raved over the new production. It was the most costly and most magnificent thing ever seen there. It had life and color, beautiful girls in handsome dress, excellent music, a splendid chorus, wonderful stage pictures and magnificent scenery. It was more gorgeous than *The Wizard of Oz*, at that time the criterion of scenic display.

Herbert was gratified with reports from the inland city; but not until the fourth week did he have a real opportunity to improve the performance. In Chicago that week he conducted several times,[6] and seems to have marked his score with directions for his friend Hirschfeld. It is well known that Herbert could obtain effects from his own music which were the despair of other conductors. He, and he alone, knew what he wanted and how to extract from his players the type of response which would vitalize the music—sometimes faster, sometimes slower. In his original manuscript he wrote repeated directions for Hirschfeld, who was obviously racing some of the phrases too fast. For instance: "Bitte! *etwas langsamer!* mein lieber Hirschfeld!" and again: "Bitte, bitte, etwas mässiger in Tempo, sonst kann es *nicht* piquant klingen." Also for the conductor he indicated how two of the instruments were to be played: "Die Cornets absolut ppp!" and "Violas deutlich nachschlagen! und sehr kurz!"[7]

Successful from the start, *Babes in Toyland* still yielded to adjustments, revisions, and curtailments which increased its general effectiveness. Each week saw a steady improvement. When it left Chicago one enthusiast wrote that it would "be such a vision of beauty and such a finished example of high art in extravaganza" that all New York would bow before it.[8]

Having left this happy impression in its wake, *Babes in Toyland* opened in New York at the Majestic Theatre on October 13, 1903, with the following cast:

Alan, nephew of Barnaby................William Norris
Jane, Barnaby's niece.....................Mabel Barrison
Uncle Barnaby, a rich miser, in love with
   Contrary Mary.....................George W. Denham

The Widow Piper, a lonely widow with
  fourteen children.........................Hattie Delaro
Contrary Mary, the Widow Piper's eldest daughter..Amy Ricard
Tom Tom, her eldest son...................Bessie Wynn
Jill, who helps Jack..........................Nellie Daly
Bo-Peep, who is a careless shepherdess..........Nella Webb
Red Riding Hood, who is devoted to her
  grandmother.............................Susie Kelleher
Sallie Waters, who wants to get married........Mary Welsh
*Curly Locks, who wants to wed a title..........Elizabeth Roth
Miss Muffet, who is afraid of spiders..........Irene Cromwell
Simple Simon, who is fond of fairs............Virginia Foltz
*Peter, who has a passion for pumpkin pie.....Bertha Krieghoff
Tommy Tucker, who sings for his supper and
  everything else..........................Doris Mitchell
*Jack, who does chores......................Mae Naudain
*Boy Blue, who wants to be a farmer.......Stella Beardsley
Bobby Shaftoe, who wants to be a sailor......Myrtle McGrain
*Roderigo, a sentimental ruffian................Frank Hayes
Gonzorgo, his hard-hearted partner.............Charles Barry
Hilda, maid-of-all-work in the Piper household..Hulda Halvers
Gertrude, who knows the legend...............Frances Marie
*The Master Toymaker, who designs the toys of
  the world...............................Dore Davidson
Grumio, apprentice at the Master Toymaker's
  workshop...............................Charles Guyer
Inspector Marmaduke, of the Toyland police.......Gus Pixley
Max, the Toymaker's apprentice.........Margaret Sutherland
The Brown Bear.........................Walter Schrode
The Sun Queen..........................Georgia Baron
The Spirit of Maple..................Margaret Sutherland
The Spirit of Oak..........................Mae Naudain
The Spirit of Pine.....................Katherine Howland
The Spirit of Willow......................Mabel Frenyear
The Moth Queen.......................Albertina Benson
Mima.......................................Grace Field
The Volcano Queen......................Minnie Murray
The Giant Spider..........................Robert Burns

In addition to this remarkably long cast—not all of whom sang, fortunately—there was a stunning array of decorative personages: butter-
flies, dandies, flower girls, French dolls, Dutch dolls, "Punches," toy

* In Chicago, other actors had played the roles marked with an asterisk, as
follows: Curly Locks, Belle Robinson; Peter, Edith Browning; Jack, Catherine
Flynn; Boy Blue, Bertha Krieghoff; Roderigo, Elmer Tenley; The Master Toymaker, Mark Smith.

soldiers, trumpeters, drummers, widows, and justices. The New York program called the work "an original musical extravaganza in a Prologue and Three Acts," described as follows:

Prologue: Scene 1, exterior of Uncle Barnaby's house; Scene 2, electrical storm at sea and wreck of the "Galleon."

Act I: Scene 1, country fête in Contrary Mary's garden; Scene 2, garden wall back of the garden; Scene 3, the Spider's forest; Scene 4, the floral palace of the Moth Queen.

Act II: Scene 1, the Christmas Tree Grove in Toyland; Scene 2, a street in Toyland; Scene 3, the Master Toymaker's workshop; Scene 4, exterior of the Master Toymaker's castle.

Act III: the courtyard of the Toyland Palace of Justice.

The synopsis of scenes clearly shows two things: the opportunity given to the composer for descriptive, fanciful music; a series of glittering locales with an appeal to viewers of all ages. A toymaker and his minions, the best loved characters from Mother Goose, fairy spirits, villains, and ordinary people—these were the ingredients that went into the extravagant fantasy. For the librettist the mixture, ending in an unreasonable riot of kaleidoscopic color, was really too rich; for the composer it was a stimulant to captivating sounds that would induce joyfulness beyond the power of words. The plot was negligible, but it sufficed as a thread on which were strung in wondrous succession musical pieces long and short, wistful and saucy, lyric and dramatic.

The Prologue[9] exhibited wordless action on the stage and music equivalent to a symphonic poem. Jane and Alan survive a shipwreck, in which their miserly uncle hopes they will die. They find their way to the garden of Contrary Mary, meet various Mother Goose characters, invade Toyland where a wicked Toymaker is unusually cruel, and finally circumvent the evil designs of the uncle. Happiness awaits them after all their troubles.

From the very opening to the end the pageantry of the stage and the color of the situations afforded Herbert more than ample inspiration for his best and most characteristic music. It could be artfully simple, as in "Never Mind, Bo-Peep," or piquantly gypsyesque, as in Alan's "Floretta." It could appeal to children of all ages, as when Jane complains "I Can't Do the Sum" (not part of the show as originally planned), or it could flaunt the flavor of Ireland, as when Mary fancies herself in love with "Barney O'Flynn." The orchestra enhanced the sweetness of the lullaby, "Go to Sleep, Slumber Deep," and then elaborated the delicacy of the butterfly ballet.

The music for the Christmas Tree Grove pulsated with life and gayety, and Gertrude's "The Legend of the Castle," the most ambitious number of the play, showed anew Herbert's genius for tone color and contrast. "The March of the Toys," pungent and brassy, quickly became immortal, but the ingenious music for the military ball remains practically unknown. There were so many opportunities, of course, for Herbert to splash his colors and his rhythms that a reexamination of the score today brings much of the satisfaction of a fresh discovery.

The plot did not bother the public, which was enraptured by the spectacles and the music. Perhaps the best over-all criticism was voiced on October 24 by the *Dramatic Mirror,* which was quite overcome by the whole production. It also recognized the book as the one weakness, charitably saying that the spoken dialogue was rather tiresome. The costumes defied description, the stage pictures were dazzling, the handsome girls "in one continual, bewildering succession of movements, dazzlingly attractive and immensely pleasing." Each new scene surpassed the preceding one, and the assembly of toys in Act II was wonderful. The music was warmly spoken of, and most of the cast were praised for their clever, spirited, and charming performance. The soundest compliment of all was: "It will prove a perfect dream of delight to the children, and will recall the happy days of childhood to those who are facing the stern realities of life."

The theatrical journals were conventionally pleased with everything, but the daily press seemed more appreciative of the music. The newspaper critics at last had something they liked, and they were not hesitant in voicing their satisfaction. Among the happiest critics were Henry Finck and J. G. Huneker, both of whom were fearful that Herbert's symphonic career might interrupt his writing for the stage. When *Babes in Toyland* bowed to New York, their relief can easily be imagined. Finck, in the *Evening Post* found the show brilliant, yet an hour too long. It would be difficult to make cuts, however, for where could the concocters begin? "Certainly not in the music, for there is really nothing that can be spared. Mr. Herbert has come back to theatrical composition after a rest which has been beneficial, and in song and ensemble he has added greatly to his reputation. Every bar is melodious, while some of the incidental and melodramatic music betrays Mr. Herbert's position among the leading American composers."

The zest and spontaneity of the show were duplicated in Huneker's review in the *Sun.* Here was a critic who enjoyed what he saw—and heard. "But the songs, the dances, the processions, the fairies, the toys, the spiders and the bears! Think of them all, set in the midst of really amazing scenery, ingenious and brilliant, surrounded with light effects which counterfeit all sorts of things from simple lightning to the spinning of a great spider's web, with showy women and costumes which show them, costumes rich and dazzling as well as tasteful, and all accompanied with music a hundred times better than is customary in shows of this sort. What more could the spirit of mortal desire?"

An agent of the staid *Tribune* came back twice to *Babes in Toyland,* dwelling upon its features which might escape a more hurried observer. The first criticism, short but wholly favorable, called the music "charming and appropriate"—"musician's music that does not pain by obvious orchestration, that is dainty and poetic at occasion or ambitious for a chorus, or tuneful, brisk and merry, as Toyland music ought to be." The following Sunday, however, he raised a question which belonged in the realm of psychology: Was not a wicked Toymaker harmful to children? No other character could appeal so to little folks, yet here he became evil and destructive, and his downfall carried terror and brutality. The smaller children were frightened; the older ones, deeply pained. Here is exactly the same spirit of criticism which, in a later time, has rebuked Walt Disney for making some of his wicked creatures more frightful than the innocent young should see.

The music critic of the *Tribune,* pondering the musical values of the score, gave vent to no such feelings. Six days after the New York première he issued an appreciation that still applies to Herbert's notable work:

Mr. Herbert has taken advantage of all the episodes which have a poetical mood to write poetical music; of the picturesque scenes to write picturesque music; of the sentimental scenes to write sentimental music, and of the humorous scenes to write music which is bright and catchy and full of quaint conceit. Always he remains the musician, respectful toward his art, even when it has no more dignified purpose than to keep the feet of marchers and dancers in motion. The march of the toy soldiers is a capital piece, and its Norse color, with just a suggestion of the grotesque, harmonizes charmingly with the scene, while the ballet which follows with its sounds from Toyland—tiny cymbals clashing, drums stiffly beating, puny trumpets blowing and stiff armed fiddlers sawing across the open strings of their instruments—is as dainty a notion as one could wish. Of course the scene is one that was bound to appeal to Mr. Herbert, as similar scenes have appealed to excellent musicians before—Adolphe Adam, Delibes and Offenbach, for instance. There is excellent fooling, obvious even to the musically illiterate, in his parodies on the styles of Sousa and Verdi [i.e., Donizetti] in the setting of "Rock-a-bye, Baby," and many pretty effects of instrumentation in the ambitious "Legend of the Castle" and the music which introduces the highly unnecessary prologue. After the intolerable stuff which weighed down "The Wizard of Oz," this music of Mr. Herbert's, on which the play floats buoyantly as a cork, is a blessed relief to the lovers of extravaganza.

Babes in Toyland had a New York run of 192 performances, then took to the road where it was enormously popular, several companies traveling several years. It became part of our culture, part of our Christmas heritage; but it also posed a problem which still defies a ready explanation, a problem which attached to Herbert all the rest of his life.

Babes in Toyland was the first of Herbert's operettas, except the ill-fated *The Gold Bug*, not written for a traveling company. The Bostonians, Alice Nielsen, Frank Daniels, Francis Wilson had interpreted the earlier operettas. They welcomed long stays in New York, but their itineraries kept them moving. *Babes in Toyland* was planned and produced as a "permanent" New York attraction, to stay in the metropolis as long as possible and then take to the road. How did this, and subsequent similar works of Herbert, compare with rival New York productions? Not too well, it must be confessed; and *The Wizard of Oz* affords a case in point—while critics and public alike conceded the superiority of Herbert's opera, the *Wizard* lasted through nearly 300 performances. As the years rolled by, some of Herbert's best works were "outdistanced" by operettas and musical comedies that are now totally forgotten. Herbert shows never suffered from inferior casts or inferior direction; they certainly never suffered from inferior music (though some were more fortunate than others). Did the greater success of an inferior production depend upon the book? If *The Wizard of Oz* is an indication, the answer is Yes. This story was an American juvenile classic—it is as fresh today as when it was written—and the characters could live on the stage because the audience knew them and loved them for themselves alone. That the same cannot be said of *Babes in Toyland*, in spite of its extraordinary music, is illustrated by the observation during its fifth week in Boston (May, 1904) that, while it was a tiptop show, it lacked the drawing power of *The Wizard of Oz*.[10]

It would be ridiculous to encourage sympathy for a misunderstood Herbert. From his first entry into operetta he was one of its best, most successful practitioners; but it is well to remember that he had formidable competitors. The situation today, of course, tells the final result: The (detachable) music of Herbert reigns supreme; the music of his contemporaries and most of his successors is gone, forgotten, even that which enlivened the immortal characters of L. Frank Baum. All of which increases the regret that Herbert never found a proper literary collaborator. If he had, an incalculable wealth of unknown Herbert music would be added to the present generous, yet somewhat restricted, repertoire.

While *Babes in Toyland* was attracting happy throngs in Chicago, Herbert began a new operetta which also had to meet extraordinary requirements. This was *Babette*, written for the still young Charles B. Dillingham (1868–1934), who lured Fritzi Scheff from grand opera to lighter entertainment. *Babette,* although not long-lived, was triply important: for itself, for bringing Herbert and Dillingham into association, and for launching Fritzi on her operetta career. She became Herbert's greatest, if not most amiable, singer, and America found her volatile, mischievous, and irritating personality absolutely irresistible.

Obviously quite different from Herbert's most satisfactory singer, the equally gifted and more intelligent Alice Nielsen, Fritzi was unique. She was beautiful, and she could sing; she was bewitching, and she liked attention; and she was temperamental. All of which leads to a slight digression.

A year and a half before *Babette,* Fritzi began to toy with the idea of entering operetta. In the spring of 1902 it was announced she would "probably be starred next season by Shubert Brothers in a new DeKoven-Smith light opera."[11] Five months later the same source announced she had changed her mind and would remain with the Metropolitan Opera Company.[12] But during the ensuing winter an announcement similar to the first was issued, and the public began to anticipate a new luminary.[13] She was to be under the management of Dillingham, and her first vehicle would be an operetta adapted from the French. More time elapsed, and the public learned she would be heard in a new comic opera called *The Duchess of Dantzig* with music by Ivan Caryll, founded on the story of *Madame Sans-Gêne.*[14] Fortunately the announcement was inexact, and Fritzi made her light opera début in Herbert's new work.

Investigating this phase of Herbert's activity, I was more than anxious to talk with Miss Scheff—still attractive, still vital, and potentially gracious. This proved to be no easy matter. Letters of appeal were ignored, and three visits to her apartment obtained no more than a startling rebuff and a door slammed so abruptly as almost to hit me in the face. Friends interceded, however, and at last I secured an audience which was all of five minutes long. We met on October 1, 1948, at the stage entrance of the Belasco Theatre in New York, where she was rehearsing for a play. The talk wearied neither of us—its brevity assured that—and it was apparent that the former star little relished my queries about her brilliant past. Certainly she had no words of kindness or gratefulness for Herbert or the music he wrote for her (newspaper publicity to the contrary notwithstanding).

Her abandonment of grand opera for rôles in operetta had stirred up great excitement, and so I asked, "Miss Scheff, what caused you to leave the Metropolitan to go into musical comedy?" Almost in a snarl, she snapped back, "I wish to God I knew!" Then she quickly modified her tone and more gently added that money was the deciding factor: Dillingham had offered her $1,000 a week to enter light opera, and "that was a lot of money in those days." I could have added that it was a lot of money today, too, but I felt my remark would have been unwelcome (as I was) and unappreciated (as I was). She practically denied all personal recollections of Herbert, but remembered having met him first when she was soloist at a Pittsburgh concert.

I asked if she could tell me why her début in light opera happened to be in a Herbert work. This she remembered, and her account made sense. Once her decision was made, she tried out the music of three leading composers for the stage—Herbert, Ludwig Englander, and Reginald de Koven. Englander, she recalled as a remarkable pianist who could make his own strains sound rich and sonorous; but when his music was orchestrated it was thin and failed to carry. To De Koven's music she remained cold. Herbert's music was the best (her judgment was good), and she chose it for the beginning of her new life. She recalled, too, that she sang in four of Herbert's operettas: *Babette, Mlle. Modiste, The Prima Donna,* and *The Duchess* (or *Mlle. Rosita*). In her opinion the last two were no good because they had bad books; at least they failed to sustain any love interest—an essential requirement in Miss Scheff's mind. Who can say that she was wrong?

Wanting to say something especially pleasant before we parted, I referred to the time when Miss Scheff still graced the Metropolitan stage. "You were a remarkable singer in those days," I remarked. "Why, I remember reading of a performance of Mozart's *Die Zauberflöte* in which you literally stole the show from Marcella Sembrich." (This was no figment of my imagination; the story is easily accessible to all who wish to read it.[15])

She was pleased with what I said—why should she not be?—but I was hardly prepared for her response: "Yes, that wasn't hard to do."

"No," I ventured, in what was supposed to be a dry tone. "I suppose not." I wondered what was coming next.

Then she continued in a very positive, semiconfidential way:

"You see, in those days I could sing, and I was dainty and small and petite—and when you were like that, you could take anything away from Sembrich!"

"And now," she went on, "I must get back inside to rehearsal. You will be coming to New York again, and we'll get together for a good long talk about Victor Herbert. You just let me know when you're coming. There's nobody I'd rather see. So now, goodbye!" Whereupon she beamed a radiant smile, blew a kiss to me from the tips of her fingers (in best of operetta style), and whirled away into the dark recesses of the Belasco Theatre. Repeated requests for another talk brought no response. I can only believe that she cordially detested *serious* recollection of the days when she had no rival.

But Fritzi Scheff retained many characteristics of her earlier self. She irritated and she charmed, she annoyed and she beguiled. She had an air and an accent thoroughly Viennese, and a personality which flashed forth mementos of her youth. I was disappointed in my five minutes with her, but I caught a glimpse of the captious Fritzi who had held audiences in thrall. It was the petite and dainty Fritzi, the girl who feared not Sembrich, that enlivened the stodgy play Herbert set to music as *Babette*.

With *Babette*, Herbert again had Harry B. Smith as libretto writer. It was not so farcical as some of Smith's books, but it was devoid of humor and lumbering in structure. Nevertheless it achieved an auspicious opening in Washington on November 9, 1903, at the New National Theatre, and a brilliant audience roared approval. President Theodore Roosevelt and family occupied a box opposite Herbert's, and the rest of official Washington was heavily represented. The music and Fritzi overwhelmed everyone, and the future of the show and the new star was confidently predicted. There was no hesitation in taking it to New York the next week.

In the metropolis *Babette* was produced at the Broadway Theatre on November 16. It was presented as a "romantic comic opera," and the cast was as follows:

Babette, a village letter writer, afterwards a
    Court prima donna.........................Fritzi Scheff
Mondragon, a soldier of fortune.............Eugene Cowles
Marcel, a painter, in love with Babette............Richie Ling
Baltazar, a professional conspirator.........Edward J. Connelly
Vinette, his daughter..........................Ida Hawley
Van Tympel, a clock maker...................Louis Harrison
Eva, his wife............................Josephine Bartlett
The King of France..........................Erroll Dunbar
Guzman, a Spanish officer...................Madison Smith
Schnapps, a tavern keeper...................William Sissons
Captain Walther............................Alfred S. Ely
Jan   } Apprentices.................... { Frank Boyle
Quentin }   { James Beals
Margot }   { Rosa Earle
Greta   } Village girls.................... { Edna Luby
Joan   }   { Adele Nott
Coachman................................J. T. Chailee
Footman..................................Charles Emerson
Mlle. de le Motte   { Bertha Willoughby
Mlle. de Rohan   } Maids of honor { May Seeley
Mlle. de Fontanges }   { Mildred Forrest

A Court lady, with solo........................Mary Smith
Marquis de Villette ⎱ ⎰ George Williamson
Count de Courville ⎬ Courtiers.........⎨ Arthur Blanchard
Duc de St. Michel ⎰ ⎱ Henry Wilkinson
François ⎱ ⎰ Georgia Campbell
Henri ⎮ ⎮ Rita Dean
Gaston ⎬ Pages....................⎨ Helen Planche
Jacque ⎮ ⎮ Aline Redmond
Laurent ⎰ ⎱ Gertrude Adams
Teresa................................Emily Montague
Katrina..............................Florence Belleville
Peasants, Courtiers, Maids of Honor, etc.

The production was in the very competent hands of Fred G. Latham
and A. M. Holbrook. The musical director was Herbert's old friend
John Lund.

The play unfolds[16] in seventeenth century Belgium and France:
Act I, garden of Van Tympel's house, near Ántwerp; Act II, a road-
side inn, near Brussels; Act III, Versailles. The Lowlands are suffering
under Spanish tyranny, and the sixteenth century should have been
the time period. However, that would have made it scarcely possible
to bring in the sumptuous court of Versailles, which flowered only in
the latter half of the seventeenth century.

The play concerns the plight of the villagers under Spanish rule.
Babette and Marcel are loyal Flemish patriots; but they and their
fellows need a leader if they are to win free of the tyrants' yoke.
Mondragon supplies the lack, and they completely foil the plans of
the Spanish sympathizers, even to the point of enlisting the aid of
the King of France. Beauty and charm and vocal ability, naturally,
are the strongest weapons in Babette's arsenal.

The libretto of *Babette* was not the worst that ever came to Herbert,
and some critics approved it in a half-hearted way; neither was it the
best, and other critics condemned it in tones of no uncertainty. A
review of the former type conceded the lyrics were in a rather happy
vein, the book itself being only a peg for the features of a brilliant
performance.[17] The opposite view lamented Fritzi Scheff's appearance
in a production so dramatically unworthy of her talents: Not only was
the plot void of all originality, it was awkwardly constructed and
boringly conventional; indeed, "the construction was so crude and
painfully obvious as to suggest an amateur rather than a professional
achievement."[18]

But the music was an entirely different story. It was rich and satisfying, descriptive and dramatic, melodious and alive. Even the opening
bowling scene was aptly pictured with sweeps of scales for all the
world like the course of a well rolled ball. There was less occasion

for pantomimic music here than in *Babes in Toyland,* but some of the short introductions to scenes were symphonic in style.

Early in the play Mondragon and Vinette (Vinetta in the printed score) sing their duet "On the Other Side of the Wall," a delightful interchange of coquettishness wherein harmonic subtlety adds to its natural delicacy. Babette's first song, "Letters I Write All the Day," is also a notable accomplishment. In her refrains she illustrates the kinds of letters she must write: for the lover who pleads for more attention (a querulous, complaining air); for the miserly landlord who insists on squeezing the poor (crabbed, monotonous, harsh music); for the boyish soldier only too anxious to avenge a fancied insult (a high-spirited galop). It is a most engaging piece which seems to be doomed to oblivion because it is so intimately a part of the drama it enlivens. Another duet, quite different in mood and style from the first, is Marcel and Babette's "I'll Bribe the Stars"—a passionate love avowal with all of Herbert's lush sentiment which our less romantic day finds somewhat onerous.

The best choral and concerted scene comes at the beginning of the second act. The kermess music is gaily ebullient, and the short peasant dance following is thoroughly characteristic.

The opening chorus of the third act brings out all the stately grace of Versailles, with fine antiphonal effects between soloist and chorus. It is surpassed, however, by the irresistible Spanish number ("It's a Way We Have in Spain"), sung by Van Tympel, Eva, Mondragon, and Marcel when they arrive at Court. Herbert loved to write Spanish music, and in this piece he outdid himself, particularly in the refrain. Its lilt, its syncopated rhythm, its unexpected repetition at a different pitch are qualities which cannot fail to delight. And almost as remarkable, though more prosaic, is the madrigal quartet called "My Lady of the Manor," which is a part song of distinction. The *pièce de résistance* of the opera is the waltz song, "Where Fairest Flow'rs Are Blooming," written of course for Fritzi and planned to exploit all her talents. It is a long, difficult, and brilliant aria, moments of coloratura alternating with *bel canto*—a dazzling number which, if properly executed, can electrify an audience into cheers of acclamation.

As Fritzi Scheff romped through the show in completely inimitable fashion she more than fulfilled expectations. She had "unlimited vitality" and proved herself a "wondrously voltaic little woman"[18] who won her audience with every note and action. Her costumes were many, and in her last one "she sang something about spring and flowers that you wanted to take home with you and put in water. It was fragrant with melody and from her throat it blossomed like a rose. She sang much—thanks be to Herbert—and always beautifully;

so finely, in fact, that half [the] time the chorus forgot its own charms and stood looking at her open-eyed and open-mouthed."[19] Only an artist can reap such undiluted praise. After the second act she called Herbert to the stage to share her bows. Unexpectedly she gave him a hug and a kiss which made him beam and glow and blush. This gesture was particularly to the fancy of the onlookers, who roared their approval of the composer's merited reward.

The music was also unanimously approved, vociferously in fact. Some felt that it was his best work to date,[20] while others were too pleased to make any comparisons. The warmest accolade came from Finck in the *Evening Post*, who literally rhapsodized over what he saw and heard:

> Mr. Herbert is, like Johann Strauss, a high-class musician, who can adapt his style to popular taste without ever becoming vulgar; and underlying his pretty tunes there are orchestral touches which rejoice the heart of lovers of the best in music. Some of the choruses, too, are excellent; but the gem of the whole score is a quartet in the last act which got two encores and deserved a hundred. There is nothing more admirable in the whole range of operatic concerted music, and it deserves to become as famous as the quartet in "Rigoletto," to which, in fact, it is far superior. It was sung, as nothing on the operetta stage has perhaps ever been sung here, with perfect intonation, mellowness of tone and refined shading. . . . "Babette" is really, for New York, an epoch-making production, not only because it is so well done, but because it is practically an *opéra comique*, a *genre* that has long been a desideratum on this side of the Atlantic. The Broadway Theatre is only a block from the Metropolitan Opera House, and lovers of good music and singing will find them not too far apart musically either.

In varying degrees other reviews agreed with this, rejoicing that Herbert's second operetta in a month was so wholeheartedly satisfying. Only a year before, the composer had defended himself against the charge of no originality. One critic remembered this and used *Babette* as a reminder of the ordeal by trial. With this operetta the composer had "not only written a charming opera which will live, but he has completely vindicated himself of the cruel and malicious charges which were made against him a few years ago. The opera is nothing if not original. Although abounding in popular airs it still received so classic a treatment that one well-known critic called it a miniature grand opera."[21]

But *Babette* did not live; it disappeared, another casualty of poor librettos. The excellent music, harnessed to trite words and boring situations, could not be extricated from its surroundings. The production went through 59 performances in New York,[22] then toured in the East and the Middle West for the remainder of the season. The early departure from New York, however, cannot be wholly interpreted as the result of failure. Just as it began its run on Broadway an announcement was made that it would stay there only through the week of January 4, 1904, when a successor would be ushered in.[23] This proves conclusively that a long stay at the New York theater was not possible and mitigates the charge of failure which is sometimes still heard. On the other hand there was no attempt to revive the show in New York, even though Herbert wanted it done.[24] Dillingham evidently had other plans for Fritzi Scheff when the new season arrived; and he used her in four different operettas during 1904–1905: *The Two Roses, Fatinitza, Giroflé-Girofla,* and *Boccaccio.*[25] None of them ran as long as *Babette.*

On the afternoon of February 24, 1904, the Pittsburg Press Club presented in the Alvin Theatre for its own benefit Julian Edwards' comic opera *Dolly Varden,* featuring Lulu Glaser. The Herbert family occupied a box and were happily surprised when the composer was honored with a lifetime honorary membership in the Club.

The elaborate program of the occasion made no mention of Herbert, else the award would have been no surprise. It was, however, an unusual publication and contained an important contribution from a rising young newspaper reporter, Wilmer M. Jacoby. Then a lad of eighteen, Jacoby was a devoted admirer of Herbert and played a prominent part in the attempt to restrain Herbert from leaving the city.

The emotional climax was reached on March 18, date of the final evening orchestra concert, when the audience gave a vociferous demonstration to the conductor and witnessed the presentation of a huge sterling silver loving cup. It bore the simple inscription:

TO VICTOR HERBERT
From His Many Pittsburg Admirers
March 18, 1904

Ernestine Schumann-Heink was the soloist, and at intermission she added her own tribute by saying: "I do not know what the difficulty is relative to Mr. Herbert and the orchestra. But it is a great pity that he should be allowed to leave. He is a great musician and a fine artist."[26]

Before leaving for the East, Herbert composed—rapidly, but with extraordinary care—an Easter anthem. Called *Christ Is Risen* and based on biblical words (which Herbert probably arranged himself), it was written for one of his closest friends, Hobart Weed of Buffalo. Weed was a businessman, but also chairman of the Music Committee of St. Paul's Episcopal Cathedral. In the latter capacity and as a friend, he had asked Herbert for an Easter work.

Herbert did not stint himself in complying with the request. He set the jubilant words for solo voices, chorus, and orchestra (with which the organ could join), and produced a work which deserves to be known today. It is not an unusual piece of religious music, but it is highly effective and entirely free of bombast. Especially interesting are the soft and subdued passages, which reveal a personal absorption in the task which was wholly praiseworthy.[27] The anthem was sung in St. Paul's Cathedral on Easter Sunday, 1904, and Herbert conducted the choir and the specially engaged orchestra. The reporters of church news enthusiastically described the composition and the appearance of the composer, which had been kept secret in order to avoid unseemly publicity to the event.[28]

Herbert's return to New York was preceded by a rumor that he might resume leadership of the Twenty-second Regiment Band;[29] but it is doubtful that he gave this any consideration. Nor was there need to, for he had announced his intention to maintain an orchestra and to continue creating operettas. He did both, with tremendous success, and became more firmly entrenched than ever as an American institution.

The New York début of the Victor Herbert Orchestra—new, yet not new, because about half of the Pittsburgh players followed him—was sequel to an event which had a touch of irony: On September 19, 1904, Herbert and his men won a rousing ovation when they appeared at the Pittsburgh Exposition, which prompted a New York reporter to castigate the gentlemen of Pittsburgh who had permitted the favorite to slip away.

The New York concerts quickly assumed a pattern, but this did not lessen the pleasure they gave. The big city had keenly anticipated his reappearance: "Now New York is to have Mr. Herbert at the handsome new Majestic Theatre in a series of performances that should fill the house and bring out whole troops of those who, while loving real music, are not averse to a tinkling tune in the menus of musical endeavors."[30]

The concerts were on Sunday evenings—the first was on October 9—and became what one observer called a permanent and worthy feature of New York's amusement life. The fifty players, all highly proficient, offered programs which spanned a wide gamut of style and mood. Herbert's lighter music figured prominently, but this was counterbalanced by overtures, symphonic movements, dances, and suites. Although Victor Herbert's Orchestra had ample opportunity to tour, it maintained its roots in New York City; it was never a touring organization like Sousa's Band.

Long before the orchestra season opened—in the spring as a matter of fact—Herbert made his return felt among a select group of New York associates, the Lambs. On November 29, 1903, the Lambs had staged their annual Thanksgiving Gambol, featuring a skit called *Some Babes from Toyland* with music by Herbert. This was a burlesque of the wall episode in the operetta. Six months later, on May 10, he conducted a related skit, entitled *Lambs in Toyland*—his own music being applied to new lyrics by Grant Stewart. The occasion, long remembered, was the Ladies Annual Gambol, which the gallant members observed in the precincts of the Lyric Theatre.

Herbert was indeed back on the Rialto, and his next stage production was not far off. It was one of his greatest, and most annoying, successes, and bore the declarative title of *It Happened in Nordland*.

A slight mystery attaches to the origin of this vivacious operetta. The spring of 1904 produced rumors that Herbert was writing an opera entitled *The Enchanted Isle*, the scene of which was an imaginary country.[31] By summer the score was reported finished, and a group of Herbert's friends, hearing a private piano rendition, were said to have declared the music was in his "most sparkling vein." The firm of Hamlin, Mitchell & Fields, moreover, was to produce it early in the season.[32] Meanwhile, *It Happened in Nordland* was also taking shape, and it, too, displayed action in an unknown land. There is a temptation to identify these works as one and the same. Two more announcements, but no proof, reveal the hazards of such identification. The aforesaid firm deferred *The Enchanted Isle* until September of 1905, and named the librettist as Frank S. Pixley;[33] and Witmark, the music publisher, declared it would issue Herbert's opera for the new Lew Fields Theatre as well as *The Enchanted Isle*.[34] The former was *It Happened in Nordland*, the author of which was Glen MacDonough. This is the extent of knowledge about *The Enchanted Isle*, which is probably a lost Herbert operetta.

Curiously enough, *It Happened in Nordland* was conceived under another title, *The American Ambassadress*. A perusal of the book quickly explains the earlier appellation, but no amount of study makes one think of a magic or bewitched island. Yet doubt still lingers over the alleged contemporary piece.

It Happened in Nordland was almost the direct result of a theatrical rupture. For years the Weber and Fields Music Hall had been one of New York's entertainment landmarks. Joseph Weber and Lew Fields were an inimitable pair; but they separated in 1904, and their Music Hall closed down.[35] Fields joined forces with Hamlin and Mitchell, organized the Lew Fields Stock Company, and arranged to open the new Lew Fields Theatre in the fall. In July, Herbert agreed to supply music for its productions.[36] At the same time Glen MacDonough received the task of writing the book of the opening piece, and Marie Cahill was signed as the female star. Rehearsals were to begin in September, leading to the theater's inauguration on November 29.[37] Practically everything proceeded as planned; but in one respect Herbert had not protected himself sufficiently, and his unexplained carelessness (his original contract seems to have been lost) brought him torment.

The first performance on any stage took place at the New Lyceum Theatre, Harrisburg, Pennsylvania, on November 21, 1904. It made a powerful impression on the audience as Herbert conducted an auspicious première. The reporter for the *Patriot* conceded it was musically and scenically magnificent, that the cast was fine and well balanced. But at the same time he voiced a feeling which boded ill for the future of some one or something. He did not like the feminine lead, and wrote quite frankly: "There was entirely too much of Marie Cahill. The management must give some one else besides their pet star a chance if they wish to hold the favor of their audience to the end. She is clever, undoubtedly, and has a fresh, pleasant voice, but there can be too much of even a good thing and last night certainly showed it." Not only was she omnipresent, but she was objectionable: "While most of her songs were amusing enough 'Kitty' is distinctly objectionable and not even clever. It might possibly take in the Bowery, but it is offensive anywhere else."

I have not been able to discover that Herbert wrote "Kitty," which the strong-willed Marie was insistently using. From the very opening performance, therefore, she adopted the practice—which was to plague Herbert as long as she remained with the company—of interpolating songs by other composers. He was powerless to prevent it, and a few months later a bitter controversy developed in New York. It was unusual, but not unheard of, for Herbert to permit the interpolation of another composer's song; the present instance led to a wrangling feud between him and a flinty, uncompromising character. Fortunately the show went on long after the obnoxious Marie was gone, if not forgotten.

The production was scheduled to open in New York on November 29, but Fred R. Hamlin died on the 27th. As a member of the producing firm he commanded considerable respect, so that the opening was deferred until December 5. Then the public trooped joyfully to see a new operetta in a colorful new theater. Several hours later it departed feeling that the one was as pretty as the other.

The show was announced as a musical comedy in a prologue and two acts. The cast was as follows:

Hubert, the long lost brother of Katherine Peepfogle	Lew Fields
Prince George of Nebula, who is ordered by the Czar to marry Queen Elsa of Nordland	Harry Davenport
Duke of Toxen, Prime Minister of Nordland	Joseph Herbert
Baron Sparta, Minister of War and Police and enemy to the Duke of Toxen.......	Harry Fisher
Captain Slivowitz, his chief assistant......	Joseph Carroll
Princess Aline, Queen Elsa's aunt........	May Robson
Dr. Otto Blotz, dermatologist and proprietor of Blotz's pain killer.................	Julius Steger
Parthenia Schmitt, a country girl, maid to the Princess Aline...................	Bessie Clayton
Hugo von Arnim, Lieutenant in the Royal Body Guard........................	Charles Gotthold
Mayme Perkins, personal secretary to the American Ambassadress..............	"Billie" Norton
Dr. Popoff, proprietor of Popoff's Sanatorium	William Burress
Captain Gatling, of the United States Navy	
Duchess Helene, sister of the Duke of Toxon	Rosemary Glosz
Rudolf, a peasant, Parthenia's sweetheart	Frank O'Neill
Prince Karl, in love with Queen Elsa	
Miss Hicks, first secretary of the American Embassy at Nordland	Pauline Frederick
Countess Pokota, lady-in-waiting to Queen Elsa	
Katherine Peepfogle, American Ambassadress to the Court of Nordland........	Marie Cahill

In addition to these there were girls and boys galore, including **Dr.** Blotz's "samples," detective girls, Nordland boys and girls, flower girls, water girls, matinee girls, masqueraders, and ineffective characters to fit into the pageantry and pantomime of the action.

The prologue showed the railroad station in Kronenberg, capital of Nordland. The first act unfolded on a promenade in Elsa Bad, also in Nordland. The second act, again in Kronenberg, revealed the terrace of Queen Elsa's palace, the time being the next day.

The ingenious Julian Mitchell supervised the staging. Max Hirschfeld was the musical director and conductor, but Herbert led the orchestra through the first act on opening night.

Though slight, there is an undeniable relationship between *It*

Happened in Nordland and a musical comedy of 1950, Irving Berlin's *Call Me Madam*. Both plays revolve around a feminine diplomat representing the United States in a foreign land. There the resemblance ends, but it is unusual enough not to pass unnoticed. The two female ambassadors are subjected to vastly different treatment, and the political inspiration of the later play was wholly lacking for the earlier, which was incoherent to a degree.

Herbert's ambassadress happens to look exactly like the Queen of the country in which she represents the United States. Because the Queen has disappeared in order to escape an unwelcome marriage, the American girl must impersonate her, else Nordland will fall apart. Everything develops successfully, with the Queen at last eloping with her true love and the ambassadress finding her long-lost brother (why he should be found remains a mystery) and returning him to America.

Even with a minimum of love interest *It Happened in Nordland* enjoyed a run of 154 performances in New York,[38] played two weeks in Boston early in May, 1905, a solid ten weeks in Chicago, and returned to the same theater in New York on August 31 for another 100 performances. It was a veritable sensation, thanks to the music and an extremely capable cast.

In some ways it was a lighter work than Herbert usually wrote. The separate numbers were shorter, there were fewer concerted pieces, the choruses and finales were less massive. Most of the reviews praised the score without emphasizing excerpts, and they all agreed on its sparkling quality and infectious tunefulness. The sophistication of Prince George was well characterized in the lilting "The Woman in the Case" and "Absinthe Frappé," and the latter was one of the most popular melodies Herbert ever wrote. Katherine's most popular solo came in the first finale, "Commanderess-in-Chief," and as a spirited march it set the feet of all who heard it tapping.

A curious feature appeared at the beginning of Act II. In the spring of 1904 Herbert had published through Witmark the gay and clever piano piece *Al Fresco*—under the pseudonym of Frank Roland, for both the composer and publisher wished to see how much or how little Herbert's name meant on a sheet of salon music.[39] They were satisfied with the sales, and in November the piece was reissued with the composer's own name on the cover. In arranging the second act of *Nordland,* Herbert wanted a lively number which could support a carnival scene, and he adapted *Al Fresco,* for chorus and orchestra, with conspicuous skill. It was followed by the lyrical hit of the show, "The Knot of Blue," a smoothly flowing waltz of undeniable charm.

In the course of its fortunate run *Nordland* witnessed some noteworthy events. It was a production which attracted personalities, and a roving reporter was pleased to comment on the appearance of two box parties there on January 23, 1905, headed by Marcella Sembrich and Andreas Dippel, both luminaries of the Metropolitan Opera Company. Another party was entertained by Daniel S. Lamont, a recent Secretary of War.[40]

Late in May, Lew Fields honored his recent partner Joseph M. Weber with a special Thursday matinee. It was important by virtue of the occasion and also for another reason. Fields, superb comedian and hardened veteran, could not make an ordinary speech. Knowing he would have to address remarks to Weber, he had recorded his words; and the phonograph record was played at the proper time.[41] This must have been a very early use of the phonograph in a practical application.

Additional happenings were interesting, but definitely worrisome. Chief among them was the quarrel between Herbert and Marie Cahill, which culminated in her leaving the company. In spite of undoubted ability she had displeased some people from the very beginning in Harrisburg. The New York opening called forth similar comments, a few of which cast doubt on her vocal powers. One listener thought she "showed a tendency to sing too much, instead of sticking to the Yvette Guilbert method of half-talking her songs" which first had made her prominent.[42] Another keen-eared critic declared "she should abandon her efforts to become a prima donna."[43] Meanwhile she ruthlessly continued to interpolate non-Herbert songs into the play, and the composer could not stop her.

As long as Herbert had no direct contact with the show he could probably forget Cahill's brashness; but Max Hirschfeld fell ill near the middle of April, and the composer had to conduct most of the performances for several weeks. Seeing and hearing her across the footlights was no sedative for his overwrought nerves, and when she sang an interpolated song he refused to conduct the orchestra, handing the baton to Henry Burck, the concertmaster. This was not conducive to harmony on any occasion. The last performance of the New York run brought the matter to the boiling point.[44]

It was Saturday night April 29. Cahill was singing the non-Herbertian "Any Old Tree," which Herbert had allowed, but for which she had obtained many extra stanzas. In the middle of the song she stopped, began to cry, and left the stage. Soon returning, she finished the song, but insisted on doing it with no accompaniment! She complained that the orchestra purposely made discords to hinder her singing. The company was to open in Boston two days later, and the singer refused to go along. Herbert of course laughed at her allegations. Whether he conducted or not, he said, the orchestra always did its best for her; and the real trouble lay in her lapsing from pitch. He admitted anger over her inserted songs.

There was no regular understudy for the part, and more than one person played Katherine Peepfogle during the next few weeks. When the show returned to New York for its second run the part was filled by a notable figure, Blanche Ring; but more trouble lay ahead. This time the outcome was to provide a steppingstone to a great actress in the American theater whose association with Herbert operetta is well-nigh completely forgotten.

This was Pauline Frederick,[45] who, from the beginning of the stormy history, had played two parts in *Nordland* and played them well. The opportunity added to her grace and dignity, and her clear soprano voice attracted much favorable notice. *Nordland* also gave her invaluable experience in the art of make-up. She witnessed Cahill's ungracious departure from the cast and watched the procession of substitutes who impersonated Katherine. When Blanche Ring assumed the leading rôle Miss Frederick was appointed understudy. It is doubtful that she anticipated assuming the part herself; yet the temperamental Blanche more or less imitated the headstrong Marie, and the young Pauline put on the mantle of the American Ambassadress.

It happened in the second half of the second New York run. During a Saturday night performance Ring, ignoring recent history, interpolated foreign material. Lew Fields was angry; they quarreled, and the prima donna left the theater in a huff. The next day she announced she would not appear on Monday unless he apologized. Fields evidently thought he did, for he canceled a special rehearsal called for Frederick's benefit. But the offended Blanche was not so easily placated, and when Monday night arrived she had disappeared and taken her costumes with her! There was turmoil backstage, and Fields was frantic; only Pauline Frederick was calm. She was thoroughly familiar with the songs, her clear soprano covered three octaves, and she was ready for the responsibility. Donning costumes which were hastily assembled at the last minute, she rose nobly to the occasion and was wholly successful. This was on October 16, 1905.[46]

The role of Katherine was much coveted, and when Ring's defection became known more than a dozen actresses clamored for it. Fortunately Fields was highly satisfied with Pauline, and she continued as the star for the remainder of the run—five weeks of unexpected prominence. This was her first and last period of operetta glory. After the play closed she developed a throat ailment which seriously impaired her singing, although her speaking voice was not affected. She went on to an enviable career on the dramatic stage, unquestionably the richer for her year with Victor Herbert's music.

On January 9, 1905, Herbert resumed his appearances at the exclusive Bagby musicales in the Waldorf-Astoria.[47] Toward the middle of March he began another series of Sunday night concerts in the Majestic Theatre.[48] On April 9 he conducted the New York Symphony Orchestra in a Carnegie Hall concert which featured the farewell appearance of a fabulous boy violinist, Franz von Vecsey.[49] And on Easter Sunday (the 23rd) he led his own orchestra in a special Easter program.[50] The New York *Evening World* had commissioned him to compose an Easter song, and it was sung on this program for the first time by Frieda Stender: it was an effective solo, with words by Glen MacDonough, and was published at once in a rather ephemeral form. Two years later it was reissued by Witmark. The usual Willow Grove engagement came in June, followed by the more glamorous stay at Saratoga's Grand Union.

The summer also had its moments of recreation. At Lake Placid, Herbert indulged in boating and won a prize which was small, but highly treasured. It might have been larger if his wife had been more amenable to the judges' request.

He was passionately fond of boats and had a number of them during his years in the Adirondacks. In 1905 he entered the *Handy Andy II* in a contest for decorated craft. Dressed in Japanese lanterns and pine boughs, the little launch brought him a copper and white-metal trophy cup, six and a half inches high, with this inscription: "Lake Placid, 1905—Decorated Launch Parade, Second Prize."

The first prize was so near! The choice lay between this and one other boat, and the judges wanted to inspect both carefully. They called to Mrs. Herbert to circle the course once more in the opposite direction so that they might see the other side. Convinced of the boat's beauty, she proudly shouted back, "It's just so good on the other side!" and refused to turn around. The remark became famous throughout the resort—and probably bestowed first prize on the chief competitor.[51]

Another humorous incident occurred at this time.[52] In the repertoire of Herbert's orchestra was a gay and colorful piece called *Spanish Rhapsody,* seemingly by a composer named Simbinghi (or Zimbinghi). Curious about the unknown composer, a reporter extracted from Herbert a somewhat sheepish confession. Herbert and orchestra had been engaged to give a concert for a ladies' association. Discussing program selections with the fair sex, Herbert was soon at his wit's end because they were so hard to please. They wanted no Wagner, no Beethoven, no Mozart. In desperation he coined the name of Simbinghi, and the allure of its strange sound captivated the ladies into acceptance! Later Herbert told his young Pittsburgh friend Wilmer M. Jacoby the story and disclosed how he had overshot the mark. The ladies had clamored so vigorously for the unknown composer that he had not had the heart to disillusion them. He had to compose the piece himself![53]

At this time, too, a most important announcement appeared. Herbert would conduct two more pairs of concerts for the New York Philharmonic Society during the 1905–1906 season.[54] This august body was still seeking a permanent leader and continuing to engage, as guest conductors, the most distinguished artists available. Again, as two years earlier, Herbert was the only American so honored. There was no reason why he should not accept the engagement; but he might have acted differently had he foreseen—which was impossible—the trap being laid by his old enemy, the *Musical Courier.*

Meanwhile Herbert remained loyal to the stage and produced two operettas in the fall—actually, late summer—of 1905. Neither was a great success, and one was more troublesome than most. The first was the two-act musical comedy *Miss Dolly Dollars,* which had its real première at the Lyceum Theatre in Rochester, New York, on August 30, then opened in New York at the Knickerbocker Theatre on September 4. Once again Harry B. Smith was the librettist. The producer was Charles B. Dillingham.

Announcements of the show were issued early in the spring, together with the name of the star, Lulu Glaser. A cynical reporter slyly added, "Mr. Herbert is not only a good musician, but a brave man,"[55] no doubt remembering her vocal problems in *Cyrano de Bergerac.* But the composition was promptly done, and rehearsals began on July 24.[56] It developed normally and was soon ready for the upstate tryout.

The Rochester audience liked it hugely, the chief recommendation being for curtailment since the creators had been overly generous in their initial display. The music was "brilliant," and the book seemed to be the work of "some phenomenally witty and skillful Englishman."[57] A few similar sentiments were voiced in New York, but there were others of contrary view.

The program of the New York opening listed the following cast:

Dorothy Gay, an American heiress known as
"Dolly Dollars"............................Lulu Glaser
Lord Burlingham, in favor of an Anglo-American
alliance................................Melville Stewart
Finney Doolittle, an educated fool...............R. C. Herz
Samuel Gay, a condensed soup magnate.......Charles Bradshaw
Mrs. Gay, his better fifty per cent..............Carrie Perkins
Guy Gay, who pays a fellow to study for him
at Oxford..............................Carter DeHaven
Bertha Billings, Dorothy's maid, with a fondness
for romance................................Olive Murray

Celeste.....................................Elsie Ferguson
Lieut. von Richter, of the German Army..........Henry Vogel
Miggs, Lord Burlingham's valet...............Byron Ongley

The Hon. Percy Fitzboodle		William Naughton
The Marquis de Baccarat		James Leahy
Baron von Rheinheister	Members of the	Carl Hartberg
Count Runoffsky	Club of	James Reany
Count Chianti	Friendly	Enrico Oremonte
Duke de Bolero	Rivals	John Ardizone
Prince Umskyvitch		Sidney Harris
Captain Sheridan Barry		Edward Leahy

'Arry		J. Leahy
Bobby		E. Oremonte
H'Alfred	Costers...................	S. A. Harris
'Arriet		Lillie Van Arsdale
Jane		Minerva Hall
Matilda		Beatrice Anderson

Hon. Montague Bank		Bessie Holbrook
Hon. Mayland Bank	Eton Boys.......	Sadie Probst
Hon. Algy Sydney		Eliza Doddridge
Hon. Reggy Chumpley		Mildred Cecil

Margery...................................Lilian Spencer
Millicent.............................Queenie Hewlet
Vera Vane.............................Marion Chase
Vashti Pearl.........................Gladys Zell
1st Bailiff.............................Joseph Frohoff
2nd Bailiff...............................L. F. Sampson

Freda Dressler		Elsa Rheinhardt
Estelle DeLange		Vida Whitmore
Greta Giltedge	The Summer Girls..	Aline Redmond
Ruth Delamere		Helen Marlborough
Vena Rodriguez		Leila Benton
Miriam Odell		Susanne Parker

The scene of the first act was a villa on the Thames at Henley; the second act, the garden of a hotel in Paris. The staging was in the hands of Al. Holbrook, the musical direction under Sig. A. de Novellis.

The story is that of a wealthy American family seeking a titled European son-in-law and of an impoverished nobleman looking for a rich American wife. Dolly and Lord Burlingham, the principals, find themselves suited to each other after they skirt disaster in the near-bankruptcy of her father. A touch of contemporaneity was added by frequent reference to the new art and sport of automobiling. The situations offered many an opportunity for social satire of a delicious sort; but the author ignored every possibility.

As usual the music was better than the story; but most critics felt that Herbert failed to do himself justice. The solo songs were not as engaging as in earlier operettas, and they lacked that sensuous persuasiveness which he generally exuded. His previous experience with Lulu Glaser had taught him her limitations, and he could not write as freely as he would have done for a genuine singer. In addition, the play was not exactly a romance in spite of the final union of the lovers. "An American Heiress," presented by Dolly and her suiters, was a charming bit of flirtation; the long opening chorus of Act II was cleverly animated; and the "Ollendorff Duet" (Dolly and von Richter) was a delightful conceit on travelers' use of foreign language dictionaries.

The best song was delivered by Lord Burlingham, cynically reflecting on the affections of women. The music and the words were well mated, and the title (drawn from Kipling's "The Betrothed") became a proverbial expression. This was "A Woman Is Only a Woman but a Good Cigar Is a Smoke." The unusual waltz in the Entr'acte remained instrumental, although it appeared in the opening scene of Act II and again in the finale.

As a production *Miss Dolly Dollars* was lively and infectious and seemed destined for a long run. Lulu Glaser had a part admirably suited to her, and Herz (as Doolittle) aroused enthusiasm. He rendered his rather trite song, "An Educated Fool," to perfection and gave such naturalness to the part that Fritzi Scheff, occupying a box, said to a companion: "Isn't it lovely to be brainy and helpless?"[58] The rest of the cast performed well, and the show's prospects were bright. The adverse judges, however, were the better prophets, and New York tolerated it only for 56 performances, including a move to the New Amsterdam Theatre on October 16.[59] One critic remained loyal to the very end. When it was in the second theater he declared it was much the best offering in New York, and the instrumental waltz was "a melody of such infinite pathos that it produces an actual physical effect on the hearer"; the show was indeed "worth going to see for the mere delight of hearing the music."[60]

Other critics and the public did not agree, and so *Miss Dolly Dollars* took to the road for the rest of the season. A short revival in the fall of 1906, still under Dillingham, brought it back to New York on October 8 with Blanche Ring in the title rôle; but it endured only 16 performances. By this time, however, it had heavy competition from later productions by Herbert, who rarely waited to see how successful his most recent score would be before launching another.

Two weeks after *Miss Dolly Dollars* was revealed to Rochester, another Herbert creation made its bow, also in upstate New York. This was *Wonderland*, which had its very first performance at the

Star Theatre in Buffalo on the night of September 14, 1905. Searchers in the past would look in vain for this title, for its label then was the vastly different *Alice and the Eight Princesses* (Herbert had simply called it *Placid* as he worked on the score at his summer home[61]). And hereby hangs a small tale—of exasperation, frustration, and ultimate disappointment.

Babes in Toyland, a piece of pure fancy, had been extraordinarily successful. It suggested a pattern to be tried again. Consequently there was agreement that Julian Mitchell, master of stagecraft, should direct a similar effort, and that the same composer and the same librettist (Glen MacDonough) should provide the materials. The reasoning was unassailable, but the results were deplorable. More emphatically than ever the blame lay on the book, although Herbert's music was not of the best.

MacDonough accepted the responsibility of concocting a story to combine Lewis Carroll's *Alice in Wonderland* and *Through the Looking-Glass* and Grimm's fairy tale "The Dancing Princess" (also known as "The Twelve Dancing Princesses"). Imagination kindles at the mention of all these titles, but MacDonough's did not kindle enough. And when he added facetious episodes of his own, they were completely foreign to the spirit of the admirable originals.

The story,[62] if such it can be called, does have a girl named Alice, a waif who sells matches. On a cold Christmas Eve she is befriended and lodged before a comforting fire, where she literally dreams her way into Wonderland and watches the fantastic adventures of the vanishing princesses. She also helps to solve their mystery. But the audience was more mystified at the end than at the beginning.

Buffalo extended a cordial welcome to the piece. An enormous audience watched Herbert conduct the orchestra, looked approvingly on the scenic grandeur, and forgave the usual first-night awkwardness. It realized the production was one of great difficulty. After more work and steady rehearsing everything would flow smoothly and freely.[63] Moreover, the outstanding cast included Bessie Clayton (Mrs. Julian Mitchell) as Alice; Sam Chip as The Mad Hatter; Eva Davenport as Phyllis; Lotta Faust as Miss Figgers; Bessie Wynn as Prince Fortunio; D. L. Don as King of Hearts; James Smith as Tweedledee; and James Cook as Tweedledum.[64]

Three days later the play opened in Chicago at the Grand Opera House; and it was in trouble from the very beginning. One hostile critic condemned the "dream play" as a genre, and bitingly declared: "Herbert and MacDonough seemingly did their utmost to induce sleep in all present, but they did not quite succeed, and the waking on-lookers found little save unreasonableness and confusion in all that the 'dream play' contained." As usual the luckless librettist aroused the highest degree of ire. In spite of its superior sources the book had "not a hint of imagination, poetry, or beauty in any of the scenes, and the lines are woefully lacking in wit or humor."[65]

Something had to be done, and quickly. While the unsatisfactory version struggled along, MacDonough was making a drastic revision which was presented to the public of Chicago on October 8. Nearly all of the Lewis Carroll characters were dropped, including even Alice; new characters were added; some of the early music was tossed aside, and new pieces were composed. And the title was changed to *The Eight Princesses.*

The improvement was hailed with pleasure; but much had to be done before the show opened in New York at the Majestic Theatre on October 24. By now it bore its third and final title, *Wonderland,* and its so-called plot had been "simplified" to an astonishing degree.[66]

When New Yorkers looked at the program they noted that the production was called "a fantastic musical play, in three acts." They noted, too, the alleged indebtedness to "The Dancing Princess" by the brothers Grimm. Then they read the following cast:

Dr. Fax, a specialist in love and its cure; head
    of the Hospital for Broken Hearts . . . . Sam Chip
Phyllis, a Dresden Shepherdess . . . . Eva Davenport
Gladys, Dr. Fax's daughter . . . . Aimee Angeles
Hildegarde Figgers, a teacher at the Asylum for
    Children of the Homeless Rich . . . . Lotta Faust
Prince Fortunio . . . . Bessie Wynn

Capt. Montague Blue | Two professional heroes, recently employed as the | Charles Barry
James, the stoker | crew of the airship "Peekaboo" . . . . | George McKay

King of Hearts, disguised as Perrico, a gypsy
    musician . . . . J. C. Marlowe
Leander . . . . Doris Mitchell
Margot, the favorite daughter of the King of Hearts . . Sue Kelleher
Gertrude . . . . Hulda Halvers
Rollo, Dr. Fax's horse . . . . { James Harris / Eugene Kelly
Chief of Gendarmes . . . . William McDaniels

Margaret | | Emily Fulton
Marguerite | | Helen Hilton
Meg | Daughters of the King | Alice Eis
Marjorie | Hearts . . . . | Lucille Eagen
Margherita | | Phoebe Loubet
Madge | | Adele Gordon
Maggie | | Minnie Woodbury
Romeo . . . . Marie Franklin

Antony..............................Kathryne Howland
Orlando................................Georgia   Baron
Lothario................................Louise Burpee
Paolo....................................Sadie Emmons
Giovanni...............................Madge Burpee
Bassanio...............................Rose   Fredricks
Monitors.............................. { May Leslie
                                         Lillian Devere
Students in the nature classes
Freshmen—8 girls
Sophomores—8 girls
Companions of Prince Fortunio—19 girls

There was a change of setting with every scene. Act I: Scene 1,
Dr. Fax's cottage in the King's Park; Scene 2, the Painted Desert;
Scene 3, the Square of the Houses that make Faces. Act II: Scene 1,
the King's Park; Scene 2, the exterior of a department store; Scene 3,
a department store; Scene 4, the Lake of the Enchanted Castle. Act III,
Ballroom of the Enchanted Castle. The stage manager was Robert
Fairchild, the musical director Carl Styx.

At first New York seemed to like *Wonderland*; but, once the novelty
had worn off, the patronage declined. The *Times* calmly announced
that it was little more than an elaborate vaudeville show which would
please those who liked pretty girls, pretty costumes, pretty songs,
pretty music. The most hopeful critic was from the *Evening Post,* and
he thought the show might become a rival of *Babes in Toyland.*
Admitting that Herbert had written better scores he consoled himself
with this truism: "Victor Herbert at his worst is better than most of
his rivals at their best."

There was unanimous agreement on just one thing, the marvelous
performance of Rollo. This artificial quadruped was operated by strings
pulled by the two men concealed within it, and his expressions and
gyrations were the hit and feature of the evening. One critic archly
suggested that the horse should have written the book so that the
audience could detect the semblance of a plot.[67]

The music was neither Herbert's best nor his worst. The opening
chorus ("Until We Meet Again") was graceful. "The Nature Class"
was excellent and sparkling. "Jografree," although cute and effective,
failed to match "I Can't Do the Sum" from *Babes in Toyland,* which
it obviously resembled. "Love's Golden Day" (Fortunio's love song)
was characteristic, and "The Only One" (also Fortunio) was a very
singable waltz.

The troublesome history of the show affected Herbert as it did
others concerned. Julian Mitchell, the producer, knew this, and he

also knew that some of Herbert's best music had to be sacrificed. Describing the rough path traversed, he commented on the changes and problems:

It was "Alice in Wonderland" [*sic*] when we opened in Buffalo and played in Chicago.

There was a prologue with some of the prettiest music Victor Herbert has ever written. Chip's part, Dr. Fax, was then the hatter. We had the Mad Tea Party, the Dormouse, the March Hare and all. But it wouldn't hold together.

Alice wandered through the scenes, but it would not do.

Buffalo accepted it, but Chicago would not stand for it. So we cut out the prologue with Mr. Herbert's pretty music; Alice, the Hare, the Hatter, the Red Knight, the Duchess—all the "Alice in Wonderland" characters, except the King of Hearts; rewrote, reshaped the play as you see it now.

Why, last Saturday night we were rehearsing in Lyric Hall, while Mr. McDonough was writing the new lines, new situations and new business, and sending it over to us by messenger, page by page.

"Alice in Wonderland" is a classic to read, but it can't be dramatized— it is a dream too delicate. There are not twenty lines in this edition that we used in the first.[68]

Nevertheless *Wonderland* had 73 performances in New York before it moved on to other places.[69] It was popular on the road as it toured for the remainder of this and all of the following season, so that what failed to advance Herbert artistically at least brought him some reward materially.

With one exception which, nationally considered, belongs to the following year, 1905 was not one of Herbert's outstanding operetta periods; but he maintained his industry and zeal. At the same time he maintained his conducting activities, including benefit performances, and his social connections with the musical great. On Sunday afternoon October 29 he was one of four conductors directing a special orchestral concert for a new tuberculosis hospital in the Adirondacks.[70] On November 12, also Sunday, he helped Nahan Franko open a new home, other guests being Willem Mengelberg, Andreas Dippel, Antonio Scotti, Enrico Caruso, Heinrich Conried, and Alfred Hertz.[71] His Sunday evening concerts were again in full swing, and the critics commented approvingly on the judicious programs which mixed Herbert's lighter classics with the most advanced Wagnerian excerpts.[72]

As far as the concert world in general was concerned, the end of the year brought to Herbert a combined triumph and disaster, neither of which he could surmount. The triumph was of his own making, the disaster stemmed from his old archenemy, the *Musical Courier*. Absolute proof is lacking, but there seems to be no reason to doubt that the resentful journal was responsible for Herbert's losing a post which he must have desired greatly.

The Philharmonic Society of New York was still seeking a permanent conductor. Its policy of guest conductors yet prevailed, and notable figures from abroad were striving for its leadership. During the 1905–1906 season Herbert was on its podium for two pairs of concerts, the first occurring on December 1 and 2. His success was unquestioned, and it was the more significant because he was the only American conductor awarded a hearing.

Herbert's program for the first pair of concerts was not exceptional, but the familiarity of the music tested his capacity all the more:

New World Symphony	Dvořák
Piano Concerto	Grieg
Raoul Pugno, soloist	
Variations from "Death and the Maiden" Quartet	
(for strings)	Schubert
Les Préludes	Liszt

In rendering this program, indeed, he elicited unprecedented praise and seemed to be in a favored position for the appointment to conduct the Philharmonic Society. Pugno was so delighted with the accompaniment that he tried to embrace Herbert on the stage. A calmer judgment, but with no less conviction, was this: "The benignant and invigorating personality and the driving musical force of the conductor communicated themselves to the orchestra of capable and earnest musicians that he led, and through them to a sincerely delighted and enthusiastic audience."[73] Even the hard-to-move Krehbiel was pleased as he compared Herbert with other leaders from foreign lands: "In strong contrast with most of the visiting conductors, Mr. Herbert made no effort to force the mere muscularity of the gigantic Philharmonic band upon the attention of the audience. Instead he seemed chiefly desirous to show its euphony as well as its virility, and in that he succeeded most admirably. He challenged the admiration of an audience that knew the music, and won a fine guerdon of praise."[74]

Just before Herbert's Philharmonic concerts, however, the *Musical Courier* took a hand in his destiny. It had not forgotten the victory he had won over it in 1902, and it was waiting for a chance at revenge. Since the famous trial the paper had almost totally ignored his existence, and the absence of his name in its pages seemed to be definitely the result of editorial policy. Suddenly, on November 29, there appeared an excellent photograph of Herbert and this amazing statement:

A man is known in the musical world by his musical deeds, and Victor Herbert's musical deeds are the basic element of the fame which he has deservedly won and now so properly enjoys. . . .

Herbert's reputation as a composer of classical music followed fast in the footsteps of his fame as a 'cellist, although he wrote comic operas also, which are very successful. His two concertos for his favorite instrument are models of their kind, filled with sprightly melody and of exquisite workmanship, and thoroughly modern in facture and technic, while retaining all the established dignity and impressiveness of the orthodox concerto form. Other 'cellists soon realized the worth of the Herbert concertos, and they have been performed repeatedly at the best symphony concerts in Europe and America. . . .

Of all Herbert's orchestral works, perhaps the finest is the symphonic poem, "Hero and Leander," which the composer himself led at a Philharmonic concert last year . . . "Hero and Leander" is a work of serious mien and facture, steeped in rich orchestral color, glowing with imagination, and embellished with all those arts and artifices of modern orchestration which characterize the work of our best latter day composers. . . .

. . . His remarkable work in Pittsburg, where he led for five [sic] years, as head of the Symphony Orchestra there, is too well remembered by THE MUSICAL COURIER readers to need repetition at this moment. Herbert trained and developed the raw material which he found in Pittsburg, and laid the foundation for the finished work which the Pittsburg Orchestra now is able to accomplish under its present leader. A glance over the Pittsburg programs of Herbert will show that he has at his fingers' ends all the entire representative musical literature for orchestra.

The qualities which he displayed in Pittsburg were all in evidence here when he led the Philharmonic concert last season, exuberant temperament chastened by scholarly sobriety, warm imagination tempered by dignified musicianship, and a fine perception of the most subtle niceties of phrasing, orchestral combination and instrumental shading and coloring. Also he revealed all the executive powers without which no conductor can hope to be great.

Gifted with all these advantages, Victor Herbert seems to be the logical choice as permanent conductor of the Philharmonic Society when that body gets ready to choose such a counsellor, guide and friend. . . .

Victor Herbert is the man for the place, by all means, and it looks to those on the inside as though the Philharmonic Society is already contemplating his engagement when it makes its final choice.

What must Herbert's feelings have been as his eyes fell on these astonishing words? How must his friends have reacted as they at last read the truth about Herbert in the *Musical Courier*? If they derived any satisfaction at all, it was short-lived; another quarter was affected by this outburst of praise; namely, the Philharmonic Society itself.

Selecting a permanent conductor was a serious matter which could not be taken lightly. For some years the *Musical Courier,* notwithstanding its reportorial activity, had lost the respect of all decent musical forces in the city. It was an evil which had to be tolerated; but it was held in obloquy, and it influenced no one of importance or stature. If Herbert should now be chosen conductor of the Philharmonic, the *Musical Courier* could actually boast of the part it had played in the selection. Consequently the directors of the Society had no choice as far as Herbert was concerned—he could not be appointed!

Perhaps two motives prompted Blumenberg—for who else could it be?—to write as he did. If Herbert were chosen, the *Courier* could claim credit for the appointment. Or, if Herbert were repudiated, the *Courier* (i.e., Blumenberg) could claim credit for that, too, for it knew full well how cordially it was disliked by respectable people. I feel very strongly that the second motive persuaded Blumenberg to take his ingenious step. He realized that his support would bring about Herbert's defeat, and he phrased and timed it so cleverly that there could be no reply from any adversary, least of all from Herbert himself. For what could Herbert possibly retort? It is strange indeed that laudatory truth can injure the object thereof; but in this case it did, and the victim was powerless to strike back.

The *Musical Courier* was not satisfied with just one amazing outburst. Figuratively, it turned the knife in the wound. After the Philharmonic concerts of December 1 and 2 it blandly ranged itself on the side of the angels, reporting: ". . . the concerts of last week brought forth artistic results which not one of the imported conductors had been able to achieve . . . The orchestra played with a measure of spontaneity, of care, of precision, and of finish that was delightful. The strings have never sounded more smooth and well balanced, tonally and dynamically, than at the two Herbert concerts, and the brass and woodwind choirs were a revelation in their evenness, accuracy and lovely quality of tone." Then back to its new theme: "If any further substantiation were needed of THE MUSICAL COURIER claim that Victor Herbert is the conductor par excellence for the Philharmonic, then such demonstration was amply furnished at Carnegie Hall last Friday and Saturday."[75]

History unhappily records that Blumenberg's strategy worked to perfection. When 1906 was a few weeks old Vassily Safonoff was appointed permanent conductor of the Philharmonic. Once the news was made public, the *Musical Courier* retreated on March 14 from the side of virtue and revealed its true self in a very long and pointless editorial that gave mocking sympathy to Herbert and recapitulated much of the 1902 trial including the jubilant banquet which had followed it. Why had Herbert failed to secure the conductorship? "Because," said the editor, "the support of the daily paper music critics in itself was sufficient to annihilate every chance he had." And he proceeded to blast New York's critical coterie with meaningless, bombastic phrases. He admitted, too, that he had supported Herbert's candidacy only to show that the critics' collective influence over important musical matters was nil and that he hated to see Herbert offered as a sacrifice to their venal schemings. Only in the closing paragraph of his senseless statement did he reveal his pent-up rancor. He set forth two melodies and wrote:

In view of this and in view of certain preceding events, THE MUSICAL COURIER herewith reproduces two specimens of compositions . . . the first specimen being from a song copyrighted in 1902, and second from [a] comic opera copyrighted in 1904.* . . . This paper would be pleased to have Walter Damrosch's opinion now, after more than three years after a former opinion had been officially given by him. This only shows that different composers have the same ideas at different times.

Not long afterward, this appeared on the *Courier's* editorial page: "The picture of a comic-opera composer has been hung in a New York clubhouse. We thought that hanging for thievery had long ago been abolished."[76]

The implications were obvious. Protected in his own scurrility, Blumenberg was able to prevent Herbert from receiving the Philharmonic conductorship, and practically at the same time to suggest theft in one of Herbert's most famous melodies. (Friends of Herbert need have no fear over this little known accusation: after similar beginnings the two melodies are entirely different—and Herbert's is infinitely superior.) But the damage was done, and the loss of the conducting post was irretrievable. Actually, of course, Blumenberg probably performed for Herbert a service in disguise. Had Herbert become a symphonic conductor again, his career would have been vastly changed; and it would be unreasonable to regret today his failure to get the post. But it would be just as unreasonable to say that Blumenberg was acting for the good of music. His writings were based on personal spleen, and his execution was diabolically effective.

Herbert gave no sign that he was disturbed by the surprising support of the *Musical Courier*. Indeed, he and his wife royally entertained one of his rivals for the appointment—Max Fiedler, who conducted the Philharmonic on December 15 and 16—at a luncheon party on December 17, and made music with him and Maud Powell in a thoroughly *gemütlich* way. Theodore Steinway was one of the contented listeners.[77] The end of the year found the composer calm, charitable, and unruffled—moods which were augmented by merriment

---

* The two were respectively Oley Speaks's "When Mabel Sings," and "The Absinthe Frappé" from Herbert's *It Happened in Nordland*.

as he conducted a special "watch night" concert on New Year's Eve in Carnegie Hall. The concert began at 9:30; his own orchestra was augmented for the occasion, and Maud Powell was the soloist.[78] Herbert was his most buoyant self, for one of his masterpieces had just opened in New York a week before.

13

Triumphs and Vexations

ON THE 27th of October, 1904, Victor Herbert signed a contract with Charles B. Dillingham obligating himself to compose an "original music score" for a comic opera in which the leading part would be played by Fritzi Scheff,[1] to deliver a completed piano-vocal score not more than four months after he received the libretto, and to have a full orchestra score ready in time for rehearsal. Dillingham pledged, among other things, to produce the comic opera "in a first class manner" and to reward the composer with royalties totaling 3 per cent of the gross receipts. Such was the beginning of *Mlle. Modiste*, the opera which immortalized the dynamic Fritzi and won for itself an unique place in American affections. Who can say that any Herbert operetta surpasses it, or that any singer (provided she can sing) ever had a more ingratiating role?

Henry Blossom was selected as librettist, and he proved to be the best such collaborator the composer ever had. Though not brilliant or strikingly clever, he had a sense of proportion and consistency which Herbert needed.

Presumably Herbert wrote most of the music in the summer of 1905. Fritzi returned late in August from a vacation in Europe and inspected the new work with Herbert and Blossom on the 26th.[2] In less than two weeks the rehearsals were under way; and the first performance on any stage occurred at the Taylor Opera House in Trenton on Saturday night October 7. The New Jersey capital saw only a single performance, but the patrons knew that something special was being launched. They learned from the advertisements three things: eighty-five persons would be on the stage; three carloads of scenery would decorate the stage; the "free list" was suspended.[3]

The company moved southward over the week end to Washington, where, on October 9, *Mlle. Modiste* bewitched President and Mrs. Theodore Roosevelt, a large share of United States officialdom, and a brilliant society gathering who packed the Columbia Theatre. They were richly rewarded for coming, and called vociferously for the composer and author, both of whom appeared on the stage after Act I and spoke brief words of thanks.[4]

After a week which was completely triumphant, the company embarked on an extended tour of two and a half months before it ventured into Broadway. Winning friends in New England it swung westward across the State of New York to Detroit, Cleveland, and Chicago, which gave it a special welcome intensified by the unhappy memory of the ill-fated *Wonderland*. The caustic critic on the Chicago *Tribune* was glad to say that Herbert in this fine score had fully redeemed himself.[5]

When *Mlle. Modiste* finally reached New York City it was a smoothly operating production. It was a happy Christmas present to Herbert's admirers—the metropolitan première being on Christmas night at the Knickerbocker Theatre. The splendid cast was as follows:

Henri de Bouvray, Comte de St. Mar.........William Pruette
Capt. Etienne de Bouvray, his nephew........Walter Percival
Hiram Bent, an American millionaire.....Claude Gillingwater
Gaston, an artist, Mme. Cécile's son................Leo Mars
General Le Marquis de Villefranche.........George Schraeder
Lieut. René La Motte, engaged to Marie
    Louise...............................Howard Chambers
François, porter at Mme. Cécile's..............R. W. Hunt
Mme. Cécile, proprietress of a Parisian
    hat shop...........................Josephine Bartlett
Fanchette ⎫ her daughters............⎧   Edna Fassett
Nanette ⎭   ⎩ Blanche Morrison
Marie Louise de Bouvray, Etienne's sister.....Louise Le Baron
Bébé, dancer at the Folies Bergères............Miss La Mora
Fleurette...................................Ada Meade
Mrs. Hiram Bent..........................Bertha Holly
Fifi.......................................Fritzi Scheff
        Milliners, Guests, Dancers, Soldiers, Servants, etc.

The stage director was Fred G. Latham; the music director, John Lund.

The first act transpires in Mme. Cécile's hat shop, Rue de la Paix, Paris. The second act, a year later, has two scenes: the private dining room of the Comte de St. Mar; the charity bazaar in the gardens of the Château de St. Mar.

Fifi, a fetching employee in the hat shop, falls in love with Etienne, but it seems that their romance will be short-lived. She is expected to marry the son of her employer, while Etienne is forbidden to wed outside his own aristocratic circle. A democratic American millionaire becomes interested in Fifi and helps her realize her ambition, to become a great singer. After a successful period of study, she returns to sing at the home of her beloved's uncle, breaks down the irascible old Count's opposition, and is claimed by Etienne as a worthy addition to the family.

For this trite but not unreasonable story, Herbert provided a score of unusually high consistency and refinement. It sparkled and sang, and it fitted the dramatic situations in near-exemplary fashion. His particular gifts were never better in evidence—gracefulness, piquancy, martial exuberance, and rich tonal color. Almost every number was distinguished of its kind, from the opening scene to the fall of the closing curtain.

Etienne's "The Time and the Place and the Girl" well characterizes the young officer's regret in never finding the three elements together. Fifi's "If I Were on the Stage" is an equally convincing statement of what she would like to do if she had the opportunity. Part of this song is the famous "Kiss Me Again," in which the clever girl shows how she would play an emotional love scene. In its context it is a gem of dramatic propriety and justly the most celebrated air in American operetta. When she appears later as a finished artist, her "The Nightingale and the Star" is a flashing concert waltz that attests the hard work she has recently done.

The crotchety Count is just as well characterized in his gruffly boisterous "I Want What I Want When I Want It," and the spirit of the French officers, shared by Fifi, is brought irresistibly to life in "The Mascot of the Troop." This is one of the best marches the composer ever wrote, with a quotation from "La Marseillaise" that lends authentic color. Even the comic songs ("The Keokuk Culture Club" and "The English Language") contributed to the judgment that the music was "as sparkling as champagne," and that it placed Herbert "in a class by himself."[6]

Critical opinion in New York was unanimous in one respect and divided in another. Fritzi Scheff was hailed as a sheer sensation, but Herbert's music aroused conflicting views. Both reactions were reflected in the daily press as well as in the theatrical journals. Her voice and technic were "eminently superior to anything a comic-opera audience has any normal right to expect,"[7] and she proved to be the brightest luminary of the New York season. Her acting and stage deportment were continually improving, and with the help of the music her "piquant personality" "no longer at odds with her environment, but yielding all her charm to the creation of character and atmosphere,"[8] bewitched every spectator. Another onlooker, more satisfied with her earlier performances, had to admit that she here surpassed all previous efforts. "She gave evidence of her gifts in such parts as Zerlina, and the gypsy in Paderewski's opera; she showed among other things, how much can be made of the action in so small a part as the first Rhine daughter in Wagner's trilogy. Since her grand opera days, she has become more subtle, saucy, pointed, amusing, and her Fifi is her masterpiece."[9] Thus was created one of the most important, effervescent, and convincing rôles in the entire operetta literature.

Herbert's music fared less well with some of the critics, but the public proved the carpers were in the wrong. The reviewers of the *Times* and the *Tribune* were not overly favorable, but the *Herald* and the *Evening Post* reported with undisguised enthusiasm. The *Evening Post* writer was quite perspicacious in stating that Herbert's "music does not contain so many individual numbers as some of his earlier operettas, but there is the same refreshing absence of the common and commonplace as in the libretto. Whether he writes for solo voice or chorus, Mr. Herbert is always interesting, and in the orchestra, too, there are clever bits for those who listen. He has a genuine and seemingly inexhaustible sense of musical humor, which is one of the secrets of his immense success." And he commented approvingly on *Mlle. Modiste* as a whole, implying clearly that it was on a far higher level than similar productions: it was free of vulgar traits, and should serve as a lesson to managers "who think that in this kind of entertainment the public likes only what it has always had, changed only by being turned to a lower key of coarseness and stupidity."

It is curious how scant was the attention paid to the famous "Kiss Me Again." Once its full beauty was realized, however, a supply of legends grew up telling either of its origin or of the first time it was ever heard. One story is that the melody came to Herbert on a hot summer night in 1905 after conducting a concert at Saratoga. Unable to sleep and plagued by the tune, he rose and jotted it down in rough outline, then crawled back to bed and fell asleep. The next morning he wrote it out in full.[10] Another story, romantically elaborated, has Herbert walking in the hotel gardens at Saratoga of a summer evening, and inadvertently overhearing the remarks of lovers. He was struck by the soft request, "Kiss me," and drew his inspiration from his accidental eavesdropping.[11]

The story I like best and believe authentic, because it has no frills and sounds professional, was told me by Herbert's old friend W. M. Jacoby of Pittsburgh. A couple of years before *Mlle. Modiste* (this would be in 1903) Herbert returned from Lake Placid to Pittsburgh, and Jacoby visited him. The composer said that a particularly beautiful melody had occurred to him one night at his summer home. Would the young reporter like to hear it? Of course. So Herbert played the still nameless air on his cello. When Jacoby asked what he would do with the melody, the composer replied he would use it some day in an operetta.[12]

Jacoby certainly heard the tune very early; but he did not claim to have been the first so privileged. This rash statement was put forth by the actor Lionel Barrymore, who asserted that he and a small group of friends including Herbert and Henry Hadley were the first to hear it—in an upstairs room of the Lambs' clubhouse, played by Herbert and Hadley from a "complicated orchestra score."[13] It would seem that his claim was based on wishful thinking nearly half a century later. Herbert would hardly have completed the full score of *Mlle. Modiste* without some one having heard its most effective theme.

There is ample reason to believe that Fritzi Scheff heard it well before Barrymore, for in the fall of 1905 Herbert went over it with her at the piano. There is reason also to believe that she did not like it, protesting that it began too low for her voice (although the starting note was only a half-tone lower than notes she sang elsewhere). Herbert told her she need hardly more than breathe its rapturous beginning; but she disliked the entire piece, and so did Blossom and Dillingham. Only Herbert's obstinacy—this time very fortunate—kept the song in the show,[14] where it became the epitome of tender love. There was irony in this result, for "Kiss Me Again" was in a sense a parody on love; it is what Fifi *would* sing *if* she were on the stage in a romantic rôle, not what she does sing after experiencing the grand emotion.

With its glamorous music and superlative star *Mlle. Modiste* enjoyed a New York run of 202 performances,[15] to the end of the season. During the summer Fritzi Scheff vacationed in Europe, but on September 1, 1906, she and the operetta were back at the Knickerbocker Theatre[16] for three more weeks, after which they went on tour. (They had to leave this particular house because Herbert's next smash hit was coming in; it was *The Red Mill!*) Metropolitan New York had them for another fortnight in Harlem and in Brooklyn, however, before other cities were visited. The company was on the road the entire season. With the 1907–1908 season Fritzi and *Mlle. Modiste* were again at the Knickerbocker Theatre on September 9 for three weeks.[17] The tour which followed this third New York appearance extended to the West Coast and ended with a four-week stand in New York's Academy of Music. It is no wonder that Fritzi is perennially identified with Herbert's Parisian comic opera. After her first year as Fifi, in fact, reports circulated that she would appear in a sequel to *Mlle. Modiste* to be called *The Mascot of the Troop*,[18] with music by Herbert. Unfortunately this intriguing possibility never materialized.

It would not be fair to pass on without answering the curious allegations that Herbert had pilfered the two most popular melodies in *Mlle. Modiste*. One commonplace remark is that the opening of "Kiss Me Again" is nearly identical with the beginning of Albéniz's *Cordova*. It is just as obvious, however, that after this beginning the two pieces have nothing in common, musically or spiritually. It is an injustice to both composers to maintain that there is more than a fortuitous relationship between them.

The other allegation is less well known; but it came to the composer's attention and aroused his ire to the point of writing a letter to the editor of the New York *Evening Telegram* (printed October 28, 1907), which explains the matter in full sufficiency. More important is the revelation of his feeling toward a gifted composer who had recently produced a masterly operetta. Herbert wrote:

In your issue of the EVENING TELEGRAM dated October 25, 1907, under the heading entitled "Did 'Mlle. Modiste' and 'The Merry Widow' Compare Notes," you publish a statement to the effect that "that march septet, 'The Women! Oh, the Women,' in the second act of 'The Merry Widow' is almost identical with the well known drum song* that Fritzi Scheff sings in 'Mlle. Modiste.'" This statement is followed by an insinuation that either my drum song was copied from 'The Merry Widow' or that both were copied from a common source.

I most emphatically protest against that insinuation as utterly unfounded. The drum song was absolutely original with me. 'Mlle. Modiste' is now running in its third year and was written before 'The Merry Widow' was produced. A comparison of the two pieces will show that melodically there is absolutely no resemblance between them.

A grave injustice is done to both Mr. Lehar as well as myself by printing in your columns such a malicious statement, purporting to have been made by an alleged informant whose identity is concealed.

It is not fair to print in your columns irresponsible drivel respecting works of acknowledged merit.

Herbert was completely right in expressing his indignation. It only remains to add that *The Merry Widow* was produced in Vienna on December 30, 1905, nearly three months after *Mlle. Modiste* was introduced in Trenton.

With *Mlle. Modiste* a huge success Herbert resumed his usual duties as a conductor. Early in 1906 his orchestra appeared again in the famous Bagby musicales at the Waldorf-Astoria, and in the spring he and

---

* "The Mascot of the Troop."

the orchestra presented Sunday evening concerts in the new and wondrous Hippodrome. On March 2 and 3 he made his final appearance as candidate for the leadership of the Philharmonic Society. A new aspect of his interest in nationalism appeared when he directed his orchestra, also in the Waldorf-Astoria, at a concert arranged as a benefit for the Society of Italian Immigration.[19] Surprisingly enough, it occurred on March 17, St. Patrick's Day!

On Sunday April 1, Herbert and his men nearly suffered disaster. There was an afternoon rehearsal on the mechanical stage (a marvel of ingenuity) of the Hippodrome. Something suddenly went wrong with the valves controlling the water supply for the great tank underneath, and when the center portion of the stage itself abruptly sank several feet into the inundation, everyone had to scramble to safety. A number of players were drenched; but the music and instruments were saved, and the concert took place as usual.[20]

Several unexpected but urgently needed benefit performances resulted from the San Francisco earthquake and fire, which occurred on April 18. On the 29th Herbert helped the afflicted by conducting an orchestra of 350 men in the Hippodrome, many of the players being volunteers from the Aschenbrödel Verein.[21] The largest and most glamorous benefit, however, took place on May 4 in the Metropolitan Opera House. Again Herbert and his orchestra constituted one of the many attractions which presented a continuous program running from eleven o'clock in the morning until eleven o'clock at night.[22] It was a most peculiar affair. Others appearing were Emma Eames, David Bispham, Adele Aus der Ohe, Lillian Blauvelt, Rafael Joseffy, Ernestine Schumann-Heink, Yvette Guilbert, and several dramatic companies in scenes from their current plays. For this marathon performance 32,000 tickets were sold at one dollar each, but the audience, once inside, would not leave. At six o'clock the manager had to ask those in seats to go out so that the thousands still in line could enter. Additional thousands were told, by large conspicuous signs, that their tickets would be honored at other theatres located from downtown to Harlem. The climax of the day came when the manager auctioned off a souvenir program autographed by all the participants. Amidst loud applause it went for $1,000 to the famous actress Lotta Crabtree.

Among the sufferers in the San Francisco catastrophe was the Bohemian Club. The Lambs had to do something for their West Coast friends, and their annual Ladies' Gambol was accordingly turned into a benefit. A highly attractive program was presented on Friday afternoon May 18 in the Broadway Theatre. An important feature was a well developed musical skit entitled *The Song Birds,* written by George

V. Hobart and composed by Victor Herbert. It had first been presented five days earlier in the clubhouse.[23]

This skit, subtitled "A Musical Fancy in One Flight," was significant and prophetic. Oscar Hammerstein, ingenious impresario of theater and opera, had let it be known he would be at the head of an opera company in the fall. He was seriously threatening the sacred precincts of the Metropolitan, and he was far from timid in declaring his intent. (An intense rivalry developed and lasted four years, during which time Hammerstein's company achieved greatness.) Herbert's skit, never published in its entirety, was a clever satire on the predicted struggle between Hammerstein of the Manhattan Opera Company and Heinrich Conried who directed the Metropolitan Opera forces.

The promise of the program was realized in the performance. The impersonators of Hammerstein and Conried were so convincing that the onlookers thought they would come to blows. Like wise impresarios, however, they settled their dispute less violently. They lined up their respective singers on opposite sides of the stage and let them sing each other hoarse. There was a roar of sound, and "every note, from the high C of Nordica to the sub-basement guttural of the man who tried to look like Edouard de Reszke. Then Victor Herbert, who conducted the orchestra, developed a clever idea. Each of the 'artists' began to sing a familiar number from one of the grand operas. Mr. Herbert had arranged these in such a way that they harmonized, and the curtain descended on an impressive finale."[24]

Best of all was the announcement by Clay M. Greene, Shepherd of the Lambs, that some $6,000 would go to the Bohemian Club of San Francisco.[25]

About the same time Herbert participated in a benefit which must have exerted a peculiar appeal: a mammoth concert in memory of Patrick S. Gilmore, with whose name at least he had been so closely associated. Arrangements were begun early in April, and everything was planned in typical Gilmore fashion—grandiose, lavish, magnificent. There were to be 1,000 voices in the chorus, 1,000 players in the orchestra, and no fewer than four conductors (Herbert, Sousa, and Walter and Frank Damrosch). The date was May 15,[26] and the proceeds were intended for Gilmore's widow and daughter.

The concert took place in Madison Square Garden and was a tremendous popular success. Fully 12,000 persons attended and paid homage to the cherished band leader. Unfortunately the Musical Mutual Protective Union, which had agreed to furnish the vast number of extra musicians, suddenly demanded full union pay for every player.[27] They justified their stand on the very illogical ground that the concert had been insufficiently publicized! As a result, when all the bills were paid, the beneficiaries received nothing at all and continued their cramped existence in one room in Boston.[28] The generosity of the four conductors, who appeared for nothing, saved the affair from complete disaster.

Somewhat different were the results of another benefit for which Herbert and his men appeared gratis: a testimonial "variety" program to aid the beloved comedian Henry Clay Barnabee of *Bostonians* fame and Mrs. W. H. MacDonald, widow of his old colleague. This occurred on Tuesday December 11 in the Broadway Theatre and netted more than $22,000[29]—a fact which must have given Herbert untold satisfaction. He was never happier than when helping someone else.

In midsummer Herbert went to Willow Grove for his usual stay (three weeks beginning July 8), and on September 24 he opened a week's engagement at the Pittsburgh Exposition. The Pennsylvania town welcomed him as one of its own and kept him busy with luncheons and dinners all the time he was there. His friends discovered he was working on a new opera,[30] which was always the case, and watched with special interest the one which had just been launched. It was among his best, and America quickly took it to its heart. The title was *The Red Mill*.

This perennial favorite was planned as a starring vehicle for Fred Stone and David Montgomery, the luminaries of the remarkable *The Wizard of Oz*, and Dillingham, the producer, displayed rare judgment in securing Henry Blossom and Victor Herbert to create the words and music. The composer did most of his work from June to August, a sweltering period which led him to write on the title page of the overture: "(Aug. 22nd 1906) Hot as the devil."[31]

The title was announced well in advance of production, and one speculative reporter wondered if *The Red Mill* "alludes subtly to the scenes of diluted dissipation and affected wickedness which were obtained at the famous 'Red Mills' of Paris, or whether the reference is flatly rural and domestic."[32] Herbert did not answer the query, and so the writer had to wait to discover that the new work reflected neither the sophistication of Le Moulin rouge nor the open countryside of the land of dikes. It was healthfully and hilariously different. Blossom did advance the claim, nevertheless, that *The Red Mill* would be the first piece ever staged in America with a scenario confined to Holland.[33]

The first performance on any stage occurred at the Star Theatre, Buffalo, on the evening of September 3, 1906. Herbert, Blossom, and Dillingham sat together in a box and saw a well rehearsed show give infinite pleasure to an immense audience.

The Red Mill met with equal success in New York when it opened at the Knickerbocker Theatre on September 24. The program called it "a musical play in two acts" and gave the following cast:

"Con" Kidder ⎱ Two Americans "doing" ⎰ Fred A. Stone
"Kid" Conner ⎰ Europe..............⎱ David Montgomery
Jan Van Borkem, Burgomaster of Katwyk-
    aan-Zee.................................Edward Begley
Franz, Sheriff of Katwyk-aan-Zee.............Charles Dox
Willem, keeper of the Red Mill Inn...........David L. Don
Captain Doris Van Damm, in love with
    Gretchen..............................Joseph M. Ratliff
The Governor of Zeeland, engaged to Gretchen....Neal McCay
Joshua Pennefeather, Solicitor, Lincoln's Inn
    Fields, London (automobiling with his
    daughters through Holland)...............Claude Cooper
Gretchen, the Burgomaster's daughter......Augusta Greenleaf
Bertha, the Burgomaster's sister.................Aline Crater
Tina (barmaid), Willem's daughter............Ethel Johnson
Countess de la Tere, automobiling with her
    sons through Holland......................Juliette Dika
Flora.................................Constance Eastman
Dora.....................................Kitty Howland
Lena....................................Paula Desmond
Anna....................................Cleo Sweninger
Phyllis..................................Estelle Baldwin
Madge.....................................Sadie Probst
        Peasants, Artists, Aides de Camp, Burghers, etc.

The music director was Max Hirschfeld; the staging was in charge of Fred G. Latham.

The play unfolded in the little Dutch port of Katwyk-aan-Zee, and the time was the present. The first act transpired "at the sign of the Red Mill"; the second showed a hall in the home of the Burgomaster.

The Red Mill was happily fated from the start. It was well-nigh perfect of its kind, maintained an extremely high level of entertainment, and exhibited no song or tune which would not bear repetition. It was light, bright, cheerful, and merry. Herbert had attempted things which were more romantic, more ambitious, but he never achieved anything which blended better with the action and story or which afforded more genuine satisfaction.

The fairly well known story centers in the adventures of two Americans, stranded penniless in Europe, who try various subterfuges to get back to New York. Looked upon as suspicious characters and appearing in outlandish disguises, they help forward the romance of the lovers

(Gretchen and Doris), who cannot marry because the Burgomaster is not satisfied with his daughter's suitor. Only when an English lawyer, member of a strange touring party, discloses that the sea captain is heir to a large fortune does the Burgomaster relent. The Americans are vindicated at the same time, and everyone's suspicious confusion is changed to hearty rejoicing.

Again the score exhibited Herbert's best qualities. In "Mignonette" Tina coquettishly tells whom she will imitate when she is an accomplished actress. Willem and the Burgomaster, perplexed by their daughters, lumberingly philosophize in their "You Never Can Tell About a Woman." Doris and Gretchen have an impassioned love duet as they plan to sail to "The Isle of Our Dreams" that very night. The extended finale of the first act, with Gretchen's sweetly plaintive "Moonbeams," is remarkable for its atmospheric effectiveness and its dramatic suitability. The musical ejaculations are singularly impressive.

The second act is closer to burlesque, but the music continues to entertain. "The Legend of the Mill," sung by Bertha, repeats the fable of its being haunted; "Good-a-bye, John" (possibly not by Herbert) shows the two Americans disguised as Italian street musicians; and "Every Day Is Ladies' Day with Me" is announced by the Governor in rollicking style as he anticipates marriage to the unwilling Gretchen.

The Red Mill pleased everyone with its finish, its beauty, its animation. Before it opened in New York expectation was high; after it was seen, satisfaction was complete. "Musicians of note and composers of ability were among the auditors . . . and no one was more enthusiastic in their applause than they were; they know Mr. Herbert's art, and they know its value."[34] The entire production, in fact, was a commendably unified whole, and the staging and the acting supported the music in exemplary fashion. Unquestionably Montgomery and Stone walked off with the greatest distinction. Their antics, their breeziness, their acrobatic dancing were irresistible; but their confreres lagged not far behind. "From Mr. Stone's first entrance down a ladder to his comic assumption of the character of Sherlock Holmes in the last act, this funny fellow, all joints and legs and angles, and his funny companion keep the merriment at unflagging pitch, and without the aid of grotesque makeup, either." So wrote the show's severest critic, who went on to reflect that Herbert had "written better music, and music that was better—very much better—sung. But his music for 'The Red Mill' has frequent moments of rhythmic felicity, especially in the dances, and on the rare occasions where a touch of something more is called for he has not been unwilling to respond."[35]

This was a judicious opinion, for in spite of its popularity the music was not the most impressive Herbert ever wrote. It happened to be an integral and satisfactory part of one of the best operettas ever seen on the American stage. It served its purpose admirably, and that was enough. Another shrewd observer asserted that Herbert had written "better things," "but there can be no question of the popularity of this music. It has a swing that is irresistible, is tuneful and original —quite good enough for the occasion. Once in a while a delightful bit of orchestration is heard, and some of the ensembles are in his best vein. Generally, however, it belongs to the 'popular' type, easily learned. The audience passed out of the house humming the airs which had caught their fancy."[36] There is no reason to doubt that the music was exactly what the composer intended it to be—simple, melodious, direct; and therein lay its strength. How he must have rejoiced at this summation of total effect: " 'The Red Mill' will grind its grist of mirth, music and melody for a long time to come and those who go to see it should wear loose collars, tight buttons and be prepared to whistle or hum its airs without a rehearsal."[37]

This critic was prophetic, for the mill ground ceaselessly and, in a sense, still grinds today. Once in operation it gave New York a run of 274 performances[38]—an exciting figure for those days—and then toured the country for years. It became an American institution, and gives no sign of yielding up its distinctive position.

Certain of Herbert's operettas are revived from time to time, but this happens generally under auspices which preclude expert or even adequate presentation. The most brilliant revival of all was reserved for *The Red Mill* when it was presented in New York at the Ziegfeld Theatre on October 16, 1945. The public, to be sure, evinced more than polite interest, especially because one of the producers was Fred Stone's daughter Paula and one of the cast was her sister Dorothy; but this sentiment changed to gratified amazement as the show ran on and on for more than a year and a quarter. It proved to be vital enough for 531 New York performances in the mid-1940's;[39] and it was the music which wrought this near-miracle, music which suited the action so well that the results were unforgettably beautiful.

The Red Mill, too, enjoyed some success in London—an unusual achievement for Herbert, who never found favor with the English. This presentation occurred somewhat accidentally, substituting for plans which could not be carried out:

In 1919 the Russian ballet season at the Empire Theatre ended on December 20. Sir Alfred Butt, managing director of the house, intended to reconstruct it at once, but found this could not be done for some weeks. Rather than have an idle stage, he arranged to import *The Red Mill,* which was announced to Londoners as having met "with considerable success" in New York some years before.[40] It opened on Boxing Night, December 26, and made a favorable impression.

How effective it was may be judged from the fact that Con Kidder and Kid Conner were two Englishmen [sic] helping a lady in distress! This was considerably different from two brash Americans impersonating, among others, Sherlock Holmes and Dr. Watson. It was admitted, nevertheless, that "some of the music is distinctly good," and the public came to see it up to February 14, 1920.[41] *The Fortune Teller* fared better in London, but *The Red Mill*, practically unheralded, made a brave showing which should not be forgotten.

Apart from its supreme importance in American operetta, *The Red Mill* presents a mystery which still clamors for solution. It centers around one of the most popular songs in the score: "Good-a-bye, John," the delightful dialect novelty which Stone and Montgomery used so cleverly. Evidently Blossom and Herbert were only indirectly responsible for it, and then were sufficiently careless, or unconcerned, to leave the matter unclarified.

"Good-a-bye, John" was a constituent part of the piano-vocal score of *The Red Mill*, as published in the fall of 1906 by M. Witmark and Sons. The song was also published in the customary sheet music edition, registered for copyright on September 24, 1906. It contained one stanza and refrain; Blossom appeared as the author, Herbert as the composer. Now it so happens that almost a year earlier, on October 7, 1905, Jerome H. Remick & Co. published and registered for copyright a song called "Good-a-bye, John" which was an excerpt from the musical comedy *The Belle of Avenue A*, with text by Harry Williams and music by Egbert Van Alstyne. This had two stanzas and refrain, and the words of the first stanza and refrain were the same as the words in the song from *The Red Mill*. Equally strange is the fact that although the melodies of the stanzas of the two songs were different (but decidedly similar), the airs of the refrains were identical!

How did Blossom and Herbert fall into such a trap? It could not conceivably be theft. Herbert never stole anything, and *The Red Mill* was too well known and too widely circulated to permit it. Moreover, Williams and Van Alstyne were celebrities in the popular song field and would surely have put a stop to any infringement of their rights. No record that has come to light shows that they objected in the slightest. Incidentally, there is no evidence that *The Belle of Avenue A* ever received a stage production in New York City. The manuscript score of *The Red Mill*, part autograph, part copy, in the Library of Congress includes a copyist's script of "Good-a-bye, John" which is of the same appearance as the other numbers indisputably Herbert's own. What is the answer?

The matter is complicated still further by an anecdote put forward in 1910 as fact by the theatrical journalist Rennold Wolf. Herbert was known to resent violently interpolations into his operettas. In the summer of 1906, after rehearsals of *The Red Mill* had started, Montgomery and Stone still wanted a number better suited to their peculiar specialties. They had a particular song in mind, but were fearful of approaching Herbert on the matter. Stone finally ventured to broach it one day when he met Herbert on the street:

"Victor, Dave and I want to do a certain kind of a song and dance in this piece, and in a rough kind of a way we've planned out the music. We wish to introduce some peculiar steps and so have to have a certain style of tune. Now, Dave and I know in a general way what we want, and probably you can pattern something after it."

Stone thereupon hummed something to give the general outline and the rhythm. He hummed it a second time and was pleased to hear Herbert say he could do something with it. Thus was born the "Good-a-bye, John" of *Red Mill* fame, but—according to Wolf—Stone knew all the time whose piece it was: a song and dance written by William Jerome and Jean Schwartz! And as late as 1910, wrote Wolf, Herbert still had no idea that Stone had slily effected an interpolation.[42]

The first part of Wolf's story may be correct, but Schwartz was not the composer. He wrote as much to me on March 22, 1952, adding that Stone did wish to use the song in *The Red Mill*. Probably Herbert did not compose it. If he found himself victimized by Stone he never disclosed his feelings, but allowed the song to be identified with his name. It was a harmless subterfuge which was none of the public's business.

Three months after *The Red Mill* opened in New York, the city welcomed another Herbert production which seemed at first destined for equal popularity. This new entry was *Dream City* and *The Magic Knight*—actually a "two-in-one" show, the two parts being closely related and belonging together—first publicly performed at Weber's Theatre in New York on Christmas night, 1906. So peculiar was its nature, however, and so high were the hopes for it, that a special dress rehearsal for the critics was presented on the afternoon of December 24. The conductor at the critical preview was Herbert himself.

Dream City and *The Magic Knight* was an experiment which failed, but not for musical reasons. The famous Joe Weber was running a music hall which provided excellent entertainment to a nonfastidious audience. It was the best of its type, but Weber waxed desirous of purveying a show of higher class. Who but Herbert should supply the necessary music? The Herbert-Weber contract, signed at Lake Placid on the 19th of June, 1906, described the production as consisting "of two sections as, for instance, a complete comic opera for the first act and a burlesque for the second act."[43] This stipulation was faithfully followed, although the burlesque was preceded by a two-act opera. The libretto, not brilliant but thoroughly serviceable, was written by Edgar Smith, Weber's regular penman.

Announcement of the project was released at once, only to stir up the ire of an aggrieved person. This was Maurice Levi, director of music for Weber's enterprises, who protested publicly, claiming that he had already contracted to provide music for all of Weber's shows. His statement augured ill, and he caused plenty of trouble later on. Meanwhile plans were pursued with enthusiasm: an excellent cast and chorus were assembled, an augmented orchestra was hired, and the usual out-of-town testing was abandoned.

Weber capitalized as much as he could on the higher entertainment level he had in mind. When he and Herbert were interviewed together he said: "The tired business man and his untired wife can . . . find amusement in real, made-to-order humor and entertainment in music that has more than three notes and was not written in the dark." And the sympathetic Herbert, first saying that "the days of the music hall have passed," continued with: "As you know, Joe, when you and Lew Fields were together you approached me on several occasions to write the music for your burlesques, and you also know, I refused each time because you ran a 'music hall.' I am willing to write light music, but I will not write the score for a music-hall show."[44]

Sober-minded purists may find it difficult to distinguish music-hall songs from musical comedy excerpts, but Weber, along with Herbert, had conceived something definite. The resultant *Dream City*, was, therefore, a perfectly respectable and hilarious operetta which should rank high among the composer's works. The pendant *The Magic Knight* was a truly extraordinary burlesque or satire or travesty on grand opera which should have been inserted into the action of the operetta, but which was presented as an afterpiece because of production problems. Good musical satire is a rare thing. Herbert's intentional caricature of Wagner's *Lohengrin* is one of the best examples of the species; if it were performed today it would be just as effective as it was in 1906—possibly more so. Its chief requirement is a brilliant soprano who can sing floridly, lightly, and heavily. Lillian Blauvelt fulfilled these conditions in the original cast and delighted the critics. As a matter of fact, *Dream City* and *The Magic Knight* received as much critical acclaim and enthusiasm as any work Herbert ever wrote; yet none of his scores is now more forgotten and ignored.

The New York program called *Dream City* "a dramatic 'pipe' in two puffs," the stage direction being under Al. Holbrook, the music under Louis F. Gottschalk. The cast was as follows:

Wilhelm Dinglebender, a Long Island truck farmer, with a dreamy disposition and a chronic distaste for labor............	Joe Weber
J. Billington Holmes, a real estate boomer, with the plans of an ideal city........	Otis Harlan
Henri D'Absinthe, an artist seeking rural atmosphere	Maurice Farkoa
Seth Hubbs, village hackman and the oracle of Malaria Center.................	Will T. Hodge
Henry Peck, a city flat-dweller, spending the week-end with his family in the country	W. L. Romaine
Willie Peck, his restless offspring	Lores Grimm
Old Man Platt, a relic................	Major Johnson
Joe Snediker ⎫	W. D. Stevenson
Hank Scudder ⎬ village romeos........	Ernest Wood
Hen Conklin ⎭	James McCormack
Tuffie, an incubator chicken............	David Abrams
Big Bill Hankins, a farm hand.........	Will Lodella
Nancy, Dinglebender's daughter and the belle of Malaria Center..............	Cecilia Loftus
Marie Dinglebender, his wife, with energy enough for two and a "bossy" disposition	Lillian Lee
Amanda Boggs, the "help" at the Dinglebender farm......................	Madelyn Marshall
Mrs. Henry Peck, with alleged society connections in the metropolis..........	Cora Tracy
Mabel ⎫	Billy Norton
Maude ⎬ her daughters..............	Lois Ewell
Gladys ⎭	Lillian de Lee
Sarah Smith, a villager...............	Ella Tate

"Puff I" showed the Dinglebender farm at Malaria Center, Long Island; "Puff II" revealed the principal square of Dream City and its newly erected opera house. The time was given as "the immediate future, according to current real estate advertisements."

The program offered a separate listing for *The Magic Knight,* defining it as "a dash at grand opera" and "incidental to Puff II":

Elsa, a typical grand-operatic maiden in the usual distressing predicament............	Lillian Blauvelt
Ortrud, her contralto aunt, given to dabbling in the art of magic..................	Cora Tracy
Frederick, her hen-pecked uncle...........	Otis Harlan
The King, a base monarch...............	Frank Belcher

Lohengrin, a professional rescuer of distressed
    maidens . . . .   Maurice Farkoa
The Herald, a mediaeval news announcer. . .   W. L. Romaine

The Swan ⎱
Godfrey ⎰ an item in a foul conspiracy. . .   Lores Grimm

Lastnite ⎫   ⎧   Billy Norton
Tunite ⎬ three knights. . . . .⎨   Lois Ewell
Tumaronite ⎭   ⎩ Lillian de Lee

Knights, Maidens, Men-at-Arms, Pages, Vassals and
other minor details of grand opera

Dream City tells of a suburban real estate development planned for rural Long Island. Dinglebender, owner of a farm, dreams of great wealth and what this will mean to him and his family. In the course of his dream he goes to the newly built opera house and becomes a disillusioned man. If wealth means opera, he would rather be poor, and he refuses to allow the real estate operator to take over his property.

For this peculiar mélange of rustic and urban humor Herbert penned some exceedingly charming music. The play was sheer comedy, and the songs and dances were tuneful, square-cut as country airs should be, and vigorous. Languorous melodies were reduced to a minimum, and the slower pieces exuded an outdoor atmosphere. If not startlingly original, the music was certainly characteristic of roles and situations; if no number stood out above the others, nearly all were highly effective and spontaneous.

The Magic Knight was obviously the spectacle witnessed by Dinglebender *et al.* in Dreamtown's opera house. Weber, perhaps fearing that some of his audience would not grasp it, inserted the following (semiserious, semifacetious) in the program:

Argument

Elsa and her brother Godfrey have been left orphans under the guardianship of their uncle and aunt, Frederick and Ortrud, and the latter conspire to defraud them of their estates.

The brother has disappeared, and Elsa is accused before the King of having made away with little Godfrey, and is about to be condemned when, as a last resource, she demands to have the herald ask for some knight errant to appear and champion her cause against her uncle.

Lohengrin appears, sailing down the river in a boat drawn by a swan, and in answer to Elsa's appeal, fights and defeats Frederick, whereupon Ortrud confesses that she used her magic arts to change little Godfrey into a swan, and Lohengrin, being something of a magician himself, changes him back again and returns to Fairyland.

If the audience will listen intently it is possible that the shade of Richard Wagner may be heard to turn over.

There were no conversational interludes, no spoken dialogue in this magnificent burlesque. Spoken words were limited to a few exclamations and ejaculatory phrases as the music continued without interruption. The prevailing style of the music was Wagnerian, with sudden outbursts of musical comedy airs, Italian coloratura and dramatic recitative. Some of the best known themes from *Lohengrin* were used with telling effect (especially Ortrud's dark motive, the introduction to Act III, and "Mein lieber Schwan"), yet it was a good burlesque on all opera, not Wagnerian alone.

The public was delighted with *Dream City* and *The Magic Knight*, and so were the critics, even the most conservative, who lavished fulsome praise upon it. The *World* called the show "high art" and its parts "models of satire and farce"; in its opinion Herbert never had done a better score, and *The Magic Knight* was "fine, keen, subtle and consistent. Its full value will only be appreciated by devotees of grand opera, but its smashing choruses, wondrous ensemble and dainty melodies will appeal to the public generally. The story runs close to the original text, but the score is as full of tricks and gymnastics as a pine wood is full of needles."

The critic from the usually cautious *Times* went beyond this. It credited Weber with doing the impossible, for he had brought forth "a new type of popular entertainment." It liked the book because "for once in a blue moon a man of average sanity will understand the reason for the laughs." The music was "the best of its kind, light, pleasing, and melodious, with the quaint little Herbert touches to give it individuality." Regarding *The Magic Knight*, it observed: "Mr. Herbert retains the best-known motives of the original, and with a simple twist of his musical wrist changes them about to suit his own fancy. The result is capital musical fun." With an equally rare outburst of humor it concluded: "As light entertainment, 'Dream City' and 'The Magic Knight' ought to know many tunites and tumaronites. Lastnite the typical firstnite Weberites went wild with delite."

The reviewer for the *Tribune* (undoubtedly Krehbiel) was more venturesome. He described the satire, with considerable success; but first he exclaimed: "Blessings on Joe Weber's head! At his Music Hall last night he played Santa Claus and made the town a present of one of the most entertaining, the most diversified, and in some ways the most nearly new shows that the town has had for many a day. . . . The result is a novelty and a joy." Then he got down to business:

"The Magic Knight" comes last (though it should be introduced into the second act of "Dream City" in some way, for it naturally belongs there). But it must be first in attention. . . . It is a burlesque in the best sense of the word, thoroughly musical, entirely charming and convulsively funny. . . . It is grand opera in form, but grand opera made deliciously ridiculous. Even the costumes are operatic as well as charming. The muscular chords of the overture—and how Mr. Herbert gets so much noise out of Weber's little orchestra is a marvel—slide from Wagner into a popular tune as the curtain rises; themes from the opera glide into Irish jigs or even the strain of "Ach, du lieber Augustin" as the opera progresses; Miss Blauvelt, for her entrance song, shouts Wagnerian declamation, only to end up by pursuing the flute up the chromatic scale in the style of "Lucia," and declaring that it is "up to her to make good as a human canary." Lohengrin enters in a hansom cab drawn by a swan, and sings "Mein lieber Schwan," to be greeted by a "Quack, quack" from Frederick. The bass monarch takes his throne and thunders forth in recitative "Now I am here. Cut out all that orchestral tone coloring and get down to business. What is the first case on the docket?" Otis Harlan, as Frederick, husband of Ortrud, dressed in comical chain mail, convulses the house by refusing to fight in the words and music of the popular song, "My Wife Won't Let Me." The Herald holds his trumpet six inches away from his inflated cheeks when the calls are sounded in the orchestra, and you think of Siegfried and his pipe and smile. The burlesque, too, has instilled an astounding lot of musical life into the chorus, and is full of pretty tunes that, if not Wagner, are surely Victor Herbert. It is just long enough, ceasing before you are tired. It is a triumph of musical fooling.

These reviews were not exceptional; they were characteristic, and they also agreed on the generally splendid performances by the principals. It looked as if New York had received an epoch-making show. But in spite of the enthusiasm, easily rekindled when the music is examined today, *Dream City* and *The Magic Knight* lived through a New York run of only 102 performances.[45] Late in March it took to the road and toured for the rest of the season. In the midst of the tour Weber withdrew *The Magic Knight* and used Lillian Blauvelt for songs between the "Puffs" of *Dream City*.[46] No satire can be appreciated unless the original has become commonly familiar to beholders; it may be assumed, therefore, that *Lohengrin* was not well enough known to operaless cities to justify the continuation of the travesty.

The following season brought additional complications. Weber sublet the show to Messrs. Wells, Dunne and Harlan, who began to produce it around the middle of September. They wanted none of Herbert's music, however, and substituted for it compositions by Maurice Levi, who had originally protested Weber's connection with Herbert. Naturally Herbert was angered by this repudiation of his work and entered suit. He obtained an injunction against the perpetrators of the outrage, and a court ruling that forbade the presentation of *Dream City* with any music except his own.[47] Moreover, the erring producers confessed their fault, negotiated a new contract with Herbert, and agreed that after the 15th of November, 1907, the opera would be performed only with Herbert's music. Finally they agreed to pay Herbert 2½ per cent of the gross receipts from September 12 to November 15—the period during which Levi's music was used.[48] Having encountered this much difficulty, the show declined thenceforth, never regaining the favor of the public and never realizing the promise of the Christmas opening.

Still another Herbert production was launched during the 1906–1907 season, and the fact confirmed his ceaseless activity, but also caused some doubt about the wisdom of his industry. It was a popular comic opera, but one which cannot be included among Herbert's better works. *The Tattooed Man,* in two acts, had its first real performance on February 11 in Baltimore at the Academy of Music and its New York première on February 18 at the Criterion Theatre. Charles Dillingham was again the producer. In addition to securing Herbert's music he had engaged Frank Daniels whose appearances in Herbert's earlier Oriental farces were well remembered. The mere announcement of Daniels' name foretold the nature of the show—riotous burlesque, with little time or mood for romance, wit, or subtlety.

Before Herbert was committed to supplying the music, the play was known as *Omar.* Dillingham had purchased it in the summer of 1905,[49] intending to produce it after the approaching holidays. He was forced to change his plans, however, and it was nearly a year before he could inform the public that Herbert would write the score.[50] The new and final title was announced only shortly before the first performance.[51] The libretto was the joint product of A. N. C. Fowler and Harry B. Smith, the two together writing the book, the latter the lyrics.

The cast of the New York opening was as follows:

Omar Khayam, Jr., astrologer, poet and sworn
    foe to temperance........................Frank Daniels
Abdallah, an Arab chief.................William P. Carleton
Algy Cuffs, a matinee idol...................Harry Clarke
Hashish, janitor of the Shah's Harem..........Nace Bonville
Muley, inspector of the mint..............George O'Donnell
Ali, court nuisance........................Gilbert Clayton
Yussuf, bad news specialist...................Charles Drew
The Shah, who travels for his health until
    very late every evening.................Herbert Waterous
A Muezzin, who calls the people to prayer, but
    they don't come.........................Harold Russell
Leila, beloved by Omar, but nothing doing........Sallie Fisher
Alma, daughter of Omar....................Gertie Carlisle

Fatima, a wall flower.........................		May Vokes
Miss Vandergilt, of New York		Maida Athens
Miss Penn, of Philadelphia		Jessie Richmond
Miss Lakeside, of Chicago		Almeda Potter
Miss Beacon, of Boston	Imported	Lottie Vernon
Miss Bridge, of Brooklyn	American	Gertrude Doremus
Miss Frisk, of 'Frisco	bridesmaids..	Josephine Karlin
Miss Vine, of St. Louis		Jane Rogers
Miss Charles, of Baltimore		Leila Benton
Miss Mint, of Washington		Gene Cole
Star of Evening	Being translations of the Ori-	Reina Swift
Blush of Dawn	ental names of Omar's four	Mabel Croft
Rose of Summer	wards	Daisy DeVere
Bird of Paradise		May Field
Mutti..................................		Maida Athens
Ahmed		Edna Birch
Selim	Omar's nephews, educated in Amer-	Bessie Holbrook
Hassan	ican colleges	Claudia Clark
Canem		Jessie Carr

Snake charmers (8 girls), Dancing slaves (10 girls)

The time was the present; the scenes were laid in Persia. Act I took place in the courtyard of the Regent's palace; Act II in the rose garden of the Shah.

The musical director was Arthur Weld. The stage director was Julian Mitchell, and he did another magnificent job.

The barely discoverable plot, as the critics called it, relates to the troubles of Omar as he rules Persia loosely while the Shah is away. Omar has a peculiar birthmark, and Fate has decreed that if he meets any other man with a similar mark they must die together. Fatima, vainly pursuing Omar, tattoos these marks on Abdallah and Algy, and Omar has to see that they come to no harm. They marry the girls they want, and Omar himself, punished by the Shah, has to accept Fatima as a bride.

This was not an inspiring tale, and the music Herbert wrote for it, though better than the story, left much to be desired. The beginning of the operetta was unusual, but the promise which caught the ears of many was left unfulfilled. He dispensed with the conventional over-ture, being satisfied with some forty introductory bars which prepared the way for the opening scene, the Muezzin calling the faithful to prayer. His summons and its slight accompaniment form a brief passage of artistic simplicity; but it is very short and yields quickly to livelier strains of conventional contour.

Even with its paucity of first-rate material the New York critics had to admit that the music was poor only for Herbert; compared with the efforts of other composers it bore the stamp of excellence. The judge from the *Tribune* expressed it best: "Mr. Herbert's music is so much better than that of most unmusical comedies—especially orchestrally— that, from one point of view, it is thankless to quarrel."

A more elaborate pronouncement appeared in the *Evening Post*: "While it is true that Mr. Herbert has written much better music, notably in 'The Babes in Toyland' and 'Nordland,' that which he has furnished for the new operetta is far in advance of most of the combinations of notes of different value which pass as music in the average operetta of the present day. At times last night the music was in Mr. Herbert's happiest vein; it had a swing and character to it, was helped along by charming orchestration, and was thoroughly enjoyable. At others it was evidently composed for the masses and accomplished its purpose."

The critic from the *Times* liked the music, but his support was ineffective, and it was planned to end the run on April 20. Actually it ended a few days earlier, for on the morning of the 16th the Criterion suffered heavy water damage caused by a fire in the neighboring New York Theatre.[52] The New York run, therefore, was limited to 59 performances.[53]

The usual tour followed, broken by a summer vacation for the players and resumed in Boston in September. When *The Tattooed Man* reopened in the Massachusetts capital, a stock company was presenting there Herbert's *The Wizard of the Nile*. A fortnight earlier the stock company had performed *The Serenade*. This juxtaposition of operettas inspired H. T. Parker to compare the 1907 product with the scores of 1895 and 1897. His findings were not flattering to the new composition, and he sadly referred to Herbert as "a composer in a hurry." He regretted that Herbert was so busy, and he hazarded the guess that "the pile of commissions on his table must be almost as high as the pile of manuscript that is to discharge them." The composer might be the "ablest composer in America of musical plays"; but he was writing too fast, and was in no position to take the pains necessary for artistic work. Parker softened his criticism with plenty of praise for Herbert's abilities and achievements; he was simply sorry to see the squandering of such talent in situations where it could not be deployed wisely and well.[54]

14

The Champion of Composers

THE most important theatrical event of early 1907 was the formation of the well known society calling itself "The Friars." This was a coterie of theater press agents who banded together first for protection, secondly for recreational pastime. These busy and unusual people organized at a midnight meeting on February 9[1] at the Café des Beaux Arts and immediately began a history of beneficent cheer. The seeds, however, had been sown three years earlier.

In the fall of 1904 Charles Emerson Cook, attached to the Belasco Theatre, was imposed on by a man purporting to be assistant dramatic editor of the Washington *Post*. Realizing he had been duped, Cook warned all New York theater press agents about the sharpster and requested similar information on like offenders. He and his colleagues quickly formed a group which agreed to investigate the legitimacy of requests for passes and theatrical courtesies and to maintain a blacklist of unethical importuners. For two years this "Press Agents' Association" (Channing Pollock, president) clarified the New York atmosphere; then they relaxed for a few months until stimulated to regroup and function again.[2] In little more than a year they had their own clubhouse, aptly called the Monastery (the president just as aptly being called the Abbot).

The Friars immediately adopted a broad social program which called for monthly dinners honoring the most distinguished persons of the theatrical world. Among these, of course, was a special dinner for Victor Herbert on the evening of May 3, 1907. His orchestra provided musical selections, but the main musical event was the first singing of "The Friars," a song which he had composed in honor of the congenial press agents.[3] It was promptly adopted as the Monastery's official "hymn."

Not long after this celebration Herbert's name appeared in the press in connection with a most astonishing report: Oscar Hammerstein, the intrepid impresario, was in Europe, and word went forth that he would not return to America until he had secured permission from James M. Barrie to convert *Peter Pan* into an opera. Herbert was to be the composer. Charles Frohman was to be consulted about the production, for he had brought *Peter Pan* to America in 1905 and had given Maude Adams her most famous role. Hammerstein, Frohman, and Barrie were said to have confidently agreed that Herbert's music would guarantee an opera to delight old and young alike.[4] It is not known whether the report ever amounted to more than rumor; but it is interesting to speculate on what might have happened. Herbert loved to write for children, and the brilliance of *Babes in Toyland* and of sections of other works gives reason to regret his failure to compose a *Peter Pan*. Hammerstein wanted something to rival Humperdinck's *Hänsel und Gretel*, and Herbert might have supplied it.

In the summer, after long and strenuous work at Willow Grove, Herbert withdrew to his Adirondack retreat, where he was supposed to begin work on the Hammerstein opera.[5] He probably gave some attention to the project; but it was quite different from *Peter Pan* and was ill-starred, even losing the support which Hammerstein was initially so eager to give. However, that was some years off, and disappointment quite unthought of.

In autumn there were continued rumors of Herbert's plans for grand opera; but to inquirers he gave no satisfaction. The best the New York *Sun* could offer its readers was a secondhand report on October 17 that his latest production was as serious a work as *Ivanhoe* (Sullivan's?) and was already in the hands of a prima donna. This was pure guesswork and was quite wrong; but the paper complimented him on letting grand opera seek him out rather than chasing after it.

If Herbert thought of tackling a new art form, he never lost sight of what was happening around him. About this time some music by a wholly unknown composer impressed him favorably, and the encouragement he offered to the boy led to the career of one of America's leading musicians. Deems Taylor, who finds Herbert "equal to Bizet" in musical stature, describes the scene effectively:

Herbert did start me, in a way, on my musical career. In 1907 I wrote a musical comedy for the senior show at New York University. It was presented at Carnegie Lyceum, and one of the actors, who was a friend of the Herbert family,* blackmailed Herbert into coming to see it. Between acts he sent for me. "You know nothing about music theory, do you?" he said. I admitted that. "Then you must study. You have real talent."

* The musical comedy was *The Oracle*, and the actor was Jack Scannell.

You can imagine what that did to a timid beginner who had never dreamed of being taken seriously![6]

In this case Herbert's judgment was more than vindicated.

The year 1908 brought Herbert one of his most gratifying distinctions and initiated him into one of his most congenial activities. The former was election to membership in the National Institute of Arts and Letters; the latter, his long association with the Society of the Friendly Sons of St. Patrick in the City of New York.

The National Institute was established in 1898 by the American Social Science Association "for the furtherance of literature and the fine arts in the United States."[7] From its very inception it showed a praiseworthy selectivity, so that membership was indisputably a badge of high achievement. According to its own statement: "The Institute tries to select the most worthy and demands the highest standard of artistic achievement. It chooses its members not from those who may win temporary applause, or even the praise of the critics, but rather from those whose sustained creative output has demonstrated its permanent value."

Along with Herbert the Institute elected three other musicians— Frederick Shepherd Converse, Henry Kimball Hadley, and Charles Martin Loeffler, all outstanding. I have been unable to discover the citation attached to Herbert's election (if one exists), but he doubtless owed his elevation to a combination of many practices. As a serious composer, as a symphonic conductor, as a popularizer in the best sense of the word, as a writer of unique operettas, he merited the award beyond question. Yet today this particular distinction is largely forgotten, and so are some of the achievements which led up to it.

Membership in the National Institute was a passive thing, a recognition bestowed, accepted and lost sight of. Not so was participation in the Society of the Friendly Sons of St. Patrick, an activity that seemed to be measured only by the zeal of the Sons themselves. All his life long Herbert was passionately devoted to Ireland and had a romantic fondness for the shamrock-studded isle. There can be no doubt of this, for a rational appraisal would have saved him from a few ill-advised political appearances in later years; but it was an honest emotion, and he had a wonderful time in championing everything Irish. Among his creative efforts were several marches and choruses which were fervent outbursts of Irish patriotism. The vocal numbers were written for the Glee Club of the Friendly Sons, which he founded in 1913.[8]

The Society of the Friendly Sons of St. Patrick was organized in 1784 by Irish veterans of the American Revolution. With astonishing vitality it has flourished down to the present, undoubtedly owing its inherent vigor to the "lost cause" of Irish independence and the centuries-old mistreatment at the hands of the British. Obviously no group could seize Herbert's fancy more firmly than this one. To it he devoted much time and energy, and through it he had a curious and enigmatic political career.

It is not certain when Herbert became a Friendly Son. Although the Society's records do not show, the Recording Secretary in 1949 thought the year was 1909;[9] but he was elected a member at least one year earlier and possibly in 1907. Annually on March 17, the Society would hold a festive dinner, printing for the occasion an elaborate booklet-program. The program for March 17, 1908, contains the first printed reference to Herbert's membership I have seen, and already he was listed as an officer: one of the six "Stewards," and the provider of a set of six Irish folksongs printed for the banquet with a foreword by himself.

The parties of the Friendly Sons were gala affairs, and the 124th anniversary dinner at Delmonico's was no exception. Among the speakers were William Howard Taft, Charles Evans Hughes, and Augustus Thomas. The food and drink were calculated to please the most epicurean of tastes. It may well be that Herbert prepared the set of six songs (the third was a piano solo) as a voluntary offering to celebrate his own admittance to the Irish company.

The six pieces, reproduced from the manuscript of Herbert's beloved librarian and immaculate copyist, Henry Boewig, were "The Minstrel Boy to the War Is Gone," "Remember the Glories of Brien the Brave," "Lament for Owen Roe O'Neill," "Believe Me, If All Those Endearing Young Charms," "Tho' the Last Glimpse of Erin," "The Harp That Once Thro' Tara's Halls." The words were taken from Thomas Moore, so that it is clear that Herbert relied heavily upon Moore's *Irish Melodies* for his sources. The authenticity of these has long since been questioned, but he would have given scant consideration to such a matter; he was intent only on rendering a tribute to what he looked upon as the Irish spirit.

Herbert's foreword was, however, startlingly unusual. It was printed in a peculiar type imitative of Gaelic characters:

THE BARDS OF IRELAND

From ancient times Ireland has been famous for its music, for in the writings of Diodorus Siculus, Ammianus Marcellinus, Strabo, and Julius Caesar we read of the honours, wealth and power bestowed upon our bards. Centuries later Giraldus Cambrensis, A.D. 1185, singing the praises of Irish music, tells us that "In Ireland bishops, abbots, and holy men are accustomed to carry about their harps and take a pious delight in playing on them." Under the names of Filea and Fear-Dana, the bards of Ireland are mentioned in its history from the earliest periods down to the year 1738, when died the famous Carolan of whom Bunting said that he seemed "to have been born to render the termination of his order brilliant."

The profound love of music which has always been a dominant trait of the Irish race has given to us a wealth of beautiful melodies of which no other people can boast. The variety exhibited by Irish music is astounding, its classic examples ranging from the gentle lullaby to the inspiring war chant and the heartbreaking lamentation. Some of the oldest and best known of these I have arranged upon the pages which follow this brief introduction. To the great skill and proficiency of our harpers was due the early development of the system of harmony and artistic instruction, characteristic of our music, and to these harpers, Cambrensis A.D. 1185 pays this tribute:

"The attention of this people to musical instruments I find worthy of commendation, in which their skill is beyond comparison, superior to that of any other nation I have seen. It is wonderful how, in such precipitate rapidity of the fingers, the musical proportions are preserved. In the midst of their complicated modulations and most intricate arrangement of notes, by a rapidity so sweet, a regularity so irregular, a concord so discordant, the melody is rendered harmonious and perfect." etc. etc. (Bunting.)

From Brompton, writing in the reign of Henry II, we learn that "The Irish harpers taught in secret, committing their lessons to memory." Probably because of this fact all the original words of the exquisite melodies which I have attached to this little sketch have been lost in company with the words of thousands of songs, contemporary with them. The names of the composers shared the fate of the lyrics, for not one has escaped oblivion. Their music, however, is one of the eternal glories of Ireland, a thought which I find most poetically expressed in the following lines from a poem written in praise of the Irish harp by my grandfather, Samuel Lover:—

> "The beauty whose sway
> Woke the bard's native lay
> Hath gone to Eternity's shade,
> While fresh in its fame
> Lives the song to her name
> Which the minstrel immortal hath made."
>
> VICTOR HERBERT

Thus did Herbert declare, with burning intensity, his attachment to Ireland, her music and her bards. Let no one think that his fondness for things Irish grew from his sociability or was fostered for the sake of publicity. It was genuine and profound, and sentimentally he never ceased being a subject of the Emerald Isle.

When Herbert and his orchestra were ready to present Sunday evening concerts again in the fall of 1908, the repertoire of his own music was surprisingly enlarged. A period of about six weeks saw the production of no less than three operettas, all major works.

The first was the curious and short-lived *Algeria*, which had its first performance on any stage in Atlantic City at the Apollo Theatre on August 24, 1908, and opened in New York at the Broadway Theatre exactly one week later. The librettist was Glen MacDonough, who again rendered Herbert a distinct disservice; the producer was Frank McKee, and the supervisor was George Marion. It quickly proved to be a failure and was one of Herbert's greatest disappointments. The fact that the music was completed months before production[10] only whetted anticipation and made the disappointment the more severe.

The New York program announced the following cast:

Zoradie, Sultana of the Barakeesh, the ruler of a powerful Desert tribe (seen in Act I as Miriam, Mistress of the Bayaderes)	Ida Brooks Hunt
General Petitpons, Governor General and uncle of Captain De Lome..........	William Pruette
Captain De Lome, in command at the oasis of Sidi Ahmoud..............	George Leon Moore
Millicent Madison, M.D., an American girl who is practicing medicine in the East	Harriet Burt
The following three characters are three soldiers of fortune who have enlisted in and deserted from the Foreign Legion of the French Army:	
C. Walsingham Wadhunter, a straggler from Bohemia....................	George Marion
Van Cortlandt Parke, an ex-cotillion leader out of work......................	Ernest Lambart
Trainor Crewe, a college athletic instructor in hard luck...................	William Cameron
The following two characters are a recently married couple from Paterson, upon their honeymoon and bound for nowhere in particular:	
Mrs. Billings F. Cooings..............	Florence Nash
Mr. Billings F. Cooings...............	Eugene P. Arnold
Ali Kohja, chief of police to the Sultana of the Barakeesh (seen in Act I as the Arab story teller).................	Joseph Carey
Mimi, of the Latin Quarter...........	May Willard
Nella, the Sultana's confidante........	Grace Rankin
Zaphirie ⎫ Ladies in waiting to the Aouda ⎬ Sultana .... Mirzah ⎪ Lakme ⎭	⎧ Katherine Howland ⎨ Madge Richardson ⎪ Carolyn Barber ⎩ Jane Grover

Lieut. Bertrand..................... Richard M. Dolliver
Lieut. Dubonnet.................... Franklin Foster
 Bayaderes and Nurses, Artists' Models, Grisettes, Candy
Sellers, Flower Sellers, Hasheesh Vendors, Kabyle, Fruit
Sellers, Rug Merchants, Jewel Merchants, Pottery
Merchants

The first act showed the walled oasis of Sidi Ahmoud in the Sahara;
the second revealed the exterior of an old palace at Mustapha Superieur,
Algiers, two days later.

The musical director was John McGhie; the stage manager, Eugene
P. Arnold.

What poses as a plot[11] presents a Sultana who wants to wed a poet
she has never seen, and a French Captain (actually the poet) who
wants to marry a girl of the desert (actually the Sultana in disguise).
A threat of war is in the air, and the Sultana has announced that the
price of a peace treaty with the French is the discovery of the elusive
poet. Various impostors are presented to her, but to no avail. At last,
however, the Sultana and the Captain reveal their true identities and
their love, and the danger of war is a matter of the past.

The music was incomparably better than the story, and a few numbers were superb; but they could not live alone. "The Boule' Miche"
(De Lome singing of his Paris days) was captivating and zestful. "Rose
of the World" (Zoradie singing the words of the poet) was one of
Herbert's best and most extended declarations of passion. "You'll Feel
Better Then" (Millicent prescribing to the General) was clever and
tricky, with some delicious bits of musical imitation in the refrain. The
finale to the first act was short, but it included a most effective scene
of the American nurses receiving overseas mail and an extraordinarily
beautiful waltz to describe the love messages their mail contained.

The most brilliant number was the opening chorus of Act II. This
provided the substance for the Algerian carnival scene, which glittered
and sparkled from beginning to end. Following it came a placid but
very charming song, "Love Is like a Cigarette" (De Lome musing over
Miriam), which Herbert had written originally as a 1905 addition to
It Happened in Nordland. "Twilight in Barakeesh" (Zoradie's reflections) was attractive and somewhat atmospheric, but it fell short of some
of Herbert's attempts at local color.

The New York critics disagreed as to which songs were best, but
they all condemned the story and many of the principals. One said
that a new cast and a rewritten book would turn the show into a success.[12] Another said the show had "a book which lacked humor and
dragged badly in spots, comedians who were not funny and a prima

donna with a voice in bad condition"; these drawbacks "combined to make a failure of it in spite of the beauty of Victor Herbert's score."[13] Still another Herbert admirer tried to make the best of a bad situation by declaring that the music was charming, "but it is wedded to a stupid book, and if the melodious songs and artistic and beautiful ensembles are to survive it must be solely on their own merit, for the dialogue and plot are the feeblest and most foolish imaginable."[14] In spite of excellent staging and a pulchritudinous chorus *Algeria* was withdrawn after only 48 performances in New York.[15]

But *Algeria* was far from dead: it only hibernated, and when summer returned plans were formulated to revise and restage it. Lew Fields acquired the rights of production, Ned Wayburn was made responsible for the staging, MacDonough rewrote the book, and Herbert revised the music, though not significantly. Also a new cast was assembled, headed by a German girl who was hailed as the nightingale of Berlin.[16]

It was decided that a new title must be affixed to the show, and the new and hopeful version was first presented at the Grand Opera House in Wilkes-Barre, Pennsylvania, September 11, 1909, as *The Rose of Algeria*.

After a week in Philadelphia the bolstered production moved on to the Herald Square Theatre in New York, September 20, 1909. The new cast gave a glimpse of the extent of change and similarity:

Zoradie, Sultana of the Barakeesh (seen in Act I as Miriam, a fortune teller)..	Lillian Herlein
Millicent Madison, M.D. (an American doctress who has brought out a corps of trained nurses for the French government)	Ethel Green
Mirzah ⎫ Ladies in waiting to the Sul-⎧	Edith Ethel MacBride
Zaphirie ⎭ tana ....⎩	Marion Wynne
General Petitpons (Gov. Gen. of Algeria and uncle of Capt. de Lome)......	Eugene Cowles
Barnum Sells ⎫ Two young American circus men, forced by the failure of their circus in Algeria to enlist in the Foreign Legion of the French Army .... Bailey Ringling ⎭	⎧William Gaston ⎩James Diamond
Capt. de Lome (in command of the military post seen in Act I).......	Frank Pollock
Mrs. Billings F. Cooings ⎫ ....⎧ Mr. Billings F. Cooings ⎭ ....⎩	Anna Wheaton Ralph Nairn
A recently married couple on their	

honeymoon and bound for nowhere in
particular

Lieut. Bertrand, aide to Capt. de Lome..	Maitland Davies
Mimi, of the Latin Quarter..........	Belle Pallma
Pierre, an artist....................	Edward Tabor
Philippe, another.................	Carl Kahn
Sergeant Georges.................	Ralph Watson
Fanchon ⎫	Carrie Poltz
Camille ⎬ Cafe chantant girls.............⎨	Florrie Poltz
Toni ⎭	Nellie Poltz

Bayaderes and nurses, flower and candy girls, artists'
models and grisettes, staff officers, soldiers and merchants

The setting was divided in this fashion: Act I, Scene 1, a French military post near the seacoast of Algeria; Scene 2, a gully on the coast; Scene 3, the open sea; Act II, terrace of an old palace in the outskirts of the city of Algiers.

The musical director was Theodore Stearns, but the opening night in New York (as well as in Philadelphia) was conducted by Herbert himself. To increase the assurance of complete success, an augmented orchestra of about fifty players was in the pit.[17]

It would be pleasant to record that *The Rose of Algeria* was a sensation; but such, alas, was not the case. There were, of course, new scenic effects,[18] and a much better cast. Unfortunately the story, rewritten or not, was fundamentally the same, and Herbert's additions were not notable.

Herbert's severest critic had this to say: "No one would have had the courage to revive and revise it if Victor Herbert's music had not been so good. The dialogue was uninteresting, and there was little real comedy. The songs and the orchestral numbers were the redeeming features."[19] And a judicious observer reflected thus: "The reconstructed libretto raised no storms of applause last night. There were no roars of laughter, but the book served the purpose of a framework for the music. The score, as was remarked a year ago, is one of Herbert's good efforts. It is full of color, rhythm and melody. There are catchy marches and waltzes, fascinating bits of incidental music, and through it all a beauty of orchestration which contributes much to the charm of the work."[20] The optimism of those responsible for the new version was quickly vitiated as they watched the New York run terminate after 40 performances.[21] A very short life on the road did nothing to buoy their spirits, and they let it expire without protest.

Long before he knew what the fate of *Algeria* would be Herbert was preparing another operetta which was gorgeously ambitious not only for himself but for its producers, entitled *Little Nemo*. It marked an innovation in Herbert's approach to the musical stage. More than that, it was a landmark in the development of America's musical theater; but its producers' ambition was the reason for its ultimate failure.

Little Nemo was a three-act musical comedy derived from pure child-like fantasy. It was inspired by a remarkable series of cartoons in the New York *Herald,* drawn by Winsor McCay, a master draftsman, an imaginative author, and a virtuoso in the employment of perspective and color.

In the cartoons Little Nemo was a boy of indeterminate age who reveled in adventures in Dreamland; on the stage the strange experiences of this same small boy were enhanced by music and made audible by song. About the cartoons Coulton Waugh writes:

Nemo is a blurred and uncertain figure, although he is at times capable of rising to self-sacrificial heights. But he is the dreamer, and in a dream, is the dreamer himself ever very clear? It is when one turns to the full panoply of the dream itself that McCay makes his lasting impression.

Nemo's companions are more sharply focused than he is, and are gay and amusing. Flip is a squat earthy clown with green face and aggressive cigar, who supplies a practical viewpoint and tempers the sentimentality of some of the other actors. A cute little brown cannibal reinforces the occasional note of pathos. Those three play against a vast procession of others: a certain Dr. Pill, and queens, princesses, giants, policemen without number. McCay draws animals with an avid enthusiasm which shows what a wonderful time he is having; and his page overflows with processions, circuses, court scenes, banquets, and festive occasions of every kind, done with bewildering detail.[22]

Such was the atmosphere, and such were the extremes of delineation, which the musical comedy had to expose.

Reports of the musical version began to be heard in the summer of 1907. George V. Hobart was expected to prepare the book Herbert would set; but he was soon supplanted by Henry Blossom,[23] who in turn dropped out of the project and was replaced by the faithful Harry B. Smith. Klaw & Erlanger were to be the producers.

Marc Klaw issued several statements about *Little Nemo* which not only had publicity value but persuasively supported his claims. It would be "absolutely novel," he said, for it would "combine the qualities of fantasy and sentiment"; and he ventured the opinion that they might have to spend $100,000, an unheard-of sum in those more reasonable days, because "the idea of dream illusion has got to obtain throughout, and the scenes must be presented so effectively that the auditor will believe in the reality of dreams."

On the same occasion Herbert also had an opportunity to express his views, and he seized it eagerly:

The idea appeals to me tremendously. It gives opportunities for fanciful incidents and for "color." It's all in Dreamland, you know, and that gives great scope for effects, the writing of which appeals to me immensely. Besides there is an excellent story—the love between Nemo and the Princess—and there are chances for humor, too. I can only say that I approach my part of the task with enthusiasm and I hope to furnish an interesting musical setting for the story. It will not be all easy, for while the opportunities for going to great fantastic extremes are presented, it must be remembered that the mood of childhood must prevail, too, and the music must be of the popular order.[24]

He exaggerated slightly in attaching so much importance to the love of Little Nemo for the Princess. It was not love in the sophisticated sense, and *Little Nemo* is a Herbert operetta totally bereft of the usual love interest. Quite properly, there is no ardent love song in it.

Plans finally developed according to schedule, and "the largest musical production ever attempted in this country"[25] was presented for the first time on any stage at the Forrest Theatre in Philadelphia on September 28, 1908. The "marvel of scenic investiture" was "dazzling" and "confusingly kaleidoscopic" to the audience; but it also had "the delicious soothing effect that is part of dream life; something suggestive of total irresponsibility, of that physical and mental lassitude that lends itself unconsciously to the banishment of care." They were convinced that McCay's "color-riot-ridden mind" had been fittingly transplanted to the stage in music, incident, characterization, and device.[26]

Little Nemo remained in Philadelphia for three successful weeks, then had an auspicious opening at the New Amsterdam Theatre in New York on October 20. Great public interest had been aroused, and society was out in force. Special traffic problems were created, ticket speculators were reported doing a thriving business, and there was a general resemblance to a grand opera première at the Metropolitan.[27]

The carefully chosen cast was as follows:

Dr. Pill, physician to King Morpheus . . . . Joseph Cawthorn
Flip, nephew of the Guard of Dawn . . . . Billy B. Van
The Dancing Missionary . . . . Harry Kelly
Little Nemo . . . . Master Gabriel
Morpheus, King of Poppyland . . . . W. W. Black
An Officer of the Continentals . . . . A. H. Hendricks
Gladys, the cat ⎫
Teddy, the bear ⎬ . . . . Dave Abrams
Nutty, the squirrel ⎭
Mons. Roma ⎫ Olympian wrestlers . . . . ⎧ Louis Hart
Mons. Graeso ⎭ ⎩ Sim Collins
Aide to Officer of the Continentals . . . . Edward B. Kramer
Ruler of the Isle of Table d'Hote . . . . Louis F. Barnes

The Candy Kid, messenger of King Morpheus. . Florence Tempest
The Little Princess. . . . . .Aimee Ehrlich
The Valentine Fairy ⎱
The Barometer Girl ⎰ . . . . .Albertine Benson
The Weather Vane. . . . . .Elphye Snowden
Mrs. Nemo. . . . . .Rose Beaumont
Sally, a traveler in Slumberland. . . . . .Madeline Marshall
Tilly ⎱ likewise travelers in Slumberland . .⎰ Mildred Manning
Betty ⎰   ⎰ Sunshine Ijames
    Pages, Attendants to the Princess, Guards of Slumber-
    land, Children, Teddy bears, Cannibals, Toy soldiers,
    Jungle animals, Soldiers, Continentals, English officers,
    Naval officers, Midshipmen, Sailors, etc.

The stage director was Herbert Gresham; the musical director, Max Hirschfeld.

The nature of the production, adventures in a world of fantasy, minimized the importance of plot, notwithstanding claims to the contrary, and the program described the scenes elaborately. A mere scenic synopsis shows the involvements on the stage:

Act I, Scene 1, the playroom of the little Princess in Slumberland; Scene 2, a playground in a city park; Scene 3, Little Nemo's bedroom; Scene 4, the land of St. Valentine; Act II, Scene 1, the Weather Factory office in Cloudland; Scene 2 (a) wreck of the Ship of Dreams, (b) the Isle of Table d'Hote; Scene 3, the amusement park in the jungle; Scene 4, Little Nemo's bedroom; Scene 5, a dream of the Fourth of July; Act III, Scene 1, deck of a battleship; Scene 2, Slumberland.

An excellent cast sang, danced and acted well. Master Gabriel, who played Nemo, was critically compared with the hero of McCay's cartoons and judged to be eminently satisfactory. As the dreaming child he was found amusing, manly, and serious at the proper time and to the proper degree. It should be noted that Master Gabriel was not a child. He was reported by a critic to be a midget thirty-one years of age with the stature and voice of a boy of ten.[28] Thus he could pursue his role with great naturalness and objectivity. The three comedians—Cawthorn, Van, and Kelly—were also highly satisfying, and Cawthorn won credit for enlarging the American language. Sometime during the New York run, probably soon after the first performance, Cawthorn was suddenly obliged to ad-lib a monologue, which he did admirably. He referred to a mythical water-dwelling creature as a "whiffenpoof" and described its habits of gobbling food or bait.[29] The next year the famous singing society of Yale University was formed, calling itself the Whiffenpoofs and adopting the Whiffenpoof Song as its official anthem.

Herbert was confronted by a real problem in composing music for a hodgepodge like *Little Nemo,* and he solved it to the best of his ability. Nevertheless the score will never rank among his best works, although it has some remarkably fine parts. Being childlike, careless, and fanciful, the songs were too much alike; and the music preserved this similarity. Of course there were marches and waltzes and topical songs, but it would be difficult to select any one as especially distinctive.

But those episodes which needed instrumental music—pageants, pantomimes, ballets—told another story. Here Herbert was not restrained by text, and he let his fancy soar. The first long pantomime was the park scene, for which Herbert provided some delicious musical phrases. Extremely skillful and effective was the use of an underlying musical figure to which new and characteristic motives were added (and continued) as park visitors enjoyed the grounds. The dignity of the policeman, the rocking of baby buggies, the ardor of lovers, the twittering of birds—these build up to a score of fascinating interest. The music for the dance of the Valentines is both spritely and graceful, with instrumental effects which are masterfully accomplished. Finally, the incidental music for the cannibal island scene and the Fourth of July celebration are likewise highly effective.

The superiority of the instrumental music may not have been noticed at the time, for the critics received the entire play with loud acclamation. One called it "a superb spectacle, as bright as a silver dollar in its comedy, and with music that instantly caught the public favor, but that from end to end was as refined and wholesome as it was beautiful and merry."[30] Another defined it as "a three hour panegyric, in music and picture, of the charms of childhood" for which Herbert wrote music "that is peculiarly adapted to the dream of childhood. Now it is tender in tone, again melodious, and suddenly, when the scene changes, a military march or a pretty waltz falls upon the ear."[31]

In spite of warm approval *Little Nemo* did not survive long. After 111 performances in New York[32] it went to Boston and Pittsburgh and finally to Chicago, where it played for two months and ended the season. It enjoyed a second season on the road, but its influence and glamour waned. Expensive to produce, it was also expensive to transport, needing a special train for its extra large company and heavy equipment;[33] and this contributed to its early disappearance.

Some interesting figures show the unique but unenviable position *Little Nemo* occupied. Lehar's *Merry Widow* (1907) was produced for less than $35,000; *The Rose of Algeria* and *Old Dutch* (both 1909) cost about $30,000 each; Leo Fall's *The Dollar Princess* (1909) required somewhat over $50,000, a high amount for a time when the average production was probably between $20,000 and $30,000. But before the first curtain went up on *Little Nemo* $86,000 had been spent;

and much more was doubtless put into it as it improved. It was staggeringly expensive for its time because of the number of scenes, the weird lighting, manifestations through trapdoors, and a vast array of exotic costumes. Up to 1910 it was supposed to be the most expensive production ever placed before the public, and after two years of performance the original investment had not been returned.[34]

With his usual prodigality Herbert had no sooner launched *Little Nemo* than he was ready with yet another comic opera, a new vehicle for Fritzi Scheff. After the undisputed triumph of *Mlle. Modiste* it was inevitable that she would be offered a successive work. Even in 1906 it was reported that Herbert and Blossom would again join talents to provide her with a show. The reports were unusually definite, informing the public that all the earlier scenes would be laid in Austria and the last would expose the interior of New York's Metropolitan Opera House.[35] The only accurate part of the advance information, however, concerned the principals, and when the composer and librettist began work on the new operetta they were once more under the aegis of C. B. Dillingham. They tried hard to make it a worthy successor to *Mlle. Modiste,* even including a French military atmosphere; but success rarely comes on order, and their efforts were not long appreciated.

The new work was *The Prima Donna,* and the title rôle was assigned to Fritzi. The first performance on any stage took place in Chicago at the Studebaker Theatre on October 5, 1908. In New York it opened at the Knickerbocker Theatre on November 30, with an apparently healthy future in front of it.

The Chicago reception was enthusiastic. The Midwesterners found the play light but plausible, and the music "a masterly production of a man who easily stands without a peer among the light opera writers of America . . . and whose superior has yet to be heard among the foreigners. . . . Mr. Herbert's fine refined melodic gift never has been more admirably in evidence . . . and his orchestration is nothing less than masterly. Such exquisite handling of the instruments has not been met with in light opera score in years, for Herbert has not only absolute knowledge of his orchestral medium but he has the priceless sense of true musical humor. Witness the wood winds in the accompaniment to 'Something Always Happens'—this alone is a master stroke and there are countless others of similar worth."[36]

Preceded by a reputation like this, *The Prima Donna* was eagerly awaited in New York. For some reason Dillingham wanted his audiences to know that this operetta with a foreign milieu was a distinctly American product, and the program stated, "Made in America"—in itself scarcely a guarantee of artistic excellence. It gave the following cast:

Colonel Dutois.........................St. Clair Bayfield
Captain Bordenave.....................William K. Harcourt
Lieut. Armand, Count de Fontenne..........William Raymond
Lieut. Fernand Drouillard.....................Donald Hall
Lieut. Gaston de Randal.....................Martin Haydon
Lieut. Prosper Rousseau...............George W. McNamara
Lieut. Eugene de Beaumont.................Robert E. Clark
Mons. Beaurivage, Athenée's father...........W. J. Ferguson
Herr Max Gundelfinger, known as "Pop".....James E. Sullivan
Signor Giuseppe Ciucicini....................Phil Branson
Baron de Pompal........................Herbert Ayling
First waiter.............................Armand Cortes
Second waiter...........................Peter Canove
Mother Justine, proprietress of the café.......Josephine Bartlett
Mlle. Athenée, prima donna of the Opéra
    Comique, Paris............................Fritzi Scheff
Margot, her maid....................Gwendolyn Valentine
Mlle. Mathilde ⎫ Café chanteuses...... ⎧ Grace Delmar
Mlle. Désirée ⎭   ⎩ Renee Dyris
The Dancer................................La Noveta
The Duchess of Montrose...............Ruth Holt Boucicault
Countess Helene........................Blanche Morrison
Marquise du Perrifonds...................Katherine Stewart
Celeste..................................Margaret Ross
Mignon..............................Gertrude Doremus
Clairette................................Virginia Reed
Bebe..................................Marguerite May

Other characters—18 girls, 14 men
Entertainment in Act II by the Metropolitan Octette:
Soprani, Margaret MacKenzie, Margaret Harrison; Con-
tralti, Florence Fisk, Evelyn Jackson; Tenori, Albert A.
Denny, Fred. Killeen; Bassi, Walter White, Virgil
Holmes.

The stage director was Fred G. Latham. The musical direction was
entrusted to John Lund.

Act I was in the Pomme d'Or Café, St. Germain; Act II, in the Club
House at Ile de Puteaux in Paris.

The story of *The Prima Donna* is reasonable but dull—particularly
the latter half. Athenée sings anonymously for an ailing café girl. She
performs a song written by Armand, and they fall in love with each
other. A jealous superior officer (Bordenave) disciplines the young lieutenant and makes improper advances to Athenée. A modest scandal
ensues, and Athenée must overcome the hypocritical opinion of society. This she does by her wit and art, and so secures the esteem of her
critics; no further obstacles separate her and her lover.

If Herbert's achievement in *The Prima Donna* is gauged by that operetta's present-day popularity, it cannot be highly rated. If, on the other hand, it is estimated on a musical comparison with his other products, it is very high indeed. His lovely score sparkled and laughed and sighed, delighting all the listeners. They specially anticipated the soprano songs, for Fritzi Scheff was a unique singer and personality. First came "Dream Love," which is extraneous to the story despite its title. It is a broad, lyrical rhapsody of a maiden singing of the land of dreams where she lives in regal splendor and has a score of lovers. Elaborate and perhaps a trifle too ambitious, it is beautifully written and builds up to a semiclimax. In singing Armand's song, Fritzi presented a most appropriate mixture of tenderness and amorousness. Called "A Soldier's Love," it is exactly what Armand claims it to be—a simple effort by an amateur composer; but the real composer's professional ability allowed no amateurishness to show through. The refrain proved to be the best waltz theme in the piece.

The first finale was unusual in that no choral effects were attempted. Here Athenée has her fight with Bordenave, and Herbert rightly kept the music in a vein to support the dramatic action. It was surprisingly turbulent and completely suitable for a scene not common to the operetta stage.

The musical opening of the second act was noteworthy for a contrivance that occurs rarely. The chorus and regular orchestra performed a spirited number in 6/8 time. On the stage another band (entertaining the guests at the club) simultaneously played a dance in 2/4 time. The results were excellent. Satisfactory if not outstanding were "Everybody Else's Girl Looks Better to Me than Mine" (Gaston forever discontented in love) and "If You Were I and I Were You" (Helene and Fernand in an innocuous duet), and these were followed by two numbers for the unaccompanied vocal octette: "What Is Love" and "The Man and the Maid." Some of Herbert's most felicitous touches were to be found in his *a cappella* part-songs, and these were highly attractive pieces which would grace any program today. The final number before the close was Athenée's jubilant outpouring of song to reveal her general happiness. Herbert gave her a brilliant Spanish air ("Espagnola") which was dancelike in rhythm and coloratura in style. Only a singer like Scheff could cope with its difficulties.

New York was immensely pleased with *The Prima Donna*, "a comic opera with a consecutive plot, real music, no vaudeville, and no horseplay."[37] Scheff admittedly dominated the show, but the supporting cast was more than adequate. Most onlookers thought it would be a strong rival of *Mlle. Modiste*. As the heroine, she "was her old self—dainty, bewitching, impetuous, and loving, and sang as well as she ever did in her life."[38] Higher praise could hardly be given, but Herbert fared equally well. The play had some innovations, and one observant critic wrote: "By way of variety there is a turn, now and then, into a sort of dramatic motive which serves to vary the movement and to furnish an opportunity for spirited composing."[39] One such incident, of course, was the moment when Athenée mauled the too attentive French captain and injected plenty of realism into her actions. This was "a rather startling episode for comic opera,"[40] but the spectators found it to their liking. Herbert could always write effective descriptive music, although his operettas rarely gave him the chance. More comprehensive was this observation: "Victor Herbert writes music for the people, yet it is the music of a master, and this was never more clearly shown than . . . last night. The marches were stirring, the waltzes had an irresistible swing, the songs were dainty and sweet, and the ensembles were built up into beautiful and musicianly climaxes."[41]

While the audience feverishly applauded Fritzi in the New York première, she brought the composer and the librettist before the footlights for their share of the loud approval. Then she thanked the audience and said she would be pleased to see them every evening in the same place at the same time. Unfortunately she herself did not return too many times, for *The Prima Donna* had a New York run of only 72 performances.[42] It went on the road for the remainder of the season and all of the next, suffering somewhat from Scheff's recurring illnesses and fainting spells. Without or with her presence, audiences heard some of Herbert's most beguiling if not most memorable music.

Extraordinarily prolific as an operetta composer in 1907 and 1908, Herbert still found time to write music and make programs for his favorite club, the Lambs. In 1907 he was their "Boy" (Vice President) and a member of the Entertainment Committee. For the spring gambol —they solemnly called it "Sprink Gimble"—he provided the music of a sketch entitled *Miss Camille,* presented on April 14, 1907. It received wider approbation on April 23 at the Annual Gambol held for ladies in the Astor Theatre. The program defined it as "a grand opera—pocket edition," confirming the pleasure Herbert experienced in parodying the serious musical stage.

On the 8th of the following March the Lambs heard and sang "a new Club song" entitled "To the Lambs," Herbert's setting of a text by Augustus Thomas; and on April 12 they relished another musical gem from his inexhaustible supply: "She Was a Hayseed Maid." When it was performed at the Astor Theatre on April 24 for the Ladies' Annual Gambol, the program referred to it as "a dreadfully refined song and dance introducing the Ladies Home Journal Octette."

Once in a while, however, even Herbert's patience with the Lambs might be strained. Such incidents, naturally, were solely club affairs, not to be known or discussed outside, but one violent disagreement was aired in the press. In the fall of 1908 Herbert admitted he had resigned from the club, because, while he was attending operetta rehearsals out of the city, several persons of whom he disapproved were elected to membership. From available reports Herbert deserved some sympathy. Two of the new members were young men commonly known as "The Hall Room Boys,"[43] and the name had various connotations. Another was an unnamed music publisher, and his election was especially irritating to Herbert, who had unsuccessfully supported the candidacy of a music publishing friend a few years before (music publishers were not generally welcome as members, lest they take advantage of their position to further their own trade).

A reporter learning of Herbert's indignant resignation, immediately badgered him and persuaded him to make a statement which included a shaft of Herbert wit:

It's a club matter and shouldn't be discussed outside of the club. The fact is, however, that I tendered my resignation because of certain recent elections that took place in my absence. In the list of men admitted I believe there was one music publisher; but I did not object to him on account of his business. In fact, I have every reason to be fond of music publishers, because they pay me large royalties. Just now the matter is at a standstill, and I can't say what the outcome will be. I did feel very bitter about the thing, but it may all be adjusted satisfactorily, and I hope it will not create any more unpleasantness.[44]

Fortunately for himself and the Lambs, Herbert altered his decision to leave the club and remained one of its most energetic workers.

Herbert left tangible evidence of his affection for one music publisher: Isidore Witmark of the firm which published so many of his operas, for whom he had promised to compose a special wedding march whenever the publisher decided to marry.[45] After waiting several years Witmark was finally ready to take the step; and, in Chicago for the première of *The Prima Donna*, he informed Herbert of his intention. The composer finished the promised march on the day before Christmas. On the title page of the manuscript, now in the Witmark Collection at Columbia University, he wrote: "Wedding Music composed expressly for my friends Viola Cahn and Isadore Witmark Victor Herbert Dec. 24th 1908."[46] Never published, it is a highly respectable piece of music with two main themes standing respectively for Isidore (*energico*) and Viola (*amabile*). It served its purpose on January 19, 1909; only its ultrapersonal application has prevented its being printed and used for subsequent matrimonial fêtes.

Throughout the fall of 1908 Herbert continued to direct his Sunday evening orchestra concerts. The character of the programs—light classics, operatic and popular solos, excerpts from his own stage works—did not change; but one important event should be noted: He began to feature a young cellist named Horace Britt who remained with him for a number of years. Britt later became one of the leading chamber music artists of his time, but he never lost his deep respect and affection for Herbert. (Britt's wistful reminiscence to me on February 28, 1952, in Washington, is itself unforgettable.)

Herbert and his orchestra made their customary society appearances, chiefly as participants of the Bagby musicales at the Waldorf-Astoria. An unusual engagement, however, at this hotel was in a concert sponsored by the New York Anti-Vivisection Society on November 11. Sharing the program were Albert Spalding and Emma Eames, who was heard to remark after the concert, for want of something better to say: "All of us love some animal or other." But at the beginning of the concert Herbert unburdened himself of much more intelligent words in this instruction to his players: "Gentlemen, in view of the nature of the association under whose auspices this afternoon's entertainment is to be held, there will be no cuts in the music of the programme."[47]

Herbert began 1909 auspiciously by becoming a member of the Bohemians, whose roster sooner or later included the greatest artists living in or visiting America. The Bohemians (New York Musicians' Club), thus the official designation, was instigated by Rafael Joseffy in April, 1907, at an intimate farewell party tendered to Moriz Rosenthal in Lüchow's restaurant. Knowing that earlier social-fraternal-professional organizations had lacked an essential vitality, Joseffy proposed a new body with specific yet broad aims. "Good-fellowship, *camaraderie* were to be promoted, the too common feelings of envy and jealousy frowned on, the art and its practitioners, lofty and lowly, encouraged."[48] Joseffy's suggestions fell on fertile soil, and the club was incorporated on May 26, 1908. Officially it declared itself set up "to promote social intercourse among its members, to further the cause of music and the interests of musicians," purposes allowing a wide latitude of corporate activity. After a few years of operation it broadened its scope to include well directed charities to needy musicians, a function it still performs to this day.

Herbert's membership in this remarkable and glamorous society dated from January 1, 1909.[49] In this year he was elected vice president; he held the office until 1915, and for the rest of his life he was one of the most distinguished members.

Another event early in 1909 was of vital concern to Herbert, who for some years had been working on its development. This was the passage of a new copyright law (still existent) which was of incalculable significance to all composers. The writers of music failed to obtain all they wanted or thought they should have, but they secured some rights they never had had before. Herbert was in the forefront of the legislative battle, which ultimately benefited all composers, popular and serious alike. It is impossible, perhaps, to determine exactly the extent of Herbert's influence; but the very impossibility increases the importance of examining his actions in detail. He was concerned chiefly with only one provision—a major provision, which came into being with the law of 1909 and immediately changed the fortune of hundreds of composers.

The law of 1909 permits the copyrighting of musical compositions. The owner of such a work (generally the composer or his publisher) has exclusive rights "to print, reprint, publish, copy, and vend" it; "to arrange or adapt it"; "to perform the copyrighted work publicly for profit," and for this purpose as well as for the purposes mentioned in the first quotation "to make any arrangement or setting of it or of the melody of it in any system of notation or any form of record in which the thought of the author [i.e., composer] may be recorded and from which it may be read or reproduced." The last clause includes the control of making sound recordings—still called, in this law, "the parts of instruments serving to reproduce mechanically the musical work." To the owner of the musical copyright is thus given the exclusive right to say when his composition may be recorded, but with a very special condition: "Whenever the owner of a musical copyright has used or permitted or knowingly acquiesced in the use of the copyrighted work upon the parts of instruments serving to reproduce mechanically the musical work, any other person may make similar use of the copyrighted work upon the payment to the copyright proprietor of a royalty of 2 cents on each such part manufactured, to be paid by the manufacturer thereof."[50] In other words, the copyright owner alone can give permission to a manufacturer to record his piece; but, once he has given that permission, any other manufacturer may record the same piece and sell the recording by paying to him the stipulated royalty—two cents per disc, piano roll, etc. In this matter the copyright owner's right is exclusive only as long as he does not exercise it; once the first record is made, he is compelled to license his work to any record maker, who in turn must pay him a fee set by law on all "parts" made.

It was not always so. America's first copyright law in 1790 extended protection only to maps, charts, and books. Music was not copyrightable until the Act of 1831, which limited the composer's exclusive right to "printing, reprinting, publishing, and vending."[51] By 1891 that right was enlarged to "printing, reprinting, publishing, completing, copying, executing, finishing, and vending," some of which seem to be more applicable to other products now subject to copyright.

Naturally nothing was said about sound recordings. Even in 1891 the recording industry was in its merest infancy, and no legislator or composer was imaginative enough to foresee how science would revolutionize the music world. But between 1891 and 1905 conditions changed radically, and the manufacturers of phonograph records and piano rolls found themselves doing a land-office business at the composers' expense. Mechanical instruments were not mentioned in the copyright law, and composers had absolutely no right to control or prohibit the recording of their compositions. Their music was copyrighted, the provisions of the law were complied with, but their best and most popular pieces were making fortunes for manufacturers, not for themselves. In December of 1905 the need for protection in the intellectual field attracted the attention of President Theodore Roosevelt, who emphasized the significance of copyright in his annual message to Congress. Music of course was only one item among many calling for consideration, but the recording problem was probably in his mind as he wrote: "Our copyright laws urgently need revision. They are imperfect in definition, confused and inconsistent in expression; they omit provision for many articles which, under modern reproductive processes, are entitled to protection; they impose hardships upon the copyright proprietor which are not essential to the fair protection of the public." He told his legislators that an appropriate bill had been framed by the United States Copyright Office, and that it deserved "prompt consideration."[52]

The Copyright Office, a part of the Library of Congress, had indeed framed a bill which was influenced by conferences of interested organizations held in June and November of 1905 and in March of 1906. Included in the bill (designated S. 6330) was a provision guaranteeing to the composer-owner of a musical work the exclusive right "to make, sell, distribute, or let for hire any device, contrivance, or appliance especially adapted in any manner whatsoever to reproduce to the ear the whole or any material part of any work published and copyrighted after this Act shall have gone into effect, or by any means of any such device or appliance publicly to reproduce to the ear the whole or any material part of such work."[53] In these words the framers of the bill sought to give the composer full and absolute control over the recording of any music he might thenceforth publish and copyright. Public hearings on the bill opened in the Library of Congress on June 6, 1906, and lasted four days. It was immediately apparent that there was determined opposition to granting the composer any exclusive recording right.

Victor Herbert helped to make recording history, and during his lifetime his orchestral records were among the most popular releases of any manufacturer. Prior to legislative protection, however, he abstained from recording, for he steadfastly believed that the composer was entitled to a fair recompense. He demonstrated his conviction one day in New York, in a manner which left no doubt about it.

After the success of *The Red Mill* a party of friends arranged a sumptuous dinner in the composer's honor. They told the restaurant keeper to spare nothing in preparing for the occasion; it was to be a delight for eye and ear as well as palate. Unaware of Herbert's intense dislike of mechanical reproducing instruments, the restaurateur erected a miniature red mill on a table close to the seat the composer was to occupy. Concealed in the mill was a phonograph, its horn so located that the sound would go directly into his ear. Herbert being waved to his chair, a waiter was signaled to work the machine. "Instantly the metallic voice from the record began to hand out 'mutilated melody' by way of 'Red Mill' popular airs, played at a most terrific tempo." Herbert was dumbfounded, but only for an instant. He turned, saw the mill, seized it and the phonograph within, and dashed them both to the floor in a fit of hearty anger. Then he started to leave. His good humor quickly returned, however, and he saw the humor of the situation. He made amends to the proprietor and explained how the music machines made money for their manufacturers but not one cent for the composers whose music they appropriated.[54]

The proprietor expressed his sympathy, but he was more enterprising than could have been imagined. When Herbert casually entered his restaurant the next day the little red mill had been patched up and remounted on a table. Once more it evidently contained a phonograph, for it bore a bold sign: "Selections from 'The Red Mill,' Revised Personally by Victor Herbert."

When the first hearings on the 1906 copyright bill were held, Victor Herbert and John Philip Sousa journeyed to Washington to testify on behalf of composers. Both were effective, but the former, this time and at subsequent hearings, was always more idealistic than the latter.

Forgathering in the old Senate Reading Room of the Library of Congress, the witnesses got down to business at once. Sousa testified:

I would like to quote Fletcher, of Saltoun, who said that he cared not who made the laws of the land if he could write its songs. We composers of America take the other view. We are very anxious as to who makes the laws of this land. We are in a very bad way. I think when the old copyright law was made, the various perforated rolls and phonograph records were not known, and there was no provision made to protect us in that direction.

Since then, the talking machines have come out, and the claim is made that the record of sound is not a notation.

. . . The claim that is made about these records is that they can not be read by any notation—simply that no method has been found to read them up to the present, but there will be. Just as the man who wanted to scan the heavens discovered a telescope to do it. No doubt there will be found a way to read these records.

We are entirely in favor of this bill. The provisions satisfy us, and we want to be protected in every possible form in our property. When these perforated roll companies and these phonograph companies take my property and put it on their records they take something that I am interested in and give me no interest in it. When they make money out of my pieces I want a share of it.[55]

Sousa's insistence that the grooves cut in the surface of a record would eventually be readable (and thus constitute a new form of musical notation) is worthy of note. He adopted this novel argument because the writings of an author, according to the Constitution, are entitled to protection, and he thus hoped to prove that a record (disc or cylinder) was a composer's writing. The argument availed him nothing, but he was not the only person to use it.

Herbert was the next to speak and made a modest, though firm, first appearance. Remarking that Sousa's statement had made the question "very plain and clear," he continued:

I would like to say this, that both Mr. Sousa and I are not here representing ourselves as individuals and our personal interests, but we stand here for many hundreds of poor fellows who have not been able to come here— possibly because they have not got the price—brother composers whose names figure on the advertisements of these companies who make perforated rolls and talking machines, etc., and who never have received a cent, just as is the case with Mr. Sousa and myself.

I do not see how they can deny that they sell their roll or their machine, because they are reproducing a part of our brain, of our genius, or whatever it might be. They pay . . . the singer who sings a song into their machines. They pay Mr. Caruso $3,000 for each song—for each record. He might be singing Mr. Sousa's song, or my song, and the composer would not receive a cent. I say that that can not be just. . . . Morally, there is only one side to it, and I hope you will see it and recommend the necessary law.[56]

The Victor Talking Machine Company conceded the composers' case readily enough, even agreeing that a record contained on its surface the writing of an author. This writing, said Horace Pettit, the company's representative, was "audibly to be read through the medium of a vibrating pencil engaging in the record groove." However, he insisted that, if composers are to be paid, then the manufacturers also were entitled to protection; they should be permitted to copyright the contrivances they made.[57]

This was not unfriendly testimony, but the temper of the manufacturers' witnesses changed very quickly. An astonishing presentation was offered by G. Howlett Davis, an inventor who had obtained many patents on mechanical music devices. He was unalterably opposed to the proposed legislation because it would give composers control over records which were solely the result of inventive genius. Such a law would discourage invention and give the composers a monopoly to the detriment of inventors and the public. Asked if he thought he was entitled to record a Sousa piece, he replied emphatically: "Yes, sir, I do; because outside of a possible minor and remote ethical or equity right, he possesses not a vestige of a statutory or legal right to stop me."[58]

Davis also had a queer appreciation of the composer's value to mankind. He reasoned that the composer created music, but never produced the means of conveying that music to the ear. This great benefit was reserved to the inventor, and the inventor alone. "The farmer or the workingman in all the small towns of this country, who are possessed of an electrical piano player or an automatic piano player, or a graphophone or a phonograph, which serves to relax the tension of their daily labor and fill their souls with music, is not because of the composer, for he rarely reached them, but it is the direct result of the inventor of the mechanical contrivance with which music may be conveyed. Yet this law attempts to reach out and take away from the inventor the product of his brain and to deliver it over to the composer."[59]

In the course of his remarks Mr. Davis expressed fear of a new monopoly, developing through the cooperation of one manufacturing company and the composers. The reference was to the Aeolian Company, maker of piano rolls, which was signing exclusive contracts with music publishers for the reproduction of what they published. He intimated that most composers were tied up with particular publishers, with the result that if this bill became law the composers would acquire a new property right in recordings of their music, and the new monopoly would be unbreakable. (The Aeolian Company was acting precisely as described—a fact which tended to confuse the proceedings of this and subsequent hearings. Justice to the composer, however, was not contingent upon Aeolian's policy.)

Herbert reacted violently to this part of Davis's speech, protesting:

Mr. Davis has made a statement which is absolutely untrue. He said, speaking of the Aeolian Company and this contract which they have signed, or made the publishers sign with them, that "They control the publishers and the publishers control the composers." That is absolutely untrue in my case. Nobody controls my works, the works that I am going to write. I am going to bring out a work in September, of which I have only written a few notes so far. I do not even know what I am going to write, and nobody has a contract with me to-day. I want to state most emphatically that I have not even been approached by any firm for the future.

. . . I have a perfect right to go around to my friends and get the best offer I can, have I not?

There must be competition. But I want to state most emphatically—and I know that these gentlemen are going to try to make the point that arrangements have already been made—that there have no arrangements been made in my case—absolutely none. I have not been approached by any one of the companies—not even by the company, for instance, that is in favor of paying the royalty, the Victor Talking Machine Company. They have never spoken a word to me about the future, and I have not made a contract for my next work with Witmark & Sons yet. I may publish it with somebody else; I do not know. So I am perfectly free to say that his statement in that respect was absolutely untrue.[60]

Ten independent manufacturers of automatic piano rolls had banded together and sent John J. O'Connell to the hearings as their legal representative. He was opposed to the composers, to the Aeolian monopoly, and to Sousa's theory that a record contained some form of writing. He told the Congressional committees that the proposed law would benefit Herbert and Sousa, but would damage the manufacturing industries to the extent of many millions of dollars. In contradicting the theory that writing of a sort could be found on a record, he drew an observation from R. R. Bowker, a tried and true friend of literary authors. Bowker wanted to aid the composers and gave his support to the writing theory: "May I say that the character of the phonograph record which uses the very word 'graph,' meaning 'writing,' represents the earliest form of writing, that of incised character writing."[61] His good intentions were of no avail.

Then S. T. Cameron (American Graphophone Company) infuriated Sousa by suggesting a completely irrelevant analogy:

You ask me if I would use Sousa's march, make that record and sell it, and not pay him any royalty. I answer, "Yes; I would"; because I have paid him royalty. Whenever Mr. Sousa publishes one of his pieces of music and puts it out upon the market and I pay the price of that music, that sheet of music passes from under the monopoly, just as when I patent a cornet and sell the cornet to Mr. Sousa, and he pays the price for it, it passes out from under the patent monopoly, and he has the right to use it. Suppose I should come here and say to you that every time one of Mr. Sousa's cornet players played the cornet that I had sold to him that he should pay me royalty for having played it! That is what he is asking of you.[62]

The initial hearings set the stage for more ardent hearings. The composers had much to gain, the manufacturers much to lose—or so they thought. The next hearings were held on December 7, 8, 10, and 11, 1906, and the testimony became more bitter as well as more animated. Herbert was present but did not testify—which does not mean that he was inactive. He lobbied, cajoled, persuaded, and teased, trying constantly to convince legislators and their friends that the composers were being victimized by the selfish and conscienceless manufacturers.

Early in the second hearings one of the manufacturers' representatives, F. W. Hedgeland, voiced the expected plea that compensation for the composers was not in the public interest because it would raise the cost of the product. He declared he wanted no special privilege, only what was fair and equitable to the public, but the trend of business was to reduce costs, not increase them. Under questioning he admitted he did not know just what would be fair and equitable—probably "any measure that will not force the entire population of this country to pay tribute to one or two individuals."[63] This remark seemed to be pointed directly at Herbert and Sousa.

To offset the pressure of the opposition R. R. Bowker again tried to help the composers. He referred with scorn to the American Musical Copyright League, in which the manufacturers had banded together, and he drew upon his personal experience in purchasing mechanical devices. He was convinced that the margin of profit on each roll of music entitled the composer to a fair return.[64]

Finally another composer of national reputation entered the fray with a passionate statement on the mechanical devices clause. This was Herbert's operetta rival of days past, Reginald de Koven. Unfortunately he was ill, and the following was read for him:

This clause, as you doubtless are aware, was inserted in the bill to give a long-needed protection to composers, who for years have suffered from the depredations of a number of mercantile companies and corporations like the Aeolian Company, the Victor talking machine, the Edison phonograph, and others too numerous to mention, who have taken—I had almost said stolen—their copyright works without so much as saying "by your leave," and grown rich on the sale of them. Of late, with the most stupendous impertinence and unblushing effrontery, they have not only not paid for the single copy of such works necessary to make their reproductions, but have actually demanded a free copy from the publishers in order that they may plunder the more easily and at the least possible expense. Their right to do this is that of the aboriginal man with a club—the same right that I should possess to knock down a man, were I strong enough to do so, and forcibly take possession of his watch and chain. But here the law intervenes to protect him, and the object of this bill is for the law to intervene to protect the unfortunate composer.[65]

An outburst like this had little effect upon the manufacturers. They countered with the proposition that, far from robbing or depriving the composer of anything, they were actually enlarging his income. Any composer popular enough or fortunate enough to have a piece of music put upon a record received that much free advertising. People who heard the record would flock to the stores to buy the music. The composers, said A. H. Walker, "stand up here and invoke these sacred ethical principles and reflect severely upon us as being pirates; whereas, instead of being pirates, we are the best friends they have." He approached tearfulness as he told his small audience: "What have we done in order to accomplish this beneficent work for these gentlemen? We have made hundreds of inventions, we have invested millions of dollars in producing automatic musical instruments, and we have put a vast amount of labor and ingenuity into the work, with the result of conferring upon them a large share of the fruits of our investment, our genius, and our labor."[66] The composers were not impressed.

Curiously enough, the counsel for the Rudolph Wurlitzer Company, George W. Pound, offered a compromise solution. Unwilling to see the mechanical devices themselves made the object of copyright, he thought the composer should be paid something for the use of his music; and he suggested a royalty of two cents for each reproduction of a work used in connection with automatic playing instruments.[67] His words seemed to fall on deaf ears, but this was the rate which was finally adopted three years later.

As 1907 wore on, the strife steadily increased. The original copyright bill was lost sight of and was supplanted by others, but the point of contention remained very much the same: Should the composer have mechanical control of his compositions, or should he not? On January 29, 1907, Representative Currier introduced a bill hostile to the composer, and Senator Kittredge submitted one completely friendly to the composer.[68] This peculiar situation actually helped the composers in their struggle by concentrating their attention on two objectives: the defeat of Currier's measure, and the triumph of Kittredge's. But they were unorganized, handicapped by weak support, and innocent of Congressional negotiation. More than anyone else Herbert became the composers' spokesman and champion. He almost commuted to Washington to lobby in their interests; he wined and dined Congressmen in an effort to gain sympathy, and he wrote eloquent arguments to win the backing of the public. He even accepted the presidency of the Authors' and Composers' Copyright League of America, which was organized to fight on behalf of the writers of music. Fellow officers were John Philip Sousa, treasurer, and Reginald de Koven, secretary.

The new League hurriedly issued proclamations and literature throughout the country in an effort to obtain popular support. Herbert drafted letters to strengthen the composers' following, and carefully explained that the fear of a monopoly arising from a manufacturer-publisher-composer combine was irrelevant and groundless. Here is the major part of a typical communication:

Dear Sir:

No doubt you are familiar with the fact that there is pending in Washington a copyright bill—the Kittredge bill, S. 2900—favoring the payment of royalties to the author and composer on mechanical instrument records.

This bill is being strongly opposed by the mechanical instrument trust, who, because they have not been paying royalties in the past through a discrepancy in the present copyright law, do not want to do so in the future. To this end, they have trumped up a number of false charges, which, however, will be readily and successfully explained away before the joint patent committee in Washington in the near future.

One of their meanest cries is that of "monopoly," they claiming that the music publishers have signed exclusive contracts with the Aeolian Company of New York, and that, in the event of the passage of the Kittredge copyright bill, the said Aeolian Company would have a monopoly, to the exclusion of other perforated roll manufacturers.

As a matter of fact, the contracts that certain publishers have made with the Aeolian Company are not contingent upon the passage or defeat of any copyright bill, but rather upon the litigation that is now pending in the Supreme Court of the United States, and which is liable to be lost, thus abrogating and nullifying all such contracts.

On the other hand, if the Kittredge bill is passed, every author and composer, including the many, many thousands not tied by exclusive contracts to any publisher or publishers (there are hardly twenty-five in all so signed) will be justly benefited.

We need your assistance in this connection, so that we can prove to those men sitting in Washington that there can be no monopoly on brains, and that the smallest minority possible have signed contracts with the Aeolian Company, which they did in the best of faith.[69]

In addition Herbert wrote articles to inform the general public of the impasse wherein the composers found themselves. A major appeal —an essay in which Herbert championed the composer artistically as well as economically—appeared in *The Circle* for March, 1908.

The just-quoted letter refers to litigation pending in the United States Supreme Court. This was the culmination of *White-Smith Music Publishing Company* v. *Apollo Company,* on which the impatiently awaited decision would be handed down on February 24, 1908. The composers hoped that the results would help them achieve their copyright objectives.

Several years previously, the Apollo Company, maker of piano rolls, had made records of two musical compositions published by the White-Smith Company, Adam Geibel's "Little Cotton Dolly" and "Kentucky Babe." The publisher sued Apollo on the grounds of infringement of copyrighted material, and lost in the lower courts. The Supreme Court consented to hear the case, and future copyright legislation would undoubtedly be affected by the outcome. If the publisher won, then manufacturers would think twice before appropriating copyrighted music; if Apollo were victor, manufacturers would be upheld in the practice they were regularly following.

Herbert was no party to this action, but he felt it was of vital concern to all composers. Therefore he submitted a petition to the Supreme Court to file a brief which was presented on October 14, 1907. It contained the following testimony: "During the last ten years your petitioner has suffered great loss and injury by reason of the unauthorized use made of your petitioner's copyrighted compositions by persons and corporations engaged in the sale of perforated music rolls and of other devices adapted to the automatic reproduction of music."[70]

The Supreme Court, of course, could judge the case only in the light of existing law; and in its decision the record manufacturer was the winner. Justice Day wrote the decision, which included the historic opinion that perforated rolls were not "copies within the meaning of the copyright act."[71] He explained: "When the combination of musical sounds is reproduced to the ear it is the original tune as conceived by the author which is heard. These musical tones are not a copy which appeals to the eye. In no sense can musical sounds which reach us through the sense of hearing be said to be copies as that term is generally understood, and as we believe it was intended to be understood in the statutes under consideration. A musical composition is an intellectual creation which first exists in the mind of the composer; he may play it for the first time upon an instrument. It is not susceptible of being copied until it has been put in a form which others can see and read."[72] Therefore, if the mechanical device was not a copy no infringement had been committed, and the composer, under law, had not been harmed.

Justice Oliver Wendell Holmes concurred in the decision; but he was impelled to write a separate opinion which also became famous.

Among its abstruse, though sympathetic, phrases was a definition of a musical composition which has no parallel in all of music literature:

The notion of property starts, I suppose, from confirmed possession of a tangible object and consists in the right to exclude others from interference with the more or less free doing with it as one wills. But in copyright property has reached a more abstract expression. The right to exclude is not directed to an object in possession or owned, but is *in vacuo,* so to speak. It restrains the spontaneity of men where but for it there would be nothing of any kind to hinder their doing as they saw fit. It is a prohibition of conduct remote from the persons or tangibles of the party having the right. It may be infringed a thousand miles from the owner and without his ever becoming aware of the wrong. It is a right which could not be recognized or endured for more than a limited time, and therefore, I may remark in passing, it is one which hardly can be conceived except as a product of statute, as the authorities now agree.

The ground of this extraordinary right is that the person to whom it is given has invented some new collocation of visible or audible points—of lines, colors, sounds, or words. The restraint is directed against reproducing this collocation, although but for the invention and the statute any one would be free to combine the contents of the dictionary, the elements of the spectrum, or the notes of the gamut in any way that he had the wit to devise. The restriction is confined to the specific form, to the collocation devised, of course, but one would expect that, if it was to be protected at all, that collocation would be protected according to what was its essence. One would expect the protection to be coextensive not only with the invention, which, though free to all, only one had the ability to achieve, but with the possibility of reproducing the result which gives to the invention its meaning and worth. A musical composition is a rational collocation of sounds apart from concepts, reduced to a tangible expression from which the collocation can be reproduced either with or without continuous human intervention. On principle anything that mechanically reproduces that collocation of sounds ought to be held a copy, or if the statute is too narrow ought to be made so by a further act, except so far as some extraneous consideration of policy may oppose. What license may be implied from a sale of the copyrighted article is a different and harder question, but I leave it untouched, as license is not relied upon as a ground for the judgment of the court.[73]

The composers, disappointed in the action of the Supreme Court which is still invoked today, looked forward to the next set of public hearings. These were held in Washington on March 26, 27, and 28, 1908, and Herbert was there as usual. He attended this time in a threefold capacity—for himself and his fellow composers, as president of the Authors' and Composers' Copyright League of America, and as representative of the American Federation of Musicians, sixty thousand strong.

At the beginning of his testimony[74] Herbert tried to show the falsity of the manufacturers' claim of freely advertising a composer's printed work. He presented a mass of phonograph advertising material which told prospective purchasers that only the most popular pieces (i.e., works already widely known and distributed) were put on discs.

Asked if he would be satisfied with a stipulated royalty on each piece of his that might be recorded, he replied with remarkable candor: "In the first place, all my works do not command the same price, and I do not think it would be fair to me to have the same price for all the work I have done." Then he complained of the manufacturers' artistic irresponsibility and told the Congressmen: "But I think I ought to have the supervision over the thing, with reference to the artistic side of it. That is the very thing I have been speaking about. As a matter of fact, they simply do not perform on their machines at all what they claim it to be. I deny that the compositions they put on their machines are my works." He pleaded for both artistic and economic control of his music, and when told that he desired something which would appear very drastic he posed the reasonable question: "How is it drastic when they steal my works?" He explained that he simply wanted the same relationship between record maker and composer as existed between publisher and composer.

The manufacturers were in no mood to yield, and their most eloquent spokesmen fought doggedly to counteract Herbert's influence which was considerable. Paul H. Cromelin, vice president of the Columbia Phonograph Company, and John J. O'Connell, counsel for the National Association of Piano Manufacturers, replied vigorously to the composers' arguments. Cromelin cited the decision of the Supreme Court in *White-Smith* v. *Apollo,* contending that mechanical devices were entitled to no copyright consideration; O'Connell charged that the composers were conducting a campaign of misrepresentation and were misleading the public. At the conclusion of the hearings no one knew what the outcome would be or to what extent the new copyright bill would recognize the effect of reproducing machines upon musical economics.

The aftermath was well described by O'Connell as soon as the bill became law.[75] He admitted readily the influence exerted by Herbert and Sousa, and he used the same Supreme Court decision to show that the composers were entitled to some relief. In fact, Justice Holmes's opinion said as much. When the hearings were over, the Congressional committees entertained two sets of views: one favored the extension of copyright protection to cover mechanical devices; the other favored payment to composers on a universal royalty basis. The possibility of giving composers no relief had totally disappeared. O'Connell was instrumental in assembling the various parties and working out the agreement which set two cents per mechanical device made as the legal royalty rate. Herbert signed the agreement, but protested that the rate was too low. On the other hand the "talking-machine people" refused to sign on the ground that the rate was too high, especially for the cheaper records. It was definitely a compromise dénouement, but the composers were much better off than before, and the manufacturers' suffering was imperceptible.

With the bill (now labeled H.R. 28,192) finally drafted it was reported on by the House Committee on Patents. The report admitted that the section "which deals with the reproduction of music by mechanical means has been the subject of more discussion and has taken more of the time of the committee than any other provision." It continued:

> Your committee have felt that justice and fair dealing, however, required that when the copyrighted music of a composer was appropriated for mechanical reproduction the composer should have some compensation for its use and that the composer should have the further right of forbidding, if he so desired, the rendition of his copyrighted music by the mechanical reproducers. How to protect him in these rights without establishing a great music monopoly was the practical question the committee had to deal with. The only way to effect both purposes, as it seemed to the committee, was, after giving the composer the exclusive right to prohibit the use of his music by the mechanical reproducers, to provide that if he used or permitted the use of his music for such purpose then, upon the payment of a reasonable royalty, all who desired might reproduce the music.[76]

To an appreciable extent this, and the law, reflected the objectives the composers were striving for, although Herbert's dissatisfaction with the amount of compulsory royalty is easily understood.

In all fairness it must be pointed out that Herbert was not alone in his fight for increased legislative recognition of the composer. He and his friends rallied considerable support for their cause, and in addition to Sousa, Isidore Witmark and Nathan Burkan were powerful allies. The former was a silent partner, so to speak, but the latter valiantly argued legal points and constitutional possibilities at the hearings. There were also others, both individuals and organizations (notably the Friars); yet Herbert's voice was the most influential and his effort to persuade the committees to give the composer a modicum of justice was the most consistent. When the bill was signed on March 4, 1909, and went into effect on July 1, the musical profession owed him a vast debt of gratitude.

The story has a short postlude. After the compromise was reached, there seemed to be no disposition to push the bill through Congress. The composers felt they could do no more, and if the bill were not passed, their efforts would have been in vain. An impulsive reaction on the part of Mrs. Ethelbert Nevin, widow of the famous composer, helped save the day. Knowing how much the composers wanted the bill to pass, realizing that she herself could not benefit from the bill because her husband's works generally fell outside its scope, she decided to go to Washington early in 1909 and agitate for its passage. She consulted with Herbert and obtained his approval. Then she called a meeting in her New York home and explained her intentions. Herbert supplied her with documents and suggested persons to see in Washington. Armed with his and other assistance she journeyed to the Capital and insisted that the bill must be passed at once.[77] It is difficult to estimate her success or the effectiveness of her plea, but she subsequently received letters of congratulation from Herbert Putnam, Librarian of Congress, and Oscar Sonneck, of the same institution.

15

A Masterpiece and the Reverse

ONE immediate result of the settlement of copyright for mechanical devices was Herbert's willingness to make phonograph records. He was engaged by Thomas A. Edison's concern, the National Phonograph Company of Orange, New Jersey, which proudly announced the fact to the world. Edison himself was cognizant of its importance, and he sent the composer a warm, personal note:

My dear Mr. Herbert

I was greatly pleased to learn that our Phonograph people have obtained the services of your great orchestra, and your personal advice and criticism in our record making.

From now on we ought to reach a still higher standard in the recording of music.

Yours
THOMAS A. EDISON

May 1, 1909

Herbert replied with equal warmth on May 3:

Dear Mr. Edison

I thank you for your kind letter of May 1st, and hope that the assistance my orchestra and I may lend in making Edison Records, will meet your expectations and further approval.

The capabilities of the Phonograph in spreading culture, instilling a sense of appreciation and discrimination of the best in art, and musically educating the people are beyond conception, and I am eager to do what I can to enlarge the scope of your truly wonderful invention.

Very sincerely yours
VICTOR HERBERT[1]

346

Edison's company had reason to be proud of its conquest. It asserted that its announcement was of "very great importance to the talking-machine trade and to the great public the world over." It issued special advertising and publicity which showed that Herbert was to be far more than a recording artist. He was to conduct his own orchestra in recording sessions, of course; but in addition he was to be the company's artistic adviser and recording supervisor. An advertisement to phonograph dealers carried these passages:

We have just secured the exclusive services of Mr. Victor Herbert as adviser in connection with the making of Edison Records.

He will suggest plans for further development of our Record business; will aid in the selections of compositions and the artists to sing or play them and will act as critic in making master Records.

The arrangement also includes the exclusive right to have the famous Victor Herbert Orchestra make Records for the Edison Phonograph.

You, as a dealer in music and musical instruments, must realize the importance of this connection which is bound to put the Edison Phonograph and the entertainment it offers on a plane even higher than it is at present.

With the Amberol Records, offering selections beyond the limits of all other records; with the world's best talent at its disposal and with a man of Mr. Herbert's ability as adviser and critic, the Edison Phonograph stands pre-eminent and alone as an instrument for discriminating lovers of musical entertainment.[2]

The Amberol record, incidentally, was the most modern Edison cylinder. Up to about 1908 the company made cylinders which played for about two minutes and were cut 100 "threads" to the inch. In 1908 the four-minute cylinder was issued, with 200 "threads" to the inch, and this was called the Edison Amberol.[3] It was a tremendous improvement.

Herbert's association with the National Phonograph Company stimulated great interest, whetted perhaps by his recent antagonism to the manufacturers. To one interviewer he made quite a declaration of faith in the still novel instrument:

I have long advocated that the composer should be connected in the arrangement and interpretation of his work for use upon the phonograph, and now that the National Phonograph Co. has given me the opportunity to see that my own works shall be interpreted by my own orchestra, led by myself, and we have also agreed upon an artistic supervision by me of important compositions in musical literature, modern and classic, I am very pleased. I shall enter upon this work with genuine enthusiasm and interest, because I believe that there are endless opportunities for the spread of musical culture through the phonograph, which enters every corner of the world.

I regard my new connection with the National Phonograph Co. as in the nature of a public service. My friends know that my income is such that I am not taking this action for individual profit.[4]

The National Phonograph Company was equally sanguine over the new relationship, and the June and July, 1909, issues of the *Edison Phonograph Monthly* were filled with anticipation and expectancy. In the middle of June, Herbert spent three days on orchestral recordings in the Company's laboratory; and the first record—"Selections from *Mlle. Modiste*," Amberol No. 195—was released in July. For three years a steady stream of Herbert records came out under the Edison label. He performed both his own and other works, and initiated a recording career unique in American phonographic history.

Neither anxiety over the copyright law nor the responsibility of making records could interfere with Herbert's established activities. Concerts, dinners, and social obligations kept him interminably busy. If the Lambs was not using his services, the Friars claimed him, as on May 14, when he directed the music for their second annual festival, helping them raise more than $8,000 and making it a huge success.[5]

In 1909 the treasury of the Lambs, too, was running low, and Herbert and his men took to the road in another All Star Gambol. A grueling week was divided as follows: May 24, New York; May 25, Hartford and Boston; May 26, Brooklyn and Philadelphia; May 27, Washington and Baltimore; May 28, Cleveland and Pittsburgh; May 29, Chicago. When the entourage returned to New York the players gave an extra performance on May 31 at the Metropolitan Opera House for the benefit of the Actors' Fund, which alone brought in some $8,000. The tour netted the club $100,000, which was its objective, and everyone was happily satisfied.[6]

With the advent of autumn Herbert again conducted Sunday evening concerts in New York and made his usual bid for operetta honors. The revival of *Algeria* (now *The Rose of Algeria*) came first. It was followed in a few weeks by the comedy of dubious merit *Old Dutch*.

This peculiar combined work of three men was first seen on the stage of the Grand Opera House at Wilkes-Barre, Pennsylvania, on November 6, 1909. After two weeks in Philadelphia at the Adelphi Theatre, where it was cordially received, it had its New York première at the Herald Square Theatre on November 22. It was not wholly successful; the story was mediocre and again, particularly in this instance, Herbert exposed his failure to appreciate textual suitability for an effective operetta.

The featured player was the popular comedian Lew Fields, who had been directly responsible for the valiant if futile effort to prolong

Algeria. Herbert may have felt especially indebted to him, but there is an additional strange story about the origin of *Old Dutch* which may be unique in light-opera history.

As early as February, 1908, Herbert had contracted with Fields to compose music for an opera to be called *Regina*, giving him the exclusive right to produce it between November 15, 1908, and May 15, 1909.[7] Fields, working for the Shubert interests, pledged that no part of the resulting work (i.e., book, lyrics, etc.) would be produced apart from Herbert's music. Quite evidently the experience with *Dream City* still disturbed the composer.

Regina never materialized. Instead, a German farce was brought back from Europe by Lee Shubert late in 1908, and Fields asked Herbert to write the music for an American adaptation. Herbert learned that the book was to be prepared by Edgar Smith, one of his opponents in the *Dream City* controversy, and refused; but he changed his mind when a concession was made. The lyrics would be provided by a third man, a friend and fellow Lamb, George V. Hobart.[8] Thus Herbert fell into the anomalous position of writing music for acceptable (?) lyrics for a play by a man whom he cordially despised and would not speak to.

This strange product opened in New York as "a musical farce in two acts." The program innocently stated, "Book by Edgar Smith, lyrics by George V. Hobart," and no spectator divined the harsh feelings concealed. Lew Fields was one of the producers, along with Sam S. and Lee Shubert. The cast was as follows:

Ludwig Streusand, absent-minded inventor; familiarly known in his native town as "Old Dutch"	Lew Fields
Liza Streusand, his daughter	Alice Dovey
Leopold Mueller, an adventurer	John E. Henshaw
Alma Villianyi, a Viennese music hall singer	Ada Lewis
Joseph Cusinier, proprietor of the "Hotel Schoenwald"	Charles Judels
Franz von Bomberg, a wealthy Viennese manufacturer, touring in the Tyrol	John Bunny
Rosa von Bomberg, his wife	Eva Davenport
Alfred von Bomberg, his son; lieutenant in the Royal Light Infantry ...	William Raymond
Hon. Algernon Clymber, in the Tyrol for his health	Vernon Castle
Jean, head porter at "Hotel Schoenwald"	Mark Johnston

The Girl with the Hair Lip. . . . .   Irene Russell

Gwendolyn ⎫
Maude   ⎪
Mabel   ⎬ Sisters of Hon. Algernon
Kate   ⎪   Clymber . . . .
Margaret ⎪
Julia   ⎭

Jane Grover
Marion Whitney
Billee Cuppia
Josephine Karlin
Elsie Le Boy
Marise Naughton

Wilhelm ⎫
Franz   ⎪ Brother officers of Alfred
Adelbert ⎬   von Bomberg . . . .
Oskar   ⎪
Rudolf   ⎪
Gustave ⎭

George Lynch
Harry Harrington
Thomas McCormick
Wood Gobel
Fred Roberts
Joseph Norwich

Freda . . . .   May Willard
Lois . . . .   Ruth Rider
Maid at the Schoenwald. . . . .   Gertrude Grant
Grenwald, a mountain guide. . . . . . .   John Donnelly
Messenger . . . .   Victor Hyde
Gendarme . . . .   George Dowling
Gendarme . . . .   Joseph Torpey
Allan . . . .   Victor Hyde
Olga . . . .   Nettie Hyde
Fleurette . . . .   Rhea Hess
Babette . . . .   Hannah Hess
Little Mime.   Helen Hayes
Lightning Charlie. . . . .   By himself

Tourists, Soldiers, Guides, Peasants, Waitresses, Guests,
Children, Mountain Climbers, Cafe Maids, Gypsies,
Dignitaries, Wives of Dignitaries, Titled Ladies, Orien-
tals, French Dancers

The show was staged by Ned Wayburn; the musical director was
Louis F. Gottschalk.

Act I had a single scene: the exterior of the Hotel Schoenwald in
the Tyrol (time, afternoon). Act II had two scenes: the Palm Garden
of the Hotel Schoenwald (time, evening), and the second floor corridor
of the hotel (time, night).

The very thin story, with a lukewarm romance, is of an inventor
who, with his daughter, takes a vacation to get away from fame. At
the resort hotel Liza meets Alfred, and they fall in love. The main
action, however, centers in the loss of the inventor's wallet, his inability
to identify himself, and the humilities he and Liza undergo when
two rascally impostors (Mueller and Alma) find the wallet and pose
as the honest pair. Justice, of course, triumphs in the end.

The musical score for *Old Dutch* was uneven, but it had several
excellent numbers and one which was unusual. The opening scene

and chorus were fine. It was an animated, colorful introduction and provided a background in keeping with the hotel, the countryside, and the guests. With genuine zest Herbert depicted the regional yodeling, the enthusiasm of the mountaineers, the military "zip" of the visiting soldiery.

The finale to the first act was equally good, with felicitous musical touches that emphasized the drama. In this scene Streusand becomes the temporary outcast, and the course of action is supported by music throughout. The bombast dies away and the stage is empty. To very soft music Liza enters, quickly followed by Alfred, who simply kisses her hand in token of faith not wholly lost. Then poor Streusand emerges from behind a rose bush and, weary in body and spirit, limps to a seat under a tree. He utters only a long expressive sigh, and a sudden flourish in the orchestra heralds the fall of the curtain and the end of the act. This closing scene was played entirely in pantomime and gave an uncommon touch of seriousness.

The critical reaction in New York was mixed. As usual the greatest amount of praise was allotted to the music; but some of the principals were highly commended. Fields, who had no singing role, gave general satisfaction, and Alice Dovey was found to be pleasing. Two members of the cast became world-famous in later years: Vernon Castle who, said one observer, deserved a better opportunity to display his ability and agility;[9] and Helen Hayes, who was making her New York début. Only nine years old, she was one of a pair of children who "stole the show" for the moments they were on the stage. Following the love duet by Alfred and Liza ("U, Dearie," not among Herbert's best) the children solemnly pantomimed the action and emotions of the lovers, with such success that the audience wanted more and more. The talented girl received this special attention: "Miss Helen Hayes, a wee miss, won the favor of the audience by a bit of acting that was refreshing."[10]

One criticism, probably merited but fortunately having no connection with the play's musical aspect, had to do with a minor character. Among the *dramatis personae* was "The Girl with the Hair Lip," obviously included as a contribution to slapstick effect. The use of such a character to increase the comedy was unhappy, and a sensitive reviewer commented on it in no uncertain terms: "It is all very well to laugh at misfortunes of a Lew Fields Dutchman— that is what the world is expected to do—but even the Tenderloin does not laugh at the deformities of children, or animals, even if a portion of it thinks certain vulgarities are the height of fun."[11] When the program for the second week was printed, the pathetic creature was no longer listed.

With its indifferent qualities *Old Dutch* enjoyed a New York run of only eighty-eight performances. Then Fields took it on tour for eight weeks which ended with the close of the season.

If Herbert was vexed by the comparatively short life of *Old Dutch*, he was far more irritated by developments five years later when Fields converted the play into a motion picture. He had thought he was protected from a repetition of the *Dream City* incident, where his music was separated from the drama and completely disregarded, and only discovered his error in court.

The motion picture, *Old Dutch*, with Lew Fields again in the title role was made by the World Film Corporation and released on February 22, 1915. The story was cheapened considerably in the transfer to the screen.[12]

Herbert tried desperately to prevent the picture from being shown and instituted legal action; but the judge, while sympathetic, failed to rule in his favor. There were two obstacles Herbert could not overcome. One was the fact that *Regina* was never created. For that work he and Fields had a definite agreement that the play should never be produced apart from the music; but by no stretch of the imagination could *Old Dutch* be considered as an extension or ultimate manifestation of *Regina*. The second obstacle resided in Herbert's refusal to set any book written by Edgar Smith. The compromise arrangement—to set lyrics provided by Hobart—meant, in the judge's mind, that between the music and Smith's play there was no formal connection; consequently the play could be taken away from the music and used in any way Smith and Fields wished. As a result Herbert had the bitter experience of seeing the picture publicized as a version of Fields's musical comedy triumph of previous years. His hostility to Smith had been an expensive emotion to indulge.

The year 1910 for Herbert was a period of both accomplishment and anticipation, in which he produced his best known operetta, a masterly score, and waited impatiently for the production of his first grand opera. Plans were also laid for an extended tour of his orchestra, the kind of tour he had not embarked on since conducting the Gilmore Band.

In the summer he worked on plans for the orchestra tour of the following spring, and by autumn advertisements were informing the country of his availability: "Victor Herbert and His Orchestra (Fifty Musicians) Assisted by a Quartette of Eminent Vocalists and Grand Opera Celebrities" sought engagements for a "Southern spring tour, April and May, 1911."[13] This announcement created considerable interest, for Herbert's orchestra was not a touring organization in the usual sense.

Another matter of anticipation which, unfortunately, failed to develop, was the proposed reorganization of the Pittsburgh Symphony Orchestra with Herbert resuming leadership. He was in Pittsburgh on November 18 and 19 to discuss the possibility and to learn about the proposed $1,000,000 endowment to assure the orchestra a satisfactory permanent income. The musical situation there was very bad, owing to the orchestra's collapse under Emil Paur. There was no meeting of minds, however, and the city remained without an orchestra for years to come.[14]

Prior to resuming his own operetta output Herbert, in the latter half of 1910, cooperated in an important project which has never been publicly known, trying to save a rather weak musical comedy from collapse. For this thankless service (which may well have been gratuitous) he received not even an acknowledgment. The show was *The Slim Princess,* a three-act comic opera with book by Henry Blossom and music by Leslie Stuart of *Floradora* fame. Based on a story by George Ade, it is concerned with a country where obesity is the idea of female beauty.

The first performance of *The Slim Princess* on any stage occurred in Buffalo at The Star Theatre on September 8, 1910. It was a Charles B. Dillingham production, and the brightest star was the dainty, vivacious Elsie Janis. The next morning the Buffalo *Express* told its readers that the music was entrancing, the book clever, the heroine irresistible; but this was an exaggeration.

In the first act of the "complete" vocal score (published 1910) is a gay, hopeful song entitled "My Yankee Doodle Girl." The words are by Henry Blossom, but the music is by John Golden. Golden, later one of America's greatest theatrical producers, was a song writer of no mean experience, although he occasionally needed a bit of musical assistance. His autobiography readily concedes that Victor Herbert supplied this aid. This particular song is the only one in the vocal score not by Stuart; but among the sheet-music excerpts there were more not written by the creator of *Florodora.* New York eventually witnessed a show which was not so exclusively by Stuart as announcements indicated.

This is especially true if the New York première at the Globe Theatre, January 2, 1911, contained the second act finale written by Herbert and preserved in the collection of Herbert autographs in the Library of Congress. Still unpublished, it is an elaborate dramatic close, full of dramatic effects in the orchestra, snatches of recitative and sung dialogue, short dance episodes, a choral ending, and a heavy flourish by the orchestra alone. There are two autograph versions of this finale: the piano-vocal score and the full orchestra score. The former bears, entirely in Herbert's hand, the names of the characters or actors sharing the scene, bits of the dialogue (spoken as well as sung), many hints of the instrumentation, and allusions to stage action. It was more generously marked up by Herbert than most of the manuscripts of his own operettas.

The finale begins and ends in the key of E flat major. At the point of highest climax (i.e., entrance into the choral ending) the music swings into an arrangement of the refrain of Golden's "My Yankee Doodle Girl," quite spirited enough to ring down the curtain with bursts of applause. When Herbert was working on this strange finale, he had before him a copy of the Golden song on which he furiously penciled the changes and improvements he deemed necessary. The song was originally in C major, and so he wrote, "(fuller and higher)," as he contemplated the transposition to E flat. He altered accompanying chords and sketched new harmonies on the printed sheet "when in E flat." He gave some directions for performance and indicated a cut for the second delivery. All his plans for utilizing Golden's cheerful song were faithfully carried over to the manuscript of the finale, and provide an illuminating example of professional *expertise.*

It remains strange, however, that Herbert consented to write an elaborate finale for a show which was not his, and for which he never received credit. The labor probably involved no more than a few hours; but he was going through one of the busiest periods of his life, and such a chore could hardly exert much attraction. Did he do it for a fee, or merely out of friendship? An appeal to John Golden for his recollection brought a response which does not allay all curiosity. Mr. Golden wrote me on April 30, 1947, that Herbert incorporated the song into the finale at Dillingham's request.

Herbert certainly acceded to Dillingham's request, but the resultant finale was far more than a mere incorporation of Golden's song. It is not unreasonable to suppose that the show needed a great deal of help. Elsie Janis's autobiography, in describing *The Slim Princess,* makes it clear that all was not well when the Buffalo presentation took place. The chief comedian had to be replaced, and things went badly until Joseph Cawthorn was engaged to guarantee hearty laughter. She does not refer to the music, but it takes little imagination to believe that it likewise needed change. Dillingham's request and the interpolation of other songs bear this out rather strongly.

Herbert's great achievement of 1910, and one of the greatest of his life, was that classic of American operetta *Naughty Marietta,* which with its sensuous beauty, romantic charm, and virile energy remains a distinguished landmark in American culture. He wrote music which equaled that of *Naughty Marietta,* but he never wrote an entire score which so seized the minds and hearts of his countrymen and became so firmly entrenched in operetta literature. With it also Herbert won posthumous distinction as the only American operetta composer selected by the highly critical historian Curt Sachs for bracketing with the European masters, Suppé, Strauss, Offenbach, and Sullivan.[15]

Naughty Marietta was performed for the first time on any stage in Syracuse, New York, at the Wieting Opera House on October 24, 1910. The New York première occurred on November 7. The combination of its music-stars-story made history.

In May, 1910, a contract[16] was drawn up between Herbert and Oscar Hammerstein, the fabulous opera impresario who, in April, had been forced out of grand-opera production by the thoroughly frightened Metropolitan Opera Company. The inhabitants of the Thirty-ninth Street house compelled the flamboyant Hammerstein to forsake grand opera for a period of ten years in any territory where the Metropolitan itself might be operating. His rivalry was more than it could stand; his artistic standards seemed higher, and his repertoire was far fresher. However, he was always in financial difficulties, and the Metropolitan's greater wealth proved the deciding factor. But he did not have to abandon comic opera or operetta, he still possessed the Manhattan Opera House, and he controlled some amazingly valuable singers.

Herbert agreed to compose the music for a comic opera entitled *Little Paris,* and to deliver a completed piano score by the 1st of October. Just when the title, and presumably the concept, changed to *Naughty Marietta* is not known—perhaps not until he was hard at work with the librettist, a Mrs. Rida Johnson Young. He probably had met her when she came to New York to work in the office of his publisher, Witmark.[17] They worked hard together, and in the middle of June she visited him at Lake Placid.

Hammerstein was proud of securing Herbert's services. He was also proud of having one of his star sopranos, from the Manhattan Opera Company, on hand to create the title role. This was little Emma Trentini, the third of the three great singers immortalized by Herbert's music (the other two being Alice Nielsen and Fritzi Scheff). If she was not the best of the three, she was certainly the most troublesome: a compact bundle of flaming temperament, she did as much to hinder *Naughty Marietta* as to make it an incredible sensation. It is alleged that Hammerstein discovered her in 1906 by accident at a cabaret in Milan where he was relaxing after a day of tiresome auditions. Before the evening was over she was signed to an opera contract, and in the next few years she became one of New York's favorite singers.[18]

Another highly publicized singer in *Naughty Marietta* was the tenor

Orville Harrold, also from the Manhattan Opera Company. He, too, had been discovered by Hammerstein, and was rising rapidly to operatic heights.

In addition to these the Manhattan Opera Company provided other singers, the chorus, part of the orchestra, and the regular conductor. *Naughty Marietta* was certainly not introduced to America by a typical Broadway company. Every audience that heard the brilliant original production was enraptured by the vocal capacity of the cast and the richness of sound coming from the orchestra pit.

This characteristic audience reaction began with the very first performance in Syracuse, whither the company had gone with some misgivings. The final rehearsal was less than satisfactory, and everyone was happily astonished by the smoothness of the première. Herbert conducted, and shared with Trentini the honors of the evening. Oscar Hammerstein was not present; but Arthur was, and wired to his father when the show was over, "Who's looney now?"[19] This cryptic message was sent because it was Arthur that had insisted that Trentini had a special talent for light opera. He even addressed the audience to this effect, saying: "It has taken me four years to convince my father that this little girl belonged in the place that she occupies tonight." The listeners agreed with him because her vocalization was "uncommonly brilliant," her high notes were clear and birdlike, and her manner was "sprightly, magnetic and vivacious."

The music exceeded expectations, and even the librettist, Mrs. Young, came in for praise. She was present and encouraged questions. When asked about the period of the play she replied: "We don't know ourselves. You see, we selected one date, and then the costumer decided that another would give him more latitude in the designing of his costumes, so it is all a little indefinite, but it is some time during the eighteenth century."

The operetta moved westward to repeated triumphs in Rochester and Buffalo. The opening night at Buffalo, October 31, Herbert was again on the conductor's stand; but he had to vault over the orchestra rail before the end in order to catch a train to Chicago. There he conferred on the forthcoming production of his first grand opera.[20] He was having the time of his life!

Naughty Marietta had its New York première on November 7. Anticipating its arrival, Hammerstein proclaimed that its music was the best ever written by an American composer. When this was repeated to Herbert he blushed; whereupon the reporter wrote the delightful lines: "Did you ever see Victor Herbert blush? It is worth twice the price of admission. A rosy sunrise hue mounts to his ever ruddy cheeks, rambles aloft to his broad brow—that brow that sends phrenologists into spasms of delight because it spells music and individuality in every bulging bump—and creeps around his ears and down the back of his neck until it is lost behind his collar."[21]

The Broadway première was at the New York Theatre, and even this fact is a reflection of Hammerstein's curious career. The impresario had built it and lost it, and now returned to it as an unwilling tenant.[22] The program exhibited the following cast:

Simon O'Hara, Captain Dick's servant..	Harry Cooper
Etienne Grandet, son of Lieut. Gov. Grandet, who is also the famous buccaneer "Bras Priqué".............	Edward Martindel
Lieutenant Governor Grandet.........	William Frederic
Sir Harry Blake, an Irish adventurer, friend to Captain Dick...........	Raymond J. Bloomer
Rudolfo, keeper of a marionette theatre.	James S. Murray
Florenze, secretary to the Governor....	Edward Morgan
Manuelo, a pirate..................	William Mack
Night watchman...................	Eugene Roder
Indian	Thomas Reynolds
East Indian.......................	Bert Leslie
Knife grinder.....................	Philip Hahn
Marietta d'Altena.................	Mlle. Emma Trentini
Lizette, a casquette girl.............	Kate Elinore
Adah, a quadroon, slave of Etienne Grandet	Mme. Marie Duchene
Nanette, a flower girl...............	Louise Aichel
Felice, a flower girl................	Blanche Lipton
Fanchon	Vera De Rose
Graziella, an Italian girl............	Sylvia Loti
Franchesca, an Italian girl............	Myrtle Randall
And	
Captain Richard Warrington, an American known as Captain Dick........	Orville Harrold

Quadroon belles, Spanish girls, San Domingo girls, French girls, Flower girls, Quadroons, Dancers, Captain Dick's Adventurers, Pirates, Street sweepers, Mexicans, Spaniards, Indians

Arthur Hammerstein was announced as the manager of the show, produced under the direction of Jacques Coini of the Manhattan Opera House. The musical director was the celebrated Gaetano Merola, also from the Manhattan, and the concertmaster of the enlarged orchestra was Frederick Landau.

The place is New Orleans, the time 1780—but a typewritten libretto gives 1750, more accurate because in 1780 Louisiana was under

Spanish rule, not French. The single scene of Act I is in the Place d'Armes of New Orleans; the first scene of Act II, in a marionette theater; and the final scene, in the ballroom of the Jeunesse Dorée Club.

No Herbert operetta is more familiar than *Naughty Marietta*. The girl of the title, of noble descent, has escaped from an unhappy marriage in Europe with a group of casquette girls, sent to America to wed the Louisiana planters. In this new land she falls under the protection of Captain Dick, a stalwart Kentuckian in pursuit of a troublesome pirate. Their friendship seems to be entirely platonic, Marietta vowing, moreover, that she will give her heart only to him who can complete her fragmentary dream melody. Etienne, in reality the pirate, tires of Adah, and becomes Marietta's suitor. He very nearly wins her; but Dick intervenes in time, and simultaneously completes the dream melody. This is all Marietta has been waiting for.

What is there to say today about the music of *Naughty Marietta*? It has made the opera a classic of the American stage; it contains five numbers which are perennial favorites, besides others which almost rival them; it exudes the lavish and lush melody and harmony which popularly represent romance in its most untrammeled form. But it is more than all this. With the score of *Naughty Marietta* Herbert seems consciously to have reverted to the broad framework that he had used in *The Serenade*. The ensembles are expansive and solid. The solos, for the most part, are long and wide-ranging (as they could be, in view of the singers at his command). The orchestral effects are rich and symphonic (as they could be, also, in view of his enlarged ensemble). A glance at the opening scene in the printed score with its pictorial and dramatic devices, not to mention the street cries and dramatic ejaculations, is enough to make one realize that Herbert was writing in his most vivid style. And the fluidity of the flower girls' choruses speeds the long, colorful scene to a splendid climax.

Captain Dick and his troop march in to the stirring strains of "Tramp! Tramp! Tramp!" which promptly became a model for male choruses in march guise. It has a vigor and pulsation which, once heard, are never forgotten. They sing of their valor, call themselves the Rangers, and boast of the regions whence they come. A delicate flirtatious number is the choral interchange between the casquette girls and the men, who want their favors; the wise little maids are on their guard and insist that marriage is their goal. The next two pieces feature Marietta. In the first, a solo called "Naughty Marietta," she characterizes herself as a mischievous, fun-loving lass who can be either affectionate or horrid. The music follows her every whim. Then she and Captain Dick sing their duet and pledge only friendship to each other. Entitled "It Never, Never Can Be Love," it has a kind of mock solemnity which fools no one.

When Adah questions fortune on whether her beloved will prove true, she sings an intense love song which is passionately somber. This is " 'Neath the Southern Moon," a beautiful poem of tropical warmth, of which the refrain is well known; the stanza is far less known but has a melody of strange nobility set forth over a starkly bare accompaniment—an exquisite piece of music. Another operetta masterpiece comes next, Marietta's exciting "Italian Street Song," sung as a reminiscence of dear Napoli. Here again the refrain is well known, the stanza less so, and the lilting air that precedes the chorus is irresistible in its own right. Both of these songs are very difficult to sing properly. The first demands a contralto with the ability to sustain and control long lines with deep feeling; the second requires a flashy, agile coloratura which can skip and run with purity and precision.

For the first finale Herbert resorted to his best broad style, which translated into music the dramatic excitement of the stage. Snatches of recitative, choral responses, arioso phrases, and energetic choruses follow one another as Marietta makes her escape under Rudolfo's protection. This is the kind of finale, splendidly organized, which earned for Herbert the reputation of composing light opera in the grand-opera manner.

The musical richness of the second act comes in the last scene, beginning with the dances at the ball. The choral-dance music is magnificent, with a riot of color and rhythm and fetching melody in "New Orleans Jeunesse Dorée" and "Loves of New Orleans." Again it is the latter that calls for special note. The song of the quadroons, the lilting waltz of the girls from Spain, the quieter gait of the San Domingo girls, and the piquant verve of the French lasses make a gorgeous panorama. The next notable piece is a concert waltz of surprising amplitude, "Live for Today." It is not unlike some that Herbert had written earlier; but here he abandoned the solo form and wrote it as a quartet, with equally prominent parts for Marietta, Adah, Captain Dick, and Etienne.

At last the main love song is heard—Dick's immortal "I'm Falling in Love with Some One," almost as firmly associated with tenors as "Kiss Me Again" is with sopranos. It is a remarkably beautiful number, with striking effects in the chromaticism of the opening and the unusual leap of a ninth in the refrain. Dick sings the song as he allows his friendship for Marietta to be supplanted by the ardor of romantic attachment.

Dick's final outburst of song is equally felicitous: the rapturous "Ah! Sweet Mystery of Life," one of the two or three most famous melodies Herbert ever wrote. With it Dick indisputably wins the heart of Marietta as well as the affection of everyone in the audience. The melody is artfully simple, unique in the extraordinary alternation of very long and very short notes at a slow tempo, controlled by a rhythm that is firm and precise. It is among the best of all operetta airs.

As with other Herbert songs which are popular enough to inspire legends, the story has arisen that "Ah! Sweet Mystery of Life" (also known as the "Dream Melody") at first had no text—that it was used only instrumentally and incidentally, that the first audiences liked it so much the creators had to find a way to work it into the structure of the play. This story, too, has no foundation in fact; it was sung from the very beginning of the operetta's career.[23]

There was such a high degree of unanimity among the New York critics that it is almost pointless to survey their reactions. First of all, it was a triumph for Herbert, who had produced a score full of beautiful melody, tenderness, humor, resounding choruses, and singable songs.[24] One observer not a music critic, thinking there was a noticeable lack of catchy numbers, remarked that in some ways Herbert had never done better.[25] The most perspicacious judge declared it was difficult to praise the music sufficiently. The composer had fully considered the circumstances of the production and had eliminated every concession to Broadway banality. Even the scant amount of comic music had more substance than was commonly the case. The opening was a finely wrought tone picture of dawning day, and the first-act finale was an ensemble of exceptional skill. Between the scenes an orchestral intermezzo was played. It was "scored with a warmth and musicianly insight of which many a composer of more pretentious reputation might well be proud. The entire orchestral part is replete with felicitous touches better than anything of the kind their writer has yet done. Mr. Herbert himself wielded the bâton on the first night with the result that everything went for its full value."[26]

There was lack of unanimity on two matters: the libretto and the comic elements it contained. Rida Johnson Young may not have produced a literary masterpiece, but it was certainly better than many a book the composer so uncritically accepted. The comic rôles (Simon O'Hara and Lizette) were possibly superfluous, but they were relatively unimportant. Their near-burlesque performances found few onlookers sensitive enough to be disturbed.

Unanimity was reached again with respect to the production and the performance. The former was brilliantly, colorfully perfect; the latter, uniformly excellent. All the principals gave distinguished portrayals, and Orville Harrold—still lacking some finish as an actor—was a sensation as the handsome ranger. His rendition of "I'm Falling in Love with Some One" was encored four times. But next to Herbert, of course, the greatest measure of praise went to the vivacious Trentini, whose voice and personality perfectly fitted her part—or perhaps it should be said that she received music which perfectly fitted her voice and personality. The New York *Times* critic noticed this and issued a warning: "Mr. Herbert has written a part for her which would tire any prima donna to sing every night, and those who would hear all the high notes, roulades, and trills which are in the score now, had best hurry to an early representation of the piece . . . because sooner or later it will probably be found expedient to take some of them out."

This remark was semiprophetic, for Trentini herself complained of her arduous assignment. The production was so successful that she was persuaded to sing eight performances a week, though her contract called for only seven, and she undoubtedly felt the strain of the constant exertion. She kept to this schedule for a considerable period, and business prospered phenomenally. During the seventeen weeks in New York the show averaged $20,000 weekly, at a time when a $2.00 top still prevailed. Herbert's royalty, incidentally, was 3 per cent of the gross receipts.[27]

Naughty Marietta departed on the inevitable tour after 136 performances.[28] There is evidence, however, that the move was planned well in advance, for the final metropolitan presentation was announced weeks ahead. Merola retired as conductor before it left New York, being succeeded by William Axt, a young man who was to become one of the most prominent musicians in Hollywood. Considerable prominence was given to the appointment. Axt had studied in Berlin and was publicized as the youngest conductor in the United States. He was also looked upon as one of the factors in Hammerstein's rivalry with the Metropolitan Opera, for he won the rather enviable nickname of "Oscar's Toscanini."[29]

The subsequent history of *Naughty Marietta* with Trentini as star is an incredible hodgepodge of a prima donna's eccentricities which finally ended in a clash with Herbert himself. They are soberly related in George Blumenthal's interesting memoirs.

The first season was triumphant throughout. The summer of 1911, Trentini spent in Italy; but she returned early to head the company for another tour covering the eastern half of the United States. During her vacation at home she had forgotten all the English she knew, and her language lessons started all over again. This was not so bad, but as the performances were given she became more and more a law unto herself and subject to whims which led to embarrassment. She would refuse to give encores, and sometimes whole numbers, and her managers wondered occasionally if she would come to the theater at all. It was not unusual for them to go to her hotel as late as 7:30 and practically drag her to the theater. She had to be teased and flattered and pampered in every conceivable way, including the payment of all her tips. Although she was earning $1,000 a week she was extremely parsimonious. Blumenthal wrote with touching simplicity, "I surely did have a terrible time with this woman"; and he was probably guilty of an understatement.

Nevertheless Trentini could sing magnificently when she wished, and plans were afoot to give her a new show for the 1912–1913 season. Herbert agreed to write the music, and Otto Hauerbach (he now spells it Harbach) was selected to do the book. This arrangement was publicly announced early in March of 1912.[30] But the company returned to New York for a final fortnight of the 1911–1912 season and went to the West End Theatre in Harlem. It was the first week in April, and a gala performance was planned, Herbert being persuaded to conduct. Blumenthal recalled it as the five hundredth performance of *Naughty Marietta*; but Philadelphia had celebrated that event on March 11 with Herbert on the podium.[31] The New York celebration observed the twenty-fifth anniversary of Oscar Hammerstein's theater building career.[32]

Everything was ready for a stunning performance. Herbert had heard of Trentini's unpredictable tantrums, but he paid them little heed. He knew that all prima donnas occasionally followed their whims and fancies. Before curtain time on the festive evening Herbert asked Blumenthal how she was feeling, and he replied that he wished she were in a better humor. The composer then went backstage to pay his respects to the singer and proceeded to the pit to conduct.

The show went beautifully until Trentini came to the "Italian Street Song." She sang it gloriously and reaped tremendous applause, whereupon Herbert signaled for an encore. She merely returned to the stage and bowed a couple of times to the audience. Again Herbert signaled her to sing the encore and even started the orchestra. This time Trentini looked at him, deliberately ignored his motions, and walked off the stage. Herbert laid down his baton and left the orchestra pit. Backstage, he told Axt to conduct the balance of the performance, as he was through. The next day he told Arthur Hammerstein that never in his entire career had he been so insulted as by Trentini. He would have nothing more to do with her, and most emphatically would not compose the music for her next show.

Trentini was remorseful over the incident, but it was too late.[33] She was fortunate in the show she thus stumbled into—*The Firefly*, with music by Rudolf Friml; but it was no match for *Naughty*

Marietta. Her break with Herbert, it may be assumed, was the occasion for real loss. He wrote his best music when he had singers of genuine ability at his disposal; the works for Nielsen, Scheff, and Trentini prove this beyond a doubt.

Only a few weeks after *Naughty Marietta* was produced in Syracuse, Herbert conducted the world première of his next operetta which was almost as ill-fated as anything he ever wrote. This was *When Sweet Sixteen* (otherwise known as *Victoria*), and it was neither youthful nor victorious. He might have been wise to withhold it from production; but it gave many people pleasure, and it gave some persons a bit of work. No further justification was needed.

When Sweet Sixteen was produced for the first time on any stage in Springfield, Massachusetts, at the Court Square Theatre on December 5, 1910. It then toured in Canada and the Middle West, suffered many changes in cast, had a summer recess, and opened in New York at Daly's Theatre on September 14, 1911. Then it faded from sight almost at once.

George V. Hobart wrote the libretto, and again the book was the composer's worst enemy. The two were reported at work on the operetta—it was called a "song play" for no apparent reason—in 1908, and it was supposedly scheduled for early production by Joseph Brooks. Another early report was that the popular Marie George was being brought from England to star in the show.[34] These hopes came to naught, and a new producer was seemingly found in Lew Fields who signed a contract with Herbert on July 7, 1909.[35] This document referred to the work—under the title *Victoria*—as already written, and pointed to production sometime during the 1909–1910 season. A few months afterward the title was changed to *Sweet Sixteen*, then, when rehearsals finally started, to the title it bore permanently.

Fields was slow in exercising his production privilege, organizing his company, and starting rehearsals in the fall of 1910. Early in November came reports that the players were disbanded; and five weeks' hard work resulted in nothing but disappointment and vexation. One reason given, in fact the only reason, was that Fields's poor health had forced him to give up all professional activity.[36] However, he was an astute showman; he probably saw so little possibility of success in the production that he was willing to sacrifice what had gone into the project rather than to proceed to likely disaster.

Herbert was not so willing to accept defeat. He found another producing company which was agreeable to the venture, and he himself reassembled the scattered players for a rehearsal which could also serve as a demonstration. The producing firm was the Ever-Wall Co.,

Inc.—a partnership of Harry J. Everall and Samuel H. Wallach—and its first production was to be the new operetta.[37]

When Sweet Sixteen as a title is somewhat misleading, for there is no young miss in it at that milestone of life. The heroine is young and sweet, but already a pawn in matrimonial scheming, which hardly takes place so flagrantly with juveniles—at least in light opera. The day before the première the Springfield *Sunday Republican* explained the prominence of the number: there were sixteen principals in the cast, sixteen girls in the chorus, sixteen musical numbers, and a medley of sixteen songs from sixteen of Herbert's most popular operas. It is safe to say that this was an exaggeration, but it made good copy; moreover, there was no better explanation for the title.

When the first performance was finally given, Herbert conducted the orchestra, and the enthusiastic audience demanded a curtain speech from him. But a fantastically long press review, two full columns and a half, was so tempered with qualifications that the provincial critic must be credited with unusual perception. While conceding that Herbert's music had its characteristic tunefulness and suavity, he also wrote paradoxically: "The story of the play . . . is not specially promising, but this is not necessarily to its detriment."[38]

Western New York, Canada, and more American cities were visited, and on February 12, 1911, the Chicago Opera House welcomed the show for a period of a month and a half. Here it seemed that things were looking brighter, although Percy Hammond stated frankly that the book was nothing at all. He also noticed that there were sixteen musical numbers and assumed that the "Sweet Sixteen" of the title "must come from Mr. Herbert's score, since there was no other excuse for it." Two more of his observations reflected the country's attitude toward Herbert rather than any intrinsic merit in the show itself: "It was Mr. Herbert, however, who pulled the entertainment through with his pretty music and made it one of the most enjoyable little song plays that has been sung here this season. The audience was overjoyed with Mr. Herbert, who conducted the orchestra, and also addressed them from the stage. Theatergoers, it seems, care not who compose the book of musical comedy so long as Victor Herbert writes the music." "But the apex of the evening's pleasure was reached when all the principals gathered in the Forest of Arden, where they were rehearsing 'As You Like It,' and engaged in a medley of a score of the popular songs from Mr. Herbert's older operas. The 'Absinthe Frappé' and the 'Put Down Six and Carry Two' numbers from 'Nordland' and 'Toyland' were sung . . . and there were tunes from 'Mlle. Modiste,' 'Algeria,' 'The Wizard of the Nile,' 'The Prima Donna' and many others until it became quite evident that Mr. Herbert is the com-

poser of nearly all the pretty comic opera music of America."[39] He
should have added that *When Sweet Sixteen* was weak musically if the
musical climax depended on a series of interpolated pieces from earlier
scores.

New York quickly proved the Chicago success was an illusion. The
cast for the metropolitan opening was as follows:

John Hammond	Frank Belcher
Mrs. Hammond, his wife	Josie Intropidi
Victoria, his daughter	Harriet Standon
Jefferson Todd, his friend	William Norris
Stanley Morton, Todd's secretary	Roy Purviance
Zeke, his valet	Harry S. Fern
Gertie Greene a manicure	Eva Williams
The Laird of Loch Lomond	George Ridgwell
Monsieur Beaucaire, a fashionable faker	Arthur Lipson
Eleanor Bradford, Victoria's cousin	Mable Mordaunt
Mabel Bradford, her other cousin	Belle Taylor
Gridley, a butler	R. M. Dolliver
Friends of Victoria from the Young Ladies Seminary:	
Emma	Esther Hall
Annabelle	Cecelia Pink
Mary	Edith Williams
Rose	Helene Miller
Marion	Rose Munroe
Louise	Mildred Sanford
Geraldine	Elinor Carrol
Florence	Monte Menden
Edna	Ludovica de Beau
Helen	Harriet Carter
Carol	Ada Blair
Margaret	Virginia May

The staging was directed by George V. Hobart and R. H. Burnside,
who was also a recent addition. The musical director was Frederick
Schwartz, in succession to Louis F. Gottschalk.

The first act took place on a Wednesday morning in September
in the living room of the Hammond country house. The second unfolded in the pine grove on John Hammond's estate at eight o'clock the
following evening.

The apology for a plot presents Victoria (more than sixteen), whose
father wants her to marry for money, and whose mother wants her to
marry for a European title. She actually falls in love with Stanley,
who, pretending to be a poor secretary, is in reality a novelist absorb-
ing new experiences. The most curious thing in the play is the

Hammond family's venture into amateur theatricals and their attempt to do Shakespeare's *As You Like It*. True love triumphs at last, and the obstinate parents are reduced to a degree of common sense.

The score of *When Sweet Sixteen* had no really distinctive numbers. The two most ambitious came at the end of Act I, "In the Golden Long Ago" and "Laughs." Other songs and ensembles had tunes which were honestly pleasing; but they lacked the weight and fervor which characterized Herbert's better pieces.

The show received remarkably little critical attention; as if condemned in advance, it failed to draw the reviewers. Of the few listeners who expressed opinions, one readily conceded that all the credit had to go to Herbert, who had supplied entrancing music;[40] another suggested that Herbert's unceasing skill with an orchestra concealed the paucity of genuine airs.[41] Consequently *When Sweet Sixteen* had only twelve performances in New York and then quietly disappeared. There is no reason to suppose that Herbert experienced more than a mild disappointment over its fate. He was busy with other things, and he was still relishing his additional celebrity as a composer of grand opera.

16

The Grand Operas

LIKE all good musicians Herbert often ridiculed the pretentions and conventions of grand opera. Though his wife had been a successful prima donna, though he had played in the best of opera orchestras and learned the repertoire thoroughly, he knew that opera was a bastard art which appalled the intelligence of all thinking people. But, as a good musician, he also recognized the unique power of grand opera and admired the emotional effectiveness of music supporting drama. Opera might be silly and fantastic and impossible, it might be contrary to nature and offensive to good sense; yet it had an incredible eloquence in presenting human conflict which abstract music could not share and the spoken word could not approach.

Herbert's friends—which meant the American public—also wanted him to compose a grand opera. Many of his best operettas had shown flashes of grand-opera fullness and breadth. They contained episodes and finales which approached the grand-opera idiom, and they had many orchestral passages which were more than adequately descriptive of physical and environmental background. His experience in the lighter musical theater, his virtuosity in scoring for orchestra, his thorough training in composition were encouraging factors. They made him a man from whom an opera was not only expected but demanded.

Little or no thought was given to Herbert's ability to write a serious music drama, sustained in mood and style. No one had any doubts as to whether America had a native genius for opera; no one wondered what would really be accomplished if Herbert should create an operatic masterpiece. Once it was known that he was writing a grand opera it was blithely assumed that he had undertaken a more important task than operetta, and that the result would give America leadership in operatic development. Herbert optimistically and innocently shared these convictions.

It is quite impossible for Americans of the mid-twentieth century to realize how eagerly the production of Herbert's first grand opera was awaited, how closely the reports of progress on it were followed, how newsworthy was its development from inception to completion. American opera was no new thing, nor was opera in English; but the time was apparently ripe for a concerted effort to promote both. An American who could do this would be the champion of both and a creator destined for immortality. The Metropolitan Opera Company was a source of national pride, for it boasted the greatest singers in the world; but it had done nothing for American opera. (Its first gesture in this direction would be on March 18, 1910, when it presented Frederick Converse's *The Pipe of Desire.*) The Manhattan Opera Company was just starting and had had little opportunity to disclose either its path or its influence. However, it was immediately a rival of the Metropolitan, and the respective managers amused the public with their fight for supremacy.

The struggle of the two companies was of more than local moment. It made the population of the entire country opera-conscious, and it made many music lovers feel that opera had a hitherto unrecognized validity. Oscar Hammerstein's first season at the helm of the Manhattan Company was 1906–1907, and he demonstrated promptly the highest artistic standards. To thousands of music lovers opera was the highest form of musical art; and if New York could support two major establishments they could draw but one conclusion, that opera was essential to healthy aesthetic experience.

Oscar Hammerstein was negotiating with Herbert for an American grand opera. He knew that Herbert wanted to write such a work; and he knew he himself had the facilities to promote it. His hopes were summed up in a statement to the press, which he addressed volubly on every conceivable occasion:

I have always wished it to be understood that in founding this opera house I had other aims than merely financial profits. I stated this on the occasion of my first night. And I adhere to it still. Fundamentally, my aims have been artistic, and will continue so.

Now that my opera house is launched and standing fair and square upon its own legs, I have determined to go a step or two forward. . . . I desire to tread the virgin fields of grand opera, and to discover something that is more novel than novelty. I want to be an operatic Columbus. . . .

Certainly our American operatic composers never would set the operatic world on fire unless they first caught hold of a torch or were provided with a match. The Manhattan Opera House is the torch and I have offered its resources to Victor Herbert, whose eminence as a composer and whose representativeness of America no one can deny. I have asked him to compose opera.

Mr. Herbert listened to my proposal . . . He will compose. I will produce.[1]

Under the circumstances, and at the time of utterance, this was exciting news. Herbert was ready to attempt a full-scale opera, and he was surrounded by friends who urged him to dally no longer. His thoughts had veered in this direction even before Hammerstein held out the match. In 1906 Herbert's Pittsburgh admirer, Wilmer M. Jacoby, had taken the playwrights John Luther Long and Edward C. Carpenter to him to discuss opera possibilities.[2] They talked with him about a music drama to be based on their *The Dragon Fly,* but without musical materialization.[3]

Early in 1907 Herbert had admitted that he wanted to do an opera, but recognized the exclusion of the American composer from the operatic marketplace. "It is my ambition to write a grand opera, and I will not deny that in a vague way I have already begun one. Just as soon as the opportunity arrives when the American composer can with dignity find a market in this country for an opera he might write I will be among the first to present my claims." He paid tribute to what Hammerstein was doing in New York, but there was not the slightest suggestion that the Manhattan Opera Company would produce an American work. He thought that Hammerstein was going to facilitate the careers of American singers who, even after European training, were unacceptable to the Metropolitan management.[4]

If Herbert was surprised by Hammerstein's approach, he was no less gratified. The public was obviously pleased to see its musical hero gain admittance to music's inner sanctum; only a few persons expressed skepticism. Krehbiel refused to take seriously Hammerstein's announcement that Herbert's opera would be the chief novelty of the 1907–1908 season. Admitting that Herbert was a "prolific and marvelously ready writer of comic operetta scores," the somewhat austere critic thought it "not likely that he will ever attempt to find a suitable grand opera book and set it to music within six or eight months, while occupied, as he is, with a multitude of other enterprises."[5] Krehbiel was right about the time limit, but wholly wrong about Herbert's determination.

There was a slight embarrassment attached to the Hammerstein-Herbert opera. Although the impresario had secured the composer, neither of them had secured a libretto; consequently neither knew what kind of opera would be written, what the requirements might be, or when it would be ready for production. The lack of a libretto, of course, was a detail that bothered Hammerstein very little—he would simply buy one; and he declared himself ready to pay $1,000 for a suitable text, preferably by an American.

Herbert could reveal no intentions until he had the indispensable libretto. He was warm, of course, in his praise of Hammerstein "for making it possible that an opera by an American . . . be produced. The activity, the enterprise which he has stimulated in the American operatic field, and the avenues of opportunity that he has opened to musicians of all sorts, are in striking contrast to the conditions and apathy and stagnation that have hitherto prevailed."[6] There was no exaggeration in these words. When Hammerstein was forced out of grand-opera production three years later, the country suffered a major artistic casualty.

Want of a libretto seemed only to increase the public's curiosity in Herbert's solution of operatic problems. Reporters besieged him, pestered him with questions, forced him into utterances which could have little meaning. He loved to talk, especially about something as exciting and innovating as an American opera, and he dwelt at length on his hopes for the work. As early as April 8, 1907, he made a fulsome speech to a reporter from the New York *Morning Telegraph*:

Of course, it is impossible in any way to outline an opera, the basis of which—the libretto—I know and can know nothing.

The musical inspiration of an opera is derivable from the passions, the dramatic situations and the emotional crises, which the composer is called upon to comment on and to illustrate by means of music.

For instance, I have been asked whether I shall open my opera with an overture or a prelude. By an overture is meant a resume—a condensation of all the dramatic music of the opera; by a prelude, an independent piece of music, the aim of which is to put the hearer into a proper mood for understanding and enjoying what is to follow.

Now, I am not much of a believer in overtures. They tell the whole musical story and often much of the dramatic story before the musical and dramatic story has begun—no very tasteful thing to do. I much prefer a prelude, though it is just within the bounds of possibility that I might receive a libretto of such a nature that to begin with an overture might not be the worst of procedure. This is to show the nebular uncertainty of it all.

My inclination is to a prelude, but not so short a prelude as the one bar or so with which "Salome" opens, such being far too short a space of time in which to accomplish the physical necessity of getting a large curtain up. Whatever may be the libretto, however, I am more certain of my general method of treatment. I shall use every resource of the modern orchestra. My music will be polyphonic. My inclinations are in all directions to the moderns. It will also be symphonic: by that I mean my opera will not consist of a series of musical numbers loosely conjoined by elementary modulations. There will be a continuous, logical and well knit stream of orchestral development of the dramatic action and comment on it. . . .

I shall endeavor, above all things, to set my music to my action. . . .

What I should like is a vigorous, picturesque and entirely human story arising out of our civilization. . . .

I should like my opera to be such a genuine and such a successful work that it would go over all the world as the output of American brain and the inspiration of American surroundings. . . .

But I do repudiate absolutely the idea that an infusion of popular or folk songs reproduces the spiritual and intellectual or romantic atmosphere of the country to which those folk songs belong.

The libretto which will satisfy me most is one in which there will be plenty of contrast, of diversified action, of strong character differentiation.[7]

There was good sense and bad in this peroration. Herbert was not so tacitly assuming the role of founder of American opera; also he hopefully (nay, confidently) expected to produce a work of international effect and influence. Obviously the press encouraged him to make such utterances, which sometimes exceeded the bounds of plausibility, and fired his imaginative longing all the more. A few weeks later he reiterated some of his sentiments and added: "My only prayer is that I may produce such an opera as will merit the approval of the American people."[8] His enthusiasm for the project was refreshing, but it was also somewhat naïve. Had he tempered his ardor with a cold analysis of history, he might have avoided some of the subsequent disappointment.

The search for a libretto continued. Hammerstein considered *The Rose of the Rancho* (1906) and *The Girl of the Golden West* (1905), plays by David Belasco, but deemed neither suitable. (Eventually Puccini made the latter into an opera, and it proved to be a dismal failure.) At this time, too, came the rumors of converting Barrie's *Peter Pan* into a musical production, but it was not suggested as the great American opera.

In October of 1907 announcement was made that a fitting libretto had been found, but only the barest information was forthcoming. Herbert would reveal neither the title nor the author; nor would he say anything beyond the fact that the theme was historic and the setting American.[9] This was the real beginning of *Natoma*, Herbert's first grand opera, which in spite of setbacks and obstacles and its lack of influence on later native music drama must be recognized as a major landmark in American musical history.

The libretto, which was certainly finished in 1907 and probably elicited no money from Hammerstein, was by Joseph Deighn Redding, a most unusual person—far different from the type of literary assistant with whom Herbert generally worked. Unfortunately, his collaboration was no more successful than that of Herbert's lighter co-workers.

Redding (1859–1932) was a man of many parts—sociable, witty, handsome, wealthy. A native of California, he became a distinguished lawyer and maintained contacts in both San Francisco and New York. He was prominent in the Bohemian Club of San Francisco and wrote music as well as words for some of its plays. In the East he was acquainted in theatrical circles and was a member of the Lambs. Here no doubt he met and became intimate with Herbert; and the two were soon wrapped up in creating the anticipated opera. Redding's musical ability was considerable—he even composed an opera (*Fay-Yen-Fah*) which was produced at Monte Carlo in 1925—and there was every reason to believe that, as a librettist, he would have special understanding of the composer's need. He supplied Herbert with California Indian themes (which Herbert readily acknowledged), and he strove his utmost to provide a drama which would be psychologically accurate as well as musically stimulating. He could also be petulant and jealous; and after the libretto of *Natoma* was so savagely attacked he began to feel that he should make more claim to his musical suggestions. This feeling, apparently, developed to a mania, for in a biographical sketch approved by his widow the following strange passage occurs: "It is stated by those intimately acquainted with the history of the opera, and generally accepted in a wide musical circle, that he was the composer of all the Indian music of the score, only the Spanish arias having been written by Victor Herbert."[10] Needless to say, this astonishing statement was unsupported by any evidence and presumably was never issued during Herbert's life. I believe it was only the defensive protest of a sorely hurt man; it deserves no credence today.

Redding was imbued with western and Indian lore. He was much impressed with the success of the play *The Girl of the Golden West* and deeply affected by one of the Bohemian Grove plays, *The Man in the Forest*, for which he had composed the music.[11] The latter, incidentally, had an Indian theme, dealing with the threatened encroachment of the white invaders. It was all very placid and symbolic. Learning of Herbert's desire for an American opera book free of banalities, Redding very likely suggested the story of *Natoma* as one satisfactory to all concerned.

The two men were rather slow in embarking upon the actual chore of creating. It was not until the 16th of January, 1909, that a contract for an opera specifically named *Natoma* was signed,[12] by Victor Herbert, Joseph D. Redding, and Oscar Hammerstein. Herbert and Redding had submitted an acceptable scenario, and they pledged themselves to complete and deliver the finished libretto and score not later than January 15, 1910; Hammerstein promised first-class production by a thoroughly competent cast and orchestra—the latter to number as many as 65 men.

Within a few weeks the first act was completed, the second well begun, and the third roughly sketched. The composer was besieged with appeals for information; but he maintained a discreet silence except for general remarks. He gave no hint of the nature of the plot or of his score, saying that such talk would be premature. He expressed great satisfaction with Redding's book and described it as having episodes from a most interesting period of American development. The text was suggesting to him wonderful tone pictures which he hoped to paint with all the color and wealth implicit in the words.[13]

Meanwhile Redding worked arduously upon the book. Two surviving letters to his daughter Josephine,[14] in San Francisco, dated September 20, and November 5, 1909, tell of his artistic strivings and his concept of the Indian maiden Natoma. They also reveal his attitude toward Herbert and toward the responsibility of a composer to an opera poem. In the first he wrote:

No one can tell whether absolute success will perch upon our banners or not, but I am confident that many elements are combining to give an unusual production. In the first place, I have confidence in my own work as not being amateurish, pedantic, heavy, lugubrious or lacking in action. Sometimes I feel more elated than at others, but I realize the tremendous difficulties of attempting to bring out a great novelty. The story is new, the locality is new, the types are new and I am asking the public to stand for all these creations and to take them in the spirit in which they were written.

If the opera were written on familiar lines, it might be a success sustained by the music, even if the critics merely said it was a good imitation of other similar efforts, but going out into the waste places of the earth and turning over new soil and asking the public to declare that what I have found is a precious metal, means either that I am wholly right or wholly wrong, so that I do not expect there will be any half-way verdict.

Many people question the ability of Victor Herbert to write grand opera music because his reputation is confined almost entirely to light opera work. I have considered this feature of the matter carefully. In the first place, he is a very complete and thoroughly equipped musician in the modern broad sense. He has practically lived in the orchestra for thirty years and has studied and familiarized himself with all the works of all the great composers. Personally, he has a very keen dramatic sense. I have noticed that in all of his light operas, the music always aids and assists the action. You can see the stamp of his individuality throughout all of the scores; that is why his operas, however trivial the subject, are successful: because they hold the attention of the audience and the music builds up the scenes with vigor.

The chief cause of the failure of many efforts in grand opera as well as light opera is the lack of dramatic action of the composers. However mellifluous and charming a theme or melody may be, if it merely dawdles along and does not assist the progress of the drama, the audience becomes bored and the whole thing fades away.

In watching Mr. Herbert's work, I have observed how invariably he adds to the situation, builds it up and gives virility to what is going on in all that he writes. He is not writing in the ultra modern school; that is to say, he is not following in the steps of Debussy and Richard Strauss. These two composers who are considered to give a new expression to music, while they are very effective for certain purposes, are really driving music off the earth. There are many critics who rave over Debussy and Strauss and they undoubtedly will accuse Mr. Herbert of being trivial and cheap. They also accuse Bizet and Verdi of being clap-trap and old-fashioned. These two last composers, however, will live after Strauss and Debussy have been forgotten.

The second letter dwelt more upon the librettist's own work. He was obviously eager to have the opinions of his daughter and his wife, as well as the thoughts of others:

I am sending you by registered post or by Wells Fargo a manuscript copy of Natoma, which I shall be very glad to have you read over with your mother . . .

You will understand that although a great deal of the recitatives are not in lyrical form, yet everything is sung from beginning to end. That is the distinction made in grand opera. There is only one exception in the last act for a few lines where Father Peralta, the priest, mounts the pulpit in the church. Even this, however, is accompanied by a pedal point on the organ or a sustained chord in the orchestra. Perhaps it would be agreeable and I certainly would be pleased to have you and your mother invite Dr. and Mrs. Younger to the reading. They are . . . thoroughly imbued with the California atmosphere.

With reference to the construction of sentences, the use of rhythms and lyrical forms, I am glad to say that Mr. Herbert has found no occasion to change any of them on account of false accents or unmusical phrasing. Being a musician myself and possessing what may be called the vibratory make-up, it comes natural to me to construct the sentences so that the attack of the voice, the stress upon syllables, of words and all that applies to musical phrasing, are in singable form. One of the greatest difficulties musical composers have to labor under is in attempting to compose to the work of a librettist who is not a musician or musicianly.

There are between twenty or thirty different forms of meter used throughout the entire work. In fact, I suppose I have probably made use of almost every form of versification, such as classic, rondeau, ballade, six-, seven- and eight-line stanza, broken stanza, quatrain, heroic, triolet, rondel, chant-royal, vilanelle, etc., etc. It has been a most delightful, although laborious effort. I have worked on it early in the morning, late at night, Sundays, on the train, in the mountains, in the office, and at odd moments whenever they could be spared.

The character of Natoma I believe to be an absolutely new type and, although mystical and ideal, yet logical and human. I have a basis for giving her beauty, simplicity and ideality: in a letter written by Vescanio (one of the early Spanish explorers) to the King of Spain in 1603, he speaks of the California Indians, particularly those from the mountains, and refers to the beauty and dignity of the Indian women. In several of the letters written by the early Mission Padres to the Viceroy of Spain and to the Pope himself, they refer to the comeliness, the cleanliness and the intelligence of the California Indian girls. To me Natoma is somewhat allegorical in that she epitomizes the pathos and heartache of the disappearing race as against the influx of the Aryan tribes. Again, the work shows that two characters are virtually obliterated: the devil-may-care and romantic Spaniard and the Indian.

The libretto of the opera in this country and its importance are but little understood by the public. This is because most of our operas are sung in foreign languages understood by but a minority of the audience and the chief interest lies in the personality of the singers as well as the music of the composer. Few people know that the great dramatist Scribe wrote librettos for Meyerbeer or that Victor Hugo was the author of several of Verdi's librettos like *Ernani* and *Rigoletto*. Verdi also had a wonderful man for his librettist by the name of Boito, who was also a great musician. I am ambitious to have the public recognize the importance of the libretto for the first time in grand opera.

It will be produced in English at the Manhattan Opera House and we expect to have the very best artists in the roles including Mary Garden, Reynaud (your favorite) and others of equal prominence. We expect that it will be done in German both at Munich and Berlin sometime next year and also at Milan in Italian and in Paris in French.

The two collaborators expected production early in 1910, but suddenly the newspapers were filled with stories of a dispute with Oscar Hammerstein. Herbert claimed the work was ready by January 15, the impresario being accordingly notified; Hammerstein declared he had seen not one note of the opera, but he was still going to stage it.[15] This last remark was a rejoinder to Herbert's assertion that he would seek other means of production.

The specific reasons for the impasse are unknown, but it is reasonable to assume that Hammerstein was financially unable to put it on the boards. By the close of the 1909–1910 season he was losing $25,000 a week as he continued his frantic (and artistically successful) rivalry with the Metropolitan, and he was fast approaching the end of his grand-opera career. He made no secret of his financial condition, however, and even tried to turn it into a show of virtue and righteousness. The night before the season closed he addressed the audience in the Manhattan Opera House and grandly said: "While my losses have been enormous, I am proud of knowing that those of my adversaries have been much larger. My efforts in the great cause, however, will not relax, and I am planning for the next season the greatest and most sublime opera for the pleasure of my audience and the honor of myself."[16] Unfortunately the Metropolitan forces had all the money, and they forced Hammerstein out of grand opera in America. He never had his sublime fifth season, and Herbert had an opera with no stage to receive it. The only person who rejoiced in the situation was Herbert's old enemy Marc Blumenberg, former editor of the *Musical Courier!*[17]

Herbert offered *Natoma* to the Metropolitan, where a new interest had been evinced in American opera (undoubtedly the result of the Herbert-Hammerstein activity). Here, on March 29, 1910, the second act received an orchestral tryout,[18] followed by Gatti-Casazza's rejection of the work. Eleven days earlier the Metropolitan had presented its first American opera, Converse's *The Pipe of Desire,* and stage works by native composers were considered to be a bad risk. Hammerstein's retirement from the scene, however, led to the formation of the Philadelphia-Chicago Opera Company, and it took over his musical resources—repertoire, singers, and conductor. It was directed by the singer Andreas Dippel, who had been an unhappy co-director of the Metropolitan. He promptly agreed to produce *Natoma* even though he incurred the displeasure of Gatti-Casazza;[19] and excited planning started at once.

There was also stimulated a renewal of the public's extraordinary interest in the work and what it was supposed to effect. There were articles attempting to define an essentially American opera; there was speculation concerning the Americanism of the *Natoma* story (which had gradually become known); there were new efforts to persuade the creators to explain their motives and objectives. When it was learned that southern California of 1820 was the setting of the opera an editorial in the New York *World* brought a reply from Redding, defending his choice of place and period as legitimate American features.[20]

The selection of Mary Garden to sing the title role was hailed with anticipation. Comforting, too, was her comment after she heard the music for the first time: "It is a beautiful opera, and it will be a pleasure to sing in it."[21] Shortly afterward, with her penchant for publicity, she issued a disconcerting blast which fanned the flame of argument still brighter:

I don't believe in opera in English. I never have believed in it and I don't believe that I ever shall believe in it. Of course, I'm willing to be convinced. You see, in the first place, I think that all music dramas should be sung in the language in which they are written; well, that makes it impossible to sing anything in the current repertoire in English, doesn't it?

Well, then, the only hope for opera in English, so far as I can see it, lies in America or England producing a race of composers, and they haven't it in them. It isn't in the blood. Composition needs Latin blood or something akin to it—nothing Anglo-Saxon or American. The American man hasn't it in him to produce great music—not yet at least, and I doubt if any of us alive to-day will hear a great work written to a libretto in our own language.

Now, I am going to sing in Victor Herbert's "Natoma" in spite of what I have just told you, because I don't want to have it said that I have done anything to hinder what is now generally called "the cause." For the first time a work by a composer who may be regarded as American is to be given a chance with the best singers, with a great orchestra, and a great conductor in the leading opera house in America—perhaps the leading opera house anywhere.

It seems to me that everybody ought to put his shoulder to this kind of wheel and set it moving. I shall be the most pleased of anybody if "Natoma" proves a success and paves the way for the successful production of other American works. Of course, "Natoma" is not exactly what may be regarded as a "grand opera." It is not music like "Tristan" for instance. It is more like the lighter operas-comique which are heard in Paris, but it possesses much melodic charm, and it may please the public. I shall sing it, and I shall sing it in English and try to do it just as well as I have tried to do *Salomé* and *Thaïs* and *Mélisande*.[22]

This had the desired effect, for the reaction was prompt and clear. An important editor referred to it as tragic; otherwise, he said, it would be amusing. He also suggested that it might be fairer to give the role to a singer who had more confidence in *Natoma* and its chances of success.

The most entertaining response came from a light-opera star, Christie MacDonald, who had no patience with Mary Garden's views. Two years later she would be the featured player in Herbert's *Sweethearts*; now she was simply furious as a matter of principle and said to a reporter on the *World*:

If Mary Garden will forgive a light opera prima donna for mentioning her name, I should like to say that it is unfair to talk against American opera as Miss Garden has done. She says Americans haven't it in them to produce great music, but they tell me that this same talk was heard when Offenbach and Audran and Donizetti works were thought to be the last word in comic opera. Since then America has produced a De Koven, a Victor Herbert, and others.

All this beating-about-the-bush talk concerning opera in English makes me indignant. If the introduction of light opera in this country had been managed in the same way as grand opera, I would be singing in German to-day and "The Spring Maid" would be advertised as "Die Sprudelfee." Furthermore, we would be hearing the same foolish argument that the real beauty of the original is lost in the translation. You may have noticed that we hear this talk only when those interested in keeping out opera in English fear they are going to lose their grip on the situation.

It would be just as sensible to give "The Spring Maid" in its original German as it is to sing "Madama Butterfly" in Italian. Both are plays set to music, and to be thoroughly enjoyed they must be understood. That's why light opera is a success in English, and that's why American composers write light opera in preference to grand opera. The masses give their support to musical performances that they are able to understand without the aid of a book of the opera. Every foreign singing opera company that ever attempted a tour of America came to grief. If American singers were able to learn rôles in a foreign tongue why shouldn't we insist upon foreign artists learning rôles in our tongue? Heaven knows they're paid enough![23]

As production day drew near, Herbert was asked more and more questions. He admitted to using a modification of Wagnerian leitmotiv, to symphonic treatment of certain themes, to the introduction of unanticipated melodies when the drama called for them. His fundamental approach to the opera remained melodic, for he had little sympathy for the methods of Strauss and Debussy. Except for the organ in Act III there were no unusual instruments in the orchestra. Of special interest were his observations on Indian themes, for, in his eagerness to explain, he risked the charge of some exaggeration. He did, however, specify what he had taken from Joseph Redding.

I have composed all of "Natoma's" music, at least the greater part of it, out of fragments of Indian music, which I have collected and studied for some time past. However, I have pursued none of these melodies to their logical conclusion. If I used Indian music with all its original intervals and cadences it would become very monotonous, and so, of course, I have adapted it. But I have fashioned melodies by using fragments of this and that Indian theme.

There is also the question of harmonization. Indian music is not harmonized, and the moment a musician harmonizes it he has made it into something different. I hope, however, to have achieved the result I was striving for, to suggest the Indian character. In two instances I have introduced Indian tunes almost verbatim, of course with my own harmonization. The first of these occurs in the dagger dance, and the other is a melody which Natoma sings in the third act. In one song of Natoma's I make the accompaniment lean heavily upon the flute, as I think that instrument more than any other suggests the nature of Indian music.

These two Indian melodies which I have mentioned were brought to me by Mr. Redding. I do not think they exist in any published collection. In one other instance I have borrowed a theme—when the Spanish colors are being hoisted the brasses play a melody, which I am told has been used for this purpose in Spain for several centuries. I got this tune from a Spanish bandmaster now living in Brooklyn.[24]

Herbert also insisted that the opera was American "in every particular." He wanted it to be successful, so that the future of the American composer would be easier. And although he hoped *Natoma* would be produced in other languages he wanted people to feel that it honestly sounded better when sung in English.

He tried to give each personage in the opera music which was individualized according to character. Here he took Mozart as his model, his operas being "the most glorious examples of characterization."[25]

Less than a week before the first performance a feature newspaper story, trying to summarize the full importance of the pending event, maintained the aura of "chosen man" around the composer, which was neither healthy nor wise. It called Herbert the man of the hour, referred to him as a symbol of patriotism and democratic life, claimed that he was to American music what Emerson and Whitman were to American literature. The production of *Natoma*, it stated, was a matter of national concern, with the whole world eagerly awaiting the results. Indeed, "the presentation will furnish an opportunity instinctively wished for by every man or woman who desires to see the United States take its proper place in the great world of art."[26] It was absolutely impossible for any work of art to be as great, as wonderful, as significant as the four-year-long build-up would have it; but the advance enthusiasts threw caution to the winds as they prepared the country for the phenomenal day. Neither Herbert nor Redding was responsible for these conditions; they were simply victims of well-meaning admirers and a national psychosis.

After rehearsal sessions in Chicago and Philadelphia *Natoma* was at last produced in the latter on February 25, 1911, at the Metropolitan Opera House. Everything about the event was brilliant and glamorous —a splendid cast, a superb conductor, a socialite audience. The program, the printed vocal score, and Redding's own typewritten libretto provide the following cast and additional information:

Natoma (dramatic soprano), an Indian girl of pure blood. She is of the same age as Barbara and has been her confident, half playmate and half maid, since childhood ....   Mary Garden

Barbara (soprano), only child of Don Francisco. A beautiful Spanish girl, just coming of age—18; she is the last of her name and has just finished her convent days ....   Lillian Grenville

Lieut. Paul Merrill (tenor), a young officer on the Brig "Liberty" of the U.S. Navy,

which has dropped anchor in the bay of Santa Barbara......................	John McCormack
Don Francisco de la Guerra (basso), a noble Spaniard of the old régime; of great dignity, courtesy and simplicity........	Gustave Huberdeau
Father Peralta (basso), the Padre of the Mission Church; likewise a Spaniard of high character and having supreme power over the inhabitants................	Hector Dufranne
Juan Bautista Alvarado (baritone), a young Spaniard of fiery temper, ambitious to marry Barbara, the only daughter of Don Francisco. He is her cousin, being the son of her mother's brother...........	Mario Sammarco
José Castro (baritone), a half-breed; part Indian and part Spaniard; a fellow of low cunning and vicious hatred of Spaniard and American alike.............	Frank Preisch
Pico (tenor) ⎱ Bravos, comrades of ⎰	Armand Crabbé
Kagama (basso) ⎰ Castro ....⎱	Constantin Nicolay
Chiquita, a dancing girl...............	Mlle. Nandina
A Voice...........................	Minnie Egener
Sergeant	Desire Defrere

Two American officers, an inn-keeper, alcalde, milk-boy, ladies, dignitaries, soldiers, friars, acolytes, nuns, convent-girls, vaqueros, market-women, Spanish dancers, reapers, vineyardists, shepherdesses, sailors

Act   I—On the Island of Santa Cruz, off the Coast of California
Act II—In the Plaza of the Town of Santa Barbara (on the mainland) in front of the Mission Church
Act III—Inside of the Mission Church

Epoch—1820, under the Spanish régime

Cleofonte Campanini was the conductor as well as the general musical director of the company; he led the orchestra at the first performance. Fernand Almanz was the stage director, and for this production he had the assistance of George Marion. The sketches and designs for the stage sets, costumes, and properties were painted by Alexander Harmer of Santa Barbara and were supposed to be historically correct. The production as a whole was executed under the supervision of Edward Siedle, technical director of the Metropolitan Opera House, New York. The scenery was painted by Gates and Morange; the costumes were by E. S. Friesinger (after plates furnished by H. A. Ogden); the properties came from the Siedle Studios.

Herewith, a synopsis of the opera:[27]

Barbara returns to her island home after convent school on the mainland. Her widowed father awaits her impatiently. Employed on the estate is the Indian maiden, Natoma, who has been Barbara's companion since childhood. Alvarado and his cronies come to the estate this same day; he is anxious to marry Barbara and gain control of the wealth she will inherit. An American naval vessel is in the vicinity, and Paul, one of its officers, visits the island and encounters Natoma. He is much impressed by her dignity, her simplicity, and her tale of hardships experienced by her people. When Barbara actually arrives, she is smitten with Paul and obviously avoids Alvarado, who becomes angry and vows vengeance. He decides to kidnap his lovely cousin on the morrow, when the great fiesta will be held in Santa Barbara. Natoma overhears his plan. Barbara and Paul exchange vows of love as the day draws to a close.

The festival on the mainland is in honor of Barbara's coming of age. Gaiety, happiness, and dancing are supposed to predominate. Barbara sings a song of joy, Alvarado dances a minuet with her, and a special contingent from the American ship offers a tribute from the United States. Paul sings an ode, which is really meant for Barbara, and Alvarado's wrath is noticeable. As the tension increases, Castro hurls a dagger into the ground and dares anyone to dance with him the ancient dagger dance of the primitive Californians. Natoma, who has been watching silently, accepts the challenge. While the crowd is fascinated by the barbaric dance, Alvarado attempts to drag Barbara away. Natoma rushes to him and kills him with one savage dagger thrust. Pandemonium ensues, and Father Peralta, appearing on the church steps, restores calm as he declares that vengeance belongs only to God.

Natoma meditates in the mission church. She is still sullen and unrepentant. Injustice has always been her lot and the lot of her people, and she calls for the destruction of all the strangers. Her passion is calmed by Father Peralta, who appeals to her goodness and her love for Barbara. Natoma succumbs to the priest's words, she is filled with the love of God, and she enters the community of nuns attached to the mission. Barbara and Paul watch her disappear into the convent garden.

As soon as *Natoma* was seen and heard the critics were unanimous in attacking the book and story. They were, in fact, unusually savage, calling it undramatic, non-American, antimusical. Paul at first is on the verge of loving Natoma, then is attracted to the prettier Barbara. Alvarado is a villain, or close to it, because he wants Barbara for himself. Castro is more villainous because he is a half-breed, a quality which Natoma despises even though the poor fellow is certainly not responsible for it. Don Francisco is a hospitable patriarch with no interest outside his daughter, and Barbara is a simple maid who seems surprised that her cousin wishes to marry her. The Indian girl, proud of her pure ancestry, dances with Castro for no apparent reason, kills Alvarado so that the officer who jilted her can have Barbara, prays for the destruction of the white people in their own church, and then is converted to the Christian faith with no sign at all of spiritual conviction. Moreover, after the tempestuous climax of Act II, reached in the assassination of Alvarado, the drama is concluded. Natoma's mental conflict is wholly artificial, and her state of unhappiness has no reasonable connection with the persecution of her dwindling people. Improbable as most opera plots are, melodramatic and thunderous as they may be, the story of *Natoma* seems uniquely feeble because it has nothing for which one can feel sympathy and no character who appears even slightly credible. Redding, who had labored with exceeding care, produced a book the effects of which were in inverse ratio to his hopes and ambitions.

The charge that the story was non-American, of course, was unimportant. The cultural background was Spanish and Indian, but geographically the tale was just as American as if it had been laid in Puritan New England or Cavalier Virginia. In two ironic ways it was really typically American: an American officer wins his girl, and an Indian is chosen to be the sacrifice.

The music of *Natoma,* however, was another matter. It was good —effective, fluent, dramatic (as the book allowed), melodious, and convincing. It was not the great American opera for which public and press had clamored; it started no school of American opera composition; it failed to sustain the claim that Herbert was the man of the hour. Yet it showed that Herbert was more than adept in writing serious music and gifted in the writing of large-scale dramatic music. The music was not particularly original, for Herbert knew only one tradition for his serious efforts—the idiom of German romanticism; but it sounded well, was coherent, and had plentiful color. Had he been able to infuse his music with American characteristics (they are still ill defined), he might have succeeded in starting the influence he wished to; and in realizing this he was bitterly disappointed.

The musical high lights of *Natoma* are several. In the first act the scene between Natoma and Paul is outstanding, especially her dramatic narration of the history of her people. Her descriptions of the famine, of her own obligation to her tribe, of the Great Spirit's gift of food are presented with telling intensity, and her rippling portrayal of Barbara's beauty is a most effective contrast in musical declamation. Alvarado's serenade to Barbara is likewise most effective. With its gay lilt and syncopation, not to mention its strumming accompaniment, this was one of the pieces, according to critics, which Herbert had derived from his operetta experience. He had done similar things in light opera undoubtedly, but it was thoroughly in keeping with the situation here. No one should have caviled at it. Somewhat more obvious is Alvarado's love song to Barbara which, undeniably tuneful, is not as adroit as the serenade. Herbert may have done this intentionally in order to heighten the contrast with the love scene between Barbara and Paul at the end of the act. Beginning with Barbara's apostrophe, "Oh, wondrous night!" and her dreamlike reverie, it exudes a passionate warmth which rises to a tumult of amorous emotion.

Before the glittering fiesta scene of the second act Natoma sings her long soliloquy at dawn. Happy for Barbara, sad in losing Paul, she pledges to preserve the happiness of her mistress by frustrating the plot against her. Her tones are solemn and excited, then exalted as she calls upon the Great Spirit of her own people to give her strength. The day advances, and the square fills with animated folk and soldiers. The holiday fever is reflected in every bar as the shouting, shifting crowd assembles. The vaqueros are headed by Pico, and he sings the celebrated Vaqueros' Song, which, in both stanza and refrain, is persuasively forceful. This number comes closer to light-opera style than any other piece in the opera; yet it, too, is in keeping with the situation, and *Natoma* would be poorer without it. The dance excerpts, excepting the Dagger Dance, are atmospheric pieces which add color to the scene and supply the ballet element. The Dagger Dance is different. This underlines a real dramatic incident in the plot and is pregnant with suspense. The heavy, remorseless, emphatic succession of chords, stark harmony, and unyielding rhythm create a terrific effect as the tension mounts to the point of Alvarado's death. The two unfortunate musical events of this act are the solos of Barbara and Paul. The beautiful maiden sings of her happiness in springtime, a long and elaborate hymn of praise, because she is home again among her loved onces. Musically it is tedious and boring, as ineffective as the Vaqueros' Song is gripping. The other questionable piece is Paul's declamation in honor of Columbus, which is bloated and pompous.

Unlike the preceding acts, the third opens with a short prelude, a brief symphonic presentation of the most emotional themes heard so far. Herbert calculated well in bringing them in at this place. They now meant something to the audience and they recapitulated Natoma's plight before the curtain rose. This music was independently organized, and Herbert (as well as others) used it frequently as a separate concert excerpt, usually with great success.

Natoma's lullaby and scene open the third act, which is essentially religious from beginning to end. The first part of her long solo is wistful and pathetic; the second part begins forlornly, changes to delicious remembrance, then waxes stormily bitter as she determines to expel the white intruders. Its terrific climax is even increased by the sudden appearance of Father Peralta with his mild but firm counseling of peace and forgiveness. His comfort and guidance are given with dignity, and Natoma yields to his words. Once she has declared her love for Barbara, has signified her willingness to let this love expiate her crime, she plays out the remainder of the scene in pantomime. Peralta speaks again, but the main effects come from the choir of the church. As Natoma disappears behind the doors of the convent garden, her own fate theme swells to prodigious volume, and the curtain falls as the doors close upon her. Musically the third act is the best of the three.

The critical reaction to *Natoma* was not far different from the response to the operettas except that it was more penetrating. The Philadelphia critics were more charitable and laudatory, the New York judges more severe. A number of New York critics attended the Philadelphia première and reported it faithfully as a matter of important news. Most of their criticisms, however, were reserved for the New York presentation three nights later—a rare opportunity for hearing a large work twice before writing a critical estimate.

The opera house in Philadelphia was festooned and decorated as if a national celebration were taking place. Some people equated the opera just this way, for "at last we have it—the American opera by an American composer, and it was sung in English."[28] The fact that most of the English was hard to understand failed to quell the enthusiasm of the auditors. Telegrams of congratulation were showered on Herbert from all parts of the world, and two of his potential rivals sent special messages. These came from Puccini and Mascagni. Mrs. John McCormack cabled from Dublin that the Irish capital was proud of Victor Herbert and her husband.

For a short while Herbert was indeed the man of the hour. He knew, however, that the success of the evening was attributable to more than one person. He felt especially indebted to the conductor, and after the first performance he released a letter expressing his gratitude to the Italian musician:

On the production of my first serious opera I desire to publicly express my deep and grateful acknowledgement to Maestro Cleofonte Campanini for his extraordinary labors in the preparation and production of our opera, "Natoma," tonight, for his unwearying patience, for his vital interest in this

American opera, and in everything pertaining to American music and musical life, for his invaluable suggestions and for the honor he is doing me by conducting the first performance.

How much of its success, if any, will be due to his commanding influence, few will ever know. I can never forget his work in this production, because I can never repay him.

In New York the critics who so often have the final say went into action, with results which irritated Herbert, mortified Redding, and tempered the innocent enthusiasm of the people. On the whole they were remarkably fair to Herbert; but his hopes had been pitched too high: like any creator completely absorbed in his intended masterpiece, he was in no mood for a judicial appraisal of his score. Moreover, he felt keenly the savage attacks upon the libretto. He considered these unfair to Redding, who had labored conscientiously on the script, and he knew they reflected on his own dramatic judgment. The qualified praise of the critics did not satisfy him.

Krehbiel, toward whom Herbert developed a violent dislike which was not wholly justified, explained the harm done by the extravagant advance publicity. He punctured the belief that opera in English was new. He thought the libretto was terrible and regretted that it had been written by an American. He did not accept *Natoma* as a masterpiece, but he recognized the indisputable merits it contained. Not long before, Puccini's much-heralded *The Girl of the Golden West* had received its world première in New York. Although composed by an Italian, it, too, was considered as an American opera because of its theme; and *Natoma* was its rival. Krehbiel compared them. He thought that *La Fanciulla del West* would be much more effective without Puccini's music, but that *Natoma* would be completely impossible without Herbert's! Thanks to the score, Redding's play achieved a "semblance of a lyric drama" wherein the inanity of the characters was obvious only at moments. He missed the carefree, happy melodist of the operettas, but admitted that the composer had "succeeded better than we could have wished at times in divorcing himself from himself." There were color and life in the harmony and orchestration, there was vitality in the themes allotted to the heroine: "he does it so well that, aided by the skill of Miss Garden in characterization, he makes Natoma . . . a figure of considerable interest." Krehbiel felt the lack of a "sustained and passionate Cantilena" and was unimpressed by the ambitious love duet in Act I; but in the last act Herbert had produced "results of dignity and value in the solemnities of the final scene." The score was the product of "anything but a 'prentice hand."[29]

The most savagely expressed opinion of the book was: "The libretto of Joseph Redding should go down into operatic history as one of the most futile, fatuous, halting, impotent, inane and puerile ever written. Its dramatic development is totally wanting in sense and logic, its situations have been worn threadbare by convention, its characters are sawdust-stuffed marionettes and its verbiage, cheap colloquialism or jingling balderdash." This, said the writer, posed a handicap on the composer, who had nevertheless produced surprising excellencies. The music exhibited bizarre and fascinating effects, his use of instrumental color was striking, his thorough musicianship was unmistakable even though some persons may have been disappointed by the lack of fluent melody.[30]

Lawrence Gilman was rather severe. In choosing the worst libretto ever set to music the composer had disappointed his admirers and had written an opera which had no real excuse for being. But even Gilman was forced to admit that *Natoma* was "smoothly constructed, the work of a deft and well-trained musician. It betrays a true instinct for the stage, a keen sense of theatrical effect." He could not resist a few ridiculous phrases of complete irrelevancy, such as his declaration that Herbert was not a Mozart, Wagner, or Verdi! No one ever had claimed he was, least of all the composer himself. Gilman also disliked the effect created by Mary Garden. He thought her make-up deplorably unbecoming and forgave her on the ground that no singing actress who ever lived could make the role interesting or credible.[31]

This differed considerably from the opinion of an equally astute observer, Carl Van Vechten, who had warmest praise not for the music but for Garden's willingness to assume a drab make-up and costume (moccasin-shod, buckskin-clad, long braids of black hair) and to vitalize a role resembling nothing she had done before. The music suited her voice, and "the vapid speeches of Mr. Redding tripped so audibly off her tongue that their banality became painfully apparent." She accomplished her task so beautifully that out of "the hodge-podge of an opera book which stands unrivalled for its stiltedness of speech, she succeeded in creating one of her most notable characters."[32]

The critic of the New York *Times* reached the same conclusion as Krehbiel regarding comparison with *The Girl of the Golden West*. Of the libretto he wrote: "This is an amateurish production . . . The prose is bald and conventional, and the lyrics are of the most hopeless operatic type, of the bad old kind, constructed on Voltaire's theory that what is too foolish to be said is appropriate to be sung." He was kindly disposed toward the music, crediting Herbert with skill, melodic inventiveness, and seriousness of purpose. He liked the treatment of the Indian themes in the Dagger Dance and the third-act lullaby: "Mr. Herbert has been ingenious in his use of these

Indian elements, to make their rhythmic and melodic characteristics count for their utmost." He also liked Garden's achievement and was pleased by the work of John McCormack.

The critic of the *Sun* agreed about the soprano, but took issue on the tenor, casting aspersions on the libretto as he did so: McCormack was not equal to his part, "for bad as the role was he was even worse." The other principals of the cast were generally excellent, although Lillian Grenville left much to be desired. The reviewer also was eager for Herbert to write another opera, advising him to seek "a libretto of artistic merit containing the essential emotional plot for the development of an operatic score."

One critic only had a kind word to say for the libretto. This was Henry T. Finck of the *Evening Post,* and even he admitted it might have had a better plot, more action, more signs of stagecraft, more poetic skill, and less sentimentality. He showed his charitableness by saying it would be difficult to find one with more musical opportunities and chances for a picturesque setting. He praised Herbert's music lavishly and took the optimistic view: "American opera is launched. Godspeed its voyage."

Special attention must be paid to a delayed criticism by Arthur Farwell, excellent musician, who all his life long was a champion of American and Indian music. The production of *Natoma* meant much to him, for it seemed to illustrate the principles he had been enunciating. The following phrases were among his observations:

The quality of musical thought throughout the opera is in general fresh, vigorous, and characteristic. Moreover, the composer shows himself capable of subtleties for which the field of comic opera writing could give him little or no scope. There is true musical impulse behind the development of the themes, and the music is everywhere straight-forward and logical. Where the composer wishes to produce an effect of mystery, as where Natoma, in Act I, tells of the origin of her forefathers in the clouds, he inclines to resort to the harmonic scheme contributed to the world's music by the modern Frenchmen. Where the text has lyrical qualities of rhythm, Mr. Herbert is at his best in the music. He is hampered, however, by that great part of the text which is written in a totally unrhythmic prose, which would be the despair of the musician were he really dependent on it for musical inspiration. Fortunately, Mr. Herbert is not. He composes from his sense of the musical needs of the scene, and does the best that can be done for the words. He cannot at all times, however, free his musical wings from the burden of the text. . . .

The orchestral garment in which Mr. Herbert has clothed his musical thoughts is of rich color and skillful weave. The score is nothing less than masterly. The first part of Act I is rather overlightly scored, and gives at first the impression that the composer has overestimated the power of the

instruments and underestimated the size of the house. It is apparent later
that this must have been done purposefully, for the sake of climax. The
composer's knowledge of the character and capacities of the instruments,
and his intuitive certainty of orchestral effects previously untried by him,
serve him well in making a score beautiful in tonal balance and color, and
effective in a multitude of ways, according to the occasion. There are many
fanciful details for the delectation of the careful observer, as where Natoma
in Act I calls Castro "Half-breed," and the orchestra for several moments
spits out an echoing "half-breed!—half-breed!" in unmistakable accents.

Farwell used restraint in pointing out the weaknesses of the libretto,
but he was aware of their existence. He was more concerned with
the composer's treatment of Indian themes, genuine or synthetic:

The question of Indian music in "Natoma" has been touched by Mr.
Herbert in no equivocal way. His Indian themes, whether borrowed entire
or simulated, are authentic in their quality. He has shown remarkable sympathy in devising a scheme of development for these themes which retains
their peculiar character and "color," and his music in this *genre* is both
impressive and convincing. Three melodies of Indian character in particular
are employed; one, a gentle theme suggesting Natoma's love; another of
stern character indicating her Indian nature; and the third the highly
barbaric "dagger dance." The first two are extensively and effectively employed throughout the opera.

It is not to be overhastily admitted that the use of Indian music in
"Natoma" is the greatest which can be made of it. It can, however, be said
that Mr. Herbert's successful and convincing employment of it is a thorough
justification of the arduous and much-contested development of this department of American music, and that it is the most important example of it, on
a large scale, yet placed before the American people.[33]

The only publication which afforded outright amusement in criticizing the opera was, naturally, the *Musical Courier*. It praised the
libretto, but— "Musically, the Herbert work does not rise to the
dignity of grand opera, and consequently cannot be treated analytically
by THE MUSICAL COURIER, as this paper does not run any department
for light or comic opera."[34] The legal defeat of a decade earlier evidently still rankled.

On March 11, a week and a half after the New York première, a
dinner in Herbert's honor was sponsored by the Bohemians, at Louis
Martin's. Speeches were made by Rubin Goldmark, Henry T. Finck,
Walter Damrosch, H. E. Krehbiel, Carl Hauser, and Herbert himself.
Joseph Redding, of course, was among the guests. It might have been
better if the dinner had been postponed a week, for Herbert was still
smarting from the attitude of the critics and he was human enough
to betray his displeasure. The critics had not changed their opinions,

and Herbert (protesting his appreciation of the honor extended to him) said they should be fair, tell the truth, and stay until the performance was over. *Natoma* had been performed a second time in New York on March 7, and Krehbiel reported that the audience was small. Actually, said Herbert, the house was sold out, and the report was inaccurate. Herbert was also mindful of the abuse Redding had suffered, and the librettist showed a certain satisfaction when the composer began these remarks. Krehbiel came to the defense of the critics, and the toastmaster (Goldmark) had to make peace in an exchange that seemed to be tinged with bitterness.

Redding spoke willingly of his work on the libretto, saying the attacks on it troubled him not at all. He claimed to be rewarded sufficiently by two years of collaboration with Herbert, and ready to do another for the same composer.

Then Finck arose to say a few words, calculated in effect, which enjoyed local currency for a long time to come. He began: "There are two or three things I want to talk about seriously. The first is a certain well-known libretto. I have here a few of the things five of the best-known critics said about it. 'It is the most unfortunate choice of a text-book ever made by a really prominent composer.' 'The first act is intolerably tedious.' 'The love duo reveals a hopelessly poetic impotence.' 'Considered purely as a poem, few will be able to read it without comic emotions.' 'The poem is in every respect an absurdity.'" The guests were uncomfortable and embarrassed. With Redding present, what on earth was Finck trying to do? Unperturbed, the speaker continued. "Now, gentlemen, do not think that I am ill-mannered. There will be no dagger dance for Mr. Redding and myself. For two reasons —first, I did not write any of those criticisms; secondly, they were not written about 'Natoma.' They were written about what is now considered the most poetic and passionate of all opera texts—'Tristan und Isolde.'" At once the tension was broken, and Finck's words were greeted with applause and laughter.

When the banquet was over, Herbert regretted his remarks about critics, and he explained his stand to a representative of *Musical America*:

I did not mean to attack critics in my speech, but only intended to make an appeal for fair play. Good criticism is courted by the composer and musician. It is necessary; but the critic should tell what happened in his review, which should be a real review and not pick to pieces one or two sections of an opera which displease him. He should take into account the hard work that is done by the composer and the librettist. I worked sixteen hours a day on "Natoma" and have almost ruined my eyesight. I do not want flattery nor nothing but honeyed words. Many critics are men of splendid education and can point out defects in a score that the composer never thought of. But this should be done kindly.

I do not believe that in a serious opera, such as "Natoma," a person can write a fair review upon hearing it once. And, knowing this, see how absurd it is to write a review when one has heard only a snatch here or there of a work, leaving, for instance, before the last act.[35]

All the publicity given to *Natoma,* plus the very real merit of the music, enabled the Philadelphia-Chicago Opera Company to keep the opera in its repertoire for three seasons. Chicago heard it for the first time on December 13, 1911, with the same scenes of excitement as had occurred in the East.[36] Here, too, the critics gave the same qualified approval, and Herbert accepted it ungraciously. One unpleasant tiff occurred between Herbert and the leading Chicago critic, Felix Borowski.

Borowski met Herbert the day after the performance and, knowing him well, said: "Victor, where on earth did you get that libretto? I should think that with all your experience in writing for the theater —after all, you've been doing that almost since you came to this country—you would know how to choose a book for stage presentation better than the one last night." By now these were fighting words to the composer, and Herbert retorted angrily: "You fellows just don't like my music. I consider that a damned good libretto, and if you don't like what I put on, it's just too bad for Chicago and the people here." He was jumping to conclusions, for there were some portions of the opera which Borowski thought were very fine, especially the Dagger Dance and the third-act prelude.[37]

Other cities hearing the opera in the three-year period were Baltimore, Cincinnati, Pittsburgh, St. Paul, Washington, Los Angeles, and San Francisco. On November 29, 1913, the company gave its thirtieth and final performance in Chicago, with Herbert conducting. This is the only performance I know of, which was led by the composer. Beginning April 13, 1914, *Natoma* was presented for a week at the Century Theatre in New York by the Century Opera Company.[38] Then it lapsed into neglect and became a legend in American musical history.

Herbert should have been content with the criticisms *Natoma* inspired, for it was an outstanding opera generously endowed with beauty and showing much of his phenomenal skill. This was readily admitted. But the work lay too close to his heart for him to see any of its faults or to accept calmly the varying judgments. However, it was not epoch-making, and there was nothing in it to encourage an "American school" of opera.

There was no lack of recognition of the composer's achievement, and on June 14, 1911, Villanova College bestowed upon him the honorary degree of Doctor of Music—an honorable award for an honorable accomplishment. Two years later Herbert F. Peyser summed up the American opera situation by comparing the four best known products of the genre—*Natoma, Cyrano de Bergerac* (Damrosch), *Mona* (Parker), and *The Pipe of Desire* (Converse)—concluding that Herbert's work was the best—a judgment that is valid today.[39]

In the early 1920's a young lady named May Valentine began to attract favorable notice by conducting touring companies giving light opera. She was offered a chance to lead a revival of *Natoma* and went to New York to confer with Herbert. The interview seemed to be successful and promising; but while she awaited the formulation of final plans the composer died, and the project expired.[40] It is known that about a month before his death Herbert was looking at a copy of *Natoma* with unusual attention. At last he remarked that the first act was poor and that he intended to rewrite it during the summer. By so doing he hoped to issue a vastly improved work.[41] But death put a stop to all such thoughts, and America has to be satisfied with the score of 1911.

Although Herbert was never satisfied with the critics' reaction to *Natoma*, his first grand opera had been treated seriously, respectfully, and on the whole fairly. Moreover, it increased the interest in English-language opera, which really meant American opera, and hastened the formation of the National Society for the Promotion of Grand Opera in English, Herbert being a member of the Advisory Council.[42] Organized late in 1911, this group started out with high ambitions which were frustrated at the very beginning. It discovered that American opera could not be promoted by wish, and Krehbiel recollected: "My impression is that it talked itself to death in a single meeting."[43] Fortunately composers really interested in opera did not wait on the fate of the Society.

Herbert was willing to try his luck again in the serious opera field, and numerous writers encouraged him to write a second work, begging only that he examine more carefully the librettos submitted. As soon as *Natoma* proved itself popular with the public Herbert indicated that he might soon make his next attempt. His interest in English opera remained lively; only his eagerness for a nationalistic subject suffered a decline.

When the Bohemians gave a supper to Leopold Godowsky on March 9, 1911, at the Hotel Astor, Herbert (as a guest) listened to a short opera in English which was part of the evening's program. It was composed by Atilio Parelli and produced on an improvised stage in the north ballroom. The music is totally unknown today, but it created a pleasant impression which Herbert shared. At the evening's end he remarked: "When you see what a welcome this charming little opera got to-night, it is plain that the American people want an opera of their own. And why shouldn't we have it? We have our own language and we have our own music. We can have a National opera just as easily as Italy, France, or Germany, but not until the people really know they want it. I believe we are soon to have our own English opera, because I believe there is a demand for it."[44] At the time he said this his second opera was almost finished. It was *Madeleine*, a short, uniquely peculiar piece in one act which lasted but fifty minutes in performance.

One might have guessed, upon serious reflection, the kind of opera *Natoma* would be—colorful, melodious, rhythmical, with set numbers either instrumental or vocal. No one could have guessed in a century the kind of opera *Madeleine* would be, for Herbert intentionally turned his back on every type of writing he knew and favored. In view of the composer's work and his apparent aims it remains an anomaly and a "freak" in operatic literature. This is not to say that it has no merit—it is actually fascinating. But for Herbert it was a pure experiment, an incredible one for him to undertake. Its failure was due partly to the challenge he accepted, partly to circumstances beyond his control.

Again he chose—inevitably, it seems—a questionable book. His subsequent defense of it did not alter its weakness, especially in view of the musical treatment he accorded it. *Madeleine* is based on the short French play *Je dîne chez ma mère* by Adrien Decourcelle and Lambert Thibaut. As a play translated into English by Evelyn Clark Morgan, *I Dine with My Mother* was produced on August 14, 1904, at New York's Proctor's Theatre.[45] It was an attractive novelty, but neither weighty nor important. In the opera the leading character is Madeleine Fleury, singer at the Paris Opéra; in the play it is Sophie Arnould, an historical personage who did sing at the Opéra, but who was also one of the most famous prostitutes in history. This aspect of her career is not reflected in either the opera or the play, both of which present the same action.

Herbert may not have known the English version of the play. He told an interviewer he had discovered an old copy of the French text and had translated it himself, giving his translation to the playwright Grant Stewart to fashion into an opera libretto.[46] Stewart fulfilled his assignment with indifferent success.

The composer's autograph vocal and full scores are in the Library of Congress. The latter is dated at the end as follows: "Fine. Saturday

May 3rd 1913. (95 in the shade.) V. H. Fine." A month and a half before this act of completion Herbert signed a contract on March 18 with the Metropolitan Opera Company[47] whereby the Company pledged to produce the opera during the 1913–1914 season and to give the first performance in its New York house. By this time Herbert had secured sole rights to the libretto, and Stewart henceforth figured in the production as a name only. His part was in no way analogous to Redding's in *Natoma*.

There was widespread interest in Herbert's new opera, but it failed to approach the excitement stirred up by *Natoma*. That had been phenomenal and could only happen once. In *Madeleine*, moreover, there was absolutely no aspect of nationalism and consequently no chance of fomenting patriotic fervor. Herbert wrote it apparently as a labor of love, beginning it with no assurance that it would be produced anywhere. Naturally he hoped he could attract the Metropolitan Opera Company, which had been showing a slight concern for American compositions, and he was pleased when the director, Gatti-Casazza, invited him to run through the piano score. This took place on March 6, 1913, and the decision to produce it was reached some days later after a conference by the composer, the impresario, and Otto H. Kahn, chairman of the Metropolitan's Board of Directors.[48]

At this time Herbert had not yet started the instrumentation which he began at once. An interviewer found him hard at work in his home studio, comfortably attired in slippers and smoking jacket, minus collar and tie, and presumably puffing his companionable cigar. Herbert told the reporter:

Something over a year ago I began working on the score of "Madeleine," and I continued the work of composition at odd intervals between my labors on other operas. On some occasions I wrote only a few measures at a time. There was lots of inspiration in the little story, for its combination of lightness and a very human quality made a strong appeal to me, as I hope it will to the public. The period of the opera is about that of 1760 and the place is Paris, with the scene laid at the salon of Madeleine Fleury, prima donna of the Opéra. This gives a chance for delightful costume effects.

Without anticipating that *Madeleine* would have a noble destiny or exert a path-breaking influence, he touched upon his aims and procedures:

Leading motives I have used, not in imitation of Wagner, of course, as Beethoven, Weber and others had followed a similar system before him. I have tried to place the drama above everything in my treatment of the story. It seems to me that the operatic composer should make it his aim to give the most adequate representation of the dramatic themes, first of all. Thus I have fashioned the score with the idea of giving the singers a chance to deliver the lines with all the effectiveness of a great actor. While the composer of an opera should handle his themes in the instrumentation so as to make the most of them, just as much as if he were composing a symphony, he should not let his orchestra get away from him so much that the dramatic action is left sagging and the singer with nothing to do. This is one pitfall which I have tried to avoid in "Madeleine."[49]

Giorgio Polacco, who was to conduct the first performance of *Madeleine,* tried to spread its reputation in England, where he was directing opera at Covent Garden. With true Latin flamboyance he told the English that *Madeleine* would place Herbert among the world's greatest composers of opera and would provide an inspiration for future composers using the English language. He also predicted that Herbert would have no further need of composing light operas. He was wrong on both counts.[50]

Late in 1913 Herbert returned to New York from a brief rest period at French Lick Springs. It was time for *Madeleine* to go into rehearsal —and at once he ran into difficulties with the prima donna, Frances Alda. Her autobiography gives a graphic account of the situation which is probably correct in all essentials. To her surprise she discovered that the opera had no real vocal melody and had an astonishing minimum of instrumental melody; and she was faced with an experience new in her career. She finally ventured to reproach Herbert for writing her an ungrateful part. She insisted that she be given something melodious to sing and convinced him that she was not entirely wrong. He promised to bring her a suitable passage the next day. Overnight he sketched out a lovely solo, more arioso than aria, which became the most appreciated section of the work.[51] In the manuscript of the full score this insertion is clearly seen; it begins with the phrase "A perfect day" and extends to the noisy entrance of the Duke. It is not in the earlier-written piano-vocal score.

Madeleine received its first performance on Saturday afternoon January 24, 1914, in New York's Metropolitan Opera House, Polacco conducting. It was ill-fated from the start. First of all, it was a short opera and had to share the afternoon's bill with something else. Thus the attention of the audience was divided. Secondly, the effect would depend upon the companion piece, which turned out to be *Pagliacci* with Caruso singing one of his star rôles. Thirdly, a matinée performance could never be as propitious as an evening staging, the glamour of which may have nothing to do with musical value but affects the atmosphere in which a new opera is launched.

The cast was small:[52]

Madeleine Fleury........................Frances Alda
Nichette...............................Leonora Sparkes
Chevalier de Mauprat...................Antonio Pini-Corsi
François, Duc d'Esterre.................Paul Althouse
Didier................................Andres de Segurola
Coachman..............................Marcel Reiner
Servants.............................. { Armin Laufer
                                         Stefan Buckreus
                                         Alfred Sappio

The chorus was almost non-existent, although there was a small group of supposed lackeys and retainers.

The story is as inconsequential as the chorus. It is New Year's afternoon, 1770 (not 1760, as Herbert has been quoted as stating). Nichette, Madeleine's maid, arranges the presents her mistress has received. A succession of admirers come to pay their respects, and Madeleine asks each one to stay for dinner. She becomes increasingly angry as each refuses—this being the one day of all the year that he must dine with his mother. Didier, the humble painter, brings Madeleine a portrait he has painted of her mother, and when her fits of temper have subsided she decides that she too will dine with her parent—and props the portrait in front of her and gazes on it with contentment.

Herbert's treatment of this placid little story was as curious as the tale itself. He wrote a miniature opera, narrow and concentrated and far less ambitious than the expansive, colorful *Natoma*. He attempted to be modern and fluent in the same manner as Richard Strauss and Wolf-Ferrari. The subject of *Madeleine* might have been treated lyrically, but the composer, perhaps against his better judgment, rejected lyricism for a style of music which was explosive, dynamic, disjointed. In view of his musical predilections and what he had done in the past, *Madeleine* was extremely unexpected, for it represented a conscious effort to create something quite foreign to all his previous work. It was indeed a "conversational" opera, with the few principals delivering most of their text in rapid recitative. The music was also strange harmonically, for it was (relatively speaking) clashing and dissonant. Herbert was striving very hard to be a representative composer of 1913!

This is not to say that the score was unpleasant or ineffective; on the contrary, it was astonishing. It is safe to say, too, that the Metropolitan had put on very few things like it—and it posed nasty problems for singers accustomed to lyric phrases and passionate declamation. Within a restricted compass, of course, Herbert endeavored to give musical characterization in both voice and orchestra. The music for the Chevalier is light and *scherzando*; that for the Duke, a little firmer and more dashing, and that for Didier, restrained, *parlando*, and reserved.

Madeleine's sentiments are delivered in a variety of styles, depending on her fleeting moods, and Nichette has a part of no strong feeling. It is true that Herbert avoided melody in the usual meaning of the term. On the other hand, there are short phrases, vocal and orchestral, which are thoroughly charming. They come and go so quickly, however, that an audience can easily miss them altogether. This is not the case, naturally, with the interpolated *scena* for Madeleine or with the short and exquisite "portrait theme" which is heard several times, and which tenderly brings down the curtain at the end. This melody is a gem of rare beauty, whether hummed by Madeleine or issuing from the pit of the orchestra.

Madeleine was not a success—a fact which should surprise no one. It was not the equal of Strauss's great operas; it was not grateful to listen to or to sing; it was very artificially contrived and lacked the traits which made *Natoma* a favorite with the public for several years. Yet it had no fair trial and might well be given again to a public more inured to novelty than the crowds of forty years ago. It has strange features which a present-day audience might find highly acceptable— speed, fluency, dexterity; and it could be produced with a minimum of expense.

Few of the critics of 1914 took kindly to *Madeleine*; but in their surprise at Herbert's offering they were undoubtedly less fair than they had been to *Natoma*. Moreover, the new opera inspired one of the most stupid opinions in the annals of musical criticism, expressed by no less a person than H. E. Krehbiel, whom Herbert now cordially disliked. Krehbiel frowned upon the modernism of contemporary opera, including the masterpieces of Strauss, and found no good in Herbert's modern experiment. His concluding judgment was that Herbert had thrice achieved a dramatic climax, "and each time with as little provocation as suffices Richard Strauss in 'Der Rosenkavalier.' "[53] This might be taken as a profound compliment, but its writer intended just the opposite.

Henry T. Finck, always faithful to Herbert, thought the plot was too tenuous and suggested it should not be set to music at all. However, Herbert had gone about it in the only way that could possibly give satisfaction, and had treated the orchestra so that it mirrored textual details "as does the piano accompaniment to a Liszt song." *Madeleine* was also, he thought, too small an opera to be effective in the Metropolitan's huge auditorium; but he liked Herbert's usual orchestral mastery and the piquancy of harmony and rhythm. The speed of the dialogue, which Herbert maintained, afforded little opportunity for melodic invention, and this, he thought, was unfortunate.[54] Later Finck revised his opinion of *Madeleine* downward, asserting that Herbert "had made the fatal mistake of adopting as a model 'Le Donne Curiose' and similar works by Wolf-Ferrari into which Toscanini had infused a brief span of life in New York."[55] It was well known that Herbert admired this Italian opera and its creator; he had publicly remarked of *Le Donne Curiose*: "No one could enjoy that work more than I did. It is skillful, tasteful, tactful, and delicious. I take my hat off to its composer; he is a master among masters. I wish I could ever hope to become half as big a man."[56]

One friendly critic who enjoyed the performance greatly was percipient enough to note the ill pairing of *Madeleine* with the Caruso-*Pagliacci*; and by implication at least he censured the formation of this double bill. He was also dissatisfied with the Metropolitan's mounting of *Madeleine*, for he found the one scene (Madeleine's salon) common, garish, and undistinguished. But the performance was wholly satisfactory, including the orchestra, which was competently directed by Polacco. As in *Natoma* the enunciation of the singers struggling with English remained a problem. Of the necessity to dine with one's mother, he wrote:

The laughter of the audience at each reiteration of this excuse was wrongly interpreted by some observers, for the provocation of this laughter was exactly what Mr. Herbert intended in his treatment of the successive episodes.

. . . It is inevitable that much of the Gallic flavor of such a *comédie intime* should be lost in its adaptation into our tongue. Mr. Herbert has sought to make his new work an opera in understandable English. The libretto is therefore in the conversation style, with consequent elements of the colloquially commonplace. That there is literary distinction in Mr. Stewart's adaptation can scarcely be maintained. Mr. Herbert has aimed, however, to write an opera of comedy adorned by sentiment, and the auditors recognized a goodly proportion of both qualities in the performance.

Mr. Herbert's music is modern in style and in some instances he has joined the realists, as in his depiction of the Duc d'Esterre's unloosing Madeleine's steeds and in her writing of the letter. The noted American composer has given some of his most beautiful melody to Madeleine's aria . . . Another episode of melodic charm is the Duc's scene with Madeleine, while the picture theme, which is utilized most effectively to embellish the pretty sentiment of the ending, is in Mr. Herbert's happiest vein. One must admire the technical skill of Mr. Herbert as manifested in this score and the numerous excellences of workmanship in the instrumentation. His scoring bespeaks consummate mastery of instrumental means.[57]

Still more light is thrown upon Herbert's methods and strivings by Richard Aldrich, who had taken his place among the country's leading critics. Aldrich was learned and impartial, by no means enamored of *Madeleine*, yet he gave this intimate opera an appraisal which was far from superficial. The very severity of his strictures attests the serious attention he focused upon it:

> The conceit is pretty. Mr. Stewart's text has not a fine literary quality and is not notable for the skill with which he has brought out those potential elements of the drama. But it has probably all that would be expected in an operatic libretto. At all events, it is serviceable; and the character of the English diction heard in the performance was not such as to bring the literary quality of the text home to the listeners, or make it matter much what that quality was.
>
> Mr. Herbert has before now shown an ever-ready ability to turn an expert hand to any kind of music that may be required. Few musicians are more fluent, few can more readily assimilate to his own uses the forms and manners of musical expression that are current in the musical world. The idioms of modern music, melodic, harmonic, orchestral, in form and substance, are quite familiar to him. He knows the orchestra intimately from long years of experience inside and out of it, as player, conductor, and composer. And until this opera was heard it would have been said that he was never at a loss for a tune, sometimes a good one; that he could shake tunes from his sleeve. Nobody could fill the land with successful operettas as he has done without this useful facility. . . .
>
> Indeed, it seems as if Mr. Herbert had been carefully observing the methods of Strauss, with a memory for much that appertains to Beckmesser; but it appears also that he has not the cleverness and the capacity of a Strauss, and the result of his efforts to be not musical but descriptive, is a score restless, uneasy, but without a real impression of vivacity or animation, lacking musical beauty and refinement and with a false ring of cleverness. . . .
>
> Mr. Herbert has shown great ingenuity in his orchestration, a desire to write in the most "modern" vein, especially when he wishes to be descriptive. He seems to have bestowed his greatest care and attention upon this rather than upon the substance of his music. He is incessantly seeking after "effects" of one kind or another, and his scoring shows a resolute determination to be another Strauss. In this his success is but partial.[58]

The constant comparison with Strauss is just, instructive, and amusing. In composing *Natoma* Herbert had declared he would not follow the procedures of the daring German, yet in *Madeleine* he surely tried to write in the same descriptive way. Aldrich was right in holding that Strauss excelled as a writer of grand opera, but it is also true that Herbert had picked a model worthy of emulation. And the opera was more musical and its lyrical phrases less arid than Aldrich thought.

Herbert was again sorely displeased by the critics' reaction to *Madeleine*. Perhaps this second experience was even more painful, for he had written the shorter work voluntarily, had valiantly striven for a new mode of expression, and had been solely responsible for the choice of story and text. On Tuesday evening January 27, *Madeleine* was performed in Brooklyn, and afterward Herbert rushed back to the Hotel Plaza in Manhattan, where the National Society for the Promotion of Grand Opera in English was enjoying an annual banquet. (Krehbiel underestimated its longevity if not its effectiveness!) He was one of the speakers, and he again reproached the critics for hindering rather than furthering the cause of American opera. "An opera," he said, "should not be judged from one hearing. In Europe each country encourages its composers and treats new productions with sympathy. Here it is different, and . . . I will say that their attitude is not fair."[59] He was wrong only in his blanket condemnation of all critics.

Madeleine had practically no history subsequent to its première. The Metropolitan Opera Company performed it six times in the first three months of 1914—four times in New York, once in Brooklyn, once in Philadelphia—then dropped it from the repertoire. In the fall of 1916 it was put on the stage in Chicago, Herbert conducting; and it was included in a series of revivals which the Society of American Singers presented during the season of 1918–1919 at the Park Theatre in New York. But it was neither exciting nor ingratiating enough to hold any place for any length of time. Furthermore, there was not a single section of it which could be extracted and presented as a concert selection. The swift-paced, non-melodic recitative and the descriptive, sometimes repellent accompaniment lent themselves not at all to abridged treatment. Thus there was no chance to popularize the music through presentation of excerpts. Yet one unique distinction belongs to it. The full orchestra score was published by G. Schirmer of New York—and it was the first full opera score by an American composer to be published in the United States.[60]

What remains to be said of Herbert as a composer of grand opera? By his two products he achieved a special, though short-lived, eminence which was shared by none of his colleagues. In the light of world history his contributions to grand opera were not of major significance; but, appearing when and as they did, they were vastly important to America. The academic conservatory composer could write operas from now until doomsday, and no one would know or care about them; but when Herbert attempted the form every one took notice and reflected on it. This was particularly true of *Natoma*, which made the country conscious of American opera. Its representation was front-page news, and its performance meant something to the man in the street. Herbert gave great encouragement to American opera composers when they needed it badly. Had his two works been bad products, this would not have been so, for no amount of enthusiasm can make up for incompetence. Fortunately *Natoma* and *Madeleine,* though appreciated below the composer's own estimate, were good works which should still be considered as outstanding in American opera. Two factors, however, still operate against them. One is the fact that, the composer notwithstanding, they are not American expressions, either stylistically or artistically. The other is Herbert's supreme position as a composer of operetta: that fame completely obliterates the real esteem due him as a composer of serious music drama. Only the creation of an undisputed masterpiece could have altered this condition—and this he did not do.

In 1924 the David Bispham Memorial Fund awarded Herbert its gold medal for his services to American opera; but his sudden death prevented personal acceptance of the trophy. Other recipients have been Charles Wakefield Cadman, Frederick S. Converse, Henry Hadley, Deems Taylor, Howard Hanson, John Erskine, George Antheil, Walter Damrosch. It takes no special pleading to maintain that none of these surpassed Herbert's own operatic achievements.

17

The Romantic Vein

IMMERSED in the production of *Natoma*, Herbert was working at the same time on a new operetta (with a French background) for Fritzi Scheff. There was something in her personality which prompted Herbert and his writers to give her French parts. (*Babette* was French to all intents and purposes; *Mlle. Modiste* and *The Prima Donna* were strictly Parisian.) The new comic opera, *The Duchess,* was first produced as *Mlle. Rosita*—a sure indication that its sponsors hoped for a real successor to *Mlle. Modiste.* Preliminary announcements referred to the piece under three additional titles, namely, The Rose Shop (the working title), Rosita and Mlle. Boutonniere.

Some of the early announcements were premature and misleading, and one, which appeared several times, still raises speculation. The chief librettist was the familiar stage figure Joseph Herbert (no relation). In the summer of 1910 he was reported visiting the composer at Lake Placid, where they were collaborating on a musical version of George Du Maurier's famous novel *Trilby.* Rumor had it that Paul Potter's dramatization would be the basis of the libretto, and that William A. Brady, who owned the dramatic rights for the United States, would allow its utilization.[1] If any plan supported this musical rumor, it was quickly dropped; and we can only regret today that Herbert failed to set that ultraromantic story of love, music, and hypnotism.

The contract for the new operetta, drawn between Herbert and the Shubert Theatrical Company, specified that the composer would receive the libretto and lyrics by December 15, 1910, and that a complete piano score would be ready two months later. This schedule was adhered to, Joseph Herbert doing the major amount of work on the libretto and Harry B. Smith assisting with the lyrics. Rehearsals were reported well under way before the end of February,[2] and it was ready for the public late in the following month.

After several irritating delays the first performance on any stage took place in Boston at the Shubert Theatre on March 27, 1911. Herbert was present as a spectator and watched the opening of a show which was beset with misfortune and riddled by bad reviews. As usual the charge of a weak book was heard; but some of the music also fell under censure. The redoubtable H. T. Parker, for instance, said the music was good to hear, yet was certainly not of Herbert's best: it lacked brightness and grace, and failed to show his customary fancy and adroitness.[3] There were opposing opinions, one being that the music was the best Herbert had written in years;[4] but these formed the minority as the operetta became better known.

The early mishaps were caused by illness. Fritzi Scheff herself was ailing after the initial performance, and several presentations had to be canceled. The first Saturday performance brought the collapse of the chief comedian (Walter Jones), and the understudy who replaced him read his lines from script![5] Preparation, evidently, was not as thorough as it should have been. The show did not play its allotted three weeks in Boston, and it was drastically overhauled before it visited Philadelphia, Washington, and Pittsburgh. Then in Chicago mechanical trouble developed in the theater's lighting system, with results both amusing and tedious.[6]

In mid-summer Scheff had to take her usual vacation. As *The Duchess,* the show resumed its tour at the Opera House in Providence, Rhode Island, on September 25. Every seat was filled as the city observed the fortieth anniversary of that theater. Most critics in smaller communities wax rhapsodic over new stage presentations, their views being generally deflated by New York critics a few days or weeks later. Not so in Providence, however, where the *Journal* carried as hostile a review as Herbert ever received.

At last *The Duchess* was deemed ready for New York, where it opened at the Lyric Theatre (Reginald de Koven, proprietor) on Monday evening October 16. Changes were still being made in the company, and almost on the eve of the New York première John McGhie was succeeded as conductor by Oscar Radin, who from his later prominence in Hollywood looks back on this early association with Herbert with pride and satisfaction.[7] The cast (greatly altered since the Boston première six months earlier) was as follows:

Aristide Boutonniere, proprietor of a flower
    shop in Paris............................Wilton Taylor
Rose (Mlle. Rosita), his daughter...............Fritzi Scheff
Angelique Boutonniere, her aunt.................May Boley

Marianne, her cousin	Lillian Spencer
Philippe, Marquis de Montreville, a soldier	George Anderson
Adolphe, Comte de Paravante, a butterfly	John E. Hazzard
Boni de Francellas	George Graham
Alfonso Castelet } Men about town {	Madison Smith
Comte Gaston Gerome	Raymond Bloomer
Lieut. Prosper de Merimee	Robert Milliken
Picotte, foot-boy	M. Berenson
Duchess de Greadfre	Ida Bernard
Notary	Robert Flynn

Shoppers, Flower-girls, Gentlemen of fashion, Artists, etc.

The production was staged by J. C. Huffman.

The unhappy story, which one reviewer called simply "bad,"[8] centers on Rose, working in a flower shop, who consents to marry a marquis, sight unseen. Thus having a title, she will then divorce him and be in a position to wed a wealthy, middle-aged count. When the time for the divorce arrives, however, Philippe and Rose discover each other's identity and realize they are in love. The irritating romance culminates in their merely remaining wedded, much to the Count's discomfiture.

The music of *The Duchess* is far better than the Providence critic wanted his readers to believe, although it cannot rank with Herbert's best scores. The dramatic scenes (the opening, and the finales of Acts I and II) were carried off with characteristic fluency and skill, and two of the ensemble numbers were well geared to further the stage action. The waltz song of Rose, "Cupid, Tell Me Why," is a notable number, suave and lovely, but scarcely equal to "Kiss Me Again" in *Mlle. Modiste*. Philippe's march song, "The Land of Sultans' Dreams," wholly refuted the charge that the score lacked catchiness, but it was surprisingly short. There was one odd feature in the score, a comic recitation ("It's the Bump"), delivered by Angelique as she praises herself and criticizes Rose, against a very slight and unusual musical accompaniment. This well-nigh obscure little number especially caught the fancy of Henry T. Finck, who praised it highly in the *Evening Post*.

The majority of critics did not condemn the music, but failed to find it as entrancing as Herbert usually wrote. One of them commented: "Herbert's score fell somewhat below expectations. His orchestration was novel and brilliant as always and his ensembles were stirring; but those who waited for melodies that would be remembered discovered and carried away only a few." Conceding the effectiveness of Scheff's waltz song, this reviewer suggested that her exquisite manner of singing it might alone carry the show to success.[9] There was general agreement on two things: the pictorial prettiness of the stage settings, and the superb performance of the star.

Act I showed the flower shop of Aristide Boutonniere; Act II, the grand salon in the Chateau de Montreville; Act III, the hunting lodge of the Duc de Montpensier at Versailles. The scenery of the last act was especially impressive. It "reproduced the effect of an old English hunting print—green turf, russet boles of trees, and huntsmen in hunting pink, to say nothing of huntresses in habits of brown and Lincoln green." Here the stunning Fritzi appeared clad in a riding habit of shining white, and the pair of graceful wolf hounds accompanying her only accentuated her charm.[10] The company surrounding her was adequate, but without distinction.[11]

Scheff remembered the difficulties the show had already encountered. On opening night in New York the friendly audience applauded her warmly and called on her to make a first-night speech. Between the second and third acts she said: "You know that since 'Mlle. Modiste' we have had nothing but bad luck. Do make this a success. If you only knew how hard we have worked—Mr. Herbert and the actors and orchestra and every one else. Mr. Herbert is such a good man that he deserves some encouragement. Please give it to him."[12] Sitting in the audience, Herbert was also summoned to make a few remarks; but he limited them to an expression of thanks to all concerned.

Neither Herbert's music nor Fritzi's plea was able to bring *The Duchess* success. In New York it played only 24 performances,[13] and on the road failed to last out the year. The sudden announcement of Scheff's departure from it and of its collapse was startling; this alone was enough to cause regret, and reference to the music as "a score of exceptional merit."[14] But it was too late, and *The Duchess* became one of Herbert's unhappiest casualties. A further casualty was embraced in the fact that Herbert never wrote another production in which Fritzi Scheff would star.

The spring of 1911 was marked, for Herbert, by increased activity in his Irish associations (he was now a vice president of the Society of the Friendly Sons of St. Patrick and a member of the American Irish Historical Society) and by a six-week orchestra tour through the South starting on April 17.

Musically, the tour was not greatly different from those Herbert had made in the old band days, except that amusement numbers were less conspicuous; but his stature had increased tremendously, and he was freer to chide his listeners when they were inattentive. In Nashville, for example, Governor Hooper was in the audience and, with others, started to leave after the orchestra had begun the final number. Herbert stopped the music. Turning, he said to the audience: "It will take ten minutes to play this piece, and those who are in a hurry to leave had perhaps better go now." The embarrassed individuals, including the Governor, meekly resumed their seats and listened to the end.[15]

After the southern tour Herbert was ready to offer the public the first fruits of a new association. In 1909 he had begun making phonograph records for the Edison company. Now he transferred this activity to the Victor Talking Machine Company, and its recordings of the Victor Herbert Orchestra (conducted by Herbert) flooded the land. The years 1911 and 1912 were his most active as a recording artist, but the connection with Victor was maintained until his death. Four records were released in July of 1911, and by the end of the year sixteen were available.[16] They and their successors were phenomenally popular, and they circulated Herbert's music and interpretations over wider areas than ever before.

For the Victor Company, too, Herbert recorded no fewer than six cello solos, all released in 1912 from April to November. In spite of primitive recording conditions these few records give a very fair approximation of his ability as an instrumental artist. He was excellent —and they give cause for regret that there could be no reproduction of his playing twenty-five years earlier, when he was at the height of his powers. It was characteristic of Herbert that his first cello record released was his own arrangement of Samuel Lover's *The Low-Back'd Car*. And it remains an attractive record today.

Coincident with Herbert's first Victor records was the announcement that a new operetta would be ready for the fall season of 1911. As a matter of fact two were announced; but only one materialized— or perhaps the first was metamorphosed into the second. The earlier report had Herbert composing music for *The Girl and the Canary*, in which the star was to be the beauteous Lina Abarbanell; the author of the book was the light and fluent Fred de Gresac[17] (who as Mme. Victor Maurel was the wife of the famous French opera baritone). This report came to naught, but it was quickly followed by the news that Herbert's forthcoming light opera would be *The Enchantress*.

The Enchantress also had a book written by Fred de Gresac (lyrics by Harry B. Smith), which justifies the theory of a change of plan rather than the abandonment of an already begun play. First performance on any stage occurred at the National Theatre in Washington on October 9, 1911; the New York première took place at the New York Theatre on October 19. The producer was Joseph M. Gaites, who luckily found himself in charge of one of the best things Herbert ever did. The score was filled with sumptuously beautiful music, and its neglect today is both unpardonable and unreasonable.

The title-rôle was taken by the English actress Kitty Gordon, whose most famous attribute was a beautiful back. She was not a great singer; but she was intelligent, clever, charming, and regal, and she triumphed magnificently in the opportunity Herbert gave her.

Either by accident or by design Herbert used *The Enchantress* as an excuse to offer the public many opinions and explanations. A rather long peroration touched upon various topics, but in it the composer suggested that the new work might be his "masterpiece in every way": he had "never had so many varied inspirations to bring forth the best" he could express.[18] He was very nearly right.

On another occasion, when talking of America's potential greatness in light opera, Herbert revealed that the cost of *The Enchantress* was $60,000.[19] His contention was that the material support could be found in this country, but that a school of light-opera composition was lacking. Another noteworthy remark was: "We need an American School of Music in order to give our young composers a chance to develop and drive out the quacks. Our young composers are too prone to get their ideas from the old world, and their work naturally will fall into the style of foreign composition. They do not get into their music that freshness and vitality so characteristic of this country. And yet on the other hand American musical taste has developed to a point where it demands something that is native. I believe that one reason why 'The Enchantress' has had so huge a success in New York, and wherever it has played, is that I determined, when I started its composition, to disregard absolutely every foreign impulse and to write in a frank, free American style."[20]

These remarks show the trend of Herbert's efforts; and *The Enchantress* itself shows the mistaken notion he entertained of American style. The score did indeed have an extraordinary freshness and vitality; but musically it was European to the core. Herbert was no doubt disappointed in his most recent operettas, *When Sweet Sixteen* and *The Duchess*; he was no doubt determined that his newest work should be an improvement over them; but the final product was a combination of French and Austrian styles which wholly belied what Herbert said and thought he was trying to do. The music was so beautiful that nobody cared.

In early September, when Kitty Gordon returned two weeks behind schedule from a vacation in England, *The Enchantress* had been in rehearsal for some time.[21] It was supposed to open on October 1, but not until the 9th did the first curtain go up on the lavish spectacle, which the critic of the Washington *Evening Star* described as "one of the most gorgeous assemblages of wonders from all parts of the civilized theater world ever placed on exhibition under the roof of a playhouse."

With this accolade, and more, to its credit *The Enchantress* moved into New York ten days later and immediately won an enthusiastic following among both public and critics. It is worth noting that this was the third Herbert operetta to appear on Broadway within thirty-five days: *When Sweet Sixteen,* on September 14; *The Duchess,* on October 16; and now *The Enchantress,* on October 19. The first-named had already vanished, but Fritzi Scheff was still struggling for the support she pleaded for. With the arrival of a much better show the days of *The Duchess* were definitely numbered—and Fritzi watched Kitty take her place in the limelight.

The New York program, calling *The Enchantress* a "new opera comique," announced the following rather small cast:

```
Vivien Savary, an opera singer................Kitty Gordon
Mamoute, her aunt..........................Hatti Arnold
Marion Love, an American heiress.............Nellie McCoy
Princess Diana, of Russia.....................Ida Fitzhugh
Princess Stellina..............................Louise Bliss
Princess Stephanie........................Venita Fitzhugh
Princess  Poppy...........................Nina  Barbour
Princess Floria..............................Mabel Berra
Princess  Berenice.........................Dorothy  Berry
Princess Hortensia.......................Clarice Gilberte
Prince Ivan of Zergovia....................Harold H. Forde
Troute, head of the Secret Service..............Ralph Riggs
Poff, the Prince's tutor....................Gilbert Clayton
Miloch, Regent of Zergovia.............Harrison Brockbank
Ozir, Minister of War......................Arthur Forrest
Prince Zepi...............................Bertram Fox
Mina, maid to Vivien...................Katherine Witchie
           Other characters: 20 girls—16 men
```

Frederick G. Latham was in charge of the staging. The musical director was Gustave Salzer.

There were only two acts. The first showed the Royal Palace of Zergovia; the second, Vivien's villa on the Danube.

The tale unfolds in the country of Zergovia, where Ivan (after some carefree, flirtatious years) is about to ascend the throne. Now he must marry and settle down, but his mate has to be a lady of royal rank. If Miloch and Ozir can persuade him to fall in love with a commoner, he will have to abdicate and leave the nation in their hands. They use Vivien (a veritable enchantress) for this purpose, and are nearly successful. At the last moment, however, royal ancestors are discovered in Vivien's family tree, and so the lovers can come together in wedded, monarchical bliss.

Curiously enough, this inevitable operetta ending was not in the libretto as originally written. The typewritten libretto deposited for copyright in the Library of Congress does not include the discovery of Vivien's royal descent. Instead, she remains adamant, convinces Ivan that he must give her up, and persuades him to wed Stephanie, his childhood sweetheart. Vivien will go to Vienna to sing in the royal opera, and the duchy promised to her by Ozir will be bestowed upon her aunt. In view of the play's general frothiness it can scarcely be maintained that the sterner ending was much more appropriate; but its very existence attests a short-lived willingness to be unconventional.

Unquestionably the music of *The Enchantress* was superior to any operetta strains Herbert had recently written. In many respects it was the equal of *Naughty Marietta* and could stand comparison with *Mlle. Modiste* and earlier masterpieces. Within its genre it was unusually rich and piquant in harmony, vivacious and enchanting in melody, captivating in rhythm, and expansive and complicated in general design.

The very opening number, with the six Princesses singing of their chances with the Prince, is alive with deft phrases and musical repartee. The interchange of phrase, the constantly scurrying accompaniment, the suave apostrophizing of the God of Love make it a brilliant curtain raiser. The Regent's entrance and ensuing solo ("If You Can't Be As Happy As You'd Like to Be") are also more than usually ambitious, without being padded, and the entrance scene of Prince Ivan is masterly. Here the fickle Prince, with a delightful air, recounts his experiences with girls, then sings to several in the ballroom how he must dance with them. Without interruption the music shifts from one dance to another—a charming waltz, a mazurka, a polka, a pseudo minuet, a two-step, and a stately polonaise. This last theme, dignified yet fiery, is used for the entrance of Vivien, who has a dramatic scene with Ivan followed at once by her first solo. She expounds herself with considerable dignity and then, ready to confess her inner romantic world, sings a waltz ("The Land of My Own Romance") that ranks with the best of Herbert's love melodies. Vivien's and Ivan's first love duet ("Rose, Lucky Rose") is of extraordinary design. It has the expected declaration of passion, but also unexpected dramatic dialogue followed by melodic conversation, another lovely waltz theme, and a repetition of Vivien's principal air. This is a far cry from the customary duet of musical comedy which is so frequently boring and dramatically inactive. The finale of the first act maintains the charm of all that has gone before, furthers the stage action impressively, and adds two more themes that match the standard already set.

The opening chorus of Act II is a dynamic creation with the chorus singers tossing opinions back and forth. There follows soon another elaborate, equally effective duet by Vivien and Ivan ("One Word from You") in which both dramatic action and amorous effusion are emphasized. Just before the closing finale, which only serves to bring the curtain down, is a so-called duet between Vivien and Ozir. It is really the solo wherewith the enchantress has to charm the Minister of War. Entitled "All Your Own Am I," or the "Champagne Song," it is one of the loveliest, most seductive pieces in all operetta literature. Surprisingly short, with great contrast between stanza and refrain, it is a gem, a true inspiration of its kind.

For the most part the New York critics judged *The Enchantress* to be superb and gave it unstinted praise. Most of them, too, found the book to be exceptionally good. Perhaps it was, comparatively speaking, even though it can arouse little sympathy today.

Most of the reviews were specific, and rightly so, for the careful listener found plentiful cause for rejoicing. "Musically, Mr. Herbert seems simply to have revelled in the score. Nothing better has rippled off his pen for a long time. He has written waltzes that would be applauded, even in Vienna, and in addition he has snappy, truly American, dashing march numbers and some graceful dances."[22] Another observer thought *The Enchantress* "a musical entertainment which will appeal to people who do not object to hearing music that is good even if it is light," and called attention to the unusual variety of the score by remarking that Herbert "has repeatedly written in his most charming vein—or veins, for he is a versatile musician—he has scored some of his melodies so delightfully that no small amount of the pleasure is derived from the orchestra."[23]

Up in Boston the crotchety H. T. Parker saw *The Enchantress* when it was on tour. He also heard Herbert conduct it. In the past he had not hesitated to criticize Herbert's music or the composer himself when he seemed to be writing too fast; but the music of *The Enchantress* Parker could not praise too highly. It was so good, he remarked, that it deserved Herbert's expert conducting, which was uniquely competent in light opera. In fact, he thought as he watched the portly but agile composer on the podium, if Herbert conducted operetta regularly he would be worth his weight in gold!

Parker found in this score all of Herbert's real musical skill, not only in the graceful melodies, but also in quaint modulations, choral sonorities, orchestral fancy, and constant lightness void of cheapness. "At his best—and he sustains his best through much of his newest operetta—we Americans may justly match him against the more vaunted composers of Vienna." It would indeed be difficult to find a more judicious, laudatory review than this from the sometimes hostile

Parker, who was also perceptive enough to tear the libretto to pieces and to speak with reservations of the actors in the cast. He bewailed the fact that Herbert so rarely had a worthy book at his disposal and insisted that Herbert, writing for the orchestra, was a better humorist than the comedians cavorting on the stage.[24]

Most critics found the entire company acceptable, but there was no doubt that Kitty Gordon was the star. She was beautiful and stately, an enchantress through dignity and intelligence rather than through siren tricks and lack of restraint. Although she was not a great singer Herbert had judged her voice well and had given her passages within her vocal capacity. Her success as Vivien Savary was genuine. Herbert was pleased with her work, for after the 75th performance of the operetta he gave a dinner in her honor as an expression of his appreciation.[25]

After 72 performances in New York[26] *The Enchantress* departed for a brilliant career on the road. This departure was not precipitate, even though the run was short, and it was announced well in advance. Almost, but not quite, like *Mlle. Modiste,* it became for nearly three full seasons a traveling institution with Kitty Gordon at its head. Its vitality was finally exhausted on the West Coast in November, 1913, and then it faded into a neglect from which it should some day recover.

The year 1912 opened with Herbert receiving what he especially loved: recognition of his love of Ireland and acknowledgment of his promotion of Irish culture. It must be admitted that some of his Irish contributions were rather vague; but there was never a moment when he did not believe he was aiding the cause. This was particularly true since he had become a Friendly Son of St. Patrick.

The welcome citation came to Herbert at his home on January 11. It was awarded by the Gaelic Society of New York and assumed the form of an engrossed and illuminated document referred to as an address. Highly decorative, it was a faithful reproduction of the lettering, color, and tracery of the famous Book of Kells, the national treasure of Ireland which has been described as the most beautiful manuscript in existence. A special committee bore the document to Herbert, and as he read it he discovered he was lauded for devotion to Irish ideals and for special service to the Society in its efforts to revive the Irish language, music, and literature. The citation concluded with the words:

Years ago your illustrious grandfather, Samuel Lover, distinguished and immortalized himself as an Irish patriot by the true Nationalism of his work in prose and poetry. In you, Sir, the hereditary trait finds its expression in matchless music. While awakening a musical spirit in America you are also perpetuating the spirit which had lived and will live forever in the music and songs of Ireland. For this we thank you heartily and sincerely.[27]

Herbert was intensely gratified by this testimonial, which he acknowledged graciously, seeming to be inordinately pleased by the mention of his mother's father.

The previous year's spring tour had proven so successful that another was undertaken in 1912, beginning on Easter Monday, April 8. It was accomplished without special incident except that Herbert himself missed the special train taking the orchestra from Kansas City to Des Moines! He finally caught up with it, however, and made his scheduled appearance.[28]

Back in New York in June, Herbert once more enjoyed some satisfaction at the expense of his old and permanent enemy, Marc Blumenberg of the *Musical Courier*. It was an indirect satisfaction, but it was certainly genuine. This time the unwise but intrepid Blumenberg had crossed swords with the noted copyright attorney Nathan Burkan (also Herbert's friend and lawyer), attacking him for his work in the hearings on the copyright bill of 1909, and calling him a legal fourflush and an attorney of obscure origin. Not unreasonably Burkan had objected to this and had sued Blumenberg for damages. As one of Burkan's witnesses Herbert explained the lawyer had assumed a stand in Washington which he (the composer) had directed and approved. When the verdict was handed down, on June 13, 1912, Burkan found himself awarded $5,000, and Blumenberg was again bested by Herbert and his friends.[29]

In the fall Herbert had his own tiff with the law, of quite a different nature, showing that the life of a composer in New York, even in 1912, left something to be desired. His home on 108th Street was surrounded by more and more noise. Knowing that he had to spend a good many hours at home composing, and realizing that he could not "compose operas to the accompaniment of hurdy gurdies and tin-pan piano,"[30] he engaged the United States Gypsum Company to construct a "soundproof, padded composing cabinet" which would shut off all sounds from outside and leave him undisturbed. It was built on the top floor of his house, but when he tried it out the sounds came through just the same. Consequently he refused to pay the $242.55 which the contracting company claimed was due. The first judgment went against him, and he was ordered to pay; but this only strengthened his resolve to stand firm and yield not a nickel. He appealed, and delighted the whole of New York when he won the case on the ground that the United States Gypsum Company had not fulfilled its part of the agreement.[31] Unfortunately the judge could not tell Herbert how to achieve solitude in the midst of street noises, city turmoil, and neighborhood singing.

Pending settlement of this litigation Herbert made a somewhat unusual appearance at a smoker given by the Bohemians at Lüchow's, November 9, 1912, in honor of the famous conductor Karl Muck. Herbert was one of the speakers at the supper, and dwelt upon his favorite topic: help for the American composer of opera. In 1910 Arthur Nevin had seen his opera *Poia* produced in Berlin, and Herbert praised Muck for making the production possible; and even though *Poia* was unsuccessful the encouragement it had received was what other American composers needed. Herbert rather cryptically remarked that Nevin's opera was not as bad as the German critics declared it to be—one of the few instances in which he expressed himself ungracefully.

The year closed happily for Herbert because he had a chance to compose another devastating skit for the Lambs. After the spring tour of the orchestra he and his men had embarked again on one of the All Star Gambols; but it covered less ground and occupied less time than usual. The new skit was performed on Sunday evening December 29, 1912, at the Lambs' Christmas Gambol in their own clubhouse. It was called *The Village Blacksmith,* with words (or "nonsense") by George V. Hobart. The program defined it as "a bit of topsyturvyism written in an effort to show that all the nuts do not come from Brazil." It was a light-hearted burlesque from beginning to end, and so successful that the Lambs, including Herbert, presented it a few months later at their annual Ladies Gambol in the Metropolitan Opera House on May 9. Again it made a hit, but the feature chiefly remembered was DeWolf Hopper singing a lullaby accompanied by the soothing strains of hammer and anvil.[32]

The noises which led Herbert to order his soundproof studio plagued him most as he was composing part of his next operetta, *The Lady of the Slipper.* This was a brilliant success as a show, though somewhat less successful as a musical composition. In spite of this reservation it must be ranked among Herbert's notable triumphs, for it blazed in New York and across the country for two full years. The real première occurred at the Chestnut Street Opera House in Philadelphia on October 8, 1912; the New York première was at the Globe Theatre on October 28.

The Lady of the Slipper, based on the story of Cinderella, was another venture into the realm of childhood lore; but it was more sophisticated than his *Babes in Toyland, Wonderland* or *Little Nemo.* The adoption of the Cinderella theme was decided by the producer, Charles B. Dillingham. According to one rather cynical but honest commentator Dillingham, doubtful as to what he should bring forth, followed Charles Frohman's adage: "When in doubt, do Cinderella."[33]

Dillingham knew at least that he wanted something grand and grandiose, and he produced it—a spectacle which would surpass all his previous efforts. Herbert was his composer. His next concern was the cast, and he set about assembling a company which would be unprecedented in fame, in ability, in variety. Indeed *The Lady of the Slipper* was announced and advertised as having the greatest cast in the history of the theater; and, once it was launched, the principals were vaunted as constituting the first all-star cast of modern times.

This may have been a slight exaggeration, but not much. A trio of stars headed the cast: Dave Montgomery, Fred Stone, and the sparkling Elsie Janis. In addition the public was promised the great comedian, Joseph Cawthorn, Allene Crater, Queenie Vassar, and a scintillating ballerina, Lydia Lopokova; also Mr. and Mrs. Vernon Castle, whose marriage had taken place on May 28, 1911,[34] and whose great days of stardom were still ahead. Others of the cast were chosen accordingly. Although there were a few defections, the public saw for many months a remarkable assemblage of talent, surrounded by all possible physical splendor in fanciful scenery, costumes, lighting and stage effects.

The story of Cinderella was excellent, but it was vitiated by the text prepared for this play. The book was written by Anne Caldwell and Laurence McCarty; the lyrics, by James O'Dea. Fortunately the scenes on the stage were so gorgeous that no one seriously minded the inept and humorless lines.

Rehearsals were under way by the middle of September, and they were long and arduous. After one ten-hour session Miss Caldwell told a roving reporter: "Everything has gone beautifully so far. Though the rehearsals are long, they never tire me, as the music is so absolutely gorgeous. I don't think there's another man in the world as wonderful as Victor Herbert. His numbers are one joy after another." Then she added this reflection: "The biggest puzzle in the play to me is which is the greatest personality, Fred Stone, David Montgomery, Elsie Janis, Lydia Lopokova or Charles Dillingham, who had the courage and diplomacy to bring such a coterie together."[35]

Miss Caldwell was right about the need for diplomacy in handling so many individual temperaments. Apparently she was right, too, about Dillingham, for the forthright reminiscences of that diminutive darling of the American stage, Elsie Janis, mentioned the same quality and gave some interesting sidelights on the preparation of *The Lady of the Slipper*, which she described as something new in the way of all-star entertainment.

With refreshing honesty Miss Janis airily dismissed the musical problems: "Of all the stars in the profession Dave Montgomery, Fred Stone and myself were the least fitted to sing Victor Herbert's music. Fortunately, we could always go into our dance, and we did!" When the company assembled for the first rehearsal she was struck by the extreme politeness of Montgomery and Stone, of Allene Crater (Mrs. Stone), of Joseph Cawthorn and Queenie Vassar. Elsie herself felt like an ambitious puppy and, though striving to be pleasant, looked at once for the thickness of her part. Dillingham, she recalls, was the prince of diplomats, and her mother—seemingly inseparable from Elsie—was the soul of tact. The script was read through, and equal parts were assigned to Montgomery-Stone-Janis. Cawthorn was unhappy with an insignificant role as husband of Cinderella's step-mother, a novel twist but no improvement on the legend. After cooperating for one week Cawthorn withdrew. This was a loss to the show; but his part vanished with him, and this was for the better.

Another pleasant memory was the appearance of Vernon and Irene Castle whom Dillingham had engaged during the summer in Paris. In their Paris clothes they made the girl think of tall and slim young palm trees. They were already developing their peculiarly individual style of dancing, then called ultra-modern, but even the imagination governing musical comedy could not fit it into the "glorified pantomime atmosphere" of *The Lady of the Slipper*. After the Philadelphia opening their dance was eliminated, but Vernon Castle remained in the cast for several weeks.

Perhaps another reason for Irene Castle's departure appears in the following episode, told with some relish by Elsie Janis:

> Irene's greatest success the summer before in Paris had been her simplicity, the afterward famous Dutch Bonnet, the modest chiffon skirts that covered her slim shapely limbs, but Irene had "gone Paris" in a big way. She had seen some Parisian *danseuse* wearing a clinging directoire gown, which at a certain moment in her dance she would lift high above her hips, displaying the shortest pair of "shorts" ever glimpsed. Nothing would do but that "La Castle" must introduce this innovation to America. Innovation is hardly the word! At the dress rehearsal in Philadelphia, when Irene, who had always rehearsed in practice clothes, suddenly pulled up her skirts like a naughty little girl, showing her "complete understanding," Charley* groaned, Fred Stone looked the other way, and Mother's gasp of dismay must have been heard in Trenton![36]

Dillingham begged "La Castle" to retreat to the Dutch Bonnet and the chiffon skirts, but the darling lady was adamant. She was soon out of the show and dancing at the Café Martin in New York, where her husband arranged to appear with her nightly. He had to commute from Philadelphia to do it.

* Dillingham.

Produced with remarkable smoothness, *The Lady of the Slipper* was warmly welcomed. The next morning's paper reported that rarely had "anything quite so beautiful in stage furnishings, costuming and brilliant ensembles" been seen in Philadelphia. The audience had been enchanted by "the prismatic changes of costume, the glitter of the groupings and the beauties of the dances," and had heard music "so delicious . . . that the talented composer, who was seated in a stage box, was called to the stage at the close of the second act and compelled to make a brief speech of thanks."[37]

The representation was so impressive that Philadelphia supported it for three weeks. It then went to New York, where the program called it "a musical fantasy in three acts" featuring Montgomery and Stone and Elsie Janis. The full title was "The Lady of the Slipper or A Modern Cinderella." The cast was as follows:

The Crown Prince Maximilian	Douglas Stevenson
Prince Ulrich, his brother	Eugene Revere
Captain Ladislaw, aide-de-camp to Maximilian	James G. Reany
Baron von Nix, Cinderella's father	Charles A. Mason
Atzel, the Baron's butler	Vernon Castle
Mouser, the Baron's cat	David Abrahams
Albrecht, a shoemaker	Samuel Burbank
Louis, his assistant	Harold Russell
Joseph, a milliner	Edgar L. Hay
Matthias, a furrier	Ed. Randall
Punks } From the cornfield	David C. Montgomery
Spooks }	Fred A. Stone
Cinderella	Elsie Janis
Romneya	Allene Crater
Dollbabia } Cinderella's step-sisters	Lillian Lee
Freakette }	Queenie Vassar
The Fairy Godmother	Vivian Rushmore
Valerie, maid at the Baron's	Peggy Wood
Sophia, Albrecht's wife	Florence Williams
Irma, Joseph's wife	Edna Bates
Clara, Louis' wife	Helen Falconer
Ludovica, Matthias' wife	Gladys Zell
Maida	Lillian Rice
Gretchen	Angie Weimers
Première danseuse	Lydia Lopokova

Courtiers, soldiers, ladies-in-waiting, Oriental women
of the harem, etc.

The stage director was R. H. Burnside; the stage manager, Clyde Mackinlay; the musical director, W. E. McQuinn.

The scenic synopsis was unusually elaborate: Act I, Scene 1, kitchen in the castle of Baron von Nix; Scene 2, on the way to the palace. Act II, ballroom in the palace of Prince Maximilian. Act III, Scene 1, the Baron's kitchen; Scene 2, throneroom of the Prince's palace.

The main thread of the Cinderella legend is recognizable throughout. Made a drudge by her two wicked half-sisters, the charming girl makes friends of two characters from the cornfield (obviously suggested by the similar characters in *The Wizard of Oz*) and, with the aid of her Fairy Godmother, goes to the ball. The slipper incident takes place in time to help the Crown Prince save his throne. Virtue is rewarded when Maximilian finds that Cinderella is the only girl who can wear the dainty object.

The show was designed as a spectacle for certain individual stars and was consistently organized with this end in view. According to one observer, neither the book nor the lyrics nor the music could have carried the show alone;[38] and he was probably right. The music is excellent from the point of view of utility (dances, pageantry, ballet), but it is neither vocal nor melodious in the way that vocal operetta music should be. Of course there was not a real singer in the cast, so that what Herbert wrote he wrote intentionally; as a result the music was subordinate to the over-all effect and had little life of its own.

The best parts of the score were undoubtedly the descriptive sections and the ballet numbers, with an occasional "characteristic" excerpt (e.g., the duet of Cinderella and the cat, "Meow! Meow! Meow!") showing real musical cleverness. The "Witches Ballet," the music for Cinderella's entrance at the ball, the ballet suite, the "Punch Bowl Glide" (which Fred Stone immortalized), the "Drums of All Nations" and the music for the "Harlequinade"—these constituted the music which paralleled the brilliance on the stage. It efficiently supported the action and the dancing and the pantomime, and in never becoming obtrusive it contributed to the undisputed triumph of the whole.

One safe critic wanted to know what show would not be good with such a cast, such a composer, such directors, such everything. He felt that all the possibilities of Cinderella had not been realized, and that Vernon Castle and Lopokova had too little to do; but the talents of Stone and Montgomery in comic pose and acrobatic dancing, of Janis in exuding charm and performing her inimitable imitations, of Herbert in composing, even though no single melody might be hummed or whistled, had coalesced into a remarkable entertainment.[39] Montgomery and Stone obviously had roles patterned after their great success in *The Wizard of Oz*, which gave great pleasure; and Janis, it was noticed, half sang, half talked her way through her vocal numbers, which bothered no one at all.

More than one person appreciated the pantomimic nature of the production and greeted it with satisfaction. The reporter from the New York *Times* thought the show had a little of everything and was excellent of its kind. Of the music he wrote:

> In this case, however, Victor Herbert having had charge of that important detail, there is more occasion for enthusiasm than sometimes happens, even if, as some people are sure to say, he has done better in the past. . . .
>
> Incidentally there are stirring marches to bring on the comely chorus, and enough of melody or discord to properly emphasize the successive passage, sentimental or comic, of an entertainment which is nearer English pantomime than anything we have had for years.

The Lady of the Slipper remained in New York through the season, closing in early May after a run (remarkable for the time) of 232 performances.[40] The starring trio were exhausted and demanded long vacations, but they returned to it in the fall for another successful season which included two months each in Chicago and Boston. In every way it was a major achievement in the American musical theater, not to mention the financial rewards to composer and producer. While it played in New York, Herbert was reported receiving between $400 and $500 weekly from it;[41] and it allegedly saved Dillingham's theatrical career. The producer had lost on several of his recent ventures, and it was believed he would retire from the theater if *The Lady of the Slipper* failed. Actually it made a fortune for him and his associates.[42]

In 1913 Herbert celebrated his 54th birthday. He was young in spirit, but he had produced so much, had delighted so many for such a long period that he was considered as a national institution. Furthermore, he had an almost precocious inclination, as a young man, to paternalize himself by calling his band and orchestra players "my boys." Thus it was a joy to honor him, a pleasure which the Society of American Dramatists and Composers gave itself when it sponsored a Victor Herbert dinner at Delmonico's on January 5, for its own twenty-first birthday.[43]

The composer was the guest of honor, and the occasion was marked by good cheer, good speeches, good companionship. The Society spared no effort in arranging festivities. The only embarrassment to Herbert sprang from the compliments showered on him. Augustus Thomas presided over the ceremonies and delivered a eulogy of his own. Herbert said that Thomas's tribute made him feel like King Lear, but roguishly added: "Bore on, I will endure." Other speakers who heaped the honors high were John Philip Sousa, Marshall P. Wilder, and Rachel Crothers. A brief summary of the affair applauded the distinctions awarded to the popular Irishman. It recognized that he had set up certain ideals and had maintained them, had brought real artistry to the American musical stage, had never shirked his tasks or skimped on his productions. His operettas were likened to whisky as described by an imbibing Kentuckian: "All is good but some is better!"[44]

The desire to honor Herbert this year seemed to be contagious, and a motley group trooped to his home on his birthday (February 1) to pay its affectionate respect or respectful affection. Enrico Caruso was among the visitors—"politicians, opera singers . . . bankers, billiard players, amateur card trick experts, librettists, lawyers, not to speak of any number of stray musicians." Why did they come? Because Herbert, more than anyone else in America, had elevated the standard of light music, had established artistic operetta over inane musical comedy, and was beloved of his fellow men. Every one shared the wish, "May he live to be a hundred!"[45]

All the while, Herbert's Irish ardor flamed more brightly than ever, and on Easter Sunday evening (March 23) he and his orchestra appeared in Carnegie Hall at the thirty-fifth annual Feis Ceoil Agus Seanachas (Irish Musical and Literary Festival) of the Gaelic Society. The soprano soloist, Idelle Patterson, sang, in addition to several Irish songs, the only non-Irish item on the program, "Caro Nome" from Verdi's *Rigoletto*![46] Herbert conducted music by William V. Wallace, Charles V. Stanford, Swan Hennesy, and himself. The program included a speaker, Professor Joseph Dunn of the Catholic University of America, who gave a lecture on ancient Gaelic literature.

Early in June, Herbert and his orchestra made another unusual appearance when they gave an afternoon concert for the New York State Music Teachers' Association meeting in Saratoga. There were two guest vocalists—Mary Carson, soprano, and Ellison Van Hoose, tenor; but the instrumental soloists were from the orchestra—Fred L. Landau, concertmaster, Horace Britt, cellist, and Albert Chiaffarelli, clarinetist. The program was designedly light, and it produced the desired effect, even in the extra numbers. "Mr. Herbert, in his encores, dared to give the audience what it desired by playing smaller works of real musical value. Other conductors might take their cue from him."[47]

Beginning July 6, Herbert was back in Willow Grove, where it was rumored he was working on an opera called *The Coquette*: another stage work which never materialized, although it may have changed into something else. As usual he rhapsodized over the Grove's attractions and reiterated that it was the most wonderful park in the world for music. Moreover, he wanted to keep it that way. Certain interests were trying to introduce liquor into the Park, and certain other interests were trying to keep it out. Herbert heartily endorsed its exclusion, asserting that intoxicants must be prevented from lowering the artistic atmosphere which the resort legitimately fostered.[48]

But long before the summer activities started, at the very beginning of spring, Herbert had again turned to the stage and produced a work which would provide music for summer programs for many years to come. Another operetta had appeared, and it was one of his best. *Sweethearts*, a comic opera in two acts (produced by Werba and Luescher), had its real first performance at the Academy of Music in Baltimore on March 24, and its first New York performance at the New Amsterdam Theatre on September 8, 1913. In addition to its fine quality, it had, indirectly, a profound effect upon the history of music in the United States.

Sweethearts, like *The Lady of the Slipper*, had a story supplied by three writers. Harry B. Smith and Fred de Gresac were responsible for the book; Robert B. Smith, brother of Harry, penned the lyrics. Their combined output was not notable, but it failed to dull the composer's best instincts. Like several of Herbert's operettas, *Sweethearts* was composed with one particular singer in mind. This was the popular Christie MacDonald, who had ventured to reprimand Mary Garden for her views on opera in English. Christie was young and pretty, a more than fair singer, a fetching, winsome girl who could grace a stage even if she lacked the personality to dominate it.

The first association of Victor Herbert with Christie MacDonald seems to have been as early as 1910. In midsummer it was announced that she would appear in a new operetta in the fall, with the music almost certainly by Herbert.[49] This came to naught, and two and a half years passed before she became a Herbert prima donna. In October of 1912 the association was revived, and Herbert, who wanted to be absolutely sure, went to Syracuse, where Christie was appearing in *The Spring Maid*. Satisfied with what he heard, he discussed at length with her the score he was ready to write and promised to finish it by the first of the year.[50]

Herbert conducted the first performance in Baltimore and received a rousing ovation. So did the operetta, which, nevertheless, revealed some perplexing faults. People were bothered not only by the length of the show—practically every stage production has to be cut and trimmed—but by apathetic action and a strange belief that the music was lacking in tunefulness.[51] By the end of the week, a complete overhauling had been accomplished, to such an extent that on Saturday the performance was well-nigh flawless. It was shorter and faster, the action had been quickened, the entire presentation was spirited and delightful. On second hearing, the music also gained greatly; and it seemed to be safe to conclude that another great success was on the way.[52]

After the opening week in Baltimore *Sweethearts* played five weeks in Philadelphia, and then five weeks in Boston, where it could have continued indefinitely. The star, however, insisted on a summer recess, which meant a new series of rehearsals before opening on Broadway. Herbert watched the preparations for New York and found everything so well arranged that he decided not to attend the metropolitan première. "The piece went fine . . . and they don't need me any more." This was his unusual expression in penning his decision to his friend and assistant, Harold Sanford.[53] The heat of summer probably persuaded Herbert to stay out of New York on September 8 (it was before the day of air-conditioned theaters); but the New York first-nighters missed him sorely as they succumbed to the charm of a beautiful score.

The New York program presented the main information dramatically in the following style:

Characters

The story of the opera is founded on the adventures of Princess Jeanne, daughter of King Rene of Naples, who reigned in the fifteenth century. Time has been changed to the present, and the locale to the ancient city of Bruges, to which the little princess is carried for safety in time of war, and is given the name of

Sylvia. . . . . .Christie MacDonald

As an infant she is found in the tulip garden one morning by

Dame Paula. . . . . .Ethel Du Fre Houston

who conducts the Laundry of the White Geese, and who is known as "Mother Goose." Sylvia is brought up as the daughter of Paula, although the latter has six daughters of her own:

Lizette		Nellie McCoy
Clairette		Cecilia Hoffman
Babette	Known as the White Geese	Edith Allen
Jeannette		Gertrude Rudd
Toinette		Gene Peltier
Nanette		Gretchen Hartman

Mikel Mikeloviz. . . . . .Tom McNaughton

who, disguised as a monk, left Sylvia when an infant in Dame Paula's care. Knowing that Sylvia is the Crown

Princess of the little kingdom of Zilania, Mikel is conspiring
to restore her to the throne, which is about to be offered to

Franz, the heir presumptive.................Thomas Conkey

who, in traveling incognito, has fallen in love with Sylvia,
and who finds a rival in

Lieutenant Karl............................Edwin Wilson

a military Lothario, betrothed to Sylvia. Mikel's plans are endangered by the schemes of

Hon. Percy Algernon Slingsby................Lionel Walsh
Petrus Van Tromp.........................Frank Belcher
Aristide Caniche..........................Robert O'Connor

who wish to purchase, for their own purposes, Prince Franz's
estates in Zilania.

Liane, a milliner............................Hazel Kirke

has sought temporary employment in the Laundry of the
White Geese, and is mistaken by Mikel and Slingsby for the
lost Princess.
Other characters introduced are:

Captain Lourent............................Briggs French
First Footman............................Edward Crawford
Second Footman..........................William Wilder
        Laundresses, the Military, Wedding-Guests, Servants

The production was staged by Frederick G. Latham, and the
orchestra was directed by John McGhie.

Act I reveals the Laundry of the White Geese in Bruges; Act II,
the Château of Prinz Franz in Zilania.

The unusually expository list of characters fails to say that Franz
is in danger of losing his throne to Sylvia, who had been removed
years previously, and that Sylvia is reluctant to give her hand and
heart to Franz. Karl's fickle nature helps her reach her decision, which
brings happiness to the lovers and the country they will jointly rule.

A glance at the score of the opera confirms what most people felt
who heard the music. It is one of Herbert's best compositions—fresh
and spontaneous, varied and clever. A few critics, it failed to please;
but they were in the minority, and the majority who praised it did so
extravagantly. From the opening chorus ("Iron! Iron! Iron!"), with its
suggestion of a monotonous chore, to the closing finale, which
exceptionally carried as much action as the first finale, the music
exuded warmth and color, high spirits, romance, and occasionally
serious contemplation.

Sylvia and Franz have each a love song to sing, and neither of these, when first delivered, is a personal declaration. The heroine's song is the immortal "Sweethearts," its waltz refrain rightly among the most famous of Herbert's melodies. Perfectly regular in its rhythm, it covers a surprisingly wide range (a half-step short of two octaves) which is probably responsible for its compelling charm. There is an interesting unknown fact about this melody. Years before, Herbert used a tiny music sketch book which is now in the Library of Congress. It is crammed full of drafts of tunes and harmonizations, some fairly complete, some hardly deserving the name of fragments. It is impossible to guess how long he used it, but on one page is written the date 1896; from the appearance of the book he may have used it some years previously. On another page appears the air which became the waltz refrain of "Sweethearts"; but across the melody are two heavy pencil marks as if the composer were decisively repudiating it. At some time, fortunately, he had a change of mind or heart, turning it into one of America's favorite songs.

Two sharply rhythmical numbers are Sylvia's "Mother Goose" and the famous wooden-shoe dance, "Jeannette and Her Little Wooden Shoes," sung by Liane, Slingsby, Caniche, and Van Tromp. In the former, both verse and refrain capturing the spirit exquisitely, the Princess is led to describe the lovable storybook personage and what she means to children. The latter tells of a little girl who could never walk silently because her shoes were so noisy, and the *Ländler* style of the music makes it irresistible.

The "Angelus" sung by Sylvia, who is later joined by Franz, has a quiet radiance which even the addition of the Prince's love song could not quite dispel. Sylvia prays simply and softly when she hears the tones of the Angelus, and her long phrases of melody, artistically varied, are impressive. The strains of Franz's song admittedly have an incongruous effect, but they creep in so adroitly that the prevailing atmosphere is unchanged.

Between the two acts Herbert provided an "Entr'acte" which was also well received. It was based upon a portion of the opening chorus, the air from "Angelus," and Franz's love theme. The following opening chorus of Act II was as gay as its title ("Waiting for the Bride"), and the next song was as pretty as its title ("Pretty As a Picture"). In one way Herbert seems to have missed his goal in this song, which was supposed to be a comic number. Van Tromp expounds a lady's enslavement to cosmetics in order to become as pretty as a picture, but the refrain of the song is so arch, without being roguish, so graceful, and so lilting, the comical effect is lost. Real roguishness, however, is to be heard in Sylvia's "In the Convent They Never Taught Me

That," which, with choral interjections, shows that the girl suffered no depression behind the cloistered walls. Highly effective, too, was the conversational duet between Sylvia and Franz, "The Cricket on the Hearth," which has a curiously neutral and colorless melody in the middle, but which closes with a refrain as comfortable as the fireplace on which the tiny cricket chirps. One comic piece which did not miss fire was the male quartet, "Pilgrims of Love," sung by Mikel, Van Tromp, Caniche, and Slingsby. The four reprobates pretend to be monks and sing a solemn, pseudo-religious part song which is a masterpiece of musical burlesque.

The finale of Act II was highly unusual because it was more than the ordinary repetition of the main tune to cover the descent of the curtain. The waltz, to be sure, was the last music heard; but before that the whole dramatic denouement was set to recitative, choral ejaculation, and orchestral unrest. As a result there was an excellent climax for which the music alone was responsible.

The New York critics were enthusiastic about the music, pleased by the performers, apathetic about the story. They looked upon the book as the Cinderella legend with a new twist which failed to remove it from the commonplace. The comedians were funny, the "straight men" were satisfactory, and Christie MacDonald had a refined charm and daintiness which cast a spell over the spectators. Her singing was adequate because Herbert had kept the music within her capacity.

It is strange that the critic who liked it least was Herbert's old admirer on the *Evening Post.* He liked much of the music, but felt that it added little to the composer's reputation.

The *Times* reporter certainly left the theater feeling much more satisfied:

. . . it is time to emphasize the fact that Mr. Victor Herbert, as is often his habit, has provided a very well written score in which there are many numbers of excellent quality, several of them graced with those delightful touches of unexpectedness which (if the bull be excused) one has come to expect of him . . .

Mr. Herbert has provided hardly a number in the piece, however, in which the chorus does not participate, and the resultant ensembles, with the association of fresh, well-trained voices, make for spirited climaxes all through.

Another reviewer who vastly enjoyed himself was from the *Tribune.* He hailed the production as "an operetta to rejoice over," writing in more detail:

Victor Herbert has given us one of his best, most melodious and most musicianly works thus far. That he has written it con amore is proved by the delicate care he has bestowed upon his orchestration, which at times rises to the level of grand opera. There is an "Angelus" here . . . that is beautiful, and an orchestral prelude to the second act that is worth listening to in attentive silence.

And then the songs! One charming melody succeeds another in rapid succession. To mention them all would be to print the titles of the whole eighteen numbers of the programme. With the "Angelus" may be mentioned, however, "Sweethearts," "Mother Goose" and "In the Convent They Never Taught Me That," all sung by Miss MacDonald, with chorus—and such a chorus!—and the captivating "Cricket on the Hearth," with its charming change from youth to old age before a glowing fire effect, rendered by the star with Mr. Conkey.

Good as these reviews are, the best was written by a musical journalist signing himself H. F. P.—undoubtedly Herbert F. Peyser. He expressed the usual opinion of the book, thought it neither entertaining nor edifying, suggested additional condensation, and said it fell far short of what a first-class libretto should be. Apparently he feared for the success of *Sweethearts*, for he mentioned how a fine score can be endangered by a mediocre book. To leave no doubt with his readers, he explained the merits of the music:

From first to last this music is utterly free from any of those suggestions of triviality that have now and then crept into portions of certain of Mr. Herbert's other scores. The abundant melodic flow is invariably marked by distinction, individuality and a quality of superlative charm. The scoring, exquisite in its piquancy, finesse and deftness, fairly glows in its varied colors. Only a specialist, however, can appreciate to the fullest the very subtle touches of beauty and humor with which Mr. Herbert's instrumentation is replete. It is scarcely possible to enumerate the "gems" of this work for the mere reason that practically every number could qualify as such. Especially worthy of mention, though, is the ravishingly beautiful "Angelus" duet, striking in its harmonic and orchestral coloring, the splendidly constructed first act finale with Wagnerian suggestions and a quartet of monks—a capital musical burlesque of ecclesiastical effects with bits of strict imitation and plagal cadences.[54]

No one could begrudge Herbert this hard-earned praise; every one hoped *Sweethearts* would be a phenomenal success. This it was not; but it fared passably well and had a run of 136 performances in New York City.[55] After nine weeks at the New Amsterdam Theatre, however, it had to move to the Liberty Theatre to make way for an incoming production. At the latter house it played eight more weeks, then moved on to Washington and the road, where it continued well into the spring.

But there is no doubt that *Sweethearts* became an American treasure, trailing scarcely at all behind *Naughty Marietta* in popular affection. This was affirmed in 1947, when Paula Stone and Michael Sloane effected a special revival in New York at the Shubert Theatre on January 21. It had a surprising run of 288 performances,[56] and the music was as fresh as ever. The star of this production was Bobby Clark, and he convincingly dominated proceedings; but even his magnificent antics and side-splitting cavortings could not obscure the fact that Herbert was the creator of a beautiful, romantic work.

By 1913 America had no better known individual than Victor Herbert. His operetta music was universally loved, and his lighter orchestral pieces (*Badinage, Panamericana,* etc.) were universally popular. His grand opera *Natoma* was also popular at this time and persuaded the populace that he was a serious composer of weight and importance. It was the operettas, of course, that brought him the greatest fame.

There could have been little surprise, therefore, when a summer announcement told the country that New York was going to have a "Victor Herbert Opera House" dedicated to the production of the composer's best works. The real promoter of the project was Frederick G. Latham, who had directed some of the most successful of Herbert's operettas. He claimed as his assets a site on Broadway near the Metropolitan Opera House, a set of plans and a program of bookings, two new Herbert scores (undoubtedly *Sweethearts* and *The Madcap Duchess*), and the support of, as well as $5,000 from, the composer himself.[57] Of course the scheme was without results, and it was probably fortunate for the principals involved that the project never materialized. It is a poor way to champion (or memorialize) an individual and his achievement, for it depends upon national prosperity and is the prey of fluctuations of national taste. The phenomenal position of Gilbert and Sullivan, obviously the prototype of the Herbert proposal, stemmed from the coalescence of words and music which led to a unique manifestation of nationalism (poetry, wit, music, psychology). Herbert never had a chance to parallel Sullivan, for two very good reasons: he had no literary collaborator like Gilbert, and his music had no specific American characteristics.

Herbert's second important production of 1913, *The Madcap Duchess*, a two-act comic opera, had its first performance on any stage at the Lyceum Theatre in Rochester, New York, on October 13, and its New York première at the Globe Theatre on November 11. It was an unusual piece which deserved better treatment than it received, but the reactions to it were as varied as the styles of music Herbert employed.

Like many of Herbert's operettas *The Madcap Duchess* was first reported to the public erroneously, or else the early plans went completely awry. The title announced in the summer was *The Coquette,* with book and lyrics by Harry B. Smith, and with Ann Swinburne as star.[58] Only the last proved to be accurate. Smith did not provide the literary work, and *The Coquette* was not the title, though it might have been suitable. The plot was taken from a novel by the Irish author Justin Huntly McCarthy, who had gained a sizable following for his light, historical romances. (David Stevens assisted in preparing the book and lyrics for the stage.) McCarthy had won his chief fame from the novel, *If I Were King,* which was to be the basis of the popular operetta, *The Vagabond King.*

The novel serving Herbert was also set in France of 1720, when Louis XV was still a boy and the great Watteau was an ornament of the court. Published in the United States in 1908, *Seraphica* received its name from the madcap duchess; but in the musical version she was more euphoniously called Seraphina.

Ann Swinburne was a young and attractive American girl endowed with grace, good sense, and musicality. The previous season she had made a notable success in *The Count of Luxembourg*; the season before that, she had shown great promise in a revival of *Robin Hood.* Herbert evidently had full confidence in her vocal ability, which meant he could use a free hand in writing her songs and ensemble pieces.

The producer was H. H. Frazee, who had every right to be satisfied with the Rochester opening. Herbert was on the conductor's stand and moved the auditors to rapt enthusiasm. Every detail seemed to be excellent; the ensemble work showed exceptional merit; and Ann Swinburne lived up to expectations.

What specially pleased Herbert in Rochester, however, was this judgment: "So long as such operas as 'The Madcap Duchess' are being written and produced we may feel assured that the American stage, as a whole, is not deteriorating, in spite of a few examples to the contrary."[59] Words like these were honey to Herbert; he always felt he was improving, then maintaining the American musical theater—and to a large extent he was, although he did it in a reactionary European way.

The Madcap Duchess visited several intervening cities before New York, where the opening performance was also conducted by Herbert, and the cast was as follows:

Renaud, Prince of St. Pol in Artois . . . . Glenn Hall
Vidame de Bethune } Guardians of Seraphina { Russell Powell
M. de Secherat } { Gilbert Clayton

Master Hardi, manager of the Regent's
    Players.............................Harry Macdonough
Louis XV, King of France..............Master Percy Helton
Philip of Orleans, the Regent...............Francis K. Lieb
Watteau, court painter......................David Andrada
Duc de Pontsable, Marshal of France........Edmund Mulcahy
Canillac, captain of the King's Musketeers......Henry Vincent
Adam, proprietor of the Windmill Inn..........Herbert Ayling
Panache, sergeant of the King's Musketeers....Herman Holland
Stephanie, Marquise de Phalaris..........Josephine Whittell
Gillette, serving maid at the Windmill Inn.......Peggy Wood
Seraphina, Duchess of Bapaume in Artois.......Ann Swinburne

Spavento		Mario Rogati
Tartaglia	of the Regent's Players	Alexander Gibson
Coraline		Virginia Carewe-Carvel
Zerbine		Virginia Allen

	Kathleen Breen
	Billie Williamson
	Glen Ellis
Watteau Shepherdesses and Shepherds	Minna Martrit
	Morris Avery
	J. Elliott
	Sven Erick
	H. B. Foster

Musketeers, Players, Courtiers, etc.

The stage manager was Fred. G. Latham; the musical director, Robert Hood Bowers (succeeding Max Hirschfeld).

The time was the autumn of 1720. Act I revealed the garden of the Windmill Inn, early morning; Act II showed Watteau's theater in the garden of Versailles, evening.

The romantic spectacle[60] tells of Renaud's banishment from Paris because he has incurred the jealousy of Philip over Stephanie, and of Seraphina's determination to avoid a marriage decreed for reasons of state. Meeting accidentally at an inn, Renaud and Seraphina begin their unanticipated courtship. Their youth brings them plenty of trouble and adventure, even to going to Paris in a troupe of strolling players and appearing at the theater of Versailles. Renaud learns of Stephanie's unworthiness, and vows he will wed no one but the little servant girl who bravely followed him to court. This is Seraphina in disguise, of course, and when she discloses her identity the lovers realize that happiness lies ahead.

An excellent summary of the entire production appeared in *Theatre* for December, 1913, with the comment:

"The Madcap Duchess" is more of an opera comique than a comic opera. This is not a distinction without a difference. The French distinction means something of a higher kind than that which a mere translation of the words would convey. If there is a public, therefore, which cares for a romantic love story, placed in a romantic period, with capable singers to interpret an admirable score, then they will find what they want at the Globe Theatre. For the music which runs through "The Madcap Duchess" is, in his lighter vein, Victor Herbert at his best.

This criticism hints at the reason *The Madcap Duchess*, as well as other Herbert operettas, had a relatively short life. It was a complacent love story, no better than many others appearing season after season, without any distinctive spark to attract special favor. Herbert did well by the story, one of the best he ever had; but it was only ordinary, and the humor supplied by comic characters was feeble. The differentiation between opéra comique and comic opera is also rather hard to maintain, at least in this country where there is no tradition for the former as a product of the French theater. In America it is a difference of degree rather than kind, and the complimentary critic doubtless considered *The Madcap Duchess* as a more refined example of comic opera than Broadway was accustomed to view.

But the music was most attractive, ranking near the top of Herbert's compositions. The opening scene of musketeers in the inn, flirting with Gillette, is adroitly done; Renaud's romance, "Aurora Blushing Rosily," is an unusual combination of arioso, recitative, choral interpolations, and violin solos. Seraphina's first song, "Love and I Are Playing," is a whimsical delight which perfectly characterizes the madcap girl on the threshold of her romantic adventure. This is followed by a duo for Seraphina and Renaud, "The Deuce, Young Man," which is dramatic and exciting. Here there is no hint of love, only well turned phrases which further the action and a jubilant conclusion as the boy and the girl decide to go to Paris together. Two excerpts involving the players are clever and amusing. In the first ("That Is Art") Hardi defines the art they practice, with gesture, pantomime, and special musical effects; in the second ("Companions, I Have Summoned You") Seraphina "tries out" for a part in the troupe and sings a mock lament and a mock dramatic scene which joyously returns to "That Is Art" after her histrionic test is over.

A quiet chorus of genuine charm ("Now Is the South-Wind Blowing") opens the second act. Interpolated in it are sung exchanges between Seraphina and Renaud; and Hardi declaims an explanation of the dramatic scene the players give. Soon Renaud sings a love song of great yearning, "Goddess of Mine," which has an unusual degree of dignity. A few weeks after *The Madcap Duchess* opened in New York Herbert substituted a new refrain in this song and changed its title to "Star of Love." This brightened the number noticeably and made it the most popular in the show.

Surely the most curious piece in the opera is a conversational duet ("Far up the Hill") sung by Seraphina and Watteau while shepherds and shepherdesses tread the same measures in a stately dance. The conversation in gavottelike phrases gives way to a strict two-part canon in the octave (eight measures) which in turn yields to eight more measures of part singing, four independent parts over an ostinato bass. So much musical science in such a short piece was probably lost on the audience—as it should be, for skill which obtrudes is not skill at all; but there it stands, delightful in its effect and successfully simulating the period of Louis XV.

There were a few qualifications in the approval bestowed upon *The Madcap Duchess*. Some accused it of being mirthless; some of being old-fashioned. One writer called it "as old-fashioned as a bunch of garden pinks, and as sweet," the last phrase removing any sting of opprobrium. He modified his apathy toward the music by a similar device: "It is obviously the work of an experienced music maker, who knows what his public likes, and gives it to them. Some of it is banal, and some of it is so slightly rehashed from previous offerings that it was no wonder that people all over the house were humming the familiar airs along with the singers. But, on the other hand, there was much of it which, while not especially fresh and inspired, yet was tuneful and musicianly and more than delighted the big audience."[61]

A contrary opinion hailed the music as beautiful, of delicate texture, and the very opposite of banal. It found, too, that the wittiest remark of the entire evening was delivered by Herbert, who had to make his usual speech of thanks after the first act. Apologizing for McCarthy's absence the composer said: "We hoped to have Mr. Justin Huntly McCarthy with us this evening, but he is the only Irishman I know who is happy in London."[62]

The New York *Times* called it "far and away the most pretentious musical offering of many seasons and unquestionably one of the greatest hits in a year when successes are much sought after and much to be desired"; and the dependable *Evening Post* published its usual panegyric:

Under Mr. Herbert's bâton everything went with a swing. He radiates energy like a pound of radium, and how he must have enjoyed composing that music! The score is one of the finest things he has done in years; in the delicacy, richness, and variety of his orchestral coloring and harmonization he has perhaps never done anything quite so good. Much of this refinement is, to be sure, wasted on an ordinary audience at a first hearing, but it makes connoisseurs feel like shouting bravo! bravissimo! And for those to whom the voice alone appeals, there are plenty of pleasing numbers, among them a gem of the first water, the Duchess's entrance air . . . with an enchanting accompaniment. Among the ensemble numbers there are two which one longs to hear again—a Hunting Song . . . and an entrancing madrigal . . . which cannot be too highly commended to singing societies the world over. Victor Herbert is a great, an original, music master, and lovers of light music must deem it a piece of rare good luck that he, like Johann Strauss, chose to devote his genius to their cause.

But in spite of its refinement and delicacy and spirit *The Madcap Duchess* was not a great success. It ran for only 71 performances in New York[63] and made no lasting impression on the road. Perhaps the qualities prized by connoisseurs were its undoing; perhaps its old-fashionedness failed to win the public, which, in matters of entertainment, likes the new and the thrilling. Yet no one can dispute the fact that the score has much choice music that should be made to sound again.

18

A S C A P

AT 575 Madison Avenue and at 110 East 14th Street, New York City, there are two monuments to Victor Herbert. The first is the home of the indispensable group known as ASCAP (American Society of Composers, Authors and Publishers). The second is a bronze plaque in Lüchow's restaurant which ASCAP dedicated on June 27, 1951. The latter reads:

This plaque is erected by
THE AMERICAN SOCIETY OF COMPOSERS,
AUTHORS AND PUBLISHERS
To the memory of the beloved
VICTOR HERBERT
composer, conductor and cellist
born in Dublin, Ireland, February 1, 1859
died in New York City, May 26, 1924

It was here at a dinner at Luchow's restaurant
in February, 1914, that Victor Herbert and
eight associates drafted plans for the
performing rights organization, which became
THE AMERICAN SOCIETY OF COMPOSERS,
AUTHORS AND PUBLISHERS

He served as director and vice president
of the Society from its inception in 1914,
until his death in 1924.

Composer of such beautiful melodies as
"Kiss Me Again," "Ah, Sweet Mystery of Life,"
"Gypsy Love Song," "Sweethearts"
and many others—

Victor Herbert holds a unique position not only in
the hearts of his fellow composers and writers,
but in those of all lovers of good music.

New York City—June 27, 1951

The unveiling of the plaque was the main feature of a festive
banquet which I had the honor of attending and enjoyed to the full.
It was a noisy occasion, and the tributes to Herbert from the speakers'
table were lost in the hubbub and excitement resulting from extraordinary libations and marvelous food. The chief stimulation for the ears
was the singing of "Kiss Me Again" by the seventy-one-year-old Fritzi
Scheff, whose voice, soaring on the amplification system above the
tumult, sounded remarkably fresh. The song vanished into the air,
largely unheard by the happy guests, but the plaque remains, "placed
on the wall above the table at which Victor Herbert dined almost
daily for many years and at which he composed many of his treasured
works. For more than a generation this table has been known as
the Victor Herbert table."[1] In spite of one serious error the plaque
stands as a reminder of one of the most important events in American
musical and sociological history: the establishment of ASCAP through
Herbert's sense of justice and his determination.

In size and scope, and perhaps in operation, ASCAP is far different
from what Herbert visualized. He died at the very moment it was
ready to burgeon, and he could scarcely anticipate the economic power
and cultural influence it could wield a quarter-century after. He might
have foreseen the frequent phases of unpopularity it has gone through,
for its very inception was hostilely opposed; but his own popularity
and sense of humor might have mitigated some of the attacks it sustained and became inured to. Much of the bitterness directed against
it was engendered by unfortunate public relations. In the main
ASCAP was set up to adhere to a righteous principle, the following
of which gave composers an earned revenue they would never have
had if the Society had not come into being. Even more important was,
and is, its impact on the public mind which is now conditioned to the
fact that composers are entitled to remuneration for the pieces they
write—as much remuneration as the traffic will bear, which is no
different from the situation prevailing in every other walk of life. For
this concept, revolutionary in America before ASCAP, Victor Herbert
and a small group of friends were responsible.

ASCAP is a performing rights society, an association formed to see
that its members derive from the public performance of music for
profit all the financial gain to which the law entitles them. The
statute on which it relies is the United States copyright law of 1909,

which clearly guarantees to owners of musical copyrights the exclusive right of public performance for profit. Much of the copyright law is in complicated language, but it would be difficult to find a simpler phrase than this, which promises to the owner of the copyright the exclusive right "to perform the copyrighted work publicly for profit if it be a musical composition." There are no qualifications, only an exception which the law presents as follows:

> . . . nothing in this title [act] shall be so construed as to prevent the performance of religious or secular works such as oratorios, cantatas, masses, or octavo choruses by public schools, church choirs, or vocal societies, rented, borrowed, or obtained from some public library, public school, church choir, school choir, or vocal society, provided the performance is given for charitable or educational purposes and not for profit.

Strictly interpreted, this provides no exception, for even these charitable-religious-educational performances must be wholly devoid of profit.

Also outside the phrase furnishing ASCAP its *raison d'être* is the provision guaranteeing copyright owners exclusive right of public presentation of dramatic works irrespective of the involvement of profit. "Dramatico-musical compositions" (operas, operettas, musical comedies, etc.) in our law are linked together with straight plays for the stage, and the owner's control over their public performance is absolute. But the owner's performing right in a musical composition —from song to symphony—extends only to public performance for profit. His success in benefiting from this right depends upon a universally accepted definition of "public" and "profit," an agreement which is still astonishingly difficult to achieve.

Three categories of persons are intimately concerned with the lawful protection of musical compositions: the composers of the music (who frequently retain the ownership of the copyright); the authors of the words (for the newly written text of a song is a copyrightable component part of a composition); and the publishers, to whom the copyright is usually assigned for exploitation subsequent to issue. All three expect to derive profits from the combination of their skill and resources. It is possible, of course, that a single individual may function in a threefold capacity and produce a work usually coming from a cooperating trio. Nevertheless, the composer, the author, and the publisher have mutual interests in a musical composition and stand to profit by the enforcement of the copyright law.

It has been suggested that the inspiration for ASCAP stemmed from Puccini's visit to America in 1910. The Italian composer came here to attend the world première of *The Girl of the Golden West,* and as he made the rounds of New York with George Maxwell (representative of his publisher, Ricordi) he continually heard his melodies being played in restaurants. Ever a sharp businessman, Puccini asked how much additional income resulted from these renditions. When Maxwell had to admit that they produced no money at all, Puccini criticized the difference between Europe and America. In the old country performance rights had been recognized and remunerated for many years. Maxwell was widely acquainted in New York's music circles and, the legend continues, discussed it with musicians and composers.[2]

There were no immediate results, but a seed was planted, then or soon, which came to fruition after the passage of several years—and this is not legend.

A young and increasingly successful composer from the Midwest, Raymond Hubbell, was interested in securing protection against unauthorized performances of his music, and so were other composers and friends of composers. In 1913 Hubbell and Nathan Burkan and George Maxwell felt the time was ripe to take steps which would insure the protection so badly needed. The task confronting them, however, was no slight one; it was imperative to enlist all possible support and sympathy. Absolutely essential was the aid of Victor Herbert, a tower of strength among American composers and the only one who bridged the gap between the creators of popular and of serious music.

During the summer Hubbell, on the advice of Burkan, went to Philadelphia to win Herbert's support. He was considerably taken aback when he found the Irishman decidedly cool to the scheme for establishing a mutual protective society. Evidently Herbert was not too eager to subscribe to any plan promoted or approved by a typically sedate Englishman like Maxwell. But Hubbell's optimism was finally convincing. They parted, after a two-day conference, in complete agreement, and Hubbell left Willow Grove with these words of Herbert ringing in his ears: "Count on me, my boy! We'll have the best Society in the world and nothing will ever stop us."[3] Herbert kept his word, and nothing did stop them, although amazing and unforeseen obstacles loomed ahead.

No single person can be described as *the* founder of ASCAP—or of any other major organization which changes the status of an entire professional group. Hubbell's own subsequent testimony explains why Herbert bears the title so gracefully:

Through all the ups and downs of turbulent years, of adverse court decisions and victories, of distracting internal desertions . . . there stood Victor, 100 o/o American Society every minute of every day, up to the day he died. . . .

Looking back now . . . I realize how big a part Victor really played in the building up of ASCAP. It never could have been done without him—he just didn't recognize setbacks. The cause which he knew was just became the dominating part of him. He just simply forced it through a cloud because he didn't see or feel the cloud.[3]

Thus neither the Society nor the musical profession exaggerates in recognizing Herbert as the ASCAP founder.

Enthusiastic plans were laid for an organizing meeting, in a private dining room in Lüchow's restaurant. Thirty-six leading composers, authors, and publishers had promised to attend the magnificent dinner ordered by Glen MacDonough, a repast to match the anticipated results. But on this October, 1913, evening it was raining, and the proposed society was unprecedented and ill defined; even the food and the companionship failed to induce the entire company to assemble. Only nine appeared.

The nine faithful founders of ASCAP were: Victor Herbert, Silvio Hein, Louis A. Hirsch, Raymond Hubbell (the sole survivor as this is written), Gustave A. Kerker, Glen MacDonough, George Maxwell, Jay Witmark, and Nathan Burkan, who as attorney was to see ASCAP through so many of its legal conflicts. Raymond Hubbell confirmed to me in personal conversation the dismay and discouragement of the nine deserted by the twenty-seven. They were severely disappointed by this apparent lack of interest, and they seriously considered abandoning the project then and there.

In Hubbell's words, Herbert saved the day:

But Herbert! there it is again—that spirit of his! "Come on. I'm here—let's get started—Glen's ordered a good dinner—with Berncastle Doctor—what more do you want? Come on—let's eat! Nathan—tell us about this society! Let's start it!" etc., etc. Well, we sat and ate and drank Lüchow's grand moselle wine and in no time, the nine of us were giving a grand imitation of a victorious high school football team.[4]

And so the nine founders listened to Burkan and determined to forge ahead regardless of the support or interest their missing colleagues might give. These nine were the founders of ASCAP, and they showed a courage which was more properly rewarded when they took the next step: calling another meeting, on February 13, 1914, but this time the response was different. Bolstered by the influence of the founding nine, their own spirit and enthusiasm now waxing strong, more than a hundred persons came together in the Hotel Claridge to organize ASCAP formally and to declare war on all who profited from illegal performances of their songs and compositions.

What was the real need of ASCAP? Why could not a composer by his own efforts maintain the exclusive right vouchsafed to him in the copyright law? ASCAP itself has supplied the answer, but it is reasonable and worthy of acceptance at face value:

. . . prior to 1914 it was the universal practice throughout the United States on the part of proprietors of places of public resort operated for profit . . . to perform publicly for profit duly copyrighted musical works without the let, leave or license of the composers and authors . . . of such works and the publishers thereof, to the great and irreparable injury, detriment and damage to such writers and publishers . . .

Throughout the length and breadth of the nation, in nearly every hotel, restaurant, motion picture theater, vaudeville theater, cabaret, dance hall and other place of public amusement, the most successful works of American authors were seized and appropriated and publicly performed for the profit of the proprietor of such establishments in violation of the copyrights of the author of such work . . . ; that such legal performances were fugitive, fleeting and momentary and multiplied in every part of the United States, and the illegality of such performances was extremely difficult to establish and prove unless a trustworthy and responsible person located in the vicinage where such illegal performance took place was on hand to witness and hear the same and could notify the infringer of his wrongful act, coupled with a demand that he cease and desist from such further unlawful use of such work; that in order for an individual to protect his lawful rights against infringement by this means, it would have been necessary for him to maintain an inspection service at more than thirty thousand different establishments located in practically every city in the United States, which was wholly impossible . . .

The users were organized into trade associations whose chief objects were to resist the demands of music writers and publishers that their performing rights be recognized and respected, and to defend by the paid counsel of each such association those of their members who might be sued for piracy.

With the development of powerful, rich, and influential trade associations of users of such performing rights, the individual unorganized music writer and publisher was helpless to prevent the piracy of his works and could not obtain just, fair, and reasonable compensation for the public performance of his works by others for profit. . . .

The . . . Society was organized under the necessities of the situation arising out of the new style of entertainment offered to the public. There was introduced a species of entertainment in restaurants, hotels, inns, and other public resorts, which was advertised as an inducement to the public to patronize these places under the names of "cabarets," "tea dansante," "after-theatre revues," "midnight revues," "dinner dancing," "dinner and music" and similar slogans to acquaint the public with the fact that a musical program was the distinctive feature and main attraction of the establishment. While no special admission fee was charged for these entertainments, it was expected that those who patronized them would purchase food and drink. In some establishments "couvert" or other charges were added to the patron's check. The patrons paid for the entertainment by a direct or indirect charge, and the entertainment was given for direct or indirect profit.

The cabaret or revue entertainment consisted of the rendition of music and the singing of songs and dancing to the accompaniment of music. In some of the establishments, the performances were given in make-up and costume, and on a platform or stage. The entertainment was advertised in the daily newspapers . . .

In its most developed form, the cabaret or revue is a regular show, with appropriate intermissions indicated by a suspension of action instead of lowering a curtain.

Cabaret, motion picture and vaudeville shows and revues were presented in nearly every city in the United States, the dominant, distinctive, and principal features of each such entertainment being the vocal and instrumental numbers of the current grand and comic operas, musical plays, as well as standard and popular compositions.

A leading and attractive feature of the larger hotels in the United States was the orchestra and the musical and dance programs.

Dance halls which relied entirely for their operations upon music sprang up like mushrooms . . .[5]

Nathan Burkan thus described the conditions facing composers (chiefly of popular and theatrical music, but in principle of all music) in 1914 America. There was no exaggeration when he declared the impossibility to a single writer of protecting musical property. Should he succeed in licensing one performance, there would be thousands of other performances, perhaps in as many places, beyond his control or even knowledge. Superficially the composers were in much the same position toward the users of their music as they had been a few years earlier toward the manufacturers of records and rolls. When the manufacturers boldly took any music they desired and gave the composers no consideration they had a legal right, which was stopped only by a drastic change in the law. The users of music in food and pleasure resorts, however, were flagrantly defying the law and felt thoroughly at ease in doing so. The law provided no means of enforcement, and the outraged composers could only shout puny and ineffective protests.

Herbert gladly took the lead in the only course: to organize and develop resources (of personnel, money, and opinion) sufficiently strong to hale infringers into court and make them obey existing laws. The organization meeting was completely successful, with enthusiasm high and a determination to make ASCAP "the most powerful organization in the world for the control of the music business."[6] The ex-

pression of such a sentiment, official or unofficial, was a mistake, for
it implied a desire for power rather than justice. George Maxwell,
who was elected president, offered a more reasonable explanation:
"The society has not been formed to make a fight upon any one or
to stir up any trouble. The writers and publishers are given protection
under the copyright laws of the United States, and until now that
protection has never been carefully brought into use. When orchestras
play the music of our members they will have to pay for the right to
do so. That is only fair, and the laws of the country make it possible
for us to see that the collections are made. There is really nothing
new in our plans, except the getting together of the men interested to
protect their rights. The rights have always been there, and now we
are going to enforce them." He also predicted that within the coming
year $1,000,000 would be collected in New York alone.

The other officers were: Victor Herbert, vice president (he refused
the presidency and would never accept it); Glen MacDonough, secretary; John Golden, treasurer; Raymond Hubbell, assistant treasurer.
Herbert, incidentally, was the second member, his payment of dues
being acknowledged on March 6, 1914. Of his compositions, listed on
his application, he named only nine operettas—*The Wizard of the
Nile, The Serenade, The Fortune Teller, The Red Mill, Babes in
Toyland, Mlle. Modiste, The Lady of the Slipper, Sweethearts,* and
The Madcap Duchess—writing after the last, perhaps with a touch
of humor, "etc. etc." His two grand operas and various orchestral works
were likewise included.

ASCAP was organized under its Articles of Association for a term
of ninety-nine years. There were at first four types of membership—
publisher, composer, author, and probationary—with eligibility defined
as follows:

A. Any person, partnership, association or corporation regularly engaged in
   the music publishing business.
B. Every person who is the composer, either alone or in collaboration with
   others, of at least six musical compositions which have been publicly
   performed or published in customary form.
C. Every person who is the author, either alone or in collaboration with
   others, of the text or lyrics of at least six musical works which have
   been publicly performed or published in customary form.
D. Any person who shall have composed or written less than six works
   either alone or in collaboration with others.[7]

Today membership is broader and eligibility is less strict, but the 1950
Articles contain one unintentionally amusing phrase: Composers and

authors may apply "who shall have had not less than one work . . . regularly published."

The purposes of ASCAP were also firmly declared in 1914:

(a) To protect composers, authors and publishers of musical works against piracies of any kind;
(b) To promote reforms in the law respecting literary property;
(c) To procure uniformity and certainty in the law respecting literary property in all countries;
(d) To facilitate the administration of the copyright laws for the protection of composers, authors and publishers of musical works;
(e) To abolish abuses and unfair practices and methods in connection with the reproduction of musical works;
(f) To promote and foster by all lawful means the interests of composers, authors and publishers of musical works;
(g) To grant licenses and collect royalties for the public representation of the works of its members by instrumentalists, singers, mechanical instruments, or any kind of combination of singers, instrumentalists and mechanical instruments, and to allot and distribute such royalties;
(h) To adjust and arbitrate differences and controversies between its members and between its members and others, and to represent its members in controversies, actions and proceedings, involving the right of public performance of any work of any member, or the question of authorship in any work of any member;
(i) To promote friendly intercourse and united action among composers, authors, publishers and producers of musical works;
(j) To acquire, own and sell real and personal property, and to accumulate and maintain a reserve fund to be used in carrying out any of the objects of the Society;
(k) To enter into agreements with other similar associations in foreign countries, providing for the reciprocal protection of the rights of the members of each society;
(l) To do any other acts or things which may be found necessary or convenient in carrying out any of the objects of the Society or in protecting or in furthering its interests or the interests of its members.

By 1950 the only real change in these purposes was the addition, in section (g), of radio broadcasting stations as performers of musical works.

Fundamentally the operations of ASCAP are simple. The members assign to the Society the performing rights in their own works, and the Society in turn licenses the use of such works in return for royalties. The royalties are divided among the Society's members according to a scheme which is a completely confidential internal arrangement. There are always dissatisfied members; but human nature has its limitations, and the small earner invariably feels he receives less than he deserves.

It may be safely assumed that all royalty recipients had the full sympathy of Herbert, whose interest in the welfare of the "boys" was very real. At board meetings he militantly and characteristically demanded that all members receive their just reward. E. C. Mills, a former general manager of ASCAP, has expressed Herbert's attitude very clearly: "It was always Herbert's feeling that these men and women were very inadequately rewarded by the amusement business for their enormous contributions toward making profitable operations possible."[8]

Of more personal interest was an early revelation of Herbert's monetary desires respecting ASCAP. It was essential to work out a method whereby each composer would receive a just recompense—the composers and authors had to be "classified" so that they would get a fair share of the profit from public performance. The prevailing method was based on popularity of works and frequency of performance, but Herbert was opposed to it from the start. He wanted no discrimination, and thought the members should share and share alike in the Society's receipts. He was vociferous about this and repeatedly said: "We're all writers—one's as good as another—Put the money all in one pot and divide it up, every three months, equally—I don't want any more than any other member!"[9]

He also felt that ASCAP had as much to offer to the serious composer as to the composer of popular songs, and he unhesitatingly bewildered his colleagues in pleading the cause of a creator of symphony or opera.

"He's a damn fine musician," Herbert would say and his growls were stentorian as he saw the classical writer go to Class C while the writer of "Mama's Got Red Hair" would perch up in Class A. The usually untalkative MacDonough, who was strong in his likes and dislikes, turned to Gus Kerker during one of Herbert's pleas for a "high brow," and remarked, "that guy's past reminds me of a trip through Greenwood Cemetery!" (Meaning Herbert's candidate)

He was advancing an impossibly ideal concept which was wholly impracticable, but it showed his loyalty to music and was typical of his generosity.

People, especially in the musical profession, watched the beginnings of ASCAP with keen interest. Such a development was almost without precedent in the United States, and its effectiveness was debatable. Maxwell was asked for additional statements of hopes and expectations, and there were plenty of voluntary evaluations of the new society's chances of success.

ASCAP had taken as its model the French Société des Auteurs, Compositeurs et Editeurs de Musique, which had opened a New York office on or about January 1, 1911, and had invited American composers to use it as a collecting agency.[10] This effort was fruitless, perhaps fortunately: there was something incongruous in action by a French society to uphold an American copyright law. But if it was ASCAP's admitted model the public wondered how ASCAP would be more successful.

A typical editorial, about as neutral as possible, appeared February 21, 1914, in *Musical America*:

The course of the American Society of Authors, Composers and Publishers, organized in New York last week will be watched with interest. The Society has the same object as similar societies in Europe, which is the collecting of royalties from the artists for public performances of music. At least one of the European societies organized for this purpose has attempted to extend its work into America on the plane of the higher class of music, but without success, for the range of musical appreciation in America is so broad that artists have no difficulty whatever in making up satisfactory programs from among works beyond the society's control. French singers in Paris must sing French songs, including modern ones, and cannot well contrive to escape the tax levied by the society.

In regard to music on the highest plane, we have in America scarcely arrived at a point of public recognition which would make it possible to carry out very fully the purpose for which this new Society is organized. It is significant, therefore, to note that the founders of the new Society are the leaders in those fields of American music which have achieved an absolute and unequivocal success, and for which there is no possible substitute in the popular favor. That is to say, it is the field of light opera and the music of the vaudeville theater, popular music in general, and the music having the widest circulation through the phonograph, that is chiefly represented, although, according to accounts of the organization, operatic and chamber music also find a place within it. Although the foundation for the Society seems to have been well laid and extensive preparations appear to have been made for its organization, it is certain that neither news nor rumors of the formation of the new Society have been generally current among the American composers of more serious music.

In proportion as American music of the higher class prevails it will probably become necessary to extend the work of the Society into that field, but this can scarcely be expected until the makers of programs can absolutely not dispense with the performance of such American works. And, in fact, we are already at the threshold of such a condition. As to the desirability of such an organization it is certain that the way of the musician in the world is more difficult than that of many persons in more distinctly commercial fields of endeavor, and he should be allowed to reap what reward he normally can from the performance of his work.

It is strange that an officer of the Society should state, at least as reported in the papers, that "writers and publishers are given protection under the copyright laws of the United States." As a matter of fact they are not "given protection." The United States, for a fee, merely allows them to register their publications in Washington, so that they may have proof of such publication and the date of it, should occasion arrive on the author's part to prove the facts.

The final paragraph was somewhat limited. The editor should also have said that the copyright law guarantees to anyone complying with the provisions of the law (which includes publication with notice of copyright) certain exclusive rights. One of them, for music, is public performance for profit. Maxwell was on fairly sound ground as he explained how the law protected the Society's composers and publishers—or any other composers and publishers, for that matter.

The editorial was sensible and prophetic in its mention of serious and popular music. For the former there was little commercial market in 1914; for the latter there was great and insistent demand. ASCAP has owed its success to popular music, without which it might expire overnight; but it recognized serious music from the very beginning, and its first articles of association, in determining apportionment of royalties, specifically acknowledged overtures, concertos, symphonic poems, symphonies, sonatas, and instrumental trios, quartets, quintets, sextets, etc. Today ASCAP is in a position to exact payment for the modern serious composer who stands to gain some remuneration he should have had long since. And Herbert fought for the serious composer from the start.

The passing reference in the editorial to French singers was important, for it implied that the performer himself would have to pay the "tax" when ASCAP called for the money. That impression was a general one. Consequently President Maxwell had to state firmly that the Society sought only to collect from the proprietors of the music-using establishments. "We shall not burden the musician," he said; "we will make arrangements with the owners of the hotels to pay so much a month for the privilege of playing various publications and will require them to furnish us with programs of the music played daily, so that we can check matters up and give composer, author and publisher his fee.[11] Nevertheless, more assurance than this was necessary before the performing musicians' fear of assessment subsided.

The first annual dinner of ASCAP was held at Lüchow's on November 29, 1914. With Herbert presiding, both the prominent and the not-so-prominent talked about the large royalties which they hoped to receive, but which had not yet arrived. Obviously the beginning was slow. George Maxwell announced that eighty-five hotels had acceded to ASCAP's demands and were paying an average of $8.23 a month. On an annual basis this was less than $10,000 a year, a far cry from the happy estimates at ASCAP's birth. He remained optimistic, however, prophesying that within a few years one hundred thousand users of music would be paying nearly $10,000,000 annually. Even if half of this treasure were spent for operating expenses, there would be nearly $5,000,000 for division among the members.[12] It is not recorded whether any members shuddered over the prospect of 50 per cent of income being needed for operating expenses, but probably some did. Thirty years after its inception ASCAP boasted that its total overhead amounted to less than 20 per cent of its gross receipts, which some members felt was too much; and at the same time ASCAP divided among its members $6,060,668.02 collected from American performing rights, a sum that was substantial, but considerably under Maxwell's halcyon total.[13]

An amusing sidelight on the first annual dinner is furnished by the music for the entertainment. Flute, violin, and harp formed the combination, and the musicians were instructed to play nothing in which performing rights still subsisted. When they began the effervescent *Funiculi Funicula,* Herbert stopped them at once. He told the leader of the tiny orchestra to go back to *The Blue Danube,* for the Italian song was much too recent for this occasion!

The growth of ASCAP was much slower than desired. One reason was the difficulty of establishing its identity and purpose; another was the fear of performing musicians that proprietors of music-using resorts would pass along to them the cost of playing copyrighted music. Related to this was the uncertainty of what new music they could buy and safely play. Herbert was called upon to write an open letter to the musical profession, which appeared in the December, 1914, *Metronome.* It turned out to be a rather elaborate essay containing some remarkable disclosures, these being the complete accord with the musicians' union and the leisurely pace at which ASCAP (surely unwillingly) intended to spread beyond New York City:

New York, Nov. 12th, 1914

To My Brother Musicians:—

In view of the campaign of misrepresentation that has been waged by certain hostile interests against the American Society of Composers, Authors and Publishers, of which I am the vice-president, I feel it my duty to place before you the true facts concerning the movement of the American Society.

This Society was organized last year out of sheer necessity because of the great reduction in the earnings of the musical authors and composers of this country since the advent of the cabaret in restaurants and the introduction of public dancing in the hotels, restaurants and public resorts.

The sale of sheet music has substantially decreased in recent years because the public instead of finding recreation in the private musicale at home spend their evenings in the cabarets and in the dance rooms of the hotels. For the same reason the runs of musical plays in the cities have in great measure been reduced.

It became necessary for the composers and musical authors to protect themselves against the loss of revenue caused by these conditions, and that could only be done by organization. A society was organized on a basis similar to the French Society known as "Société des Auteurs, Compositeurs, et Editeurs de Musique," which was organized in 1851 and is the most influential society of the kind in Europe. Similar societies have been organized in Italy, Germany, Austria and England. These societies collect license fees from hotels, restaurants and cabarets for the privilege of playing the copyrighted music of their members.

The American Society of Composers, Authors and Publishers has a membership of over two hundred, and is also affiliated with the Austrian, Italian and English Societies, so that any establishment procuring a license from this Society may play not only the music of the members of this Society, but also of the members of the English, Italian and Austrian Societies. Negotiations are now pending to make a similar arrangement with the German Society.

The license fees exacted by our Society are $5.00, $10.00 and $15.00 per month (17, 25 and 50 cents a day), the amount depending on the location, business and advantages of each establishment. This fee covers the entire building from roof to cellar and all orchestras and musicians employed in each establishment.

The constitution of our Society provides that this fee shall be collected *only* from the proprietors and managers of the establishments, *and not from the musicians or leaders of the orchestras playing in those places.*

Our Society absolutely refuses to receive any fee from any musician or leader or make any license agreement with any musician or leader.

We have strictly lived up to this principle. Whenever leaders have offered to pay the fee themselves and have the license agreement made with them, we have refused to do so.

We have never brought any suit against any musician or leader.

It is the intention of our Society *to prevent the proprietors and managers of these establishments from shifting the license fee to the musicians or leaders by corresponding reductions of salaries.* In order to enforce this rule licenses will be refused to those proprietors and managers who attempt to make the musicians or leaders pay the license fee.

The license fee asked by this Society is small, being only 17 cents a day in the case of the $5.00 license, and only 50 cents a day in the case of the $15.00 license, the highest amount charged in any case.

Managers and proprietors cannot complain because they are asked to pay so small a compensation for the privilege to use the best copyrighted works of American and European composers and authors.

The fairness of such a charge is recognized all over Europe and it is universally accepted and complied with as a just demand.

In New York City the justice of our demand is gradually being recognized by the proprietors. We have thus far in New York City issued fifty-eight licenses to various places, among which are some of the leading establishments.

Our Society was determined from the beginning to maintain friendly relations with the musicians. Many of our members are members of the American Federation of Musicians and they certainly would not be parties to any movement which would threaten to injure or interfere with the interests of the musicians.

At a conference held by our Board with representatives of the American Federation, namely, Mr. Weber, the former president, Mr. Carruthers, the president, and Mr. Maloney, the counsel of the Federation, we pledged our friendship to the American Federation. We assured them that our movement *did not contemplate the molesting or interfering to the slightest extent with any member of the Union or any other musician,* and that our campaign was directed toward the proprietors of these establishments who were using our works for the purpose of attracting patrons for their own profit; that we would not directly or indirectly collect any fees from any leader or musician nor prosecute any leader or musician for using our works, but limit our proceedings to the prosecution of the owner of the establishment.

For the present our operations are limited strictly to New York City and we have not taken any steps against the use of our music outside of New York. *We have pledged ourselves to the Federation to give it sixty days' notice before extending our activity to any place outside of New York City.*

I feel that this Society will accomplish a great deal of good in placing the composer on an independent footing and will encourage the writing of good music, and I feel that the musician and orchestra leader will in the end be benefited, and will cooperate with us in every way.

Fraternally yours,

Victor Herbert

In the next issue of *Metronome* Herbert's letter won approbation from the editor, who pointed out that ASCAP would not function outside of New York for some time to come, and therefore "musicians in all parts of the country need have no hesitancy in buying and playing compositions by members until further notice." However, the playing musicians were slow to be comforted by this assurance. More than a year later no less a person than Meyer Davis tried to rally them to defeat legislation which would make payments to ASCAP mandatory. He shortsightedly felt that the players themselves would be compelled to pay the tribute, and that "thousands upon thousands of musicians will be thrown out of employment." He cried, moreover, that "mechanical instruments will be employed in greater number because they contain fewer selections and consequently a smaller royalty would be charged for their use."[14]

These fears were groundless and proved to be no obstacle to the growth of ASCAP. A different danger was rearing its head, and before it was subdued ASCAP had some very black moments. Herbert again led the way to ultimate victory, clearing the path to a brilliant future. In so doing he was responsible for one of the most important and trenchant decisions ever to emanate from the United States Supreme Court.

In the summer of 1914 a case of great moment to ASCAP was heard in the United States District Court for the Southern District of New York. The John Church Company, publisher of John Philip Sousa's music, brought an action against the Hilliard Hotel Company which was operating the Vanderbilt Hotel. In the dining room of the Vanderbilt the orchestra had played Sousa's march, *From Maine to Oregon,* for the pleasure of the diners. Permission to play it had not been obtained, and the publisher claimed it was an unauthorized performance for profit. Judge Lacombe agreed and decided in favor of Church and Sousa; his opinion stated: "The place was public, although all the public could not gather in it, and I think . . . that the hotel would not have paid for the playing of the piece unless in some way or other they were to gain thereby."[15] This decision was eminently to ASCAP's liking.

But the case was appealed to the Circuit Court of Appeals, Second Circuit, where on February 9, 1915, Judge Ward ruled in favor of the hotel. He let his imagination play rather free as he reversed the lower Court:

It does not make a performance any less gratuitous to an audience because some one pays the musicians for rendering it, or because it was a means of attracting custom, or was a part of the operation of the hotel. There is more in . . . that persons could not go into the saloon without buying something to eat. Still such persons primarily go into the saloon for refreshment and pay for what they order, and not for the music. We are not convinced . . . that the defendants played "From Maine to Oregon" for profit within the meaning of those words in our copyright act. If the complainant's construction of it is right, then a church in which a copyrighted anthem is played is liable, together with the organist and every member of the choir, not only to injunction, but in damages in the sum of $10 for each performance [allowed by statute], and the individuals perhaps to fine and imprisonment in addition, because there is an expectation that the congregation will be increased by making the service more attractive.[16]

This seemed like a tragic blow against ASCAP. The satisfaction of the first decision was completely nullified, and the second decision, appealed no further, carried with it the finality of doom. If performances of music in hotels were not deemed to be for profit, then the very foundations of ASCAP were destroyed and its future was definitely wiped out. ASCAP admitted as much, and Nathan Burkan conceded a complete cessation of activities after Judge Ward's fateful decision.[17]

The users of the music were naturally happy, but they reckoned without Herbert and the legal skill of his friend Burkan. The prevailing circumstances and the blow sustained by all composers when the Hilliard Hotel Company bested John Church made more imperative than ever a society protecting the valuable performing rights in music. Herbert and his friends prepared a new case, emphasized a new aspect of the problem, and after a pair of dramatic reverses carried it through to complete victory. Had it ended otherwise ASCAP would not have survived.

It is important to remember that the famous case of *Herbert* v. *Shanley* involved far more than the vindication of a single composer's rights, which were, to be sure, of paramount importance; it established principles for the benefit of all composers and gave life to the association they themselves had brought into being. ASCAP as such did not figure in the case, but years later Burkan testified that the members helped defray the cost of litigation. He asserted that the successful conclusion could not have been attained by Herbert alone.[18]

Shanley's was a well known restaurant on Broadway between Forty-third and Forty-fourth streets, furnishing music to its patrons during certain parts of the day. Here in 1913, according to legend, Herbert entered and heard his "Sweethearts" performed, whereupon he became angry and brought suit against the infringing proprietor. Nothing could be further from the truth. Shanley's was but one of many restaurants illegally providing music for diners, and Herbert's assault upon it was carefully planned and executed. His case depended on no accidental hearing.

Herbert charged that "Sweethearts" was heard at Shanley's, in an unauthorized performance, on April 1, 1915. In the formal bill of complaint he never said that he had heard the piece played there. This significant testimony came from one John Leffler, a theater manager, who swore to an affidavit that he was the person hearing and recognizing the piece. Herbert was not alone in the suit; with him as complainants were the three authors of the operetta (Harry B. Smith, Robert B. Smith, Fred de Gresac Maurel) and the publisher, G. Schirmer. But there was never any doubt that Herbert was the aggressor, or that to him was due the credit of championing a seemingly lost cause.

A word of explanation is necessary to clarify Herbert's chief hope of victory. He maintained, of course, that his was the right to control the public performance of his music for profit, but since the Church-Hilliard case had established a public dining-room performance as not for profit, he had to find a different point of attack. This was discovered under another clause of the copyright law, which declares that a copyright owner has the exclusive right (regardless of profit) of public performance of a dramatic work. An operetta is a dramatic work, and if a whole work is protected, then any part of it must be equally protected. Because *Sweethearts* was a dramatic production, for the stage, the Shanley performance of the waltz-song "Sweethearts" (an integral part of the whole) was illegal and was an infringement of the owner's rights. This contention was featured in the plaintiffs' bill—and to their dismay it backfired on them; but by the time the case was permanently settled it had become a matter of no importance!

Burkan drew up an elaborate bill of complaint for his clients, the "orators" to the Court. Among many prosaic items it included the following:

XIV. Upon information and belief that the defendant [Shanley] on the 1st day of April, 1915, and at other times subsequent thereto, without the knowledge, consent, permission or approval of your orators, and against the will of your orators and in infringement of the said copyright in the said dramatico-musical composition "Sweethearts" and of the said copyright in the said vocal score of said composition, and in violation of the right of your orators in the said dramatico-musical work produced, performed and represented publicly in the defendant's restaurant and place of public entertainment on said premises known as "Shanley's," Broadway 43rd and 44th Streets, New York City, the said vocal number "Sweethearts" and caused the said number to be played and performed by professional singers upon a stage maintained by the defendant in the dining hall of said premises accompanied by an orchestra. That the said vocalists and orchestra were engaged by the defendant to perform and play upon said premises for compensation; that the said performances of the said vocal number on the said premises were public and were not given for a charitable, religious or educational purpose, but were given for the purpose of the defendant's business and as part of the service rendered to the patrons of the defendant's said establishment who purchased and partook of meals or refreshments at said establishment, and said performances were given as one of the special features of the said business.

XV. That the defendant advertised the business conducted on said premises in the New York Review, the New York Times and other papers published and circulated in the City of New York, in the manner following, to wit:

Shanley's
Broadway—43rd to 44th St.
Perfection in Food and Service,
Inimitable Entertainment
Cabaret Extraordinaire
Twenty Acts Every Evening   7 to 1

Superior Seven-Course Luncheon, 75c (Music)

Famous

for

Dinners

and

Suppers

XVI. On information and belief: That the said performance of said vocal number of said opera by the orchestra and the professional vocalists employed by the defendant were given by the defendant for the entertainment and amusement of the patrons patronizing said establishment, and purchasing food for refreshments of the defendant, and for the purpose of attracting patrons to said establishment, and in order to make the business of the defendant possible.

XVII. On information and belief: That the said performances of said vocal number of said opera were part of a theatrical entertainment given by the defendant upon said premises in order to attract patrons to its said establishment and for the entertainment and amusement of its patrons gives a theatrical entertainment which consists of a series of theatrical exhibitions, the performers of which acts or exhibitions are under the pay of the defendant, and the weekly cost of the entertainment offered to the public during each week is upwards of One thousand ($1,000.00) Dollars. That the defendant did and does advertise the said theatrical entertainment as an inducement to patrons to dine and partake of refreshments in defendant's restaurant.

XVIII. That the said wrongful public performances and representations by the defendant of said vocal number "Sweethearts" have attracted and are attracting many persons to the defendant's place of business to hear the said vocal number, and the defendant threatens to continue the unlawful and wrongful performances of the said numbers.

XIX. That the acts of the defendant are causing great injury and damage to the business and profits of your orators, because they are thereby deprived of the exclusive right to publicly perform and represent the said dramatico-musical composition "Sweethearts" and to grant to others the privilege to publicly perform and represent the said composition on the payment of royalties. That no proprietor, lessee or manager of any place of entertainment or amusement will make a contract with your orators for the privilege to publicly perform the said musical comedy in public upon the payment of a license fee or royalty, if the defendant is permitted to continue the unlawful acts hereinabove set forth, and it will further seriously injure your orators in the profits to be derived from the public performances of the said opera and will further diminish the value of said opera and that the injury cannot be accurately ascertained or computed, and that your orators, by reason of the aforesaid unlawful use of their property, are irreparably injured, all of which acts are contrary to equity and good conscience, and tend to the injury and wrong of your orators.

And your orators further show that they have no adequate and available remedy at law against the said continued violation of their rights, inasmuch as the injury is a continuous one and involves endless litigation and further-more, is of such a nature that the extent of your orators' loss could not be measured or estimated or proved to the full measure thereof produced.

Thus the orators prayed the Court to demand an answer from the defendant and to make him cease and desist in his nefarious practice. Several important affidavits were also submitted by the Herbert forces. The most significant was John Leffler's, which exactly identified the infringing performance of "Sweethearts" in Shanley's restaurant. Another came from Samuel W. Tannenbaum, now one of the nation's leading copyright attorneys but then a young lawyer in Nathan Burkan's employ. Tannenbaum swore that he clipped a typical Shanley advertisement from the New York *Times* of April 8.

Still another came from Herbert himself, a most interesting state-ment in which the composer foresaw loss of artistic as well as economic control of his music. Herbert's affidavit asserted:

I am a composer of a number of copyrighted operas and the value of my copyrights depends largely on my exclusive right to control the public presen-tation of the works copyrighted.

The methods resorted to by the defendant of attracting patronage to its establishment, by giving performances of copyrighted works, have been widely adopted by other proprietors of hotels, restaurants and places of public accommodation.

Appended hereto are advertisements [more than a score] appearing in the daily press showing that regular theatrical performances are being given nightly in hotels, restaurants and places of public accommodation, although no direct pecuniary charge or fee is made, in order to attract patronage.

The legalizing of the practice complained of will cause a diminution of the attendance at licensed performances of the complainants' opera "Sweet-hearts" and will deprive us of the power to prevent the inferior rendition of our works and the injury to the artistic reputation of the works that would result from such inferior rendition.[19]

On April 14, 1915, Shanley's received a notice to appear in court. On April 22 it submitted an answer to the bill of complaint. This interesting document readily admitted the performance of Herbert's song, but denied that it was performed as a dramatic work or any part thereof. The performance, said the defendant, was merely an activity incidental to the restaurant business; it was not for profit, and no extra charge was imposed on the patrons who heard it.

More interesting than the formal answer was an affidavit sworn to by John J. Moran, secretary and general manager of the Shanley Company, for it accurately reflected the custom and practice of leading restaurants of the period:

The defendant conducts a hotel and restaurant known as "Shanley's" on Broadway between 43rd and 44th Streets, in the Borough of Manhattan, City of New York. The restaurant is on the ground floor and is used as any high class restaurant in the city is used, to wit, for the purpose of serving food and drink to patrons who pay the price therefor. No charge is made for admission to said restaurant or for the privilege of listening to any performance of music therein, and the only remuneration received by the defendant from any of the patrons who enter said restaurant is from the sale of food and drink that is ordered by said patrons. There is no rule requiring the patrons to order or pay for a minimum amount of food or drink. A person who only desires a sandwich has as much right to enter said restaurant and receives as much attention from the management thereof as a person who desires to order an elaborate meal.

In the said restaurant is erected a platform on which platform an orchestra is seated at certain hours of the day during which a musical program is given for the benefit of the patrons of the restaurant. This platform is not a stage. It has none of the appurtenances that are necessary parts of a stage, that is to say, it has no foot lights, side lights, border lights, scenery, wings, curtain or flies. No theatrical performance is given in the premises. None of the singers who appear ever appear in any costume other than the ordinary conventional evening dress costume. None of the songs that are sung are ever sung in character. Shanley's restaurant serves about twenty-five hundred (2500) people each day. The musical entertainment is, however, only given during limited hours. At the lunch period, to wit, from about noontime to 2 P.M. the orchestra plays. From six o'clock until closing time at about 1:30 A.M. the orchestra plays, and at intervals during that time singers appear who sing various selections of a diversified character. Some of the songs are popular melodies, some are selections from the operas, and some are musical compositions of a little bit higher musical quality than the popular songs and yet not part of a musical composition as important as an opera.

The musical entertainment that is given in "Shanley's" is what is popularly known as a cabaret. The word "cabaret" has a significance purely local in character and is to be distinguished entirely from what is known as a "cabaret" in Paris. In Paris the word "cabaret" was intended to mean a volunteer performance given by patrons of a restaurant or cafe, while in New York the word "cabaret" has been extended to include every form of musical entertainment that may be given in a restaurant. The form of musical entertainment now given in Shanley's restaurant is the same kind of entertainment that has been given in restaurants for many years past. The character of the entertainment now given is somewhat more elaborate than was given in restaurants fifteen or twenty years ago, but in substance it is the same. The music, however, was never the principal business of a restaurant keeper. It has always been and now is purely incidental to the restaurant business, and the price charged for food and service is the same without as with the music.

. . . ["Sweethearts"] was sung on those [mentioned] occasions by a young lady who was not an actress; who had never been employed in a theatrical production; who never appeared on the stage; and who is not what is known as an actress. At the time she sang this song she did not sing it as a part of the dramatico-musical composition known as "Sweethearts." The song "Sweethearts" as sung by her is published as a separate musical composition by G. Schirmer, Inc., in the form ordinarily known as sheet music form, and the song as so published is a complete musical composition in itself. . . . The said song . . . was sung in the defendant's restaurants for the purpose of the entertainment of the guests then dining in said restaurant. No admission was charged to any of such guests to hear the said song or any other music in said dining room. . . .

The advertisement attached to the affidavits [of the plaintiffs] stating that a cabaret consisting of twenty acts is given, does not indicate, nor was it intended to indicate, that a theatrical performance is given in the restaurant. Each singer is known as an act and instead of stating that twenty singers are employed in the restaurant, it is stated that twenty acts are given there.[19]

The lines of the dispute were clearly drawn. Herbert wanted to stop the unauthorized performance of his music. He knew it should bring him some profit, but he also knew the formidable precedent set by the Church-Hilliard case. Therefore he relied upon the fact that the performed song was part of a dramatic work over which he was entitled to practically complete control. Shanley, on the other hand, insisted there was not the slightest dramatic inference in the manner of performance of the song, and that no motives of profit could be deduced from the presentation.

The Court, in the person of Judge Learned Hand, reached a decision promptly. On May 1, 1915, he decided against Herbert, and in so doing astonished the complainants by his reasoning. He cited Church-Hilliard as a now accepted authority for establishing the principle that music in a restaurant like Shanley's was not performed for profit. He agreed with the plaintiffs that the performance of an operetta excerpt was a performance of a dramatico-musical nature, even though only the words and the music were heard. These two elements were sufficient to constitute an infringement. But he also decided that, because the song, "Sweethearts," was published as a separate piece and copyrighted as such (i.e., as a musical composition and not as a dramatico-musical composition), the owners had lost the dramatic rights they once had in it. He even criticized the plaintiffs for trying to secure a double protection to which, in his opinion, they were not entitled. "There can be no justice," said Judge Hand, "in preserving their dramatic rights at the expense of the public's rights arising from taking out a musical copyright. Had they wished to retain a complete dramatic monopoly, they had it in their power to do so."[20] Because the plaintiffs had abandoned their dramatic control of the song, and because the Church-Hilliard precedent precluded the profit question, there was no infringement in the performances cited. Because of the unfortunate copyright claimed in the excerpt as a musical composition, "singing the words to the music, accompanied by the orchestra, is therefore within the musical rights so dedicated" or abandoned or lost to the public. The Judge admonished the plaintiffs by saying they were "really trying to eat their cake and have it" and reproved them for wanting full benefits while yielding the public none. Consequently the motion for an injunction against Shanley was firmly denied.

Herbert immediately appealed this decision, and the case was taken to the Circuit Court of Appeals which had ruled for Hilliard against John Church. Here Judge Rogers decided against Herbert on January 11, 1916. In upholding Learned Hand's decision he agreed that the dramatico-musical rights in the separate song, "Sweethearts," had been lost because—this was important— the sheet-music version (a republication from the complete score) failed to state "that the comic opera from which the song was taken was itself copyrighted."[21] This led to the same conclusion Judge Hand had reached; but it was a technicality somewhat outside the spirit of the case. Because there was no such statement, continued Judge Rogers, the complainants could find no benefit in the earlier copyright for the whole opera. With an exasperating disregard of what might have happened otherwise, the Judge went on: "Whether, if they had inserted a notice of the previous copyright, they would have retained the advantages of it as to the republished song, we need not now consider."

Naturally the profit aspect received little attention in the Court, which had favored the Hilliard Hotel Company; but the Court's attitude was reiterated in Judge Rogers' two conclusions:

(1) That complainants can not claim the benefit of the copyright of the dramatico-musical composition for that portion of the composition which they republished separately and without notice of the copyright previously obtained.

(2) That the copyright of the song "Sweethearts" as a separate musical composition, even if valid, is not infringed by its being rendered in a public restaurant where no admission fee is charged, although the performer is privately paid for rendering it by the proprietor of the resort.

With these words the Court of Appeals affirmed Judge Hand's decree. The composers along Broadway and the members of ASCAP saw no hope after such a disastrous decision. "The recent decision of the United States Court of Appeals in the case of Victor Herbert against the Shanley Restaurant Company ended the campaign of the authors and composers to collect royalties from restaurants as far as the courts are concerned, with a complete defeat of the authors."[22] Such was the interpretation of the musical press, and few could be found to argue differently. ASCAP was even urged to initiate changes in the copyright law, this being the only course seemingly left open if composers were to benefit at all from public performances of their music. As a matter of fact, ASCAP started to move in this direction, but the objective happily proved unnecessary.

Herbert appealed once more, this time to the United States Supreme Court, and Justice Oliver Wendell Holmes achieved a musical immortality by reversing the two lower courts and deciding in Herbert's favor. Burkan prepared an elaborate brief and attained a rare degree of eloquence in approaching the highest court in the land. Holmes's decision was as succinct and short as the opposing presentations were long and involved. It was also sardonic, scornful, and sparkling with a wit which pierced the pretensions of restaurant keepers who claimed to provide free entertainment for their patrons. Judge Lacombe, who originally favored Church years earlier should not be forgotten; Holmes completely vindicated this neglected jurist.

The Supreme Court adjudged Herbert victorious on January 22, 1917. Holmes's classic decision plunged to the heart of the matter, which was the profit element in public performance. With scant courtesy he brushed aside the secondary thoughts of Judges Hand and Rogers and concentrated on essentials. Herbert in coming to the Supreme Court, and the Court in deciding, permanently changed the fate of every composer in America.

The Supreme Court's ruling also embraced the Church-Hilliard case which had come to the high tribunal in the wake of Herbert's determination. In both cases the composer was upheld as Justice Holmes declared:

. . . The plaintiffs were the composers and owners of a comic opera entitled "Sweethearts," containing a song of the same title as a leading feature in the performance. There is a copyright for the opera and also one for the song, which is published and sold separately. This the Shanley Company caused to be sung by professional singers upon a stage in its restaurant on Broadway, accompanied by an orchestra. The district court, after holding that by the separate publication the plaintiffs' rights were limited to those conferred by the separate copyright, a matter that it will not be necessary to discuss, followed the decision in [*Church* v. *Hilliard*] as to public performance for profit. . . .
If the rights under the copyright are infringed only by a performance where money is taken in at the door, they are very imperfectly protected. Performances not different in kind from those of the defendants could be given that might compete with and even destroy the success of the monopoly

that the law intends the plaintiffs to have. It is enough to say that there is no need to construe the statute so narrowly. The defendants' performances are not eleemosynary. They are part of a total for which the public pays, and the fact that the price of the whole is attributed to a particular item which those present are expected to order is not important. It is true that the music is not the sole object, but neither is the food, which probably could be got cheaper elsewhere. The object is a repast in surroundings that to people having limited powers of conversation or disliking the rival noise give a luxurious pleasure not to be had from eating a silent meal. If music did not pay, it would be given up. If it pays, it pays out of the public's pocket. Whether it pays or not, the purpose of employing it is profit, and that is enough.

Decree reversed.[23]

The composers were jubilant, and they had a right to be. With Herbert at their head they had snatched victory from seemingly total defeat, and ASCAP at last found itself in a bargaining position which was unassailable. Their opponents recognized this and lost no time in making adjustments. Acknowledging the Supreme Court's ruling, the New York City Hotel Men's Association set the pattern for the future by promptly coming to terms with ASCAP. No difficulties were encountered as the two sides deliberated on the amounts to be paid for the performance of copyrighted works. ASCAP, indeed, accepted the rates which the hotel men proposed.[24]

ASCAP's troubles were not over simply because of Herbert's hard-won triumph. By its own admission it existed for seven years before it could pay royalties to its members.[25] Then radio appeared on the scene, followed by talking pictures and television, and a mass market for copyrighted music developed which guaranteed to the Society's members a constantly increasing annual revenue. Neither did the Herbert case put an end to ASCAP's legal struggles. The world of commerce, reluctant to pay cash for tunes which a man could whistle on the street with impunity, opposed ASCAP stubbornly, even to the creation of a rival establishment which would "sell" protected compositions at lower rates. A large fraction of ASCAP's career has been spent in the courtroom defining "public performance," even "performance," and defending the rights of composers who have created something worthy of remuneration. Yet it is no exaggeration to say that without Herbert as the founder, without Herbert's zeal in the case to define "profit," ASCAP would have amounted to nothing, and the situation of the American composer would have been vastly different today. Rarely does such a strong organization—for its strength increases notwithstanding rivalries and government supervision—owe so much to a single individual.

ASCAP is of incalculable significance to the American composer;

but it was still more to the original nine stalwarts who founded it. The launching and developing of the Society provided a bond which was toughened by the ensuing trouble and adversity. With the passing of the years the little band grew smaller; but as each founder died the memories of the early days burned brighter for the companions that remained. They had been through something that no mere charter member knew. It was this intangible something, this realization of an unique experience shared in common, that led Raymond Hubbell to write a beautiful expression when only two of the Founders were still alive:

Once in a while I close my eyes and in memory I go back to that rainy October night, in 1913, at Lüchow's Restaurant. I see that long table with places set . . . and vision the little group of which only Jay Witmark and myself remain. Reverently I raise my glass to dear old Victor, Glen, George, Nathan, Lou, Gus and Sylvio and whisper, as I think of all the blessings God has showered on ASCAP, if you fellows were here, I know we'd do it all over again![26]

19

The Irish Patriot

THE opening of 1914 found Herbert eager and impatient. The production of *Madeleine* was an event of first importance, and the establishment of ASCAP was an event of prime but untested significance. Immediately after the latter there were rumors that he would compose a new opera based on a play of which he had secured the operatic rights.[1] This was *Maria Rosa,* by the well known Catalan playwright, Angel Guimerà.

Herbert also continued his activity at the Lambs, conducting an orchestral performance of selections from *Sweethearts* on April 5 and composing another musical skit entitled *What Twenty Years Will Do* (*to Some People and a Tune*). The skit was performed on Sunday evening May 3—while the composer was in England on a European trip which was transformed from sheer delight into near disaster—with the violinist Max Bendix as conductor.

Herbert's trip was planned as a real adventure. Accompanied by Mrs. Herbert and his young daughter, he expected to combine business with pleasure. He and his wife had not been abroad since their summer visit of 1887, and he could now return to his old haunts as an artist of substantial achievement. The pleasure would come from his rediscovery of Europe; the business, from opportunities of securing performances of his works. One extremely important performance seemed to be assured: a presentation of *Madeleine* at the Théâtre des Champs Elysées in Paris. Henry Russell, manager of the Boston Opera Company, was directing a season of grand opera at the famous Paris house, and appeared to be completely willing to stage the piece. Horace Britt, Herbert's close friend, agreed to conduct the opera, although the composer himself expected to lead the première.[2]

The little family group sailed on the *Mauretania* and arrived in

England on April 13.[3] Proceeding to London, which Herbert had not seen since childhood, they settled themselves at the Hotel Métropole and embarked on a round of energetic sightseeing. In London, as in New York, Herbert was good copy for newspapermen, who lost no time in making him talk on any number of subjects. He thought the English capital had changed enormously since his last view of it, and he expressed pleasure in the condition of London's streets. In his opinion they were wonderfully clean, and their smooth surfaces put to shame Broadway's pockmarked asphalt. He was sure this was the reason for the relative scarcity of "autocar accidents" in the British metropolis.

Herbert had made no plans to visit Ireland on this European trip, his schedule evidently permitting no departure from very definite arrangements, but the interviewing reporters soon extracted from him an expression of political feeling against Edward Henry Carson, a prominent Ulsterman who was opposing Irish home rule. He also gave his listeners a glimpse of his intentions:

I have always been anxious to come over here, but I have been so busy in America that I could not find time before. I am going to Paris and Berlin— yes, partly on business. I expect to meet several managers in London and Berlin who have asked me to see them. I shall probably give a concert from my works in London. I have also been invited to conduct one of the leading orchestras in Paris.

The only fly in the foreign ointment is that I am afraid I shall not have time to visit Ireland as the Old Country ought to be visited to satisfy my own sentiments and those of my countrymen.[4]

On his musical expectations Herbert ventured only vague and cautious remarks. He made no reference to *Madeleine,* but he had crossed the ocean with its Paris performance very much on his mind. He had also brought the necessary materials. Britt had preceded him and was waiting in Paris for the preparations to begin.

Almost as soon as he was in London, Herbert sent an important letter to Henry Russell in Paris:

April 14, 1914.

My dear Mr. Russell

I am sending you today two piano scores of "Madeleine" with the French translation and hope you will be able to select a cast at your earliest convenience so that the respective artists can begin to study their parts. I am sure that your Mr. Horace Britt would be delighted to study with the artists until my arrival in Paris.

I can well imagine that your hands are full with preparations for your season, but hope you will find time to drop me a line here.

This minute I received a cable from New-York telling me of the great success of "Natoma" last night at the Century Theatre.

Wishing you all success in your great venture I beg to remain yours

Very sincerely

VICTOR HERBERT[5]

Evidently he sent a letter to Britt at the same time, for the next day he wrote:

April 15th

My dear Horace

I sent you a letter to the Theatre des Champs Elysées yesterday before I could find your private address. Please get the letter and act accordingly.

Drop me a line here, please, as I expect to remain here for about two weeks before coming to Paris.

How are you?

Best regards to Madame

Yours very sincerely

VICTOR HERBERT[6]

Suddenly, the Paris performance of *Madeleine* was canceled, and no definite reason was given. According to Horace Britt a prominent American musician in the French city was influential in stopping the presentation; but his identity remains uncertain.[7] Britt himself was disappointed. Herbert, wanting very much to appear before a French audience as a creator of serious music, at once asked details as to the cost of an orchestra concert devoted to his own works. These Britt gave him; and on the 19th of April Herbert sent the following warm letter of appreciation[8] which counseled caution with respect to expense. He was completely ignorant of the reason for dropping *Madeleine*; apparently the idea of a jealous colleague never entered his mind, for he seemed friendly yet toward Russell although not amiable toward his suggestion of a London staging:

Sunday

My dear Britt

It is very kind of you to go to all this trouble in finding out the cost of a concert in Paris.

After all I hardly think it would pay to spend in the neighborhood of a thousand dollars for one concert, especially at this time of year. It would be just as well to conduct a number or two at one of your Sunday concerts and I will try to get an invitation to do so.

Mr. Russell is trying to get "Madeleine" produced here, but I am (entre nous!) not very enthusiastic about Covent Garden, and really don't care much wether [sic] they do it, or not.

As Madeleine will not be done in Paris (but I don't know why not) I will change my plans somewhat and probably go to Berlin after a short stay in Paris. I will inform you of our time of arrival there, of course, and will write you again before leaving London. We will probably stay here another week or a week and a half.

So far I haven't heard or seen anything remarkably good here and the general conditions of things musical and theatrical is undoubtedly better in the U.S.A.

Thank you again, my dear friend, for your great kindness and willingness to help me. I assure you that I deeply appreciate your loyalty.

Very sincerely yours

VICTOR HERBERT

Best regards to Madame B!

Resigned to his disappointment, Herbert set about making new plans; but they were changed for him, and most dangerously. While going through Buckingham Palace on April 22 he was stricken with appendicitis of the severest sort. Two days later four physicians decided he must undergo surgery at once. His appendix was removed on April 25, and for twenty-four hours his life hung in the balance.[9] Three more days elapsed before the crisis was over.

Fortunately Mrs. Herbert and their daughter were present to give him indispensable care and attention. Mrs. Herbert at last had to go to Frankfort for a rest cure herself, while he quietly recuperated at Brighton.[10] In June the trio of Herberts, together again, sailed from England on the *Imperator* and arrived in New York on the 25th.[11] The composer seemed to have regained his hearty good health, but he was sorely disappointed over the outcome of his trip.

Herbert's major task, of course, was composing operettas, and he had to prepare two for presentation in the fall. Knowing his habits of work, one may seriously doubt if he had written a note of either before he sailed for England, but announcements of the first appeared while he was convalescing from the operation. *The Débutante* was a musical comedy in two acts featuring Hazel Dawn, who had already been seen in *The Pink Lady* (1911) and *The Little Café* (1913), both composed by Ivan Caryll. The book and lyrics were written respectively by Harry B. and Robert B. Smith.

The first performance on any stage of *The Débutante* occurred at the New Nixon Theatre in Atlantic City, September 21, 1914. After playing in several large eastern cities, including three weeks in Philadelphia, it opened in New York at the Knickerbocker Theatre on December 7, the composer leading the orchestra that night. A better operetta of Herbert's, *The Only Girl,* was already a month old on Broadway, and the short life of *The Débutante* was partly the result of this curious arrangement. Other factors responsible for its brief career were a stupid libretto and a lack of spontaneity in the music.

The Débutante was produced by John C. Fisher and staged by George Marion, with dances by Allen K. Foster. Carlo Edwards was the musical director when the show reached New York, but he had been preceded by Joseph Sainton. The first audience at the Knickerbocker saw the following cast:

The Hon. Spencer Mainwaring Cavendish,
    Midshipman...........................Sylvia Jason
An Old Sailor..............................Cyril Smith
Bo'sun, H.M.S. Scorpion.................Thomas Reynolds
The Cook, H.M.S. Scorpion..............J. Abbott Worthley
Lieutenant Larry Sheridan, British Navy......Robert G. Pitkin
Mildred....................................Dolly Alwin
Annabel....................................Peggy Parker
Mrs. Zenobia Bunker, wife of Ezra Bunker......Maude Odell
Ezra Bunker, composer of the music of the future....Will West
Godfrey Frazer, an American captain of
    industry..............................William Danforth
Wiggins....................................Jack Hall
Elaine, daughter of Sir Francis Vane...........Hazel Dawn

Marie ⎫		Marie Baxter
Elsie ⎪		Elsie Schneider
Dorothy ⎪		Dorothy Landers
Irene ⎬ School girl companions of Elaine..⎨		Irene Hopping
Harriet ⎪		Harriet Dubarry
Mae ⎪		Mae Doherty
Eva ⎪		Eva Stuart
Frances ⎭		Frances Ramey

Armand, Marquis de Frontenac.................Stewart Baird
Philip Frazer, son of Godfrey..............Wilmuth Merkyl
Irma, a Russian dancer........................Zoe Barnett
Teslavitz, a famous violoncellist...........Theodore Heinroth
Nina, a future ballet girl.....................Sylvia Jason
Paul Masson, a famous sculptor.............J. Abbott Worthley
English Ambassador..........................Frank Travers
German Ambassador..........................Jack Heisler
French Ambassador..........................William Gibney
Footmen.......................Robert Waite, Owen Jones
    Officers, Midshipmen, Sailors, Society Buds, Masqueraders,
        "Call around again" girls.

Act I showed Godfrey Frazer's villa, Mt. Edgecombe, near Plymouth, England; Act II, the reception room of Paul Masson's studio in Paris.

In *The Débutante* Elaine and Philip have been childhood companions. Philip's father, who is also Elaine's guardian, wants the two to marry; but the boy fancies himself in love with the exotic Irma, a Russian dancer, and she has also attracted the amorous attention of the father. Elaine follows Philip to Paris and arouses his jealousy in various ways, but succeeds in winning his love and in defeating Irma's charms.

For this mélange of misadventure Herbert wrote an elaborate and fairly complicated score. Many of the solo numbers, however, lacked the freshness of his best work, and the chorus had little to do except sing refrains. Two facts seem to be plainly ironical: the first part of Elaine's entrance song ("Professor Cupid") is not even attractive; and the most musical number, a solo of real charm and extended development, is allotted not to hero or heroine but to Armand ("All for the Sake of a Girl"). It is much better than the two main waltzes of the play, "The Golden Age" (duet for Elaine and Philip) and "The Love of the Lorelei" (for Philip, Larry, and Elaine). Most unusual, of course, and very effective when well done, are cello and violin solos, fitted into the stage action. Theodore Heinroth was an accomplished cellist, and Hazel Dawn herself played the violin more than acceptably.

The reviewers one and all praised Hazel Dawn unreservedly—a response heartily approved by Herbert. In his customary remarks of appreciation he described her as an "apparition of beauty, sweetness and talent" and voiced his deepest pleasure in her performance.[12] Neither was there any noticeable disagreement about the lavish production or the cast in general, which performed well; but there was great variety of opinion about the music. The critics who were less perceptive musically bestowed high praise on the score; the more sensitive had more judicious things to say without liking, or disliking, the same pieces. One sensible review called the whole evening a mild diversion, pleasant but not memorable.[13] In the eyes (or ears) of the critic of the *Evening Post* Herbert seemingly could do no wrong; but even he had some reservations about this particular score. He happily found a way, however, to turn his column completely to Herbert's advantage:

It cannot be denied that among the twenty numbers of the score there are several which are the result *of savoir faire* rather than of inspiration; but most of them are genuine "Herbert's," and several of them are gems . . . Mr. Herbert's mastery of the orchestra is indeed manifested throughout the whole score, as always. Many of the fine points doubtless escape the audience at a first hearing, but they will help along the success with music-lovers. It was a treat to see Mr. Herbert conduct—a veritable Toscanini in his skill in securing delicate effects. At the end he had some fun parodying the futurists in music.

A more satisfied listener contented himself with the following: "Altogether 'The Debutante' seemed as near typical of Mr. Herbert's best work as anything we have heard in some time. He conducted last night and drew forth a terrific exhibition of energy and devotion from the players in the orchestra."[14]

Any qualifications attached to an estimate of *The Débutante* should not lead to a conclusion that it was an unimportant work. On the contrary, it was pretentious and large in scope, and the composer's effort was obvious. The music simply lacked the freedom and grace of some of his better works. The public seemed to react accordingly, for the New York run extended only to 48 performances,[15] and it failed to achieve conspicuous success on the road. Like *The Madcap Duchess*, it was called old-fashioned by one observer;[16] and this was more significant in 1914 than in 1913. The brash and talented and limited young Irving Berlin produced in New York on December 8, 1914, the musical comedy *Watch Your Step*, which was hailed as the first work of its kind to be written in ragtime. Whether such a definition can be maintained is beside the point. The musical stage, outside serious opera, was about to adopt a style quite at variance with Herbert's manner of writing, and for the first time he found himself in the position of being "dated" by his contemporaries.

The Débutante almost had a twin. Less than two weeks after Hazel Dawn's promising appearance in Atlantic City as Elaine, the same house presented to the same public the world première of Herbert's next musical production, *The Only Girl*, which had its first performance on any stage at the New Nixon Theatre on October 1, 1914, the composer conducting. On November 2, it opened in New York at the Thirty-ninth Street Theatre, five weeks ahead of *The Débutante*. It became one of Herbert's greatest successes and also, in its totality, one of his most individual creations. Nothing like it, moreover, had flowed from his pen before.

Herbert was fortunate in having Henry Blossom again as librettist. For a text Blossom turned to a pleasant play which had enjoyed only an indifferent success on Broadway two years earlier. He added a few characters to give the composer more latitude, but adhered fundamentally to the American original, which was based on a German comedy by Ludwig Fulda. Before it achieved fame as the inspiration of Herbert's score the play experienced quite a history in a comparatively short time.

In 1897 Fulda had brought out the comedy *Jugendfreunde* (The Friends of Our Youth), which the German Emperor was said to have called the funniest play ever written.[17] Fourteen years later, Helen Kraft submitted a literal translation of it to Isidore Witmark, who liked it but felt it needed emending. The music publisher tried to interest a number of people in it—including Paul Wilstach, Rida Johnson Young, Otto Harbach, and Harold Atteridge—without avail. Finally Harbach suggested that Witmark seek the aid of Frank Mandel, who was working for Belasco. Mandel was interested, and he cooperated fully with Witmark who, however, never took any credit for sponsoring the play.[18]

The result was the three-act play *Our Wives,* by Frank Mandel and Helen Kraft, which was produced in Hartford, Connecticut, on July 1, 1912, and in New York on November 4. On Broadway it had 40 performances and was no great success; but Chicago responded warmly enough to hold it for four months. Henry Blossom saw *Our Wives* in a Pennsylvania town and recognized its possibilities as a musical play. When he reached New York he won Herbert's interest and cooperation; and together they brought it forth in a musical version as *The Only Girl.*

The Only Girl was described as "a musical farcical comedy."[19] It was announced to the public just as Herbert was beginning his European trip, the two creators planning to concentrate on it later in the summer. There is a story, and it may be true, that Herbert composed all the music in seven consecutive days.[20] The only dates, in the composer's hand, on the manuscript in the Library of Congress are September 9 and 11, both written at Lake Placid.

Every care was exercised to insure an outstanding production. Joe Weber was the producer, and the reliable Fred G. Latham was the stage director. Robert Hood Bowers was in charge of the music. Early reports referred to the show as an elaborate production, but the reference must have been to its over-all excellence because, in the usual sense, it was not elaborate at all. It was simple in plot and execution, modest in its musical demands, economical in its personnel requirements. All these factors added to its charm and spontaneity.

Before reaching New York *The Only Girl* excited considerable speculation. Professional reviewers were deprecating the season's prospects, especially in musical plays. Their pessimism was darker than usual as they emphasized the scarcity of good musical productions. Managers were thought to fear the increasing investment required by a good show, and a public demand which could not be satisfied by the supply. As one journalist wrote: "It has long been a well-known fact that, with the exception of Victor Herbert, there is no one in this country who seems to understand musical comedy requirements."[21] With *The Only Girl* Herbert helped to quell the demand; and at the same time he showed how a fine musical show could be staged with a minimum of expense.

The cast at the New York opening was:

Alan Kimbrough (Kim), a librettist...........Thurston Hall
Sylvester Martin (Corksey), a broker.........Richard Bartlett
John Ayre (Fresh), a lawyer.....................Jed Prouty
Andrew McMurray (Bunkie), a painter.......Ernest Torrence
Ruth Wilson, a composer...................Wilda Bennett
Saunders, Kimbrough's valet...................John Findlay
Birdie Martin.............................Louise Kelley
Margaret Ayre........................Josephine Whittell
Jane McMurray...........................Vivian Wessell
Patrice La Montrose (Patsy), a soubrette........Adele Rowland
Ruby..................................Estelle Richmond
Violet..................................Marjorie Oviatt
Vida...................................Jane Hilbert
Paula..................................Claire Standish
Pearle.................................Gladys Schultz
Renee..................................Jeanne Darys

The time was the present, and the scene was Kimbrough's New York apartment: Act I, the living room; Act II, the same—six weeks later; Act III, the dining room—same evening.

The merry tale concerns Kim, a librettist, who is seeking a composer to set his newest show to music. He finds one in Ruth, but warns her that their relations will be strictly artistic and platonic. He is one of a group of four bachelors, who have sworn to preserve their single state. One by one, however, his three male friends succumb to feminine wiles, Kim alone resisting; but at the end he admits that Ruth is "the only girl" for him, and he is eager to follow the example of his companions.

The Only Girl is really neither an operetta nor a musical comedy. It is a play with music, but the music is more than incidental to the action. There are no dramatic scenes with musical emphasis, no passages of recitative or declamation, no passionateariosos, no choruses in the accepted sense. The score is predominantly a series of solos and part songs which are utterly charming and characteristic of the moods expressed. Perhaps none of them is particularly original; but the lively ones have the best of Herbert's verve and animation, and those that are slower-paced have his inimitable caressing grace. The artistic integrity and consistency of the score as a whole set it apart from the bulk of Herbert's output.

Patsy's "The More I See of Others" is saucy and impudent. Ruth's melody, which catches the librettist's ear, is the famous "When You're Away"—one of that group of Herbert airs now firmly lodged in America's mind and heart. It is a surprisingly simple waltz; yet by its avoidance of phrase repetition, and by its gradual rise to a higher melodic level, it is one of the composer's most effective and best balanced tunes. Its frequent appearance in the score gives it the aspect of a theme song for the entire work. It is not, however, the culminating song of love. This distinction goes to Ruth's and Kim's duet, "You're the Only Girl for Me," which has a quiet dignity far removed from the lushness of Herbert's usual romantic writing.

In the second act Patsy sings a song ("Personality") which is captivating in its piquancy and delicate syncopation. Here, too, there is uncommonly good matching of stanza and refrain, the contrast being vivid without change of spirit, rhythm, or style. Were it not for "When You're Away," Jane's "Tell It All Over Again" would probably be known as *The Only Girl* waltz. It is exceptionally attractive and is enhanced by the interpolation of chromatic tones which add to its smoothness and suavity. A sparkling ensemble number is the sextet "Connubial Bliss," sung by the three couples so recently married. The rapid conversation is succeeded by a refrain for all six together as they praise the happiness found in married life.

The third act opens with a waltz chorus wherewith Patsy and her girl friends drink a toast to Kim. It is energetic in the style of vigorous carnival music, as effective in its way as the march in Act II. Patsy has another good song in "You Have to Have a Part to Make a Hit," but it is overshadowed by a male trio sung by Fresh, Corksey, and Bunkie, "When You're Wearing the Ball and Chain." The three new husbands have discovered some of the drawbacks of marriage, and sing of them in a popular vein which delightfully mocks the state into which they have plunged. In its female counterpart ("Why Should We Stay Home and Sew?" or "Equal Rights") the trio of wives, with equal spirit, take umbrage with the men and express the feminine point of view. An orchestrally dressed-up reference to Ruth's waltz leads to the final duet, and the play closes with a grandiose repetition of "When You're Away."

The Only Girl, with not a single dull number, at once captured the fancy of public and press alike, and they responded to its merits in spite of the fact that no great star was in the cast. The men and women on the stage did a superb job, their naturalness and versatility standing them in good stead. If any person should be singled out for special notice it might be Wilda Bennett, Ernest Torrence, and John Findlay. Torrence, who subsequently became one of the silent screen's best character actors, was an accomplished musician, having trained for opera and studied at the Stuttgart Conservatory.[22] Findlay made a favorable impression by acting alone, for his role as valet was completely nonmusical. As Saunders he had an opportunity to observe and react rather cynically to the courting troubles of his master and friends; and he won many accolades for the way he did it.

The New York *Times* termed the play "as refreshing and delightful" as one could wish for, full of "genuine, splendid fun and pretty, tuneful music." It would have been better to call it a "farcical comedy with music" than to apply the phrase the authors had used. It was free of cheapness and vulgarity, and was certainly not for the tired businessman. "It is instead an entertainment for the very wide-awake person, young or old, who goes to the theatre for a thoroughly enjoyable evening."

Another critic expressed pleased surprise that *The Only Girl* was an exception to the usual failure of stage comedies converted into musicals.[23] The Herbert-Blossom opus turned out to be one of the brightest, most pleasing spectacles in many a season, a result of the best work both men were capable of. To be sure, they had started with a comedy rich in possibilities; but they could only be congratulated on what they had added to it.

It was noticed that Herbert had a book far different from the kind usually foisted on him, and there was a genuinely felt pleasure in observing the way he rose to the occasion.

In conception and execution *The Only Girl* was a modest undertaking. After a few days, however, Joe Weber realized he had an unusual success on his hands, and he abandoned the smallish theater, moving on November 16 to the Lyric Theatre, which afforded more room for the orchestra and more seats for the public. Here the play remained for the rest of its New York run, which totaled 240 performances,[24] lasting into June of 1915. (Let it not be forgotten that *The Débutante* had long since come and gone.) Two prosperous years on the road followed.

The Only Girl was one of the few Herbert productions to be staged in England. In the spring of 1915 Weber disposed of English production rights to Messrs. George Grossmith and Edward Laurillard who presented it in London at the Apollo Theatre on September 25. There it ran for almost three months and won the approbation of the stolid British.

The *Times* was restrained but not reluctant in its good words. The *Daily News and Leader* declared that success was assured by the end of the second act, and it referred to the music as "well made and suave if in no sense original."

The reviewer in the *Daily Telegraph* was completely enthusiastic and, in one place, amusing. He began with the exclamation, "Pleasant comedy and pretty music!" and commented on the rarity of such a combination. He told his readers that the play came from America, "though nobody would have guessed it"—a cryptic remark for any American perusers; but he furnished a just appraisal of the score:

> With the music . . . it is a case of quality rather than quantity. As already hinted, the musical numbers are never dragged in to the detriment of the play's action. Rather, indeed, do they tend to lift it up at the right moment. In Mr. Victor Herbert, who enjoys a high reputation in America, the lighter lyric stage boasts a composer of indubitable taste and accomplishment. If one cannot claim for the tunes he has penned for "The Only Girl" any remarkable freshness or distinction, he almost invariably steers clear of obvious commonplace, and his scoring throughout is as deft and dainty as you could wish. Even a ragtime song heard early in the piece—and conceived apparently in a spirit of parody—derives a measure of refinement and grace from its treatment, and when it comes to writing a downright "popular" number, as in the case of the extremely amusing . . . march duet—a thing of uncommon lilt and swing—the composer shows that . . . he can do it when he chooses.

This review was probably the friendliest that Herbert ever prompted from the British press. It, and others, indicated that *The Only Girl* might have attracted the British public longer than three months; but the engagement was limited at the outset, and the show was withdrawn after December 18. The New York press noted the London success with gratification and complimented the London critics who found it a welcome relief to ragtime. This it was, "and so, indeed, is the very name of Victor Herbert, which is associated with all that is best and most dainty and purely musicianly and melodious in the world of music, operatic or otherwise."[25]

The Only Girl offers a lesson to anyone exploring the present-day absence of Herbert's music from the stage. When it was revived in New York on May 21, 1934, at the Forty-fourth Street Theatre it lasted for only 16 performances.[26] The reason? The book. Relatively, the libretto which Blossom fashioned was one of the best Herbert ever had, and was more than satisfactory to audiences of 1914. But the passage of twenty years brought changes in dramatic taste which persuaded both professional and lay judges that Blossom's work could attract no longer. Robert Benchley wrote in a serious moment: "The Herbert music is, of course, perennially lovely, but those Henry Blossom librettos need a cold winter's night and an attendant air of excitement in the theatrical district to make them bearable. Even in its heyday, the book to 'The Only Girl' was not so hot, and in the not-so-very-merry month of May, 1934, you could go clamming in it."[27]

A colleague of Benchley's, Robert A. Simon, seized upon the revival to compose a little essay on Herbert and his works. Classifying the Blossom libretto with all the others Herbert had used—which was not quite fair—Simon wrote: "Whatever you may think of the libretto . . . there is so much vitality in the Herbert tunes that they will remain in circulation after the libretti have had their final revivals." He found in many of the melodies "the ring of permanence"; and, while he deprecated the lack of dramatic composing in *The Only Girl*, he added: "A glance at the published scores of 'Mlle. Modiste' and 'The Red Mill' will prove that he was more than a facile melodist and a practical orchestrator." He warmed to his subject and even reverted to *Natoma*: "Duller operas than 'Natoma' continue in the standard repertoire, and if the piece were sung in Italian, thus obscuring its textural peculiarities, it might still have a hearing now and then." He proceeded next to call for performances of some of Herbert's unknown serious works and explained how certain specific songs in *The Only Girl* must be executed to have their full effect.[28]

Thus did *The Only Girl* affect listeners a generation after its birth and a decade after its composer's death; it was at least a positive influence which has not been exploited as it should be.

On the 1914 visit to Europe Herbert regretted the lack of time to visit Ireland. His Irish interests and sympathies were, if possible, increasing, and he probably fancied himself as a leader of Irish thought in the United States. He was certainly a leader in Irish feeling, and missed no opportunity to further the "cause" when music or musicians were needed. Two such occasions appeared early in 1915: the first on January 26, when he conducted the Glee Club (which he had founded) of the Society of the Friendly Sons of St. Patrick in the Hotel Astor;[29] the second on February 5, when he played some piano accompaniments for an Irish singer, Thomas Egan, in Carnegie Hall.[30]

These were mere gestures, however, compared with his elevation to the presidency of the Society of the Friendly Sons of St. Patrick, on November 16, 1914, at the annual business meeting of the Society.[31] His real activity began the following year. His continuous loyalty to this organization was both curious and touching; it revealed a quest for emotional satisfaction which could be found only in a society inspired by the political misery and legendary wealth of a famed land.

On St. Patrick's Day, 1915, the Friendly Sons gathered at the Hotel Astor for their 131st anniversary dinner. Naturally President Herbert was represented in the musical part of the program; but his duties as presiding officer and toastmaster were more important. He opened the proceedings with these graceful remarks:

Gentlemen, it is my privilege as President of the Friendly Sons of St. Patrick to offer you a most cordial welcome, a *Cead Mile Failte*—a hundred thousand welcomes. On this day when the hearts of all Irishmen throughout the world are beating faster, and the little sprig of shamrock is worn by every son of our beloved Isle, we renew and reincarnate the everlasting love and undying devotion we feel for our old Home across the Sea. [Applause.]

I do not wish to brag about the achievements of the Irish race, but is it not a fact that on every page of the World's history and particularly the history of this country, you will find the names of some of the most illustrious sons of Erin, and have we not in generous measure helped to build up this wonderful country since its earliest development? But we have become grateful sons of the Goddess of Liberty, enjoying the blessings of Freedom denied us in our own land. [Applause.] Unbounded as is our loyalty to the country of our adoption—and we have done our best to reward America for opening her maternal arms to us—we are still fond lovers of that Green Isle beyond the Sea. [Great applause.]

I could continue at length, gentlemen, but I must remember that I am only Toastmaster on this occasion. I will, therefore, content myself with asking you to give your fullest attention to the speakers that have kindly consented to address us to-night.

Gentlemen, I ask you all to rise and drink to the first toast of the evening —The President of the United States.[32]

The toast was drunk with a will, and the Sons all sang "The Star-Spangled Banner." Then Herbert introduced the speakers, prefacing each one with a few well chosen phrases. The first was a prominent lawyer from Detroit, Joseph F. Monaghan; the second was the Governor of New York State; the third, the Mayor of New York City. After Mayor Mitchel had spoken of the city's bright future Herbert remarked:

I am sure you all love the roseate outlook for autonomy that our worthy Mayor has painted to you. I do hope that this Legislature at Albany if they do pass a Home Rule Bill for New York City will pass a better one than the English Parliament passed for our country. [Loud applause.] No matter what people will tell you about the Irish Home Rule Bill, and even if it be His Honor, the Mayor, I beg to disagree with him. The Irish Home Rule Bill is a check without a date. [Continued applause.]

Herbert always felt he was fighting for the Irish as victims of English injustice. He was equally willing to come to the support of Americans when he thought they were shabbily treated. Later in 1915 he had an opportunity to vent his wrath on the San Francisco Symphony Orchestra, which had just dropped Henry Hadley as conductor. Personal feelings also influenced Herbert, for Hadley had long been one of his closest friends; but there was a real issue quite outside the realm of friendship.

Hadley, an excellent musician, was the first regular conductor of the San Francisco Symphony, leading it from 1911 to 1915. But as so frequently happens, to this day, the Musical Association supporting the orchestra decided it needed the glamour of a foreign name. Hadley was released, although his success was conceded, and Alfred Hertz was engaged. Hertz, too, was a friend of Herbert's, but the Irish composer was sure an injustice had been committed. Late in the summer, in Chicago for the opening of *The Only Girl,* he was interviewed by the press; and he explained his feelings on the matter with harsh eloquence. One interviewer reported that some of Herbert's language was unprintable as he castigated the San Francisco organization for the choice it had made. He termed Hertz's appointment a burning shame, and added:

I remember when I was in Berlin I answered an advertisement for first cellist in one of the orchestras. I entered the competition and was successful against a number of other cellists. Two days later I received notice that my contract had been cancelled because I was a British subject. The director said merely that it was the policy of the orchestra to give preference to Germans. I agreed that he was right.

But out here in San Francisco, after an American and a good conductor had built up an orchestra, they go and get that German Hertz.[33]

As a forceful parting shot Herbert exclaimed: "You may tell them [the public] what I say. They thought they had to have somebody with a foreign name."

It must be pointed out that the Hadley incident attracted considerable attention: its significance was neither local nor confined to the feelings of his Irish friend. Many Americans were under the impression that qualified native talent was wilfully neglected in favor of foreign importation. Herbert happened to be the most prominent individual to protest it. Two months later he went to San Francisco and, in an unimportant way, reaped a harvest from the words uttered in Chicago.

For most of 1915 San Francisco played host to the world as people flocked to the Panama-Pacific International Exposition. Lasting from February 20 to December 4, the gala celebration honored the completion of the Panama Canal (the first steamer having passed through on August 3, 1914), and the city on the Golden Gate won the right to house the exposition over the claims of several other communities.[34] All kinds of exciting events were arranged, and musicians and musical organizations of the first magnitude were brought to the California town. Herbert and his orchestra, augmented by special players, were engaged for a week of daily concerts beginning on November 1.

Mr. and Mrs. Herbert, with their daughter, registered at the St. Francis Hotel on October 21. It was the composer's first visit to the Far West, and he anticipated his stay keenly. Reporters besieged him as usual with queries ranging from his personal finances to his musical beliefs. He denied possession of the former and said that "most folks who have money have it because they are a little bit 'close.' " But on the latter he was willing to be more expansive:

How do I regard my different musical creative efforts as, for instance, my grand operas, as compared with my light operas? There is only one kind of music. That is good music. There is only one kind of art, and that is good art. Shakespeare wrote comedies; he conceded the point that artists sometimes forget; it is the matter which governs the form. A musician and a conductor should be like a minister. He should be human, and not try to frighten folks to death. The masterpiece of all stage music is a comic opera, "Meistersingers." False notions regarding good music are fostered by three classes: poor interpreters who fail to bring out the beauty of good music; conductors who are pedants before they are musicians, and ragtime performers who discourage the belief that there is good music which everybody can comprehend.[35]

Relieved of this sentiment as well as others, Herbert began a strenuous week of concert preparation, sightseeing, and socializing. The newspapers gave him as much attention as they accorded Thomas Edison or Henry Ford, and his friends made him the center of society and club life.[36]

There was one critic on the West Coast, unfortunately, who wrote an essay-length report on Herbert's conducting and musicianship: a carefully studied attack on all he did and all he stood for. This was Alfred Metzger, who damned with faint praise as he objected to Herbert's interpretations, the content of his programs, and the nature of his audiences. He found fault with Herbert's talks with the press and denied that the conductor was qualified to define good music. He summarized his cautious and subtle attack so: "To sum it all up, Mr. Herbert is a very skillful and a very ingenious composer of the lighter style of music and a conductor that exhibits much routine and thoroughness as a musician, but to say that he is a great composer or a great conductor would be stretching one's imagination to the breaking point."[37] In itself this was not a bad statement; but its concessive psychology following a series of uncharitable opinions intensified its hostility. Furthermore, the question of greatness was irrelevant, because Herbert never had claimed to have it.

There were two reasons for Metzger's attitude. One was the contempt for musical highbrows which Herbert freely expressed; the other, the dismissal of Henry Hadley, which had so aroused Herbert's anger. Metzger, perhaps unconsciously, made this clear when he posed the rhetorical question: "Can it be possible that the absence of the 'highbrows' at the Victor Herbert concerts is responsible for his sneering attitude, and at the same time for his numerous expressions regarding the remarkable musical achievements of Henry Hadley, and the San Francisco musical delinquency in permitting that wonderful conductor to return to his eastern haunts?" This foolish question was never answered, and if the highbrows had come to the concerts they would have found the Festival Hall long since sold out.

When he returned to New York, Herbert was pleased to find his newest operetta a decided success. It had been launched late in the summer, long before he went to California, and had quickly proved itself to be a work of grace and charm, almost if not quite as vital as his very best.

The Princess Pat was a comic opera in three acts, strictly modern and American in setting and story. The librettist was Henry Blossom. The producer was John Cort; the stage director, Fred G. Latham. The first performance on any stage took place at the Cort Theatre in Atlantic City on August 23, 1915, the composer conducting. The New York première, with Herbert again on the podium, occurred at the Cort Theatre on September 29.

Like many a similar piece, *The Princess Pat* had a rising star in the title role. This was Eleanor Painter, an American girl of talent and charm who had won her spurs the previous season in *The Lilac Domino*. Another interesting person in the cast was Al Shean, principal comedian, who became nationally famous a few years later as the second half of "Mr. Gallagher and Mr. Shean."

Although the Atlantic City opening was on schedule, the New York opening was delayed two days by a tragedy which upset everyone connected with the production. The first performance was supposed to be on September 27, but an incident on the night of September 26 made postponement unavoidable.

A girl named Pearl Palmer had the second feminine lead (the role of Grace Holbrook). On the night of the 26th, her fiancé, Herbert Heckler, who also was a light-opera singer, visited her in her room on the top floor of a small music conservatory. She sent him on an errand, and he then revealed to a friend that he was emotionally disturbed and fearful of the future, admitting his worry over Pearl and attributing a change in her attitude to her recent success on the stage. He burst into tears as he voiced his worst apprehension: "Something's the matter. I'm losing Pearl's love. She isn't the same as she was. She's very successful and ambitious, and I think she's forgetting me in her pride in her work. If I can't have her love I don't want to live."[38] Heckler returned to the girl's room, and about eleven o'clock four revolver shots were heard. A passing patrolman rushed into the house and found each of them with two bullet wounds in the head. It was obvious that the man, already dead, had shot the girl and then killed himself. Pearl tried to speak, but she lost consciousness and failed to rally. She died early the next morning.

The company of *The Princess Pat* was stunned. Herbert and the principals were completely shocked by the happening, and a two-day postponement seemed to be the only way out of the dilemma. A substitute for Pearl Palmer also had to be found, who could go on with a minimum of preparation, and who would continue in the cast permanently. They were fortunate in obtaining Eva Fallon. Understandably nervous on her first appearance, she performed admirably and won the praise of the critics who knew the trying circumstances of her assignment.

The entire cast which opened in New York was:

Marie	Leonora Novasio
Thomas	Martin Haydon
Bob Darrow	Sam B. Hardy
Tony Schmalz, Jr.	Robert Ober
Si Perkins	Alexander Clark
Grace Holbrook	Eva Fallon
General John Holbrook	Louis Casavant
Anthony Schmalz	Al Shean
Princess di Montaldo (née Patrice O'Connor)	Eleanor Painter
Prince Antonio di Montaldo	Joseph R. Lertora
Bertie Ashland	Ralph Riggs
Gabrielle Fourneaux	Katherine Witchie
Anne Winthrop	Clare Freeman
Bella Wells	Charlotte La Grande
Coralie Bliss	Doris Kenyon
Dorothy Pryme	Lyn Donaldson
Elsie Smith	Kathleen Errol
Frances Hedges	Una Brooks
Hester Lisle	Clara Taylor
Maude Van Cortlandt	Lilian Charles
Reggie Calthorpe	Este Morrison
Sidney Gray	Jack Hagner
Duncan Arthur	Sven Eric
Teddy Thorne	William Quinby
Lee Bainbridge	Carl Drury
Jack Wickham	William Collins
Nat Franklin	Irving Fast
Achille Mazetti	Mario Rogati

The musical director was Gustave Salzer.

The action was in the present on Long Island, as follows: Act I, garden of General Holbrook's home, forenoon; Act II, living room in

General Holbrook's home, evening, same day; Act III, smoking room at the Westmoreland Hunt Club, the following night.

The substance of the story—far from the worst at Herbert's disposal —centers in the cooling affection of Prince Antonio (Toto) for his wife (Pat). A new romance develops between Tony, Jr. (of Yale) and Grace. Her family is in dire financial straits, and the Schmalz fortune is needed to remedy the situation. Grace and Pat are intimate friends, and they help each other with their respective problems. Pat makes her husband jealous and wins back his full affection. Grace escapes the importunings of the elder Schmalz by giving her heart to the son. Both young couples look forward to pure happiness.

In the score of *The Princess Pat* Herbert wrote a wealth of charming, cheerful music. There was no departure from the style of previous operettas, but the individual solos, ensemble numbers, and dramatic episodes paralleled many of his best efforts. There was also a quantity of entrancing instrumental music, for which the house party with its dances gave full opportunity.

Some of the vocal numbers are shorter than those in earlier scores; but they are no less bright and, for savorers of romance, no less flavorful. A short chorus heralds the entrance of Pat, who then sings "Love Is the Best of All," which has a stanza with characteristics of the mazurka and a refrain forming one of the best waltzes Herbert ever wrote. The theme of the waltz is itself distinguished, but Herbert added choral responses and then a solo obbligato to a choral presentation which are highly impressive. Quite unusual is the female duet ("For Better or for Worse!") in which Pat and Grace wonder what the future holds for two girls in their predicaments. The similarity of phrases, the careful differentiation of range, and the easy flow of melody made it a part song of rare quality.

Near the opening of the second act a rather sad waltz called *Estellita* emanates from a phonograph on the stage. Herbert had written this piece earlier in the year, and he incorporated it into the score as part of the musical background. The operetta's only real love song comes in this act: the "Neapolitan Love Song," wherein Toto, the Italian prince, looks forward to holding his loved one close again. The irresistible Italian style of both stanza and refrain make it a vocal gem. It is characteristically popular, yet the artistry of the composer is reflected in every phrase. "I Wish I Was an Island in an Ocean of Girls," sung by Mr. Schmalz is as captivating as its title, neither more nor less; and the duet of Pat and Toto, "All for You," is romantic enough for them to be wooing while, actually, they are thinking of happier times and are puzzled by their present estrangement. A musical high light of the act comes at the end of the finale, with the humor of Pat's advances to

Mr. Schmalz and his reactions faithfully represented in the music. Exaggerated ardor, ill concealed restraint, and coy archness are as evident in the orchestra as on the stage.

The best music in the last act is that for dancing; but Tony and Grace sing an attractive duet ("I'd Like to Have You Around"), and Pat sings "Two Laughing Irish Eyes," which has the lilt and flavor of the Old Country itself. The musical opportunities, however, have already been exhausted, and the play ends abruptly on a repeated fragment of "All for You."

The public showed unanimity in applauding *The Princess Pat*, the press nearly so. But one critic, who signed no name, burst forth with a splenetic attack which is ridiculous even today. It was so contrary to prevailing opinion that preservation seems mandatory:

> Mr. Herbert's music was not inspired. Its lack of distinction was emphasized by the pretentiousness of its form. There was the usual pompous and inflated imitation of operatic style, the overorchestration which is characteristic of his operetta music, and with it all no suggestion of the fact that operetta is not opera reduced to the terms of the most popular music. There are composers who recognize that there is a distinctive genre for operetta, but Mr. Herbert applies to a score such as a light work ought to possess all the forces which could be brought into use for a five act opera.[39]

Badly written to begin with, this statement can be refuted in every part. Other reviewers did refute it as they expressed gratitude for the existence of Herbert and his work. The following passage is typical:

> With pretty definite recollections of all the music that Victor Herbert has written in the last fifteen years, it is hard to recall a comic opera score by him more genuinely delightful, more even in quality or more characteristic of his best mood than "The Princess Pat."
>
> There may have been individual numbers of more striking beauty and finer musicianship. There is, for instance, the unforgettable "March of the Toys," and one of the lyrical numbers in "Mlle. Modiste." But for even excellence, persistent charm and sparkling vivacity, "The Princess Pat" comes close to his best.[40]

Another review expressed similar sentiments while giving an equally kind account of the singers and performance:

> No American composer has better knowledge of the art of color in orchestration; none has as great ability in creating atmosphere—that much abused theatrical term—in his music; none can shake such a wealth of delightful melodies out of his sleeve, and none can produce a more enjoyable operetta than Victor Herbert at his best, and he was in his most delightful mood when he wrote "Princess Pat" . . . It was not alone the music,

however, for the company, which had been carefully selected, was equal to any seen in years in light opera in this city, and all, even to those having the least important parts, could sing, and sing well. The acting was all that could be desired, and the chorus was pretty, well and modestly dressed, and could sing and dance. Henry Blossom's book was weak in spots, but never offensive or dull, so everything combined to bring about a pleasant evening.[41]

Two reviews call for special notice, for, both enthusiastic, they were unusual. The New York *Times* declared the honors of the evening must be shared by the composer and Eleanor Painter. He had provided music which was "dainty, sweet, gay, spirited and rich in melody"; and, "among all those who sing in light opera and musical comedy in America, none has a voice as good as hers. Also she dances beautifully. And she can act." The show was an occasion for "honest rejoicing," for it was Herbert "at his best." Then a welcome suggestion which was not exactly new to Herbert: "If ever New York is so happy as to possess such an institution as the famous London Savoy there are few American composers who would care to dispute Mr. Herbert's right to write the scores." And the reviewer went on to proclaim that Eleanor Painter should be, nay, "must be," the prima donna at the American Savoy, but "the quest of the librettist . . . must go on." Blossom was admittedly brighter than most of his contemporaries, but even he had not "produced sufficient credentials" to earn the lofty appointment.

The review in the *Tribune* was by Heywood Broun, who apparently had the time of his life. "The pen may be mightier than the sword," wrote the truthful Broun, "but the baton beats it hollow, that is, if Victor Herbert wields it. There is ever so much more humor in the music of 'Princess Pat' . . . than in the libretto by Henry Blossom. But even the lesser contribution is pleasant enough to make the new musical comedy . . . an eminently successful production." Broun joined his colleagues in praising Eleanor Painter, but was more interested in the music and how Herbert applied it to the action on the stage, remarking, "The music at the end of Act 2, which accompanies the love scene between the Princess and Schmalz, is quite the wittiest thing in the play."

The Princess Pat did not greatly differ from other Herbert operettas in its subsequent history. It had 158 performances in New York,[42] was highly successful on the road, especially in Boston, and had a thriving career the following season. Thus it lasted practically up to America's entry into World War I, when Herbert operettas, as an art product, seemed to come to the end of their period.

As the year 1916 began Herbert was pursuing activities as ordinary as they were varied. On the 8th of January he conducted the orchestral part of a dinner program with which the Bohemians honored the great violinist Mischa Elman.[43] On the 17th occurred the first New York performance of a play by Edward Childs Carpenter, *The Cinderella Man,* for which Herbert composed an incidental song, "Out of His Heart He Builds a Home."

Less than a month later occurred an event to which Herbert made an important contribution: a rare testimonial to one of his most treasured friends, the singer Enrico Caruso. The exclusive Lotos Club of New York, rendezvous of many famous artists and musicians, sponsored a dinner in Caruso's honor on February 5. Herbert was asked to pay an oral tribute to the tenor, who had no equal in this country or abroad. The composer took his assignment very seriously, and the careful draft in his own hand is preserved among the Herbert papers in the Library of Congress. Its pleasant humor is surpassed by the deep affection which he felt for Caruso, and the profound generosity in the homage of one artist to another. Herbert's words reflect a genuine eloquence:

I am glad of this opportunity of paying my respects to the guest of the evening.

Too seldom the Lotos Club honors *artists* of exceptional achievements, although its membership consists of artists and men who love the Arts and their prophets.

Being an old member of this club I feel that I am entitled to the making of this remark, not only to give to the *"Powers that be"* this hint but also to impress our *guest* with the fact, that *his* is a *rare honor.*

"Alas for those that never sing, But die with all their music in them!" So says *Oliver Wendell Holmes* somewhere! Evidently Holmes was not referring even prophetically to our friend when he penned those lines! For he has given practically the whole world a chance to admire him and, believe me, a "Caruso night" in Paris, in Berlin, in Vienna, not to speak of his own Italy, is as great an event as it is with us, here in America.

Of him *cannot* be said what Franz Liszt once wrote to a titled lady friend, asking her what she thought of his poetic gifts. He wrote: "Ich kraxle auf der Leiter, und komme doch nicht weiter!" or in "English," freely translated: "I'm clambering up the ladder—but I don't seem to be gaining."

It is not easy to praise a man to his face and it may be like carrying "coals to Newcastle" or "owls to Athens" to *proclaim* that for us here there is *only one, our Caruso!* standing today at the *top of that ladder,* in the glory of his Godgiven, golden voice, his supreme art, and last, but not least, in *the warm glow* of his democratic modesty and his personal charm. It has been my misfortune never to have been *"sung"* by him. I have been *drawn* by him though, that is true, not only to the Metropolitan but on paper— Even in his delightful *caricatures* he shows the sweetness of his nature—he has never drawn me as *fat* as others have.

Not to have had the good luck, to have been sung by him, is only a matter of circumstances, however, and I must hope for better luck in the future! *But I gladly thank* him in the name of all those *brother composers* whose good fortune it has been to have their works illuminated and idealized by his wonderful gifts. Long life to him, and in closing I would address him in his own tongue: *thus*

A te O Caruso, che con la tua voce d'oro sollevi all' enthusiasmo più ardente e trascini alla commozione più profonda tutte le folle, alzo il bicchiere e bevo alla tua *salute,* alla tua *gloria,* a quella della tua *Italia*—grande nel Pensiero, nell' Azione, immortale nell' Arte.

Evviva!

The Italian passage may be roughly rendered as follows: "To you, O Caruso, who with your golden voice can arouse the most ardent enthusiasm and can inspire the crowds with deepest emotions, I raise my glass and drink to your health, to your glory, to the glory of your Italy—great in thought, in action, immortal in art. Hail!"[44]

Caruso was at the height of his powers and fame, and it was easy to pay him the homage he deserved. Tribute followed tribute as the great tenor was fêted far and wide. Another celebration was organized, and again Herbert was among the speakers who lauded his accomplishments. The hosts were the Friars, who invited Caruso to be guest of honor at a clubhouse dinner late in November, 1916. Also among the distinguished speakers were Giulio Gatti-Casazza, Antonio Scotti, Giorgio Polacco, Edward Ziegler, and William J. Henderson. On this occasion Herbert delivered his warm praise of the Metropolitan's chief attraction in Italian.[45]

Herbert's willingness to glorify Italy and Italian song was as nothing, of course, compared with his constant glorification of Ireland and her cause. And it was in 1916 that he made his deepest penetration into Irish-American affairs, feeling no doubt that Erin's future was to be affected permanently by the sympathy sweeping eastward across the Atlantic.

The feeling of the American Irish (or the Irish in America) was fanned to a feverish pitch, and Herbert did his full share of propagandizing for the Celts. In retrospect many of the manifestations and demonstrations appear to be of slight moment; but the participants were intensely pro-Irish and anti-English—which sentiment flamed the brighter, it would be hard to say. There is something infinitely appealing in the spectacle of Herbert throwing himself into this semi-political arena, furiously striving to further a cause which appealed to his imagination and to advance the liberty of a people he was proud to call his own. He reaped considerable criticism for his actions, he found himself completely repudiated in England, he paved the way to one of his greatest musical disappointments, and he was forced to change sides when the First World War finally encompassed the United States as an ally of Great Britain. Yet throughout 1916 Herbert, unwavering in his devotion to Erin, was a conspicuous leader of Irish interests and an actor in events such as rarely engage the attention of musicians.

Irish history of the early twentieth century was a conglomeration of mistreatment, misunderstanding, bloodshed, and futility. The possibility that the British Government would confer home rule aroused discontent in Ireland that varied between south and north, and national feeling ran extravagantly high as the desired goals remained elusive. The Gaels at home expected aid and comfort from their brothers in America, and the Irish in the United States did their best to supply at least the comfort. With the outbreak of World War I the Irish republicans thought their great moment had arrived. They hoped that England would be soundly thrashed by Germany, that their own independence would be permanently won, and that, from being Britain's despised dependency, they would take their place among the nations of the world. Herbert vociferously shared all these hopes and dreams, which seemed realizable in 1916 but vanished as the course of events determined differently.

On Saturday March 4, there was an assembly of patriotic Irishmen in the ballroom of New York's Astor Hotel. Nearly 2,000 delegates from places as distant as Alaska and Florida came together to plan the achievement of Irish independence. They called themselves "The Friends of Irish Freedom," and they decided to "encourage and assist any movement for the national independence of Ireland and to aid in the industrial development of the country as well as in the revival of the language, the literature, the music, and the customs of the Gaels."[46] One of the leaders of the meeting was Victor Herbert who, "standing under a decoration made by twining American flags and the green Irish banner with the golden harp," rapped for order and called for the election of Irish-born John W. Goff as temporary chairman. Goff was a Justice of the Supreme Court of the State of New York. The militant spirit of the assembly was shown in the opening prayer of Monsignor Henry A. Brann, who addressed the Deity so: "God save Ireland! Make her free and punish her enemies!"

New officers were nominated, and Justice Goff was elected president, Herbert becoming one of five vice presidents. On the following day the meeting continued in the George M. Cohan Theatre, where Goff resigned as president and Herbert was elected to succeed him. The delegates adopted a Declaration of Freedom, which they claimed was based on American ideals and institutions, and one ardent patriot boasted that every soul in Ireland was disloyal to England. The most fanatical Irishman present was unquestionably Jeremiah O'Leary, a pro-German agitator who wanted the Irish to stand whenever *"Die Wacht am Rhein"* was played or sung!

March 17 followed handily on March 4 and 5, and Herbert, still president of the Friendly Sons of St. Patrick, officiated cheerfully at the 132nd anniversary dinner at the Hotel Astor. Political and patriotic concerns failed to suppress music, joviality, and good-fellowship. Herbert introduced the first toast of the evening: The President of the United States.[47]

The Friendly Sons wished to have a souvenir of the occasion, and they decided to reproduce in miniature a famous art treasure in the National Museum in Dublin. It was the Ardagh Chalice, richly ornamented with metal and enamel and bearing Celtic tracery of exquisite interlacing designs. George Noble Plunkett, eminent Irish author and director of the Museum, learned of their intention and sent a felicitous message which ended with this greeting: "Kindly convey my greetings to the Friendly Sons of St. Patrick, and in particular to your President, Mr. Victor Herbert, my fellow citizen, who so brilliantly maintains the traditions of his family and of our race."

At this banquet Herbert laid no stress on the Irish-English situation; but he was soon again in the political fray. The press was allotting much space to developments in Ireland, especially to the efforts of Sir Edward Carson and John Edward Redmond. Irishmen, they both were interested in home rule, but they failed to satisfy their countrymen, at home or abroad, who were bent on breaking every tie with England. Carson and Redmond felt, moreover, that home rule or quasi independence should not be granted during the war, that Ireland should aid England first, then embark on her new career as a self-governing community. A large number of Irishmen were convinced that this was a betrayal of their cause, another Anglican subterfuge to maintain Hibernian subjection.

Herbert, the best known if not the wisest Irish leader in America, was asked to express his views on the matter and to state Ireland's position in what was truly building up to a crisis. He responded by writing an eloquent and fiery essay for the New York *Sun* (March 26, 1916) which was quite a remarkable document. He castigated England in no uncertain terms, heaped opprobrium on the head of Redmond, denied the sincerity of Carson's interest in Ireland. He wanted Germany to beat England expeditiously, and he hoped America would take no part in the war. There was one glaring paradox in his article: he pleaded for a neutral opinion in this country, but wrote the most unneutral words conceivable!

The seriousness of the situation was not exaggerated by Herbert, although his solutions were open to question. The Irish at home did not want to fight for England, and they did want help from Germany. In fact, they fully expected aid from Great Britain's adversary, and Sir Roger Casement, a leading Irish rebel, went to Berlin to negotiate it. A German vessel carrying arms to the Irish was captured by the British, and so was Casement, who returned from the Continent in a German submarine. He was condemned as a traitor and hanged on August 3, 1916.

Meanwhile, as part of the chain of events, the violent Irish planned a revolution which broke out on April 24 (Easter Monday). In the fighting that lasted about a week over a hundred British troops were killed. When the Government regained control it executed fifteen of the rebels, who immediately became heroes to their countrymen.

On Sunday night May 14, the capacity of Carnegie Hall in New York was taxed by an Irish mass meeting to honor the executed rebels and to protest the action of the British Government. There was more cheering than mourning as the patriots advanced the cause of their native land. Stimulating their fervor was an orange-green-white flag of the "Irish Republic" which was spread over the speakers' table; it was presented to the crowd as a banner which had been carried in the Dublin fight.

Herbert opened the meeting formally by asking all present to rise in memory of the "Irish martyrs of 1916," then announced that a fund would be collected in New York for the families of the men England had put to death. He introduced New York State Supreme Court Justice Edward J. Gavegan, who made the astonishing statement: "We may safely predict that the battle of Dublin will go down in history as the first and only victory in the world's great war which was won by English troops."[48]

But human memory is short-lived, and a struggle across the ocean sometimes needs more than words to sustain American interest. This was proved by the Irish Relief Fund Bazaar, which opened at Madison Square Garden on Saturday night October 14. It was a curious affair, sponsored by Irish and Germans jointly. Only a fraction of the expected crowd appeared for the opening, and half were of the Teutonic race. Herbert officially declared the Bazaar open and extended a hearty welcome, rejoicing to see the great assemblage before him; but he had written his remarks well in advance, and he chose not to depart from his paper. He explained the purpose of the Bazaar and paid tribute to the brave men who had died in the Irish rebellion: "Those men paid the penalty of their convictions and have won for themselves imperishable fame."[49]

The Bazaar itself was outstanding. It had been carefully planned and arranged, and in addition to amusement features it presented many useful articles and displays. The layout, moreover, was artistic and visually attractive. There was clear evidence, however, that German propaganda was taking precedence over Irish sympathy, and in none too subtle a manner. German booths paralleled the Irish; in the basement was to be seen the model of a huge German submarine; portraits of George Washington and Roger Casement were offered for sale, but so, too, were pictures of Kaiser Wilhelm II conferring with his generals and bronze reproductions of the German imperial coat of arms with Hindenburg's likeness in the center. The mixture of Irish and German sentiment was nowhere more clearly shown than in the announcement: "Tomorrow night Mme. Gadski, wife of Capt. Hans Tauscher, the Krupp agent in America, will sing Irish songs." Her husband was subsequently deported as an enemy alien.

The Bazaar marked the climax of Herbert's flirtation with political Irish nationalism, although he never wavered in devotion to the Irish cause. The patience of the United States toward Germany was fast running out, and Herbert had never a thought of opposing American policy. He was undoubtedly regretful when the United States became allied with England, but his allegiance to America was stronger than his affection for Ireland. There was no weakening of this, however, and he championed Irish art and culture to the end of his days.

20

Motion Pictures and the Irish Operetta

IRISH affairs did not occupy all of Herbert's attention in 1916. He also encountered and entered into several new experiences, for each of which he displayed his usual zest and interest. One was of the utmost importance.

In the spring he arranged to make some piano recordings for the Aeolian Company, the rolls to be issued as Duo-Art products. He was to play only his own selections. The records were desired not as examples of expert pianism, which Herbert could never have done, but as personal utterances of a composer playing his own music.[1]

Almost simultaneously he accepted an invitation which, had he reflected upon it, would have convinced him of his approaching venerability. Newtown High School (Elmhurst, L. I.) decided to call April 14 Victor Herbert Day, and asked the composer to come as guest of honor. The school chorus and orchestra prepared a special program, and Herbert led the orchestra in his popular *Serenade*. The school principal introduced him to the students, and he entertained them with a witty talk which prefaced a plea that they should always love the best in music.[2]

As summer drew near the public waited with intense curiosity for a new manifestation of his genius, a work which, though almost totally forgotten today, remains a landmark in musical history: his symphonic accompaniment to the full-length feature motion picture *The Fall of a Nation*.

It is difficult to assess the full value of this achievement, artistically or historically. The annals of motion picture composition are so incomplete, the determination of events is so dependent on definition, that one cannot safely decide exactly what Herbert did, at least with respect to priority and chronological precedence. If common agreement can be reached on a few terms he should be considered as the first composer in America to write an original symphonic score for a full-length feature film. In Europe Engelbert Humperdinck alone is alleged to have preceded him with the musical accompaniment to the near-contemporary *Sister Beatrice.*[3] Even in 1916 critics were careful not to assign absolute priority to any individual for innovations in movie music; and it is more hazardous to advance such claims today. Most such music has disappeared; it was composed by musicians of questionable attainment for temporary and utilitarian use, and had no meaning with respect to the screen drama itself. Herbert's composition, however—this can be asserted with no fear of contradiction —was by far the most important product of American movie music written in the first two decades of the twentieth century, perhaps in the third as well.

It is also difficult to recall how primitive and incongruous were the musical accompaniments of films as late as 1916. Neither content nor medium of performance was standardized, and audiences might be subjected to the most extravagant and the most shameless of adaptations. But protests were beginning to be frequent, and demands were made for better, more appropriate music. Cecil B. De Mille raised his voice against bad music, warning exhibitors of *Carmen* (which featured Geraldine Farrar) that trashy music could ruin it.[4] Carl Van Vechten related an incredible experience. Dropping into a movie theater in New York, he saw a film entitled *The Woman Next Door* and heard some kind of orchestra play the whole of Beethoven's first symphony! Of course the symphony ended before the picture, and the next composition was Waldteufel's *Les Patineurs.*[5] By way of commendation Van Vechten referred to Herbert's *The Fall of a Nation,* with the qualification that the score failed to take full advantage of movie technic. This was hardly a fair criticism, because no one knew what this technic was.

Metropolitan critics were pleased to see the disappearance of the movie pianist. Any theater with a degree of respectability had to have at least a small orchestra which could supply the public with good and appropriate music. These critics derived considerable satisfaction from a new profession springing up overnight, "that of writing music for the movies"—an activity in the development stage, but of infinite possibilities.[6]

The musical accompaniment of the classic *The Birth of a Nation* (1915) was an early product of the new profession, but it was far from an original work. Even the composer, or compiler, of this accompaniment, Joseph C. Breil, admitted that only half was original, the other half being arrangements of familiar songs and pieces. He expressed the hope in 1916 of some day writing the perfect music score, which would be completely original in composition and construction. He did not admit that Herbert had done so, perhaps because his rival had incorporated into *The Fall of a Nation* familiar strains of taps, "Lead, Kindly Light," and national airs. Let it be said at once that Herbert did this consciously and for specific dramatic effects, just as Puccini employed "The Star-Spangled Banner" in *Madame Butterfly*. Herbert's score was none the less an original work. The genius of D. W. Griffith had created *The Birth of a Nation*, and his sagacity had called for a special musical accompaniment. Breil implied, however, that he was still looking for the artist-producer who would leave the composer free and in a position to exercise complete independence of judgment.[7]

Herbert found such a producer in Thomas Dixon, author of the novel *The Clansman* on which Griffith had based *The Birth of a Nation*. And once again, it must be regretfully admitted, Herbert erred in his estimate of a story or "book." It is doubtful if a sillier, more puerile, more fantastic book than *The Fall of a Nation* was ever penned. Consequently Herbert's music was coupled, as usual, with a story which could not possibly survive as such and with a motion picture, which, as cinema art, had no chance of being a major achievement. *The Clansman* was far from earning any literary accolades, but Griffith's directing genius had converted it into a film of lasting significance. The book *The Fall of a Nation* was even less good as a story, and the author guided the film-making himself, evidently feeling that he had learned enough from Griffith to produce a picture without professional assistance.

Thomas Dixon (1864–1946) was a curious and not wholly admirable individual. He was a North Carolinian who espoused the reactionary Southern creed of absolute white supremacy and illustrated it by writing novels of a lurid and sensational type. A Baptist preacher remarkably endowed with oratorical eloquence, with years in a New York pulpit, he was also a lecturer with a national following. In his writings and talks he was something of a rabble-rouser; but he took himself very seriously, and so did his readers and listeners.

The Fall of a Nation, issued in 1916 both as a novel and as a film, departed from Dixon's usual utterances. It was a badly written tract on the subject of America's unpreparedness for war and its inability to withstand the invasion of a foreign power. The time was that of the war in Europe, and the invading power, although unnamed, was obviously Germany. Under the stress of a fast-approaching national emergency Dixon had, perhaps, a legitimate theme; but his treatment of it, the sheerest and most impossible make-believe, was unbelievable.

He had to deny that the invaders were Germans. In this respect his statement was weak; but it ended with an assertion of democratic principles no one could quarrel with.[8]

One observation is unavoidable. If Herbert's Irish activities made him seem to be pro-German, he was never so with respect to the position of America and her allies. He recognized at once the meaning of *The Fall of a Nation* and underlined it musically with skill and vigor.

Before accepting Dixon's commission Herbert carefully read the story and the film scenario. It contained, in his opinion, all the elements of grand opera—the tragedy of a great nation's collapse and the splendor of its return to power, the faith of noble women in hours of despair, and the ardent love story of a good man and a good woman.[9] Villainy was present, too, but it met its just deserts. Herbert approached his task with the utmost seriousness, striving for unity of design by using special themes for individuals and events. He also suspected the importance his work might have in motion picture annals, and he was guilty of no exaggeration as he justified his act:

For the first time in the history of American pictorial drama a complete accompanying score will be played that has never been heard anywhere else. When listening to music that marks the flight of cavalry you will not say, "Oh, that is 'The Ride of the Valkyries,' " nor in scenes of stress and storm will you be regaled by the strains of "In the Hall of the Mountain King."

In brief, the musical program will not be a mosaic or patchwork of bits of Wagner, Grieg, Beethoven, Schumann, Mendelssohn, Gounod, Verdi, Liszt, Bizet, Berlioz and other writers. It will be as strictly new.

Hundreds, I almost said thousands, of music-lovers have told me their pleasure in picture presentations was to a large extent spoiled by patchwork music. When the orchestra played they heard bits of "Faust" or "Tannhäuser," "Carmen" or "Traviata"; the hearing of the music flashed pictures from those operas on the minds of the spectators, and attention was distracted from the characters in the story. I believe Humperdinck did write an original score to the pictured miracle play, "Sister Beatrice," but with that exception cinema music has been unoriginal.

The good example of Humperdinck led me to collaborate with what must seem to many people a revolutionary departure from the older fields of musicianship.[10]

The first public showing of *The Fall of a Nation* occurred at the Liberty Theatre in New York City on June 6, 1916. (General exhibition on a country-wide scale did not begin until fall.) The advertisements already reflected the future Hollywood tradition of linguistic hyperbole. Here are some of the phrases which enticed the public to buy tickets: "Thomas Dixon's Stupendous Spectacle"; "the first grand opera cinema"; "a big vital throbbing message to the American People"; "a bugle call to arms for national defense."[11] And it must be admitted that both Dixon and Herbert did their best to keep the phrases within the realm of truthful description.

The leading roles in the film, a product of the National Drama Corporation, were:

Charles Waldron..........................	Percy Standing
John Vassar...............................	Arthur Shirley
Virginia Holland.........................	Lorraine Huling
Tommaso.................................	Philip Gastrock
Angela..................................	Flora MacDonald

The official description stated that *The Fall of a Nation* was

produced in a prologue and two acts [i.e., two parts]. The theme of the play is the eternal conflict of autocracy and democracy—and the necessity for the preparedness of democracy against the aggressions of autocratic rule.

The Prologue is a series of historical scenes, showing the reasons for the early settling of America, the subsequent aggressions of Kings against the Colonies, and incidents of continued conflict after they have become a nation. The desire to escape the tyranny of monarchical rule and find freedom in a new soil brought our forefathers to America's shores. Here the evidences of autocratic aggression still continued even after we became a nation, and only Eternal Vigilance will award us continued liberty, for the menace of monarchical aggression still exists.

Act One presents the dangers to which our country is exposed, the plots and intrigues of the enemies within who take advantage of our state of unpreparedness and combine with enemies from without. The Advocates of Peace at any price, both men and women, unwittingly assist the enemies of our country. The result is a combined attack from both domestic and foreign foes and the country is over-ridden and conquered.

In Act Two the country is under the heel of the conqueror and the people drain the bitter cup of defeat. In the dark hour of adversity there arises a modern Joan of Arc, the former leader of the women's party that strove for peace at any price. She organizes a secret clan of women who assist their brothers in throwing off the yoke of the conqueror. The power of democracy is returned and a greater nation rises fully prepared to assert itself in any crisis.[12]

This sets forth only the theme, not the story whereby the theme was developed and personalized. The theme is unobjectionable. Democracy does have difficulty in maintaining itself, and America must be vigilant in order to repel foes at home and abroad. Liberty is to be had at precious cost, and its enemies have more than one way of committing aggression. Dixon's acceptable theme was, unfortunately, completely vitiated by the fable in which he wrapped it.

Waldron, a man of great wealth and apparently a patriotic American, is the villain. He connives with European enemies and facilitates their invasion of the United States. Vassar is a young Congressman whose legislation for increased armaments is defeated, partly through the efforts of Virginia, leader of a suffragist-peace group. With America overrun by the conquerors, she realizes her error, mobilizes a secret band of militant women, and wrests the land back from the brutal foreigners. She yields her pacific principles and her heart to the noble Vassar.[13]

The Fall of a Nation was spectacular and exciting, but it was also a bad picture. The success it enjoyed was momentary, for no one could long give credence to its fundamental plot. It was also a lengthy picture, Dixon not forgetting to insert a bit of comic relief, a few scenes of pathos (the Italian dying for his adopted country), and expressions of scorn for Americans who wanted to negotiate with the enemy. Among the last were figures "unmistakably intended to represent William J. Bryan and Henry Ford, carrying flowers to a conquering army where they are given the task of peeling potatoes."[14] Some critics conceded a certain effectiveness to the scenes of crowds and battles, but even they admitted that audiences liking the picture would be the victims of patriotic emotion. The implausibility of the picture, plus its inferior direction, prevented acceptance as a work of significance.

One itemized review, arranged in tabular style, was brutal in its brevity:

Story	National defense propaganda. Very bad story, poorly constructed, ridiculous in action, and lacking in elementary dramatic values. . . .
Direction	Bad throughout.
Action	Wearisome. Full of inconsistencies.
Situations	Silly.
Thrills	Miss fire.
Atmosphere	Poor.
Continuity	Jagged. Story lacks sequence and rambles along foolishly.
Suspense	Absolutely lacking.
Detail	Bad.
Costumes	Accurate.
Photography	Fair.
Lighting	Average.
Exteriors	Several badly photographed.
Interiors	Unconvincing.[15]

And yet there was the accompanying music by Herbert. It aroused an entirely different response, commanding admiration, and lending a measure of respectability to the picture. The score was universally praised, not only for its over-all effect, but also for the reasonable manner in which it linked scene to scene, episode to episode. A symphonic orchestra established each mood, intensified the terrors, heightened the comic parts of the twelve-reel film. There was universal agreement that the score provided an "operatic accompaniment" which would prove more popular than the picture. And Dixon was credited with one inspiration: the engaging of Herbert to do this work. Their collaboration set an important precedent in "cinema-symphony productions"[16] and opened a new path for composers seeking new outlets. The Mayor of New York was present at the première, as were Thomas H. Ince, Jesse L. Lasky, and Mary Pickford; but most of the audience seemed to be from the music, not the movie, world. It was apparent from the outset that the music rather than the picture was the center of attraction. Both Herbert and Dixon had to make short speeches of appreciation to the large and friendly crowd.

The New York *Times* was not ready to condemn the film in its entirety. It was "an unbridled photo play . . . full of thrills," wrote the critic; moreover, "many stretches of the film are fairly spectacular and it is full of battlefields and such pictures of avenging cavalry sweeping along moonlit country roads as the movies always do particularly well." But he had to admit the presence of a "few points that offend against good taste and several points that outrage the intelligence." He was completely happy about the music. In pointing out its great virtue he clearly exposed the vast difference between Herbert's objective and the ends achieved by other composers who had written picture accompaniments. "Mr. Herbert's score is effective. It helps a lot. It is easy enough to find miscellaneous musical motifs to accompany a photoplay, but here we have a score adjusted also to its rhythms."

In a more penetrating estimate a different music critic asserted that the film was "about the weirdest conglomeration of impossibilities that 'film fans' have been asked to witness in many a day":

But without a doubt the most important and valuable element in "The Fall of a Nation" is the music, especially composed for the picture by Victor Herbert. The incredibility of many of the scenes is considerably lessened by the effective score that Mr. Herbert has provided. He has not merely written an orchestral accompaniment with a series of "motifs." His score is interesting and worth while from a purely musical standpoint. Of course, there are typical Herbert melodies, light and buoyant, in his most characteristic style. In the Prologue the national airs, "Star Spangled Banner," "Columbia, the Gem of the Ocean" and "America," are skilfully interwoven; the bassoon sounds a note of doom as the enemy is plotting; good, honest "rag-time" is used for the music of the carnival celebrating the end of the European war; the scarlet blare of the brass, marking the din of battle, is positively thrilling; for the death of the loyal Italian strains of "Lead, Kindly Light," cleverly scored for woodwind, are employed; there is a beautiful theme for strings for the love scenes, and many other original touches too numerous to mention.

The music is not only perfectly synchronized with the picture, but its rhythms are in absolute accord with the tempo of the action.

Mr. Herbert's stimulating score clearly indicates the marked advance that music is making in the domain of the photoplay and should prove encouraging to composers who have not yet tried their hand at this type of work.[17]

Another critic offered the novel suggestion that one could better judge the music by hearing it apart from the picture, but mentioned no way of doing this. He was convinced that some of the best writing of Herbert's entire career had been done in this score, the chief reason being that the composer had stipulated, upon accepting Dixon's commission, he must have complete independence to write what and as he pleased.[18]

It is still well-nigh impossible to examine or hear the music apart from the picture; to hear it with the picture is virtually impossible. The complete score has disappeared, and will probably never be recovered. Estimates of its importance, which I heartily subscribe to, must be obtained from secondary sources and criticisms and from fragments of the music long since detached from the complete score. The "Love Theme" was published as a piece of sheet music for piano solo by Witmark in 1916. The melody itself seems warmly suited to its purpose, but it is placed in an incongruous setting which prevents any judgment respecting its original use. More interesting are several excerpts which were published posthumously by Carl Fischer, Inc. These constituted only a small portion of the original work; they were, moreover, arrangements for small or salon orchestra prepared by Herbert's friend and long-time assistant, Harold Sanford. Fortunately those portions of the original score from which they are derived are preserved in the Library of Congress, as well as their preliminary piano sketches, and they offer a glimpse of what the composer wrote for the film.

First and foremost, the music is descriptive and atmospheric. Some of it is melodramatic; some, exciting; some, playful. The themes are well shaped, the orchestration full, the harmonies rich and occasionally biting. From the strictly musical point of view there is nothing new here, no unexpected revelation of Herbert's genius or of any change in his manner of composing. It is, nevertheless, very serious music, written with extreme care and carefully plotted for the purpose it was to serve. The most important thing about it was the fact that it existed for a purpose for which composers in 1916 had little respect, a function which at that time scarcely fell within the realm of conventional music making. Herbert was unusually bold in venturing to supply a score for such use. That it was the best part of the composite production, the only part which enjoyed success, heightens its significance and increases the debt to Herbert of the music and cinema world.

Viewed from any angle, and notwithstanding its unfamiliarity today, the music of *The Fall of a Nation* was extraordinary; but once again the drama it was attached to brought its rapid downfall. In New York the picture ran about six weeks and then was withdrawn. The general release occurred in September, but theaters able to assemble an orchestra capable of playing Herbert's score were few and far between. If the music could help the picture, it had practically no opportunities to do so; when it did, the glaring faults of the picture still prevented any hope of popularity. It was not like an operetta with a weak book, whither people came only to hear the music. Audiences visited the picture primarily for the images on the screen: if these were not satisfactory in themselves or in sequence, no amount of inspired music could fill the void.

After the exciting and certainly important experience with *The Fall of a Nation* Herbert passed the summer in the usual way. He conducted at Willow Grove for three weeks beginning late in June. He vacationed at Lake Placid where his motor launch *Natoma* won a trophy. He wrote more music for the stage, about which there are some unsettled questions. Among the pieces composed were several for an operetta named *The Garden of Eden* (book by Harry B. Smith); yet this never materialized.[19] There were also reports that Joe Weber had brought Herbert and Otto Hauerbach together to create an operetta; but this was abandoned in favor of a different project.[20] In the autumn people heard another rumor to the effect that New York would have a permanent theater where only the productions of Herbert and Henry Blossom would be given.[21] This plan was apparently different from the earlier one, but it lived no longer, which was perhaps fortunate for all concerned.

Somewhat removed from the usual course of events was a theatrical production for which Herbert wrote only half of the music. The other half was by Irving Berlin, working independently, and the result was the gorgeous revue *The Century Girl*. There was no collaboration on any of the pieces or numbers.

Although *The Century Girl* was not of primary importance in Herbert's total production, it was a magnificent show which set new standards of opulent luxury and scenic display. It derived its title from presentation in the Century Theatre in New York, a house so huge that suitable productions were hard to find. Grand opera had failed there, and the combined genius of two great impresarios was necessary before a success evolved. In the spring of 1916 Charles B. Dillingham and Florenz Ziegfeld, Jr., leased the house and announced they would make it the home of high-class musical comedy.[22] On the 12th of July these gentlemen, on behalf of the Century Amusement Corporation, signed a contract with Herbert, who agreed to write and orchestrate as much music as might be needed.[23] From the beginning of the venture Dillingham and Ziegfeld wanted a spectacular and lavish production. Two composers were better than one (at least quantitatively), and Berlin was invited to share in the musical creation. The producers also thought the music would exhibit two sharply contrasting styles.

Berlin was just twenty-eight, and the prospect of sharing responsibility with the fifty-seven-year-old Herbert, at the height of his fame, was frightening. Moreover, the younger man, who needed no apologists for his talent and originality, was musically illiterate. He could feel and play and conceive music, but he could neither read nor write it. By his own admission he was like a man who could talk but knew not how to spell or write what he said.[24] Compared with Herbert, who towered above Broadway composers through his command of musical "science," Berlin was handicapped; and he was somewhat disturbed. Characteristically Herbert put the young man promptly at his ease; and the two proceeded to turn out the music expected of them. Berlin felt the results did show a contrast in musical styles, but he doubted if the audience was ever aware of it.

These two composers worked together on no other occasion, but this one was sufficient to make a lasting impression on Berlin's mind. While *The Century Girl* was in rehearsal Herbert would have to play some of his music on the piano; and, being no expert pianist, he failed to approximate the wanted effects. The innocent Berlin expected the same unsatisfactory results when the music was transferred to the orchestra. But when Herbert took up the baton and led the ensemble in the same music he had played on the keyboard, its rich, sensuous fullness sounded (in Berlin's own words) as if it were falling from heaven.

Sometimes Berlin was concerned about his musical illiteracy, and he once expressed worry over the future as he and Herbert were talking at the Lambs. Confessing his ignorance, he asked Herbert if he should study and gain a modicum of technical knowledge. The older man's answer was wise. Berlin had already shown the proper musical instinct for successful writing, and the discipline of formal training seemed unnecessary. However, added Herbert, should Berlin submit to regular instruction, his easy flow of inspiration would in no way be curtailed—which was the doleful prediction of a number of uninspired illiterates. Berlin did not enroll for study, and years later he was still wondering what might have happened if he had. He only knew that his respect for note-reading ability declined when his six-year-old daughter took piano lessons and acquired it!

Herbert was always a great man in Berlin's eyes, kind and helpful and, when occasion demanded, firm and unyielding. And he wrote great music, music which never changed, which remained as fresh in the 1950's as the day it was written. Furthermore, he was America's unique example of the composer who, in the theatrical world, functioned as creator-arranger-orchestrator, the one person who maintained the European tradition of Strauss and Offenbach and other masters of the romantic operetta.

As the two composers labored on *The Century Girl,* the management worked on the cast and production. Economy was no object, and the final company seemed like a roster of the most glamorous names in the field of entertainment. When the show opened on November 6, 1916, in the Century Theatre the following were only a small fraction of a star-studded cast: Marie Dressler, Hazel Dawn, Leon Errol, Sam Bernard, Elsie Janis, Gus Van and Joe Schenck, Vera Maxwell, Harry Kelly, and Frank Tinney. (Hazel Dawn, be it noted, was the beauty who had the honor of impersonating "the Century Girl.") Having no plot to speak of, the show became a sequence of pageantry, music, ballet, comedy and vaudeville specialties, each principal performer displaying his peculiar skill. The public was astonished and delighted, and marveled at the cost which was apparent in every number. Herbert conducted most of his own music on opening night, when the performance was much too long.[25]

Herbert wrote the music for some of the songs, much of the pageantry and dancing, and some of the comedy. This included "The Birth of the Century Girl" and "The Toy Soldiers" in Act I, "The Stone Age," also called "The Ballet Loose" (Act II), "Uncle Sam's Children" (finale, Act II), and "Under the Sea" in Act III. The songs were good, but the scenic music was more important and won much the greater share of approval. One gathers from the program that the big scenes were entrusted to Herbert; the smaller ones or skits, to Berlin. Among the latter, however, was an episode entitled "The Music Lesson" wherein the two composers were impersonated on the stage. Arthur Cunningham and John Slavin portrayed Herbert and Berlin respectively, and for this little sketch the real Berlin concocted a counter melody to "Kiss Me Again."

As a whole *The Century Girl* was "spectacle and vaudeville, glorified beyond anything we have had in the music hall world and multiplied by ten."[26] If one thing stood out more than another it was probably the second-act finale, a patriotic vision of action, drill, and dance devised by Ned Wayburn. The stairs and the revolving stage were used ingeniously, and Herbert's music swept the audience to wild enthusiasm.

Herbert's music enhanced everything it touched, but "his especially valuable contributions" were "descriptive in nature, such as the accompaniment for a promenade of girls representing famous women of the different centuries; the setting for a ravishing 'Under the Sea' scene, and the Stravinskyesque score for a burlesque, 'The Ballet Loose,' a convulsive bit of choreography from the Stone Age."[27] The friendly writer here quoted also mentioned two of Herbert's songs as deserving special notice: "You Belong to Me" and "When Uncle Sam Is Ruler of the Sea." The latter is, incidentally, one of Herbert's best marches, virile and sweeping and inciting true patriotic fervor.

The Century Girl enjoyed a run of 200 performances[28] which carried it to the end of the season. It was not taken on the road because its very elaborateness was deemed unsuitable for any other theater. Expense, too, was undoubtedly a consideration. Its positive success, however, presaged well for the future, and plans were made for *The Century Girl of 1917,* Herbert contracting to supply music for it. Unfortunately the show was never produced.

As *The Century Girl* was getting under way Herbert was already looking forward to a new operetta which, when completed, might be his greatest work. The story of *Eileen,* first known as *Hearts of Erin,* was not distinguished; but it had a plausible ramification in history and a background which excited his feelings and imagination. It was Irish throughout, and it dwelt upon the struggle between Ireland and England at the close of the eighteenth century. Fate decreed that with it Herbert was to experience one of his severest disappointments. Its failure was due to circumstances, not to inferior music; actually it is one of Herbert's most important works and certainly his last work of real significance for the stage.

For *Eileen* he wrote a score of genuine distinction and of extraordinary dramatic potency. The Irish theme seemed to call for extra effort, and the composer responded nobly. Every piece and incidental number in the printed score of this "romantic comic opera" testifies to special affection, but in addition he prefaced the score with the note: "In this score I have not made use of any traditional Irish airs, but have endeavored, to the best of my ability, to write all 'Irish' numbers in the characteristic spirit of the music of my native country—Ireland." He succeeded admirably, as everyone who heard the music agreed, yet today *Eileen* is known only through one excerpt; the best of its music remains unplayed and unsung.

Herbert's most ardent Irish activity occurred in 1916. It was natural, therefore, that he apply musically some of his stimulated nationalism. There could have been little surprise when Klaw and Erlanger announced in the spring of that year that they would produce a new romantic opera by Herbert, laid in Ireland.[29] Composer and producer, however, failed to reach agreement on certain production details,[30] and in the fall Joe Weber secured the production rights. This was at a time when Weber was laying ambitious plans. He intended to erect in New York a theater which would specialize in American musical comedy, and, because he wanted nothing but the best, he allegedly engaged Herbert and Henry Blossom to supply two works a year for a period of six years.[31] But these plans fell through, a not infrequent happening in the world of the theater. Apparently *Eileen* was not one of the contemplated twelve works, although Herbert wrote the music and Blossom the book. The contract between Herbert-Blossom and Weber for the Irish opera was not signed until November 5, 1916, when most of the music was already finished.[32] The terms were not unusual except for one thing: Herbert was to approve the person selected as conductor, and no musician was to be engaged without the composer passing on his name. This condition prompts two suggestions: either Herbert had been dissatisfied with recent musical performances, or he wanted superlative results in this Irish production. I prefer the latter explanation.

Hearts of Erin was performed for the first time on any stage in Cleveland, Ohio, at the Colonial Theatre on Monday January 1, 1917. Because it was New Year's Day there were two performances, and Herbert conducted both. Rehearsing had continued past midnight on New Year's Eve, but no one connected with the show had any thought of conviviality. Wearing a sweater, Herbert was perspiring freely at the hour of twelve, when Weber called to him to stop directing. The producer announced the time and wished everyone a Happy New Year. Every person present calmly returned the greeting, whereupon Herbert raised his arm and the final practice was resumed.[33] Shortly before midnight there had been a pause for rest and coffee and sandwiches. Blossom was there, and the three creators of the show talked excitedly about its prospects. Enthusiasm ruled them all. Herbert proudly declared, "I'm Irish, you know, Irish to the core," and betrayed his feeling for the opera by saying: " 'Hearts of Erin' is the effort of my life." He confirmed this, unnecessarily, the next day at the première when he told the packed audience of his long-held desire to write an opera worthy of his native land. The reaction of his auditors persuaded him to add: "My dream has been realized; this is the happiest day of my life, and I thank you from the bottom of my heart."[34] He was so overcome with emotion he did not speak well, but his halting speech only intensified the meaning of his words.

Herbert was elated by Cleveland's reception of *Hearts of Erin.* He read in the following day's papers, that his music was not Irish, but actually Ireland; that he enjoyed a privilege granted to few—to sound the very heart of a nation; that "a wealth of history, of tradition, of emotion and ambition had found musical expression."[35] Even a person less swayed by Herbert's ardor was forced to write: "Its music is of the most infectious, rollicking sort, interspersed with a few sentimental bits, but made up for the most part of catchy reels and jigs and folk-like tunes, so true to the type that one can hardly realize that here is no adaptation of collected folk melodies, but new and wholly fresh lyrics from the brain of the composer."[36]

The composer remained in Cleveland several days, winning another ovation when he conducted again on Thursday night. During his stay he was given a chance to express his views on the musicality of Ireland and on national music in America. He felt that the characteristic traits of Irish music had provided the inspiration for *Hearts of Erin,* and he disclaimed any personal credit for the opera's many beauties. Insisting that he had only done his duty as an Irishman, he observed:

> There is no place in all the world where there is more music than in Ireland. Why shouldn't an Irishman make an opera of it? He deserves no special credit for it, because he has the material at hand and in abundance. The Irish sing when they work, and they sing when they suffer—unluckily they've never known much but work and suffering. Song, too, they've had, and song they have kept through all the centuries, as pure and sweet as ever it was. It has meant an Irish national music, which I have tried to express and reflect in my opera.[37]

He went on to assert the need of an American national music which should parallel the Irish. He did not think it would come from either Negro or Indian strains, but he was farsighted enough to encourage the collecting of such music ere it be irretrievably lost. What American music should or would be like, he did not know—and we are groping similarly today.

After the week in Cleveland *Hearts of Erin* started on a tour of eastern cities, but it was not supposed to enter New York this season.[38] A substantial run developed in Boston, where it was rechristened *Eileen.* The only reason advanced for the change was that the earlier title suggested a drama rather than a musical play, but the theatrical world conceded it was a shrewd decision. In Boston, too, the leading tenor of the company (Vernon Stiles) departed because of a disagreement with the management, and was replaced by Walter Van Brunt singing under the name of Walter Scanlan. Meanwhile Joe Weber found it possible to bring *Eileen* to New York sooner than expected, and it opened in the metropolis at the Shubert Theatre on March 19—as close to St. Patrick's Day as could be arranged.

The program announced the following cast:

Captain Barry O'Day	Walter Scanlan
Sir "Reggie" Stribling	Algernon Greig
Dinny Doyle	Scott Welsh
Lanty Hackett	Harry Crosby
"Humpy" Grogan	John B. Cooke
Shaun Dhu	Greek Evans
Mickey O'Brien	Joseph Dillon
Colonel Lester	Edward Martindel
Biddy Flynn	Josie Claflin
Rosie Flynn	Louise Allen
Lady Maude Estabrooke	Olga Roller
Eileen Mulvaney	Grace Breen
Marie, her maid	Paulette Antoine
Myles, a footman	Lewis Ayer
Peter, the piper	Francis X. Hennessy
Sergeant	Roger McKenna
Corporal	Eric Block

Fishermen, Redcoats, Smugglers, Guests, Tenantry,
Servants, etc.

It was staged by Fred G. Latham, Arthur Kautzenbach was the musical director, and Harold Sanford was given special mention as concert master.

The three acts had as many different scenes: Act I, at the sign of the Black Bull—morning; Act II, interior of the Castle—afternoon; Act III, Gardens of the Castle—evening.

The action of *Eileen,* on the west coast of Ireland, stems from the ill-fated rebellion of 1798. Barry O'Day returns from France to help his homeland and to lay the ground for expected French assistance. Informers tell the British of his arrival, and a price is put on his head. He is befriended by Lady Maude, and falls in love with her beautiful niece, Eileen. Colonel Lester finally captures him at Lady Maude's castle, and tells him that the French fleet has been routed and the chief Irish leader has been seized by the Government. An unexpected message from Dublin, however, announces that a new administration there is granting a general amnesty to all rebels. The smugglers are pardoned, and Eileen and Barry face a happy future together.

The story of *Eileen* is certainly among the better books Herbert set to music, but just as certainly it falls short of the possibilities inherent in the theme. It opens with much promise, then trails off into an improbable love affair, an awkward pursuit of a foolish hero, and a collapse of all tension by the unexpected pardon. The Irish dialogue is effectively colloquial, but there is very little humor in either words or situations.

One thing about the book has remained unrecognized It seems to have a definite though not close relationship with Samuel Lover's novel *Rory O'More*. The story by Herbert's grandfather deals with the Irish rebellion, and Rory himself is peculiarly similar to Dinny Doyle. The novel has no character like Barry O'Day, but the young Frenchman who befriends Rory has all the gentility which Blossom's hero has acquired in France. It may be that these points of relationship are entirely fortuitous; yet they are too prominent to be ignored. Of course Lover's book was superior to Blossom's.

In composing the music for *Eileen* Herbert was probably unaware of the story's shortcomings. However, it was legitimately Irish, presented a legitimate romance (plausibility being no factor), and was anti-British, even though Colonel Lester had vestiges of gallantry. It stimulated him to write some of his very best music, not only in the songs, but also in the dramatic scenes and ensembles. Furthermore, he consciously made many of its melodies Irish in style and flavor, and he harmonized them with great skill and appropriateness. He used the orchestra for dramatic purposes more than in any other of his operettas and again forced comparison with grand-opera procedure.

Undoubtedly Herbert spent an unusual amount of time on the score, lavishing special care on it and making changes for improvement. Both the manuscript in the Library of Congress and the two printed editions (one called *Hearts of Erin,* the other *Eileen*) confirm this. There were important alterations between the Cleveland première and the New York opening, these being far more significant than the usual curtailment of material after a tryout. He worked on it more or less continuously. In the autograph score the end of Act I is dated "Sept 16th 1916 Lake Placid," and the last bar of "Eileen! (Alanna, Astore)" is followed by "Sat. Dec 9th 1916. 'Tutto finito!' V. H." Apparently this was the piece last finished before the performance in Cleveland. Other dates in the manuscript, however, are "Febr 9th 1917" on the opening of Act II and "Sat. Febr 24th 1917" on "Love's Awakening" ("When Love Awakes")—substituted in the post-Cleveland period. Evidences of this sort are rare in Herbert's work.

The opening chorus, "Free Trade and a Misty Moon," gives a foretaste of the music to follow. Tense, mysterious, and sharply defined, it is an excellent smugglers' chorus which exemplifies the spirit of the hardy outlaws. Barry's song, "When Shall I Again See Ireland," is in reality an ode of homage to his native land. Its broad sweeping phrases are reminiscent of many of Thomas Moore's Irish melodies, and its general mood is noble and exalted. The finale of the first act is long and continuously filled with recitative, descriptive orchestral passages, and patriotic choral work. A clever anticipation of the love duet in Act III is heard when Barry has his first glimpse of Eileen, but there is no pause in the musical dialogue of the personages on the stage. The people sing a chant of victory ("Glad Triumphant Hour") as they listen to Barry's exhortation, and this gives way to Grogan's sneaky theme when the spy's evil work becomes manifest. The redcoats are announced in a stirring fashion, and the act ends in a climax of excitement and confusion.

The opening round in Act II ("Come, Tom") is a masterly bit of writing, with the three voices intertwining skillfully. Here, too, the Irish flavor is unmistakable. Lady Maude's musical request for a French pavane leads to Eileen's Gallic "Too-re-loo-re," as stately a measure as one could desire. In this act Barry reflects on Eileen's loveliness and sings his slow waltz, "Eileen! (Alanna, Astore)." The refrain is less Irish than the stanza, with its minor cadences and characteristic intervals, but the whole is a piece where beauty and popularity easily combine. Later Eileen sings of her suddenly realized love for Barry. Her "When Love Awakes" is a full-blown and extended confession of rapture in Herbert's most passionate manner. When the chorus amplifies her song, the resulting effect is extremely convincing.

The third act has an elaborate opening wherein a religious atmosphere at first prevails. It is the hour for an "Ave Maria," which is sung in solemn calm; and also fittingly Dinny sings the praises of Lady Maude for helping Barry get away. His eulogy has great dignity, and she responds with a musical recognition of the patriots' devotion to Ireland. The chorus repeats her hymnlike song and closes a scene of genuine artistry. When Barry recklessly reappears he meets Eileen, and they sing the duet which today keeps *Eileen* alive. This is the admittedly beautiful "Thine Alone," again suggestively Irish by virtue of its intervals and harmonic implications. It is a fervent avowal of mutual love which loses some of its effect when sung—as it generally is today—as a solo. When the two voices sing together they are in unison, beyond question intentional; but they have characteristic individual phrases to sing separately, and the timbre of the combined voices is far different from that of one voice singing alone. As Dinny tells his countrymen of Barry's plans he climaxes his talk with the song, "The Irish Have a Great Day To-night," a rousing call to action which ought to free any nation from oppressive bonds. Vigorously amplified by a male chorus, it is a noteworthy example of Herbert's preserving the Irish idiom in the guise of a typical American march. The closing hymn, broad and sturdy, reflects the hope of all Irishmen as they face the future. It is aptly entitled "When Ireland Stands Among the Nations of the World."

There was almost a surfeit of musical enjoyment in *Eileen,* a fact readily acknowledged by the New York critics. There was the customary disagreement over the book, some finding it unusually good for an American libretto (which it doubtless was), others ridiculing it as monstrous and unbearable (which it was not).

Surely the most satisfying expression was in a letter from a close personal friend, a supremely gifted artist who knew the value of theatrical music and who wrote from a full heart. It was never communicated to the public:

March 20th 1917

Dear Mr. Herbert;

It gave my husband and me so much pleasure to hear the first performance of your opera-comique "Eileen."

The music is really extremely lovely and original and was rendered with true artistic spirit, so that we enjoyed every bit of it immensely.

We were delighted too, to see the enthusiastic audience give this charming work the appreciation it deserves.

Hoping to see you all soon and with much love in which my husband joins,

Yours sincerely
MARCELLA SEMBRICH[39]

Partly opposing this view, but only because of the libretto, was a young man destined to become a brilliant critic of drama and literature. Alexander Woollcott was percipient and sensitive to all artistic values, and, as he briefly praised the music in no uncertain terms, he roundly condemned the contribution of Henry Blossom:

Though you would never guess it from the curiously capitalized program, Victor Herbert, and not Joe Weber, is the star of "Eileen." He has seldom written a more thoroughly characteristic and delightful score. If, as you might have gathered from his amusingly expansive curtain-speech at the première, he feels it satisfies at last his ancient desire "to write an Irish opera which would be worthy of the traditions of a great race and its literature," it is a pity he could have found no more inspiring a libretto than the awkward and diluted shillalah drama which Henry Blossom has compiled.

The book of "Eileen," with its threadbare stage properties and its jests that have seen better days, is simply preposterous. It is not Irish but Irish-American. Mr. Blossom of St. Louis doubtless gathered his material and atmosphere by reading for quite half an hour in some public library.

"Eileen" is rich in melody. It is fairly well sung, and, thanks particularly to one Scott Welsh, well enough played. But as far as it betrays any knowledge of or feeling for Irish custom, Irish spirit, and Irish lore, it might have been written by a young man from Wyoming whose sole impressions of the Emerald Isle were derived from two visits to a theatre where Andrew Mack was playing and one conversation with a man who had once (long ago) seen a play by Dion Boucicault.[40]

Woollcott's strictures cannot be wholly denied, but he may not have seen many of Herbert's earlier works. Some of their books surely would have completely paralyzed his powers of description. The regular reviewer for the New York *Times* agreed with Woollcott because the story did not matter anyway. On the other hand the Irish setting provided special and unusual interest, and the score was bursting with rich melody. He noticed how characteristically Irish the music was and conceded that much of the charm stemmed from this national flavor. The composer's technical skill and his ingenious orchestration were evident as usual, and the dramatic use of the orchestra called for special comment. As a production *Eileen* was more than satisfactory, fortunate in having good singers, and steeped in visual and aural beauty. The orchestra, too, was excellent, and Herbert, who conducted the New York première, directed it brilliantly.

Another intelligent criticism admitted there was a plot, but at the time of going to press no infringement suits had been started!

The principal feature, of course, is the music, and of this one has his money's worth. Mr. Herbert's score is altogether charming and well up to his usual melodious standard. It is a trifle heavy for its subject, making it smack, at times, of grand opera. Edward Martindel sang well and acted with distinction the part of the British officer. Grace Breen was a sympathetic, but somewhat colorless heroine. Walter Scanlan, as the hero, lacked the dashing personality the part required. Algernon Greig contributed the only light touch of the evening with a humorous song most cleverly done.

The chorus sings remarkably well as do most ill-looking chorusi. They do themselves credit by their harmonious rendering of the two best songs in the piece. One of these, "Free Trade and a Misty Moon," which is by all odds the most captivating bit of the entertainment, is led by Greek Evans in the rôle of Shaun Dhu. His voice with its vibrant power and beauty of tone lends grateful relief to the usual piping of actors and others usually found in Irish song plays.[41]

Opposed to the reviewers condemning the book were just as many and more who were not at all disturbed by it, and who found *Eileen* praiseworthy in every respect. One such critic not too slyly referred to the generation-old rivalry between Herbert and Reginald de Koven, who had just seen his serious opera *The Canterbury Pilgrims* produced by the Metropolitan Opera Company on March 8. The critic lavishly praised *Eileen* and then declared that Herbert was turning out light opera of grand-opera impressiveness while de Koven had shown he could write grand opera of musical comedy caliber![42] Herbert would have been more than human if he had not enjoyed this gibe at the pretentious composer of *Robin Hood*.

Reviewers who found the libretto better than average were correct, but even they had to admit that only the music commanded attention. One briefly summarized it by saying it would set the standard of operetta music "for generations to come";[43] another declared that it surpassed Herbert's earlier efforts and established him, "without exaggeration, as the leader of light opera composers in the world."[44] Still another enthusiastically set forth:

If ever there was a labor of love performed by a composer, it was Victor Herbert's writing of . . . "Eileen" . . . As Mr. Herbert said in his curtain speech: "I have lived in America for many years; for a long time I have been a citizen of this country, and believe I am a good American citizen. But I was born in Dublin and I have always wanted to write an Irish comic opera which would add to Ireland's wealth of beautiful music and would be worthy of the traditions of the race.

That the eminent composer has richly succeeded in realizing his wish we herewith testify. "Eileen," however, is more than an opera—it is a bit of propaganda . . . Indeed, when one listens to Mr. Herbert's music . . . how could one deny the Irish anything? Faith, they plead for it so sweetly![45]

It would be hazardous to deny that Herbert had realized, at least within limits, his ambition to write a great Irish operetta. At the same time it was "one of the most distinctive comic opera triumphs on the American stage" and certainly not unrelated to Ireland's travail and longing to achieve a national destiny.[46]

Eileen enjoyed a run of 64 performances in New York,[47] which took it to the end of the season. During the summer plans were made to launch a two-year tour in the fall: all the large cities of America were to be visited. Evidently Herbert wanted to spread his Irish gospel as far and as wide as possible. Late in September *Eileen* began its cross-country trek in Hartford, Connecticut. In fairly rapid succession it was presented in different eastern cities (four weeks in Philadelphia), then moved on toward the Middle West. One of the shortest stops—two days only—was in Dayton, Ohio, where, at the Victoria Theatre on January 16, 1918, it was completely destroyed by fire.[48] Scenery, costumes, properties, electrical effects and musical instruments perished, and all thought of reconstituting the show was immediately abandoned.

Three years later, a valiant attempt was made to revive *Eileen*, and Herbert conducted the opening in Cleveland, where it played the week of March 28, 1921.[49] But its new life was short, partly because the international situation was different, partly because the American public craved new fare. Infrequent presentations since then have given America no real chance to learn its beauties and its charm.

No operetta of Herbert's is more deserving of revival than *Eileen*. It is his most earnest attempt at light opera, and may be his greatest. Beyond question *Eileen* "marked the last truly characteristic, genuine effort of his long and brilliant career."[50] Such was the true, yet rather sad judgment of Gustav Klemm, talented American composer and devout admirer of Herbert's genius. *Eileen* should be better known in America and in one other place—the present realm of Ireland, whose independence would have gladdened Herbert's heart.

Naturally the creation of *Eileen* brought no halt to Herbert's Irish activities. A concert in Carnegie Hall on the evening of April 8, 1917—sponsored by Clan-na-Gael and Cumann-na-mBan, Inc.—celebrated the "Irish Republic Anniversary," and a small regiment of performers, singers and speakers took part.[51]

On May 7 the Society of the Friendly Sons of St. Patrick held a quarterly meeting at the Hotel Astor. Herbert retired as president and received a large silver loving cup (actually a punch bowl) for the services he had rendered. He was happy to welcome as a new member John McCormack, who sang to his fellows with Herbert playing the accompaniments. Both received a tremendous ovation. A full measure of reasonableness also crept into the Sons' analysis of foreign affairs. They pledged full loyalty to the United States Government, now an ally of Great Britain, with no reservations concerning Ireland's freedom.[52]

Nine days afterward Herbert, still starry-eyed over any Hibernian manifestation, created a mild sensation in the Grand Central Palace. The Actors' Fund Fair was in progress, and prominent personalities of the stage were more or less on display. Herbert was among them, and as he circled the booths he spied an enclosure all draped in green and Irish atmosphere. Here sleeping peacefully as if in the parlor was a tiny white pig which caught the composer's fancy. He stopped, waved his baton over the little pig's head, and pronounced: "I dub thee Princess Pat—no, Eileen—no, that won't do either. Well, then Victor you shall be."[53] And he tied a green ribbon to the animal's neck and carried it around for the rest of the evening.

So successful had been Herbert's contribution to the revue, *The Century Girl,* that he was looked upon thenceforth as a source of music for similar productions, at least for those of Florenz Ziegfeld, Jr. He was never the sole composer for any of the Ziegfeld Follies, nor could he be called one of the characteristic composers; but for the rest of his life he wrote for them a considerable quantity of music. It was as functional as it was effective. A musician like Herbert was needed for the spectacles and pageants which Ziegfeld and his lieutenant, Joseph Urban, loved to stage; and he injected a flavor of tonal artistry that paralleled the visual beauty of the producers.

Herbert's first participation in the Ziegfeld Follies was in 1917, when he composed the music for a special finale to Act I which was designedly patriotic. The show opened at the New Amsterdam Theatre in New York on June 12, and was hailed as a continuation of Ziegfeld's best work. There was the usual succession of comedians and singers and beautiful girls, but above all was the patriotic finale which glorified America and promised victory over the Central Powers. Admittedly flamboyant, it was none the less effective as George Washington, Abraham Lincoln, and Woodrow Wilson appeared on the stage; as smartly attired girls "in costumes more artistic than historic" paraded before an awesome eagle; as a fleet of American battleships seemed to roll right up to the footlights; and as a gigantic American flag waved over the audience, which stood to the strains of "The Star-Spangled Banner."[54] Herbert's music included a rousing song entitled "Can't You Hear Your Country Calling," which helped to whip the crowd to a high pitch of excitement but was equally appropriate to the gyrations on the stage.

A few months later New York received another revue which owed much of its music to Herbert: *Miss 1917,* produced at the Century Theatre on November 5, 1917, by Dillingham and Ziegfeld. *Miss 1917* was the real successor and sequel to *The Century Girl* of the preceding season; but, whereas the earlier show had been brilliantly glamorous, this one was a dismal failure. Its rapid decline was due to financial difficulties, not to inferior talent or music. The stringencies of wartime economy, plus another crazily expensive roster of attractions, doomed the enterprise and forced it into early bankruptcy. Only 48 performances were given.[55]

Miss 1917 was not highly important, but neither was it devoid of interest. Its music, like that of its forerunner, was the work of two composers, Herbert's colleague this time being Jerome Kern. The semblance of a book, vastly insignificant, was prepared by Guy Bolton and P. G. Wodehouse. For *The Century Girl* Herbert had written both scenic music and songs; for *Miss 1917* he wrote much more of the former. "The Society Farmerettes" was the only new and original song by him listed on the opening-night program. Quite unusual was "The Singing Blacksmith of Curriclough" which he based upon songs of his grandfather, Samuel Lover. Arranged for double octet, this was a labor of love as well as of entertainment.

The most ambitious contribution to the score was Herbert's music for a ballet scene ("poem-choreographic") designed, staged, and danced (with others) by Adolph Bolm. Its title was "Falling Leaves." The sylvan surroundings, the rustic atmosphere, the Grecian touches and mythological allusions left an impression of exquisite fancy and imagination.

Between the Ziegfeld Follies of 1917 and *Miss 1917* Herbert composed another operetta, the first of the post-*Eileen* productions which constitute his final group of works for the stage. None of these was particularly outstanding. They have flashes of Herbert's inimitable charm and grace, but they also show a lack of zest, a reluctance to write a big scene, a tendency to fill a score with popular songs which would have been too slight for a Herbert light opera of an earlier day.

The new operetta in three acts, *Her Regiment,* was based upon a story supposedly romantic but pitifully weak. The book and lyrics were by William Le Baron, who more or less replaced Henry Blossom. Herbert and Blossom seemed to have come to a parting of the ways—a rift which caused comment all along Broadway.[56] But Le Baron was not Blossom's equal, and his association with Herbert was scarcely momentous. The producer of *Her Regiment* was Joe Weber, who made his final arrangements with the composer in July, although the piece was well publicized earlier.

Herbert composed most of the music at Lake Placid between the middle of August and the middle of September. The first performance on any stage occurred in Springfield, Massachusetts, on October 22, 1917, and the New York opening followed on November 12 at the Broadhurst Theatre. Under the expert guidance of Fred G. Latham the production was expertly handled and staged, its lack of success resulting from inner weaknesses that no stage manager could overcome.

The New York program announced the following cast:

Colonel Pontsable	Hugh Chilvers
André de Courcy	Donald Brian
Blanquet	Frank Moulan
Eugene de Merriame	Sidney Jarvis
Sergeant Sabretache	Frederick Manatt
Carabine	George Averill
François	Frank Meyers
Estelle Durvenay	Audrey Maple
Lisette Berlier	Josie Intropidi
Madame Guerriere	Paulina French
Jeanette	Norma Brown

Georgette.................................Cissie Sewall
Fifi.....................................Edythe Mason
Soldiers, Peasants, Girls, Guests, Servants, etc.

The musical director and the concert master were special friends of Herbert's: Fritz (or Frederik) Stahlberg, associated with him since the Pittsburgh Symphony days; and Harold Sanford, now his music assistant.

The setting was a French military encampment in Normandy in 1914: Act I, outside the "Pomme d'Or"; Act II, reception room of the Château Belleville; Act III, officers' quarters at the barracks.

In spite of its time and place, *Her Regiment* was not a war play. André de Courcy, the hero, has enlisted in the army under the name Jolicœur. He is in trouble from a youthful escapade in Paris. Estelle, home from schooling in America, is staying with her aunt in a neighboring château. She is supposed to marry Colonel Pontsable, the commander of the regiment. Love finds a way, however, and the Colonel, after blustering misunderstanding, relinquishes her to André.

The musical score of *Her Regiment* was effective and adequate, but had no qualities that could convert a dull book into anything resembling a success. There were no outstanding numbers, the choruses were abbreviated, and even the inevitable waltz was, for Herbert, somewhat pedestrian. The most attractive pieces are: "Soldier Men" (Estelle), piquant and flirtatious; " 'Twixt Love and Duty" (André), with a military refrain; "Art Song" (Eugene and girls), carrying on a pretty dialogue.

Nevertheless the music was tuneful, and the critics detected in it no waning of Herbert's powers. If it failed to enhance his reputation, it was only because he had been so generous in the past.[57] Moreover, the book was "generally highly dull," and the operetta as a whole was somewhat old-fashioned. All the critics agreed that the music was the best thing about it; but this was a customary judgment, not likely to prolong the life of a mediocre play. After 40 performances[58] it departed from Broadway and left few regrets behind it.

21

Aftermath and Twilight

As HERBERT entered the world of revues and less concentrated musical productions he lost none of his interest in serious music. Just as steadfast was his concern for musical conditions in America; and he tried to give support to worthy causes. Late in 1917 he lent encouragement to his old friend John C. Freund, who was establishing the Musical Alliance of the United States, designed "to unite all interested in music and in the musical industries."[1]

The listed aims of the Musical Alliance were an expression of nationalism resulting from the World War; but they were admirable in principle, particularly in their repudiation of nationalistic discrimination and their call for a national conservatory of music.

The World War had more immediate effects upon musical conditions in America. It prevented some musicians from coming to America, but it also forced certain artists to leave these shores. German musicians were especially suspect, and our unenviable patriotic fervor led to the deportation of notable men. The most celebrated case was that of Karl Muck, conductor of the Boston Symphony Orchestra. Incidentally, the great German conductor displeased some of the Boston Brahmins with the version of "The Star-Spangled Banner" used by his orchestra. The discontented alleged that it was German in character, and Muck forthwith ordered a different arrangement. The objectionable version, unidentified to the public, was Herbert's arrangement—the final portion of his *American Fantasy*; the acceptable version was the product of the Boston concertmaster, Anton Witek, who was also suspected of enemy sympathies![2]

A similar incident, nearly as important, developed in the Midwest. Ernst Kunwald, Vienna-born conductor of the Cincinnati Symphony Orchestra, became a "prominent target in Attorney-General

508

Mitchell Palmer's witch-hunt,"[3] and was interned and subsequently deported. Left leaderless in the middle of the 1917–1918 season, the orchestra had real difficulties in maintaining its schedule. Eugène Ysaÿe was eventually chosen as permanent conductor; but the broken season was successfully carried out by several guest conductors, among whom were Herbert and Ossip Gabrilowitsch.

As guest conductor of the Cincinnati Symphony, Herbert was extremely happy to be at such work again. He directed three pairs of regular symphony concerts—January 11–12 and 25–26 and February 8–9, 1918—and three "pop" concerts.[4] His programs of the three symphonic pairs are of interest:

January 11 and 12

Symphony No. 5	Tchaikovsky
Overture to The Roman Carnival	Berlioz
The Swan of Tuonela	Sibelius
Siegfried's Rhine Journey, from Götterdämmerung	Wagner

January 25 and 26

Overture to A Midsummer Night's Dream	Mendelssohn
Symphony No. 7	Beethoven
Symphonie Espagnole (Jacques Thibaud, soloist)	Lalo
Rhapsodic Dance, Bamboula	Coleridge-Taylor

February 8 and 9

Symphony No. 1—Rustic Wedding	Goldmark
Piano Concerto No. 2 (Mischa Levitzki, soloist)	Saint-Saëns
Suite, Woodland Fancies	Herbert

It is interesting to note that Herbert played German music at these concerts in spite of the unreasonable prejudice against it. He even had the courage to play Wagner, who was practically *verboten* at the time, and he probably reveled in his audacity. The large German population of Cincinnati may have encouraged his selections, but it could hardly have strengthened his conviction that this was the best music he could present.

Back in New York, Herbert quietly assumed his place among the city's leading artists and participated in different events. On March 30, 1918, the Bohemians organized a reception at Delmonico's in honor of the famous violinist and pedagogue Leopold Auer. Herbert was at the table of honor along with Auer, Franz Kneisel, Fritz Kreisler, Artur Bodanzky, Josef Hofmann, and Walter Damrosch.[5]

On May 6 the Bohemians organized a committee to cooperate in planning music for the men in the Army and Navy. Herbert was a member of the committee[6] and proffered his good will and experience to the country's fighting forces.

This spring, too, Herbert and his orchestra appeared at a huge entertainment to raise money for the Catholic War Fund. The details were arranged by his friend Nathan Burkan, and several thousand dollars were collected.[7]

In the same season Herbert and other residents in the Riverside Drive neighborhood were appalled by chemical stenches blown across the Hudson River from New Jersey. Several chemical plants on the western bank were booming, and when the wind wafted their odors eastward the New Yorkers were sadly discomfited. Finally the New York State Board of Health, on petition by the West End Association and the City of New York, received the complaints of the citizens who declared they could no longer either take walks or leave their windows open.

Herbert consented to be the principal witness of the delegation which appeared before the State Health Commissioner on April 29. He described conditions as "absolutely intolerable," as constituting "positively the worst nuisance in the world" and a serious threat to the health of every one living under their influence. The odors interfered with his composing and with the strolls he depended on for exercise. When asked on what days the odors were worst he said he could give no accurate reply because he never kept a "diary of smells." In testifying he became more feelingful on the subject and reached the height of passionate indignation in declaring:

All I can say is that it is the most awful bunch of smells I've ever smelled. We suffer terribly. I've already noticed that it was particularly bad near the Soldiers and Sailors' monument, and in that part of the drive where Mayor Mitchell lived. When Mitchell was Mayor I was always kind of happy that he had to smell them, too. It's an unbearable nuisance not to be able to go out for a little walk in the most beautiful park in the city without consulting my nose for guidance.[8]

The odors did not stop Herbert entirely from writing music, but some of his reported compositions failed to appear. One announcement was that he was making a musical comedy setting of Clara Lipman's play *Julie Bonbon,* in which Irene Bordoni would be starred.[9] Another promised a fall production of *The House That Jack Built,* the music by Herbert, the book by Edward Childs Carpenter.[10] A substantial part of the music was written, but arrangements for production were never completed.

Composed about this time, and undeservedly neglected and unknown today, was the cantata for solo, chorus, and orchestra *The Call to Freedom.* This "patriotic ode" was published in the spring of 1918 and first performed at Willow Grove the following June 27. In the première Herbert conducted his own orchestra and the excellent Strawbridge & Clothier chorus, long and expertly trained by his friend Herbert J. Tily.

The Call to Freedom is a work large in concept but of moderate proportions. Inspired by the war, it is intensely serious and is a musical expression of real dignity and power. Perhaps more than any other work it reveals the stanch ideals of Herbert and his unquenchable thirst for American liberty. This is evidenced not only by the sincerity of the music, but also by the remarkable fact that he turned poet and wrote the text. Presumably he had in mind all the oppressed of Europe, for his chorus represented "the downtrodden Peoples of the East" who were attracted to the West by the soloist, "the Spirit of Freedom." The poem has as much cogency today as it had in 1918.

The disuse of this cantata for patriotic gatherings or ceremonies is explicable only by its need of a large orchestra for maximum effectiveness. Neither the chorus nor the solos are difficult, although the range of the solos is somewhat demanding. Its revival by choral societies, now or in the future, should be quite rewarding.

In 1952 William Tufts, the enterprising leader of the Agriculture Choristers at Washington, programmed *The Call to Freedom* even though he had but twenty singers and a piano for accompaniment. Notwithstanding the inadequate resources, a critic wrote:

> Herbert's composition, dating back to 1918 and World War I, is an inspired work, designed for hundreds of voices and an orchestra. With a small group of 20 voices available, the grandiose effect could only be imagined. . . . The composition was well presented. It is quite incomprehensible that such an outstanding and timely piece of music as this should have remained in obscurity so long.[11]

At Philadelphia in the summer of 1918 Herbert wrote another patriotic piece which was a tribute to one of America's fighting services. It was the march-song *All Hail to You, Marines!* with text by a Philadelphia newspaperman, Richard J. Beamish. Herbert dashed off the melody as soon as he saw the words, hoping it would become an effective addition to the growing collection of America's war songs.[12] Unfortunately it was not very distinguished and failed to fulfill the composer's hopes.

At Lake Placid after the Willow Grove summer series Herbert found other opportunities to assist in the war effort, notably in raising funds for the Red Cross. On August 18 he joined with Billie Burke and George Hamlin in a benefit concert, appearing before the public as a cellist for the first time in about twenty years. Hamlin sang songs of Samuel Lover, with Herbert accompanying him on the piano, and Miss Burke recited one of Lover's poems. At the conclusion of the affair the Red Cross had gained some $2,500.[13]

Twenty years earlier, Herbert had wondered what role his 22nd Regiment Band would be called on to play in the Spanish-American War. That was a minor struggle, however, and nothing interfered with his becoming a symphony conductor. In the fall of 1918 his old National Guard regiment, not knowing the future, asked him to return to it and try to restore its musical superiority. At the "earnest solicitation" of Colonel H. H. Treadwell, Herbert rejoined his old outfit and received the rank of first lieutenant. Not only was he to rebuild the band, but he was to give band instruction to promising men two nights a week.[14] Fortunately the war was nearer its end than anyone surmised, and Herbert escaped the onerous task. There was, nevertheless, a gallantry in his willingness to assume a semimilitary responsibility in an occupation which had lost all its congeniality. (Let us hope that Lieutenant Herbert received, at least, a few salutes!) The incident also inspired him to write one of his best marches—*Defendam March,* which he dedicated to Colonel Treadwell.

At this time, too, Herbert found a new and pleasing diversion. Father William Joseph Finn, justly celebrated for developing boy choirs, set up his choir school at 3 Riverside Drive. Herbert was interested in the boys' work, and when time permitted he would stop at the school to visit with the youthful singers. Then he would hum certain Gregorian modes and ask the boys whether they could identify them. He hoped to catch them napping or off guard, but the boys loved it—and him, too. Strange to say, his friendship seemed to stop short of Father Finn himself.[15]

Soon it was time for this many-sided man to be in the theater once more, and the Christmas season of 1918 was brightened by a new Herbert three-act musical comedy, *The Velvet Lady,* produced by Klaw and Erlanger. The first performance on any stage occurred at the Forrest Theatre in Philadelphia, December 23; the first performance in New York was at the New Amsterdam Theatre, February 3, 1919. Herbert conducted both. The play was entertaining, and so was the music; and it enjoyed a moderate success. But again the score suffered by comparison with Herbert's earlier and greater works.

Regardless of the rumor of a break in relations, Herbert and Henry Blossom collaborated again and tried valiantly to duplicate what they had done in 1914 with the delightful *The Only Girl,* Herbert supplying a series of fairly short pieces to a libretto derived from a play. *The Velvet Lady* was based on a three-act farce: *A Full House,* by

Fred Jackson, which had been presented in New York on May 10, 1915.[16] However, the results were not as effective, and the music was less attractive.

The program of the New York opening provided the following information:

Parks		Ernest Torrence
Una	⎫	Una Fleming
Teddy	⎪	Teddie Hudson
Janet	⎪	Janet McIlwaine
Lucine	⎪	Lucine Paula
Florence	⎬ The Bridesmaids	Florence Crips
Dolly	⎪	Dolly Alwyn
Helen	⎪	Helen Borden
Mignon	⎪	Mignon Reed
Tess	⎭	Tess Mayer
Ottilie Howell, a bride		Marie Flynn
Susie		Georgia O'Ramey
Miss Winnacker, Auntie		Eleanor Gordon
Bubbles, Ottilie's sister		Minerva Coverdale
Nicholas King		Jed Prouty
Ned Pembroke		Alfred Gerrard
George Howell		Ray Redmond
Sergeant		Daniel Sullivan
Mooney, a new cop		Eddie Dowling
"Spookie Ookum"		Janet McIlwaine
Vera Vernon (The Velvet Lady)		Fay Marbe
Mrs. Pembroke		Edna von Buelow

Guests, Policemen

The musical director was Frederik Stahlberg; the stage directors, Edgar MacGregor and Julian Mitchell.

Act I is in the library of Howell's house on Riverside Drive, late afternoon; Act II, in the living hall of Howell's house, early the same evening (Halloween); Act III, in Howell's living room an hour later.

The insipid story is based upon a packet of indiscreet letters which Ned has written to a dancer, the Velvet Lady. George agrees to get them back, for Ned must have them in order to convince Bubbles of his blameless past. In going about his task, George is forced to neglect Ottilie, his new bride; and, when he does return, his suitcase with the letters has been accidentally exchanged for one filled with stolen jewels. The real thief and the police also come to the Howell home. Susie, the maid, finally settles matters to the satisfaction of all concerned.

A farce pure and simple, with not a vestige of romance or tenderness, it was not a dull play, and there were amusing situations; but the humor was labored and not calculated to inspire mellifluous music. As a result Herbert's score was chiefly a series of short, popular songs which resembled the contemporary foxtrot, waltz, or one-step. He was never comfortable in writing a typical popular song; and in a work made up of nothing else he was very much at a disadvantage. The critic for the New York *Times* could rightly say that the music lent gaiety and charm; but he was not familiar with much of Herbert's music as he wrote, about "Life and Love": "The waltz in particular seemed to delight the audience, striking the note of youthful love and longing with a freshness of romantic melody in the very best mood of the Viennese composers."

Some critics noticed that the music was weak for Herbert; they conceded its prettiness without falling under its spell.[17] Neither were they entranced by the production as a whole, for some of the principals seemed to be miscast while others had too little to do. There was a bit of paradox in the fact that the leading character was really Susie, the maid—certainly not the Velvet Lady, who had only about fifteen minutes before the footlights. Yet the show lived through 136 performances on Broadway[18] before it took to the road, where it was moderately successful.

With *The Velvet Lady* came an unhappy revelation of British feeling toward Herbert. There were reports in the middle of 1919 that the show would be produced in London, but that Herbert's music would not be used. The reason? Simply that in recent years Herbert had expressed so violently his pro-Irish, anti-British political sentiments that England would no longer welcome his music. The British animosity was "sufficient to preclude his scores from being presented in England."[19]

In the first half of 1919 Herbert made numerous benefit appearances; but two events stand out from them all. February 21 and 22 found him officiating as guest conductor of the Chicago Symphony Orchestra—an engagement which afforded special satisfaction. Chicago, a score of years before, had considered him as a rival to Theodore Thomas and had castigated him for his presumption. Now he returned as an invited guest for a pair of concerts in the regular symphony season. His soloist was an old friend, the distinguished pianist Ossip Gabrilowitsch, who played the Tchaikovsky Concerto in B flat minor. The day before the first concert the pianist, who was no mean composer, autographed one of his own songs (*Good-bye,* Op. 11, No. 1) for Herbert in the following manner: "To Victor Herbert in sincerest admiration and friendship. Ossip Gabrilowitsch. Chicago Febr. 20th 1919."[20]

The second noteworthy event was an ASCAP dinner in honor of George Maxwell, the first president of the Society, who was soon to depart for Europe. His colleagues arranged a festive evening for him at the Hotel Claridge on March 29. Herbert was toastmaster and performed his duties cheerfully and with ease. The proceedings had to open, however, with a tinge of solemnity. Herbert rose and called for a silent toast to Henry Blossom, who had died six days earlier. Blossom was the best librettist Herbert ever found, and his death was a blow to the composer as well as to ASCAP, of which he was a charter member, and a director for the last two years of his life.

During the evening there were many speeches, but two exceeded the others in importance. One was by Raymond Hubbell, an outstanding popular composer and an intimate friend of Herbert's. No one was better qualified to recount the achievements of the Society from its inception. With radio still unheard of, neither he nor his colleagues had the slightest premonition of the struggles and prosperity that lay ahead. Herbert also gave a speech, reminiscent in tone. He told of the fight for increased copyright protection and the difficulties that had had to be overcome before composers won the right to royalties on mechanical instruments. Then, at the clamoring request of the entire assemblage, he played a cello solo, choosing the ever popular *Le Cygne* by Saint-Saëns.[21]

Herbert signed another recording contract on May 27, 1919, whereby he agreed to make piano rolls for the American Piano Company (Ampico). He was to play only his own compositions, but the company had the right to select the titles from his published works.[22] The loss of business files and the abrupt demise of the player-piano have made it almost impossible to determine how many piano recordings Herbert made or what they were. It is known, at least, that he made records for both the American and the Aeolian (Duo-Art) companies, the two foremost piano-roll manufacturers. The two are now combined in the American Piano Corporation, which could name in 1952 only the following recordings by Herbert and could not say when they were made or released:

Ampico: Indian Summer; A Kiss in the Dark (key of D), from *Orange Blossoms*; I Might Be Your Once-in-a-While, from *Angel Face*; Babes in Toyland; Kiss Me Again, from *Mlle. Modiste;* Punchinello; When Knighthood Was in Flower; Yesterthoughts. Duo-Art: When You're Away, from *The Only Girl*.

Herbert again had music in the Ziegfeld Follies of 1919, which was produced in New York at the New Amsterdam Theatre on June 16.

He contributed to the second act the episode "The Circus Ballet," which was appreciated as a "ballet of real distinction"[23] and was enhanced by the inimitable grace of Marilyn Miller.

Already, however, a new Herbert operetta had been launched in the Middle West, and the country's attention was focused on it. *Angel Face* proved to be musically superior to his two previous efforts. The libretto, however (by Harry B. and Robert B. Smith), was so bad that critics either ignored it completely or confessed it was beyond their comprehension.

The composer signed his contract for *Little Miss Wise*—later known as *Angel Face*—on February 8, 1919, with the publishers, T. B. Harms and Francis, Day & Hunter (represented by Max Dreyfus);[24] but George W. Lederer became the producer of the show. The first performance on any stage occurred in Chicago at the Colonial Theatre on June 8, the composer conducting, and the audience showing marked enthusiasm. The music was called the best Herbert had written in years— a pardonable exaggeration; but the book was characterized as slipshod, puerile, and threadbare.[25] It was noticed, too, that the play seemed to be derived from an older farce called at different times *The Elixir of Love* and *Some Baby*. Still, the success of *Angel Face* seemed undoubted as it entertained a number of cities before opening in New York at the Knickerbocker Theatre, December 29, 1919, when the cast was:

Tom Larkins, a rich young man, whose fad is musical comedy, composer of "The Lemon Girl"....................	John E. Young
Arthur Griffin, a sculptor, Tom's friend who shares his apartment................	Tyler Brooks
Friends of Tom and Arthur:	
Sandy Sharp....................	Richard Pyle
Hugh Fairchild..................	John Reinhard
Rockwell Gibbs..................	Howard Johnson
Professor Barlow, an eccentric scientist....	George Schiller
Ira Mapes, a student of entomology......	Bernard Thornton
Slooch, a correspondence school detective..	Jack Donahue
Irving, Tom's servant..................	William Cameron
Mrs. Zenobia Wise....................	Eda von Buelow
Betty, her youngest daughter, aged 17....	Marguerite Zender
Vera, her eldest daughter, aged 28......	Minerva Grey
Completing the quintette of Mrs. Wise's daughters:	
Paula	Mary Milburn
Lily	Marguerite St. Clair
Pearl	Gertrude Wadelle

Mrs. Larkins, Tom's grandmother from
   Keokuk ....   Sarah McVicker
Tessie Blythe, Tom's fiancee...........   Emilie Lea
Moya, a friend of Tessie...............   May Thompson
      Members of a musical comedy company

Lederer himself was in charge of the staging, the musical numbers being staged by Julian Alfred. The musical director was Harold Vicars.

Printed in the program was a curious note which gave the spectators a false anticipation of what was to come:

Taking a gland from a young and vigorous chimpanzee I grafted it onto a man 80 years old who was virtually in a state of decrepitude. The patient showed a complete change. His shoulders became upright, he walked straighter and seemed to enjoy the physical and mental powers of a young man of 30.—Dr. Serge Voronoff, head of the physiological laboratories of the Collège de France.

This strange notice was not entirely unrelated to the drama, but *Angel Face* was scarcely concerned with rejuvenescence; had it been, it might have provided more amusement.

The first two acts are in the bachelor apartment shared by Arthur Griffin and Tom Larkins; the third and last act, in the hotel lounge across the street.

"Angel Face" is the appellation chosen by Betty as she pursues Arthur and breaks his unhappy engagement with Vera. Tom has his own troubles as he tries to convince Tessie that his popularity with the ladies is meaningless as far as she is concerned. Professor Barlow, inventor of the harmless elixir, thinks that his formula has actually reduced Tessie to babyhood; but the infant is a kidnapped child, stolen from the hotel across the street. When all doubts are resolved, Tom and Arthur are happily reconciled with Tessie and Betty.

Herbert conducted the first New York performance of this farrago of nonsense, and the audience gave him its usual warm response. It found the music tuneful and spirited, but by far the best strains were in a potpourri of melodies from past operettas. As Alexander Woollcott remarked in the New York *Times,* they reminded one of the debt really owed to the composer.

The music of *Angel Face* furnished plenty of pleasure, but it fell behind the elaborate scores of earlier years. As in *The Velvet Lady* the pieces were mostly short and separate manifestations of current popular song. They were, however, more attractive than the airs in the previous play, and they afforded some hope that Herbert might yet be successful as a composer of smart, sophisticated comedy. One song, "I Might Be Your Once-in-a-While," swept the country with its infectious lilt and happy charm. Another song—"Angel Face"—was almost as captivating, with carefree syncopation and subtly spiced harmony. But on the whole the music failed to equal Herbert's best, for it was not characteristic of what he stood for or could do most effectively.

The criticisms followed an oft-repeated pattern. The book was bad, the music was good and "even imparted vitality" to the book, so that the "excess of plot may be forgiven."[26] The thought that the book was encumbered by plot was specially stressed by Heywood Broun, who wrote: "Nobody can accuse Mr. Smith of having failed to provide . . . a plot. 'Angel Face' has dozens of plots, all jostling and elbowing each other in an effort to produce new complications. It is a very old home week of plots, and sometimes we felt that the Knickerbocker Theatre was hardly big enough to hold them all."[27] A less charitable reviewer thought the book "so tedious, useless and archaic that it is hard to imagine how any sentient being could have written it." He reported the reference to monkey glands for recapturing lost youth, and added: "The book of 'Angel Face' is an ideal subject for such an operation."[28]

Angel Face ran for 57 performances in New York[29] before it took to the road, where its success was reasonable. In the middle of 1920, however, a curious thing happened. Claims were advanced against the originality of the libretto, and Harry B. Smith had to pay $2,500 to Irwin Rosen and F. Howard Schnebbe, who owned the play on which *Angel Face* was based.[30] This was *The Elixir of Youth* by Zellah Covington and Jules Simonson, produced in New York on August 12, 1915, as *Some Baby*.

This awkward situation had nothing to do with Herbert; but two years later he was rendered unhappy by the repudiation of *Angel Face* in England. Again its failure seemed to stem from the story and not from the music. Norman J. Norman produced the work in London at the Strand on October 11, 1922, and the critical London *Times* called the story complex, the dialogue dull, the lyrics scarcely above average. It conceded some tunefulness to the music and admitted it was "like an oasis in a desert of humdrum conversation about nothing in particular." A warning was issued that success would come only after necessary and inevitable pruning. Whatever was done was insufficient, and success never arrived. It was withdrawn after 13 performances,[31] and Herbert's reputation in England was severely injured.

Between *Angel Face* and his next operetta Herbert was persuaded to write incidental music for a play. It was not the first time he had done so, but two of the songs he composed now were so good that the venture deserves special mention. As usual, he picked a bad play to embellish.

Edward Locke's *The Dream Song* was produced in Chicago at the

Central Music Hall on October 23, 1919, and ran through the 8th of November.[32] Its success was so meager that it failed to reach New York. The three acts, in London, Paris, and London respectively, tell of an exiled Polish composer who writes an opera, wants his daughter to sing the soprano lead, and is furious when she ignores his wishes and instead marries a young Russian artist. The available prima donna, however, fails in her assignment, and the daughter (Marie) returns to her father, saves the opera, and wins back her father's affection.

The plot was distinctly unoriginal and the acting in general was "frequently amateurish."[33] There was, however, special interest in the music, for Herbert occupied a niche of his own in Chicago's affections. A leading local music critic, Maurice Rosenfeld, singled it out for particular comment, and he must have astonished his readers with these few lines: "There are several special musical numbers through the drama, written by Victor Herbert. These are serious ballads, revealing little of the happy tuneful Herbert that we know in his musical comedies, and still less of the dramatic and inspired invention of the composer of grand operas, 'Natoma' and 'Madeleine.' The songs are long drawn out, with neither aim nor climax, and with just indifferent tunes."[34]

Now this particular criticism happened to be a most curious mixture of irrelevance, perspicuity, and bad judgment, the kind of statement which would make any affected composer hostile to reviewers of his music. The songs were serious, also long drawn out; but they were not without aim or climax, and they were decidedly tuneful. "Lovelight" is a gracious waltz of considerable intensity and natural charm. But more important is "Farewell," a ballad or near art song, which may rank among Herbert's best vocal solos. It is both melancholy and dramatic, passionately intense, and surprisingly richly harmonized. A rhythmic-melodic pattern occurs repeatedly in the accompaniment, leaving the solo voice free to intone around it. The alternation of major-minor modes and a completely natural climax allotted to the singer (who must encompass nearly two octaves) increase the song's emotional tension. It is also a song of great dynamic extremes, another aspect which makes it unusual among Herbert's pieces for the voice. Regardless of the play, these songs are outstanding little works and deserve to be sung and heard.

Six months after the first performance of *Angel Face* Herbert was ready with another operetta. Both the producer (Harry Wardell) and the librettist (Frederic A. Kummer) were associates new to Herbert, and the three contrived a spectacle which was pleasant and amusing. Nevertheless it was not conspicuously successful.

Herbert contracted to write the music on October 16, 1919, when the show was still without a title.[35] Nor had it received a title nearly a month later, when the public was informed that production would take place around Christmas, that it would be staged by J. Clifford Brooke, and that Philip James would be the conductor.[36]

James has become one of America's eminent composers and musical leaders. Herbert met him shortly after the close of the First World War. He heard the young man direct the famous Pershing Band at the Hippodrome, was impressed with his ability, and offered help if he needed a job after release from the army.[37] When James learned of Herbert's new show he applied for the conductor's post. Herbert, of course, was not the employer, but he offered James some good and characteristic advice: under no circumstances to take the job for less than $100 per week in New York or less than $150 per week on the road. If he consented to do the work for less, Herbert did not want to see him again! There was much argument over the conductor's salary, but—James was firm in his demands and eventually was appointed at the figures suggested. He went back to Herbert with the good news, over which there was mutual rejoicing.[38]

Prior to production there were conflicting reports as to where the new work, at last entitled *My Golden Girl,* would be introduced. Both Providence and Wilmington were mentioned as likely places. But the first performance on any stage occurred in Stamford, Connecticut (the composer conducting), on December 19, 1919, the other cities having to wait their turn as it readied itself for New York. Here it was first produced at the Nora Bayes Theatre on February 2, 1920, and the friendly audience was vociferous as Herbert walked down the aisle, received the baton from the regular conductor, and gave the signal to begin.[39] Herbert, always a good showman, was fond of this kind of entrance. The audience also liked it, and it made a great effect.

The cast at the New York opening contained several names which became fixtures in stage and screen entertainment:

Wilson, the Mitchells' butler...............Robert O'Connor
Blanche, a maid..........................Dorothy Tierney
Kitty Mason, a friend of Mrs. Mitchell......Evelyn Cavanaugh
Capt. Paul de Bazin, her fiancé.................Richard Dore
Arthur Mitchell, a dissatisfied young man........Victor Morley
Peggy Mitchell, his wife, equally dissatisfied......Marie Carroll
Martin, the Mitchells' chauffeur............Raymond Barrett
Mr. Hanks, Mrs. Mitchell's lawyer............Ned A. Sparks
Mr. Pullinger, Mr. Mitchell's lawyer..............Edward See
Helen Randolph, Mr. Mitchell's affinity..........Helen Bolton
Howard Pope, Mrs. Mitchell's affinity..........George Trabert
Mrs. Judson Mitchell, Mr. Mitchell's mother...Edna May Oliver

Mr. Clarence Swan, Mrs. Mitchell's father........Harold Vizard
Mildred Ray ⎱ friends of Kitty............ ⎰ Victoria White
Lois Booth ⎰ ⎱ Adele Boulais
    Guests: Trixie Packard, Yvonne La Grange, Gladys
Hart, Eileen Adaire, Caroline Holton, Viola Degnan, Flo
Howard, Jeannette Dietrich, Robina Davidson, Peggy
Schramm, Marci White, Loretta Walsh, Norma Eve
Warrington, Robert Archibald, Eastman McRoy,
William Strubain

Act I, Scene 1, was in the main hall, the Mitchells' country home on
Long Island, present time, on a Saturday afternoon in June; Scene 2—
The same—that evening before dinner; Act II, the Mitchells' private
bathing beach—that night.

    The play was an attempt to portray the troubles of a young married
couple, each with a hobby that claims too much time and attention.
Arthur plays the bassoon, Peggy plays golf; besides, they fancy themselves in love with Helen and Howard respectively. So they agree to
a divorce; but the complications caused by their lawyers and their
affinities make them realize how silly they have been. They reconcile
their differences while Helen and Howard discover that they, too, are
made for each other.

    It was not difficult to place songs in such a story, but there was scant
opportunity for romantic ardor or dramatic development. Herbert
contented himself with separate songs which were tuneful, bright and
pleasant, and sometimes a little wistful. The last quality inheres in the
duet of Arthur and Peggy ("Darby and Joan") as they sing of how
they might have felt had they lived in a rustic past. Rather clever in its
musical effect is Arthur's "I Want You," a bassoon love song in which
he demonstrates, by singing, his style of playing his favorite instrument.
The jerkiness of certain phrases and the chromatic deviations of the air
faithfully reflect an amateur's difficulties with a refractory tool.

    The title song, "My Golden Girl," sung by Howard to Peggy, is one
of Herbert's weaker love lyrics. Much better, and genuinely amusing,
is "A Song without (Many) Words," delivered by Helen and Arthur.
They are inspired to improvise a song without the help of words or a
bassoon, and the text consists solely of popular song rhymes. The inter-
ludial phrases are charming. The most interesting song in the show was
doubtless the intentionally blatant "Ragtime Terpsichore," sung by
Wilson and Blanche as the butler struggles with his jazz steps. The
juxtaposition of different rhythms in vocal line and accompaniment
reveals the seriousness of Herbert's efforts to write a good jazz number.
A duet of some importance is Helen's and Howard's "If We Had Met
Before," sung as they are attracted to each other. More in the style of

Herbert's earlier works, its modestly romantic vein offers a rather sharp contrast to the more flamboyant songs he was now affecting. Howard and Helen were also supposed to sing a duet, with waltz refrain, entitled "Oh Day in June," but although it was composed and even published, it was not used in *My Golden Girl*. The melody soared too high for the soprano's voice. The loss of the number was a real misfortune, for it was a characteristic Herbert lyric—in the opinion of Philip James, one of his best.[40] This was one more instance of Herbert being handicapped by inadequate vocalists.

The date of the New York opening was unfortunate. A Dillingham production (*The Night Boat*) and the return of Maxine Elliott (in *Trimmed in Scarlet*) occurred the same night, and the theater reviewers paid little attention to Herbert's latest work. Those who did see it offered pretty much the usual description: good music, poor book. The competence of the performance was accepted, vocally and histrionically, and the production as a whole seemed quite satisfactory. Its life depended entirely on the music. On April 5 it moved from the Nora Bayes Theatre, a roof spot, to the more conventional Casino, where better business was expected. Here it lasted to the end of the month, through the 105th performance,[41] when it was withdrawn for the summer. On the tour organized for the following season it was only moderately successful; and it soon joined the growing collection of Herbert's unsung works.

My Golden Girl was filled with separate songs written in the popular style of the day. As such it was like most of Herbert's later works, differing widely from the opulent, richly filled scores of his earlier productions. Many observers of his career have concluded that he was "written out," that his powers were weaker than at any previous time. There can be no doubt that the musical comedy of 1920 was different from the operetta of 1905; but Herbert was fully conscious of the fact and was striving to produce what the public wanted. Some professional critics felt that musical comedy was on the decline, and a few blamed the composers for capitulating to the public appetite. Herbert seemed to feel that this was an oversimplification of the case: mixed in were the salability of music and the problems of the music publisher. When asked to state his views he said: "One very interesting phase of the question is the growth of the music publishing business. Songs from successful plays are printed in great numbers and are the source of great profits. In order that these songs may sell, they must have words that are independent of the play—that is, on some general theme and attractive to the person that has not seen the play. I think that this may have had its effect in weaning us (the composers) away from comic opera in which the lyrics are woven into the plot and are part of it."[42]

A world of regret may be read into Herbert's words, but not an assumption that he was unable to match the masterpieces of an earlier decade.

Herbert's remarks aroused considerable interest and led to further analysis of the musical stage. It was suggested that he had been charitable, that commercialism had gained the upper hand. No longer was it necessary for composer and author to collaborate closely when the music had to sell regardless of relationship to an associated plot. This explained, said an interpreter, why Herbert now turned out a *My Golden Girl* rather than a *Babes in Toyland*. It must be admitted that, while the earlier operettas (for example, *Mlle. Modiste, The Fortune Teller, The Serenade*) contained many songs with texts well bound in with the story, they contained many others loosely if at all connected with it; but in the musical stage of 1920 the connection had become tenuous indeed.

Herbert may have thought that composers had been weaned from the lyrical, more expansive comic opera, but he longed to return to its satisfying embrace. He wanted a theater of his own (not an unfamiliar idea), and he hoped to free himself from the binding grip of current musical comedy. When asked if he desired such a theater he replied: "Yes, I do, and I'm hoping that it comes to a realization next season. I would like to have a theater that would indefinitely stand for notable musical productions, building up in time a clientele and a reputation such as have come to be identified with Mr. Belasco's playhouse. I would like to revive there my old successes as well as present there my new operettas." He cited the production of Fritz Kreisler's *Apple Blossoms* and a revival of *Ruddigore* as an indication of the public's return to genuine operetta, clearly implying his own desire to resume a more congenial type of stage composition.[43] He did not succeed, but he was certainly conscious of what he was doing and how it differed from what he wanted to do.

At the same time Herbert evinced no animosity for the librettists who wrote the "plots." He knew their lot was hard, their reward small, especially in public approval. He frankly admitted: "It is very difficult to write a plot for a musical comedy. The musical numbers are constantly interfering with the action; every time a song is introduced, the plot is thrown down on the floor like a piece of old rope, and interest in the story is interrupted. Another thing that our librettists are up against is that they have to write clean stuff—thank God! In French musical plays the author can make vulgarity pass for entertainment."[44] He would be respectively pleased and shocked by some of the books of present-day musical comedies.

Incidental tasks, some amusing, some enlightening, continued to hold Herbert's attention. Of the former category was his service as court witness in a plagiarism suit brought by Alice Smythe Burton Jay against the publishing firm of Chappell & Co. Miss Jay claimed that the composer (Harry H. Williams) of the famous song, "It's a Long, Long Way to Tipperary" had stolen from one of her own artistic efforts. In addition to lack of proximity making the theft impossible, Herbert testified on the dissimilarity of the airs; and the court dismissed the suit.[45]

More important was Herbert's service as one of two judges (the other was Percy Grainger) in a contest sponsored by Edwin Franko Goldman, who in 1920 offered $250 for a new and original band composition. No one has done more to raise the standards of band music in America than this distinguished musician. Full scores of the competing works had to be in by the 1st of May, whereupon they were sent to Messrs. Herbert and Grainger for examination.

Herbert took this assignment very seriously. After leisurely inspecting the manuscripts he wrote to the sponsor:

May 28th, 1920

My dear Mr. Goldman,

After having devoted considerable time to looking over the various band compositions submitted to me, I have no hesitation in saying that the work "A Chant from the Great Plains" deserves the prize.

It is the work of a splendid musician, and one who understands artistic band scoring thoroughly. The composer shows originality and ability in regard to form and thematic development.

Several other works were quite good and of superior quality.

The contest has proven that a greater interest is being taken in bands and band music than ever before, and also that we are developing a branch of that art that has hitherto been neglected. If a contest of this kind is the means of bringing forth only one composition of real merit and also serves to encourage our American composers, it is doing a real service to the advance of our native music and it should be repeated annually.

Yours sincerely,
VICTOR HERBERT[46]

Percy Grainger picked the same work, and *A Chant from the Great Plains* won the Goldman prize. It was composed by Carl Busch (1862–1943), eminent Danish musician who lived many years in Kansas City, Missouri, where he helped immeasurably in raising musical standards in the Middle West. A word from Dr. Goldman adds an interesting touch:

I realized in those days that if the band were to survive and be a worthwhile medium for the expression of music, it would have to acquire a repertoire of its own and not depend solely upon transcriptions and arrangements. I have been urging composers to write for band for thirty years—and am now beginning to feel that my struggle and efforts are being rewarded. Herbert said that some of the works submitted in the contest were of "good quality"—but he told me later that in most instances that it was a pity that so much good paper had been utterly wasted.

The winner of the contest was Carl Busch, of Kansas City—a fine conductor and an excellent composer who died a few years ago. . . . Both Herbert and Grainger agreed that the Busch work was outstanding—and they were anxious to know something about the composer—since he was obliged to write under a nom de plume. They were particularly anxious to know where he got his knowledge of "bandstration." It seems that when he was a student in Paris he was obliged to earn money—so he got a job at copying music for the famous Garde Republicaine band.[47]

Herbert's praise of the Goldman contest as an encouragement to the native composer was quite proper, but the judges may have been somewhat surprised to find the award going to a naturalized American. There was no question about the justice of the decision. It only showed, upon disclosure of the winner's identity, that American music still had a long way to go. This fact was illustrated by Herbert's remark to the contest's sponsor.

The summer of 1920 found Herbert contributing, as usual, to the Ziegfeld Follies. The show opened in New York on June 22, at the New Amsterdam Theatre, and the audience feasted its eyes on lavish splendor, riotous color, and female pulchritude. Herbert's music was both descriptive and vocal, words being supplied by his stanch friend Gene Buck. "Creation," the second scene of Act I, was a pictorial and musical characterization of feminine qualities (timidity, vanity, softness, cruelty, warmth, coldness, fidelity, etc.), each represented by a handsome girl. "Chiffon Fantasie," the fifth scene, contained the song "When the Right One Comes Along," and featured the lovely Mary Eaton. Act II exhibited "The Dancing School" and "The Love Boat"—the latter a fantasy of romantic Venice.

Toward the end of 1920 Herbert provided ballet music for the extraordinarily popular musical comedy *Sally,* presented at the New Amsterdam Theatre on December 21. This was not much different from a Follies assignment, and it was indeed a Ziegfeld production, under the personal direction of Florenz Ziegfeld, Jr., with scenes designed by Joseph Urban. The composer of *Sally* was the deservedly esteemed Jerome Kern, but the composer of the "Butterfly Ballet" was Herbert. The star was the lovely Marilyn Miller, who did full justice to the music she interpreted. The knowledge and skill of the older man were needed to guarantee the success of a certain type of sequence.

Two disappointing operettas or musical comedies also came from Herbert's pen in 1920. Neither was successful, and the earlier earned the unenviable distinction of never being presented in New York City. Little is known about it, and it remains almost as much a curiosity as the ill-fated *The Gold Bug,* which played a week in New York, but nowhere else. The 1920 failure, *Oui Madame,* was originally produced in Phila-delphia, at the Philadelphia Theatre, on March 22. The lyrics were by Robert B. Smith; the book, by G. M. Wright (Mrs. Smith). The pro-ducer was Alfred E. Aarons; the stage director, Herbert Gresham. The musical director was Max Steiner; the stage manager, Karl Nielsen.

More than ordinary disappointment attached to *Oui Madame,* for it was intended to be the first of a series of "art" musical comedies having a permanent home in the Philadelphia playhouse. The theater was the former Little Theatre, newly rechristened, and the players were to appear nowhere else.[48] The house seated only a few more than 300, and it was expected that discriminating audiences would support the unusual shows to be offered. The program of *Oui Madame* called the production "the ultimate in intimate musical plays," a phrase suggest-ing the kind of policy the house wanted to follow. It was a venture into the ideal which always appealed to Herbert tremendously; but Ameri-can musical comedy is probably the last form of entertainment that can adapt itself to a little-theater environment or following. The content value of a musical comedy story is slight enough even when exposed with the full panoply of a regulation stage and a house filled with on-lookers wanting fun and laughter. Hazardous indeed is the career of a show projected in surroundings of limited size and depending on a special clientele. Yet *Oui Madame* represented a courageous move; its failure, apparently inevitable, must even today be lamented.

In Philadelphia *Oui Madame* packed the tiny auditorium. The top price on the opening night was $5.00 (on other evenings $3.50) and no expense was spared in providing extra niceties. Special programs were passed out and these caused much comment. They were tan and brown made to resemble a dance program each with a little pencil which could be used to write notes and memoranda on the blank page in the back. The size of the house limited the orchestra to sixteen men who had to be carefully installed.[49] Every one in the theater believed he was witnessing the initiation of the home of intimate musical comedy.

The cast follows:

Annette Beaudet, the future great poet . . . . Emmie Niclas
Dora Meade, the future great prima donna . . . . Dolly Alwyn
Laura Briggs, the future great pianist . . . . Eleanor Sinclair
Jane Walker, the future great artist . . . . Marguerite St. Clair
Grace Sterling, the future great model . . . . Dorothy St. Clair
Margery Chase, the future great actress . . . . . . Marguerite Mason
Betty Wilson, the future great sculptress . . . . Mayre Hall

Lola Allen, the future great modiste............Patrice Clarke
Peggy Earle, the future great harpist............Violet Weller
Claudia, the future great dancer..............May Thompson
Dick Sheldon, the future great playwright......Vinton Freedley
Polly, his wife.........................Dorothy Maynard
Pansy, "Just like one of the family"..........Georgia O'Ramey
Jerry Walton, who occupies an apartment above....Glenn Anders
Steve, janitor of the Marble Bluff apts............Harry Kelly
Mrs. Sheldon, Dick's mother........Catherine Calhoun Doucet
Dot Sheldon, Dick's sister..................Marguerite Fritts
Dave Kidder, college chum of Jerry............John C. Butler
Fritz, the future great waiter..................Karl Nielsen
Joe Bixby, college chum of Jerry...............John V. Lowe
Billy Wild, college chum of Jerry...........J. Franklin Daly
Tom Smiley, college chum of Jerry.............Ralph O'Brien
Fred Harper, college chum of Jerry...........Howard Remig
Fox, Secret Service operative..................Karl Nielsen

Act I took place in the living room of the DeForest apartment (lent to
Dick Sheldon) in the Marble Bluff on Riverside Drive, New York;
Act II in the garden of Mrs. Sheldon's country home on Long Island
(leased for the season).

This frothy "intimate play" dwells upon complications besetting
Dick Sheldon and his young bride. Hoping to make headway in the
world of art-theater-music-dance-etc. they entertain a group of ambitious
girls in a borrowed apartment. When Dick's mother and sister arrive
unexpectedly the apartment's proprietor must be produced; but the
regular lodger is unavailable, and so Steve is pressed into service. He
poses as Colonel Hutt, becoming a commanding and comical fellow in
his new unsought character. Pansy the cook and maid has a vocabulary
practically limited to "Oui Madame" as she responds to her superiors.
She is convinced that the spurious Colonel Hutt is none other than a
sweetheart who threw her over some five years before. Pretending to be
a bona fide colonel, Steve tries to establish himself as a twin brother of
Pansy's former companion; but the maid disproves his claim by revealing a mermaid tattoo on his leg.

Herbert wrote a rather prodigal amount of music for this lighthearted,
lightweight tale, but only a small portion was published. It consisted
of the now-usual separate pieces which he was turning out as parts of a
conventional musical comedy. They were adroit, tuneful, skillfully
produced and pleasing to the ear; but most of them were regular in
pattern and had no trace of refreshing novelty. Two excerpts, however,
can be offered as exceptions. The stanza portion of "Play Her Something
I Can Dance to" has some surprising chromatic phrases, so delectable
indeed that the ensuing refrain, while prettier, is downright disappoint-

ing. The other exception is the slow waltz "My Day Has Come," which is considerably freer in form than the average musical comedy song; it was a post-première piece, written when the reception proved *Oui Madame* needed strengthening if it was to survive.

The immediate reception of *Oui Madame* was more than encouraging, and a friendly critic prophesied success for the "genuine merit" it exhibited.[50] Other reviewers shared this opinion, but time quickly proved them wrong. The short run in Philadelphia was followed by engagements in Atlantic City and Boston. In Boston the music was favorably received, but the book was found "meagre in charm, humor and ease": although the music contained reminiscences of Herbert in his prime, it was obviously written "hardly with the high distinction of old."[51] Few would care to take issue with this regretful judgment.

Oui Madame did not survive a month in Boston, notwithstanding valiant efforts to revitalize it dramatically and musically. Even the expert ministration of Ned Wayburn failed to get it ready for New York. During the summer it was revised and recast, and early in September it ventured forth again under the title *Some Colonel*. Springfield, Massachusetts, found it an unimpressive mixture of music, talk, and dance[52]—and its days were numbered. It expired a few weeks later in Richmond, Virginia, a total stranger to Broadway, which waited for Herbert as a matter of course.

In the original cast of *Oui Madame* was a young man named Vinton Freedley. Well known in Philadelphia theatrical circles, he anticipated an important success from the opportunity presented by the new play. His hopes were dashed to the ground.

For young Mr. Freedley the failure of *Oui Madame* may have been a blessing in disguise. Not long afterward he entered theatrical management and production, to become eventually one of the most eminent producers in America. As he reflected on Herbert's accomplishments he came to the conclusion reached by the many who have been obliged to apologize for the literary quality of Herbert operettas that he never found a writer of merit with whom to work.[53]

The unhappy fate of *Oui Madame* deterred Herbert not at all from composing another musical comedy at once.

The Girl in the Spotlight reached New York, but it was not much more successful than its predecessor. The author of both book and lyrics was Richard Bruce (that is, Robert B. Smith). Like other Herbert shows it had two titles before the final name was adopted: the composer's manuscript in the Library of Congress discloses *Molly Darling* as one, and just before the scheduled first performance in Chicago a public announcement referred to it as *The Miracle Maid*.[54] That performance did not materialize, for a local musicians' strike threatened to wreck theatrical activities and the show was rushed eastward. The first performance on any stage occurred in Stamford, Connecticut, on July 7, 1920,[55] and the first New York performance took place on the 12th at the Knickerbocker Theatre.

The metropolitan première was conducted by the composer, who—perhaps for the first time in his long career—drew criticism for wielding the baton under such circumstances. This came from a reviewer who noticed an undue amount of nervousness on the stage, for which, he suggested, Herbert was responsible.[56] Such a charge seems ridiculous, particularly in view of Herbert's long habit and experience in directing premières. If the performers were more nervous than usual, it was probably due to the emergency exit from Chicago and the hastily prepared tryout in Connecticut.

The producer of *The Girl in the Spotlight* was George W. Lederer, who also directed the staging. Harold Vicars was the musical director. The New York program announced this cast:

Tom Fielding, a young musician whose great future always keeps just ahead of him, and who shares a Greenwich Village garret with	John Reinhard
Bill Weed, a poet, misfortune's favorite son, and	Johnny Dooley
Ned Brandon, an artist. To their humble abode comes	Richard Pyle
Max Preiss, who has made in the fur business a fortune, which he has invested in the Frivolity Theatre. Now looking for a popular song which is sung by	James B. Carson
Molly Shannon, house-maid at Mrs. Todgers' lodging house, where the smallest hall-room is occupied by	Mary Milburn
Frank Marvin, formerly of the A.E.F., but just a man out of a job.	Ben Forbes
Across the court from the garret is Max Preiss's rehearsal hall. His company includes	
Bess	Minerva Grey
Clare	Jessie Lewis
June	Agnes Patterson
each of whom hopes to make a conquest of	
Watchem Tripp, stage manager, who is putting on the dances in the new opera, in which is	Hal Skelley

Nina Romaine, leading lady of the Frivolity Theatre, whose most constant admirer is	June Elvidge
John Rawlins, a western mine owner.	John Hendricks
Of the personnel of Preiss's Company, the principal dancers are	
Margot	Ruby Lewis
Julie	Lucille Kent
Laurette	Lillian Young
and the usual leading ladies of the future are	
Ethel	Flora Crosbie
Margery	June White
Kitty	Gertrude Reynolds
Dorothy	Evelyn Grieg
Mabelle	Helen Gates
Estelle	Geneva Mitchell
Berenice	Helen March
Audrey	Ann Milburn
Clarice	Elizabeth Chase
Jean	Margaret Kerr
Leila	Georgie Prentice
Natalie	Dorothy Barth
Olivia	Marguerite Daniels
Rosina	Gladys Hart
Stella	Ly Wirth

There were five scenes in the customary two acts: Act I, Scene 1, the sky-parlor of Mrs. Todgers' lodging house, near Washington Square; Scene 2, the rehearsal hall of Max Preiss's Frivolity Theatre Co., across the court from Mrs. Todgers'; Act II, Scene 1, the Green Room of the Frivolity Theatre, converted into a chorus dressing room for the first night of a new operetta; Scene 2, a corridor in the theater; Scene 3, a garden of orchids, the last scene of Preiss's opera, set for an impromptu supper after the performance.

The threadbare plot is another version of the Cinderella legend. When an emergency arises, Molly, a drab little servant, is ready to sing a role in a new operetta. She replaces the star (Nina), whose dressing room has been burglarized, and she saves the young composer's great effort from failure. In addition, she loves the composer, and her triumph on the stage is duplicated in his heart.

The Girl in the Spotlight was ambitious scenically and dramatically, but it was mechanically put together and lacking in distinction. One reviewer suggested that Lederer had said to Herbert: "Write me a musical comedy with two or three sentimental ballads, some sensuous intermezzos and a spirited march, and we'll reap large profits from the reaction which is bound to come from the horde of musical revues on Broadway." The musical results supported the theory of the reviewer, who went on to say that the book mattered not at all, that it was incoherent, naïve, seldom bright, and laboriously contrived—that it was nothing more than a framework for a series of pleasant Herbert airs.[57]

The cast was good, and the performances, individual and ensemble, were highly commendable; but the future of the show was uncertain. When it came to New York in the middle of July the experts were astonished, declaring that Lederer was taking a long chance. Hot weather ensued, and after 56 performances[58] it was withdrawn. It had only a modicum of success thereafter although it remained on the road until the following year. An attempt to rejuvenate it under the title of *Molly Darlin'* showed no appreciable results.[59] The final position of *The Girl in the Spotlight* can be estimated from the fact that it is one of the very few Herbert productions never published in piano-vocal score form.

After *The Girl in the Spotlight* Herbert brought out no new stage work for more than two years, a remarkably long period of silence for him. He was now in his sixties, however, and entitled to a break in an incredibly extended series of operettas, not one of which was inconsiderable in size. Idleness, of course, was out of the question, and among his continued activities of long standing was the composition of an elaborate comedy sketch for the Lambs, who successfully produced it at their annual public gambol on June 5, 1921: *The Tale of a Lamb: An Idiomelodic Fantasy*. This was staged, as well as suggested, by R. H. Burnside. The composer conducted the performance, in the Hippodrome.

For three weeks beginning in July, Herbert conducted the symphony concerts at the Lewisohn Stadium. Years had passed since New York had listened to Herbert as a symphony conductor, and the city welcomed him back with warm enthusiasm. He seemed to be no less elated, and when he appeared for the first concert on July 28 he donned full evening dress. His predecessor had worn a white sport suit, and Herbert's sartorial distinction did not pass unnoticed. The performances were distinguished for "the increased unanimity, surety and warmth in the playing"; the orchestra "seemed eagerly to respond to every wish of the conductor," and the music "was applauded with far more than customary warmth."[60] This success continued, as did the response of the players, throughout the short season.

The public at large was always eager to see Herbert. A number of large motion picture theaters were beginning to support quasi-symphony orchestras, and it was not difficult to arrange for appearances as guest conductor. Early in 1922 he toured across the country in this capacity, leading many orchestras in selections from his works. During his stay in San Francisco the first part of March he befriended the music teachers of that city in a way which won their warmest gratitude.

For some two years the music teachers of San Francisco had been forced to pay a tax levied by the city's Board of Supervisors: $3 per quarter on all annual incomes up to $3,000; beyond that, varying amounts graduated upward to $125 per quarter on an annual income of $150,000. The low-income teachers naturally suffered the most.

Herbert visited one of the regular meetings of the Board, and the members complacently awaited flattery for their civic enlightenment. To their astonishment he vigorously attacked them for imposing a tax on a cultural activity and for discriminating against music teachers in so doing. Full of indignation, he assailed both the idea and its execution. He minced no words as he expressed his wrath to the Supervisors. "What's this I hear about your taxing musicians?" he roared. "Why, even Julius Caesar respected the bards and refrained from taxing them. He knew they were giving the people something that would make their lives beautiful, and he was man enough to know that to tax people who do that would be idiotic."[61] He told them that Caesar had suspended taxes on makers of poetry, music, and art, adding: "I hope San Francisco will not be 2,000 years behind that time." As he enlarged on his displeasure he criticized the American inclination to measure all things in terms of dollars and cents: "We do more talking in the United States about culture and civilization than in any other place in the world, but we do the absurd thing of taxing music teachers who are furnishing the culture for our rising generation, and often at the beggarly stipend of 50c. a lesson."[62]

Headed by the Mayor, the Supervisors sheepishly explained that the suggestion for the tax had come from Los Angeles; but Herbert was in no mood for attempted justifications. He demanded abolishment of the tax, and it was repealed at this very session of the Board. In five minutes he had accomplished something for which the local music teaching profession had struggled twenty-four months.

Before going to San Francisco—where, incidentally, he and David Warfield were simultaneously made honorary members of the famed Bohemian Club—the composer filled a two weeks' engagement in February in Los Angeles. Here he was asked to comment on his guest appearances and on the orchestras being established in movie houses:

I am enjoying my present tour of the country very much. You see, I have been conducting my music at the larger cinema theaters of the leading cities. I believe much credit should be given our leading moving picture managements for what they are doing in music for the mass of the people, the general public such as attends the pictures by the millions every week of the year. The big picture houses engage large and efficient orchestras which play excellent music as well as that of lighter caliber. The theater-going public, generally speaking, are not musically cultured, and they do not attend the theater for the purpose of hearing music of the better sort. Nevertheless, they are given music as well as the lighter kind and they are learning to discriminate. They are learning to recognize and like good music.

At the same time he was asked what he thought of music written for motion pictures, particularly whether he thought a new art form would evolve from a combination of music and screen drama. He replied rather deliberately:

This may come about, but it must be through intelligent and sympathetic cooperation between the composer and his cinema collaborators.

At the present stage of development of the union of music and cinema, music suffers the disadvantage of sharing little consideration at the hands of the production manager and director. These dictators of what shall be or shall not be eliminated from a film care not that the music written for a three-minute scene will not fit that scene when it is cut to two minutes. Yet their liberal and well-scattered cutting goes ever on after the music has been carefully planned for a film.

Obviously, considered from the standpoint of art, the musical sentiment and action of the story should synchronize.[63]

The summers of 1921 and 1922 found Herbert making his usual contributions to the Ziegfeld Follies, and elaborate numbers they were. Produced respectively in New York at the Globe Theatre on June 21, 1921, and at the New Amsterdam Theatre on June 5, 1922, these two editions of the annual spectacle glowed with color and beauty, and thrilled or lulled the spectators into rapturous admiration. Much more important for Herbert, however, was a new operetta, a "comedy with music," which promised to rival his best works of past years. Neither expense nor effort was spared in its preparation, and he worked frantically to have the orchestrations ready on time.

Orange Blossoms had its first real performance in Philadelphia at the Garrick Theatre on September 4, 1922, its New York première on September 19 at the Fulton Theatre. Following his long established custom Herbert conducted the New York opening. When it was over, a reviewer posed the inevitable question: "Can a musical comedy of surpassing beauty and extraordinarily entertaining people survive a dull book?"[64]

For as long as a year Herbert had contemplated setting this particular book. In the summer of 1921, while he was conducting the

Stadium concerts, there were rumors that Dillingham was about to make him begin the composition of the score.[65] However, a year went by before he began the music, and in that interval the producer changed from Dillingham to Edward Royce; the play remained the same, a comedy drama fairly well known to French, English, and American audiences. The original form was *La Passerelle,* written by Fred de Gresac and François de Croisset. Cosmo Gordon-Lennox transformed the French to *The Marriage of Kitty,* which was presented in London in 1902 and in New York on November 30, 1903, and again on December 18, 1914. The two New York productions ran for 51 and 27 performances respectively, the famous Marie Tempest doubtless being responsible for the longer engagement. When it was finally revived as a musical comedy, lyrics were added by B. G. de Sylva, and Fred de Gresac was listed as author of the book.

Orange Blossoms in 1922 was a vision of glamor. The program announced that Norman Bel Geddes had designed special scenery, and that Paul Poiret had created the feminine costumes. The following cast appeared at the New York opening:

Lawyer Brassac	Pat Somerset
Tillie	Queenie Smith
Octave	Maurice Darcy
Baron Roger Belmont	Robert Michaelis
Kitty	Edith Day
Jimmy Flynn	Hal Skelley
Helene de Vasquez	Phyllis Le Grand
Auguste	Robert Fischer
Ninetta	Nancy Welford

Brassac's clients:

Cecilia Malba	Evelyn Darville
Christiane de Mirandol	Alta King
Julie Bresil	Dagmar Oakland
Yolande Du Pont	Emily Drange
Paulette de Trevors	Fay Evelyn
Simone Garrick	Diana Stepman
Regina Marnac	Eden Gray
Valentina Vendome	Vera de Wolfe

Gentlemen in the case

> Thomas Fitzpatrick
> Frank Curran
> Oliver Stewart
> Danny Murray
> Abner Barnart
> Jack Whiting
> Gayle Mays
> Clinton Merrill

Dancers............................. {
Queenie Smith
Nancy Welford
Elva Pomfret
Mary Lucas

The musical director was Gus Salzer.

The three acts were as follows: Act I, a lawyer's office in Paris; Act II, Kitty's villa at Cannes; Act III, the garden of Kitty's villa at Cannes.

Orange Blossoms adhered faithfully to the story of *The Marriage of Kitty*, at least in essential plot; but it had a swollen personnel for which there was no dramatic excuse. Brassac's clients were new, and so were the "gentlemen in the case," their masculine counterparts. Also new were Tillie (Brassac's secretary, a gum-chewing American stenographer) and Jimmy Flynn (an American private detective). They all were added for reasons of music and comedy, but they needlessly cluttered the action.

In main outline Roger wishes to wed Helene, a Brazilian divorcée, but his deceased aunt's will expressly forbids such an act. Yet he must marry within a year or forfeit a great fortune. Lawyer Brassac has a goddaughter, recently orphaned, and he arranges for Roger to marry Kitty. Kitty will then go to Cannes, live there a year, and grant Roger a divorce. Roger comes to Cannes to discuss the final details of the arrangement; but he discovers he loves Kitty after all, and he surrenders Helene to an earlier claimant for her affections.

The music of *Orange Blossoms,* to a noticeable degree, resembled some of the earlier works which had brought Herbert his deserved fame. It was more dramatic and more expanded, and there were fewer numbers which seemed to be just so many popular songs. The opening scene in the lawyer's office, with the catty females airing their grievances, is broadly contrived and happily varied, and Brassac's closing boastfulness finds response in the clients' satisfaction. Roger has a better than average song when he sings of his feeling for Helene in "This Time It's Love." The best song in the operetta, of course, is "A Kiss in the Dark"—also one of the best in all Herbert literature. It proved that Herbert's romantic-melodic inspiration had not deserted him. Kitty sings it to her godfather as she recalls an adventure in Deauville and the thrill of the kiss from the stranger in the dark.

Tillie and Jimmy have a racy and impudent duet in "New York Is the Same Old Place," which is followed by a longer lyrical exchange between Helene and Roger, "Then Comes the Dawning," as they look forward to the end of separation. Somewhat out of the ordinary is another song of Kitty's, "In Hennequeville," in which the winsome maiden rehearses the part she must play as Roger's wife. In artless fashion she contrasts the life of Paris with life in her home town, and the music has a rustic gaiety in character with her mood.

The second act opens with a resounding chorus, "On the Riviera," in which the girls and men visiting Kitty sing of love in a land of enchantment. In her villa Kitty sings a wistful song of her unwanted solitude in "The Lonely Nest." Besides being naturally attractive, this is unusual in that it has two refrains, the second a rhythmic variant of the first. The change is exquisitely subtle, a touch of delicacy which only a musician of fine sensitivity could accomplish. In her deliberate flirtation with the men at the villa Kitty sings with them "A Dream of Orange Blossoms"; and Helene and Roger soon sing another excellent duet, "Because I Love You So," which has impetuous and strangely urgent stanza music and a refrain that must be sung with great abandon to achieve the wanted effect. The finale of the act is brief compared with Herbert's earlier finales; but it has much of their sharpness, fullness, and energy.

The music of Act III is disappointing in view of what has preceded it. The opening is a pleasurable but undistinguished "Mosquito Ballet," and Kitty's song "Legend of the Glowworm" has the same qualities. The few succeeding pieces are not particularly noteworthy, although the militant "Let's Not Get Married" (sung by girls and men) ends with a unison chorus of military verve and vigor.

It was unfortunate that the third act fell below the others musically; but the first two had more than occasional flashes of the old Herbert, pleasing his long-time admirers.

The critics received *Orange Blossoms* with varied reactions, agreeing chiefly on the beauty of the over-all production. The cast was adequate, and the principals earned a generous amount of commendation, especially Hal Skelley and Queenie Smith. These two comedians, however, were not a basic part of the story—their parts had not been in the original play—and their conscientious antics did not dissuade one reviewer from referring to the "most unfunny" of musical comedy books.[66] There was near-unanimity on the scenic loveliness, the impeccable costumes, the feminine pulchritude. Yet all these points of excellence gave no promise of great success; they merely led to the oft repeated verdict that, if success ensued, it would be due to the music.

To a very large extent Herbert regained lost ground in *Orange Blossoms*; but he accomplished it with an older type of music which could hardly hold a strident, modern public. Consequently *Orange Blossoms* left the New York stage after 95 performances,[67] even a November slash in ticket prices (from $4.00 top to $3.50) failing to stave off closing.[68] Nevertheless, the score afforded great satisfaction to Herbert and his friends, for it brought him renewed consideration as the most important composer for the American stage.

Little concerned about past disappointments, Herbert entered 1923 as busily as any other year. New problems would rear their heads, but he was chiefly concerned with composing and conducting. Old friends could not be forgotten, of course, and one of his first efforts of the new year was to provide and arrange music for the Lambs. At their Mid-Winter Gambol in the Globe Theatre, February 18, 1923, they presented the fantasy *Toyland Today*—a parody on *Babes in Toyland,* which was twenty years old. Associated with Herbert in this happy diversion were Glen MacDonough as author and Julian Mitchell as producer, both of whom had functioned similarly for the original *Babes.* Many of the original characters were impersonated on the stage, but the most refreshing scene was a travesty on American prohibition. The mere *dramatis personae* of the "Wandering Spirits" locates the sympathies of the creators, performers, and audience: the Brothers Haig; Messrs. J. Walker and T. Collins; Messrs. Hunter and Old Taylor; Messrs. Bushmill and Bourbon; Miss Orange Blossom; Miss Manhattan; the Widow Cliquot; Senorita Bacardi; Miss Ginnette Daisy; Miss Martini; one Pussyfool; another. Played by talented members of the actors' fraternity, they must have achieved a devastatingly funny verisimilitude.

Turning to more serious matters, Herbert prepared to enter upon a new engagement which lasted the rest of his life. In the late winter of 1922 he had enjoyed conducting orchestras in large motion picture theaters across the country. Now he was offered the opportunity of conducting permanently in one of New York's best film houses under conditions which approached the ideal.

His employer was William Randolph Hearst, head of Cosmopolitan Pictures and the Cosmopolitan Theatre. In a remarkably precise letter Herbert outlined exactly what he would do and what Hearst must allow him if his services were wanted:

March 12, 1923

Mr. William Randolph Hearst,
   Cosmopolitan Studios
      127th St. & 2nd Avenue
      New York, N.Y.
Dear Mr. Hearst,—

Our agreement for my engagement as orchestra conductor at the Cosmopolitan Theatre, at Columbus Circle, New York City, is as follows:

I am engaged for one (1) year, commencing on or about May 1 1923, at a salary of Fifteen Hundred ($1500.) Dollars per week, to conduct the overture, or instead thereof a short concert of musical numbers to be selected by me, for the matinee and evening performance at such theatre, and to compose a suitable overture for each new Cosmopolitan feature presented at such theatre.

During the actual showing of the picture the orchestra shall be conducted by an assistant director who shall be approved by me.

The members of the orchestra shall at all times during my engagement consist of not less than forty (40) musicians and shall be engaged by my representative at your expense, (a reasonable allowance to be made for salaries higher than the union scale to be paid to the first instruments such as concert master, harpist and others).

The rights of publication of all music written by me shall be excepted and reserved to me.

I shall attend and conduct, whenever required, in any theatre in the United States, while there shall be exhibited at such theatre a first run of a Cosmopolitan feature picture, but I shall not be required to conduct in any such theatre for a longer period than one week at a time. Reasonable notice to attend and conduct at such theatre shall be given to me in advance of my appearance thereat.

I shall be furnished first-class transportation, travelling and hotel expenses, including drawing room on trains whenever available, in connection with each such trip to and from New York.

The number of musicians in the orchestra of each theatre so visited by me shall not be less than thirty-five (35) men.

The statement, "Victor Herbert and his Orchestra" shall be featured in all advertising matter issued by the Cosmopolitan Theatre, as well as any theatre wherein I shall appear as a visiting conductor, during the period of my appearance.

I will render my services to you exclusively, except that I shall be free to do the following:

I shall have the right to conduct concerts at Willow Grove Park, Pennsylvania, for a period of four (4) weeks during the Summer months and shall also have the right to fulfill my contract with the Victor Talking Machine Co. which calls for my appearance at the Victor Recording Studios for about a week in each year, the time being fixed by the Victor Company.

I shall be free to conduct the orchestra for the first performance of any new play the music of which shall have been composed by me. I shall be free to write and compose music as heretofore.

I shall be entitled to a reasonable vacation, with salary, of approximately two (2) weeks.

I shall receive no salary during my absence from the Cosmopolitan Theatre by reason of my Willow Grove engagement or Victor Talking Machine Company engagement.

You shall have the option to renew this agreement for another year upon the same terms as herein contained, such option to be exercised by written notice to me not later than January 1 1924.

Yours very sincerely,
[signed]   Victor Herbert

Accepted;
W. R. Hearst[69]   [signed]

In this contractual letter Herbert was firm on two main points, both of which were quite proper. He insisted on adequate remuneration and on control of musical conditions as reflected in the size and capacity of the orchestra. In the ordinary sense of the word he did not become a "movie conductor." He was orchestral director in a preeminent motion picture theater and a leader in the movement making the large film houses an important factor in the musical life of the people. The observations gleaned from his trip as guest conductor across the country were bearing fruit. This relationship with Hearst also produced five overtures, three of which remain unpublished: *Under the Red Robe* (published as *Dramatic Overture*), *The Great White Way* (published as *Golden Days Overture*), *Little Old New York, Star of the North,* and *Yolanda.*

Herbert liked this employment, although it was a confining obligation. The work was not heavy, and in the theater he had a private room containing all the comforts of home. Nor did it interfere with his usual activities.

This same winter he had to display equal firmness in another direction so that both he and his orchestra players could adjust themselves to changing times and conditions. Willow Grove Park was beginning to be a problem, and he felt the time was at hand for an adjustment of time and fee.

Normally Herbert and his orchestra played at the Philadelphia resort for a period of three weeks, the reimbursement being in the neighborhood of $5,000 per week. Typical engagements, each of twenty-one days, were fulfilled in 1920, 1921, and 1922, but the terms had to be altered before he would consent to return in 1923. Early in the year John R. Davies, president of the Willow Grove Park Company, received from Herbert the following message, which obviously required an effort, because Herbert's name and Willow Grove were well-nigh synonymous:

My dear Mr. Davies,
In order to save you any inconvenience in making your orch. bookings for the coming season at Willow Grove Park, I think it proper, that I should advise you at this time, that I couldn't accept the contract you were kind enough to offer me heretofore. Conditions have changed so much of late, that I have been compelled to take less and less from year to year for myself

personally, and in regard to the men, there are so many engagements in New York City open to them, that a season of three weeks only does not seem attractive to them.

I have always loved the engagement, but I regret to say, that unless you give more time, and a little more money, I shall be unable to be with you again this coming season.

With kindest regards
I am
[scrawled signature][70]

Again Herbert's attitude bore fruit. The 1923 contract for Willow Grove (executed on March 21) called for a four-week engagement at $6,000 per week. The same terms were kept in force for the following year, but Herbert, alas, was not present to benefit from them.

When Herbert told Hearst he must be unrestricted in his own composing he included in his thoughts compositions apart from the expected operettas. It is not known whether he wanted to experiment with new forms, receive unusual commissions, or simply write for pleasure; but during the last year or so of his life he created several unusual works which reveal an inquisitive mind as well as fine craftsmanship.

The most unusual of these, practically unknown, is a short piece of religious instrumental music to serve as a prelude to a Lenten play. It was written for a specific purpose, to open the drama *The Two Marys*, by the Reverend Joseph P. Herbert of Brooklyn. The manuscript in the Library of Congress shows a lightly scored piece of quiet contemplation and exquisite sensitivity. The composer finished the scoring on February 10, 1923. Easter of that year was April 1, so that it was ready for performance well in advance of Holy Week on which the text concentrates. It is a choice piece of music, lending itself to either church or concert environment.

Thirteen years later, *The Two Marys* was published as a play. The title page called it a "four act Lenten drama . . . written around the dramatic events, that were enacted, during the First Holy Week, between Palm Sunday and Easter Sunday, as they are described in the Gospel Narratives, written by the Four Evangelists." There is no mention of an instrumental prelude in the printed book, but Herbert's music needs no literary support to be effective if an enterprising conductor will bring it to the attention of an audience.

In the summer of 1923 it was reported that Herbert was composing music for a production of Tony Sarg, the ingenious creator of marionettes and puppet shows.[71] This was *The Willow Plate*, "a Chinese shadowgraph play," for which he supplied "The Mandarin's Garden," "The Little Gardenhouse," "Chang, the Lover," "Kongshee, the

Mandarin's Daughter," and "A Wedding Procession." The instrumentation, however, was not finished until February 22, 1924.

As Herbert began to think about *The Willow Plate* he was at a loss for genuine Chinese themes. Wanting to write in as authentic a vein as possible, he visited the Music Division of the New York Public Library, where Dr. Otto Kinkeldey, the greatest musical scholar in America, provided him with a number of themes. Genuine themes from the Far East, however, are not as pleasing, not as picturesque, not as adaptable as an Occidental imagines, and Herbert was soon bewildered by the music Dr. Kinkeldey had supplied. Some five or six days later he returned to the library and confessed his impasse. He wanted, he said, merely something that went "Chink chink-a-chink chink-a-chink," and he droned out appropriate intervals to the series of solemn *chink's*. Dr. Kinkeldey laughed and gave him some good advice, which was to go home and write his own Chinese music![72]

Herbert followed this advice admirably, turning out five short pieces which aptly suggest oriental atmosphere, yet are far removed from the cheapness usually inherent in exotic contrivings. Although they are pseudo-oriental, their flavor is unmistakable, their charm undeniable. The piano versions, which were published, give only faint approximations of the actual sound.

The 1923 Ziegfeld Follies came to New York unusually late, not opening at the New Amsterdam Theatre until October 20. This year Herbert supplied an extra amount of music for the show, the lyrics for the vocal numbers again being written by his old friend Gene Buck. The titles of scenes containing Herbert's music were: "Webbing," "Old Fashioned Garden," "Little Old New York," "I'd Love to Waltz Through Life with You," "Fencing," "Legends of the Drums." The last named was an enormous spectacle which featured European and oriental nationalities, seasonal characteristics, and a large corps of feminine drummers.

Starting 1924, Herbert composed a song, "Heart o' Mine," for Laurence Eyre's play *Merry Wives of Gotham,* or *Fanshastics,* produced in New York on January 16. It was a comedy dealing with Irish character, humor and instinct, and particularly appealed to Herbert's sensibilities.

Less than a month later a concert took place in New York which was almost revolutionary, and Herbert was one of the three most important figures actively involved: the famous concert by Paul Whiteman and his orchestra in Aeolian Hall on February 12. It was supposed to make jazz (or what then passed for jazz) respectable as serious art. It was supposed to exert an influence on contemporary instrumentation. It was supposed to introduce a new young genius, George Gershwin, playing the solo part of a new, unheard masterpiece, his own *Rhapsody in Blue*. The concert accomplished all these things and was fully as important as its promoters claimed. In fact, it grows more important in retrospect as the years go by.

Unknown to any of the auditors, however, this concert was sadly significant for another reason. It marked the last appearance of Herbert as a composer of an important work, his *Suite of Serenades* receiving its first performance that day. It served as a maturer counterpart to Gershwin's fresh young *Rhapsody*.

From a later generation's point of view Whiteman was attempting the impossible as he sought to capture jazz in a strait-jacketed form of organized notation and more or less inflexible interpretation. The very essence of jazz, as understood today, lies in its freedom, its improvisatory character, its resistance to the elements which are the backbone of art music. But in the 1920's the polite conception of jazz was based on an expansion of the idiom of popular song and ragtime; and if these forms of music could be both broadened and refined, if such themes could be orchestrated in combinations of large dance bands (played by astonishingly expert virtuosos), if they could be extended and somewhat developed without change of idiomatic expression—then the art of jazz would be that much nearer a fine art in its own right. Within this framework of thought Whiteman was correct in venturing to present his concert, which the program called "An Experiment in Modern Music." Those who heard it in New York, as well as those in other cities to which Whiteman's orchestra subsequently toured, are not likely to forget the amazing sounds, the delightful experience the program offered.

Whiteman prepared for the New York concert with utmost care. It was not to be a thoughtless or ephemeral venture, entered into by a bunch of popular music boys, but a serious experiment of musical significance. Nearly thirty patrons and patronesses were persuaded to support the concert, and among them were Heywood Broun, Walter Damrosch, Leopold Godowsky, Jascha Heifetz, Victor Herbert, Otto H. Kahn, Fritz Kreisler, Sergei Rachmaninoff, Max Reinhardt, Moriz Rosenthal, Leopold Stokowski, Josef Stransky, Deems Taylor, and Carl Van Vechten.

Whiteman's interesting autobiography tells how he felt as the concert drew near, how he both hoped and feared the results, how he lived between extremes of "dire fear and exultant confidence."[73] He tells of his temerity in asking for patrons and of his gratification in their acceptance, of the obstacles and expense involved, of the great desire to reach students and critics and practitioners of serious music. He was amazed to see the mass of people storming into the hall, then worried that he might, after all, have nothing to offer them. The support of Herbert was especially consoling.

Some days before the concert Herbert let it be known that he had declined the offer to conduct the first performance, explaining semi-facetiously to his interviewer: "The saxophones, I can write for them, but I could never conduct them. They make me nervous!"[74] Other instruments also gave him concern. Whiteman's orchestra that day consisted of twenty-three musicians who had to play thirty-six instruments (mostly woodwind and brass, although there were eight violins and two double basses), and Herbert had to write for a combination quite different from the usual orchestra and band.[75] The score he finally produced was a brilliant example of novel, experimental instrumentation.

The program of Whiteman's Aeolian Hall concert was interesting and important:

First Half

1. TRUE FORM OF JAZZ
   a. Ten Years Ago—"Livery Stable Blues"   LaRocca
   b. With Modern Embellishment—"Mama Loves Papa"   Baer

2. COMEDY SELECTIONS
   a. Origin of "Yes, We Have No Bananas"   Silver
   b. Instrumental Comedy—"So This Is Venice"   Thomas
      (Featuring Ross Gorman) (Adapted from
      "The Carnival of Venice")

3. CONTRAST—LEGITIMATE SCORING VS. JAZZING
   a. Selection in True Form—"Whispering"   Schonberger
   b. Same Selection with Jazz Treatment

4. RECENT COMPOSITIONS WITH MODERN SCORE
   a. "Limehouse Blues"   Braham
   b. "I Love You"   Archer
   c. "Raggedy Ann"   Kern

5. ZEZ CONFREY (Piano)
   a. Medley Popular Airs
   b. "Kitten on the Keys"   Confrey
   c. "Ice Cream and Art"
   d. "Nickel in the Slot"   Confrey
      Accompanied by the Orchestra

6. FLAVORING A SELECTION WITH BORROWED
      THEMES
   "Russian Rose"   Grofé
      (Based on "The Volga Boat Song")

7. SEMISYMPHONIC ARRANGEMENT OF POPULAR
    MELODIES
    Consisting of
    "Alexander's Ragtime Band"
    "A Pretty Girl Is like a Melody"   }   Berlin
    "Orange Blossoms in California"   }

Second Half

8. A SUITE OF SERENADES   Herbert
    a. Spanish
    b. Chinese
    c. Cuban
    d. Oriental

9. ADAPTATION OF STANDARD SELECTIONS TO
    DANCE RHYTHM
    a. "Pale Moon"   Logan
    b. "To a Wild Rose"   MacDowell
    c. "Chansonette"   Friml

10. GEORGE GERSHWIN (Piano)
    "A Rhapsody in Blue"   Gershwin
        Accompanied by the Orchestra

11. IN THE FIELD OF THE CLASSICS
    "Pomp and Circumstance"   Elgar

The program was plentifully supplied with commentary. One
paragraph was a general appreciation of Herbert in terms of Whiteman's objective:

Mr. Herbert has written a series of four Serenades which will be played
for the first time today. It is refreshing to keep an eye upon Victor Herbert
because of his persistent refusal to remain in one place. He is the composer
of many of our popular musical comedies, yet he is no stranger to the Metropolitan and its grand opera flavor. Although he ought to dislike modern
popular music and moan for the good old days of Viennese operetta, he is not
only open-minded on the subject, but actually composes with the best of
them. He brings to Jazz a technical mastery and a clearness of mind which
it otherwise frequently lacks. He has ingenuity and good taste, a knowledge
and freshness—qualities too rare in popular music to be sacrificed.

And of the *Suite of Serenades* in particular the program reported:

The character of each of the four pieces composing this suite is indicated
by its name. The melodic material is Mr. Herbert's own. These pieces are
his first essay in writing for the "jazz" orchestra. Besides scoring them for
the wind and percussion instruments essential to such an orchestra, Mr.
Herbert employs eight violins and the lower strings. The "Cuban" serenade,

though written in 2–4 time, introduces a peculiarity of syncopation which Mr. Herbert learned from a native Cuban, who was one of the violinists in his orchestra. The score further enlists among its exotic elements that proverbially efficacious sound-producer, the Cuban gourd. Mr. Herbert declares this adventure into a hitherto unfamiliar field a novel experiment for him. "Here I have had to remember that to the same player may be allotted three instruments, which he must have his chance to change. I might wish at a given moment the plaintive voice of the oboe, but just at that moment the gentleman who should play the oboe is busy with the bass-clarinet! I have respected the rules of the game. I might say of this suite, in the words of the Seventh Century Nun, that even if other people do not like it, it pleases me because it is I who did it!"

The public did like the Suite and tendered a real ovation to Herbert, "that master of instrumentation," when it was played. This was attested by Olin Downes, who went on to praise the entire concert for its vitality and genuineness.[76] It is doubtless true that Herbert's piece created less interest than the new work by Gershwin, who was more closely related to the spirit of the occasion and was to be a stronger influence upon composers seeking new idioms and fresh ideas; but it was keenly appreciated for itself alone—a series of exquisite tone pictures spiced with the exotic flavor of the areas they represented. None of them was long, but together the four constituted an instrumental *tour de force*, the like of which the "old master" had never done before. As H. O. Osgood wrote for the *Musical Courier*:

Then came one of the things that the whole program had been working up to, an original suite of four serenades by Victor Herbert, specially written and scored for the occasion. It proved that neither Victor's creative genius nor his orchestrating hand have lost their cunning. Each one had a typical flavor—Spanish, Chinese, Cuban (a fascinating tango, the best of the lot) and Oriental.[77]

Herbert finished the scoring of the Serenades in this order: "Cuban," January 14; "Spanish," January 17; "Oriental," January 19; "Chinese," January 20. (In the "Chinese," by the way, he used a theme which also found its way into "Kongshee" from *The Willow Plate*.) Across the top of his manuscript he wrote, "For my friend Paul Whiteman and his excellent Orchestra,"[78] a dedication which prompts an important observation. Herbert did not write a jazz suite, nor did he attempt to do so. He wrote a group of pieces for what was then considered to be a jazz orchestra, using the same combination of instruments, and to that extent alone furthering the prevalent conception of jazz. It was remarkable what he could do in this direction, yet his *Suite* was actually the least like jazz of anything on the program. The rigidly set pieces exhibited no jazz characteristics of either theme or harmony. In view of their nationalistic coloring they were not even typically American. They were, however, artistic gems of the utmost clarity, and they were properly considered to be among the high lights of the concert.

As written for Whiteman, the *Suite of Serenades* was not a very practical composition. The chances of performance by anyone else were non-existent, for where could a similar or equal band be found? Almost immediately, therefore, Herbert arranged the pieces—"rewrote" might be a better word—for regular symphony orchestra, thus making them readily available for further performance. He finished the new score, which is in the Library of Congress, on March 4, 1924. In either version the Suite should be performed oftener than now seems to be the case.

The Whiteman concert of February 12 is justly famous for its production of Gershwin's *Rhapsody in Blue,* a remarkable work which introduced a new genius to the concert halls of the world. Even this work, however, benefited from Herbert's counsel and superior musical judgment generously offered to the younger composer. Gershwin's own biographer and friend made public the incident which today is all but forgotten:

Nor should we overlook the . . . rôle played by Victor Herbert in the tale of the *Rhapsody in Blue.* The genial Irishman, who had come too late for the era of jazz, and who did not especially like its ordinary practitioners, was a great admirer of George. Early feeling the importance of sound instrumental knowledge to George's career, he had even offered, with his Hibernian generosity, to instruct the youthful composer in orchestration, gratis. George was not, at the moment, ready to accept the offer. Herbert, as the composer of the cycle of serenades on the Whiteman program, sat in on a number of the rehearsals. He was half minded, indeed, to conduct them himself, but at the last moment yielded the baton to Paul. He heard a few rehearsals of the *Rhapsody,* too, and contributed one valuable suggestion that George was quick to adopt.

The transition to the *andantino moderato* (the slow melody of the middle section) was originally a single rising passage, *rubato e legato,* in contrary motion. This passage Gershwin simply repeated. Why only a sterile repetition? asked Herbert. Why not a climactic rise to the fermata? Accordingly, the passage was changed to the version as printed on page 28 of the piano score, last four bars. The original was but a repetition of the first of these bars.[79]

The conclusion is inescapable that the Whiteman concert was one of the important events in Herbert's career. He shared in it fully, as composer, supporter, and adviser; and he helped to ramify American music with elements which were nothing if not vitalizing.

Almost immediately after this notable concert Herbert had to turn again to controversy in the matter of copyright protection in radio broadcasting. The struggle was not to be as long and bitter as the fight from 1914 to 1917, but radio's cavalier use of copyrighted music was forcing ASCAP to maintain constant vigilance.

ASCAP had willingly gone to the courts to protect the interests of its members; and in each legal fray it had emerged victorious. The fast burgeoning radio industry saw itself defeated again and again as it heard the judges decree that a broadcast rendition was a performance, a public performance, and for profit. Consequently it had to pay the copyright owner, or his representative, or use only music in the public domain. ASCAP was more than holding its own as it taught American business what "public performance for profit" meant.

New threats, however, appeared in the winter and spring of 1924 when several bills were introduced in Congress which would exempt broadcasters from paying for the use of copyrighted music. These would have amended the Copyright Act so that the composers could have no remuneration at all from the broadcasters.[80] ASCAP was up in arms at once and sent large delegations to the Washington hearings in April and May.

The April delegation—led by such famous individuals as Herbert, Sousa, Raymond Hubbell, Gene Buck, and Irving Berlin—arriving on the 16th, repaired to the National Press Club and offered an impromptu entertainment to a delighted private audience, in which Herbert played the cello and loyally presented Lover's *The Low-Back'd Car*. The next day they went to the hearings on the most feared measure, a bill presented by Senator Clarence C. Dill; and Buck took the initiative on the composers' behalf, ably supported by his colleagues. Sousa, in his usual blunt fashion, said: "The Radio Corporation of America gets money, doesn't it? If they get money out of my tunes, I want some of it, that's all."[81]

When Herbert was introduced he amused everyone with a reply he could not resist making. Asked to give his full name to the official stenographer, he demurely said, with a twinkle in his eyes, "Oh, I thought you had heard of me." Then he lent his weight to the attack on the bill and protested both its unfairness and its danger. He had heard "A Kiss in the Dark" on the radio eight or nine times in one evening, and he complained it was being played *ad nauseam*. Not only was he receiving no payment for the performances, but no one would be tempted to buy it after such persistent use.

Herbert and company returned to Washington in May to testify further in the same cause. Forthrightly the composer declared:

Authors and composers need the protection of the copyright laws. It is almost impossible to sell sheet music any more. This is our source of livelihood. In the olden days a man or a woman would enter a theatre or a music house, hear a good piece of music and then purchase it. In this way a demand was created for our product. Today these compositions are delivered daily to the homes. They are rendered in an inartistic manner and the public soon tires of them. . . .

What is to become of musical art in America if the present state of affairs continues? There can be no initiative in this field if reward is to be denied the men and women who devote their lives to musical culture. If you do not protect us it will be a sad thing for the musical art of the United States. I want to say that I was not driven here by the publishers. I came here to fight for our cause, which is a good one.[82]

The efforts of ASCAP were crowned with success, for the inimical bills were not enacted into law, and the composers began to reap their reward from the radio magnates. Had it not been for the radio, indeed, with its unique capacity of countless (literally countless) public performances for profit, ASCAP would never have attained that degree of affluence and power which aroused envy and bitterness and led to a surprising amount of Government control. That, however, is another story in which Herbert played no part. His function was to start and sustain the Society until it could be, figuratively, self-supporting; he led it into the promised land of financial plenty, then passed the leadership on to others.

Two characteristics consistently appear in Herbert's ASCAP battlings. He constantly thought of other composers, pleading for their welfare and urging just compensation for all their labors; and he sought to control the artistic standards of musical performance. In the latter he was less successful—nor could he fare otherwise in a matter quite foreign to legislative control—but he spoke of it every time he was embroiled in court and legal proceedings. Few of his colleagues in either serious or light music showed as much idealism or generosity of spirit.

Between the two hearings in Washington Herbert brought out his last operetta, *The Dream Girl*. A "musical play" in three acts and six scenes, it was a production of Lee and J. J. Shubert, the staging being done by J. C. Huffman. The first performance on any stage, conducted by A. Goodman, was in New Haven, Connecticut, at the Shubert Theatre on April 22, 1924; the first New York performance, at the Ambassador Theatre, was on August 20. The metropolitan première was, of course, posthumous—a fact which increased the public's interest and possibly its support. However, it was an inferior musical work and could neither achieve a long life nor enhance the composer's reputation. After 117 performances in New York,[83] Herbert was still lamented, but *The Dream Girl* was not.

There is some reason for believing that Herbert was reluctant to compose and release *The Dream Girl*. It was based on the play *The Road to Yesterday* (produced in New York, December 31, 1906) by Beulah Marie Dix and Evelyn Greenleaf Sutherland; but when the musical version was produced, the book was credited to Rida Johnson Young (who had written *Naughty Marietta*) and Harold Atteridge. As far back as 1919 Mrs. Young and Herbert had been working on the operetta, conferring at Lake Placid during the summer. It was announced then that New York would see *The Road to Yesterday* as a musical comedy in the fall.[84] In addition to this Herbert was negotiating with his publishers (Harms) for publication of the music as early as April 16, 1919, and the negotiation was still incomplete on May 11, 1921.[85] There is a strong suspicion that Herbert had finally found a libretto to which even he took exception! Not that the play was bad (when first given in New York it had run for 216 performances); but the interpolation of musical comedy humor was crudely done, and it contrasted sorely with the fantasylike basic concept.

The Dream Girl opened in New York with the following cast:

Elspeth	Fay Bainter
Malena	Vivara
Dolly Follis	Wyn Richmond
Wilson Addison	George Lemaire
Aunt Harriet	Maude Odell
Jimmie Van Dyke	Billy B. Van
Elinor Levison	Alice Moffat
Nora	Clara Palmer
Jack Warren	Walter Woolf
Will Levison	John Clarke
Bobby Thompkins	Frank Masters
Mr. Gillette	William O'Neal
Ken Paulton	Edward Basse
Antonio	William O'Neal
Cristoforo	Edmund Fitzpatrick

American girls, Artists' models, Gentlemen of ensemble

Act I, Scene 1, Will Levison's studio, late afternoon, in London, 1923; Scene 2, the Road to Long Ago. Act II, Scene 1, the Red Swan Inn (English inn of 15th century); Scene 2, a green before the castle (15th century); Scene 3, room in the castle of Lord Strangevon (15th century). Act III, Will Levison's studio, after midnight, 1923.

The essence of the drama is the phenomenon of reincarnation as experienced in a dream. Dreaming herself back to fifteenth century

England, Elspeth meets Jack, who befriends her and then saves her from marriage to a villain. Returned to the twentieth century, she and Jack realize that the dream has come true, she insisting that they have really been engaged for five hundred years!

In spite of many kind things the critics wrote about the music, Herbert's pieces were not of his best; and to a certain degree he realized it. After *The Dream Girl* was produced in New Haven he was in low spirits, and he told Deems Taylor that his day was over.[86] It was not a happy thought for a man of such vitality, spirit, and ceaseless enterprise.

The theme song of the play, "My Dream Girl," fortunately, is a very charming number. The phrases of the stanza are attractively wistful, and the air of the refrain has a lilting syncopation which is gently infectious. Of this piece the reviewer of the New York *Times* wrote: "It is fitting that the song hit . . . should be a waltz. 'Dream Girl' . . . carries in it all the wistful and melodious tones that a pampered world had come to demand from Victor Herbert's waltzes." The reviewer's adjectives were well chosen, but—this song was not a waltz! It was a smooth, suave foxtrot, and none the less appealing for that; but one wonders how musically accurate dramatic criticism was in the plush decade of the 1920's.

The "Bubble Song" was a waltz, and not a very good one; "My Hero" was not very heroic. Other songs suffered from being cast in conventional forms of restricted compass, with melodies fairly trite in shape and sound. The real state of *The Dream Girl* is best appreciated by the fact that some songs by Sigmund Romberg were added to it; but the program did not identify them to the public. It was kinder not to.

Yet the public and press received *The Dream Girl* with enthusiasm. Fay Bainter was welcomed with special warmth, Walter Woolf was duly praised, and Billy Van was properly recognized. Van was the comedian who had a part intended to add laughter to the play. It missed fire, however, and only drew the observation that the evening was "destitute of humor."[87] Fay Bainter was the most appreciated figure on the stage, earning plaudits by her "unforced charm" and "unrehearsed wistfulness."[88]

The music, too, received flattering comment, and Herbert would have been pleased to read it. One critic declared the score would rank high in the total production of Herbert's work;[89] another, that the show had fine melodies and fine singing;[90] still another, "The score is full of melody and color and the songs still haunt you as you leave the theatre."[91] A wise summary of the total effect was expressed in these terms: "Prospective visitors to 'The Dream Girl' are hereby notified that it is by no means the frenzied, wise cracking, explosion of jazz that abstracts shekels from the public purse in the name of musical comedy. It is leisurely, amiable operetta decidedly arresting to the ear, and well worth an evening's indolence."[92]

Thus ended Herbert's operetta career, with an attractive, amiable work that could entertain and please, but could not hold its own with new styles and more fashionable composers. Herbert need not have worried—his accomplishment made a permanent impress on the culture of his country and the lives of his countrymen.

After the birth of *The Dream Girl* in New Haven, Herbert continued to compose and to conduct at the Cosmopolitan Theatre. His immediate assignment was the 1924 edition of the Ziegfeld Follies, which opened at the New Amsterdam Theatre on June 24. It was another posthumous production and contained only two scenes with new Herbert music. In Scene 10 of Act I occurred "A Garden" and "The Beauty Contest," which coalesced into a pageant of glamorous femininity; and in Scene 6 of Act II was an unnamed choreographic sequence performed by the Tiller Girls. There was more Herbert music in the production, but this was interpolated because of the composer's unexpected death.

More important, perhaps, than any of his late music was a letter of only four sentences which Herbert impulsively dashed off less than a fortnight before he died. In all musicians' correspondence it would be difficult to match it for the qualities it shows.

A well known and ingenious New York columnist, S. Jay Kaufman, was moved to solicit opinions from Broadway personalities as to who was America's greatest composer. Then he published his replies in his column in the *Evening Telegram.* Ordinarily such an article has only local, temporary interest, but in this case an extraordinary element crept in. The audience appealed to by Mr. Kaufman was scarcely made up of people supporting the serious music of concert hall or opera house. Consequently some strange candidates were advanced for the title of America's greatest composer. Among the names suggested were Jerome Kern, Robert A. King, W. C. Handy, Harry Woods, and Charles K. Harris. Two gentlemen unblushingly suggested that they themselves should be so considered. Six nominations came in for Herbert—one being by Eddie Cantor.

The predominance of support for Herbert was not important—it was inevitable. Important was the fact that one of his nominators was the well known popular song writer Leo Edwards, who was unusually friendly with the man he was naming. The reasons he gave for his choice were sensible, not extravagant or silly like some, and he presented a good case in a rather trivial affair.

But Herbert read the column and attached importance to Leo Edwards' deeply felt statement. He could see little difference, as far as the experience of a people was concerned, between a popular and a serious composer, and he wanted to see justice done wherever it had been omitted. He wrote to Edwards:

May 13th

My dear Leo

Thanks for the clipping.

Let me assure you that I much appreciate your very complimentary contribution to Mr. Kaufman's curious enterprise.

Strange to say no one mentioned MacDowell, who, of course, is America's *greatest* composer.

But I know you meant well.

With sincerest regards

Yours

VICTOR HERBERT[93]

This remarkable letter deserves more than hasty approval; it deserves study and reflection. It is a revelation of Herbert from several points of view. His choice phrase describing Kaufman's column was eloquently understated. His surprise that MacDowell was proposed by no one was naïve, but so honest that its sincerity cannot be doubted. His own opinion of MacDowell's rank and stature was incontestable and was the very essence of selflessness. The letter as a whole is one of the finest examples of one great musician's opinion of another; as such it merits the permanent attention of the music-loving world. That it was written to a friend—and not for publication—only increases the admiration and affection which Herbert constantly attracted.

Having declared MacDowell America's greatest composer, Herbert had only a few days to live. He was apparently in the best of health as he continued his round of duties: the Cosmopolitan Theatre; the Follies; preparation for the Willow Grove season. Outwardly he seemed to be in excellent spirits. If he ever felt that the musical scene was passing him by, he gave little sign of it. But he was sixty-five years old, and an incredible amount of work showed how he had driven himself for thirty-five years. Occasionally he became reflective and reminiscent.

In May he consented to sit for a portrait painting by Miss F. Enid Stoddard, which the Irish Musical Society was to present to him on June 1.[94] (The portrait is now in private hands.) It was difficult to arrange the sittings, and when he came to the artist's studio he was impatient and anxious to be off to his next engagement.

He talked a great deal of his grandfather and his mother, affectionately describing her wonderful character and the influence she had exerted over him as he grew to manhood. He liked to talk about people in general, to express views which, unwittingly, revealed his own character. "Humanity," he told the artist, "can't be put on one dead level. A man is born with a light in his eye, with a song in his heart, with a gift for friendship, or with the power to stamp his personality on others. Nothing can take those gifts away and nothing can put them in a man but the power that made him. Some people without a penny to bless them are born aristocrats—and some aren't." The artist reported:

One could never think of him as old. He appeared so joyously young. He worried that I would make him too serious.

"Don't make me look glum," he would say when he would look at the first sketch, which necessarily has all the lines of the face blocked out first and has not yet been given freshness and color.

"I'm a very happy person, and I refuse to look serious," was the way he put it when I drove him back to the chair with the assurance that the final work would show him as happy as he felt.

Saturday May 24 was his last sitting for the artist. Two days later she learned of his death as she was giving the portrait its finishing touches.[95]

On that Saturday, Herbert went to the Cosmopolitan Theatre to discuss another motion picture overture (*Janice Meredith*) he was supposed to write. The manager told him he was looking ten years younger, and the composer replied that that was the way he felt.

On the next day, Sunday, Herbert had to attend a rehearsal of the Ziegfeld Follies which lasted into the night. When it was over he went to the home of Mischa Elman, the famous violinist, where a program of chamber music was also lasting far into the night. A rehearsal of the Elman String Quartet was in progress, and Horace Britt, cellist of the Quartet and friend of Herbert for many years, had urged him to come.

Herbert arrived between eleven and twelve o'clock, as the string players were going through Beethoven's Quartet in C minor, Op. 18, No. 4. He listened attentively, and after the players had gone through a few bars of the second movement with the sharply articulated eighth and sixteenth notes he stopped them. He told them that the staccato notes should be shorter and cleaner, and that in his younger days he had performed them so—whereupon he proceeded to show the musicians the proper manner of executing the music.

After more listening Herbert told Elman that his String Quartet had the best cellist possible to obtain. Needless to say, Horace Britt was intensely pleased and never forgot the flattering but honest opinion spontaneously rendered.[96]

Another visitor that night was the eminent pianist Arthur Loesser, who met Herbert for the first time. Herbert was delighted by this slight encounter with chamber music again; and before the evening was over he and Loesser and Elman made an appointment for the following afternoon for more chamber music. Loesser went to the appointed place and waited patiently; at last he went home, arriving there about five o'clock. His father greeted him with the words that Victor Herbert was dead![97]

Meanwhile May 26 had begun as usual, with Herbert planning an active day. He lunched at the Lambs with Raymond Hubbell and others, and seemed to enjoy a modest meal. Some imaginative persons have stated that Herbert's sudden attack was the result of a too heavy luncheon; but his lunch check, which has been preserved, contradicts this emphatically:

1	Bacon & eggs	.80
1	Pot Coffee	.15
1	Bread & butter	.10
1	Baked apple	.20
		$1.25

Across the back of the check is boldly scrawled in pencil, "Victor Herbert"—as firm and characteristic a signature as he ever wrote.[98] It gave no indication of ill health, weakness, or debility.

Telling his friends at the Lambs he would soon see them at a continuation of the Follies rehearsal, he was about to leave the clubhouse when he encountered the conductor Oscar Radin. His thoughts were only of the future as he spoke: "Radin, I'm going to Philadelphia to arrange for my concerts at Willow Grove Park. When I return I want you to have dinner with me at a new Roumanian restaurant which I discovered." He chuckled and continued, "They have the funniest combination there! A fiddle, a cymbalon, and a falsetto-tenor." And he gave a hilarious imitation of the tenor singing "Come Where My Love Lies Dreaming," then turned to the door. "Don't forget, Radin! That's a date!"[99] It was the Lambs' last glimpse of Herbert alive.

It is astonishing how quickly different stories of a great man's collapse get into public circulation, how various are accounts of the same event in newspapers published the same day. Readers of New York journals on May 27, which reported Herbert's death, may well have wondered what actually had happened, for there was ample conflict in the press accounts. It has been my good fortune, through the helpful cooperation of Dr. Edwin Franko Goldman and Nathan Settel, M.D., to talk at length with Natalie Schmidt, librarian at the New York Polyclinic Hospital.[100] I prefer to take Miss Schmidt's version of Herbert's passing as the true account.

The office of Herbert's physician, Emanuel Baruch, was at 57 East

Seventy-seventh Street. Miss Schmidt was Dr. Baruch's office attendant in 1924 and was well acquainted with the distinguished patients treated by her employer. Obviously Herbert felt ill shortly after lunch, else he would not have called at the office on such a busy day; but Dr. Baruch was a close personal friend, and the composer's unexpected visit in itself caused no surprise. Herbert greatly enjoyed the Doctor's conversation, coming to the office frequently for a chat over coffee and eclairs. His warm, friendly, and magnetic personality had made a deep impression on the young and attractive Miss Schmidt.

Early in the afternoon on May 26 Herbert trudged up the stairs to Dr. Baruch's reception room. Miss Schmidt received him, told him the Doctor was out, and showed him into the room where the "rich" patients awaited their turn for attention. (Dr. Baruch had separate waiting rooms for "rich" and "poor" patients, an arrangement that sometimes saved both types from being embarrassed or ill at ease.) She returned to the room for the "poor" whither Herbert followed her for the sole reason, evidently, that he wanted company and not solitude. No one else was in the office.

Herbert made no attempt to describe an ailment, but he did complain of feeling cold and gloomy. The weather outdoors was mild, and Miss Schmidt thought he would be more cheerful in the open air than surrounded by walls. Having no idea how ill he was—neither his appearance nor words afforded any clue—she suggested that he go back downstairs and walk around the block. When he returned the Doctor would probably be back in the office. Herbert accepted her suggestion, walked out of the office, and started downstairs. He collapsed on the way down and was dead when he reached the bottom.

Passers-by recognized Herbert at once, and the news of his death spread over the city like wildfire. The Doctor returned soon after, but he was too late—life was gone. Miss Schmidt was the last person to see Herbert alive.

Later in the afternoon Dr. Baruch gave Miss Schmidt an admonition which may explain some of the discrepancies in stories of how Herbert died. The girl was reminded of Herbert's stature and fame, that importunate reporters would be pestering her for information and testimonials. Under no circumstances, he instructed, should she tell anyone that Herbert died leaving the office. He died as he was coming to the office, not going away. Even when a doctor is out and not available to treat an emergency case, it must not be said that a victim suffered death while departing from a doctor's quarters. No doctor could risk the danger of the truth, which might be distorted or perverted to his own detriment or to the detriment of medical science. Miss Schmidt was loyal to her trust.

Days later the composer's family discovered to their dismay that he had apparently been aware of a heart condition. He had in his medicine cabinet digitalis which he had obtained by prescription from Dr. Baruch.[101] With characteristic good intent, he had been stonily silent about the medicine, pretending bravely to be in the best of health in order to alarm no one close to him. Had he confessed his condition to his family, his life and his enjoyment of it might have been prolonged indefinitely. It was an ill advised kindness, but who can find it in his heart to censure the composer for such consideration?

The whole United States was shocked and bereaved by Herbert's sudden, yet mercifully swift, death. The feelings of the family can only be imagined, but the laments of his friends and colleagues were numberless and meaningful. One brief remark made twenty-four years later transcends them all, for it reflects the reaction of thousands of persons. In September of 1948 Raymond Hubbell said to me in the clubhouse of the Lambs, "When I heard that Victor Herbert was dead, it seemed like the light of the whole world had gone out."

It would be pointless to reproduce all the testimonials and tributes immediately prompted by his death. They were legion. Most of them came from his associates in the theater along Broadway. To a certain extent the world of serious music had forgotten what he meant to the development of musical art in this country, or what he had done for orchestral playing and American opera. But much was remembered, and the following statement comprehends adequately his meaning to his countrymen:

Many American composers have mastered the technic of music, a few are blessed with taste and imagination, and once in a way an individual combines in his art craftsmanship and distinction. Victor Herbert did this and more. He wooed, with a charm as natural as it was irresistible, the popular ear, and by a caprice of art his music delights the discerning no less than the vulgar. The melodies he poured forth so prodigally are only occasionally commonplace; they have that mysterious attribute called style which makes the master-artist. He wrote too readily and too much, and inevitably not all his music is of equal worth. That holds true of greater creative men. His technical skill was uncanny, even in this day of tonal conjurers. A Herbert score "sounds"—every note tells and sparkles like the colors on a fine canvas. Partly this perfection is due to his sound training and painstaking study; yet other men have had equal educational advantages and have accomplished nothing. They lacked the quality—shall we call it genius?—that was in a high degree Mr. Herbert's.

Composer, conductor, 'cellist, Mr. Herbert's special contribution to music in this country was his light operas. He showed that the operetta form could be successfully cultivated by musicians of taste and training; that it was a form worthy of respect. As a man he was esteemed for his open and genial personality, his ready wit, his friendliness. The composer leaves a host of admirers, who mourn his passing with a feeling of personal loss. His place in American music—in the world's music—is secure and, being in a high sense unique, will always remain his very own.[102]

Deems Taylor was in the Middle West when Herbert died. Upon receiving the sad news he sent a special message to New York which spoke for himself as well as thousands of others:

Losing Victor Herbert, the musical world loses some one it will never quite replace. He was the last of the troubadours. His musical ancestor was Mozart and the family of which he was so brilliant a younger son numbered Offenbach, Delibes, Bizet, the Strausses and Arthur Sullivan among its elders.

What he had was what they all had, the gift of song. His music bubbled and sparkled and charmed, and he brought the precious gift of gayety to an art that so often suffers from the pretentiousness and self-consciousness of its practitioners.

The thirty years of his too short career have left us two grand operas and over forty operettas and musical comedies, all distinguished by an unending flow of melodic invention, harmonic and rhythmic individuality and brilliant instrumentation.

Above all he had perfect taste. Herbert's music could be trivial at times but he never wrote a vulgar line in his life. Now that he is gone there is no one left who has quite his combination of effortless spontaneity and endearing light heartedness.

He is not dead, of course. The composer of "Babes in Toyland," "The Fortune Teller," "The Red Mill," "Nordland" and "Mlle. Modiste" cannot be held as dead by a world so heavily in his debt.[103]

On the afternoon of May 26 Florenz Ziegfeld, Jr., spoke a few eloquent words:

He was the greatest musician America ever developed. He wasn't half appreciated during his lifetime, rich though his life was. The people will probably appreciate him now that he is gone. He was the greatest man in my experience that I had dealings with—a very serious man.[104]

Eddie Cantor expressed the feelings of the artists in the theater:

I wish that I had the authority to voice the sorrow of the theatrical world for one who has done so much to bring beauty and color to its people and places.

I wish that I were empowered to give him a suitable memorial; to enlist the co-operation of the theatrical world to let the world know how permanent has been our respect and affection. It need not be a monument of stone, but it might be something vital and living—a great pipe organ, a library of music, a permanent scholarship fund for struggling musicians, a pension for a promising American composer. By such a memorial we could do much for our native art.

Who will help me in this work?

Victor Herbert was so much a part of us, so intimate in work, so close to us all, that we forget how great a man he was, how permanent his work and how profound its significance.

We of the stage, art and literary world, are constantly aware or should be aware of the responsibility we have. For it is our task to make of our theatres, our music and our literature, something that will live, equal and rival the accomplishments of other nations. There are two great standards by which all artistic accomplishments are measured—by their universal qualities and by their native qualities.

Victor Herbert's relations to both these standards has been notable. Through his numerous writings, he has developed what was distinctly an American school of musical comedy composition. He established a taste. He devised melodies. He effected rhythms. He made every aspect of his work so distinctive that the whole world knew that it had one great composer who was able to and did give characteristic expression to the American spirit. And in doing this thing he complied simultaneously with universal standards. He won the approval of the world. He made people of all lands love his music, dance to its rhythms, whistle to its lilt, sing to its refrains. . . .

But Herbert did not belong to the days that have gone by. He belonged to the present. And even to-day, when the "Follies," the last word in modernity, needed a musical high spot, Victor Herbert was called on to supply it.[105]

The authors of song lyrics had their own spokesman in William Jerome, who also echoed the feelings of thousands as he said:

In his passing America has not only lost her greatest composer but has also lost the greatest pal any nation ever knew.

All song writers were big in his eyes. Big or small, that big Irish American heart of his loved them all. . . . Greater New York should give Victor Herbert a public funeral and no citizen of the greatest city of the world ever did more to deserve one.

He was everything the Master said a man should be and followed in his footsteps as closely as possible for a human being to do so. There is no doubt about Victor Herbert's destination—a greater power has already welcomed him—no place could be anything but Heaven in the presence of Victor Herbert.[106]

On May 28 New York gave Herbert the public funeral he so richly deserved; but its pageantry was solemn and grief-laden. Many of the complicated arrangements were cared for by ASCAP, particularly by his old friends Gene Buck and Silvio Hein. Those who witnessed or participated in the ceremonies never forgot the reverent homage paid to the man who had made life happier and sweeter.

The procession was formidable, beginning at the offices of ASCAP (then 56 West Forty-fifth Street) and moving slowly to Fifth Avenue and then to St. Thomas's Episcopal Church. The throng assembled there was a cross section of all humanity, while the musical fraternity ranged from the most eminent composers to a pathetic little hurdy-gurdy man standing on a simple wooden box in order to have a better view.[107] As the mourners and spectators waited, the cortège approached the church headed by the New York City Police Band. (But Richard McCann, when president of Local 802 of the American Federation of Musicians, claimed this was an erroneous impression; that the band was a special group carefully selected by Paul Henneberg, Herbert's former star flutist.[108])

Behind the leading band came the hearse, escorted by soldiers from Governor's Island and sailors from the Brooklyn Navy Yard. The family car followed; then ASCAP *en masse* and groups from the organizations Herbert was so much a part of: the Lambs, the Friars, the Lotos Club, the Friendly Sons of St. Patrick, the Bohemians, another large musical contingent recruited from New York theaters and sent by Local 802 (playing under Victor Baravalle), and a detachment of the 102nd Engineers, formerly Herbert's beloved 22nd Regiment. Swinging into Fifth Avenue, Baravalle had a strong temptation to lead his musicians in the "March of the Toys" from *Babes in Toyland*. If he had, said Raymond Hubbell later, the very heart of New York would have broken in two![109]

The clergymen officiating at the church were Ernest M. Stires and Wilbur L. Caswell, the former eulogizing the deceased in terms departing little from Deems Taylor's message from the Middle West. Anna Fitziu, eminent opera soprano, sang *Lead, Kindly Light,* and Nahan Franko, violinist, played Bach's "Air on the G String"—always one of Herbert's favorite pieces of music. The entire service was marked by a simplicity which was memorable and impressive. At its conclusion the body was taken to Woodlawn Cemetery, where a firing squad of the 102nd Engineers discharged a parting volley and a bugler blew taps.

The honorary pallbearers were: Emanuel Baruch, Gene Buck, Nathan Burkan, Calvin Child, Daniel F. Cohalan, Nahan Franko, Henry Hadley, Henry L. Joyce, Jerome Kern, Morgan J. O'Brien, James A. O'Gorman, Walter W. Price, John Philip Sousa, Colonel H. H. Treadwell, Emil Winter. As a group they represented Herbert's social, musical, theatrical, and political life, a life which was still widening at the time it was brought to a close.

On June 10, 1925, Herbert's remains were transferred to a mausoleum in Woodlawn Cemetery, and the event was seized as an opportunity for a modest memorial ceremony. The composer's societies and activities were again represented by worthy individuals, and Augustus Thomas spoke warmly of Herbert's accomplishments and the affection he inspired.[110]

Herbert's posthumous career in the hearts of his countrymen has been marked by surprisingly few tangible, visible manifestations. In one respect, of course, they have not been necessary, for every time a piece of his is played or sung—no American composer is played more —his memory is quickened and listeners are happy, even if unaware of what he did or stood for. In a very true sense he left his own memorial in his music; and no composer would ask anything better. But with the passing of the years one wonders if the bronze bust in Central Park (unveiled by his daughter in 1927), the three-cent memorial stamp issued on May 13, 1940, and the Liberty ship *Victor Herbert* launched August 22, 1943, sufficiently commemorate the man who had genius for two things: music and friendship. America has treated her composers rather shabbily in the past, and the isolation of Stephen Collins Foster in New York University's Hall of Fame only strengthens this assertion. The repeated failure of Edward MacDowell (whom Herbert considered as America's greatest composer) to win election there, the abrupt rejection of Herbert in 1950 show that the way of the musician is hard when it depends on the recognition accorded by succeeding generations. Fortunately the importance of a creative artist has no relation to remembrances erected after he is gone. What he created is his monument, and here Herbert has no fear of competition.

In a very real sense Herbert's earthly career extended well beyond the day of his death. When he married Therese Förster, in 1886, he took unto himself a wife who soon abandoned her own activities in order to further her husband's climb to fame and fortune. Self-effacing as wife, mother, and companion she formed a new world around her husband, happy in his success, proud of his achievement. When Herbert died this world was shattered with numbing suddenness, and she never fully recovered from the shock. She looked forward to the time she would rejoin him, and confessed to friends this was her strongest desire. On February 24, 1927, Mrs. Herbert passed away at her home after a protracted illness which culminated with startling speed.[111] Two days later she was placed beside her husband in the Woodlawn Cemetery mausoleum. While she lived she was an extension of Herbert's work in the world; when she died that work was symbolically closed—but she had helped direct it to the realm of lasting art.

22

The Man and His Achievement

PERHAPS no biographer ever had a more elusive subject than Victor Herbert. Chronicling his activities, recording his achievements, and listing his works are feasible, even though treacherous snares await the unwary; catching his personality, making him live again for forgetful oldsters or a younger generation that never knew him, presenting his character "in the round"—here are tasks exceedingly difficult. He was a bundle of contrasts and extremes, serious and gay, jolly and sad, and almost any description of him may be true. The affection he engendered in people about him, moreover, gave rise to legends and stories and anecdotes, many of them apocryphal, many half truthful, many completely veracious. Only a great man has the capacity to stimulate this kind of homage, and Herbert was responsible for an extraordinary amount.

Like all great men, Herbert could be naïve and occasionally vain. He exhibited both qualities in a childlike manner which betrayed an awareness of his own worth and a deep inclination to accept the worth of others. He was no paragon of virtue, yet in his ability to awaken the love of others he was virtue personified. Fritz Kreisler told me one day, "Victor Herbert had the greatest capacity for pure friendship of all the men I ever met." Could more be said by one lovable character of another?

No one adjective, no series of words or phrases can adequately describe this unique character. But he was truthful and simple, generous and kind, firm and trustworthy. He was always quick to resent injustice, and he was hot-tempered, sometimes allowing his feelings to get the upper hand. If he lost his temper, however, no rancor remained; calm was restored, and he quickly regained his normal serenity and merriment.

His generosity was fabulous. There is no exaggeration in the stories

561

of his dispensing cash to anyone approaching him with a tale of misfortune. Herbert liked money and the comforts or necessities it could buy; even more he liked what money could buy for others, and his dispensations to musical and theatrical colleagues were inestimable in extent and amount. Undoubtedly he was often victimized by conscienceless scroungers; but he never had to ask himself if he had let a needy person go by. He responded extravagantly, and "he had a singular way of bestowing benefactions without subjecting those helped to the embarrassing necessity of expressing gratitude."[1]

Herbert was trustworthy. The nucleus of men he gathered around him and who played for him throughout the years accepted his word implicitly with respect to engagements and remuneration. They had no contract, and they knew they needed none. He was loved and trusted, and a contract would have been a superfluous piece of paper. It was hardly a businesslike arrangement, but to play for Herbert transcended any business relationship.[2]

Herbert was truthful, even when he issued statements which would hardly further the performance of his own music. On March 15, 1924, *Musical America* published (in "Mephisto's Musings") a rather flattering reference to *Natoma*; but the writer made some errors which showed poor memory or faulty information. He mentioned Sophie Braslau as the creator of the title rôle and the Metropolitan as the producer of the opera. Herbert would not countenance such misrepresentation, and he wrote a characteristic letter the day the magazine appeared:

MY DEAR MEPHISTO:

As a rule your comments on musical matters are not only most interesting, but also correct in regard to facts. In your last issue, however, in speaking of the history and fate of American Grand Operas, you say that my "Natoma" was produced by the Metropolitan Opera Company and that Miss Sophie Braslau sang the title rôle. Neither of these statements is based on fact.

"Natoma" was produced by the (then) Philadelphia-Chicago Opera Company, Miss Mary Garden sang the title rôle and Maestro Campanini conducted. "Natoma" was presented at the Metropolitan Opera House by this company, which gave several request performances at that time. Miss Braslau is a very charming artist, but she never sang "Natoma." She created the title rôle in Cadman's Indian opera, however.

As far as the attitude of the American opera-going public, which you criticize, is concerned, there was nothing the matter with it in my case. This is proved by the fact that "Natoma" was produced by the Chicago Company thirty-five times, and only Maestro Campanini's untimely death stopped the continuation of the opera in the company's répertoire. Has the Metropolitan ever produced an American opera thirty-five times?

Permit me to say in conclusion that I am not trying to bring the attention of the Metropolitan to "Natoma." Even if they were willing to do the work (in English, of course), it would be impossible to cast the opera with Americans, in regard to the male rôles, simply because they have not got a sufficient number of American artists.

Excuse my frankness, but I love the truth!

VICTOR HERBERT

New York City, March 15, 1924.[3]

Herbert was prompt to give encouragement to musicians, young or old, whenever he was pleased by their performance. It made no difference where he encountered them. He once heard two young sisters playing piano and violin in an Albany hotel, and he could not leave without telling them how much pleasure their music had given him, in such a way that the delighted girls remembered it ever afterward. Thirty years later the story came back to Herbert's daughter in Lake Placid who thereby relived her own experience of her father's kindness.[4]

America knew Herbert as a large man of portly mien. He was stout but not fat, and his size was magnified by his frame. Not much under six feet in height, he preserved a remarkable nimbleness and agility for such proportions. In his younger days his hair was a curly dark brown, almost black, and it whitened beautifully in his late years. What never changed was the twinkle in his eye which betrayed the *joie de vivre* that enwrapped his whole personality.

He had religious instincts and respected sincere believers of all creeds; consequently he had friends among both Catholic and Protestant clergy and laity. Not a regular church attendant, he was nevertheless an Episcopalian, following in the footsteps of his grandfather, who, in spite of his attacks on the Anglican Church, never left it. When Herbert died many of his friends were astonished to discover that he was not a Catholic, for it seemed axiomatic that a patriotic Irishman must belong to the Roman faith; but religion was a very personal matter to him, and he probably never discussed it with anyone.

His constant industry made it difficult for him to develop hobbies or avocations. He was ill at ease if not working, and he sometimes scoffed at the virtues attributed to an avocation. When asked to name his favorite hobby he would indignantly deny having any, then retort, "What do you think I am, a businessman?" When occasion required, however, he could relax as much as necessary, by simply staying at home and idling with the family or by venting his energies on the attractions offered by Lake Placid.

On this beautiful lake, Herbert had idyllic summer quarters inspiring both work and recreation, and indulged in what might be called his favorite pastimes: working, swimming, boating. (He attempted to play golf, but failed to develop an interest in it.) He loved the water and was expert both in swimming and in operating motor launches.

Herbert's fondness for boats extended to the titles he gave them and the significance they held for him. He acquired his first boat in 1905 and promptly named it *Handy Andy*. Then came *Handy Andy II* and other craft successively called *Rory I* and *Rory II*, and at last the *Natoma*. The operatic boat was the largest and most powerful on the lake—forty feet long, with an engine of 125 horse power—custom-built to satisfy certain desires and demands. Obviously he delighted in names derived from Samuel Lover's best known characters, and felt that they, as well as the boats they adorned, belonged to him. This was exemplified in a curious way.

Herbert decided it was time to replace *Handy Andy II*, and he was pleased that a fellow Placidian was eager to buy it. Agreement was reached on all business details, and the purchaser, Wm. S. Benson, handed him the check for the stipulated amount. About to leave, Benson was amazed to hear: "You know Mr. Benson, you only bought the boat—its name belongs to me." He was thunderstruck and dismayed. He had been attracted to the boat in the first place because of its unusual name, and he had no intention of rechristening it. He protested vigorously, threatening to call the whole deal off; but neither coaxing nor argument had the slightest effect, and the chagrined buyer at last accepted the boat without the name. The best he could do was to call it the *Sarah Jane* ("Not even a good name for a girl-friend of Handy Andy!").[5] But he never tired of telling the story.

This transaction did not stop the succession of *Handy Andys* on the waters of Lake Placid. *Handy Andy III* eventually made its appearance and had the misfortune to sink in an accident. Then came *Handy Andy IV*, which still skims over the lake for the pleasure of the composer's daughter and her husband, a reminder of the composer's firmness and Lover's roguish hero.

Had Herbert enjoyed more leisure or been more sedentary his chief pleasure would have been reading. Even in the life he created for himself he was remarkably well read, and his curiosity and his interests were remarkably broad. He surrounded himself with books, and used them; but he had no time for systematic reading. The owner of countless miscellaneous and fugitive volumes, he had a special fondness for masters of German, French, and English literature. For his personal library he acquired the works of Goethe, Schiller, Heine, Scott, Kipling, Hugo, and Maupassant. He especially treasured, of course, the works of Samuel Lover. He was able to read (and speak and write) in four languages—English, German, French, Italian; the only thing he lacked was time.

As he avoided avocations, so he gave little thought to amusements.

He did not care for games and had no inclination to play cards. His favorite amusement, if it can be called such, was the theater; but he was highly selective in what he saw. He was always sensitively affected by what he witnessed and heard.

As a man of the world having taste, discrimination, and experience Herbert was an epicure in food and drink. He knew and appreciated the most savory dishes and the choicest wines and liquors, but he governed his appetites strictly and remained the connoisseur. (I wish, in this respect, to acknowledge a small debt to the composer: I have discovered through him the delectability of a fine Irish whisky!) In food, of course, Herbert was uniquely favored, because Mrs. Herbert had the faculty of preparing dishes fit for royalty.

Good food, liquid or solid, inspires sociability and a departure from professional cares and concerns. But Herbert was too much the musician to be long diverted from the art he so assiduously practiced. This was especially true with younger people who wanted to acquire more knowledge of their craft from Herbert's vast experience. Thus the composer Philip James has confessed to learning more about orchestration from Herbert over a drink of whisky than from all the textbooks on the subject ever written.[6] The artistic influence and pedagogical value of such talks cannot be measured; but neither can they be overestimated.

Just as Herbert's music was highly emotional, so was his reaction to the music of others. Certain of the master composers were like gods to him, and he knew how to distinguish between the schools they represented. He might say of Wagner's *Tristan und Isolde,* "That is the finest music in the world!" and then in equal admiration of Schubert's songs exclaim, "Not a note should be changed." One afternoon he and his prolific librettist, Harry B. Smith, together listened to Tchaikovsky's *Symphonie Pathétique,* conducted by Safonoff. After the performance H. E. Krehbiel joined them, and Smith noticed how profoundly the last movement of the symphony had depressed both the composer and the critic. Finally Herbert, who had conducted the work so often, remarked, "It is magnificent, but I wish it had never been written."[7]

Rarely, however, was Herbert led by music into a state of mental depression. He had a feeling for the art which surpassed his ability to analyze it, and on one occasion at least he gropingly tried to express the "oneness" of all music regardless of its specific manifestations. The wisdom of his observation is readily apparent:

Sit in a darkened room and leave your mind free from prejudice while you listen to a voice chanting an ancient Irish Banshee song. Give your imagination fair berth and see if it isn't the wail of a cantor in [a] synagogue

—wonderfully beautiful music—or a song of the Far East, a Grecian folk song, the shriek of the American Indian in a war dance, a snatch of Gregorian music, or even some of the Chinese music that one hears a bit of in 'Frisco. It's all the same.

During this same session of informal philosophy he set forth a series of five aphorisms which reflected his conscious thought and conduct:

The saddest thing in the world is a book full of jokes. The next saddest is an educated dunce.

There is no such thing in the world as luck, so far as human endeavor is concerned, unless the other fellow has it.

They ought to pass a law against singing "My Country 'Tis of Thee." It's about as thoroughly American as gorgonzola cheese.

Education is too cheap; it has spoiled almost as many as it has made.

The great bane of modern education is classification; there are too many card index minds.[8]

Herbert's own philosophy of music was summed up in one word: work. Any composer worthy the name, he believed, had a profession to practice like any other professional man, eight hours a day, day after day.[9] Whenever possible he would follow such a schedule, in New York or Lake Placid, working early and late to discharge the responsibility which was assumed as both duty and pleasure.

Inwardly Herbert was intensely serious; outwardly and no less sincerely he was the soul of geniality, kindness, and democratic camaraderie. This was the side the public heard about as his players and associates spread their affectionate tales of his unique personality. But he put one thing above all else: the excellence of any performance he might be conducting, be the music his own or that of another composer.

Some of his players have told me that no one could make music like Herbert, that playing under his baton was an unparalleled experience. In strict baton technic, they allege, Herbert was surpassed by a few; in making music, catching and diffusing its spirit or even adding more, he was in a class by himself. In rehearsals he was firm, even tyrannical, and unhappy was the player who failed to please him. He could release a volley of sarcasm which would wilt the strongest opponent or culprit. His precept was: "Kindness alone won't build a fine orchestra,"[10] and he adhered to it religiously. The difference between Herbert and other conductors was that when the rehearsal was over Herbert promptly became one of the boys again; other conductors, never. Hence he was loved as well as respected.

Under Herbert as a symphonic conductor the men well knew what was expected of them. The repertoire was fairly standard, and the presentations were rigorously formal. Playing in Herbert's concert orchestra, with a mixed repertoire of lighter and heavier numbers, they had to be ready for any kind of emergency, especially audience requests for a favorite piece. The music might not be in front of them; but if it was in their concert repertoire Herbert expected the men to know it, and he would tolerate no faking:

One of the violinists who played under his bâton, says that it was a stupendous experience to play under the direction of Victor Herbert since, if anything were not perfect, he had an almost uncanny knack of knowing just whose fault it was. And if the audience demanded any number, Herbert would order it, regardless of whether they had the notes or not. He took it for granted that the men would know by memory any number in their repertoire. And any luckless second violinist who attempted to bluff his way through was called to strict account.[11]

Herbert himself had an enormous quantity of music memorized, and never used a score when conducting his own orchestra (except when playing accompaniments). He might look at a score of a larger work in the afternoon to refresh his memory for night, then he would be sure of it; or, if a bit of doubt entered his mind as he mounted the podium, he would whisper to Fred Landau, his concertmaster, "Upbeat or downbeat?" The answer was whispered back, and the piece was unerringly played.[12]

The perfection attained through strict rehearsal was for the music itself and the people who came to hear it. There was never a more conscientious musician than Herbert, who would perform as carefully for ten persons as for ten thousand. This was another of his cardinal principles, based on the conviction that the ten had paid for the same degree of excellence as had the multitude. Such a minimum audience, to be sure, seldom fell to his lot.

As Herbert moved farther away from the symphonic field he became more and more closely identified as the interpreter of his own music. Naturally he was the best of the "Herbert conductors," and other interpreters are still the despair of all who heard the composer himself. It was not easy to impart his wishes to his men, and he would "sweat great gobs of desperation trying to get what he wanted." His rubato was inimitable, and so were the subtle nuances embedded in the music, which were as difficult to notate as "a gentleman's code of manners." To a greater or lesser degree all his scores had the same individuality, yet "without the magic key" of his personality "to open their tightly locked pages, they remained a closed book, refusing to yield their secret."[13] This may seem like an overstatement, for Herbert's music will always exert its particular charm; but it is just as true as the fact that those who never heard Rachmaninoff play his own concertos have no idea how effective his mind and fingers made them. It is a tragedy that Herbert died before the present-day perfection of phonograph recording.

The same spirit of perfection motivated Herbert in rehearsals of his operettas, occasions when he usually had men not from his own orchestra. What he strove for and how he affected the players made a scene worth remembering:

I have been present at some of the Monday morning rehearsals preceding the opening, that night, of one of his operettas, either new or an old one on tour. He was a tyrant—genial, witty and urbane—but a tyrant none the less. How he would plague the men, used to slouching back in their chairs and only playing what they saw. It was Herbert's task—and what a job!—to make them, as it were, read between the lines. He couldn't put into print that sly rubato and the various other Herbertisms that went into the mosaic of his music. In desperation Herbert would sometimes leave the conductor's stand, grab the 'cellist's instrument and try to show the wooden, unyielding orchestra just what effect he was after. . . . That night and for the rest of the week, the men would sit forward on their chairs, alert and eager, and the audience would hear the music as it should be played. But, alas, the next week the genial Irishman would be elsewhere spreading the Gospel of Herbert according to St. Victor, and the orchestra men would slump back in their chairs, their eyes would become glassy, and they would play only what they saw—and nothing more.[13]

Remarkably like this, written in another place and time, is Peggy Wood's recollection of Herbert's conduct at an operetta rehearsal:

Herbert usually conducted the first nights of any of his shows and, since he always did his own orchestrations and knew what he wanted out of the band and the singers, his orchestral rehearsals and premières were something to be remembered with mingled agony and delight. If things went wrong the musicians complained he had such an erratic beat they couldn't tell where they were at; and when that happened his magnificent flow of invective made them wish they weren't where they were. But they adored him, nonetheless, and the very sight of him lighted up every face whenever he trotted onto the stage (for he never walked, he moved at a sort of half run, as if in a vast impatience to get to the spot where he wanted to be faster than mortal legs could propel him by ordinary procedure). I was lucky enough to be in four shows of his and I shall never forget the electricity which seemed to crackle from his immense vitality as he would galvanize any group with chuckling good humor or coruscating criticism.[14]

From the first association with Herbert his orchestra men knew him for what he was, a strict leader and a faithful friend. When young Frederik (Fritz) Stahlberg, fresh from Germany and Stuttgart at the age of twenty-two, arrived in Pittsburgh in 1899 to play in the symphony, Herbert promptly informed him of the peculiarities of American life, warning him what he must avoid. He told the young man first of all that he should not succumb to the American habit of "treating"—rounds of drinks where everyone in the group had to buy a round at least once. It was an expensive habit and, said Herbert, a dangerous one, for it led to excessive consumption.[15] Forewarned was forearmed.

The men were always alert for evidences of Herbert's wit and sharpness, then awaited the opportunity to retell them. In Willow Grove during World War I Herbert had frequent occasion to play *Over There*. One day a man brought him a march and asked him to play it. After looking at the manuscript Herbert had to refuse the request, whereupon the disappointed amateur reminded him of the performances of *Over There*. Herbert patiently explained that *Over There* was a classic of its kind, but the man made still another effort by saying he had heard that Herbert encouraged home talent. "I do, my boy, I do," replied Herbert, "I always encourage home talent—to play at home!"[16]

He loved to play jokes, and his men never knew what to expect next. Once, when about to start on a tour in the early Pittsburgh days, Herbert ascertained beforehand that the name of his Pullman car was Darius. He casually asked his concertmaster what car his berth was in, and Kunits replied, "Darius—Darius, King of the Persians." "Yes," said Herbert nonchalantly, "King of the Persians, son of Hystaspes, born 550 B.C. and died 485—the founder of the Persian dynasty . . ." while the listeners gaped in astonishment. He had looked up his information that morning and was pleased to amaze his men with his innocent erudition.[17]

When on tour the men were understandably jealous of their privacy and were always ready to eject intruding strangers. They had, in fact, what might be called a vocal fanfare which they would sing in a way to terrify any unwary interloper. Herbert had written it for them, and it went like this:

One person they once chased from their car with this decisive chant was Jim Jeffries when he was heavyweight boxing champion. The prize fighter was surprised at the greeting, turned on his heel, and left. When Herbert heard of his men's exploit he sagely remarked: "Don't be puffed up, boys. He could've cleaned you all up at the same time —it was your singing he ran from!"[18]

Herbert was as generous with praise as he was with money if he thought the recipient deserved it. Encountering a young musician of exceptional talent, as he occasionally did when he toured with a show and drew upon extra local musicians, he would make a point of singling him out, advising him on proper training, and encouraging him to find larger opportunities.[19]

If, however, he found a person attempting to do things beyond his capacity, a musician who was a faker or a *poseur,* he was equally ready to express his indignation, sometimes bluntly. Not infrequently Herbert's orchestra, in the course of a concert, would play for a choral work, and the conductor of the choral society would lead the performance. On one such occasion it happened that the choral conductor was woefully inadequate, and his rehearsal with Herbert's expert men made everyone unhappy. The orchestra was annoyed at first, then became restive, and finally slipped beyond his control. They began throwing little things at him, such as cigarette butts, and at last a piece of sausage skin landed on the conductor's stand. The poor man survived his ordeal and complained to Herbert about the orchestra's lack of respect and discipline. Herbert gave him little consolation: "You know, it doesn't take very long for them to find out what kind of an ass is before them!"[20]

Herbert was also ready to measure up to unexpected requirements or requests which came in unexpected places at unexpected times. When he fulfilled them he sometimes received an unexpected reward. One place he visited repeatedly in New York was the home of Charles M. Schwab, the steel magnate, who had been interested in him since the Pittsburgh days. In this famous mansion was a magnificent pipe organ, presided over by Archer Gibson, and Herbert loved to sit on the bench with Gibson and improvise on the awe-inspiring instrument.

Occasionally Schwab would have Gibson assemble a symphony orchestra in the house. One evening Herbert was present at a domestic orchestra concert, another guest being a famous prima donna from the Metropolitan Opera. Everybody was delighted when she consented to sing "Kiss Me Again" if Herbert would play a cello obbligato to her solo. He seized a sheet of paper, wrote out the desired part, and played it to perfection as she rendered the beautiful melody. It was so successful that she bestowed kisses on Herbert and Schwab, leaving Gibson disappointed and neglected.[21]

One of the best Herbert stories—in fact, there is none better, and it is not apocryphal—originated in Pittsburgh some time after he had severed his connection with the symphony orchestra. For several years he returned with his own orchestra to play at the annual exposition, and during one of these engagements members of the Press Club decided to give him a dinner. The hosts, numbering some thirty-odd, had special banquet menus printed, whence came the idea that Herbert should autograph each card and write a few bars of melody at the card owner's request. The whole procedure was to be carefully worked out, for there was to be a major objective: proof of complete familiarity with all of Herbert's operetta themes. The spirit of mischief crept in at the last moment, and thereby hangs this tale.

Few of the dinner participants were well acquainted with Herbert's already astonishing output. Consequently each one received a slip of paper on which was written the title of a song and the production in which it was sung. The men were instructed to memorize these data, then at the proper moment to offer their menus to Herbert and ask him to write a few measures of so-and-so from such-and-such a work. The titles thus memorized were, deliberately, not the best known, for the diners wanted to impress the composer with their knowledge of his music and also to see how easily he could recall the countless airs he had written in the past. Here are some examples of what were asked for:

The Angelus	from	*The Serenade*
Butterfly Waltz		*Babette*
My Angeline		*The Wizard of the Nile*
Song of the Priestess		*The Idol's Eye*
Ah! Cupid		*Prince Ananias*
Oriental Dance		*Wonderland*
Birth of the Butterfly		*Babes in Toyland*
Song of the Danube		*The Singing Girl*
The Nightingale and the Star		*Mlle. Modiste*

The men learned what to request before Herbert arrived, but one man came too late to receive his instructions. Hearing about the plan, he at once clamored for a Herbert title, for he did not know a single one. He was something of a nuisance, and so to shut him up and to get on with proceedings a "friend" told him to ask for "Brown October Ale" from *Robin Hood*, Reginald de Koven's most celebrated work. The teller of this tale, also a participant in the affair, must finish the story in his own words:

This poor cluck didn't know the difference and assumed, of course, that Herbert had written it. We watched very carefully when this fellow placed his card in front of Herbert and quoted the above song. Herbert never batted an eye, but printed a few bars of music on the program, signed his name and handed it back with a smile.

This was pretty game of Herbert as he and De Koven were keen rivals at the time, and I am quite sure that neither liked the other personally, but naturally he was quite tickled that so many newspaper men in Pittsburgh knew so many of his compositions and remarked upon this when he made a little speech at the end of the dinner.

That evening when I was in Herbert's dressing room at the Exposition during the intermission of the evening concert, I told him only that part of the foregoing which related to the nuisance and "Brown October Ale," allowing Herbert to think that all of the other choices were spontaneous and out of the minds of the newspaper men who were at the dinner. I asked him what he had done and he replied he wrote a few bars of "Absinthe Frappé" from *Nordland* and let it go at that.[22]

This was Victor Herbert, whose quickness was matched by his kindness and forbearance, who made friends in all walks of life. His friend, Marcella Sembrich, phrased it well when she described him as being "so full of heart." And then she expanded her views: "A good heart, and it is only a good heart that can produce the kind of melody that Victor put into his songs. A fine character shows in music, and his was one of the finest. . . . I liked to sing when Victor was conducting."[23]

His appearance might change, but his character never altered. As he became one of music's elder statesmen "his eyes still had that merry twinkle. His wit and tongue were still keen and quick. There were changes, though. His hair was white. And he was quieter,—not as nervous as formerly,—more serene. But he was as mischievous as ever. One evening at a little party where everyone spoke German, when called upon to speak, he rose to his feet and began with great gravity, 'Verehrte Mitesser . . .' which means, strangely enough, not only 'honored co-eaters,' but also 'honored blockheads!' "[24]

Such were the traits and impressions perceived by the thousands, which led to an introduction of Herbert at a banquet in these terms: "Gentlemen, one of God's noblemen,—Victor Herbert!"[25]

What did Herbert accomplish, and what did he want to do? This book tries to answer the questions, but an afterword seems to be necessary. The astonishing number of his compositions attests only his industry, not the value of its results. The degree to which America remembers his music is a far better indication of how significant his contribution is; but even this measurement is fallible, for American memories are short; we forget more than we recollect.

Naturally Herbert is best known as a composer *par excellence* of operettas. Their happy strains bring him much closer to immortality than his frequent attempts to write serious instrumental music or formidable grand operas. It was fortunate both for him and for his public that he made operetta his specialty: for him, because it meant plentiful performance and lucrative gain; for his public, because it heard a form of music which was skillfully wrought, emotionally potent, artistically satisfying. Better than anyone else he bridged the gap (artificial yet ever present in the mind) between the lighter and weightier types of music, and he appealed to his listeners to disregard these types. By example and precept he begged his hearers to attend to quality and artistry, not kind.

Herbert's music, of course, was not all of equal worth; but no composer's is. His best scores (e.g., *Mlle. Modiste, The Enchantress, The Serenade, The Fortune Teller, Eileen, Naughty Marietta, Sweethearts, Cyrano de Bergerac*) are unsurpassed in their genre and invite a closer study of everything he wrote. Their grace and charm, their felicity of expression, their vigor and variety stamp Herbert as a master of operetta art—not for America alone, but for all countries of similar musical characteristics.

In one sense Herbert was not an American composer. His style was both eclectic and international. He had the daintiness of the French, the solidity of the German, the sensuousness of the Viennese, the playfulness of the Irish. When he exhibited an American trait it was usually by writing a specimen of ragtime, which he could do well enough, but which he scarcely favored by musical inclination. He brought to the American musical stage a freedom of expression and a grandeur of choral climax it had not known before—and the sheer force of his musical gifts made him the peer of the company boasting of Offenbach, Strauss, and Sullivan.

He liked to experiment without being the originator of any new form. Different types of stories, different sizes of casts and ensembles, different kinds of singers (from excellent to execrable) deterred him not at all; and within the operetta form as he knew it in Europe he added a vast variety of color and feeling. He "enriched the tonal palette of his countrymen; he refined the humors of musical commentary; he added robustness and ebullience to the light opera of his day."[26]

Herbert "was dynamic, impetuous, gay, romantic, inventive, cooperative and desperately hard-working. And of these qualities he gave freely in the service of the theater. The success of all his best pieces was his reward and the American theater's good fortune. But he was too lavish and too experimental by nature to turn out work that was of even merit." He perceived the value of folk elements in drama, and he recognized new talent which was about to revolutionize our musical expression (e.g., Gershwin). "He did more than any other man to organize a theatre orchestra whose instruments should be adequate for any theatre score and should serve, rather than betray, the singers." Even in writing the score of *The Fall of a Nation,* "the first original score that followed the action" of a film, he expanded the application of musical illustration. "There is, in fact, hardly a point in our modern musical theatre that does not, to advantage, show the touch of Victor Herbert's eager and resourceful mind and fingers."[27]

Herbert was the only man in America, if not in the world, who could do so many things in music and do them so well. His musical training set him apart from the usual theater composer, and his colleagues along Broadway marveled at his technical proficiency. (Similarly his colleagues in serious music marveled at his adaptability to the demands of the stage.) His orchestrations were the delight and despair of all who heard them, and his orchestral sagacity was looked on with awe. The style of today differs from that of a generation ago, and comparisons are often futile; but the achievement of Herbert stands unchallenged. This is firmly implied by Robert Russell Bennett, one of America's most illustrious musicians:

> My opinion of Victor's place in the American musical theatre would have less than no importance, but I can quote you something that you might like to include in your book. Jerome Kern once made an arrangement for orchestra of about 16 bars of one of his melodies while we were on the road together. That night, after we had played the arrangement, he said to his music director, "Did you notice the 16 bars that I arranged? They were no good—and that's why that old fellow over there was the greatest of them all," pointing to a picture of Victor Herbert on his piano.[28]

Few of Herbert's operettas are remembered today as theatrical productions. Even the modern revivals of *The Red Mill* and *Sweethearts* leave no lasting memory of book, plot, or text. The composer's failure to find a worthy literary partner has been decried so often as to become proverbial. "It's a rollicking roster—honest tunes, robust or charming, as the case called for, and usually finer to the ear when divorced from their words. Herbert belonged to the 'ifs' of operetta. If only he had had a Gilbert . . ."[29]

This lament is only partly justified. Herbert certainly never found a librettist even faintly approaching Sullivan's partner, and many of his books were of the shoddiest. But they were acceptable (for a while) to the contemporary public, and there is no record that Herbert himself was dissatisfied with them. Even had he been, where would he have turned for better? Smith and Blossom were the best the country had to offer: if they failed to suit, what could a composer do? There is doubtless some truth in the charge that Herbert failed to appreciate the faults in the stories he had to set; but an alternative has never been suggested. He had to use the writers available or compose no operettas, a choice which could be resolved without hesitation.

It is curious how readily a bad operetta text is attacked. To a lesser extent the same is true of a libretto for grand opera. Some of the best of grand operas have books quite as inane as the ones handed to Herbert, but they have succeeded nevertheless. A music drama, comic or serious, lives by virtue of its music, and the composer's genius alone will prolong its existence. Undoubtedly some (perhaps most) of Herbert's finest stage music is heard no more because it is wedded to words and situations which cannot be revived, but the cause is not limited to the words alone. Convention and taste and credibility are all contributing factors; if these, or the prejudices based on these, can be overcome, a surprising amount of the best Herbert can be restored to performance.

Gilbert and Sullivan were assuredly a unique combination. Their words and music cannot be imagined separately. Yet because of this very fact they tyrannize over each other and enjoy no individual fame or appreciation. A happier fate for a composer is to particularize his product so that even a fortunate association will not alter his artistic stature. Herbert's accomplishments depended on no one but himself. His music is loved because it is his own individual expression, not because it is indissolubly linked with a set of words it cannot cast aside. The failure of Herbert to find his Gilbert should occasion no regret—although speculation on the reverse refuses to subside. It is, moreover, a foolish speculation, for it adds nothing to Herbert's stature and tends to belittle what he actually did.

At heart Herbert was a missionary, of exemplary tolerance, who was supremely devoted to his mission: providing good music to the people. His composing, his performing, his "preaching" were pointed to this purpose, and his personality was of the kind that furthered the purpose abundantly. More than a decade before his death Herbert received an accolade from a critic he enjoyed quarreling with, but Felix Borowski was still moved to write the following: "No composer in this country has done more—not one, indeed, has done so much—to educate the people to appreciate the better art. And by better art we do not mean necessarily the symphonies that are packed with fugues and double counterpoint."[30] The same verdict can justly be rendered today.

Compositions by Victor Herbert

OPERAS

MADELEINE. A lyric opera in one act. New York: G. Schirmer, 1913 (piano-vocal score. Full score [1914?]).

1st perf., Jan. 24, 1914, New York.

NATOMA. An opera in three acts. New York: G. Schirmer, 1911 (piano-vocal score).

1st perf., Feb. 25, 1911, Philadelphia.

OPERETTAS

ALGERIA. New York: C. K. Harris, 1908 (piano-vocal score).

1st perf., Atlantic City, Aug. 24, 1908; 1st N.Y. perf., Aug. 31, 1908.

ALICE AND THE EIGHT PRINCESSES. See WONDERLAND.

THE AMEER. New York: Witmark, 1899 (piano-vocal score).

1st perf., Scranton, Oct. 9, 1899; 1st N.Y. perf., Dec. 4, 1899.

THE AMERICAN AMBASSADRESS. See IT HAPPENED IN NORDLAND.

ANGEL FACE. New York: Harms, 1920 (piano-vocal score).

1st perf., Chicago, June 8, 1919; 1st N.Y. perf., Dec. 29, 1919.

BABES IN TOYLAND. New York: Witmark, 1903 (piano-vocal score).

1st perf., Chicago, June 17, 1903; 1st N.Y. perf., Oct. 13, 1903.

BABETTE. New York: Witmark, 1903 (piano-vocal score).

1st perf., Washington, Nov. 9, 1903; 1st N.Y. perf., Nov. 16, 1903.

CYRANO DE BERGERAC. New York: Witmark, 1899 (piano-vocal score).

1st perf., Montreal, Sept. 11, 1899; 1st N.Y. perf., Sept. 18, 1899.

THE DÉBUTANTE. New York: G. Schirmer, 1914 (piano-vocal score).

1st perf., Atlantic City, Sept. 21, 1914; 1st N.Y. perf., Dec. 7, 1914.

DOLLY DOLLARS. See MISS DOLLY DOLLARS.

DREAM CITY and THE MAGIC KNIGHT. New York: C. K. Harris, 1907 (piano-vocal score).

1st perf., New York, Dec. 25, 1906.

THE DREAM GIRL. New York: Harms, 1924 (no score published).

1st perf., New Haven, April 22, 1924; 1st N.Y. perf., Aug. 20, 1924.

THE DUCHESS. New York: Witmark, 1911 (piano-vocal score; first published as MLLE. ROSITA).

1st perf., Boston, March 27, 1911, as MLLE. ROSITA; 1st N.Y. perf., Oct. 16, 1911.

THE EIGHT PRINCESSES. *See* WONDERLAND.

EILEEN. New York: Witmark, 1917 (piano-vocal score, 1st published as HEARTS OF ERIN).

1st perf., Cleveland, Jan. 1, 1917, as HEARTS OF ERIN; 1st N.Y. perf., March 19, 1917.

THE ENCHANTRESS. New York: Witmark, 1911 (piano-vocal score).

1st perf., Washington, Oct. 9, 1911; 1st N.Y. perf., Oct. 19, 1911.

THE FORTUNE TELLER. New York: Witmark, 1898 (piano-vocal score).

1st perf., Toronto, Sept. 14, 1898; 1st N.Y. perf., Sept. 26, 1898.

THE GIRL IN THE SPOTLIGHT. New York: Harms, 1920 (no score published).

1st perf., Stamford, Conn., July 7, 1920; 1st N.Y. perf., July 12, 1920.

THE GOLD BUG. New York: E. Schuberth, 1896 (no score published).

1st perf., New York, Sept. 21, 1896.

HEARTS OF ERIN. *See* EILEEN.

HER REGIMENT. New York: Harms, 1917 (piano-vocal score).

1st perf., Springfield, Mass., Oct. 22, 1917; 1st N.Y. perf., Nov. 12, 1917.

THE IDOL'S EYE. New York: E. Schuberth, 1897 (piano-vocal score).

1st perf., Troy, N.Y., Sept. 20, 1897; 1st N.Y. perf., Oct. 25, 1897.

IT HAPPENED IN NORDLAND. New York: Witmark, 1905 (piano-vocal score).

1st perf., Harrisburg, Nov. 21, 1904; 1st N.Y. perf., Dec. 5, 1904.

THE LADY OF THE SLIPPER. New York: Witmark, 1912 (piano-vocal score).

1st perf., Philadelphia, Oct. 8, 1912; 1st N.Y. perf., Oct. 28, 1912.

LITTLE NEMO. New York: Cohan & Harris, 1908 (piano-vocal score).

1st perf., Philadelphia, Sept. 28, 1908; 1st N.Y. perf., Oct. 20, 1908.

THE MADCAP DUCHESS. New York: G. Schirmer, 1913 (piano-vocal score).

1st perf., Rochester, Oct. 13, 1913; 1st N.Y. perf., Nov. 11, 1913.

MLLE. MODISTE. New York: Witmark, 1905 (piano-vocal score).

1st perf., Trenton, Oct. 7, 1905; 1st N.Y. perf., Dec. 25, 1905.

MLLE. ROSITA. *See* THE DUCHESS.

MISS DOLLY DOLLARS. New York: Witmark, 1905 (piano-vocal score).

1st perf., Rochester, Aug. 30, 1905; 1st N.Y. perf., Sept. 4, 1905.

MY GOLDEN GIRL. New York: Harms, 1919 (no score published).

1st perf., Stamford, Conn., Dec. 19, 1919; 1st N.Y. perf., Feb. 2, 1920.

NAUGHTY MARIETTA. New York: Witmark, 1910 (piano-vocal score).

1st perf., Syracuse, Oct. 24, 1910; 1st N.Y. perf., Nov. 7, 1910.

OLD DUTCH. New York: Witmark, 1909 (piano-vocal score).

1st perf., Wilkes-Barre, Nov. 6, 1909; 1st N.Y. perf., Nov. 22, 1909.

THE ONLY GIRL.   New York: Witmark, 1914 (piano-vocal score).
    1st perf., Atlantic City, Oct. 1, 1914; 1st N.Y. perf., Nov. 2, 1914.
ORANGE BLOSSOMS.   New York: Harms, 1922 (piano-vocal score).
    1st perf., Philadelphia, Sept. 4, 1922; 1st N.Y. perf., Sept. 19, 1922.
OUI MADAME.   New York: Harms, 1920 (no score published).
    1st perf., Philadelphia, March 22, 1920.
THE PRIMA DONNA.   New York: Witmark, 1908 (piano-vocal score).
    1st perf., Chicago, Oct. 5, 1908; 1st N.Y. perf., Nov. 30, 1908.
PRINCE ANANIAS.   New York: E. Schuberth, 1895 (piano-vocal score).
    1st perf., New York, Nov. 20, 1894.
THE PRINCESS PAT.   New York: Witmark, 1915 (piano-vocal score).
    1st perf., Atlantic City, Aug. 23, 1915; 1st N.Y. perf., Sept. 29, 1915.
THE RED MILL.   New York: Witmark, 1906 (piano-vocal score).
    1st perf., Buffalo, Sept. 3, 1906; 1st N.Y. perf., Sept. 24, 1906.
THE ROSE OF ALGERIA (a revision of ALGERIA).   New York: C. K. Harris,
    1909 (piano-vocal score).
    1st perf., Wilkes-Barre, Sept. 11, 1909; 1st N.Y. perf., Sept. 20, 1909.
THE SERENADE.   New York: E. Schuberth, 1897 (piano-vocal score).
    1st perf., Cleveland, Feb. 17, 1897; 1st N.Y. perf., March 16, 1897.
THE SINGING GIRL.   New York: Witmark, 1899 (piano-vocal score).
    1st perf., Montreal, Oct. 2, 1899; 1st N.Y. perf., Oct. 23, 1899.
SWEET SIXTEEN.   *See* WHEN SWEET SIXTEEN.
SWEETHEARTS.   New York: G. Schirmer, 1913 (piano-vocal score).
    1st perf., Baltimore, March 24, 1913; 1st N.Y. perf., Sept. 8, 1913.
THE TATTOOED MAN.   New York: Witmark, 1907 (piano-vocal score).
    1st perf., Baltimore, Feb. 11, 1907; 1st N.Y. perf., Feb. 18, 1907.
THE VELVET LADY.   New York: Witmark, 1919 (piano-vocal score).
    1st perf., Philadelphia, Dec. 23, 1918; 1st N.Y. perf., Feb. 3, 1919.
THE VICEROY.   New York: Witmark, 1900 (piano-vocal score).
    1st perf., San Francisco, Feb. 12, 1900; 1st N.Y. perf., April 9, 1900.
VICTORIA.   *See* WHEN SWEET SIXTEEN.
WHEN SWEET SIXTEEN.   New York: Witmark, 1910 (piano-vocal score).
    1st perf., Springfield, Mass., Dec. 5, 1910; 1st N.Y. perf., Sept. 14, 1911.
THE WIZARD OF THE NILE.   New York: E. Schuberth, 1895 (piano-vocal
    score).
    1st perf., Wilkes-Barre, Sept. 26, 1895; 1st N.Y. perf., Nov. 4, 1895.
WONDERLAND.   New York: Witmark, 1905 (piano-vocal score).
    1st perf., Buffalo, Sept. 14, 1905; 1st N.Y. perf., Oct. 24, 1905.

LIST OF COMPOSITIONS
(Excluding Operas and Operettas)

This list includes published and unpublished compositions. It does not
claim completeness, however, for hitherto unknown pieces by Herbert are
constantly coming to light. Also, much of his music has been republished in
innumerable arrangements and under new titles. As presented here the list

stresses compositions in their original form and at the time of their first appearance.

A la Mazurka. For cello and piano. (Before 1893.)

A la Valse. *See* Two Pieces for Violin.

Ah Love Me! *See* Three Songs, Op. 15.

Air de Ballet. No. 1 of Three Compositions for String Orchestra. New York: G. Schirmer, 1912. (Also for piano.)

Al Fresco. Intermezzo by Frank Roland [pseud.] for piano. New York: M. Witmark & Sons, 1904.

All Hail to You, Marines! Words by Richard J. Beamish. Text and melody (facsimile of composer's autograph) published in the Philadelphia *Press*, July 14, 1918.

All the Vogue. One-step by Noble MacClure [pseud.] for piano. New York: M. Witmark & Sons, 1915.

Allotria. For orchestra. (Undated.)

Alma Mater Song of the Catholic University of America. Words by Robert H. Mahoney. Washington: Catholic University, 1921.

American Fantasia. For orchestra. New York: E. Schuberth & Co., 1898.

The American Girl. March. For piano. New York: E. Schuberth & Co., 1896. (Also for orchestra and band.)

The American Rose. Waltz. For piano. New York: M. Witmark & Sons, 1917. (Dedicated to the American Rose Society.)

Aschenbrödel March. For orchestra, 1910.

Auditorium Festival March. For orchestra—composed 1901 for the 12th anniversary of the Auditorium, Chicago. *See* Festival March.

Aus "Liedern eines fahrenden Gesellen," Op. 20, No. 2. Berlin: Luckhardt, 1890. (Male chorus.)

Badinage. For orchestra. New York: E. Schuberth & Co., 1895.

Bagatelle. For cello and piano. (Before 1890.)

The Ballet Loose. *See* The Century Girl.

Baltimore Centennial. March. For piano. New York: E. Schuberth & Co., 1896. (Also for band; composed for the Baltimore Centennial, 1897.)

The Bards of Ireland. Folksongs arranged for voice and piano. (Privately printed by the composer, 1908.)

Belle O'Brien. Song, piano acc. Words by John Ernest McCann. New York: Harms, 1895.

The Belle of Pittsburg. March. For piano. New York: E. Schuberth & Co., 1895. (Also for band.)

Benamela. Finale to Carlo Brizzi's romantic opera or ballet, 1894. Piano-vocal score. (Later used in *The Idol's Eye*.)

Berceuse. For cello or violin and piano. New York: M. Witmark & Sons, 1912. (Probably written before composer came to America.)

Bird-Catching. *See* Vogelfang.

The Birth of the Century Girl. *See* The Century Girl.

The Birthday of the Dauphin. Scene in the Ziegfeld Follies, 1921.

Blümlein am Herzen, Op. 4. Stuttgart: Zumsteeg, 1884. (Song, piano acc.)

Bring on the Girls. Scene and song in the Ziegfeld Follies, 1922.

The Bubble. For orchestra. (Undated.)

Butterfly Ballet. For orchestra. In Jerome Kern's *Sally*, 1920.

The Call to Freedom. A patriotic ode for soprano solo and chorus of mixed voices. Piano-vocal score. Boston: Oliver Ditson Co., 1918. (Text also by Herbert.)

Cannibal Dance. For orchestra, arranged by Harold Sanford. New York: C. Fischer, Inc., 1926. (Written when Herbert was conductor of the Pittsburgh Orchestra.)

Can't You Hear Your Country Calling. Lyric by Gene Buck. New York: Harms, 1917. (Song, piano acc.; from the Ziegfeld Follies, 1917.)

The Captive. Dramatic cantata for soli, chorus and orchestra, Op. 25. Text by Rudolph von Baumbach. New York: G. Schirmer, 1915. (Piano-vocal score; composed in 1891 and published that year by Luckhardt of Berlin as *Der Gefangene*.)

The Century Girl. A Revue, music composed by Herbert and Irving Berlin. New York: Harms, 1916. (Herbert contributed: The Birth of the Century Girl, The Century Girl, Humpty Dumpty, The Romping Red Heads, The Stone Age—The Ballet Loose, The Toy Soldiers, Under the Sea, When Uncle Sam Is Ruler of the Sea, You Belong to Me.)

The Century Girl. *See* preceding paragraph.

The Championship of the World. Scene in the Ziegfeld Follies, 1921.

Chant d'Amour. For organ, written for Marcel Dupré, 1924.

Chiffon Fantasie. Scene in the Ziegfeld Follies, 1920.

Christ Is Risen: An Easter Anthem. New York: M. Witmark & Sons, 1908. (Piano-vocal score; composed 1904 for Easter service in St. Paul's Cathedral, Buffalo.)

The Cinderella Man. *See* Out of His Heart He Builds a Home.

The Circus Ballet. Scene in the Ziegfeld Follies, 1919.

Columbia. Anthem. Words by Clay M. Greene. New York: E. Schuberth & Co., 1898. (Song, piano acc.; anthem of the Lambs.)

Columbus. Suite for orchestra, Op. 35, 1903.

Concerto for cello and orchestra, Op. 8. (Composed 1894.)

Concerto No. 2 for cello and orchestra, Op. 30. New York: E. Schuberth & Co., 1898. (Dedicated to the New York Philharmonic Society.)

Confession. *See* Geständniss.

Consecrated Spot. *See* Geweihte Stätte.

La Coquette. For piano. New York: M. Witmark & Sons, 1900. (The second of a set of six pieces.)

The Corner, or Victor's Best. For orchestra. (Undated.)

Cosmopolitan March. For piano. New York: Leo Feist, 1935. (Also for orchestra; composed 1923?)

Creation. Scene in the Ziegfeld Follies, 1920.

The Crucible's Toast. Words by Arthur G. Burgoyne. Song, piano acc. (Undated.)

The Cruiskeen Lawn (Old Irish). Arranged for unaccompanied male chorus. New York: G. Schirmer, 1913. (Dedicated to Clarence Dickinson and the Mendelssohn Glee Club of New York.)

The Dancing School—Her First Lesson. Scene in the Ziegfeld Follies, 1920.

Danse Baroque. For orchestra. New York: C. Fischer, Inc., 1925. (Composed 1913.)

Day Is Here. Words by Lorraine Noel Finley. Song, piano acc. New York: G. Schirmer, Inc., 1940. (New words; cf. Three songs, op. 15, No. 2.)

Defendam March. For piano. New York: M. Witmark & Sons, 1919. (Also for band; written for the 22nd Engineers, N. Y. G. [*sic.*], and dedicated to Col. H. H. Treadwell by Lieut. Victor Herbert.)

Der Liebsten Namen schieb ich in Sand. *See* Mein Herz ist treu.

Der Schönheit Krone, Op. 5. Stuttgart: Zumsteeg, 1884. (Male chorus.)

Devotion: A Love Sonnet for Piano. New York: Harms, 1921.

Dodge Brothers March. For piano, with lyric refrain by Maxwell I. Pitkin. New York: Jerome H. Remick & Co., 1920. (Dedicated to Horace E. Dodge.) (Also for band and orch.)

Dramatic Overture. *See* Under the Red Robe.

Dream On. Words by B. G. DeSylva. Song, piano acc. New York: Harms, 1922. (Adaptation of Indian Lullaby.)

The Dream Song. *See* Farewell, Lovelight.

Du ahnst es nicht, Op. 21, No. 1. Berlin: Luckhardt, 1891. (Song, piano acc.)

Duo. For 2 violins, piano acc. New York: Harms, 1923.

An Easter Dawn. Words by Glen MacDonough. A new Easter song composed especially and exclusively for the New York *Evening World*. New York: M. Witmark & Sons, 1907. (Composed 1905.)

Einsamkeit. For 3 flutes, 2 oboes, soprano and alto saxophones, 4 clarinets, 2 bassoons, bass clarinet, and contrabass clarinet. (Composed 1898?)

Eldorado. March. For piano. Boston: Oliver Ditson Co., 1894. (Also for band.)

L'Encore. For flute, clarinet, and orchestra. New York: M. Witmark & Sons, 1910. (Written when Herbert was conductor of the Pittsburgh Orchestra.)

The Equity Star. Lyric by Grant Stewart. Song, piano acc. New York: Harms, 1921.

Estellita: Valse Pathétique. For piano. New York: M. Witmark & Sons, 1915. (Also used in *The Princess Pat.*)

Eventide. *See* Aus "Liedern eines fahrenden Gesellen."

Exile's Haven. Words by Lorraine Noel Finley. Song, piano acc. New York: G. Schirmer, Inc., 1940. (New words; cf. Home Sickness)

The Faded Rose. *See* Three Songs, Op. 15.

The Fall of a Nation. Symphonic score for motion picture, 1916. Excerpts published: Love Theme (piano, Witmark, 1916); for orchestra by C. Fischer, in 1925 and 1926: Devastation, Entrance of the Heroes, Forebodings, Heart Throbs, Karma, The Knight's Tournament, Little Italy, Mystic Rider, Punch and Judy, The Rabble.

Falling Leaves. Ballet in *Miss 1917*.

Fanshastics. *See* Heart o' Mine.

Fantasia on Mascagni's *Cavalleria Rusticana*. For violin and orchestra. (Composed 1893?)

Fantasie on "The Desire" of Schubert. For cello and orchestra. (Composed 1891?)

Farewell. Words by Edward Locke. Song, piano acc. New York: Harms, 1919. (Written for the play, *The Dream Song*.)

Farljandio. Scene in the Ziegfeld Follies, 1922.

The Fawn and the Wood Nymph. Ballet.

"Fencing" Number. Scene in the Ziegfeld Follies, 1923.

Fernher tönte Cicadensang. *See* Die versunkene Stadt.

Festival March. For orchestra. New York: C. Fischer, 1935. *See also* Auditorium Festival March.

The Fight Is Made and Won. Words by Thomas J. Vivian. Song, piano acc. New York: W. R. Hearst, The New York Journal, 1898.

The Finest. March. For piano. New York: Music Printing Co., Inc., 1918. (Also for band; dedicated to the Police Band, City of New York.)

The First Kiss. *See* Geweihte Stätte.

Fleurette. Valse lente. For piano. New York: M. Witmark & Sons. 1903.

Fliege fort, du klein Waldvögelein, Op. 18, No. 1. Berlin: Luckhardt, 1891. (Song, piano acc.)

Flower of My Heart. *See* Blümlein am Herzen.

Fly Away, Little Bird. *See* Fliege fort, du klein Waldvögelein.

For "Franz's" Wedding. For cello and organ. (Composed 1903.)

For the Flag He Loved so Well. Words by Vincent Bryan. Song, piano acc. (Undated.)

Forget-Me-Not. No. 2 of Three Compositions for String Orchestra. New York: G. Schirmer, 1912.

Fowling. *See* Vogelfang.

The Friars. Words by Charles Emerson Cook. Song, piano acc. New York: M. Witmark & Sons, 1907.

Frieden. *See* Peace.

Frühlingslied, Op. 14, No. 1. Berlin: Luckhardt, 1889. (Song, piano acc.)

A Garden—The Beauty Contest. Scene in the Ziegfeld Follies, 1924.

Gate City Guard. March. For piano. New York: E. Schuberth & Co., 1895. (Also for band.)

Der Gefangene. *See* The Captive.

Das Geheimniss, Op. 14, No. 4. Berlin: Luckhardt, 1889. (Song, piano acc.)

Geständniss, Op. 13, No. 1. Berlin: Luckhardt, 1889. (Song, piano acc.)

Get Together. Fox trot by Noble MacClure [pseud.] for piano. New York: M. Witmark & Sons, 1915.

Geweihte Stätte, Op. 13, No. 2. Berlin: Luckhardt, 1889. (Song, piano acc.)

Ghazel. For piano. New York: M. Witmark & Sons, 1900. (The 1st of a set of 6 pieces.)

Give Me That Rose. Words by Booth Tarkington. Song, piano acc. (Undated—arranged by the composer for string orch., 1922.)

Give Your Heart in June-Time. Duet, piano acc. New York: Harms, 1925. (Used in *Sky High*, a musical production by Harold Atteridge and Harry Graham.)

God Shall Guide Us! Song, piano acc. Philadelphia: Oliver Ditson Co., 1944. (From *The Call to Freedom.*)

God Spare the Emerald Isle. Words by William Jerome. Song, piano acc. New York: Harms, 1923.

Golden Days Overture. *See* The Great White Way.

The Great White Way. Overture. For orchestra, 1923. (Published in 1939 by G. Schirmer, Inc., of New York as Golden Days Overture.) Composed for motion picture.

The Hail of the Friendly Sons. Words by Joseph I. C. Clarke. For male chorus, unacc. New York: G. Schirmer, 1913.

Hast ein Blaublümelein einst mir gegeben. *See* Blümlein am Herzen.

Heart o' Mine. An Irish song, as sung in Henry Miller's production of *Fanshastics* (also called *Merry Wives of Gotham*). Words by Laurence Eyre. Song, piano. New York: Harms, 1924.

Heimweh. *See* Home Sickness.

Here Comes the Band. Melody with piano acc.; incomplete. (Undated.)

Hero and Leander, Op. 33. Symphonic poem.

Home Sickness. Song, piano acc. New York: E. Schuberth & Co., 1896.

Honeymoon. Concert waltz for orch. (Composed 1887?)

The Hostess' Daughter. *See* Wirthstöchterlein.

Hula-Lula. A "Territorial Operetta" written for the Lambs' annual gambol, 1899. Words by L. J. B. Lincoln.

Humoresque. For 3 flutes, 2 oboes, soprano and alto saxophones, 4 clarinets, 2 bassoons, bass clarinet, and contrabass clarinet. (Composed 1898?)

Humpty Dumpty. *See* The Century Girl.

I Love the Isle of the Sea. Words by Louis O'Connell. Song, piano acc. Chicago: Clinton Keithley Publications, 1935.

I Love Thee. *See* Ich liebe dich.

I Want to Be a Gambling Man. *See* Miss Camille.

I Want to Be a Good Lamb. Words by George V. Hobart. Song, piano acc. New York: Famous Music Co., 1940. (Composed 1909.)

Ice-Water Galop. For band. (Composed 1894?)

Ich liebe dich, Op. 14, No. 2. Berlin: Luckhardt, 1889. (Song, piano acc.)

I'd Love to Waltz Through Life with You. Words by Gene Buck. New York: Harms, 1923. (Song, piano acc.—from the Ziegfeld Follies, 1923.)

If Love Were What the Rose Is. Words by Algernon Charles Swinburne. Song, piano acc. New York: M. Witmark & Sons, 1907.

If You but Knew. *See* Three Songs, Op. 15.

I'll Be There. Words by Robert B. Smith. Song, piano acc. New York: Harms, 1921. (Used in the composer's operetta *The Girl in the Spotlight.*)

In Khorassan. Words by Gene Buck. New York: Harms, 1921. (Song, piano acc.—from the Ziegfeld Follies, 1921.)

In the Folds of the Starry Flag. Words by Paul West. Song, piano acc. New York: M. Witmark & Sons, 1904.

In the Sweet Bye and Bye. Words by George V. Hobart. Song, piano acc. (Composed 1906.)

Inauguration March. *See* McKinley Inauguration.

Indian Lullaby. For orch. (Composed 1922; title subsequently changed to Dream On.)

Indian Summer. An American Idyll. For piano. New York: Harms, 1919. (Also for orch.)

Irish Rhapsody. For orch. New York: G. Schirmer, 1910. (Composed 1892.)

Janice Meredith. Overture. For orch. (Incomplete; composer writing this, for motion picture, at time of death.)

Jenny's Baby. Words by John Ernest McCann. Song, piano acc. New York: E. Schuberth & Co., 1895.

The Jester's Serenade. For orch. New York: C. Fischer, Inc., 1925. (Composed 1908.)

Just for Fun. For three cornets and drums. New York: C. Fischer, Inc., 1950. (Composed 1895?)

Kiss Me Again. Words by Henry Blossom. Song, piano acc. New York: M. Witmark & Sons, 1915. (Words of the stanza different from those in *Mlle. Modiste.*)

Lady of the Lantern. Words by Gene Buck. New York: Harms, 1923. (Song, piano acc.; from the Ziegfeld Follies, 1923.)

Lambs in Toyland. Words by Grant Stewart. (A skit written for the Lambs, 1904.)

The Lambs' March. For orch. (Written for the Lambs, 1914.)

The Lambs' Star Gambol. March. For orch. (Written for the Lambs, 1912.)

The Legend of the Cyclamen Tree. Scene in the Ziegfeld Follies, 1921.

The Legend of the Golden Tree. Words by Gene Buck. New York: Harms, 1921. (Song, piano acc.—from the Ziegfeld Follies, 1921.)

Légende. For cello and orch. (Composed before 1894.)

Legends of the Drums. Scene in the Ziegfeld Follies, 1923.

Liebesleben. *See* Three Songs, Op. 15.

Liebeslied. *See* Love-Song.

Lied eines fahrenden Gesellen. *See* Aus "Liedern eines fahrenden Gesellen."

Little Old New York. Overture. For orch. (Composed for motion picture, 1923.)

Little Old New York. Words by William Le Baron. Song, piano acc. New York: Harms, 1923. (For the motion picture of the same name.)

Little Old New York. Scene and song in the Ziegfeld Follies, 1923.

The Little Red Lark. Old Irish, arranged for violin and piano. New York: M. Witmark & Sons, 1917.

Lora Lee. Words by Joseph I. C. Clarke. For male chorus, unacc. New York: Harms, 1922. (Dedicated to the Glee Club of the Friendly Sons of St. Patrick, New York, and its director, G. H. Gartlan.)

The Love Boat. Scene in the Ziegfeld Follies, 1920.

The Love Boat. Words by Gene Buck. New York: Harms, 1920. (Song, piano acc.—from the Ziegfeld Follies, 1920.)

Love Laid His Sleepless Head. Words by Algernon Charles Swinburne. Song, piano acc. New York: M. Witmark & Sons, 1907.

Love-Song. Song, piano acc. New York: E. Schuberth & Co., 1896.

A Love Sonnet. For orch. New York: C. Fischer, Inc., 1925. (Arr. by Harold Sanford.)

Lovelight. Words by Edward Locke. Song, piano acc. New York: Harms, 1919. (Written for the play *The Dream Song*.)

Love's Hour. Words by Rida Johnson Young. Song, piano acc. New York: G. Schirmer, 1912. (Composed for Luisa Tetrazzini.)

Love's Life. *See* Three Songs, Op. 15.

Love's Oracle. Words by Edward Peple. Song, piano acc. New York: M. Witmark & Sons, 1909. (Dedicated to Billie Burke.)

Love's Token. *See* Three Songs, Op. 15.

McKinley Inauguration. March. For piano. New York: E. Schuberth & Co., 1897. (Also for band; dedicated to President McKinley.)

Mädchen ging im Feld allein. *See* Schnelle Blüthe.

A Maiden Went into the Field Alone. *See* Schnelle Blüthe.

March of the 22nd Regiment, N.G.N.Y. For piano. New York: E. Schuberth & Co., 1898. (Also for orch. and band.)

The Marion Davies March. For piano. New York: Harms, 1922. (Composed for the motion picture *When Knighthood Was in Flower*.)

Mary Came Over to Me. Words by Irving Caesar. Song, piano acc. New York: Harms, 1922.

Mary's Lamb. Words by Edward E. Kidder. Song, piano acc. New York: E. Schuberth & Co., 1898. (Dedicated to the Lambs.)

Mazuma. *See* The Song Birds.

Me and Nancy. *See* Sweet Nancy.

Mein Blick ruht gern auf dir. *See* Du ahnst es nicht.

Mein Herz ist treu, Op. 21, No. 2. Berlin: Luckhardt, 1891. (Song, piano acc.)

Mein Schätzlein, froh sing ich dir. *See* Der Schönheit Krone.

Mélodie. For cello and piano. (Composed 1893?)

Merry Wives of Gotham. *See* Heart o' Mine.

Mirage. *See* Two pieces for Violin.

Miss Camille. A musical burlesque. Words by George V. Hobart. New York: M. Witmark & Sons, 1907. (Songs, piano acc.: My Toast to You, I Want to Be a Gambling Man, The Spanish Serenade.) (Composed for the Lambs, 1907.)

Miss 1917. A revue. (The composer supplied music for the following: The Mosquitos' Frolic, The Society Farmerettes, Falling Leaves, The Singing Blacksmith of Curriclough—the last named a medley of airs by Samuel Lover.)

Molly. Words by Rida Johnson Young. Song, piano acc. New York: M. Witmark & Sons, 1919. (Dedicated to John McCormack.)

The Mosquitos' Frolic. Scene in *Miss 1917*.

The Mountain Brook. For piano. New York: M. Witmark & Sons, 1900. (The 4th in a set of 6 pieces.)

My Heart Is True. *See* Mein Herz ist treu.

My Toast to You. *See* Miss Camille.

The New Ireland. Words by Joseph I. C. Clarke. For male chorus, unacc. New York: G. Schirmer, 1914.

Nina. Song, piano acc. (Undated.)

Nocturne. For cello and piano. (Composed before 1892.)

Nur du bist's. *See* Three Songs, Op. 15.

Ocean Breezes. Waltz, for piano. New York: E. Schuberth & Co., 1898. (Also for orch. and band.)

O'Donnell Aboo! The Clanconnel War Song. A.D. 1597, by M. J. McCann. Air: Roderich Vich Alpine dhu. Arranged for male chorus, unacc. New York: G. Schirmer, 1915.

Old Fashioned Garden. Scene in the Ziegfeld Follies, 1923.

Old Ireland Shall Be Free! Words by John Jerome Rooney. Traditional air: Boys of Wexford. Arranged for male chorus, unacc. New York: M. Witmark & Sons, 1915.

On the Promenade. For Piano. New York: M. Witmark & Sons, 1900. (The 5th in a set of 6 pieces.)

On Your Way. One-step by Noble MacClure [pseud.] for piano. New York: M. Witmark & Sons, 1915.

Only You. *See* Three Songs, Op. 15.

The Orange, White and Blue. Words by John P. Pine. Song, piano acc. New York: G. Schirmer, 1916. (Dedicated to the school children of New York.)

Out of His Heart He Builds a Home. Words by Edward Childs Carpenter. Song, piano acc. New York: M. Witmark & Sons, 1916. (Composed for the play *The Cinderella Man.*)

Pan-Americana. Morceau charactéristique. For piano. New York: M. Witmark & Sons, 1901. (Also for orch.)

Peace. Song, piano acc. New York: E. Schuberth & Co., 1896.

Pensée amoureuse. For cello and piano. Paris: G. Ricordi & Cie., 1906.

Persian Dance. For orch. New York: C. Fischer, Inc., 1926. (Arr. by Harold Sanford.)

Persian March. For orch. New York: C. Fischer, Inc., 1926. (Arr. by Harold Sanford.)

Petite Valse. For cello (or violin) and piano. Paris: G. Ricordi & Cie., 1906.

Two Pieces for Violin with Piano Accompaniment: a) Mirage. b) A la Valse. New York: G. Schirmer, 1915. (Dedicated to Fritz Kreisler.)

Polonaise de Concert, in A. For cello and piano. (Composed before 1887.)

Prelude ("The Two Marys" by Rev. Joseph P. Herbert). For orch. (Composed 1923.)

The President's March. For piano. New York: E. Schuberth & Co., 1898. (Also for orch. and band; dedicated to President McKinley; also published in the *Ladies' Home Journal,* July 1898.)

The Princess of My Dreams. Words by Gene Buck. New York: Harms, 1921. (Song, piano acc.—from the Ziegfeld Follies, 1921.)

Punchinello. For piano. New York: M. Witmark & Sons, 1900. (The 6th of a set of 6 pieces.)

Remembrance. For piano. Buffalo: Weed & Co., 1918. (Published in orchestral arrangement as Souvenir by C. Fischer, Inc., New York, 1925.)

Remembrance. Words by Fanny Lover (from the German of Carl Weitbrecht). Song, piano acc. New York: G. Schirmer, 1915.

The River Song. Words by Lorraine Noel Finley. Song, piano acc. New York: G. Schirmer, Inc., 1940. (New words; cf. Peace.)

Romance. For cello (or violin) and piano. Paris: G. Ricordi & Cie., 1906.

Romeo, Juliet, Johnny and Jane. Song, piano acc. (Used in *Round the Town*, a revue, 1924.)

The Romping Red Heads. *See* The Century Girl.

Rose-Briar Waltz. For violin and piano. (Undated.)

Rosemary. Waltz. For piano. New York: Harms, 1917.

Round the Town. *See* Romeo, Juliet, Johnny and Jane.

Royal Sec, a Champagne Galop. For orch. (Composed before 1885.)

Sally. *See* Butterfly Ballet.

Salute to America. March. For orch. (Undated.)

Salute to Atlanta. March. For piano. Atlanta: The Phillips & Crew Co., 1895. (Also for band.)

Scherzino. For cello and piano. (Composed before 1892.)

Schnelle Blüthe, Op. 18, No. 2. Berlin: Luckhardt, 1891. (Song, piano acc.)

Secrecy. *See* Das Geheimniss.

The Secret. Words by James Russell Lowell. Song, piano acc. (In *The Music of the Modern World*, Anton Seidl, editor in chief; New York: Appleton, 1895-1897.)

Serenade. *See* Ständchen.

Serenade für Streichorchester, Op. 12. Berlin: Luckhardt, 1889.

She Was a Hayseed Maid. Song and dance. (Composed for the Lambs, 1908.)

The Silent Rose. *See* Three Songs, Op. 15.

The Singing Blacksmith of Curriclough. *See* Miss 1917.

Sky High. *See* Give Your Heart in June-Time.

The Society Farmerettes. *See* Miss 1917.

Soixante-neuf (69). For string orch. (Composed 1902; this nameless piece was the 69th number in the encore book of the Victor Herbert Orchestra.)

Soldiers of Erin. For orch. (Undated.)

Some Babes from Toyland. A skit for the Lambs, 1903.

The Song Birds. A musical skit. Words by George V. Hobart. New York: M. Witmark & Sons, 1907. (Songs, piano acc.: Mazuma, Yankee Land.)

A Song of Spring. *See* Frühlingslied.

Two Songs, Op. 10. *See* Wirthstöchterlein *and* Vogelfang.

Two Songs, Op. 13. *See* Geständniss *and* Geweihte Stätte.

Four Songs, Op. 14. *See* Frühlingslied, Ich liebe dich, Ständchen *and* Das Geheimniss.

Three Songs with Piano Accompaniment, Op. 15. New York: E. Schuberth & Co., 1888. (1, The Silent Rose; 2, Love's Token; 3, Ah Love Me!)

Souvenir. *See* Remembrance.

Souvenir de Saratoga. *See* Under the Elms.

Spanish Rhapsody. For orch. (Composed 1905?)

The Spanish Serenade. *See* Miss Camille.

Ständchen, Op. 14, No. 3. Berlin: Luckhardt, 1889. (Song, piano acc.)

Star of the North. Overture, for orch. (For motion picture, 1923.)

Die stille Rose. *See* Three Songs, Op. 15.

Success Is Work. March. For orch. (Composed for the dedication of the new Witmark Building, Aug. 4, 1903.)

Suite, Op. 3. For cello and orch. Stuttgart: Zumsteeg, 1884.

A Suite of Serenades. For piano. New York: Harms, 1924. (Composed originally for Paul Whiteman's Orchestra; also for symphony orchestra.)

Suite romantique, Op. 31. For orch. Berlin: Simrock, 1901. (Dedicated to the Pittsburgh Symphony Orchestra.)

The Sunken City. *See* Die versunkene Stadt.

Sunset. No. 3 of Three Compositions for String Orchestra. New York: G. Schirmer, 1912.

Sweet Harp of the Days That Are Gone (To the Irish Harp). Words by Samuel Lover. Song, piano acc. New York: E. Schuberth & Co., 1898.

Sweet Nancy. Words by John Ernest McCann. Song, piano acc. New York: Harms, 1895.

The Tale of a Lamb. A musical skit. (Composed for the Lambs, 1921.)

That Old Fashioned Garden of Mine. Words by Gene Buck. New York: Harms, 1923. (Song, piano acc.—from the Ziegfeld Follies, 1923.)

The Three Solitaires. Polka. For 3 trumpets (or cornets) and piano. New York: M. Witmark & Sons, 1915.

To the Irish Harp. *See* Sweet Harp of the Days That Are Gone.

To the Lambs. Words by Augustus Thomas. Song, piano acc. (A new club song of the Lambs, 1906.)

To Thee, My Queen of Beauty. *See* Der Schönheit Krone.

The Toy Soldiers. *See* The Century Girl.

Toyland Today. A fantasy, words by Glen MacDonough. (Composed for the Lambs, 1923.)

Trinity Blue. Words by Judge Joseph Buffington. Song, piano acc. (Composed 1903?)

Tristesse. For cello and piano. (Composed before 1893.)

Twenty-second Regiment March. *See* March of the 22nd Regiment N.G.N.Y.

The Twirly Little Girlies at the End of the Line. Words by Rida Johnson Young. Song, piano acc. New York: M. Witmark & Sons. 1912.

The Two Marys. *See* Prelude (The Two Marys).

Under the Elms (Souvenir de Saratoga). For piano. New York: M. Witmark & Sons, 1903. (Also for orch.)

Under the Red Robe. Overture. For orch. (Composed for motion picture, 1923; published as Dramatic Overture by G. Schirmer, Inc., of New York, 1938.)

Under the Sea. *See* The Century Girl.

Valse à la Mode. By Noble MacClure [pseud.]. For piano. New York: M. Witmark & Sons, 1915.

The Veiled Prophet. March. For piano. New York: E. Schuberth & Co., 1896. (Also for band.)

Die versunkene Stadt, Op. 20, No. 1. Berlin: Luckhardt, 1890. (Male chorus, unacc.)

The Village Blacksmith. A musical skit. Words by George V. Hobart. (Composed for the Lambs, 1912.)

The Vision of Columbus. For orch. (Composed 1893.)

Vogelfang, Op. 10, No. 2. Berlin: Luckhardt, 1889. (Song, piano acc.)

Walzer. For orch. (Undated.)

The Water Sprite. Ballet, 1922.

Weaving. Scene in the Ziegfeld Follies, 1922.

Weaving My Dreams. Words by Gene Buck. New York: Harms, 1922. (Song, piano acc.—from the Ziegfeld Follies, 1922.)

Webbing. Scene in the Ziegfeld Follies, 1923.

Wedding Music, composed expressly for Viola Cahn and Isidore Witmark, 1908. For piano.

Wenn im Purpurschein. *See* Aus "Liedern eines fahrenden Gesellen."

Western Overture. For orch. New York: C. Fischer, Inc., 1940. (Composed 1906?)

What Twenty Years Will Do (to Some People and a Tune). A musical skit. Words by George V. Hobart. (Composed for the Lambs, 1914.)

When Knighthood Was in Flower (waltz song). Words by William Le Baron. Song, piano acc. New York: Harms, 1922. (The musical theme of the motion picture of the same name.)

When the Frost Is on the Punkin (in Junior Laurel Songs). Boston: Birchard, 1916.

When the Maytime Comes Again (in Junior Laurel Songs). Boston: Birchard, 1920.

When the Right One Comes Along. Words by Gene Buck. Song in the Ziegfeld Follies, 1920.

When the Sixty-ninth Comes Back. Words by Joyce Kilmer. Song, piano acc. New York: M. Witmark & Sons, 1919.

When Uncle Sam Is Ruler of the Sea. *See* The Century Girl.

Whispering Willows. For piano. New York: M. Witmark & Sons, 1915. (Also for orch.)

Widow Machree. For male chorus, unacc. (from the song by Samuel Lover). New York: G. Schirmer, 1915.

The Willow Plate. A Chinese shadowgraph play by Tony Sarg. For piano. New York: Harms, 1924. (Also for orch.)

The Winning of the West. A spectacle or pantomime. (Composed for the Lambs, 1916.)

Wirthstöchterlein, Op. 10, No. 1. Berlin: Luckhardt, 1889. (Song, piano acc.)

Woodland Fancies, Op. 34. Suite for orch. New York: G. Schirmer, 1928–1929. (Composed 1901.)

The World's Progress. March. For piano. New York: M. Witmark & Sons, 1916. (Dedicated to the Associated Advertising Clubs of the World.)

Yankee Land. *See* The Song Birds.

Yesterthoughts. For piano. New York: M. Witmark & Sons, 1900. (The 3rd in a set of 6 pieces; also for orch.)

Les Yeux bleus. Song, piano acc. (Composed 1890?)

Yolanda. Overture. For orch. (For motion picture, 1923.)
You Belong to Me. *See* The Century Girl.
The Ziegfeld Follies. Music for the productions of 1917, 1919, 1920, 1921,
   1922, 1923, 1924.

ARRANGEMENTS

   Victor Herbert made numerous arrangements of the works of other composers. The following list is as complete as possible from the music and
evidence available. All are for orchestra except as indicated.

J. S. Bach	Largo, from the Concerto for two violins
Alfred Bachelet	Chère Nuit
A. E. Batiste	Offertory in G
Gaetano Braga	The Angels' Serenade
Johannes Brahms	Wiegenlied
Harry T. Burleigh	Sinner, Please Doan Let Dis Harves' Pass
C. W. Cadman	At Dawning
	From the Land of the Sky Blue Water
Cécile Chaminade	Air de Ballet
	The Flatterer
	Pas des Amphores
	The Scarf Dance
Frédéric Chopin	Mazurka, Op. 7, No. 1
	Mazurka, Op. 7, No. 3
	Valse, Op. 64, No. 1
Karl Davidov	Am Springbrunnen
Claude Debussy	The Girl with the Flaxen Hair
	Minstrels
Reginald de Koven	The Knickerbockers (selections arr. for orch., for piano, for flute and piano, for violin and piano)
	Robin Hood (selections arr. for flute and piano, for violin and piano)
Luigi Denza	Funiculi-Funicula
Gaetano Donizetti	Sextet from *Lucia di Lammermoor*
Antonin Dvořák	Gypsy-Melody (Songs My Mother Taught Me)
	Humoresque
Giuseppe Ferrata	Love Song
	Valse Gentile
Ernest Gillet	La Lettre de Manon
Benjamin Godard	Berceuse from *Jocelyn*
Edvard Grieg	Erotik
	To Spring
Swan Hennessy	Ancient Clan March
	In Irish Style
Edgar S. Kelley	Chinese Song
Halfdan Kjerulf	Last Night

Fritz Kreisler	Liebesfreud
Hubert Léonard	The Cat and the Mice
	The Donkey and the Driver
Anatol Liadov	A Music Box
Franz Liszt	Liebestraum
Samuel Lover	The Angel's Whisper (arr. for cello and piano)
	The Low-Back'd Car (arr. for cello and piano; also for violin and piano)
Allan Macbeth	Forget-Me-Not
Gabriel-Marie	La Cinquantaine
Felix Mendelssohn	A Midsummer Night's Dream (including the *Spring Song* for voice and piano)
	Spinning Song
	Spring Song
John Milledge	The Bugle Call (arr. for band)
Arthur Nevin	Love Dreams
Ethelbert Nevin	Narcissus
	Oh! That We Two Were Maying (arr. for double male quartet)
	The Rosary
Gabriel Pierné	Serenade
Eduard Poldini	Poupée valsante
Franz Ries	Perpetuum Mobile
N. A. Rimsky-Korsakov	A Hindoo Love Song, from *Sadko*
Landon Ronald	Evening
Monroe H. Rosenfeld	The Sun March and Two-Step (arr. for band)
Anton Rubinstein	Kamennoi-Ostrow
	Melody in F
Franz Schubert	Der Wanderer
Robert Schumann	The Two Grenadiers
A. Simonetti	Madrigale
Charles H. Steinway	Madeleine
Johann Strauss	New York Herald Waltz (arr. for band)
Leslie Stuart	The Slim Princess (finale to Act II arr. for stage presentation)
Peter I. Tchaikovsky	Chant sans Paroles
Francesco Paolo Tosti	La Serenata
Giuseppe Verdi	The Quartet from *Rigoletto*

As editor Victor Herbert collaborated in the following publications:

THE WORLD'S BEST COMPOSERS. Famous compositions for the piano. Editors: Victor Herbert, Fanny Morris Smith, Louis R. Dressler. New York: The University Society, 1899. (4 volumes)

THE WORLD'S BEST MUSIC. Philharmonic edition, second series. Edited by Victor Herbert, Reginald de Koven and others. New York: The University Society, 1910. (3 volumes)

Phonograph Recordings Made by Victor Herbert

A. AS VIOLONCELLIST

The Angel's Whisper (Lover)	Victor 64240
The Low-Back'd Car (Lover)	Victor 64239
Pensée Amoureuse	Victor 74286
Petite Valse	Victor 64297
Scherzo, Op. 12, No. 2 (Van Goens)	Victor 65298
Simple Aveu (Thomé)	Victor 74300

B. AS CONDUCTOR OF THE VICTOR HERBERT ORCHESTRA
For the Edison Company

Air on the G String (Bach)	307
Algeria: Rose of the World	345
L'Arlésienne: Farandole (Bizet)	10456
Aubade Printanière (Lacombe)	10563
Babes in Toyland, Selections from	396
Badinage	369
Berceuse (Gounod)	10480
Le Cid: Ballet Music, Aubade, Navarraise (Massenet)	484
L'Encore	10413
The Flatterer (Chaminade)	10372
Fleurette	10380
The Fortune Teller, Fantasy from	547
Humorous Transcriptions on a German Folk-Song (Ochs)	527
Hungarian Dance in D (Brahms)	10353
Hungarian Dance in G minor (Brahms)	10324
It Happened in Nordland, Selections from	229
Jubel Overture (Weber)	761
Little Nemo, Selections from	287
Mlle. Modiste, Selections from	195

593

Mlle. Modiste: Ballet Music	330
The Nations: Spanish (Moszkowski)	10470
Naughty Marietta, Selections from	729
Naughty Marietta: Dream Melody, Intermezzo	683
Old Dutch, Selections from	453
The Prima Donna: Entr'acte	420
The Red Mill, Selections from	215
Reminiscences of Scotland (Herbert?)	
(For promotion purposes only)	D-9
Samson and Delilah: Dance of the Priestesses of Dagon	
(Saint-Saëns)	10536
The Singing Girl, Selections from	918
Slavic March (Tchaikovsky)	501
Spring Song (Mendelssohn)	10260
The Tattooed Man, Selections from	440
The Tattooed Man: Oriental March	10280
To a Wild Rose (MacDowell)	10338
Venetian Love Song (Nevin)	10297
When Sweet Sixteen: The Wild Rose	704
The Wizard of the Nile, Selections from	569
Wonderland: Oriental Dance	10217

For the Victor Company

L'Africaine: Indian March (Meyerbeer)	70068
Air for the G String (Bach)	70047
Al Fresco	60086
American Fantasy	55093
Angels' Serenade (Braga)	55040
At Dawning (Cadman)	45170
Babes in Toyland: March of the Toys	70048
Babes in Toyland: The Military Ball	70091
Babes in Toyland: Toymaker's Shop	60080
Babette: There Once Was an Owl	60088
Badinage	70053
Carmen: Suite, 1 (Bizet)	70066
Carmen: Suite, 2 (Bizet)	60067
Carmen: Suite, 3 & 4 (Bizet)	70067
Casse Noisette: Danse Arabe (Tchaikovsky)	45053
Casse Noisette: Danse Chinoise (Tchaikovsky)	45053
Cavalleria Rusticana: Intermezzo (Mascagni)	60074
Devotion	55223
Dream of Love (Liszt)	70046
Eileen, Gems from	35631
(Victor Light Opera Co., composer conducting)	
The Enchantress, Selections from	70090
Die Fledermaus: The Merry Countess Waltz (Strauss)	70082

La Gioconda: Dance of the Hours (Ponchielli)	70070
Humoresque (Dvořák)	45165
Indian Summer	55200
Kamennoi-Ostrow: Rêve Angélique (Rubinstein)	70077
The Lady of the Slipper, Selections from	55039
Largo from "Xerxes" (Händel)	55040
Little Nemo: They Were Irish	60089
Lohengrin: Bridal March (Wagner)	55048
Madame Butterfly, Fantasy from (Puccini)	70055
Mlle. Modiste: Kiss Me Again	45165
Mlle. Rosita: Intermezzo	60087
Marche Slave (Tchaikovsky)	70050
Melody in F (Rubinstein)	60051
Midsummer Night's Dream: Wedding March (Mendelssohn)	55048
Minuet (Paderewski)	45054
Narcissus (Nevin)	45052
Natoma: Dagger Dance	70049
Naughty Marietta: Intermezzo	70075
Pan Americana	70089
Pas des Amphores (Chaminade)	60047
Prima Donna: Entr'acte	70092
The Rosary (Nevin)	60050
The Rose of Algeria: Entrance of the Sultana	70056
Spring Song (Mendelssohn)	60046
Sweethearts, Selections from	55039
Träume (Wagner)	55041
Tristan und Isolde: Isoldes Liebestod (Wagner)	55041
Venetian Love Song (Nevin)	60056
Waltzing Doll (Poldini)	45170
Woodland Sketches (MacDowell)	60053
Yesterthoughts	60054

(Professional records)

Poupée valsante (Poldini)	B21927
Serenade (Drigo)	B13356

Notes

CHAPTER I

1. *Encyclopaedia Britannica*, 9th ed.; art. Dublin. 2. Letters from Oscar Faber (German grandson of Fanny Lover), 1949. 3. Interview with Herbert, New York *Morning Telegraph*, Dec. 13, 1914 (Mag. 5). 4. *Ibid.* 5. *Ibid.* 6. Letters from O. Faber. 7 *Ibid.* 8. W. Armstrong, in *Ainslee's*, Feb., 1910. 9. Interview with Herbert, *loc. cit.* 10. Armstrong, *loc. cit.* 11. A. Eames, in *Entertaining*, Feb., 1909. 12. Armstrong, *loc. cit.* 13. Interview with Herbert, *loc. cit.* 14. Armstrong, *loc. cit.* 15. Unidentified clipping, G. Klemm scrapbook in Library of Congress. Also, interview with Herbert, *loc. cit.* 16. Deposited in Library of Congress by Mrs. Ella Herbert Bartlett. 17. Carl Engel, "Charles Martin Loeffler," *Musical Quarterly*, Vol. XI, pp. 316-317 (July, 1925). Permission of G. Schirmer, Inc. 18. Interview with Herbert, *loc. cit.* 19. Unidentified clipping, Bartlett scrapbook II, deposited in Library of Congress by Mrs. Ella Herbert Bartlett.

CHAPTER II

1. K. Baedeker, *Southern Germany and Austria* (Leipzig, 1883), pp. 2–10. 2. Stuttgart directory, 1882. 3. *Adress- und Geschäfts-Handbuch der königlichen Haupt- und Residenzstadt Stuttgart für das Jahr 1882.* 4. As quoted by G. Schlotterbeck in Pittsburgh *Post*, Jan. 13, 1901. 5. *Ibid.*, Nov. 19, 1899. 6. *Allgemeine musikalische Zeitung*, Nov. 30, 1881, p. 765. 7. *Neue Zeitschrift für Musik*, Jan. 22, 1882, p. 41. 8. *Ibid.*, Feb. 24, 1882, p. 94. 9. *Allgemeine Deutsche Musik-Zeitung*, July 7, 1882. 10. E. N. Waters, in *Library of Congress Quarterly Journal of Current Acquisitions*, Feb., 1949, pp. 11–12. 11. *Allgemeine Deutsche Musik-Zeitung*, July 28, 1882, p. 266. 12. As quoted by Schlotterbeck in Pittsburgh *Post*, Mar. 9, 1902. 13. *Neue Zeitschrift für Musik*, Jan. 18, 1884, p. 38. 14. *Ibid.*, Mar. 20, 1885, p. 135. 15. Unidentified clipping in Bartlett scrapbook II (LC). 16. *Neue Zeitschrift für Musik*, Dec. 11, 1885, p. 511. 17. *Musikalisches Wochenblatt*, Feb. 11, 1886, p. 93. 18. W. Altmann, *Kurzgefasstes Tonkünstler-Lexikon*, 14th ed. (1936), ed. P. Frank. 19. *Neue Zeitschrift für Musik*, Sept. 11, 1885, p. 376, and Feb. 26, 1886, p. 100. 20. *Ibid.*, July 10, 1885, p. 297. 21. From a collection of unpublished autograph letters of Herbert, deposited in the Library of Congress by Mrs. Ella Herbert Bartlett. 22. Lucy Poate Stebbins and

Richard Poate Stebbins, *Frank Damrosch: Let the People Sing* (Durham, N.C., 1945), p. 94. 23. Boston *Transcript*, Aug. 15, 1911, and *Musical America*, Aug. 19, 1911.

CHAPTER III

1. From a collection of unpublished autograph letters of Herbert, deposited in the Library of Congress by Mrs. Ella Herbert Bartlett. 2. New York *Herald*, Oct. 25, 1886, p. 10. 3. *Ibid.*, Oct. 26, 1886, p. 5. 4. W. H. Seltsam, ed., *Metropolitan Opera Annals* (New York, 1947). 5. H. T. Finck, ed., *Anton Seidl: A Memorial by His Friends* (New York, 1899). 6. New York *Sun*, Nov. 9, 1886, p. 4. 7. New York *World*, Nov. 9, 1886, p. 5. 8. J. G. Huneker, *Steeplejack* (2 vols., New York, 1920), Vol. II, p. 16. 9. *Musical Courier*, Nov. 17, 1886, p. 310. 10. New York *Tribune*, May 30, 1886, p. 11. 11. J. G. Huneker, *New Cosmopolis* (New York, 1915), p. 79. 12. J. G. Huneker, *Steeplejack*, Vol. II, p. 26. 13. *Ibid.*, p. 10. 14. *Ibid.*, p. 38. 15. New York *Tribune*, Jan. 8, 1887, p. 4. 16. New York *Herald*, Jan. 8, 1887, p. 4. 17. *Musical Courier*, Jan. 19, 1887, p. 38. 18. W. Beetz, *Das Wiener Opernhaus 1869 bis 1945* (Zürich, 1949), p. 76. 19. *Musical Courier*, Aug. 17, 1887, p. 102. 20. New York *Clipper*, Aug. 19, 1899, p. 489. 21. G. C. D. Odell, *Annals of the New York Stage* (15 vols., New York, 1927–1949), Vol. XIII, p. 535. 22. Unidentified clippings in Bartlett scrapbook II. 23. *Musical Courier*, Oct. 19, 1887, pp. 256, 259. 24. G. C. D. Odell, *op. cit.*, p. 475. 25. Sam Franko, *Chords and Discords* (New York, 1938), p. 87. 26. *Ibid.*, pp. 66–67. 27. G. H. Wilson, ed., *The Musical Yearbook of the United States* (10 vols., Boston, 1884–1893), Vol. V, p. 68. 28. *Musical Courier*, Dec. 14, 1887, p. 388. 29. A. P. Hughes, *Music Is My Life* (Cleveland, 1947), p. 129. 30. Letter to the author from Arthur Judson, Oct. 31, 1949. 31. H. E. Krehbiel, *The Philharmonic Society of New York* (New York, 1892), p. 173. 32. *Musical Courier*, Feb. 21, 1888, p. 212. 33. *Ibid.*, June 20, 1888, p. 421. 34. *Ibid.*, Sept. 12, 1888, p. 186. 35. *Ibid.*, June 27, 1888, p. 438, and Sept. 12, 1888, p. 186. 36. Unidentified clipping in Bartlett scrapbook II. 37. O. Thompson, *The American Singer* (New York, 1937), pp. 119 ff. 38. I. Glackens, in *American Music Lover*, June, 1939. 39. Unidentified clipping in Bartlett scrapbook II. 40. G. C. D. Odell, *op. cit.*, Vol. XIV, p. 188. 41. *Ibid.*, p. 97. 42. Aguilar Free Library Society, Fourteenth and Final Report, 1902. 43. *Ibid.*, Report, 1889. 44. H. E. Krehbiel, *Review of the New York Musical Season, 1888–1889* (New York, 1889), pp. 35–36. 45. *Musical Courier*, Dec. 26, 1888, p. 468. 46. Told to the author by Fred Landau in New York, Sept. 25, 1948. 47. H. E. Krehbiel, *Review, etc.*, pp. 58–59. 48. New York *Sun*, Jan. 6, 1889, p. 11. 49. *Ibid.*, Jan. 9, 1889, p. 2. 50. *Musical Courier*, Jan. 23, 1889, p. 65, and Feb. 20, 1889, p. 147. 51. A. P. Hughes, *op. cit.*, p. 52. 52. Pittsburgh *Press*, May 20, 1889, p. 7. 53. *Musical Courier*, May 29, 1889, p. 435. 54. Pittsburgh *Press*, May 22, 1889, p. 4. 55. *Musical Courier*, May 29, 1889, p. 435. 56. Pittsburgh *Press*, *loc. cit.* 57. *Musical Courier*, *loc. cit.* 58. W. A. Fisher, *Music Festivals in the United States* (Boston, 1934), p. 26. 59. R. Morin, *The Worcester Music Festival* (Worcester, 1946), p. 12. 60. Festival program 1889. 61. Quoted in Morin, *op. cit.*, p. 60. 62. J. G. Huneker, *Steeplejack*, Vol. II, pp. 65–66. 63. Pamphlet issued by the Conservatory, ca. 1893, in New York Public Library. 64. U.S. Statutes at Large, 26, p. 1093. 65. Memorandum, Law Librarian of Congress to Librarian of Congress, Mar. 1, 1917. 66. *Musical Courier*, Jan. 29, 1890, p. 84. 67. *Ibid.*,

Feb. 19, 1890, p. 156. 68. *Ibid.*, Sept. 10, 1890, p. 255. 69. Quoted in Morin, *op. cit.*, p. 64. 70. *Musical Courier*, Dec. 17, 1890, p. 625. 71. Richard G. Appel in a letter to the author, Aug. 31, 1948. 72. *Musical Courier*, May 31, 1891, pp. 483–485. 73. P. I. Tchaikovski, *Diaries*, transl. by W. Lakond (New York, 1945), pp. 325 ff. 74. Program book, Philadelphia Symphony Orchestra, April 19/20, 1940. 75. *Musical Courier*, June 3, 1891, p. 581. 76. *Ibid.*, July 1, 1891, p. 9. 77. *Ibid.*, July 8, 1891, p. 31. 78. Sam Franko, *Chords and Discords*, p. 91. 79. Quoted in Morin, *The Worcester Music Festival*, p. 66. 80. *Musical Courier*, Sept. 30, 1891, p. 354. 81. G. H. Wilson, ed., *The Musical Yearbook of the United States*, Vol. IX, p. 58. 82. *Musical Courier*, Feb. 3, 1892, p. 10. 83. *Musical Courier*, April 27, 1892, p. 7. 84. *Musical Courier*, July 13, 1892, pp. 9–12. 85. *Musical Courier*, Dec. 7, 1892, p. 12. 86. *Musical Courier*, Dec. 28, 1892, p. 18. 87. Letter to the author from R. S. Bartlett, June 22, 1948. 88. *Musical Courier*, Nov. 9, 1892, p. 5. 89. *Musical Courier*, Nov. 16, 1892, p. 6. 90. *Musical Courier*, Nov. 23, 1892, p. 6. 91. *Musical Courier*, Jan. 4, 1893, pp. 7–8. 92. N.Y. *Tribune*, Jan. 14, 1893, p. 6. 93. *Musical Courier*, Feb. 15, 1893, p. 14. 94. *Musical Courier*, Mar. 29, 1893, p. 13. 95. P. MacKaye, *Epoch* (2 vols., New York, 1927). 96. *Ibid.*, II, p. 343. 97. *Ibid.*, pp. 352 ff. 98. *Ibid.*, pp. 378 ff.

CHAPTER IV

1. *Musical Courier*, Sept. 13, 1893, p. 15, and Sept. 20, p. 7. 2. Unidentified clipping in Bartlett scrapbook II. 3. *Musical Courier*, Jan. 1, 1894, p. 8. 4. Unidentified clipping in Bartlett scrapbook VI. 5. Buffalo *Express*, Dec. 10, 1893; *cf.* also Francis Neilson, *My Life in Two Worlds* (Appleton, Wis.): C. C. Nelson Publ. Co., 1952; II, pp. 140–141. 6. G. W. Wingate, *History of the Twenty-second Regiment of the National Guard of the State of New York* (New York, 1896), pp. 499 ff. 7. J. P. Sousa, *Marching Along* (Boston: Hale, Cushman & Flint, 1928), pp. 330-331, 133. 8. *Musical Courier*, Sept. 28, 1892, pp. 7–8. 9. *Musical Courier*, Courier, Oct. 26, 1892, p. 15. 10. Sousa, *op. cit.*, p. 127. 11. *Musical Courier*, Oct. 18, 1893. 12. *Musical Courier*, Sept. 27, 1893, p. 7. 13. New York *World*, Dec. 3, 1893. 14. *Musical Courier*, Nov. 22, 1893, p. 25. 15. New York *Clipper*, June 9, 1900, p. 334. 16. *Musical Courier*, Nov. 29, 1893. 17. Sam Franko, *Chords and Discords*, pp. 80–81. 18. *Musical Courier*, Jan. 3, 1894, p. 10. 19. *Musical Courier*, Feb. 28, 1894, p. 19. 20. Franko, *op. cit.*, p. 93. 21. Supplied by R. S. Bartlett. 22. N.Y. *Herald*, Dec. 16, 1893. 23. G. C. D. Odell, *Annals of the New York Stage*, Vol. XV, p. 790. 24. *Musical Courier*, April 11, 1894, p. 19. 25. Odell, *op. cit.*, pp. 761, 763. 26. *Ibid.*, p. 766. 27. Unidentified clipping in Bartlett scrapbook II. 28. *Ibid.* 29. Odell, *op. cit.*, p. 773. 30. *Metronome*, Sept., 1894, p. 7. 31. Clipping from the *Dominant*, Bartlett scrapbook II. 32. *Musical Courier*, Nov. 28, 1894, p. 35. 33. Rudolph Aronson, *Theatrical and Musical Memoirs* (New York: McBride Nast & Co., 1913), pp. 103 ff. 34. New York *Dramatic Mirror*, July 27, 1895, p. 2. 35. L. C. Strang, *Celebrated Comedians of Light Opera and Musical Comedy in America* (Boston: Page, 1900), p. 187. 36. Henry Clay Barnabee, *Reminiscences* (Boston: Chapple, 1913), p. 363. 37. R. Grau, *Forty Years Observation of Music and the Drama* (New York: Broadway Publishing Co., 1909), p. 270. See also A. Eames, in *Metronome*, March, 1910, anniversary supplement, p. 33. 38. *Musical Courier*, July 4,

1894, p. 10. 39. Supplied by R. S. Bartlett. 40. Unidentified clipping in Bartlett scrapbook II. 41. Barnabee, *op. cit.*, pp. 403–404. 42. Autograph letter of Herbert in Library of Congress.

CHAPTER V

1. *Musical Courier*, Jan. 30, 1895, p. 30. 2. *Ibid.*, Feb. 27, 1895, p. 28. 3. *Ibid.*, Jan. 9, 1895, p. 25. 4. *Ibid.*, March 20, 1895, p. 28. 5. Jacksonville *Florida Citizen*, March 3, 1895. 6. Unidentified clipping in Bartlett scrapbook III. 7. *Muscial Courier*, Jan. 16, 1895, p. 19. 8. *Ibid.*, Aug. 28, 1895, pp. 10, 24. 9. *Ibid.*, Sept. 9, 1895, p. 21. 10. *Metronome*, Oct., 1895, p. 15. 11. *Ibid.*, p. 17. 12. H. B. Smith, *First Nights and First Editions* (Boston: Little Brown & Co., 1931), pp. 173 ff. 13. Contract in possession of Mr. and Mrs. R. S. Bartlett. 14. N.Y. *Dramatic Mirror*, June 22, 1895, p. 4; also June 29, p. 9, and July 20, p. 3. 15. *Ibid.*, Dec. 28, 1895, p. 2. 16. *Ibid.*, Jan. 25, 1896, p. 3. 17. *Ibid.*, Feb. 8, 1896, p. 11. 18. New York *Herald*, Sept. 27, 1896. New York *Dramatic Mirror*, Nov. 21, 1896, p. 12, and May 8, 1897, p. 14. 19. New York *Clipper*, May 26, 1900, p. 288; June 22, 1901, p. 363; May 3, 1903, p. 236; Nov. 28, 1903, p. 953; May 27, 1905, p. 351. 20. F. Hadamowsky and H. Otte, *Die Wiener Operette* (Vienna: Bellaria-Verlag, 1947), p. 391. 21. New York *Dramatic Mirror*, Oct. 3, 1896, p. 16. 22. Letter preserved in Library of Congress. 23. *Musical Courier*, May 19, 1897, p. 5. 24. *The Theatre*, Oct., 1897, pp. 198–199.

CHAPTER VI

1. The Lambs, *Annual Reports, Certificate of Incorporation, Constitution, By-Laws and Rules, Officers, Members and Committees* (New York, 1899), p. 125. 2. Program owned by Broughton Tall of Baltimore. 3. C. H. Hoyt, *Five Plays*, ed. Douglas L. Hunt (Vol. 9 in the series *America's Lost Plays*) (Princeton: Princeton University Press, 1941). 4. D. L. Hunt, "The Life and Work of Charles Hoyt," *Birmingham-Southern College Bulletin*, Vol. XXXIX, No. 1 (Jan., 1946). 5. Letter to the author from May Davenport Seymour, March 24, 1950. 6. Hoyt, *op. cit.* 7. Letters to the author from Mrs. Elizabeth P. Barrett and from Miss Seymour, March 24, 1950. 8. *Musical Courier*, April 22, 1896, p. 14. 9. N.Y. *Clipper*, Sept. 26 and Oct. 3, 1896. 10. D. Gilbert, *American Vaudeville* (New York: Whittlesey House, 1940), p. 283. 11. *Musical Courier*, Nov. 25, 1896, p. 31. 12. H. C. Barnabee, *Reminiscences*, pp. 211, 419–420. 13. H. B. Smith, *First Nights and First Editions*, pp. 179 ff. 14. Contract in possession of Mr. and Mrs. R. S. Bartlett. 15. N.Y. *Dramatic Mirror*, Oct. 31, 1896, p. 13, and Dec. 26, p. 15. 16. *Ibid.*, Jan. 9, 1897, p. 11. 17. *Ibid.*, Jan. 16, 1897, p. 15; Jan. 30, p. 14; Feb. 13, p. 15. 18. N.Y. *Clipper*, Feb. 20, 1897, p. 815. 19. Prompt book in Library of Congress. 20. Alice Nielsen, "Born to Sing," *Collier's*, June 25, July 2 and 9, 1932. 21. N.Y. *Sun*, March 17, 1897. 22. N.Y. *World*, March 17, 1897. 23. *Musical Courier*, March 24, 1897, pp. 20–21. 24. N.Y. *Dramatic Mirror*, Aug. 22, 1903, p. 9. 25. Copy of letter, Aug. 3, 1903, to E. Schuberth & Co., in Library of Congress. 26. *Musical Courier*, March 3, 1897, p. 35. 27. Washington *Post*, March 5, 1897. 28. Washington *Evening Star*, March 6, 1897. 29. *Musical Courier*, April 7, 1897, p. 27. 30. *Ibid.*, Aug. 4, 1897, p. iv. 31. N.Y. *Dramatic Mirror*, Oct. 2, 1897, p. 28. 32. N.Y. *Clipper*, July 3, 1897. 33. H. B. Smith, *op. cit.*,

p. 176. 34. Prompt book and printed vocal score. 35. N.Y. *Clipper*, Oct. 30, 1897. 36. N.Y. *Times*, Oct. 26, 1897. 37. N.Y. *Clipper*, Dec. 11, 1897. 38. N.Y. *Dramatic Mirror*, Aug. 20, 1898, p. 14. 39. Letter from Harold Spivacke to R. S. Bartlett, Dec. 1, 1938. 40. N.Y. *Dramatic Mirror*, Feb. 12, 1898, p. 23. 41. *Musical Courier*, Feb. 2, 1898, p. 38, and Jan. 29, 1902, pp. 29, 89–90. 42. H. T. Finck, *Anton Seidl*, pp. 89–90. 43. N.Y. *Clipper*, May 14, 1898. 44. *Ibid.*, March 12, 1898. 45. *Ibid.*, May 28, 1898. 46. *Ibid.*, June 11, 1898.

CHAPTER VII

1. N.Y. *Clipper*, July 2 and Sept. 10, 1898. 2. *Ibid.*, Oct. 8, 1898. 3. N.Y. *Dramatic Mirror*, Jan. 29, 1898, p. 13. 4. *Ibid.*, Feb. 26, 1898, p. 14, and May 7, p. 15. 5. *Ibid.*, May 7, p. 15. 6. *Ibid*, Aug. 13, p. 14. 7. N.Y. *Clipper*, Sept. 10, 1898. 8. I. Witmark and I. Goldberg, *Story of the House of Witmark: From Ragtime to Swingtime* (New York: Furman, 1939), pp. 201–202. 9. *Musical Courier*, Sept. 7, 1898, p. 19. 10. Prompt book and printed vocal score. 11. N.Y. *Clipper*, Oct. 29, 1898. 12. N.Y. *Dramatic Mirror*, Feb. 4, 1899, p. 14. 13. N. Y. *Clipper*, March 23, 1901, p. 83. 14. *Ibid.*, March 16, 1901, p. 47. 15. Pittsburgh *Leader*, April 10, 1901. 16. *The Stage*, April 11, 1901, p. 14. 17. Letter from Herbert to Rechten, of E. Schuberth & Co., Aug. 23, 1903 (in the Library of Congress). 18. N.Y. *Clipper*, July 20, 1901, p. 438. 19. *Musical Courier*, July 17, 1901, p. 15. 20. *Musical America*, Oct. 29, 1898, p. 5. 21. *Musical Courier*, Nov. 24, 1897, p. 36. 22. *Ibid.*, Feb. 16, 1898, pp. 20–21. 23. *Ibid.*, Feb. 23, 1898, p. 20. 24. *Ibid.*, March 23, 1898, p. 22. 25. *Ibid.*, March 2, 1898, p. 27. 26. *Ibid.*, May 18, 1898, p. 18. 27. *Ibid.*, Oct. 26, 1898, pp. 31–32. 28. Pittsburgh *Press*, Nov. 13, 1898.

CHAPTER VIII

1. *Musical Courier*, Nov. 16, 1898, p. 22. 2. Pittsburgh *Leader*, Nov. 12, 1898. 3. *Ibid.*, Nov. 18, 1898. 4. Program of the concert. 5. *Metronome*, Nov., 1898, p. 16. 6. Pittsburgh *Times*, Dec. 28, 1898. 7. N.Y. *Tribune*, April 7, 1899, p. 5. 8. Unidentified clipping in Robinson Locke scrapbook (Herbert), in New York Public Library. 9. *Musical Courier*, April 12, 1899, p. 31. 10. N.Y. *Dramatic Mirror*, May 27, 1899, p. 17. 11. N.Y. *Clipper*, June 24, 1899, p. 328. 12. *Ibid.*, Oct. 8, 1898. 13. *Ibid.*, Nov. 12, 1898. 14. *Ibid.*, July 15, 1899, p. 385. 15. *Ibid.*, Sept. 16, 1899, p. 579. 16. N.Y. *Dramatic Mirror*, Sept. 23, 1899, p. 17. 17. N.Y. *Times*, Sept. 19, 1899. 18. H. E. Krehbiel, *More Chapters of Opera* (New York: Holt, 1919), p. 291. 19. N.Y. *Tribune*, Oct. 24, 1899, p. 9. 20. Burns Mantle and G. P. Sherwood, eds., *Best Plays of 1899–1909* (New York: Dodd, Mead, 1944). 21. N.Y. *Clipper*, Oct. 14, 1899, p. 673. 22. *Ibid.*, Jan. 28, 1899. 23. N.Y. *Dramatic Mirror*, June 10, 1899, p. 11; June 17, 1899, p. 15; July 22, 1899, p. 2. 24. Program of the first New York performance. 25. N.Y. *Clipper*, Oct. 28, 1899, p. 722. 26. *Ibid.*, Jan. 6, 1900, p. 940. 27. N.Y. *Dramatic Mirror*, Feb. 18, 1899, p. 14. 28. Contract in possession of Mr. and Mrs. R. S. Bartlett. 29. Prompt book. 30. N.Y. *Clipper*, Dec. 9, 1899, p. 856. 31. N.Y. *Tribune*, Dec. 5, 1899, p. 7. 32. N.Y. *Clipper*, Feb. 17, 1900, p. 1074, and April 14, p. 154. 33. Smith, *First Nights and First Editions*, p. 180. 34. H. C. Barnabee, *Reminiscences*, p. 422. 35. N.Y. *Dramatic Mirror*, April 14, 1900, p. 16. 36. *Ibid.*, Dec. 29, 1900, p. 7.

CHAPTER IX

1. Cornelia Dyas, "Victor Herbert, Musician," *Metropolitan Magazine*, Nov., 1899, pp. 495–499. 2. *Musical Courier*, Aug. 9, 1899, p. 7. 3. Pittsburgh *Dispatch*, Jan. 24, 1900. 4. Pittsburgh *Leader*, Jan. 25, 1900. 5. *Ibid.*, Jan. 28, 1900. 6. Pittsburgh *Bulletin*, Feb. 3, 1900. 7. *Musical Courier*, Feb. 7, 1900, pp. 29–30. 8. The contract, belonging to Mrs. Kate Wilson Smith, was examined by the author in the Pittsburgh Carnegie Library. 9. Pittsburgh *Leader*, Oct. 22, 1900. 10. Pittsburgh *Times*, Nov. 16, 1900. 11. Pittsburgh *Dispatch*, Jan. 20, 1901. 12. Copied by R. S. Bartlett. 13. N.Y. *Journal*, Feb. 13, 1901. 14. N.Y. *Herald Tribune*, May 27, 1924.

CHAPTER X

1. The trial information and testimony summarized or directly quoted from this point on in Chapter X are drawn from Herbert v. Musical Courier Co., 180 N. Y. Rep., 520. 2. Letter to the author from the secretary of Walter Damrosch, Oct. 15, 1947. 3. Pittsburgh *Sun-Telegraph*, Feb. 25, 1938. 4. *Concert-Goer*, Nov. 1, 1902. 5. Letter to the author from the Clerk of the Court of Appeals of the State of New York, March 30, 1949. 6. *Concert-Goer*, Nov. 1, 1902. 7. *Music*, Dec., 1902, pp. 283–285. 8. *Concert-Goer*, Nov. 15, 1902. 9. *Music Trades*, Nov. 15, 1902, p. 31. 10. *Concert-Goer*, Nov. 15, 1902.

CHAPTER XI

1. Pittsburgh *Leader*, Nov. 10, 1901. 2. N.Y. *Dramatic Mirror*, April 6, 1901, p. 17. 3. Pittsburgh *Post*, Nov. 17, 1901. 4. A. P. Hughes, *Music Is My Life* (Cleveland: World Publishing Co., 1947), pp. 54–56. 5. N.Y. *Tribune*, June 15, 1902, Sec. III, p. 8. 6. Pittsburgh *Post*, Dec. 22, 1901. 7. N.Y. *Evening Sun*, Jan. 22, 1902. 8. Pittsburgh *Post*, Feb. 2, 1902. 9. Pittsburgh *Leader*, March 23, 1902. 10. Pittsburgh *Post*, March 23, 1902. 11. Letter to the author from the Free Library of Philadelphia, June 1, 1951. 12. R. A. Gerson, *Music in Philadelphia* (Philadelphia: Presser, 1940), p. 195. 13. P. A. Otis, *The Chicago Symphony Orchestra* (Chicago: Summy, 1925), pp. 207–208. 14. Letter to the author from Julian Caster (friend of Lund), July 14, 1950. 15. Advertising circular of the Grand Union Hotel, supplied by the manager, John H. Leahy. 16. *Daily Saratogian*, June 14, 1898. 17. *Saratoga Illustrated* (New York, 1900). 18. Hugh Bradley, *Such Was Saratoga* (New York: Doubleday, Doran, 1940), p. 246. 19. E. B. Marks (as told to A. J. Liebling), *They All Sang* (New York: Viking Press, 1934), p. 137. 20. Copy of certificate of citizenship in possession of Mr. and Mrs. R. S. Bartlett. 21. Pittsburgh *Gazette*, March 5, 1903. 22. Pittsburgh *Post*, March 22, 1903. 23. Pittsburgh *Telegraph*, March 21, 1903. 24. N.Y. *Dramatic Mirror*, Nov. 7, 1903, p. 16. 25. J. G. Huneker, *The Philharmonic Society of New York and Its Seventy-fifth Anniversary* (New York: The Philharmonic Society, 1917). 26. G. Schlotterbeck in Pittsburgh *Post*, March 13, 1904. 27. *Musical America*, April 1, 1922, p. 47. 28. Letter from G. H. Wilson to editor of the Pittsburgh *Leader*, Jan. 7, 1904. 29. James B. Oliver to James H. Park, Jan. 20, 1904. 30. Letter to G. H. Wilson, from his secretary, July 3, 1903. 31. Unidentified clipping in scrapbook belonging to Broughton Tall. 32. Autograph letter of Joseph Buffington, belonging to Mr. and Mrs. R. S.

Bartlett. **33.** Pittsburgh *Times,* Dec. 10, 1903. **34.** Pittsburgh *Dispatch,* Dec. 5, 1903. **35.** Pittsburgh *Leader,* Dec. 20, 1903. **36.** Pittsburgh *Post,* Jan. 31, 1904. **37.** *Presto,* musical supplement, March 31, 1904, p. 1.

CHAPTER XII

1. M. B. Leavitt, *Fifty Years in Theatrical Management* (New York: Broadway Publishing Co., 1912), p. 591. **2.** N.Y. *Clipper,* April 18, 1903, p. 184. **3.** N.Y. *Dramatic Mirror,* May 9, 1903, p. 7. **4.** Herbert's autograph score (photostat in Library of Congress). **5.** N.Y. *Dramatic Mirror,* June 6, 1903, p. 17. **6.** N.Y. *Clipper,* July 18, 1903. **7.** Herbert's autograph score. **8.** N.Y. *Dramatic Mirror,* Sept. 19, 1903, p. 14. **9.** Prompt book, vocal score, and New York program. **10.** N.Y. *Clipper,* May 21, 1904. **11.** N.Y. *Dramatic Mirror,* March 15, 1902, p. 15. **12.** *Ibid.,* Aug. 2, 1902, p. 13. **13.** *Ibid.,* Feb. 21, 1903, p. 17. **14.** *Ibid.,* June 20, 1903, p. 14. **15.** Edward C. Moore, *Forty Years of Opera in Chicago* (New York: Liveright, 1930), p. 40. **16.** The libretto. **17.** N.Y. *Clipper,* Nov. 21, 1903, p. 933. **18.** N.Y. *Dramatic Mirror,* Nov. 28, 1903, p. 18. **19.** N.Y. *World,* Nov. 17, 1903. **20.** N.Y. *Herald,* Nov. 17, 1903. **21.** *Music Trade Review,* Dec. 5, 1903, p. 3. **22.** Mantle and Sherwood, eds., *The Best Plays of 1899–1909,* p. 445. **23.** N.Y. *Dramatic Mirror,* Nov. 28, 1903, p. 27. **24.** Unidentified clipping in Robinson Locke scrapbook (Herbert) in New York Public Library. **25.** Mantle and Sherwood, *op. cit.,* p. 479. **26.** Pittsburgh *Dispatch,* March 19, 1904. **27.** Herbert's autograph scores in Library of Congress. **28.** Buffalo *Evening News* and *Courier,* April 4, 1904. **29.** N.Y. *Morning Telegraph,* March 1, 1904. **30.** Unidentified clipping in Robinson Locke scrapbook (Herbert). **31.** N.Y. *Dramatic Mirror,* April 24, 1904, p. 13, and May 7, p. 242. **32.** *Ibid.,* July 2, 1904, p. 2. **33.** *Ibid.,* Nov. 19, 1904, p. 13. **34.** N.Y. *Clipper,* Oct. 22, 1904, p. 813. **35.** Felix Isman, *Weber and Fields* (New York: Boni & Liveright, 1924), p. 299. **36.** N.Y. *Dramatic Mirror,* July 23, 1904, p. 3. **37.** N.Y. *Clipper,* Nov. 19, 1904, p. 912. **38.** Mantle and Sherwood, *op. cit.,* p. 475. **39.** I. Witmark and I. Goldberg, *Story of the House of Witmark: From Ragtime to Swingtime* (New York: Furman, 1939), p. 213. **40.** N.Y. *Dramatic Mirror,* Feb. 4, 1905, p. 2. **41.** *Ibid.,* April 1, 1905, p. 13. **42.** *Ibid.,* Dec. 17, 1904, p. 16. **43.** N.Y. *Evening Post,* Dec. 6, 1904, p. 7. **44.** *Musical Courier,* May 3, 1905, p. 24. **45.** Muriel Elwood, *Pauline Frederick, on and off the Stage* (Chicago: Kroch, 1940), pp. 25 ff. **46.** N.Y. *Clipper,* Oct. 21, 1905. **47.** N.Y. *Dramatic Mirror,* Jan. 28, 1905, p. 8. **48.** N.Y. *Clipper,* March 11, 1905, p. 77. **49.** N.Y. *Dramatic Mirror,* April 22, 1905, p. 16. **50.** *Ibid.,* April 29, 1905, p. 21. **51.** Letter to the author from R. S. Bartlett, Sept. 4, 1949. **52.** Unidentified clipping in Robinson Locke scrapbook (Herbert). **53.** Related by Jacoby to the author, Nov. 30, 1947. **54.** Unidentified clipping in Robinson Locke scrapbook (Herbert). **55.** *Ibid.* **56.** N.Y. *Dramatic Mirror,* Aug. 5, 1905, p. 4. **57.** Rochester *Democrat and Chronicle,* Aug. 31, 1905. **58.** N.Y. *Tribune,* Sept. 5, 1905. **59.** Mantle and Sherwood, *op. cit.,* p. 493. **60.** *Standard,* Oct. 27, 1905. **61.** Letter to the author from R. S. Bartlett. **62.** The prompt book. **63.** Buffalo *Express,* Sept. 15, 1905. **64.** N.Y. *Dramatic Mirror,* Sept. 23, 1905, p. 13. **65.** Chicago *Daily Tribune,* Sept. 19, 1905. **66.** N.Y. *Dramatic Mirror,* Nov. 4, 1905, p. 3. **67.** N.Y. *Evening Post,* Oct. 25, 1905. **68.** N.Y. *World,* Oct. 29, 1905, p. 2M. **69.** Mantle and Sherwood, *op. cit.,* p. 499. **70.** N.Y. *Dramatic Mirror,* Oct. 28, 1905, p. 20, and Nov. 4, p. 2. **71.** *Musical Courier,*

Nov. 15, 1905, p. 22. **72.** *Musical America,* Nov. 18, 1905, p. 13. **73.** N.Y. *Telegraph,* Dec. 2, 1905 **74.** N.Y. *Tribune,* Dec. 2, 1905. **75.** *Musical Courier,* Dec. 6, 1905, p. 24. **76.** *Ibid.,* July 18, 1906, p. 20. **77.** *Musical America,* Dec. 23, 1905, p. 3. **78.** N.Y. *Tribune,* Dec. 31, 1905, p. 10. (I).

CHAPTER XIII

1. Contract in possession of Mr. and Mrs. R. S. Bartlett. **2.** N.Y. *Dramatic Mirror,* Sept. 2, 1905, p. 10. **3.** Trenton *Daily True American,* Oct. 7, 1905. **4.** Washington *Evening Star,* Oct. 10, 1905. **5.** N.Y. *Dramatic Mirror,* Dec. 16, 1905, p. 12. **6.** *Musical Courier,* Jan. 17, 1906, p. 28. **7.** N.Y. *Dramatic Mirror,* Jan. 6, 1906, p. 3. **8.** N.Y. *Tribune,* Dec. 26, 1905. **9.** N.Y. *Evening Post,* Dec. 26, 1905. **10.** G. Klemm, in *Etude,* March, 1939. **11.** H. Bradley, *Such Was Saratoga,* p. 247. **12.** Related to the author by W. M. Jacoby, July 31, 1948. **13.** Lionel Barrymore (as told to Cameron Shipp), "We Barrymores," *Saturday Evening Post,* Aug. 26, 1950, p. 62. **14.** G. Klemm, *loc. cit.* **15.** Burns Mantle and G. P. Sherwood, eds., *The Best Plays of 1899–1909,* p. 566. **16.** N.Y. *Clipper,* Sept. 1, 1906. **17.** *Ibid.,* Sept. 14, 1907, p. 814. **18.** *Musical America,* Sept. 15, 1906, p. 1. **19.** N.Y. *Dramatic Mirror,* March 24, 1906, p. 22. **20.** *Musical America,* April 7, 1906, p. 3. **21.** N.Y. *Dramatic Mirror,* May 5, 1906, p. 10. **22.** N.Y. *Clipper,* May 12, 1906, p. 336. **23.** *Ibid.,* May 19, 1906, p. 368. **24.** *Musical America,* May 19, 1906, p. 7. **25.** N.Y. *Clipper,* May 26, 1906, p. 394. **26.** N.Y. *Dramatic Mirror,* April 7, 1906, p. 13. **27.** *Musical America,* May 19, 1906, p. 5. **28.** *Ibid.,* Aug. 11, 1906, p. 7. **29.** N.Y. *Clipper,* Dec. 22, 1906, p. 1164. **30.** *Musical America,* Oct. 6, 1906, p. 13. **31.** Herbert's autograph score in Library of Congress. **32.** Unidentified clipping in Robinson Locke scrapbook (Herbert), in New York Public Library. **33.** Buffalo *Express,* Sept. 2, 1906, p. 25. **34.** *Musical America,* Sept. 29, 1906, p. 13. **35.** N.Y. *Tribune,* Sept. 25, 1906, p. 7. **36.** N.Y. *Evening Post,* Sept. 25, 1906, p. 7. **37.** N.Y. *Herald,* Sept. 25, 1906, p. 9. **38.** Mantle and Sherwood, eds., *op. cit.,* p. 520. **39.** *Ibid.* **40.** London *Times,* Dec. 1, 1919, p. 12. **41.** *Ibid.,* Feb. 9, 1920, p. 12. **42.** Rennold Wolf, "Chronicles of Broadway," *Green Book Magazine,* Dec., 1910, pp. 1206–1207. **43.** Contract in possession of Mr. and Mrs. R. S. Bartlett. **44.** *Musical America,* Jan. 26, 1907, p. 12. **45.** Mantle and Sherwood, *op. cit.,* p. 529. **46.** N.Y. *Dramatic Mirror,* May 4, 1907, p. 9. **47.** *Ibid.,* Nov. 11, 1907, p. 4. **48.** Contract in possession of Mr. and Mrs. R. S. Bartlett. **49.** N.Y. *Dramatic Mirror,* Sept. 9, 1905, p. 21. **50.** N.Y. *Clipper,* June 2, 1906, p. 406. **51.** N.Y. *Dramatic Mirror,* Feb. 2, 1907, p. 16. **52.** N.Y. *Clipper,* April 27, 1907, p. 280. **53.** Mantle and Sherwood, *op. cit.,* p. 534. **54.** Boston *Transcript,* Sept. 19, 1907.

CHAPTER XIV

1. N.Y. *Dramatic Mirror,* Feb. 23, 1907, p. 12. **2.** *Ibid.,* May 1, 1909, p. 7. **3.** N.Y. *Clipper,* May 11, 1907, p. 334. **4.** *Musical America,* June 1, 1907, p. 2. **5.** N.Y. *Telegraph,* Aug. 7, 1907. **6.** Letter to the author from Deems Taylor, July 20, 1949. See also Taylor, "Melodies I Know by Heart," *Stage,* Aug., 1938, p. 54. **7.** National Institute of Arts and Letters, *Constitution and List of Members,* 1950 ed. **8.** *Musical Courier,* June 17, 1914, p. 11. **9.** Letter to the author from Richard C. Murphy, Sept. 19, 1949. **10.** *Musical America,* Feb. 22, 1908, p. 17. **11.** The prompt book. **12.** N.Y. *Dramatic Mirror,* Sept. 12, 1908, pp.

2, 6. 13. N.Y. *Sun*, Sept. 21, 1909, p. 7. 14. N.Y. *Evening Post*, Sept. 1, 1908, p. 5. 15. Mantle and Sherwood, eds., *The Best Plays of 1899–1909*, p. 566. 16. N.Y. *Dramatic Mirror*, Aug. 21, 1909, p. 14. 17. N.Y. *Clipper*, Sept. 25, 1909, p. 839. 18. N.Y. *Dramatic Mirror*, Oct. 2, 1909, p. 7. 19. N.Y. *Tribune*, Sept. 21, 1909, p. 7. 20. N.Y. *Sun*, Sept. 21, 1909, p. 7. 21. Mantle and Sherwood, eds., *The Best Plays of 1909–1919*, p. 400. 22. Coulton Waugh, *The Comics* (New York: Macmillan, 1947), pp. 19–20. 23. N.Y. *Telegraph*, Sept. 19, 1907. 24. Pittsburgh *Gazette*, June 7, 1908. 25. N.Y. *Clipper*, June 13, 1908, p. 436. 26. Philadelphia *Inquirer*, Sept. 29, 1908. 27. N.Y. *Herald*, Oct. 21, 1908, p. 13. 28. N.Y. *Evening Post*, Oct. 21, 1908, p. 7. 29. Letter to the author from Prof. Ralph H. Gabriel of Yale, May 6, 1950. See also Jack Stone, "The Whiffenpoof Story," in the syndicated *American Weekly*, April 17, 1949, p. 12, and unidentified clipping (letter from Harry B. Smith to the editor). 30. N.Y. *Herald, loc. cit.*, 31. N.Y. *Tribune*, Oct. 21, 1908, p. 7. 32. Mantle and Sherwood, eds., *The Best Plays of 1899–1909*, p. 571. 33. N.Y. *Clipper*, March 6, 1909, p. 85. 34. "Plays and Players," *American Magazine*, May, 1910, pp. 105 ff. 35. N.Y. *Dramatic Mirror*, Jan. 13, 1906, p. 2. 36. Chicago *Daily Tribune*, Oct. 6, 1908, p. 10. 37. N.Y. *Dramatic Mirror*, Dec. 12, 1908, p. 3. 38. N.Y. *Evening Post*, Dec. 1, 1908, p. 9. 39. N.Y. *Times*, Dec. 1, 1908, p. 9. 40. N.Y. *Herald*, Dec. 1, 1908, p. 12. 41. N.Y. *Evening Post*, Dec. 1, 1908, p. 9. 42. Mantle and Sherwood, *op. cit.*, p. 573. 43. N.Y. *Telegraph*, Nov. 12, 1908. 44. *Ibid.*, Nov. 10, 1908. 45. I. Witmark and I. Goldberg, *Story of the House of Witmark: From Ragtime to Swingtime*, pp. 214 ff. 46. *Ibid.*, pp. 312 ff. 47. N.Y. *Telegraph*, Nov. 12, 1908. 48. H. E. Krehbiel, *The Bohemians (New York Musicians' Club): A Historical Narrative and Record* (New York, 1921). 49. Letter to the author from Clyde Burrows, Feb. 14, 1949. 50. *Copyright Law of the United States of America*, Bulletin No. 14 (Washington: Copyright Office, The Library of Congress, 1949), pp. 2–3. 51. Thorvald Solberg, *Copyright Enactments of the United States, 1783–1906* (Washington: Government Printing Office, 1906). 52. H. A. Howell, *The Copyright Law* (Washington: Bureau of National Affairs, 1942), p. 194. 53. *Arguments Before the Committees on Patents of the Senate and House of Representatives, Conjointly, on the Bills S. 6330 and H.R. 19853, to Amend and Consolidate the Acts Respecting Copyright, June 6, 7, 8, and 9, 1906* (Washington: Government Printing Office, 1906). 54. N.Y. *Clipper*, Feb. 1, 1908, p. 1358. 55. *Arguments . . . on the Bills S. 6330 and H.R. 19853 . . . June 6, 7, 8, and 9, 1906*, pp. 23–24. 56. *Ibid.*, pp. 25–26. 57. *Ibid.*, pp. 27–28. 58. *Ibid.*, p. 101. 59. *Ibid.*, p. 104. 60. *Ibid.*, pp. 108–109. 61. *Ibid.*, p. 121. 62. *Ibid.*, p. 141. 63. *Arguments Before the Committees on Patents of the Senate and House of Representatives, Conjointly, on the Bills S. 6330 and H.R. 19853, to Amend and Consolidate the Acts Respecting Copyright, December 7, 8, 10 and 11, 1906* (Washington: Government Printing Office, 1906), p. 28. 64. *Ibid.*, pp. 81, 84–85. 65. *Ibid.*, pp. 197–199. 66. *Ibid.*, p. 284. 67. *Ibid.*, p. 284. 68. *Hearings Before the Committees on Patents of the Senate and House of Representatives on Pending Bills to Amend and Consolidate the Acts Respecting Copyright, March 26, 27, and 28, 1908* (Washington: Government Printing Office, 1908), p. 313. 69. *Ibid.*, pp. 257–258. 70. N.Y. *Telegraph*, Oct. 15, 1907. 71. *Hearings*, etc., p. 272. 72. *Ibid.*, p. 271. 73. *Ibid.*, pp. 272–273. 74. *Ibid.*, pp. 188 ff. 75. *Music Trades*, March 13, 1909, pp. 5–6. 76. Howell, *op. cit.*, pp. 197 ff. 77. J. T. Howard, *Ethelbert Nevin* (New York: Crowell, 1935), pp. 348 ff.

CHAPTER XV

1. Both letters in *Edison Phonograph Monthly,* June, 1909. 2. *Music Trades,* May 8, 1909, p. 34. 3. Letter to the author from Norman R. Speiden (Thomas Alva Edison Foundation), Nov. 27, 1951. 4. *Music Trades,* May 8, 1909, p. 21. 5. N.Y. *Dramatic Mirror,* May 1, 1909, p. 19, and May 22, p. 7. 6. N.Y. *Clipper,* June 5, 1909, pp. 425, 436. 7. New York Supplement . . . Vol. 152 . . . (New York State Reporter, Vol. 186) Containing the Decisions of the Supreme and Lower Courts of Record of New York State, April 5–May 31, 1915 (St. Paul: West Publishing Co., 1915), pp. 487 ff. 8. N.Y. *Times,* March 6, 1915, p. 11. 9. N.Y. *Evening Post,* Nov. 23, 1909, p. 9. 10. N.Y. *Herald,* Nov. 23, 1909, p. 12. 11. N.Y. *Tribune,* Nov. 24, 1909, p. 7. 12. *Moving Picture World,* Feb. 13, 1915, pp. 990, 1050. 13. *Musical America,* Oct. 1, 1910, p. 19. 14. Pittsburgh *Dispatch,* Nov. 19, 1910, and N.Y. *Morning Telegraph,* Nov. 21, 1910. 15. Curt Sachs, *Our Musical Heritage* (New York: Prentice-Hall, 1948), p. 349. 16. Contract in possession of Mr. and Mrs. R. S. Bartlett. 17. I. Witmark and I. Goldberg, *Story of the House of Witmark: From Ragtime to Swingtime,* p. 348. 18. G. Blumenthal, *My Sixty Years in Show Business* (New York: F. C. Osberg, 1936), p. 131. 19. Syracuse *Herald,* Oct. 25, 1910, p. 3. 20. Buffalo *Express,* Nov. 1, 1910, p. 8. 21. N.Y. *Telegraph,* Nov. 6, 1910. 22. Blumenthal, *op. cit.,* pp. 134 ff. 23. Letter to the author from Fred L. Landau, Feb. 3, 1951. 24. N.Y. *Tribune,* Nov. 9, 1910. 25. N.Y. *Clipper,* Nov. 12, 1910, p. 977. 26. *Musical America,* Nov. 12, 1910, p. 29. 27. Blumenthal, *op. cit.,* pp. 134 ff. 28. Mantle and Sherwood, eds., *The Best Plays of 1909–1919,* p. 430. 29. *Musical America,* Feb. 25, 1911, p. 21. 30. *Ibid.,* March 2, 1912, p. 35. 31. *Ibid.,* March 16, 1912, p. 39. 32. N.Y. *Clipper,* April 6, 1912, p. 13. 33. Blumenthal, *op. cit.,* p. 148. 34. N.Y. *Clipper,* Oct. 10, 1908, p. 854, and Oct. 31, p. 930. 35. Contract in possession of Mr. and Mrs. R. S. Bartlett. 36. N.Y. *Telegraph,* Nov. 11, 1910. 37. N.Y. *Dramatic Mirror,* Nov. 30, 1910, p. 10. 38. Springfield *Daily Republican,* Dec. 6, 1910, p. 2. 39. Chicago *Tribune,* Feb. 14, 1911, p. 8. 40. N.Y. *Clipper,* Sept. 23, 1911, p. 7. 41. N.Y. *Dramatic Mirror,* Sept. 20, 1911, p. 10.

CHAPTER XVI

1. Unidentified clipping, New York, early April, 1907. 2. Told to the author by Jacoby, Sept. 25, 1947. 3. Note to the author from Carpenter, Oct. 11, 1948. 4. Baltimore *Sun,* Feb. 11, 1907, p. 14. 5. H. E. Krehbiel, *Chapters of Opera* (New York: Holt, 1911), p. 376. 6. See note 1, above. 7. N.Y. *Telegraph,* April 8, 1907. 8. *Musical America,* June 22, 1907, p. 2. 9. *Ibid.,* Oct. 12, 1907, p. 1. 10. *The Americana,* a Universal Reference Library (New York: Americana Corp., 1933); *art.* Redding, pp. 143–144. 11. Letter to the author from Redding's niece-in-law, Mrs. John E. Beck, March 21, 1949. 12. Contract in possession of Mr. and Mrs. R. S. Bartlett. 13. "Mlle Manhattan's Gossip," N.Y. *Morning Telegraph,* Feb. 11, 1909. 14. Copies supplied to the author by Mrs. John E. Beck. 15. *Musical America,* April 9, 1910, p. 5. 16. H. E. Krehbiel, *More Chapters of Opera* (New York: Holt, 1919), p. 80. 17. *Musical Courier,* Feb. 9, 1910, p. 22. 18. *Musical America,* April 9, 1910, p. 5. 19. Stated by Dippel to Redding in a letter of April 3, 1932, made available to the author by Mrs. John E. Beck. 20. *Musical*

America, Nov. 12, 1910, p. 24. 21. *Ibid.,* Nov. 5, 1910, p. 4. 22. *Ibid.,* Feb. 11, 1911, p. 15. 23. *Ibid.,* Feb. 18, 1911, p. 32. 24. N.Y. *Times,* Jan. 22, 1911. 25. *Musical America,* Feb. 11, 1911, p. 3. 26. Agnes G. Hogan in Philadelphia *Record,* Feb. 19, 1911, Sec. IV, p. 5. 27. From the vocal score, published by G. Schirmer, New York, 1911. 28. Philadelphia *Public Ledger,* Feb. 26, 1911. 29. N.Y. *Tribune,* March 1, 1911. 30. *Musical America,* March 4, 1911. 31. *Harper's Weekly,* March 11, 1911. 32. C. Van Vechten, *Interpreters and Interpretations* (New York: Knopf, 1917), pp. 84–85. 33. *American Review of Reviews,* April, 1911, pp. 441 ff. 34. *Musical Courier,* March 1, 1911, pp. 30–31. 35. *Musical America,* March 18, 1911. 36. E. C. Moore, *Forty Years of Opera in Chicago* (New York: Liveright, 1930). 37. Told to the author by Felix Borowski, Washington, June 10, 1947. 38. *Musical Courier,* April 22, 1914, p. 29. 39. *Musical America,* July 26, 1913, pp. 11, 28. 40. Letter to the author from May Valentine, Chicago, June 24, 1947. 41. Told to the author by R. S. Bartlett, Oct. 17, 1946. 42. N.Y. *Clipper,* Dec. 9, 1911, p. 1. 43. Krehbiel, *More Chapters of Opera,* p. 173. 44. N.Y. *Times,* March 10, 1913. 45. N.Y. *Dramatic Mirror,* Aug. 20, 1904; p. 15. 46. *Musical America,* March 29, 1913. 47. Contract in possession of Mr. and Mrs. R. S. Bartlett. 48. *Musical America,* March 15, 1913, p. 7, and March 22, p. 4. 49. *Ibid.,* March 29, 1913, p. 7. 50. N.Y. *Times,* May 25, 1913, Part III, p. 4. 51. Frances Alda, *Men, Women and Tenors* (Boston: Houghton Mifflin, 1937), pp. 189–190. 52. W. H. Seltsam, compiler, *Metropolitan Opera Annals* (New York: H. W. Wilson, 1947). 53. Krehbiel, *More Chapters of Opera,* p. 320. 54. N.Y. *Evening Post,* Jan. 26, 1914. 55. H. T. Finck, *My Adventures in the Golden Age of Music* (New York: Funk & Wagnalls, 1926), p. 371. 56. *Musical America,* Feb. 3, 1912. 57. *Ibid.,* Jan. 31, 1914, p. 5. 58. Richard Aldrich, "New Productions in New York," *New Music Review and Church Music Review,* March, 1914, pp. 180–181. 59. *Musical America,* Feb. 7, 1914, pp. 1–4. 60. E. E. Hipsher, *American Opera and Its Composers* (Philadelphia: Presser, 1934), p. 265.

CHAPTER XVII

1. N.Y. *Dramatic Mirror,* July 2, 1910, p. 4. 2. *Musical America,* Feb. 25, 1911, p. 6. 3. Boston *Transcript,* March 28, 1911, p. 17. 4. *Musical America,* April 8, 1911, p. 15. 5. *Ibid.,* April 15, 1911, p. 15. 6. N.Y. *Clipper,* June 3, 1911, p. 8. 7. Letter to the author from Oscar Radin, March 8, 1950. 8. *Theatre,* Dec., 1911, p. xiv. 9. N.Y. *Sun,* Oct. 17, 1911, p. 7. 10. N.Y. *Times,* Oct. 17, 1911, p. 9. 11. N.Y. *Dramatic Mirror,* Oct. 28, 1911, p. 10. 12. N.Y. *Herald,* Oct. 17, 1911, p. 12. 13. Mantle and Sherwood, eds., *The Best Plays of 1909–1919,* p. 454. 14. *Musical America,* Dec. 30, 1911, p. 31. 15. *Ibid.,* May 27, 1911. 16. Information supplied by Harold D. Desfor (RCA Victor), Jan. 18, 1952. 17. *Variety,* June 17, 1911, p. 4. 18. *Musical America,* July 29, 1911, p. 28. 19. Cincinnati *Commercial,* Oct. 14, 1912. 20. Buffalo *Commercial,* Feb. 28, 1912. 21. N.Y. *Dramatic Mirror,* Sept. 13, 1911, p. 7. 22. N.Y. *Herald,* Oct. 20, 1911, p. 11. 23 N.Y. *Times,* Oct. 20, 1911, p. 13. 24. Boston *Transcript,* Nov. 12, 1912. 25. N.Y. *Dramatic Mirror,* Jan. 3, 1912, p. 27. 26. Mantle and Sherwood, *op. cit.,* p. 455. 27. N.Y. *Times,* Jan. 12, 1912. 28. N.Y. *Dramatic Mirror,* May 22, 1912, p. 15. 29. *Musical America,* June 22, 1912, pp. 19–20. 30. N.Y. *Dramatic Mirror,* Nov. 6, 1912, p. 16. 31. *Ibid.,* Dec. 11, 1912, p. 13. 32. N.Y.

Clipper, May 17, 1913, p. 12. **33.** Elsie Janis, *So Far, So Good!* (New York: Dutton, 1932), p. 108; used by permission. **34.** N.Y. *Clipper,* June 3, 1911, p. 11. **35.** N.Y. *Dramatic Mirror,* Oct. 16, 1912, p. 8. **36.** Janis, *op. cit.,* pp. 107 ff. **37.** Philadelphia *Inquirer,* Oct. 9, 1912, p. 11. **38.** N.Y. *Clipper,* Nov. 2, 1912, p. 6. **39.** *Variety,* Nov. 1, 1912, p. 24. **40.** Mantle and Sherwood, *The Best Plays of 1909–1919.* **41.** *Musical America,* April 26, 1913, p. 22. **42.** N.Y. *Dramatic Mirror,* Sept. 10, 1913, p. 7. **43.** N.Y. *Sun,* Jan. 6, 1913. **44.** *Musical Leader,* Jan. 16, 1913. **45.** *Musical America,* Feb. 15, 1913. **46.** The printed program. **47.** *Musical America,* June 21, 1913, pp. 1–4. **48.** Philadelphia *North American,* July 7, 1913. **49.** N.Y. *Dramatic Mirror,* July 23, 1910, p. 3. **50.** *Ibid.,* Oct. 30, 1912, p. 9. **51.** *Ibid.,* April 2, 1913, p. 15. **52.** *Ibid.,* April 9, 1913, p. 14. **53.** Autograph letter of Aug. 31, 1913, in Library of Congress. **54.** *Musical America,* Sept. 13, 1913, p. 4. **55.** Mantle and Sherwood, *op. cit.* **56.** Mantle, ed., *The Best Plays of 1946–47,* p. 457. **57.** *Variety,* Aug. 1, 1913, p. 3. **58.** N.Y. *Dramatic Mirror,* June 25, 1913, p. 12. **59.** *Musical America,* Nov. 1, 1913, p. 18. **60.** The vocal score, published by G. Schirmer, New York, 1913. **61.** N.Y. *Sun,* Nov. 12, 1913, p. 7. **62.** N.Y. *Herald,* Nov. 12, 1913. **63.** Mantle and Sherwood, *op. cit.*

CHAPTER XVIII

1. The banquet program. **2.** Mark Murphy, "Play for Pay," *Hearst's International combined with Cosmopolitan,* June, 1951, pp. 137–140. **3.** Raymond Hubbell, *From Nothing to Five Million a Year: The Story of A.S.C.A.P.,* by a Founder. (Unpublished.) **4.** *Ibid.,* p. 3. **5.** Nathan Burkan, "Ascap Files Answer to U.S. Suit (Filed in the District Court of the United States for the Southern District of New York, Oct. 31, 1934)," *NAB Reports,* Vol. 2, No. 53 (Nov. 10, 1934), pp. 570–584. **6.** N.Y. *Times,* Feb. 14, 1914, p. 1. **7.** Copy of the 1914 Articles, supplied by Schwartz & Frohlich, counsel for ASCAP. **8.** Letter to the author, July 21, 1950. **9.** Hubbell, *op. cit.,* pp. 62 ff. **10.** *Musical Courier,* March 22, 1911. **11.** *Musical America,* Feb. 21, 1914, p. 1. **12.** N.Y. *Times,* Nov. 30, 1914, p. 9. **13.** *Alden-Rochelle, Inc., et al.* v. *ASCAP:* The Court's Findings of Fact and Conclusions of Law, July 19, 1948 (Vincent L. Leibell, judge). **14.** *Musical America,* March 4, 1916, p. 52. **15.** *Metronome,* Jan., 1915, p. 15. **16.** *Decisions of the United States Courts Involving Copyright, 1914–1917* (Copyright Office Bulletin, No. 18, Washington: Government Printing Office, 1918), p. 52. **17.** Nathan Burkan, *loc. cit.* **18.** *Ibid.* **19.** U. S. Supreme Court. Records and Briefs. Vol. 242, pp. 591–608. **20.** *Decisions of the United States Courts, etc.,* p. 216. **21.** *Ibid.,* p. 221. **22.** *Musical America,* Feb. 5, 1916, p. 30. **23.** *Decisions of the United States Courts, etc.,* pp. 225–226. **24.** Nathan Burkan, *loc. cit.,* **25.** *The ASCAP Story* (published by the Society, 1949?). **26.** Raymond Hubbell, *op. cit.,* p. 129.

CHAPTER XIX

1. N.Y. *Dramatic Mirror,* Feb. 18, 1914, p. 16. **2.** Information supplied by Horace Britt. **3.** N.Y. *Times,* April 19, 1914, Part IV, p. 3. **4.** *Ibid.* **5.** Autograph Letter in Library of Congress. **6.** *Ibid.* **7.** Conversation with Horace Britt, Washington, winter 1952. **8.** Autograph letter in Library of Congress. **9.** N.Y. *Times,* April 26, 1914, Part IV, p. 3. **10.** Letter to the author from R. S. Bartlett, Dec. 23, 1949. **11.** N.Y. *Times,* June 26, 1914, p. 18. **12.** N.Y.

Herald, Dec. 8, 1914, p. 15. **13.** N.Y. *Times,* Dec. 8, 1914, p. 11. **14.** N.Y. *Tribune,* Dec. 8, 1914, p. 9. **15.** Mantle and Sherwood, *The Best Plays of 1909–1919.* **16.** N.Y. *Clipper,* Dec. 12, 1914, p. 4. **17.** N.Y. *Dramatic Mirror,* July 10, 1912, p. 10. **18** I. Witmark and I. Goldberg, *Story of the House of Witmark: From Ragtime to Swingtime,* pp. 354, 261. **19.** The printed score. **20.** Gustav Klemm, "Victor Herbert As I Knew Him," *Etude,* May, 1939, pp. 296, 350, 353. **21.** N.Y. *Dramatic Mirror,* Oct. 14, 1914, p. 9. **22.** *Ibid.,* Dec. 16, 1914, p. 5. **23.** N.Y. *Clipper,* Nov. 14, 1914, p. 6. **24.** Mantle and Sherwood, *op. cit.* **25.** *Metronome,* Nov., 1915, p. 17. **26.** Mantle and Sherwood, *op. cit.* **27.** *New Yorker,* June 2, 1934, p. 28; used by permission. **28.** *Ibid.,* June 9, 1934, pp. 75–76; used by permission. **29.** *Musical America,* Feb. 6, 1915, p. 37. **30.** *Ibid.,* Feb. 13, 1915, p. 30. **31.** N.Y. *Times,* Nov. 17, 1914, p. 8. **32.** Program of the dinner. **33.** *Chicago Tribune,* Sept. 5, 1915, Part II, p. 1. **34.** L. F. Byington and Oscar Lewis, eds., *The History of San Francisco* (3 vols., Indianapolis: S. J. Clarke Publishing Co., 1931), Vol. I, pp. 453ff. **35.** San Francisco *Chronicle,* Oct. 22, 1915, p. 10. **36.** *Musical America,* Nov. 6, 1915, p. 6. **37.** *Pacific Coast Musical Review,* Nov. 11, 1915, p. 1. **38.** N.Y. *Times,* Sept. 27, 1915, p. 1. **39.** N.Y. *Sun,* Sept. 30, 1915, p. 7. **40.** N.Y. *World,* Sept. 30, 1915, p. 9. **41.** N.Y. *Evening Post,* Sept. 30, 1915, p. 9. **42.** Mantle and Sherwood, *op. cit.* **43.** H. E. Krehbiel, *The Bohemians (New York Musicians' Club): A Historical Narrative and Record* (New York, 1921), p. 38. **44.** Supplied by Mr. Pignatelli of the Library of Congress staff. **45.** *Musical America,* Dec. 2, 1916, p. 48. **46.** N.Y. *Times,* March 5, 1916, Part I, p. 7. **47.** Program of the banquet. **48.** N.Y. *Times,* May 15, 1916, pp. 1–2. **49.** *Ibid.,* Oct. 15, 1916, Part I, p. 19.

CHAPTER XX

1. Letter to Herbert from the Aeolian Co., April 12, 1916, in Library of Congress. **2.** *Musical America,* May 6, 1916, p. 64. **3.** N.Y. *Times,* May 3, 1916, p. 11. **4.** N.Y. *Dramatic Mirror,* March 4, 1916, p. 22. **5.** Van Vechten, *Music and Bad Manners* (New York: Knopf, 1916), pp. 43 ff. **6.** B. C. Cook, in *Motion Picture Magazine,* Oct., 1916, pp. 111–114. **7.** J. C. Breil, in *Metronome,* Nov., 1916, p. 42. **8.** *Moving Picture World,* June 24, 1916, p. 2211. **9.** *Metronone,* June, 1916, p. 16. **10.** *Musical America,* May 13, 1916, p. 43. **11.** *Variety,* June 9, 1916, p. 16. **12.** From the scenario in Library of Congress. **13.** N.Y. *Dramatic Mirror,* June 3, 1916, p. 26. **14.** *Moving Picture World,* June 24, 1916, p. 2256. **15.** N.Y. *Clipper,* Sept. 30, 1916, p. 33. **16.** N.Y. *Dramatic Mirror,* June 17, 1916, p. 22. **17.** *Musical America,* June 17, 1916, p. 39. **18.** *Metronome,* Sept., 1916, p. 50. **19.** Manuscripts in Library of Congress. **20.** *Variety,* Aug. 25, 1916, p. 12. **21.** *Ibid.,* Oct. 13, 1916, p. 13. **22.** N.Y. *Clipper,* May 13, 1916, p. 3. **23.** Contract in possession of Mr. and Mrs. R. S. Bartlett. **24.** Author's interview with Irving Berlin, New York, May 19, 1949. **25.** N.Y. *Times,* Nov. 7, 1916, p. 9. **26.** *Ibid.* **27.** *Musical America,* Nov. 18, 1916, p. 39. **28.** Mantle and Sherwood, *The Best Plays of 1909–1919.* **29.** N.Y. *Dramatic Mirror,* May 20, 1916, p. 7. **30.** *Musical America,* March 24, 1917. **31.** N.Y. *Dramatic Mirror,* Dec. 23, 1916, p. 8. **32.** Contract in possession of Mr. and Mrs. R. S. Bartlett. **33.** Cleveland *Plain Dealer,* Jan. 1, 1917, p. 1. **34.** N.Y. *Dramatic Mirror,* Jan. 13, 1917, p. 8. **35.** Cleveland *Plain Dealer,* Jan. 2, 1917, p. 6. **36.** *Musical America,* Jan. 13, 1917, p. 25. **37.** Cleveland *Plain Dealer,* Jan. 3, 1917, p. 12. **38.** *Variety,* Jan. 12, 1917, p. 10. **39.** Letter in Mrs. R. S. Bartlett's autograph album, in Library of Congress. **40.** N.Y. *Times,* March 25, 1917,**

Part VIII, p. 5. **41.** *Theatre*, May, 1917, p. 278. **42.** N.Y. *Dramatic Mirror*, March 31, 1917, p. 4. **43.** N.Y. *Clipper*, March 21, 1917, p. 10. **44.** N.Y. *Dramatic Mirror*, March 24, 1917, p. 7. **45.** *Musical America*, March 24, 1917. **46.** N.Y. *Dramatic Mirror*, March 24, 1917, p. 7. **47.** Mantle and Sherwood, *op. cit*, **48.** Cincinnati *Enquirer*, Jan. 17, 1918, p. 5. **49.** N.Y. *Clipper*, April 6, 1921, p. 19. **50.** *Musical Observer*, Oct., 1928. **51.** The program of the concert. **52.** N.Y. *Times*, May 8, 1917, p. 11. **53.** *Ibid.*, May 17, 1917, p. 11. **54.** *Ibid.*, June 13, 1917, p. 11. **55.** Mantle and Sherwood, *op. cit.* **56.** *Variety*, June 22, 1917, p. 3. **57.** N.Y. *Times*, Nov. 13, 1917, p. 11. **58.** Mantle and Sherwood, *op. cit.*

CHAPTER XXI

1. *Musical America*, Dec. 1, 1917, p. 27. **2.** Moses Smith, *Koussevitzky* (New York: Allen, Towne & Heath, 1947), p. 137. Also letter to the author from Leonard Burkat (Boston Symphony Orchestra), Dec. 26, 1947. **3.** Cincinnati Symphony Orchestra *Year Book*, 1950–51, p. 6. **4.** Letter to the author from Martha M. Smith (Cincinnati Symphony Orchestra), Feb. 8, 1950. **5.** *Musical America*, April 6, 1918, p. 48. **6.** Letter to the author from Clyde Burrows, Feb. 14, 1949. **7.** *Variety*, March 29, 1918, p. 11. **8.** N.Y. *Times*, April 30, 1918, p. 24. **9.** N.Y. *Clipper*, June 5, 1918, p. 12. **10.** *Variety*, June 21, 1918; p. 12. **11.** Elena de Sayn in Washington *Evening Star*, May 29, 1952, p. 13. **12.** *Musical America*, Aug. 24, 1918, p. 4. **13.** N.Y. *Clipper*, Aug. 21, 1918, p. 5, and N.Y. *Dramatic Mirror*, Aug. 31, p. 303. **14.** N.Y. *Times*, Oct. 15, 1918, p. 10. **15.** W. J. Finn, *Sharps and Flats in Five Decades* (New York: Harper, 1947), p. 243. **16.** Mantle and Sherwood, *The Best Plays of 1909–1919.* **17.** *Variety*, Feb. 7, 1919, p. 16. **18.** Mantle and Sherwood, *op. cit.* **19.** N.Y. *Clipper*, June 29, 1919, p. 4. **20.** In Library of Congress. **21.** *Musical America*, April 5, 1919, p. 55. **22.** Contract in possession of Mr. and Mrs. R. S. Bartlett. **23.** N.Y. *Times*, June 17, 1919, p. 20. **24.** Contract in possession of Mr. & Mrs. R. S. Bartlett. **25.** *Variety*, June 13, 1919, p. 14. **26.** N.Y. *Sun*, Dec. 30, 1919, p. 8. **27.** N.Y. *Tribune*, Dec. 31, 1919, p. 11. **28.** N.Y. *Herald*, Dec. 30, 1919, p. 8. **29.** Burns Mantle, *The Best Plays of 1919–1920.* **30.** Information supplied by R. S. Bartlett. **31.** London *Times*, Oct. 23, 1922, p. 8. **32.** Letter to the author from the Chicago Public Library, Jan. 17, 1953. **33.** Chicago *Tribune*, Oct. 24, 1919, p. 21. **34.** Chicago *Daily News*, Oct. 24, 1919, p. 4. **35.** Contract in possession of Mr. and Mrs. R. S. Bartlett. **36.** *Variety*, Nov. 7, 1919, p. 10. **37.** Letter to the author from Philip James, June 24, 1948. **38.** Conversation with Philip James, New York, Oct. 1, 1948. **39.** *Variety*, Feb. 6, 1920, p. 17. **40.** Letter to the author from Philip James, Oct. 3, 1948. **41.** Mantle, *op. cit.* **42.** N.Y. *Clipper*, Feb. 18, 1920, p. 17. **43.** N.Y. *Dramatic Mirror*, Feb. 28, 1920, p. 361. **44.** *Musical America*, April 3, 1920, p. 22. **45.** N.Y. *Times*, June 24, 1920, p. 25. **46.** Copy of letter supplied to the author by Edwin Franko Goldman. **47.** Letter from Edwin Franko Goldman, Sept. 30, 1946. **48.** N.Y. *Dramatic Mirror*, March 20, 1920, p. 524. **49.** Philadelphia *Ledger*, March 23, 1920, p. 9. **50.** *Ibid.* **51.** Boston *Evening Transcript*, May 4, 1920, p. 16. **52.** N.Y. *Clipper*, Sept. 15, 1920, p. 4. **53.** Letter to the author, Aug. 10, 1949. **54.** N.Y. *Dramatic Mirror*, July 3, 1920, p. 16. **55.** Letter from the Ferguson Library, Stamford, Conn., Nov. 18, 1952. **56.** *Variety*, July 16, 1920, p. 15. **57.** N.Y. *Dramatic Mirror*, July 17, 1920, p. 97. **58.** Mantle, *The Best Plays of 1919–1920.* **59.** N.Y.

Clipper, Jan. 5, 1921, p. 34.   60. *Musical America,* Aug. 6, 1921, p. 31.
61. *Pacific Coast Musician,* April, 1922, p. 4.   62. *Musical America,* March
18, 1922, p. 2.   63. *Pacific Coast Musicians,* March, 1922, p. 7.   64. *Variety,*
Sept. 22, 1922, pp. 17, 21.   65. *Musical America,* July 16, 1921, p. 16.
66. *Variety,* Sept. 22, 1922, pp. 17, 21.   67. Mantle, *The Best Plays of
1922–1923.*   68. N.Y. *Clipper,* Nov. 29, 1922, p. 5.   69. Original in possession
of Mr. and Mrs. R. S. Bartlett.   70. Pencil draft, undated, in possession of
Mr. and Mrs. R. S. Bartlett.   71. *Musical America,* Sept. 8, 1923, p. 16.
72. Told to the author by Otto Kinkeldey, Washington, Dec. 15, 1945.
73. Paul Whiteman and Mary Margaret McBride, *Jazz* (New York: Sears,
1926), pp. 87 ff.   74. *Musical America,* Feb. 2, 1924, p. 3.   75. I. Goldberg,
George Gershwin (New York: Simon & Schuster, 1931), pp. 147–148; used
by permission.   76. N.Y. *Times,* Feb. 14, 1924, p. 15.   77. H. O. Osgood,
So This Is Jazz (Boston: Little, Brown & Co., 1926), p. 139.   78. Facsimile
of autograph score in New York Public Library.   79. Goldberg, *op. cit.,* pp.
160–161.   80. Annual Report of the Librarian of Congress, 1924, pp. 190–
192.   81. N.Y. *Times,* April 18, 1924, pp. 1, 5.   82. *Ibid.,* May 7, 1924,
p. 19.   83. Mantle, *The Best Plays of 1924–1925.*   84. N.Y. *Dramatic
Mirror,* July 1, 1919, p. 1011.   85. Correspondence between Harms and Herbert,
in possession of Mr. and Mrs. R. S. Bartlett.   86. *Stage,* Aug., 1938, p. 54.
87. N.Y. *Herald Tribune,* Aug. 22, 1924, p. 6.   88. N.Y. *Times,* Aug. 22,
1924, p. 8.   89. *Ibid.*   90. *Variety,* Aug. 27, 1924, pp. 18–19.   91. *Theatre
Magazine,* Oct., 1924, p. 16   92. N.Y. *World,* Aug. 21, 1924, p. 7.
93. Herbert's autograph letter and S. Jay Kaufman's column in office of
ASCAP, New York.   94. N.Y. *World,* June 1, 1924, p. 9S.   95. N.Y.
Times, May 27, 1924.   96. Told to the author by Horace Britt, Washington,
Feb. 28, 1952.   97. Told to the author by Arthur Loesser, Washington, Nov.
15, 1947.   98. Herbert's lunch check, in possession of Mr. and Mrs. R. S.
Bartlett.   99. Letter to the author from Oscar Radin, March 8, 1950.   100. In
office of Dr. Nathan Settel, New York, April 17, 1947.   101. Told to the
author by R. S. Bartlett, April 17, 1947.   102. *Musical America,* June 7,
1924, p. 22.   103. N.Y. *World,* May 28, 1924.   104. N.Y. *Morning Telegraph,* May 27, 1924.   105. *Ibid.,* May 28, 1924.   106. *Ibid.,* May 27, 1924.
107. N.Y. *Times,* May 29, 1924.   108. Told to the author by Richard McCann,
Oct. 17, 1946, in the office of the New York Local, No. 802, of the American
Federation of Musicians.   109. Raymond Hubbell, *From Nothing to Five
Million a Year: The Story of A.S.C.A.P.,* by a Founder (unpublished).
110. N.Y. *Times,* June 11, 1925, p. 19.   111. *Ibid.,* Feb. 25, 1927, p. 21.

CHAPTER XXII

1. Robert Grau, *Forty Years Observation of Music and the Drama* (New
York: Broadway Publishing Co., 1909), p. 268.   2. Told to the author, New
York, Sept., 1948, by Fred L. Landau and Ernest Wagner, respectively Herbert's
concert-master and his first flutist.   3. *Musical America,* March 22, 1924, p. 11.
4. Letter from R. S. Bartlett, July 8, 1949.   5. *Ibid.,* Aug. 26, 1946.   6. Let-
ter from Philip James, June 24, 1948.   7. Harry B. Smith, *First Nights and
First Editions* (Boston: Little, Brown & Co., 1931), p. 186.   8. Syracuse *Post
Standard,* Oct. 20, 1913.   9. Told to the author by Irving Caesar, Washing-
ton, Jan. 16, 1953.   10. Frederik Stahlberg, *Yesterthoughts in Memory of
Victor Herbert* (unpublished), p. 6.   11. Viola B. Shore, in *Musical Observer,*
Aug., 1923.   12. Told to the author by Fred L. Landau, New York, Sept. 25,

1948.   13. Gustav Klemm, in the *Musical Record,* Aug., 1933.   14. Peggy Wood, *How Young You Look* (New York: Farrar & Rinehart, 1941), pp. 93–94; used by permission.   15. Stahlberg, *op. cit.,* p. 5.   16. *Ibid.,* p. 11. 17. *Ibid.,* p. 15.   18. *Ibid.,* p. 16.   19. Told to the author by Fred L. Landau, New York, Sept. 25, 1948.   20. Told to the author by Victor Kolar, Detroit, Feb. 20, 1948.   21. Letter from Archer Gibson, Oct. 21, 1949.   22. Letter from W. M. Jacoby, Aug. 14, 1948.   23. N.Y. *Times,* June 1, 1924, Section VIII, p. 12.   24. Stahlberg, *op. cit.,* p. 43.   25. *Ibid.,* p. 46.   26. I. Goldberg, *Tin Pan Alley* (New York: John Day, 1930), p. 196.   27. Edith J. R. Isaacs and Rosamond Gilder, "American Musical Comedy," *Theatre Arts,* Aug., 1945, pp. 465–466; used by permission of the author and *Theatre Arts.* 28. Letter from Robert Russell Bennett, June 24, 1950.   29. Goldberg, *op. cit.,* p. 193.   30. Felix Borowski in Chicago *Record Herald,* Oct. 19, 1913.

Index

613